Chinese History in Economic Perspective

This volume and the conference from which it resulted were sponsored by the Joint Committee on Chinese Studies of the American Council of Learned Societies and the Social Science Research Council, with funds provided by the Henry Luce Foundation, Inc., the National Science Foundation, and the Andrew W. Mellon Foundation.

Chinese History in Economic Perspective

EDITED BY
Thomas G. Rawski and Lillian M. Li

UNIVERSITY OF CALIFORNIA PRESS
Berkeley   Los Angeles   Oxford

University of California Press
Berkeley and Los Angeles, California

University of California Press, Ltd.
Oxford, England

© 1992 by
The Regents of the University of California

Library of Congress Cataloging-in-Publication Data

Chinese history in economic perspective / edited by Thomas G. Rawski
and Lillian M. Li.
    p. cm.
Includes bibliographical references and index.
ISBN 978-0-520-30188-7 (pbk. : alk. paper)
    1. China—Economic conditions—1644–1912. 2. China—Economic
conditions—1912–1949. I. Rawski, Thomas G., 1943–
II. Li, Lillian M., 1943–
HC427.7.C466   1991
330.951—dc20   90-42379
                                                             CIP

Studies on China

A series of conference volumes sponsored by the Joint Committee on Chinese Studies of the American Council of Learned Societies and the Social Science Research Council

1. The Origins of Chinese Civilization
   edited by David N. Keightley
   University of California Press, 1982

2. Popular Chinese Literature and Performing Arts in the People's Republic of China, 1949–1979
   edited by Bonnie S. McDougall
   University of California Press, 1984

3. Class and Social Stratification in Post-Revolution China
   edited by James L. Watson
   Cambridge University Press, 1984

4. Popular Culture in Late Imperial China
   edited by David Johnson, Andrew J. Nathan, and Evelyn S. Rawski
   University of California Press, 1985

5. Kinship Organization in Late Imperial China, 1000–1940
   edited by Patricia Buckley Ebrey and James L. Watson
   University of California Press, 1986

6. The Vitality of the Lyric Voice: *Shih* Poetry from the Late Han to the T'ang
   edited by Shuen-fu Lin and Stephen Owen
   Princeton University Press, 1986

7. Policy Implementation in Post-Mao China
   edited by David M. Lampton
   University of California Press, 1987

8. Death Ritual in Late Imperial and Modern China
   edited by James L. Watson and Evelyn S. Rawski
   University of California Press, 1988

9. Neo-Confucian Education: The Formative Stage
   edited by Wm. Theodore de Bary and John W. Chaffee
   University of California Press, 1989

10. Orthodoxy in Late Imperial China
    edited by Kwang-Ching Liu
    University of California Press, 1990

11. Chinese Local Elites and Patterns of Dominance
    edited by Joseph W. Esherick and Mary Backus Rankin
    University of California Press, 1990

12. Marriage and Inequality in Chinese Society
edited by Rubie S. Watson and Patricia Buckley Ebrey
University of California Press, 1990

13. Chinese History in Economic Perspective
edited by Thomas G. Rawski and Lillian M. Li
University of California Press, 1992

CONTENTS

LIST OF TABLES, FIGURES, AND MAPS / *ix*
WEIGHTS AND MEASURES / *xiii*
PREFACE / *xv*
CONTRIBUTORS / *xvii*

INTRODUCTION: CHINESE HISTORY IN ECONOMIC PERSPECTIVE / *1*
Thomas G. Rawski and Lillian M. Li

PART 1 • PRICE BEHAVIOR / *33*

1. Secular Trends of Rice Prices in the Yangzi Delta, 1638–1935 / *35*
   Yeh-chien Wang

2. Grain Prices in Zhili Province, 1736–1911: A Preliminary Study / *69*
   Lillian M. Li

3. The Qing State and the Gansu Grain Market, 1739–1864 / *100*
   Peter C. Perdue

4. Grain Markets and Food Supplies in Eighteenth-Century Hunan / *126*
   R. Bin Wong and Peter C. Perdue

5. Infanticide and Family Planning in Late Imperial China:
   The Price and Population History of Rural Liaoning, 1774–1873 / *145*
   James Lee, Cameron Campbell, and Guofu Tan

PART 2 • MARKET RESPONSE / *177*

6. Land Concentration and Income Distribution in Republican China / *179*
   Loren Brandt and Barbara Sands

CONTENTS

7. Farming, Sericulture, and Peasant Rationality in Wuxi County in the Early Twentieth Century / *207*
   Lynda S. Bell

8. Women's Work in the Ningbo Area, 1900–1936 / *243*
   Susan Mann

9. Native-Place Hierarchy and Labor Market Segmentation: The Case of Subei People in Shanghai / *271*
   Emily Honig

10. Local Interest Story: Political Power and Regional Differences in the Shandong Capital Market, 1900–1937 / *295*
    Kenneth Pomeranz

GLOSSARY / *319*
BIBLIOGRAPHY / *325*
INDEX / *351*

TABLES, FIGURES, AND MAPS

TABLES

1.1 Rice Prices in the Yangzi Delta, 1638–1935 / *40*

1.2 Trends of Population, Silver Stocks, and Rice Prices in China, 1650–1930 / *57*

1.3 Price Trends, Climate Cycles, and Harvest Conditions in the Yangzi Delta, 1653–1920 / *63*

2.1 Annual Trends and Seasonal Variation in Grain Prices in Zhili Province, 1738–1910 / *84*

2.2 Grain Price Increases in Crisis Years in Zhili Province, 1738–1910 / *89*

2.3 Grain Prices during the 1743–1744 Drought in Zhili Province (Excluding Baoding) / *91*

2.4 Grain Prices during the 1775–1776 Drought and Flood in Zhili Province (Excluding Baoding) / *92*

2.5 Grain Prices during the Last Years of the 1761–1763 Flood in Zhili Province (Excluding Baoding) / *94*

2.6 Grain Price Variation in Crisis and Noncrisis Years in Zhili Province (Excluding Xuanhua and Chengde), 1738–1910 / *96*

3.1 Annual Trends and Seasonal Variation in Millet Prices in Gansu Prefectures, 1739–1864 / *118*

3.2 Differences in Annual Averages of Low Millet Prices in Gansu Prefectures, 1739–1864 / *122*

3.3 Variation in Low Millet Prices in Gansu Province, 1739–1864 / *124*

LIST OF TABLES, FIGURES, AND MAPS

5.1 Summary of the Population Registers of Daoyi, Liaoning, 1774–1873 / *148*

5.2 Male and Female Life Expectancy in Daoyi, 1792–1867 / *152*

5.3 Female Life Expectancy in Daoyi during Good and Bad Periods, 1792–1867 / *153*

5.4 Male Life Expectancy in Daoyi during Good and Bad Periods, 1792–1867 / *154*

5.5 Sex Ratios by Birth Order and Completed Family Size / *154*

5.6 Correlations of High and Low Grain Prices in Fengtian Prefecture, 1774–1873 / *162*

5.7 Correlations of Grain Prices and Death and Birth Rates in Daoyi, 1774–1873 / *166*

6.1 Size Distribution of Land Owned by 1.75 Million Rural Households in China, 1930s / *182*

6.2 Size Distribution of Land Owned by Households in Huailu County, Hebei, 1706, 1736, and 1939 / *183*

6.3 Distribution of Cultivated Holdings and Incomes per Household in China, 1930s / *189*

6.4 Market Exchange in Three Hebei Villages, 1936 / *192*

6.5 Asset and Income Distribution in Three Hebei Villages, 1936 / *195*

6.6 Correlations of Factor Holdings by Households in Three Hebei Villages, 1936 / *201*

6.7 Distribution of Household Incomes in Selected Low-Income Countries / *203*

7.1 Annual Income, Production Costs, and Labor Usage per *Mu* for Rice/Wheat Cultivation and Silkworm Raising in Wuxi County, Jiangsu, 1939 / *220*

7.2 Land Usage for Rice/Wheat Farming and Mulberry Cultivation in Three Wuxi Villages, 1929 / *226*

7.3 Land Productivity in Three Wuxi Villages, 1929 / *228*

7.4 Labor Days in Rice/Wheat Farming in Three Wuxi Villages, 1929 / *232*

7.5 Labor Days in Mulberry Cultivation and Silkworm Raising in Three Wuxi Villages, 1929 / *234*

7.6 Labor Units in Three Wuxi Villages, 1929 / *236*

7.7 Labor Productivity in Three Wuxi Villages, 1929 / *238*

8.1 Farm Wages in Three Counties in Zhejiang Province, 1933 / *253*

10.1 Returns on Grain Holding in Shandong Prefectures, 1900–1911 / *300*

LIST OF TABLES, FIGURES, AND MAPS   xi

FIGURES

1.1 Rice Prices in the Yangzi Delta, 1638–1935   /   *48*

1.2 Thirty-one-Year Moving Average of Rice Prices in the Yangzi Delta, 1638–1935   /   *50*

1.3 Trends of Population, Silver Stocks, and Rice Prices in China, 1650–1930   /   *58*

2.1 Grain Prices in Zhili Province, 1738–1910   /   *77*

2.2 Grain Prices in Zhili Province, 1738–1910: Indexed   /   *78*

2.3 Annual Grain Prices in Zhili Province, 1738–1806   /   *79*

2.4 Prices of Coarse Grains Relative to Wheat in Zhili Province, 1738–1910   /   *81*

2.5 Seasonal Variation of Grain Prices in Zhili Province (Excluding Baoding), 1738–1910   /   *85*

2.6 Seasonal Variation of Grain Prices in Zhili Province (Including Baoding), 1738–1910   /   *87*

3.1 Reported Grain Reserves in Gansu Province, 1740–1860   /   *108*

3.2 Millet Prices in Gansu Province and Gongchang Prefecture, 1739–1864   /   *114*

3.3 Seasonal Variation in Millet Prices in Gansu Province and Gongchang Prefecture, 1739–1864   /   *120*

4.1 Adjusted Annual Averages of High and Low Prices for High-Grade Rice in Hunan Province, 1738–1858   /   *133*

4.2 Seasonal Variation in Prices of High-Grade Rice in Selected Hunan Prefectures, 1738–1858   /   *134*

4.3 Ways to Measure Correlations of High and Low Prices in Prefectures A and B   /   *141*

4.4 Correlations of High and Low Rice Prices in Selected Rice-Exporting Prefectures in Hunan, 1739–1805   /   *142*

5.1 Preceding Birth Interval by Order of Child in Daoyi and France, 1774–1873   /   *155*

5.2 Male Fertility in Daoyi by Family Relationship, 1792–1873   /   *157*

5.3 Low Grain Prices in Fengtian Prefecture, 1774–1873   /   *160*

5.4 High Grain Prices in Fengtian Prefecture, 1774–1873   /   *161*

5.5 Crude Birth Rates in Daoyi, 1774–1864   /   *164*

5.6 Crude Death Rates in Daoyi, 1771–1873   /   *165*

5.7 Birth Rates by Sex in Daoyi as a Function of Low Millet Prices, 1775–1840 / *168*

5.8 Female Births by Household Type in Daoyi in Periods of High and Low Grain Prices, 1792–1840 / *170*

5.9 Female Births by Family Relationship in Daoyi in Periods of High and Low Grain Prices, 1792–1840 / *171*

5.10 Male Births by Household Type in Daoyi in Periods of High and Low Grain Prices, 1792–1873 / *173*

5.11 Male Births by Family Relationship in Daoyi in Periods of High and Low Grain Prices, 1792–1873 / *174*

MAPS

1.1 Grain Trade Routes in Qing China / *37*

1.2 Rice Prices of Selected Prefectures in China, 1738–1740 and 1909 / *53*

2.1 Zhili Province in the Qing Period / *71*

3.1 Correlations and Variation of Low Millet Prices in Gansu Province, 1739–1864 / *116*

4.1 Qing Dynasty Hunan / *129*

4.2 Correlations of Annual Price Differences for High-Grade Rice in Qing Dynasty Hunan / *138*

8.1 Ningbo and Its Hinterland, ca. 1930 / *248*

9.1 Jiangsu Province, 1935 / *273*

10.1 Approximate Map of Shandong's Regional Capital Markets, 1911–1937 / *297*

WEIGHTS AND MEASURES

dan: a measure of weight equal to 100 *jin*, with local variation.

jin (or *catty*): a measure of weight, normally equal to 1.3 pounds, with local variation.

mu: a measure of area equal to 0.1647 acre or 0.0666 hectare, with local variation.

shi: a measure of volume for grain (1 *shi* of milled rice weighed approximately 175–195 pounds); also used interchangeably with *dan* as a measure of weight, with local variation. Gansu granaries recorded stocks in *jingshi*, a measure of volume seven-tenths as large as the *cangshi*, the standard granary measure used elsewhere in China. In Wuxi, *shi* was used to denote a weight of approximately 150 *jin*.

tael (or *liang*): the Chinese ounce, a measure of weight equal to one-sixteenth of a *jin*; also one of numerous units of account for uncoined silver money employed in China before 1932.

yuan (or *dollar*): refers to silver coinage issued in China from the late nineteenth century and to fiat money of the Republic of China following the demonetization of silver in 1935.

SOURCES: Han-sheng Chuan and Richard A. Kraus, *Mid-Ch'ing Rice Markets and Trade: An Essay in Price History* (Cambridge, 1975), pp. 79–98; Thomas G. Rawski, *Economic Growth in Prewar China* (Berkeley and Los Angeles, 1989), p. xv.

PREFACE

This volume is based on papers and discussions from the Workshop and Conference on Economic Methods for Chinese Historical Research sponsored by the Henry Luce Foundation, the American Council of Learned Societies, and the National Science Foundation and held in Honolulu, Hawaii, in January 1987 and Oracle, Arizona, in January 1988. In the 1987 workshop, a number of economists who work in economic history were asked to prepare seminars on broad subjects, such as choice, long-term trends, macroeconomics, international and interregional issues, and economic institutions, for which the historian-participants had prepared by doing assigned readings. The fact that none of the economists, except Thomas G. Rawski, were China specialists added an important comparative dimension to the proceedings. The economists were Jon Cohen, University of Toronto; Peter H. Lindert, University of California, Davis; Donald N. McCloskey, University of Iowa; and Richard Sutch, University of California, Berkeley. The papers they delivered at this meeting, together with additional material on monetary and labor economics, will be published separately in a volume entitled *Economics and the Historian*.

The same group of historians and economists convened at the 1988 conference. This time, however, the historians presented their papers, which they had written on the basis of guidelines and suggestions from the previous year, and the economists served as the discussants. In addition to those participants whose papers are included in this volume, I-chun Fan, Bozhong Li, and Guangyuan Zhou also attended the conference. Their participation and the contributions of the economists are gratefully acknowledged by the editors and authors of this volume.

We would also like to express our gratitude to Julius Rubin, who helped us start the whole project, to two anonymous referees for their insightful reviews of the entire manuscript, to David Arkush, Philip Kuhn, Susan Naquin, Evelyn S. Rawski, and William T. Rowe for their assistance in revising the introductory essay, to Shu-jen Yeh for helping to prepare the glossary and the bibliography, and to Eleanor Bennett, Sarah S. Fought, William Karunaratne, Debbie Kwolek, Patty Huchber, Sharon Wetzel, and Debra Ziolkowski for their invaluable efforts behind the scenes.

CONTRIBUTORS

Lynda S. Bell is Assistant Professor of History, University of California, Riverside.
Loren Brandt is Associate Professor of Economics, University of Toronto.
Cameron Campbell is with the Graduate Group in Demography, University of Pennsylvania.
Emily Honig is Associate Professor of History, Yale University.
James Lee is Associate Professor of History, California Institute of Technology.
Lillian M. Li is Professor of History, Swarthmore College.
Susan Mann is Professor of History, University of California, Davis.
Peter C. Perdue is Associate Professor of History, Massachusetts Institute of Technology.
Kenneth Pomeranz is Assistant Professor of History, University of California, Irvine.
Thomas G. Rawski is Professor of Economics and History, University of Pittsburgh.
Barbara Sands is Associate Professor of Economics, University of Arizona.
Guofu Tan is Assistant Professor of Economics, University of British Columbia.
Yeh-chien Wang is Professor of History, Kent State University.
R. Bin Wong is Associate Professor of History, University of California, Irvine.

Introduction: Chinese History in Economic Perspective

Thomas G. Rawski and Lillian M. Li

Economics and economists tend to bring out strong emotions both in the general public and among (noneconomist) scholars. How often does one encounter the sentiment, "If economists are so smart, how come they couldn't predict such-and-such [the latest round of inflation, the October '87 stock market crash, etc.]?" Economics has always been a controversial field of study, and economists often exhibit a strong professional affinity for contentiousness among themselves. Yet, while society might conceivably get along without economists, it would be difficult to imagine a world in which economics did not play a role, even the mythical world of Robinson Crusoe. Nor can historians avoid the economic aspects of history even when they would like to do so. Embedded in all their common notions of how history has developed are views, conscious or unconscious, of economic forces: the prosperity of the Italian city-states prompted the cultural efflorescence of the Renaissance, the Chinese had a rural revolution because the peasants were so poor, Europeans conducted oceanic explorations because they needed spices, and so forth. But fundamentally, historians need to know about the material side of history because they are concerned with human welfare, social development, and national histories. The classic definition of economics, after all, is that it studies the allocation of scarce resources among alternative uses. Therefore, subjects such as agriculture, money, industry, and trade compel historians' interest for a variety of commendable reasons.

It is our contention, however, that the study of such subjects in economic history has not always employed a true economic approach or perspective, at least among historians of China. This book is dedicated to the idea that the history of China's economy has been written many times in many ways but that the economic history of China has not yet been written. This, indeed, is not such a history either, but the essays in this volume are intended to illustrate how economic history is not the same as the history of an economy, and how an economic perspective involves more than an interest in some economic topic. Scholarship on China has excelled in studying the economy of China, but has barely begun to do so with a true economic perspective. The fundamental objective of this volume is to delineate and illustrate the potential contribution of systematically applying an economic approach to the study of China's economic history.

STATE OF THE FIELD

Traditional Chinese scholarship did not neglect economic topics. Indeed, in the standard dynastic histories, sections on population, land taxes, and money, for example, assumed a prominent position. Local histories also treated these topics, as well as listing or describing local products, grain storage, and the like. A well-functioning economy was the hallmark of a successful dynastic regime, a visible sign of the harmony of heaven, earth, and man. Economics and morality were linked; a prosperous economy was a sign of the essential morality of the ruler. The model of the economy, like that of society, was based on the notions of harmony and stability, and not on the desirability of growth and change. The golden age of the past was one in which men plowed the fields and women wove cloth. Wars and famines signified the disruption of stability. The goal was to restore the status quo ante, the golden age, not to surpass it, because it could not be surpassed.

In recent decades, a different paradigm, that of Chinese Marxism, has dominated Chinese scholarship. The three broad areas that receive the most attention from historians in the People's Republic of China are land tenure, foreign imperialism, and the "sprouts of capitalism." In the post-Mao era, the "Asiatic mode of production" was added to this list. Studies of land tenure are closely linked to issues of servitude and subordination among China's peasantry in each period of history. Studies of foreign imperialism stress the plundering of China's economic resources by Western powers and Japan in the nineteenth and twentieth centuries, and the obstacles to the development of a modern economy posed by the unequal treaties. Studies of the "sprouts of capitalism" focus on the signs of development in China's late imperial, or early modern, economy (roughly since the mid-sixteenth century), such as the expansion of handicraft production and the freeing of labor in the countryside, but the line of interpretation has shifted from time to time—sometimes emphasizing the sprouts themselves and, at other times, the smothering of the sprouts. The revival of interest in Marx's idea of the Asiatic mode of production highlighted the dilemma of Chinese Marxist historians: how to fit Chinese history into the scheme of world history. Previously discredited by party historians because it tended to suggest that Chinese development did not fit into a unilinear world pattern, the Asiatic mode attracted renewed attention in the 1980s in part because it helped legitimize China's recent economic policies, which may seem to transgress the stages of history normally posited in the Marxist scheme of history.

How one evaluates the Marxist scholarship on China is to a certain extent a function of one's ideological persuasion. Certainly the Marxist framework provides a compelling agenda for research. Critics think, and sometimes dare to say, that the agenda is limited and that the questions posed to some extent determine the outcome. But this criticism could be leveled at any paradigm or framework. What is striking to us, however, is the extent to which a materialist or economic interpretation of history has essentially transformed itself into social history. It is the struggle between social forces and the conflict of social classes that seem to determine the economic stage of history rather than the economic forces that determine the social. Marxist historiography has stood Marxism on its head.

Substituting modernization theory for Confucian or Marxist theory, the postwar generation of Western historians has also sought reasons for China's economic backwardness in modern times. American scholarship in the 1950s and 1960s tended to focus on treaty-port developments and the introduction of Western trade and technology into China, implying that contact with the West, even on unfavorable terms, offered an opportunity for positive change that was missed.[1] A second wave of scholarship has focused on the role of entrepreneurship and bureaucratic leadership (or the lack of it) in the nineteenth and twentieth centuries, finding in them a major reason for China's "failure to modernize" along Western lines, even when exposed to Western influence.[2] In a similar vein, scholarship in Taiwan has emphasized the institutional and bureaucratic aspects of China's economic development in the last two centuries.

In an innovative and influential interpretive history, Mark Elvin tried to break away from the yoke of Western periodization schemes to show that China's history followed a different "pattern," in which a medieval economic revolution led to a "high-level equilibrium trap" that did not prevent further growth, but did impede significant change—"economic development without technological change."[3] Yet like other Western scholars, and indeed like the Chinese scholars, his underlying preoccupation is with explaining China's poor economic performance in modern times.

Like Elvin, recent Western scholarship has tended to search back beyond

---

1. E.g., Chi-ming Hou, *Foreign Investment and Economic Development in China, 1840–1937* (Cambridge, Mass., 1965).

2. E.g., Albert Feuerwerker, *China's Early Industrialization: Sheng Hsuan-huai (1862–1874) and Mandarin Enterprise* (Cambridge, Mass., 1958); Yen-p'ing Hao, *The Comprador in Nineteenth-Century China: Bridge between East and West* (Cambridge, Mass., 1970); Wellington K. K. Chan, *Merchants, Mandarins, and Modern Enterprise in Late Ch'ing China* (Cambridge, Mass., 1977); and Sherman Cochran, *Big Business in China: Sino-Foreign Rivalry in the Cigarette Industry, 1890–1930* (Cambridge, Mass., 1980).

3. Mark Elvin, *The Pattern of the Chinese Past* (Stanford, 1973), Part Three, pp. 203–319.

the troubled modern period to find strengths and weaknesses in the Chinese economy before the nineteenth century that might help to explain its behavior after the Opium War. These studies have focused on the role of the traditional Chinese state in shaping the economy, particularly in the eighteenth century. Building on Ping-ti Ho's work on China's population,[4] these studies have, on the one hand, emphasized the positive role of the state in encouraging the settlement of undeveloped and frontier areas[5] and in maintaining granary stocks to stabilize prices and prevent famines[6] while, on the other hand, stressing the essential limitations of state power. Yeh-chien Wang's work on Qing land tax, Madeleine Zelin's work on tax surcharges, and Susan Mann's work on the merchants' role in collecting commercial taxes all tend to show how the Qing and Republican governments were unable, and sometimes unwilling, to capture a larger share of the country's wealth for their own purposes.[7]

Some American scholarship, as well as some Japanese scholarship, has shared the Chinese interest in the primacy of social forces in governing economic history. For example, standing on different sides of an ideological divide, Ramon H. Myers and Philip C. C. Huang have disagreed sharply on the extent to which the land tenure system in North China produced social inequalities.[8] The work of William T. Rowe and others on the growth of Chinese cities tends to emphasize the strength of commercial developments that took place largely outside the sphere of direct government influence.[9] And G. William Skinner's influential work on marketing and his macroregions paradigm both stress the essential independence of economic activity from political trends as embodied in the dynastic cycle.[10]

Although there are notable exceptions not captured in this broad summary, it is striking how American scholarship on Chinese economic history,

---

4. Ho, *Studies on the Population of China, 1368–1953* (Cambridge, Mass., 1959).

5. E.g., Peter C. Perdue, *Exhausting the Earth: State and Peasant in Hunan, 1500–1850* (Cambridge, Mass., 1987).

6. Pierre-Etienne Will, *Bureaucratie et famine en Chine au 18e siècle* (Paris, 1980), and Pierre-Etienne Will and R. Bin Wong, *Nourish the People: The State Civilian Granary System in China, 1650–1850* (Ann Arbor, Mich., 1991).

7. Yeh-chien Wang, *Land Taxation in Imperial China, 1750–1911* (Cambridge, Mass., 1973); Madeleine Zelin, *The Magistrate's Tael: Rationalizing Fiscal Reform in Eighteenth-Century Ch'ing China* (Berkeley and Los Angeles, 1984); and Susan Mann, *Local Merchants and the Chinese Bureaucracy, 1750–1850* (Stanford, 1987).

8. Ramon H. Myers, *The Chinese Peasant Economy: Agricultural Development in Hopei and Shantung, 1890–1949* (Cambridge, Mass., 1970) and Philip C. C. Huang, *The Peasant Economy and Social Change in North China* (Stanford, 1985).

9. William T. Rowe, *Hankow: Commerce and Society in a Chinese City, 1796–1889* (Stanford, 1984).

10. See especially "Introduction: Urban Development in Imperial China" and "Regional Urbanization in Nineteenth-Century China," both in G. William Skinner, ed., *The City in Late Imperial China* (Stanford, 1977).

somewhat like PRC scholarship, has really revolved around social and institutional history. In fact, the bulk of the work concerning the Chinese economy has been done, not by those trained in economics, but rather by social historians, anthropologists, and others. Most of these scholars—including some of the contributors to this volume—have not in the past made regular and systematic use of economic analysis to inform and structure their inquiries. In part this may be due to ideological or disciplinary predisposition, and in part it may reflect the types of sources available for the study of economic history. Traditional official records are strong on bureaucratic institutions and practices but weak in quantitative material. Even so, the tendency for researchers to neglect economic approaches in writing the history of China's economy may reflect their limited appreciation of how the economic perspective can sharpen an analysis of the historical record.

In the 1960s similar criticisms were raised by a group of "new economic historians" against the work of the earlier generation of economic historians in the West. Feeling that the traditional economic histories of Europe and the United States overemphasized the description of legal and other institutions, the new generation advocated the application of economic theory and quantitative methods to historical scholarship. With the advent of Robert Fogel and Stanley Engerman's study of slavery in the American South, and the ensuing controversies, the Cliometric revolution reached its heyday and, some have said, began to peak.[11] Nonetheless, a more quantitative and analytic approach continues to prevail in the leading journals of economic history.

Our goal is not to champion the introduction of Cliometrics into Chinese economic history but rather to advocate adopting a more self-conscious economic perspective that may or may not involve quantitative analysis. Our belief is that the use of economic theory can illuminate issues that might otherwise prove inaccessible. In addition, the contributors to this volume have reached the surprising conclusion that applying economic analysis to historical topics often enlarges the interpretive significance of phenomena that historians, and not economists, are best qualified to comprehend.

ECONOMIC THEORY

What do we mean by an *economic perspective*? We mean the application of *economic theory* and *methods* to the study of historical topics.

Classical economic theory, as developed in the West, rests on a number of key concepts, which some call principles and others may call assumptions. The most fundamental of these is the concept of *choice*. Donald N. McCloskey

---

11. Robert Fogel and Stanley Engerman, *Time on the Cross: The Economics of American Negro Slavery* (Boston, 1974). The development of the new economic history is discussed in Alexander J. Field, ed., *The Future of Economic History* (Boston, 1987), in the editor's introductory essay.

defines economics as "the study of human choice under constraints."[12] Income and wealth, the conventional measures of economic well-being, define the extent of choice available to consumers. In most economies, choice is exercised primarily in markets, which offer opportunities to sell commodities and human skills in return for income, which can be translated, again through the marketplace, into consumpion goods. Prices signal the rates at which any individual's resources of money, time, and skill can be converted into desired commodities or services. For the economist, prices demand attention because they offer precise measures of both choice and constraint that (important for the historian) are often recorded in great detail. Markets and prices thus emerge from the centrality of choice as natural focal points for historical inquiry.

Rationality is a closely related concept. Rationality means that people are motivated by self-interest, primarily pecuniary. Economic rationality means that individuals, families, and organizations have well-defined ideas about how various opportunities affect their well-being and that choice rests upon comparison of the cost of available alternatives. Economic rationality suggests that people know how to calculate costs and benefits and that they are free to act according to their choices.

The centrality of choice in economics leads to the concept of *opportunity cost*, which defines the cost of a specific action in terms of the value of alternative options rather than actual monetary outlay. Or, in McCloskey's words, "choosing one thing means giving up another, because things are scarce, constrained."[13] In the economists' view, the cost of education, for example, includes the value of income-earning opportunities forsaken by the student as well as the actual tuition she or he pays. The opportunity cost of moving to a new location must comprehend the value of wages lost while on the road as well as transportation costs. Opportunity cost is quite literally the value of "the road not taken."

Much of economic analysis revolves around the concept of *equilibrium*, which portrays economic circumstance as the outcome of a balance of conflicting forces. Market price is determined through bidding, a process of organized struggle between buyers, who seek to force the price to the lowest possible level, and sellers, whose interest is served by attaining the highest possible price. Market forces ceaselessly push price and quantity in the direction of equilibrium. If demand exceeds supply at the current price, anxious buyers will bid up the price, simultaneously curbing demand and attracting additional supplies. If price is so high that supply exceeds demand, sellers' prices will be bid down, leading toward the balance between desired purchases and sales that characterizes an equilibrium position.

---

12. McCloskey, "The Economics of Choice" (Unpublished paper prepared for the Workshop on Economic Methods for Chinese Historical Research, Honolulu, January 1987), p. 1.

13. Ibid., 1.

Together with the idea of *entry and exit*, which simply maintains that productive resources, including human labor, will abandon occupations offering low rewards and gravitate toward the areas of greatest opportunity, the economists' equilibrium notion offers a valuable tool for historical researchers. Even though the interaction of supply and demand in particular markets may not leave clear tracks in the historical record, the qualitative consequences of changes in equilibrium positions often generate shifts in the direction of resource flows that will not escape the historian's notice. As D. K. Lieu has observed, businessmen in China (and elsewhere) "are ready to clear out at any time" if they see better prospects in another trade. The appearance of new businesses and the abandonment of old trades thus become a sensitive barometer of relative profitability in different lines of endeavor.[14] Similarly, if large numbers of workers migrate from North China to Manchuria, or from the rust belt to California, no statistical analysis is required to verify the existence of regional differences in economic opportunity.

OBJECTIONS TO ECONOMIC THEORY

When thus presented as a series of abstract concepts, economic theory often provokes the deepest skepticism, if not outright hostility, among noneconomists.

Some have charged that these ideas of neoclassical Western economics are not universal principles or absolute truths but are, instead, a series of assumptions that are largely a matter of perspective or even faith, not susceptible to proof or argument. Moreover, these ideas are culturally and historically specific, a product of a particular phase of Western history, and are not universally applicable. Some, like Karl Polanyi, have argued that these ideas themselves have shaped people's behavior and the development of economic institutions, especially markets, that they have been, in short, not descriptive but prescriptive.[15]

Others object to economic theory because they believe it to rest on a view of human nature that is self-fulfilling, possibly erroneous, and certainly repugnant. "Rational economic man as a reflection of human nature is a fiction.... But it is a powerful fiction, and it becomes less and less a fiction as more and more of our institutions get pervaded by its assumptions and other paths are closed," writes one recent critic.[16] Adam Smith's notion that individuals pursuing their own self-interest are "led by an invisible hand" toward improving the society and economy in which they live is difficult to reconcile with more flattering views of human nature and human good.

---

14. Lieu, *The Growth and Industrialization of Shanghai* (Shanghai, 1936), p. 103.
15. Karl Polanyi, *The Great Transformation* (Boston, 1957).
16. Barry Schwartz, *The Battle for Human Nature: Science, Morality and Modern Life* (New York, 1986), p. 325.

There are those who believe that the classical economists' view of human nature is not only incorrect but that it can be replaced by a superior form of morality. Amitai Etzioni, for example, argues for the replacement of utilitarianism with ethical principles that stress intention, not result, for the replacement of individual calculation with collective rationality, and for the replacement of economic rationality with values and emotions.[17]

Most others who object to economic theory do so on the grounds that it is empirically invalid. They say that simple observation will reveal that not everyone is motivated by monetary self-interest above all other considerations and that the notion of economic rationality must therefore be false. The economists reply that economic rationality need not imply ceaseless calculation of cost and benefit by households and businesses, nor must economic decisions rest exclusively on financial considerations. Although economists often construct theories on the assumption that individuals and business firms pursue maximum financial rewards, the notion of rationality encompasses the possibility that a desire for prestige or perhaps stability, as well as monetary gain, may motivate economic behavior. The recent debate about the "moral economy of the peasant" highlights this controversy, with James C. Scott arguing that in peasant societies the dominant motive is survival and security, so that risk minimization, not profit maximization, is the principal goal.[18] Economists respond that peasant rationality is essentially no different from anyone else's rationality and that avoidance of risk is not inconsistent with rational calculation.

Critics also protest that rational choice implies perfect information and intelligence. But what if someone does not have all the information needed, or what if he or she is stupid or, worse still, lazy? I could increase my financial resources if I thought about my investments all the time, but I do not choose to use my time that way. The opportunity cost, measured in work or recreational time lost, is simply too high. But economists reply that decisions based on limited information and crude calculations may in fact reflect rational behavior. After all, the time and expense required to collect further information or to conduct detailed studies of opportunity costs may outweigh the anticipated benefits of prolonged search and analysis.

Finally, skeptics reject the idea that people actually have a choice in economic matters and are free to enter into or exit from economic activities as some kind of economists' wonderland, full of Mad Hatters. Surely, in real life people are not always free to change jobs, change residences, or change investments according to the dictates of rational calculation.[19] Custom, law,

---

17. Amitai Etzioni, *The Moral Dimension: Toward a New Economics* (New York, 1988).

18. James C. Scott, *The Moral Economy of the Peasant: Rebellion and Subsistence in Southeast Asia* (New Haven, 1976).

19. The Nobel Prize–winning economist George J. Stigler tells the story of an economist who carefully decided how far from the city to locate his country home by efficiently balancing the

social practice and prejudice, inertia, and any number of restrictions on behavior exist today and were even more decisive in premodern times.

Economists, however, recognize that market activity and price formation do not occur in a social or cultural vacuum. They see the institutional arrangements that circumscribe and encapsulate economic activity—the household, legal structures, customary market procedures, forms of contract arrangement, business organization, even ideology and morality—as constraining economic activity along with limitations on the stock of physical and financial resources.[20] But economists regard institutions as flexible rather than immutable. If costs exceed benefits, economists anticipate change (perhaps gradual) in the relations between individuals and social institutions, as well as between buyers and sellers. The post–World War II increase in female employment in the United States represents such an event, with the unorganized response of millions of women to altered labor market conditions leading to changes in marriage practices, family size, child rearing, educational patterns, eating habits, and many other aspects of life long regarded as determined by custom and tradition rather than the marketplace.

The clash between economists and noneconomists is perhaps best embodied in the economists' favorite term, *ceteris paribus* (literally, all other things being equal). While economists will acknowledge the importance of noneconomic factors, those bothersome factors are generally left in the background of their theories and models. Let others study politics, law, social class, injustice, and the like. Models can be pure and "elegant," a favorite expression of economists, because all those other factors can be held constant or set aside. And since such factors are not easily quantifiable, how much more convenient to leave them out. Quantification of the nonquantitative is best left to the "soft" social scientists—the sociologists, the political scientists, and the historians.[21]

It is ceteris paribus that allows economists to be optimists. Although economics is called the dismal science, in fact economists tend to maintain a rosy view of the world controlled by an invisible hand. If only the government and others would stay out of it, the rational response to opportunity could produce growth and a better life for everyone. In the field of Chinese studies, the

---

number of fresh eggs he could get against the number of friends who would still be willing to visit him. In his review of Stigler's memoirs, Robert Krulwich dryly comments, "Here, I say, is why more and more people ignore economists." *New York Times Book Review*, Oct. 23, 1988.

20. Jon Cohen, "Institutions and Economic Analysis" (Unpublished paper prepared for the Workshop on Economic Methods for Chinese Historical Research, Honolulu, January 1987).

21. In all fairness, it must be said that economists tend to recognize their professional weaknesses and know how to laugh at them. Evidence for this can be found in the rich store of economist jokes that end with the punch line, "Assume..."

optimism of the economists stands in marked contrast to the gloomy prognostications of the political scientists. The Chinese economic reforms of the 1980s inspired great hope among most economists, who tended to see the possibility for continued growth and change, while political scientists warned of bureaucratic competition, political backlash, social discontent, and other dangers, which they said might thwart the reforms.

THEORETICAL REASONING

The tendency of many economists to sweep noneconomic factors into the dustbin of ceteris paribus is indeed regrettable. Recently, however, a few economic theorists themselves have begun to question the basic assumptions of the approaches that have dominated their field. The study of macroeconomics has been described as "a religious battlefield," where the most fundamental beliefs are being challenged.[22] George A. Akerlof, who has contributed to this battle, has said

> The unwritten rules that only *economic phenomena* be considered in economic models, with agents as individualistic, selfish maximizers, restrict the range of economic theory and in some cases even cause the economics profession to appear peculiarly absurd—because, without relaxation of these rules, certain *almost indisputable* economic facts, such as the existence of involuntary unemployment, become inconsistent with economic theory.... Individualistic maximizing behavior constitutes an assumption that sharply restricts the domain of possible economic models. It is an assumption that turns out to be surprisingly restrictive.[23]

While recognizing the importance of noneconomic factors in governing economic behavior, a theorist such as Akerlof is nevertheless concerned primarily with perfecting an economic model, albeit one that he considers reasonably consistent with reality. For some economic theorists, it might be said, the model *is* the reality. Many economists tend to value work that contributes to the building of economic theory and to dismiss the study of real data as mere "empirical work." Economic historians, however, have argued for the importance of economic history to the development of theory.[24] It is our contention that just as economists need to test their theories against historical reality, historians can and should enrich their work through the use of economic theory, as well as economic methods.

Economic theory can serve several purposes for historians. At a practical

---

22. An insight attributed to Mark Kuperberg of the Economics Department, Swarthmore College, whom we also thank for the reference to Akerlof's work (see n. 23).

23. George A. Akerlof, *An Economic Theorist's Book of Tales: Essays That Entertain the Consequences of New Assumptions in Economic Theory* (Cambridge, 1984), p. 2.

24. The contributions that historical studies can make to economic theory are outlined in essays in William M. Parker, ed., *Economic History and the Modern Economist* (Oxford and New York, 1986).

level, some knowledge of economic theory can provide essential context for interpreting evidence that would otherwise be misunderstood. Upon learning of the small share of imported grain (and more generally, of foreign trade) in the economic life of late Qing China, the historian (and even the economist)[25] naturally assumes that foreign trade must have played a small role in China's economy, especially in the interior. But this assumption overlooks the economists' "marginal principle," which teaches that market prices are determined by the behavior of "marginal" buyers and sellers, who are on the brink of indifference between patronizing the local market or doing business elsewhere. If the demand for and supply of a particular commodity is "inelastic," meaning the amount people will purchase or sell is relatively inflexible in the face of changes in market price (as in the case of heating oil, milk, or insulin), then small changes in quantity may lead to relatively large changes in the price. Alternatively, if the demand for a commodity is elastic, small changes in price may lead to relatively large changes in the quantities people desire to buy or sell. Thus shifts in the behavior of marginal buyers or sellers can generate large changes in the prices or quantities available to all buyers and sellers.

Loren Brandt's study of Yangzi rice markets nicely illustrates these ideas. Despite the small volume of overseas rice trade, Brandt finds that by the end of the nineteenth century, rice prices in interior markets, like Chongqing and Changsha, were quickly affected by fluctuations in Asian grain markets.[26] This means that the daily lives of rice farmers, rice consumers, would-be rice farmers, grain merchants and shippers, the families and suppliers of these agents, their customers and suppliers, and others in interior regions, like Sichuan and Hunan, were significantly affected by what seem at first glance to be minor economic phenomena. Brandt's study shows how actions in apparently insignificant components of an economy can produce significant reactions, even in distant places, through the medium of market forces. Many people can verify this "principle" from their personal memories of the oil crisis of the early 1970s, when rising energy costs affected travel habits, auto designs, building codes, and so forth in the United States, Japan, and even oil exporters, like Canada.

The economists' campaign to win the minds, if not the hearts, of historians can probably not succeed merely by reciting economic principles as abstractions or immutable laws. More persuasive, perhaps, is the reasoning that is derived from economic theory. Economic theory can serve as a lever for increasing the power of a given set of data and a tool for squeezing as much meaning and implication from it as possible. For economists, economic

---

25. Thomas G. Rawski, "China's Republican Economy: An Introduction" (Toronto, 1978), pp. 2–5.

26. Loren Brandt, "Chinese Agriculture and the International Economy, 1870s–1930s: A Reassessment," *Explorations in Economic History* 22 (1985): 168–93.

theory will suggest a story, or sequence of implications, about sets of initial economic circumstances or facts. The predictions obtained from theoretical reasoning can range from simple propositions about the impact on relative prices of meat and fish of the Pope's decision to end the Catholic tradition of meatless Fridays to Karl Marx's grand vision of capitalist decline. The stories told by economic historians fall between these two extremes, typically using short chains of reasoning based on economic concepts to obtain predictions that can be tested with historical evidence.[27] Their method involves selecting a model, or analytic framework, based on assumptions that appear to fit the historical circumstances under investigation, studying the logical implications of the model in search of testable conclusions, and comparing these predictions, as well as the model's assumptions, with concrete evidence from historical sources.

Several examples can illustrate the value of theory-based analysis as a source of hypotheses for the historian to investigate. Consider the case of railway development, which, by reducing transport costs and transit time, creates new opportunities for trade among cities and between town and countryside. Construction of a new railway line should raise the price that farmers receive for fruit crops, which now gain unprecedented access to urban markets, and lower the cost to farmers of urban factory goods. Terms of trade (price of interregional "exports" divided by price of imports) should improve for both townspeople and farmers. But China's new railways became the focus of military strife among competing political groups, bringing death and destruction to hapless farmers caught between rival armies.

Lacking detailed information concerning changes in local production or the damage inflicted by military operations, how can the historian begin to determine the economic consequences of railway construction in rural China? Here is where recourse to economic theory, with its capacity to reveal causal links that may provide unexpected opportunities to examine the consequences of historical events, begins to display its potential. The concept of entry and exit immediately directs the researcher's attention to changes in population density and migration patterns as indicators of altered patterns of economic opportunity in regions affected by railway development. The economic theory of rent implies that trends in land rents and land prices can reveal whether, from the viewpoint of local farmers, the opportunities created by railway development outweighed the damage caused by periodic military incursions and, if so, by how much.[28] Another perspective

27. Donald N. McCloskey, *Econometric History* (Houndsmills, Eng., 1987), chap. 2.
28. The idea of using trends in land values to appraise the impact of transport innovation comes from Roger Ransom, "Social Returns from Public Transport Investment: A Case Study of the Ohio Canal," *Journal of Political Economy* 78 (1970): 1041–60. For Chinese evidence, see Ernest P. Liang, *China: Railways and Agricultural Development, 1875–1935* (Chicago, 1982), pp. 141–44.

on the consequences of railway expansion comes from Thomas R. Gottschang's finding that the coming of the railway apparently slowed the pace of out-migration from North China, despite reducing the cost of travel to and from Manchuria. Apparently the increased opportunity arising from proximity to rail transport outweighed the reduced cost of migration in the eyes of farm families in Hebei and Shandong.[29]

Further examples of how historians can benefit from thinking in terms of economic theory arise from applying the concept of *market integration*, also known as the law of one price, which postulates that the universal desire to buy cheap and sell dear attracts buyers to low-price markets and sellers to high-price outlets, thus squeezing interregional price differences toward the minimum necessitated by the costs of shipping goods between separate markets. Market integration is made possible by good and cheap transportation, adequate information about costs, and efficient commercial institutions. Consumers, as well as economists, like market integration because it gives them access to a wide range of products at low prices. Producers value market integration because it expands the actual and potential market for their goods. Historians should also be keenly interested in market integration not simply for what markets show about links among various segments of the economy but also because, as the work of Skinner copiously demonstrates, analysis of marketing relationships may affect a host of political and social factors ranging from taxation to marriage and even language.[30]

Here again, a dose of theory can help the historian to leap over documentary lacunae, as well as overcome skepticism about the heuristic value of economic principles or assumptions. Did agricultural wages, productivity, and incomes rise in China during the decades prior to World War II? To answer this question, one would hope to find reliable information on trends in agricultural production and farmers' incomes. Unfortunately, the information available to the researcher is both thin and of questionable validity. Wage data for nonfarm occupations, however, are relatively abundant. Can theory offer a useful link between agricultural circumstances and nonfarm wages?

Unskilled workers in such nonfarm industries as cotton mills and coal mines often came directly from rural villages. China's cotton and coal magnates were profit-seeking entrepreneurs operating in fiercely competitive markets that offered little chance to "pass along" rising costs in the form of higher prices. They had every incentive to keep wages as low as possible. Unless forced to raise wages by government fiat or union pressure, employers sought to avoid raising wages except when it was necessary to assure an

29. Thomas R. Gottschang, "Economic Change, Disasters, and Migration: The Historical Case of Manchuria," *Economic Development and Cultural Change* 35, no. 3 (1987): 461–90.
30. Skinner, "Marketing and Social Structure in Rural China," in three parts, *Journal of Asian Studies* 24, no. 1 (1964): 3–43; 24, no. 2 (1965): 195–228; and 24, no. 3 (1965): 363–99.

adequate work force. As long as rural labor incomes remain stable, mines and mills can attract workers without raising wages. If rural incomes begin to increase, mines and mills will find their labor supply drying up unless they offer higher wages to village recruits. Under these circumstances, a pattern of rising real wages for unskilled workers in China's cotton and coal industries can be taken as evidence of rising real incomes in the rural regions that supplied miners and mill hands and also in more remote areas linked through labor markets to the immediate supplying regions. Because interregional wage differentials induced large numbers of Chinese workers to cross provincial and even international boundaries in pursuit of economic opportunity, evidence of rising real wages for unskilled workers in the widely dispersed cotton and coal industries furnishes strong support for the view that the rising trend of labor income was national in scope.[31]

Underlying this reasoning is the economists' conception, or model, of how markets, in this case labor markets, function. Textile mills or coal mines located in city A customarily obtain unskilled workers (perhaps indirectly through the agency of labor recruiters) from rural areas B and C. The mills or mines pay wages that are higher than typical farm incomes. This premium compensates workers for the cost of journeying to an unfamiliar locale, separation from their families, and the risk of industrial accidents. If farm incomes in B or C begin to rise, mill or mine wages will look less attractive to potential recruits, who will become less willing to leave their villages. The mill or mine owners (or labor recruiters) can look elsewhere for job candidates or raise wages to encourage more volunteers from the customary locations. If young villagers elsewhere are willing to move in response to economic opportunity, nonfarm employers may prefer the cheap option of seeking recruits from alternate rural locations D and E by offering the standard wage. If the rise in farm incomes is a local phenomenon confined to B and C, this approach will prove successful in damping upward pressure on nonfarm wages for unskilled labor. If, on the other hand, farm incomes are increasing across a wide range of localities from which mills and mines might seek to recruit new workers, nonfarm employers will find themselves unable to maintain an adequate work force without raising the wages offered to unskilled recruits. If farm incomes—which provide the financial alternative against which potential miners and textile workers measure the benefit of leaving their home villages—continue to increase, wages paid by mines and mills will rise too.

Thus, once it is assumed that labor markets function in the manner specified, with employers seeking cheap labor supplies and villagers willing to migrate in response to premium wages, the theory of market integration, here

---

31. Thomas G. Rawski, *Economic Growth in Prewar China* (Berkeley and Los Angeles, 1989), chap. 6.

applied to the market for unskilled labor, encourages the historian to perceive the trend of unskilled workers' earnings in coal mines and cotton mills as a barometer of farm incomes, not only in the workers' home villages but also in other villages where mines and mills could easily have sought fresh recruits. The link between farm and nonfarm wages is not automatic. Application of this reasoning requires the historian to determine that the wage data pertain to occupations open to village recruits and to verify the historical relevance of the behavior patterns postulated in the framework, or model, outlined above. If these tasks can be accomplished, economic theory permits the historian to construct a powerful and revealing analysis of phenomena that are simply not amenable to study through conventional methods.

The theory of market integration can also help to estimate interest rates in historical situations. Interest rates are of historical significance because they are part of broader economic cycles, because they tell us something about trends in the economy, and because they influence individual choices between current and future consumption. Yet interest rates are difficult for historians to discern. Consequently Donald N. McCloskey and John Nash's suggestion that interest rates are inherent in the seasonal fluctuation of grain prices is useful for Chinese historians, since the Chinese historical record contains a great deal of detailed information about grain prices. Whoever holds grain harvested in autumn for resale or consumption in the spring sacrifices the use of the money that could be obtained by immediate sale of the autumn harvest. Whoever loans money during the winter months makes an identical sacrifice. In other words, the opportunity cost of holding grain is the cash that could be obtained from autumn sales, plus whatever interest could be earned by that cash over the winter. The law of one price, here applied to the market for money, insists that, over a suitably long number of years, the earnings from assigning funds to holding grain must match the returns from assigning funds to holding debtors' promissory notes. Thus, McCloskey and Nash explain, interest rates, and the variation of interest rates across time and space, can be calculated from the seasonal rise in grain prices that begins with the annual post-harvest trough and ends at the seasonal preharvest peak.[32]

To recognize the importance of market integration is one thing; to define and measure it is another. As some of the essays in this volume show, even with good price data, it may be difficult to discern whether and when true market integration existed in history. Even in today's world of data collection and widespread information networks, economists still have difficulty establishing what actually constitutes market integration.[33] In antitrust cases, the

32. Donald N. McCloskey and John Nash, "Corn at Interest: The Extent and Cost of Grain Storage in Medieval England," *American Economic Review* 74, no. 1 (1984): 174–87.

33. For one suggestion, see George J. Stigler and Robert A. Sherwin, "The Extent of the Market," *Journal of Law and Economics* 28 (1985): 555–85.

appropriate definition of a market includes both the "product market" (i.e., whether the product has reasonable substitutes) and the geographic market. When Mobil Corporation tried to acquire the Marathon Oil Company in 1981, Marathon brought an antitrust suit against Mobil. Mobil attempted to demonstrate that the relevant market for oil was nationwide and that hence the merger would have only a slight impact on prices. For Marathon, on the other hand, the task was to demonstrate that the markets for oil were regional and that hence the merger was likely to have a great impact on prices. Marathon won the case because, in the words of the court, "the persistence of price differentials in various areas of the nation demonstrates that motor gasoline does not move from area to area in response to price changes easily or as readily as Mobil asserts. Rather, they indicate that the relevant geographic market for motor gasoline is something less than nationwide."[34] Here the debate among lawyers and economists centered, not on the theoretical importance of market integration, but on exactly how to define and measure it.

ECONOMIC METHODS AND THE DATA PROBLEM

The second aspect of an economic perspective or approach involves *method*. Methodology in economics can mean different things. Broadly defined, it can mean a way of thinking or a general approach to hypothesis testing or problem solving. More narrowly conceived, it can refer to particular statistical techniques: the Gini coefficient, the Chow test, and so forth. Although economics often involves the use of numbers and quantification of some sort, its approach is not absolutely dependent on quantification. At least two of the articles in this volume (by Susan Mann and Emily Honig) involve little quantitative data, and yet they fully reflect an economist's way of thinking.

Historians of China may be discouraged from pursuing economic topics because of the apparent lack of data. And yet there are, as we shall describe later, many more data than meet the eye. Moreover, generations of historians have contributed fruitfully to the analysis of economic trends in Europe and North America without the benefit of careful compilation or systematic analysis of quantitative data. A generation of new economic historians, focusing its attention on the economies of North America and Great Britain, has demonstrated that better, fuller results and sounder interpretations are often available when research using conventional documentary sources is combined with diligent mining of quantitative materials, which are *always* deficient in a variety of dimensions. Before succumbing to the defeatist view

---

34. F. M. Scherer, "Merger in the Petroleum Industry: The Mobil-Marathon Case (1981)," in John E. Kwoka, Jr., and Lawrence J. White, eds., *The Antitrust Revolution* (Glenview, Ill., 1989), p. 35.

that certain data are uniquely defective, Chinese historians should consider the implication of Nicholas Crafts's new study claiming that the average annual growth of British per capita income between 1801 and 1831 should be reduced from the long-accepted Deane-Cole result of 1.6 percent to a much lower figure of 0.5 percent, implying that per capita incomes rose by 16 percent rather than 61 percent during 1801–31.[35] If British historians cannot yet determine whether industry and commerce grew slower (Deane and Cole) or faster (Crafts), or whether agriculture grew much faster (Deane and Cole) or slower (Crafts) during 1760–80 than during 1700–60, perhaps their data, which have supported hundreds of studies in what McCloskey calls "econometric history" are no better than the Chinese historians'.

Historians are particularly concerned with detecting trends and cycles. Contrary to the political scientists' old adage "In China if something happens twice, it's a trend," the identification of trends in economic history is a bit more complicated. Was the economy growing or stagnating? Were incomes rising or falling? Was land distribution becoming more equal or less equal? Was the standard of living rising or falling? Not only is this the stuff of which the truly important historical debates are made, but it should be apparent that this is also the material of present-day debates among political candidates. These are questions of measurement that are at the heart of economic methodology.

How economists can use incomplete and imperfect data in studying historical problems can perhaps be illustrated with an analysis of the fate of the traditional Chinese junk trade in the Republican period. As railways and steamships were introduced to the Chinese economy in the late nineteenth and early twentieth centuries, it has often been assumed that they displaced the traditional sailing vessels, or junks. But Thomas G. Rawski's hypothesis is that the junk trade not only survived the introduction of modern transport but actually increased its volume at the same time that modern transport grew.[36] If he can prove his case, it would be extremely significant for evaluating China's prewar economy because it would show that the rapidly growing freight carriage by railways and steamships represented *trade creation*—an important sign of commercialization and economic expansion—and not *trade diversion*—a mere substitution of new technology for old with no change in cargo volume.

Economic theory links changes in production (in this case, of transport services) to the level of capital formation (construction of new junks). Wooden sailing vessels have long service lives. If we assume that participants

---

35. N. F. R. Crafts, *British Economic Growth during the Industrial Revolution* (Oxford, 1985), as reviewed in the *Journal of Economic Literature* 24, no. 2 (1986): 683–84; and Phyllis Deane and W. A. Cole, *British Economic Growth, 1688–1959* (Cambridge, 1967).

36. Based on Thomas G. Rawski, *Economic Growth in Prewar China*, chap. 4.

in the shipping and boat-building trades display the income-seeking behavior that economists expect in any market economy (shippers do not abandon useful vessels in the absence of significant technological change; shipyards do not continue to operate if sales volume and price plummet), then we must expect any decline in the volume of junk traffic to quickly erode the demand for new ships. This is exactly what occurred on the Liao River in Manchuria, where diversion of riverine traffic to the railways prompted observers to note that "there are no new ships built for the river and [the] majority of the ships now being used are those constructed more than ten years ago."[37] Information about shipbuilding in the Yangzi Delta (including Shanghai), however, shows that the industry continued to thrive despite unrestricted competition from new carriers. A 1941 survey at Suzhou found that 14 of 36 ships were less than ten years old.[38] Another study lists over 20 places near Shanghai and along both banks of the Yangzi where shipyards continued to operate even after 1940.[39]

If evidence from shipbuilding data indicates that junk traffic did not decline prior to 1937, how can we investigate the stronger proposition that junk shipping actually increased despite growing competition from steamships, motor launches, railways, and trucks? Fortunately, we have some data showing that the junk trade expanded in several important ports and fared well in competition with rail, steamship, and cart traffic in delivering cotton to the major textile center of Tianjin. This information may be supplemented by a series of calculations that estimate the volume of wheat arriving in Shanghai by junk. Wheat was one of the most important commodities shipped into Shanghai. If junk-borne shipments of wheat increased along with the expansion of railway and steamship carriage, the overall argument about the survival and growth of the junk trade is greatly strengthened.

Our estimate rests on an equation. The volume of wheat arriving by junk was roughly equal to (1) the wheat required by Shanghai flour mills, minus (2) the net import of wheat into Shanghai from abroad, minus (3) the net inflow of domestic wheat carried by steamship, minus (4) the inflow of domestic wheat into Shanghai by rail. Gathering together various pieces of admittedly imperfect data, we reach the conclusion that junk-borne shipments of wheat into Shanghai may have risen from 139,000 tons in 1914 to an average of 244,000 tons in the 1930s. But how can we defend our estimate in the face of the known imperfections in the data we have used? The key is to look very carefully at the assumptions employed in constructing the data from which these results are derived. For example, there are several different figures for overseas wheat imports (2) during 1931–33, the end point of our

---

37. *The Manchuria Year Book 1932–33* (Tokyo, 1932), p. 284.
38. *Chūshi no minsengyō: Soshū minsen jittai chōsa hōkoku* (Tokyo, 1943), 1:26–27.
39. *Shina no kōun* (Tokyo, 1944), pp. 83–84.

time series. Our calculations employ the largest of these figures, a tactic that lowers the estimated junk inflow for 1931–33 and thus tends to undercut the working hypothesis. Second, lacking data on railway shipments (4) in 1914, the starting point of our time series, we assume the lowest possible figure—none at all. This raises the estimated inflow of junk-borne wheat in 1914, again in opposition to the proposed conclusion. Despite these two challenges, the calculations are still able to show that junk-borne shipments of wheat into Shanghai were substantially larger in 1931–33 than in 1914.

Historians unfamiliar with quantitative research may complain that this type of scholarship is no more than a tissue of assumptions, with results predetermined before pencil meets paper. Nothing could be further from the truth. Assumptions are all laid out for the readers' scrutiny and critical evaluation, and precisely to show that they do *not* control the conclusions. In a world of imperfect sources, the researcher must convince critical readers that empirical results are strong enough to overcome possible defects in the underlying data. The tactic of demonstrating an assertion to be valid even under assumptions that stack the deck against the proposed conclusion is commonly used in economics for precisely this purpose. Findings that can survive the impact even of contrary assumptions are called *robust*. Robustness is a characteristic eagerly sought by applied economists and carefully weighed by readers who find themselves suspicious of published results. If evidence favoring the proposed conclusion is so striking that it emerges even from data that are skewed in ways that suppress the very trend the researcher seeks to establish, even a skeptical audience should acquiesce.

In this way—as illustrated by the examples of using wage data to study farm incomes, deriving interest rates from grain prices, and seeking information about junk traffic by investigating the fortunes of shipbuilders—historians can use economic reasoning to assist them in separating historical fact from fiction. Although it was generally said that steam and rail transport displaced junk transport, economic theory led to the suspicion that this might not actually have been the case, and application of economic methods showed that it almost certainly was not the case.

Identifying trends can help economists and historians to distinguish how people behave from what people say. If professors complain of low incomes, we conclude that they desire higher salaries. It is only when significant numbers of teachers leave academe that we can identify professional wages as being too low in the equilibrium sense. Unlike intellectual historians, who interest themselves in conscious ideas, or cultural or social historians, who investigate attitudes and perceptions (*mentalités*) that are unconscious, economists are skeptical about words and self-perception. Because acquiring information is costly in terms of both time and money, economists believe that people tend to be well informed only about matters of direct importance to their livelihood and may not see the larger picture. Furthermore, what people say and write about their economic circumstances is often intended to change those circumstances and may not be a reliable guide to the circumstances themselves.

But in focusing on broad trends, economists may overlook cyclical events or regional variations that greatly affect the lives of those who experience them and therefore offer important material for historical studies. Thus the conclusion that junk traffic increased in China during the decades prior to World War II submerges the reality of a regional decline in junk activity along the Liao River. In a monumental and influential work on Chinese agriculture from 1368 to 1968, the economist Dwight H. Perkins estimates the expansion of agricultural output in this period on the basis of population size.[40] The key to his estimate was the assumption that everyone must have eaten a minimum diet (or they would not have been alive).

The story of a rapidly expanding population sustained by six centuries of increased agricultural productivity certainly paints a rosy picture of the Chinese economy and implies that everyone had at least a subsistence diet, contrary to a gloomy Malthusian picture that might otherwise be imagined. But in fact Perkins's calculations say only that *on the whole* people must have had enough to eat. His equation does not take into account those who may have died from undernutrition, nor does it consider patterns of regional development and decline or the possibility of extreme inequality of income and welfare. Economists seeking to define long-term trends in average income or consumption may not notice that a minority may have eaten, and lived, exceedingly well, while a larger group may have suffered from inadequate diets (since on the whole, or on average, people had enough to eat). As a result, the measurement of macroeconomic trends, while offering valuable information to historians, leaves much important work to be done in terms of investigating the distribution of gains and losses among regions, groups, and individuals.[41]

ECONOMISTS AND HISTORIANS NEED EACH OTHER

Our message, then, is not that the economic approach to historical research overshadows other types of inquiry or that economics is a panacea for scholarly problems. Indeed, the economic approach tends to have its own limitations, such as taking the whole to be the same as the sum of the parts or underrating the importance of noneconomic causation in history. Economists need to take historical realities into account. But historians need to adopt an

---

40. Dwight H. Perkins, *Agricultural Development in China, 1368–1968* (Chicago, 1969).

41. This perception is shared by economists who report that "rapid growth in underdeveloped countries has been of little or no benefit to perhaps a third of the population." See Hollis Chenery, "Introduction," in Chenery et al., *Redistribution with Growth* (London, 1974), p. xiii.

economic perspective, particularly when writing about the economy. We contend that history written without the insights that emerge from systematically applying economic theory and method will be incomplete and impoverished. If historians are willing to suspend a certain disbelief about the economists' principles and assumptions, systematic application of theory and methods may produce insights and results that will weaken the initial disbelief. The knowledge required for historians to make use of the economic approach is neither remote nor inaccessible. The successful completion of this volume demonstrates that a brief period of intensive preparation will enable historical researchers without extensive economic training to fruitfully apply the insights of economic analysis with results that will appeal to economists as well as historians. This volume stands as the proof of this assertion, and we now turn to a survey of its contents.

CONTENTS OF THIS VOLUME

The essays in this volume fall into two groups. The first group relies primarily on grain price data from the Qing dynasty to establish long-term trends in the Chinese economy, analyze the nature of market integration, and delineate the role of the Qing state. They could be described as studies of price behavior. The second group of papers focuses on the study of land, labor, and capital in more localized situations in the twentieth century. Narrower in focus and more recent in time, these papers center on the issue of market response. In different ways, these papers illustrate some of the general ideas about economic perspective and approach discussed above and point to further opportunities for work in Chinese economic history.

The essays on Qing price history make use of grain price data from the Qing period compiled from the holdings of the First Historical Archives in Beijing and the National Palace Museum in Taibei. These data form what is perhaps the richest, longest, and most detailed price series for the history of any national economy. Starting formally from the beginning of the Qianlong period in 1736, each governor was required to submit a monthly report of grain prices in his province. This included the high and low price of each major grain grown in each prefecture. This monthly provincial report was compiled from ten-day reports submitted by each prefecture (*fu*), which in turn had collected ten-day reports from each county (*xian*). Thus the high and low prices noted in the prefectural reports represent the highest and lowest prices reported by any county within a given prefecture during that month. The number of grains for which prices were collected varied with each province. In the South, as many as five or more different grades of rice were included. In North China, five to seven grains were reported, including wheat, millet, and sorghum.

Although the analysis of these grain price data has just begun, even the preliminary results have great importance for Chinese historical studies. The records of grain price behavior permit us to establish basic long-term trends in China's historical economy, as well as to identify some shorter-term cycles. Grain was the single most important commodity in the agrarian economy of imperial China and the best indicator of economic trends. Yeh-chien Wang's article, "Secular Trends of Rice Prices in the Yangzi Delta, 1638–1935," delineates two long-term cycles in that key region of China: a steep downtrend from the 1640s to the early 1680s followed by over a century of generally rising prices; and a second cycle of price declines followed by steep inflation from the 1880s until the world depression of the 1930s.

Lillian M. Li's paper, "Grain Prices in Zhili Province, 1736–1911: A Preliminary Study," shows broadly similar patterns for wheat, millet, and sorghum prices in North China, with a peak in the 1820s and another steady climb starting in the 1890s. Li's data suggest the presence of distinct short-term cycles of perhaps four- or five-year intervals for coarse grains in the eighteenth century, and possibly longer cycles for wheat prices. She also finds considerable price fluctuation in the late nineteenth century, before the steady upward climb of the early twentieth century.

Much more work remains to be done to determine whether Wang was correct in his earlier, pioneering work when he concluded that North and South China grain prices in the Qing moved essentially in a synchronic manner, thus contradicting Skinner's hypothesis of asynchronic regional cycles and also implying considerable interregional market integration as early as the eighteenth century. Also on the agenda is work that will connect the analysis of Qing grain prices with the work of Brandt, who dates China's integration with the international rice market from the late nineteenth century.[42]

Grain prices can provide insight into the functioning of markets. In particular, price data can illuminate the extent of market integration within, as well as among, regions. Peter C. Perdue's essay, "The Qing State and the Gansu Grain Market, 1739–1864," reveals that even the remote Northwest of China had achieved a considerable degree of market integration, primarily through strong state intervention. Because of the strategic importance of the Northwest, the Qing court maintained a heavy military presence there and, to support it, a granary system that kept relatively high per capita levels of grain reserves. Perdue believes that, in conjunction with private storage and commerce, public grain storage worked to support the integration of key markets of Gansu with each other and with neighboring Ningxia Province.

42. Yeh-chien Wang, "Spatial and Temporal Patterns of Grain Prices in China, 1740–1910" (Paper presented at the Conference on Spatial and Temporal Trends and Cycles in Chinese Economic History, Bellagio, Italy, 1984); G. William Skinner, "Presidential Address: The Structure of Chinese History," *Journal of Asian Studies* 44, no. 2 (1985): 271–92; Brandt, "Chinese Agriculture and the International Economy."

Although Perdue's conclusions must be described as tentative because his data series are far from complete, his Gansu data present a strong case for market integration even in relatively remote areas of China.

In "Grain Markets and Food Supplies in Eighteenth-Century Hunan," R. Bin Wong and Peter C. Perdue further pursue the issue of market integration, this time within Hunan Province, a major rice-exporting region in central China. Since the general outline and functioning of the Hunan grain markets is relatively well documented, Wong and Perdue utilize the grain price data to test whether high levels of integration actually existed among those prefectures known to be heavily engaged in the rice export trade. They find that separate analyses of high prices and low prices each tend to confirm integration among the exporting prefectures and lack of integration between them and the nonexporting prefectures. They also see in the separate reporting of high and low prices an opportunity to test for integration within each prefecture, since the high and low prices reported for any month from each prefecture presumably represent price quotations from two different counties within the prefecture. They find that, with one exception, exporting prefectures had high levels of internal integration. Intraprefectural integration was also high in relatively isolated prefectures. In short, Wong and Perdue's findings are reassuring because the "price data generally confirm the outlines of the export trade based on qualitative information."

Because there is a considerable amount of qualitative information about Hunan's rice trade, one may conclude with some degree of confidence that high correlations of prices or price differences (the difference between the price in the current period and the price in the previous period) do represent market integration. Without confirmation of trading patterns, the occurrence of high price correlations might arise from common climatic patterns or changes in the stock of money rather than from market integration. In the case of Gansu, for example, it might be argued that the strong military presence in the province produced a type of integration of prices based, not on true markets, but rather on a large measure of government intervention. Perhaps this could be seen as a kind of false or pseudo market integration, which is not to deny its historical significance. The same hypothesis could be advanced with respect to grain markets in Zhili, where the presence of the Imperial court, bannermen, and the military was so pervasive.

We can also use grain prices to examine the short-term fluctuations in periods of crises. Li, in her article on Zhili, uses grain prices to test the impact of crises in several different ways. Like Perdue, she uses regression analysis to try to measure the relative impact on prices of the passage of time, seasonality, and natural catastrophes. Overall, she finds that flood or drought did affect prices, as one would expect. But the differences between the price levels in normal years and those observed under crisis conditions were rather slight in comparison to the differences recorded during crises in seventeenth- and eighteenth-century Europe. Most likely, the operation of the government granary system helped to stabilize prices and avert catastrophes, as well as to provide relief during the crises themselves.

The topic of government grain storage raises a number of theoretical as well as historical problems. Recent scholarship on the Qing granary system has excited considerable interest. In fact, some of our contributors have completed a book describing the state granaries and offering important data on their management and holdings.[43] For Chinese historians, the state's major role in grain storage comes as no surprise, although the extent and efficiency of the Qing granary system is quite remarkable. For non-China economists and many historians, however, the notion of public storage requires considerable explanation. Economists, working from the principle of opportunity cost, will immediately question whether government effort had any significant effect on market circumstances. Private citizens store grain because they hope to profit from the regular differential between low autumn and high springtime grain prices and also from high prices that occur in the wake of disasters, such as flood, drought, and war. Government storage efforts intended to limit seasonal price fluctuations and to curtail irregular price peaks will reduce the profitability of private grain storage and lower the risk to private citizens of not holding grain stocks. Thus, economists will reason, public storage encourages a reduction of private storage, creating the possibility that energetic official intervention may have no significant effect on the total quantity of grain stored, seasonal price fluctuations, or the price consequences of periodic natural or manmade disasters.

Of course the Chinese historians have a response to the economists' skepticism. The economists' assumption that private and public grain storage are substitutes for each other is based on the premise that the private sector has the capacity to store grain as conveniently as the government. In fact, the forthcoming granary volume will show that in per capita terms, the granary stocks were highest in China's most remote and least commercialized provinces. The government, in short, appears to have intervened precisely where the private sector was least able to ensure market stability. Put another way, the government was subsidizing the storage of grain. In highly commercialized regions, such as the Lower Yangzi area, with its dense network of markets and transport arteries and extensive private commerce, the government could and did leave the job to private efforts and to the market. Larger public storage programs might merely have replaced private efforts rather than compressing the amplitude of fluctuations. The topic of grain storage thus illustrates the economic sophistication of Qing officials. It also provides a

---

43. Pierre-Etienne Will and R. Bin Wong, *Nourish the People: The State Civilian Granary System in China, 1650–1850* (Ann Arbor, 1991). James Lee, Jean Oi, and Peter Perdue also contributed to this book.

fruitful example of how the economists' approach to a problem may help to structure historical inquiry and how, conversely, understanding the historical context helps to modify the predictions of economic theories. Although much work has already been done on granaries, the availability of price data now creates an opportunity to combine economic analysis and documentary research to test and measure the impact of Qing grain storage efforts on the economy.

Another theoretical problem raised by the grain price data, also illustrated in Li's article, is that of how to define and identify markets. Do wheat, millet, and sorghum in North China belong to the same market, or do they constitute separate markets? The principle of substitution teaches that a rise in the relative price of wheat or any other commodity will increase the demand for, and hence the price of, items that provide close substitutes for the initial product as buyers seek to maintain their living standards or contain costs in the face of adverse price change. The question here is to what extent people were willing to substitute one grain for another or, elsewhere, one type of cloth for another. Such questions bear closely on the question of market integration and call for further inquiry.

While the articles of Li, Perdue, and Wong and Perdue deal only with grain prices, the articles of Yeh-chien Wang and James Lee, Cameron Campbell, and Guofu Tan show how price data can be used in conjunction with other long-term data. In his article, Wang arrays his rice price data from the Lower Yangzi region together with population data, information about silver stocks, and weather trends, to consider what factors may have influenced long-term cycles of inflation and deflation in the Yangzi Delta. Wang's preliminary, and pathbreaking, estimates of China's monetary silver stocks indicate a roughly parallel growth of rice prices and the stock of monetary silver throughout the Qing period. He finds that in China, as in England, long-term trends in food prices display a substantial correlation with changes in population and population growth. Wang describes two long swings in rice prices during the three centuries prior to World War II. In both cases, periods of rising prices coincide with relatively rapid growth of both population and monetary silver, while interludes of deflation are associated with stagnant or declining population. Wang's discussion highlights opportunities for further study of major factors underlying the long-term path of China's economy. Can we sharpen the causal interrelations among population, money stock, commercialization, climatic change, food production, and the material well-being of the Chinese peasantry? Do available studies understate the long-term significance of international money flows for China's agrarian economy? How closely were the rice markets of the Yangzi Delta linked to the farm economies of other regions within China's vast land mass?

In "Infanticide and Family Planning in Late Imperial China: The Price and Population History of Rural Liaoning, 1774–1873," James Lee, Cameron Campbell, and Guofu Tan employ price data to help analyze a unique and rich set of Qing dynasty population registers from Daoyi, a rural suburb of present-day Shenyang in Liaoning (formerly Fengtian) Province in southern Manchuria. Their major demographic findings are, first, that significantly higher levels of infant mortality were found among females than among males, although there were greater fluctuations in mortality among males; second, that most couples appear to have practiced a considerable degree of family planning; and, third, that infanticide, particularly female infanticide, was a principal means of family planning. In this article, the authors pose the question of how food prices might have influenced birth and death rates. In other words, were fertility or mortality affected by times of scarcity, as indicated by high food prices? Their answer is that there seems, on the whole, to have been little relationship between food prices and mortality, but there was a strong relationship between high food prices and infanticides, particularly, but not exclusively, female infanticides. While these conclusions are likely to be hotly debated, in part because it is unclear whether Liaoning or Manchurian family patterns are generalizable to the rest of China, Lee, Campbell, and Tan have pointed toward a direction in research that has not previously been pursued in Chinese history.

The second group of essays in this volume focuses on issues more familiar to modern Chinese history—urban and rural poverty, the economic consequences of political unrest, and economic growth or the lack of it. In dealing with the factors of land, labor, and capital in local or regional settings, these essays pursue large issues in a more focused, and perhaps more manageable, way than the first set of articles. In each case, we see the interplay between economic analysis and historical inquiry. Economic models open new avenues of inquiry for historians, while the historical context illuminates the social and institutional conditions that shape the impact of economic forces in particular times and places.

In the first of these essays, "Land Concentration and Income Distribution in Republican China," Loren Brandt and Barbara Sands—the only economists among our contributors—address the issue of land concentration and income distribution in twentieth-century China. They challenge the commonly held view that there was increasing concentration of land ownership in the late nineteenth and early twentieth centuries and that concentration of landed wealth necessarily produced wide inequalities in the distribution of income. Although the data from the 1920s and 1930s show a highly unequal distribution of land, Brandt and Sands show that shifting the statistical base from landholding per household into per capita terms narrows the gap between poor and wealthy households. They argue that without comparable data for earlier periods, there is no basis for claiming that the degree of concentration of land ownership was rising over time.

Their key point, however, is that in the complex economy of North China, the distribution of per capita income depended on earnings from the disposition of labor and goods as well as land, so that the concentration of landholdings need not have coincided with the concentration of incomes. If, as hypothesized by Peter H. Lindert, "the common folk," who specialized in producing and selling goods that embodied large components of unskilled labor, "were among the greatest gainers" from the expansion of China's domestic and international trade, the spread of commercial agriculture following the growth of trade and transport may emerge as a significant source of reduced income inequality in the North China countryside.[44]

Although Brandt and Sands analyze three villages selected for their distinct economic characteristics, skeptics will note the small size of their sample and the possible biases inherent in their principal source, the South Manchurian Railway Company village surveys, which form the basis for a number of controversial studies of peasant welfare in North China.[45] For our purposes, however, of greater interest than the ultimate correctness of their interpretation is the economic approach or perspective that they have employed. By posing a theoretical issue, then isolating a number of key variables and finding an appropriate set of data, the authors create a framework for systematic analysis of the issue at hand. Finally, by placing the Chinese issue in comparative, international terms, the authors provide a baseline or context within which to judge the issue of large or small. At what point should income inequality be considered large? Too large? Such judgments require not only quantification but also appropriate context.

Lynda S. Bell approaches the issue of rural income from another perspective: she looks at the silk industry in Wuxi, an area in the Lower Yangzi region that developed into a major sericultural and silk-reeling center in the nineteenth century after the Taiping Rebellion. In "Farming, Sericulture, and Peasant Rationality in Wuxi County in the Early Twentieth Century," Bell explores an apparent paradox: why, in one of the more prosperous regions of China, did peasants in the 1920s and 1930s experience low incomes from sericultural activity? And why should peasants continue to pursue sericulture even though, as she effectively demonstrates, the returns per unit of labor were lower for mulberry cultivation and silkworm raising than for rice or wheat farming? Does this mean that farm households were not acting rationally or that they were engaged in a kind of "self-exploitation" in the manner described by A. V. Chayanov for the Russian peasantry? The key to this paradox, Bell finds, is that women supplied most of the labor in seri-

---

44. Peter H. Lindert, "International Economics and the Historian" (Revision of a paper prepared for the Workshop on Economic Methods for Chinese Historical Research, Honolulu, September 1987), p. 30.

45. Myers, *Chinese Peasant Economy*, and Philip C. C. Huang, *Peasant Economy*, also rely on these surveys.

culture. Compared to other domestic industries they could engage in, such as cotton weaving, sericulture brought superior returns. Only factory work could have brought higher wages to women, but the opportunity cost—in terms of domestic labor lost to the family if the woman left for a factory—outweighed the extra income that might have been earned. Moreover, Bell's calculations reveal that even at the depressed silk prices of the 1930s, income from sericulture allowed Wuxi farm households to buy more rice than they could have grown on the land occupied by mulberry plants. So Bell finds peasant choices ultimately to be rational, but cautions that rationality need not imply that they were earning large profits; rather, rationality was what kept them going in an economy in which subsistence, rather than profit, was still the major preoccupation. Participation in an international market presented new opportunities, but Wuxi peasants found that it also presented new risks.

While the economic value of female labor implicitly figures in Bell's article, it is the main topic of Susan Mann's essay, "Women's Work in the Ningbo Area, 1900–1936." Using rich qualitative materials from a relatively commercialized region of China, Mann delineates the factors that affected both the demand for, and the supply of, female labor. On the demand side, she shows that there were many opportunities for female workers both within and outside the household in the Ningbo area and that the hierarchy of jobs, from the women's perspective, was less related to wage levels than to the perceptions of social respectability and the degree of personal convenience associated with each type of work. On the supply side, the availability of female labor from each household was dependent on three major factors: its size, its other resource endowments (these two were, of course, closely related), and its stage in the family cycle. Families with adult women who had no child-care responsibilities (young women before marriage or "able-bodied widows") were most likely to have labor to spare and therefore to benefit from new opportunities for female employment within the household. Factory employment, which violated social conventions that restricted respectable women to working within the household, was acceptable only to women from "poor households strategizing to keep their menfolk afloat."

In "Native-Place Hierarchy and Labor Market Segmentation: The Case of Subei People in Shanghai," Emily Honig addresses an apparent puzzle: why were people from Subei, the area of Jiangsu Province north of the Yangzi River and south of the Huai River, routinely barred from certain types of employment in Shanghai, even when they would have worked for lower wages than employers paid to natives of south Jiangsu? Regarded as inferior human beings, the Subei people in Shanghai were condemned to the least attractive and least remunerative forms of employment—rickshaw pulling, night soil and garbage collecting (literally, as she says, "shit work"), barbering, and so forth—within a clear hierarchy of jobs. Honig employs the economists' concept of segmented labor markets to show that in Shanghai, it was not race, religion, or ethnicity that formed a barrier to free entry and exit, but native-place hierarchy.

Both Mann's and Honig's articles show that the economists' notion of choice has to be tempered by the social historians' understanding of gender, class, and native-place ties. Despite the heuristic value of the economists' notion of ceteris paribus, historians find that all other things are rarely equal and in fact it is the "other things" that may hold the key to understanding the flow of events. Still, the approach of these two papers is entirely consistent with an economic perspective. To start with the assumption that there should be a unified labor market with no barriers to exit or entry and with essentially one wage scale is not wrong; what would be wrong is to stop there. Looked at from the employers' perspective, labor market segmentation rests on their need to assess the qualifications and character of would-be employees or associates. With no access to data banks or credit histories, they must seek a quick and inexpensive screening device. Discrimination on the basis of ethnicity, place of origin, linguistic background, or education, can be partly understood simply as a cost- and risk-reducing business decision.

Susan Mann's Ningbo women benefited from their reputation for diligence, skill, and gentility. Employers preferred workers from Ningbo and other south Jiangsu communities over migrants from the north not only because of their superior technical and social skills but also because kinship ties and networks of regional association were available for disciplining and controlling south Jiangsu workers, making it more profitable to hire them, even when they might require higher pay than northerners. By the same token, Subei natives were discriminated against. Businessmen preferred to deal with those whose background seemed to increase the likelihood of the successful fulfillment of agreements. When disputes arise, the existence of voluntary organizations, such as native-place associations (*huiguan*), increases the probability of speedy resolution of conflict by informal procedures acceptable to all parties. Drawing on the economic theory of clubs, Janet T. Landa has proposed just such an explanation for the tendency of Chinese businessmen in Southeast Asia to deal preferentially with Chinese whose ancestors migrated from the same district or province, secondarily with other Chinese, and only if other contacts are not available, with local non-Chinese or with foreign business partners.[46]

Finally, Kenneth Pomeranz's article, "Local Interest Story: Political Power and Regional Differences in the Shandong Capital Market, 1900–

---

46. Janet T. Landa, "The Political Economy of the Ethnically Homogeneous Chinese Middleman Group in Southeast Asia: Ethnicity and Entrepreneurship in a Plural Society," in *The Chinese in Southeast Asia*, vol. 1, ed. Linda Y. C. Lim and Peter L. A. Gosling (Singapore, 1983), pp. 86–116.

1937," illustrates how political structures can decisively influence the outcome of economic change. During the early twentieth century, Shandong Province experienced an expansion of markets and commerce similar to that in the Wuxi region of Jiangsu Province in an earlier period. As in Jiangsu, Shandong villagers were quick to avail themselves of new economic opportunities, specializing in peanuts and other cash crops in some regions and, as Pomeranz documents, exporting large quantities of underpriced copper coins whenever it became possible to do so.

Shandong's political elite found themselves torn between the gains available from encouraging economic integration and the benefits for themselves and their mercantile allies of using military force to obstruct integration and then exploit the resulting regional price gaps for pecuniary gain. With leaders in different regions responding differently to market circumstances, Shandong's economy displayed lines of demarcation that reflected the impact of political decisions more than economic, social, or geographic forces. Despite a national trend toward economic integration, the needs of state making during this turbulent period of Shandong's history prompted local authorities to restrict the movement of specie across administrative boundaries, leading to marked regional variations in both the silver-copper ratio and local interest rates that illustrate a real political constraint on the spread of purely market forces.

CONCLUSION

The essays in this volume do not fall into any single neat line of interpretation about the economic history of China over the last two or three centuries. Pomeranz's detailed work on Shandong cautions us against any broad generalizations about the extent to which the treaty ports in nineteenth- and twentieth-century China affected the hinterland economy. Pomeranz shows us that the more advanced, coastal area did interact with the hinterland but that political intervention prevented a higher degree of market integration.

The works of Bell, Mann, and Honig also contain a cautionary message. Even in the Lower Yangzi macroregion, the most agriculturally prosperous and commercially advanced area of China, the opportunities for economic gain for individual peasants or workers, although often greater than ever before, could be undercut by international economic instability, gender differences in the returns to labor, and unequal access to the urban labor market. The story that Brandt and Sands tell, however, contains the reverse message. In the much more adverse conditions of North China, all may not have been so bad as it appeared. New employment opportunities provided more channels for a family's economic gain than just landholding. Entry to and exit from these lines of work appear unimpeded in the North China world they describe.

The lessons of the articles in Part 1 are somewhat different. In some cases, the findings of these grain price studies confirm previously known trends or previously advanced hypotheses. For example, Wong and Perdue's study of Hunan's grain price series confirms commercial patterns already discerned through qualitative sources. Li's case studies of crises parallel the results of Pierre-Etienne Will's documentary study. Perdue's delineation of marketing patterns in Gansu coincides with G. William Skinner's predictions about the spatial patterns of Gansu's commodity trade. In other cases, such as Wang's study of money supply or Lee, Campbell, and Tan's study of Liaoning, new materials have generated new hypotheses about long-term trends.

These essays also contain the potential for even bolder messages, perhaps revisions of current received wisdom, about China's economic history over the last two or three centuries. Some readers may derive from the essays in Part 1 a picture of the eighteenth-century economy as more advanced in commercial development and market integration than previously thought. Certainly, the quality of the Qing bureaucracy's price data seems higher than that of its population records, the systematic fabrication of which Skinner has recently exposed.[47] Wang's compilation of information on stocks of monetary silver creates an opportunity for using the equation of exchange to investigate the implications of Dwight Perkins's long-standing assertion that, on the average, Chinese living standards, as measured by the availability of grain, experienced no long-term upward or downward trend during the Ming and Qing dynasties.[48] The essays in Part 2 all illustrate, in varying ways, the extent to which commercialization, including the development of foreign as well as domestic trade, penetrated the local economies of many areas. The story of expanding commercial networks finds a basis in these papers, but there are other stories that have been, and will be, told about the modern economy.

Despite the many insights and contributions contained in the essays that follow, we believe, however, that the real lessons of this volume are not the substantive ones. In each case, economic theories and methods have been employed to clarify the facts of history and to advance its understanding.

47. G. William Skinner, "Sichuan's Population in the Nineteenth Century: Lessons from Disaggregated Data," *Late Imperial China* 8, no. 1 (1987): 69.

48. If we assume parallel growth between silver stocks and money supply, between grain prices and the general price level, and between foodgrain production and total output, the equation of exchange can be used to derive the time path for income velocity of monetary circulation implied by Wang's data on silver, grain prices, and population together with Perkins's hypothesis of stable per capita output. The plausibility of the resulting velocity estimates and of changes that might arise from adjustments reflecting known biases in the underlying data (we know, for example, that money supply grew faster than silver stocks in the late nineteenth and early twentieth centuries) should make it possible to evaluate the degree to which Perkins's results, the grain price data, and Wang's new monetary estimates provide a mutually consistent picture of overall economic trends.

Without a fundamental understanding of the laws of supply and demand and the significance of market integration, none of the essays in Part 1 could have been written. Without an appreciation of how factor markets operate, the essays in Part 2 would have been greatly weakened. Wang's article provides an excellent example of how economic theory, in this case the quantity theory of money, can inform both the construction and interpretation of economic data to help formulate new questions and hypotheses.

In many of the essays, however, a simple economic approach in itself would lead to an impasse or a seeming contradiction. These apparent puzzles, such as Shandong's lack of monetary integration or Wuxi's apparent poverty in one of China's most prosperous regions, can only be explained with reference to the institutional and social context that historians are uniquely qualified to understand and explain. Without knowledge of the social prejudices attached to Subei people, their lowly position in Shanghai's labor force would defy understanding. Without knowing the history of the Chinese bureaucracy and the fundamentals of Confucian political theory, Western-trained economists find it difficult to comprehend why the Chinese state should have maintained a vast civilian granary system in the Qing period. Often the results of economic analysis raise questions that compel us to further noneconomic inquiry. The surprising demographic behavior of the Han Banner population of Liaoning causes us to want to know more about their ethnic background, their family structure, and their food allocation habits and in particular to understand whether they were very different from Han Chinese who lived within the Great Wall. In short, economic analysis cannot stand alone and, in almost every case, offers rich opportunities for work with other disciplines—sociology, anthropology, politics, and history.

Chinese economic history is barely coming into its own as a field of study. What this volume is intended to show, to its authors as well as to our colleagues and students, is that further study of China's economic history that systematically utilizes the theories and methods of economics can generate new hypotheses and fresh perspectives that will enrich the study of all aspects of China's history as well as deepen our understanding of the structure and evolution of the Chinese economy itself.

PART ONE

Price Behavior

ONE

Secular Trends of Rice Prices in the Yangzi Delta, 1638–1935

Yeh-chien Wang

In an agrarian society like Qing China, grains are the most important commodities in domestic trade, and food consumption makes up more than half of the average household budget.[1] Grain prices are therefore the leading indicator in the market; the direction and the magnitude of their movement generally reflect conditions of inflation, deflation, or crises of major proportion. Moreover, persistent changes in grain prices relative to prices of other commodities give rise to a process of income redistribution affecting the welfare of virtually all groups of people and eventually the social and political stability of a country. As such, a clear knowledge of the trends of grain prices will provide not only a key to understanding the state of economy and society but also a basis for further research in real wages, the standard of living, and many other areas once data on other economic indicators are uncovered.

I would like to thank the participants of the Conference on Economic Methods for Chinese Historical Research held in Oracle, Arizona, in 1988 and especially Professors Jon Cohen, Peter H. Lindert, Lillian M. Li, and Thomas G. Rawski for their comments and suggestions. Most data for this paper were gathered at the First Historical Archives in Beijing and the National Palace Museum in Taibei. I feel greatly indebted to the staffs of these two institutions for their cooperation and assistance. I am also grateful to Fang Xing of the Institute of Economics, Chinese Academy of Social Sciences, and the late Wu Dange of Fudan University, who kindly showed me additional sources of price data from published works, and to Douglas E. Lewis of Computer Services at Kent State University for his assistance in data design and graphics. For financial support I wish to acknowledge assistance from the following institutions: the Committee on Scholarly Communication with the People's Republic of China, the National Science Council of the Republic of China, the Social Science Research Council, the American Council of Learned Societies, the Foundation for Scholarly Exchange (Fulbright Foundation), the Wang Institute for Graduate Studies, and Kent State University.

1. See Wu Chengming, *Zhongguo ziben zhuyi yu guonei shichang* (Beijing, 1985), p. 253; John Lossing Buck, *Chinese Farm Economy* (Chicago, 1930), pp. 361–64, 386; Sidney Gamble, *Ting Hsien: A North China Rural Community* (Stanford, 1968), p.118.

Empirical studies in price history for imperial China are still in their infancy because of scarcity of data,[2] but the gradual opening of archival resources in both Beijing and Taibei offers us rich mines for historical exploration. What I am attempting to do in this paper is to delineate broadly the secular trends of the prices of rice, the single most important staple food of the Chinese people, in the Yangzi Delta for three centuries prior to World War II and to suggest some tentative explanations for the trends observed.

The Yangzi Delta is chosen as the focus of observation for two main reasons. First, price data for the area are more abundant and, by and large, of better quality than price data for other areas. I am thus able to construct a price series extending over three centuries. Second, because of its economic centrality, prices in the area reflected conditions of demand and supply in the national, not just regional, market. In late imperial China most of the long-distance trade used the waterways, of which the Yangzi River, the Grand Canal, and the sea route along the coast were by far the most important. Linking the eastern coast with the interior, the Yangzi River flows through China's most productive regions. Together with its tributaries and connecting lakes it provided the most efficient network of inland transportation. The Grand Canal joined the capital region to the resource-rich South, while the sea route tied together all of the coastal provinces from Hainan Island to the Liaodong Peninsula. Only the northwestern region and the southwestern corner of the empire remained relatively isolated. Before the Opium War (1840–42) there were, according to one study, more than 200,000 junks plying these waterways and other smaller rivers with a total carrying capacity amounting to 4–5 million tons.[3] Strategically situated at the focal point where the three principal arteries converged, the Yangzi Delta thus became the hub of interregional trade (see Map 1.1).

In addition to the advantage it possessed in geographic position, the industrial structure of the delta further enhanced its economic significance. It was, on the one hand, the center of the textile industry. On the other hand, its agriculture was unable to produce sufficient food to feed its inhabitants because it had the highest density of population in the country and much of its cultivated acreage was occupied by cash crops, such as cotton and mulberries.[4] These structural features of the delta economy gave rise to a

---

2. A few works may be cited: Han-sheng Chuan and Richard A. Kraus, *Mid-Ch'ing Rice Markets and Trade: An Essay in Price History* (Cambridge, Mass., 1975); Hwang Kuo-shu and Yeh-chien Wang, "Qingdai liangjia de changji biandong, 1763–1910," *Jingji lunwen* 9, no. 1 (March 1981): 1–27; Yeh-chien Wang, "Food Supply in Eighteenth-Century Fukien," *Late Imperial China* 7, no. 2 (December 1986): 80–117.

3. Fan Baichuan, *Zhongguo lunchuan hangyunye de xingqi* (Chengdu, 1985), pp. 35–83.

4. Cf. Yeh-chien Wang, "Food Supply and Grain Prices in the Yangtze Delta in the Eighteenth Century," *Proceedings of the Second Conference on Modern Chinese Economic History* (Taibei: Academia Sinica, 1989), pp. 424–27.

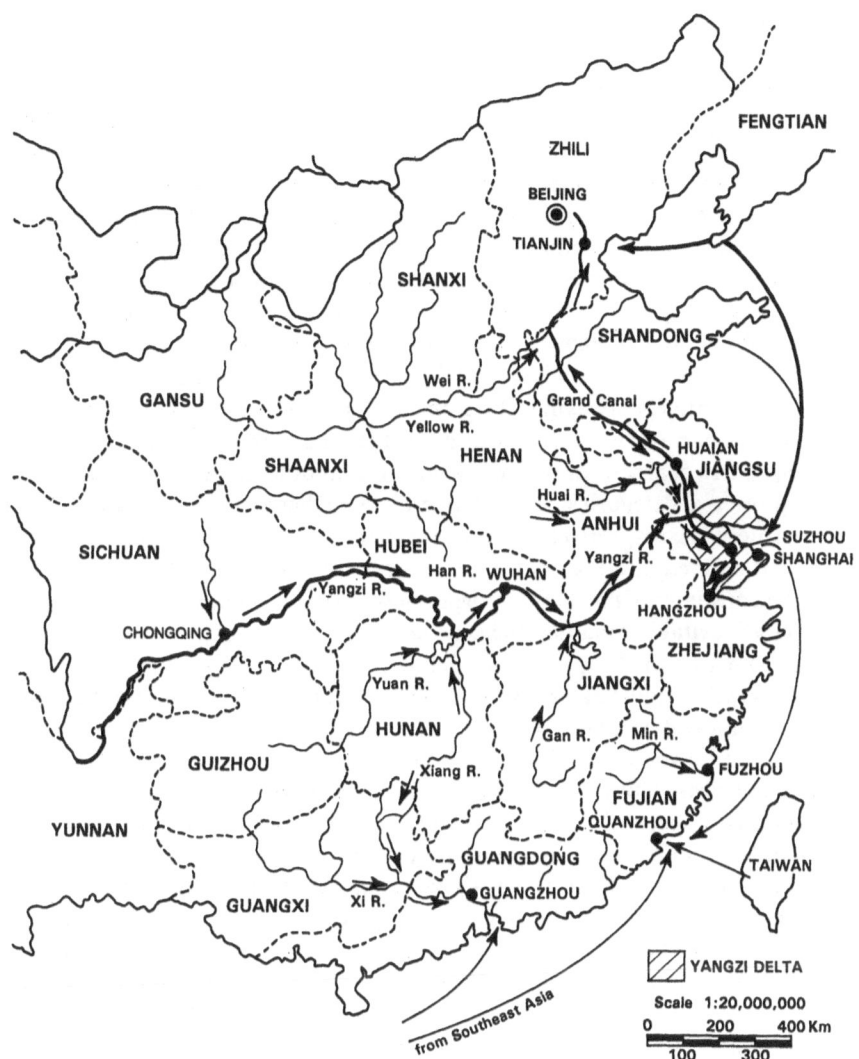

Map 1.1. Grain Trade Routes in Qing China.

growing two-way traffic in which cotton cloth and silk, the staple products of the delta, were distributed to the rest of the country while surplus food from inland and the newly developed areas came to the delta for local consumption or for transshipment to other areas where food was also in short supply. In the latter part of the eighteenth century the annual volume of long-distance trade in rice down the Yangzi River to the delta was probably between 15 million and 20 million *shi*, of which 5–6 million was transshipped to North China and the southeast coast (including 3 million *shi* as grain tribute to the capital). In addition, around 15 million *shi* of soybeans, bean products, and a variety of grains and fruits was transported from Manchuria and North China to the delta via the coastal waters and the Grand Canal. Beyond this, grain trade across provincial borders in the rest of the country was, quantitatively speaking, insignificant.[5] It must be noted, furthermore, that grains and textiles formed an overwhelming proportion of commercial cargoes carried across provinces. Before the middle of the nineteenth century, those two categories, as estimated by Wu Chengming, accounted for 42 and 31 percent, respectively, of the total value of the seven major commodities that entered interregional trade.[6] As the principal supplier of textiles to, and the consumer of most of the surplus food from, other parts of the country, the delta inevitably assumed the central role in the domestic market.

In a study on food supply in the delta in the eighteenth century, I selected for observation and analysis rice prices for 1738–89 in Suzhou and Hangzhou, the most flourishing prefectures in the delta and two principal prefectures in the Lower Yangzi Region, in conjunction with Quanzhou Prefecture of the Southeast Coast, Hanyang Prefecture of the Middle Yangzi Region, Huaian Prefecture in North China, and Guangdong Province in the Lingnan Region. My findings lend strong support to the proposition that the delta had economic centrality. First, prices show a remarkable degree of synchronized movement across all of the five macroregions linked by the three major waterways. Second, a Pearson correlation analysis of the deseasonalized, decycled, and detrended prices in these regions gives coefficients that are all positive, most of them of relatively high value (0.6 and over), and degrees of association between Suzhou and the rest that are the most pronounced. Although the data are far from complete and perfect, this survey of the grain trade nationwide and of grain price movements in a large part of the country does indicate the central position Suzhou occupied in the country's grain market.[7]

Not only was Suzhou the national market for grain and textiles, it was also

5. Wang Yejian (Wang Yeh-chien) and Hwang Guoshu (Hwang Kuo-shu), "Shiba shiji Zhongguo liangshi gongxu de kaocha" (Paper read at the Symposium on Rural Economy in Modern China, Taibei, Institute of Modern History, Academia Sinica, 1989).
6. Wu Chengming, *Zhongguo ziben*, pp. 247–51.
7. Wang, "Food Supply and Grain Prices," pp. 444–51.

the foremost emporium for many other commodities. In 1756, for example, Governor Gao Jin said in a memorial to the emperor that tung oil and black plums were produced in Huguang, white wax in Hunan and Guizhou, copper in Yunnan and Guangdong, coir fiber in Huguang, Jiangxi, and Zhejiang, and rattan in Guangdong. But all of these products were, he pointed out, shipped to Suzhou for distribution to other parts of the empire.[8]

In Table 1.1, I have compiled an annual price series for the delta from 1638 through 1935 by combining four shorter series as follows: a Shanghai series for 1638–95, a series for Suzhou City (the capital city of Suzhou Prefecture) covering 1696–1740, a Suzhou Prefecture series for 1741–1910, and a Shanghai series for 1911–35. There are, however, a number of years for which price data are missing. In such cases, I have filled out the missing data by extrapolation (marked with an asterisk in the third column); for the years 1862–64, when Suzhou was occupied by the Taiping rebels, I have used Shanghai prices.

The core of these data is the 170-year-long Suzhou Prefecture series plus the preceding Suzhou City series. Combined, these two series cover the entire Qing period except for the beginning decades. The data for the Suzhou City series are obtained from reports of governors and imperial commissioners of silk works residing in the city. Since the city was then the largest grain market in the country, to which early Manchu emperors paid close attention, more price reports came from there than elsewhere in the country. But it was not until the establishment of a nationwide grain-price-reporting system in the late 1730s that reports became regularly required of local administrations. Under this system, provincial authorities throughout the country were required to submit to the throne monthly reports on prices of major grains in every prefecture under their jurisdiction.[9] The Suzhou Prefecture series is based on these reports. My colleague and I have gathered 1,632 monthly reports for this period (1740–1910), of which 96 years are complete with 12 months of data, another 25 years with 11 months of data, and only 6 years without data at all (see column 3). Nonetheless, how reliable are these official data? Obviously we cannot proceed with our research unless we have some degree of confidence that they provide a good approximation of market prices.

For the present purpose of trend observation I shall employ two kinds of tests to evaluate the official data, first, to observe whether excessively high prices occur in, or are preceded by, years of major natural or man-made calamities in the area or other parts of the country and, second, to see whether the secular movements of prices as manifested in the official series

---

8. *Gongzhongdang Qianlongchao zouzhe* (Taibei, 1979), 15:431.

9. For monthly grain price reports, see James Lee, Cameron Campbell, and Guofu Tan, "Infanticide and Family Planning," in this collection.

TABLE 1.1 Rice Prices in the Yangzi Delta, 1638–1935
(taels of silver per *shi* unless noted otherwise)

Year	Annual Price	No. of Official Reports Available	Other Series	31-Year Moving Average	Deviation from Moving Average (%)
1638	1.90				
1639	1.90				
1640	2.80				
1641	3.90	*			
1642	5.00				
1643	2.50				
1644	2.50				
1645	2.50				
1646	3.00				
1647	4.00				
1648	3.10	*			
1649	2.20				
1650	1.80				
1651	3.90				
1652	3.30				
1653	2.70			2.18	24
1654	2.50			2.14	17
1655	2.50			2.11	19
1656	1.60	*		2.06	-22
1657	0.70			1.97	-64
1658	1.35	*		1.83	-26
1659	2.00			1.76	13
1660	1.85	*		1.71	8
1661	1.70			1.65	3
1662	1.70			1.58	8
1663	0.90			1.48	-39
1664	0.95	*		1.44	-34
1665	1.00			1.44	-31
1666	0.70			1.43	-51
1667	0.60			1.33	-55
1668	0.55	*		1.25	-56
1669	0.50			1.19	-58
1670	1.00			1.14	-12
1671	1.30			1.09	19
1672	1.10			1.08	2
1673	0.60			1.07	-44
1674	0.60			1.07	-44
1675	0.70	*		1.03	-32
1676	0.80			1.01	-21
1677	0.80			0.97	-18
1678	0.90			0.95	-5
1679	1.80			0.96	88

TABLE 1.1 *(Continued)*

Year	Annual Price	No. of Official Reports Available	Other Series	31-Year Moving Average	Deviation from Moving Average (%)
1680	2.30			0.95	142
1681	1.50	*		0.94	60
1682	0.70			0.94	- 26
1683	0.90			0.95	- 6
1684	0.90		0.90	0.96	- 7
1685	0.90		0.85	0.97	- 8
1686	1.00	*	0.90	0.97	3
1687	1.10		0.90	0.96	15
1688	0.60		0.80	0.95	- 37
1689	1.10		0.94	0.97	13
1690	1.00		0.90	0.99	1
1691	1.00		0.85	1.02	- 2
1692	0.70		0.80	1.03	- 32
1693	1.00		1.20	1.06	- 5
1694	1.10		0.75	1.07	3
1695	0.70		0.75	1.04	- 33
1696	0.70	1	0.75	0.99	- 29
1697	0.80	*	0.88	0.96	- 17
1698	0.90	1	0.85	0.97	- 7
1699	0.86	*	0.85	0.97	- 11
1700	0.83	*	0.83	0.98	- 15
1701	0.80	1	0.73	0.98	- 19
1702	0.92	*	0.73	0.98	- 6
1703	1.04	*	0.90	0.97	7
1704	1.16	*	0.95	0.98	19
1705	1.28	*	1.05	0.97	32
1706	1.40	1	1.02	0.96	45
1707	1.30	3	1.30	0.96	35
1708	1.60	4	1.40	0.97	64
1709	1.20	10	1.32	0.98	22
1710	0.90	7	1.02	0.98	- 8
1711	0.80	7	0.82	0.99	- 19
1712	0.70	2	0.80	1.01	- 31
1713	0.90	9	1.03	1.02	- 12
1714	0.90	9	1.10	1.03	- 13
1715	1.20	7	0.85	1.04	15
1716	1.00	11	1.50	1.05	- 5
1717	1.00	9	0.85	1.07	- 7
1718	0.80	10	0.76	1.09	- 26
1719	0.70	10	1.00	1.09	- 36
1720	0.80	14	0.95	1.09	- 26

(continued on next page)

TABLE 1.1 *(Continued)*

Year	Annual Price	No. of Official Reports Available	Other Series	31-Year Moving Average	Deviation from Moving Average (%)
1721	0.90	5	1.30	1.08	- 16
1722	1.00	9	1.10	1.07	- 6
1723	1.00	5	1.20	1.07	- 6
1724	1.20	7	1.30	1.06	13
1725	1.20	11	1.00	1.06	13
1726	0.90	11	1.10	1.08	- 16
1727	1.30	14	1.15	1.10	18
1728	1.20	1	1.00	1.13	6
1729	1.20	*	0.85	1.15	4
1730	1.20	*	1.00	1.17	3
1731	1.20	1	1.20	1.17	2
1732	1.30	*	1.40	1.19	9
1733	1.40	2	1.20	1.22	14
1734	1.20	1	0.90	1.25	- 4
1735	1.00	1	0.86	1.28	- 22
1736	1.00	11	0.80	1.32	- 24
1737	1.10	12	0.92	1.37	- 19
1738	1.30	12	1.20	1.39	- 6
1739	1.40	12	1.05	1.41	- 1
1740	1.20	12	1.00	1.43	- 16
1741	1.34	12	1.10	1.48	- 10
1742	1.53	12	1.25	1.51	2
1743	1.60	11	1.30	1.52	5
1744	1.55	12	1.05	1.55	0
1745	1.42	12	1.00	1.58	- 10
1746	1.37	12	1.10	1.60	- 14
1747	1.61	12	1.50	1.62	- 1
1748	2.04	12	1.60	1.64	25
1749	1.69	12	1.40	1.65	3
1750	1.64	11	1.30	1.67	- 2
1751	1.93	11	2.10	1.70	13
1752	2.31	12	1.40	1.72	34
1753	1.73	12	1.30	1.74	- 1
1754	1.64	12	1.20	1.76	- 7
1755	1.89	11	2.20	1.78	6
1756	2.73	11	1.60	1.80	52
1757	1.70	7	1.30	1.80	- 6
1758	1.75	12	1.40	1.80	- 3
1759	1.95	12	1.90	1.80	8
1760	2.18	12	1.30	1.82	20

TABLE 1.1 *(Continued)*

Year	Annual Price	No. of Official Reports Available	Other Series	31-Year Moving Average	Deviation from Moving Average (%)
1761	1.82	12	1.50	1.84	- 1
1762	1.91	11	1.60	1.85	3
1763	1.82	6	1.40	1.86	- 2
1764	1.74	8	1.60	1.87	- 7
1765	1.93	7	1.95	1.87	3
1766	1.92	12	1.70	1.87	2
1767	1.67	11	1.70	1.88	- 11
1768	1.73	12	1.85	1.87	- 7
1769	1.97	12	2.10	1.87	5
1770	2.00	11	2.10	1.88	6
1771	1.62	7	1.80	1.91	- 15
1772	1.55	11	1.30	1.89	- 18
1773	1.36	11	1.32	1.89	- 28
1774	1.63	12	2.00	1.88	- 13
1775	2.05	12	2.20	1.86	10
1776	2.09	12	1.57	1.84	14
1777	1.87	12	1.45	1.82	2
1778	1.75	12	2.00	1.81	- 3
1779	2.33	12	2.10	1.79	30
1780	1.87	9	1.90	1.78	5
1781	1.68	12	2.30	1.76	- 5
1782	1.98	12	2.00	1.74	14
1783	2.05	8	1.90	1.72	19
1784	1.77	10	2.05	1.70	4
1785	2.09	11	3.50	1.68	24
1786	2.63	9	3.50	1.67	58
1787	2.19	12	2.10	1.68	31
1788	1.62	11	2.10	1.71	- 5
1789	1.49	6	2.00	1.75	- 15
1790	1.42	9	2.00	1.79	- 21
1791	1.46	2	2.20	1.82	- 20
1792	1.37	4	2.50	1.82	- 25
1793	1.36	4	3.30	1.86	- 27
1794	1.44	5	3.50	1.90	- 24
1795	1.37	6	2.70	1.91	- 28
1796	1.23	12	2.20	1.93	- 36
1797	1.18	7	2.75	1.96	- 40
1798	1.16	10	2.18	1.98	- 41
1799	1.20	12	1.85	2.01	- 40
1800	1.26	11	2.85	2.05	- 38

(continued on next page)

TABLE 1.1 *(Continued)*

Year	Annual Price	No. of Official Reports Available	Other Series	31-Year Moving Average	Deviation from Moving Average (%)
1801	1.57	12	2.62	2.07	- 24
1802	2.00	12	2.60	2.06	- 3
1803	2.48	12		2.06	20
1804	2.69	12		2.08	29
1805	2.79	4		2.11	32
1806	2.92	3		2.14	36
1807	2.35	1		2.17	8
1808	2.98	4		2.21	35
1809	2.95	11		2.25	31
1810	2.63	12		2.28	15
1811	2.41	12		2.31	4
1812	2.64	12		2.34	13
1813	2.61	12		2.37	10
1814	2.90	11		2.41	20
1815	3.09	1		2.44	26
1816	2.78	12		2.48	12
1817	2.27	11		2.52	- 10
1818	2.37	5		2.54	- 7
1819	2.11	12		2.56	- 17
1820	2.33	12		2.55	- 9
1821	2.48	1		2.53	- 2
1822	2.49	*		2.50	- 1
1823	2.50	1		2.50	0
1824	2.50	*		2.47	1
1825	2.50	1		2.46	2
1826	2.28	4		2.46	- 7
1827	2.17	12		2.46	- 12
1828	2.18	7		2.45	- 11
1829	2.22	12		2.44	- 9
1830	2.28	10		2.42	- 6
1831	2.51	12		2.38	5
1832	2.60	11		2.35	10
1833	2.77	12		2.35	18
1834	2.96	12		2.34	- 4
1835	2.37	12		2.35	1
1836	2.25	12	1.54	2.34	- 4
1837	2.17	12	1.32	2.31	- 6
1838	2.08	12		2.27	- 8
1839	2.24	12	1.54	2.23	0
1840	2.51	12	1.61	2.20	14

TABLE 1.1 *(Continued)*

Year	Annual Price	No. of Official Reports Available	Other Series	31-Year Moving Average	Deviation from Moving Average (%)
1841	2.57	12		2.17	19
1842	2.55	12	1.61	2.18	17
1843	2.26	12		2.20	3
1844	2.38	12	1.25	2.21	8
1845	2.24	12	0.96	2.19	2
1846	1.91	12	0.96	2.21	-14
1847	1.95	12	1.04	2.27	-14
1848	1.98	11	1.04	2.31	-14
1849	2.20	7	2.79	2.34	-6
1850	2.39	12	1.43	2.34	2
1851	2.18	12	0.96	2.36	-8
1852	1.32	12	1.32	2.36	-44
1853	1.35	8		2.35	-43
1854	1.38	1		2.35	-41
1855	1.46	9	1.07	2.34	-38
1856	1.48	1	2.64	2.32	-36
1857	2.66	8	2.68	2.30	16
1858	2.79	10	3.82	2.27	23
1859	2.37	9		2.25	5
1860	1.68	3	1.75	2.22	-24
1861	2.96	*		2.20	35
1862	4.24		4.24	2.20	93
1863	3.82		3.82	2.21	73
1864	3.96		3.96	2.20	80
1865	2.84	4	2.93	2.18	30
1866	3.00	12	2.83	2.15	40
1867	2.26	12	2.69	2.13	6
1868	1.81	11	2.73	2.14	-16
1869	1.96	12	2.14	2.15	-9
1870	2.08	12	2.71	2.16	-4
1871	1.90	12	2.12	2.18	-13
1872	1.79	12	1.91	2.19	-18
1873	1.72	12	1.53	2.16	-20
1874	1.72	12	1.53	2.13	-19
1875	1.53	11	1.77	2.13	-28
1876	1.53	9	1.77	2.13	-28
1877	1.83	12	1.98	2.10	-13
1878	2.27	12	2.08	2.03	12
1879	1.81	12	2.08	1.97	-8
1880	1.50	12	1.70	1.91	-22

(continued on next page)

TABLE 1.1 *(Continued)*

Year	Annual Price	No. of Official Reports Available	Other Series	31-Year Moving Average	Deviation from Moving Average (%)
1881	1.33	12	1.70	1.90	- 30
1882	1.63	12	1.70	1.88	- 14
1883	1.79	12	1.70	1.91	- 7
1884	1.69	12	1.70	1.95	- 13
1885	1.59	12	2.26	1.98	- 20
1886	1.97	12	2.55	1.99	- 1
1887	1.96	11	1.84	2.05	- 4
1888	1.73	1	1.98	2.10	- 18
1889	1.87	12	1.98	2.16	- 13
1890	2.14	12	1.84	2.20	- 3
1891	1.88	12	2.55	2.25	- 16
1892	2.01	12	2.12	2.33	- 14
1893	2.04	12	1.98	2.40	- 15
1894	2.02	12	2.55	2.43	- 17
1895	2.11	12	3.54	2.50	- 16
1896	2.36	12	2.97	2.65	- 11
1897	2.59	12	3.68	2.81	- 8
1898	3.20	12	3.39	2.94	9
1899	2.85	12	3.39	3.01	- 5
1900	2.80	12	2.83	3.14	- 11
1901	2.65	11	2.83	3.27	- 19
1902	3.54	11	3.82	3.37	5
1903	3.52	12	3.82	3.47	1
1904	3.47	10	2.97	3.59	- 3
1905	2.87	11	3.61	3.77	- 24
1906	3.12	10	3.28	3.95	- 21
1907	3.98	12	4.11	4.17	- 4
1908	4.06	12	4.24	4.38	- 7
1909	3.34	12	3.54	4.57	- 27
1910	3.91	12	4.24	4.78	- 18
1911	6.20			5.11	21
1912	6.16			5.40	14
1913	5.60			5.60	0
1914	4.21			5.83	- 28
1915	5.74			6.17	- 7
1916	5.53			6.39	- 13
1917	5.06			6.58	- 23
1918	5.14			6.67	- 23
1919	5.39			6.82	- 21
1920	7.47			7.01	7

TABLE 1.1 *(Continued)*

Year	Annual Price	No. of Official Reports Available	Other Series	31-Year Moving Average	Deviation from Moving Average (%)
1921	7.51				
1922	8.68				
1923	8.74				
1924	7.96				
1925	8.50				
1926	12.24				
1927	11.48				
1928	8.61				
1929	10.50				
1930	13.22				
1931	9.54				
1932	8.82				
1933	6.26				
1934	7.98				
1935	9.56				

SOURCES: Ye Mengzhu, *Yueshi bian* (Shanghai, 1981), pp. 153-56, 171-72; Yao Tinglin, *Linian ji*, in *Qingdai riji huichao* (Shanghai, 1982), pp. 39-161; Li Xu, *Li Xu zouzhe* (Beijing, 1976), pp. 1-293; *Gongzhongdang Yongzhengchao zouzhe* (Taibei, 1977-79); *Gongzhongdang Qianlongchao zouzhe* (Taibei, 1979-89); grain price lists preserved at the First Historical Archives in Beijing and the National Palace Museum in Taibei; *Decennial Reports, 1892-1901* (Shanghai, 1904), vol. II, app. 1, p. 26; *Decennial Reports, 1902-1911* (Shanghai, 1913), vol. II, p. 340; Ke Wuchi, *Louwang yongyu ji* (Beijing, 1986), pp. 3-105; *Yinxian tongzhi* (1935), pp. 219-29; "Shanghai wushiliu nianlai mijia tongji", *Shehui yuekan* 1, no. 2 (Feb. 1929): 1-18; Zhu Sihuang, comp., *Minguo jingjishi* (Shanghai, 1948), p. 543; Tanaka Issei, "Shindai Settō sōzoku no soshiki keisei ni okeru sōshi engeki no kinō ni tsuite", *Tōyōshi kenkyū* 44, no. 4 (March 1986): 47-50.

NOTES: The tael is a unit of weight in Qing China, and its official standard *(kuping)* is equivalent to 37.3 grams. The *shi* (officially *cangshi*) is a unit of capacity amounting to 1.035 hectoliters.

Price data from official reports are for second-grade rice. An asterisk marks years with missing data, filled in by extrapolation. Shanghai data are used for 1862-64.

Price data from unofficial sources are presumably stated in local units of measure, of which the exact weight and capacity are unknown. The Maritime Customs data and Shanghai data for the Republican period are converted into their equivalents in Qing official standards according to rates as follows: 1 tael = 0.99 Haikwan tael = 1.10 Shanghai taels = 1.39 *yuan*, and 1 *shi* = 1.4 piculs = 0.926 Shanghai *shi*.

Prices originally stated in copper cash are converted into prices in taels according to the exchange rate between silver and cash in the respective years.

The 31-year moving average is the arithmetic average of the annual prices for a 31-year period centered on the year under observation. For example, the moving average for 1653 is the arithmetic average of annual prices for the 31 years from 1638 to 1668.

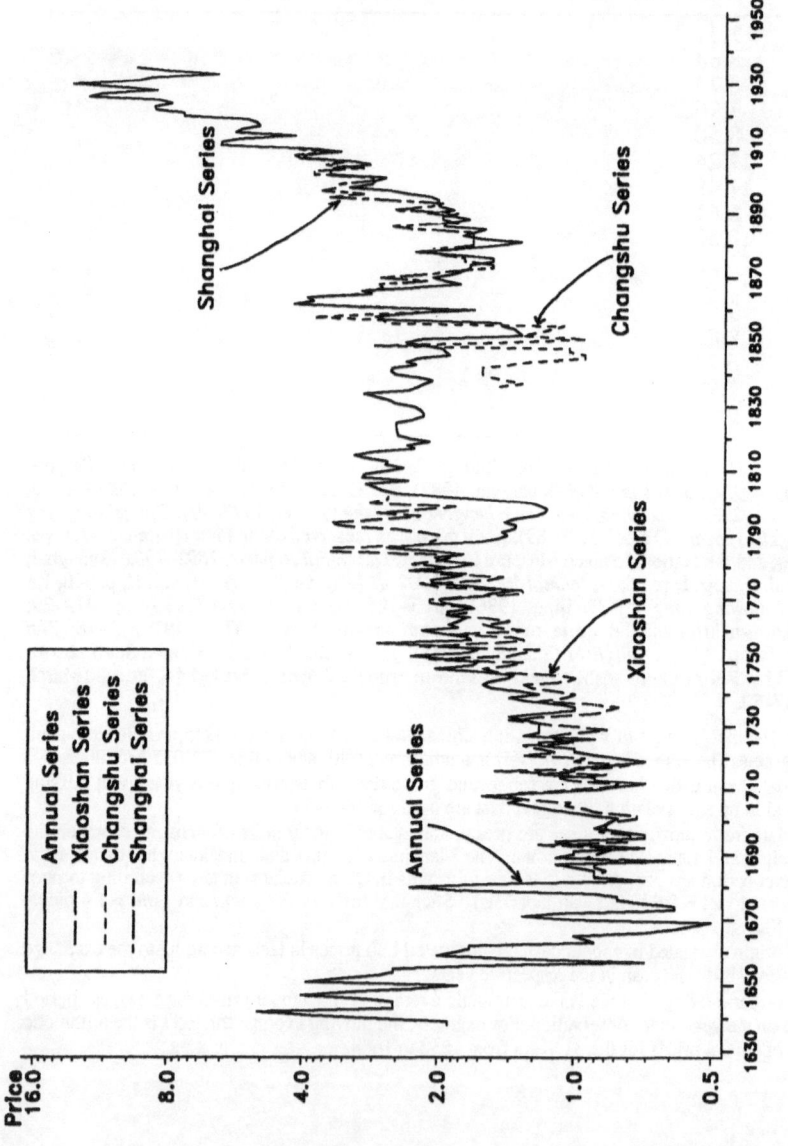

Fig. 1.1. Rice Prices in the Yangzi Delta, 1638–1935 (taels per *shi*)

are in line with those exhibited in other price series for the area that are derived from different and yet reputable sources. As indicated in Table 1.1 and Figure 1.1, rice prices peaked in 1756, 1786, 1814–15, and the early 1860s. In 1755 heavy flooding afflicted the Lower Yangzi and Huai River valleys, and in 1785 a dreadful drought blanketed the Lower and Middle Yangzi Valley, the North China Plain, and Manchuria. In 1814 the country was hit by both—flooding in Zhejiang, Fujian, and Jiangxi and drought in Jiangsu, Anhui, Henan, Sichuan, and Shanxi.[10] Finally, it was at the height of the Taiping Rebellion (1850–64) that prices skyrocketed as never before in the Qing period.

In the fourth column of Table 1.1, I have assembled three more series of rice prices of shorter duration for Xiaoshan (a county in the neighborhood of Hangzhou), Changshu (a county in Suzhou Prefecture), and Shanghai. The Xiaoshan series for 1684–1802 is derived from the records of the Lai clan in the county; the Changshu series for 1836–1860 from casual notes of a local scholar; and the Shanghai series for 1862–1910 from the decennial reports of China's Maritime Customs. As shown in Figure 1.1, prices of these shorter series move mostly in step with those of the annual series. Moreover, the linear trends fitted respectively for the annual series and for the Xiaoshan series for a whole century (1684–1788) turn out to be virtually the same, that is, an increase at the rate of 0.0131 tael per year for the former series and 0.0136 for the latter. The same can be said of the annual series and the Maritime Customs series for the last three decades of the Qing period, with respective increases of 0.0848 and 0.0860 tael. There is, then, good reason to believe the general validity of official price data for the Qing so far as the secular trend is concerned.

For the last dozen years of the eighteenth century, however, the annual series and the Xiaoshan series diverge significantly from each other (see Fig. 1.1). I suspect that something went wrong with the price reports from Suzhou Prefecture for those years because they show a sudden and drastic decrease in the extent of price fluctuations compared with any period before or after. On the other hand, not only for Suzhou but also for many other prefectures in and out of Jiangsu, the movement of prices represents a V-shape between the mid-1780s and the early years of the nineteenth century and the trough in the Suzhou series appears to be among the deepest. I cannot at the moment give a satisfactory explanation for the divergence between the two series for this short period. Perhaps a real picture will emerge with the discovery of new data.

Of all the data in the annual series, those for 1911–35 are unquestionably

10. *Zhongguo jin wubainian hanlao fenbu tuji*, comp. Zhongyang Qixiangju Qixiang Kexue Yenjiuyuan (Institute of Meteorology, the Central Bureau of Meteorology; Beijing; 1981), pp. 148, 163, 178.

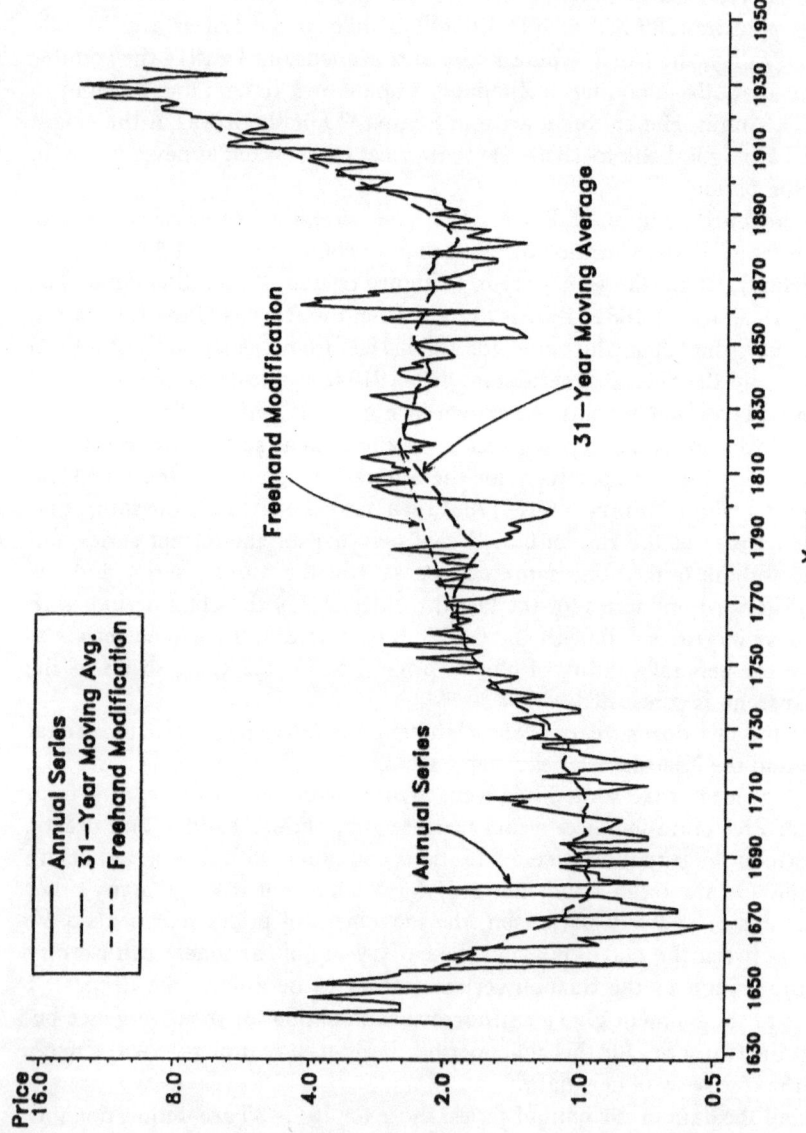

Fig. 1.2. Thirty-one-Year Moving Average of Rice Prices in the Yangzi Delta, 1638–1935 (taels per *shi*)

the most solid because they are compiled on the basis of price quotations in the *Shen Bao* and *Xinwen Bao*, two widely read newspapers in prewar Shanghai. The most rudimentary data are those for the seventeenth century, which are derived from random notes left by two contemporary local scholars. These notes do not have price entries for every year, and price data therein lack statistical uniformity in terms of product and date. Nonetheless, prices recorded by one scholar are highly consistent with those by the other. Moreover, virtually all peak prices noted by either of them coincide with years of calamities or come immediately afterward. All in all, while the quality of the four sets of data that form the annual series is uneven, the data are good enough to be taken as a general indicator of price trends in the market.

To better observe the broad trends of prices, I have, as did W. G. Hoskins for wheat prices in England, smoothed the annual series by using 31-year moving averages.[11] The results are rendered in column 5 of Table 1.1 and plotted in ratio scale in Figure 1.2. The smoothed averages fit the original series rather well. In view of the probable defects of the series for the last dozen years of the eighteenth century, which may have exerted an undue influence over the projection of the price trend, the shallow trough in the mid-1780s may well be nothing more than a statistical illusion. I have therefore smoothed it out freehand with a broken line. So modified, the figure shows prices to have moved in two broad swings over the three centuries. Beginning in the 1640s, the first swing headed steeply downward, reaching bottom in the early 1680s, then changed direction, rising at a modest rate for over a century to its peak around 1820. Then came the second swing. Prices descended gradually through the early 1850s and, after experiencing drastic fluctuations caused by the Taiping Rebellion and its aftermath in the third quarter of the nineteenth century, shot up in the early 1880s and kept rising through the 1920s.

As pointed out before, prices moved generally in a synchronized fashion in the Yangzi Delta and most other regions. Indeed, we can find few exceptions to the long inflationary trend in the eighteenth century, the slight downturn in the second quarter of the nineteenth century, and the half-century upswing before the Great Depression.[12] It may be worth noting that while broad trends in grain prices are also recognizable in premodern Europe, the turning points are much less uniform from one region to another. There were the well-observed Price Revolution in the sixteenth century, the fall of prices in the seventeenth, renewed inflation in the eighteenth. Nonetheless, the sixteenth-century inflationary period drew to an end between 1590 and 1600 in the south but between 1620 and 1640 in the north; and the seventeenth-

---

11. W. G. Hoskins, "Harvest Fluctuations and English Economic History, 1480–1619," *Agricultural History Review* 12 (1964): 28–46.

12. See also the other papers in Part 1 of this volume.

century deflationary period reached its nadir in the 1690s in Würzburg and Vienna but not until the 1730s and 1740s in England.

More interesting is the contrast in regional price differentials between the two continents. In the last half of the fifteenth century the western Mediterranean region led Europe with the highest prices, eastern Europe stood at the other end, and the northern and Atlantic regions fell in between. The ratio of wheat prices then was about 6 or 7 to 1 between the two extremes. A century later the gap was narrowed to 4 to 1 because of the growth of the grain trade on the Baltic, which brought more and more Polish wheat to the Mediterranean region. Even more remarkable was the development of the Atlantic trade in the next one and a half centuries. By 1700 the north (England, France, the Low Countries) had taken the economic leadership from the Mediterranean and turned itself into the region of expensive wheat. By the middle of the eighteenth century prices in most regions had, by and large, merged into one another, with a somewhat higher level in the north.[13] Europe thus became a highly integrated economy before the advent of the Industrial Revolution.

Early eighteenth-century China was, on the whole, comparable with Europe in terms of market integration. As shown in Map 1.2, in South China, where most people lived and where rice was the staple food, the Yangzi Delta (Suzhou and Hangzhou) had the highest prices, that is, about 1.5 taels per *shi*, around 1740. Next came neighboring Anhui and the southeastern coast of Fujian and Guangdong, where rice prices stayed at 1.0 taels or somewhat higher. The third region was the vast food-producing area of Sichuan, Huguang, and Guangxi, where rice was sold at around 0.8–0.9 tael per *shi*, the cheapest of all. The ratio between the highest and the lowest prices is 2 to 1 in the South. North China produced little rice, and most people there ate wheat, millet, and kaoliang instead. Almost all of the rice that the well-to-do consumed in the North was shipped from the South; its price was therefore much higher than in the South. Should the North be added as the fourth region for observation, the ratio between the highest and the lowest prices would increase to 3 to 1 (note that rice prices in the North vary from 1.8 taels in Xi'an to 2.4 taels in Jinan and Chengde).[14]

In the latter part of the nineteenth century, modern transportation, such as steamships and trains, was introduced into China. A narrowing of price

---

13. For European prices, cf. F. P. Braudel and F. Spooner, "Prices in Europe from 1450 to 1750," *The Cambridge Economic History of Europe*, vol. 4, ed. E. E. Rich and C. H. Wilson (Cambridge, 1967), pp. 378–486.

14. All price data come from the First Historical Archives in Beijing and the National Palace Museum in Taibei. The 1909 price for Guangzhou (2.30 taels per *shi*) is apparently unreliable. Because Guangdong had become the province with the severest shortage in food supply, the Guangzhou price should be at least as high as the Quanzhou price. The 1909 price for Tianjin is unavailable; instead I give the price of top-grade rice in Beijing for the same year.

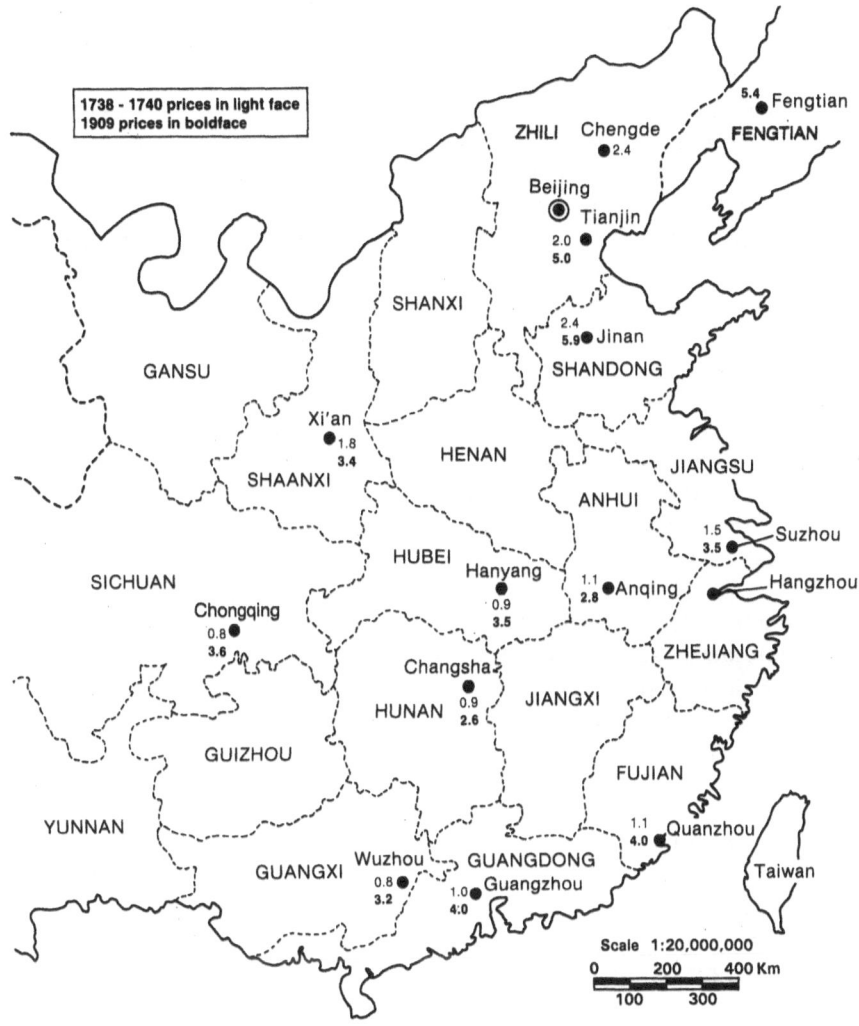

Map 1.2. Rice Prices of Selected Prefectures in China, 1738–1740 and 1909 (taels per *shi*).

differentials is observable, though the degree of uniformity was much less pronounced than in Europe on the eve of its industrial takeoff. Although in the latter half of the nineteenth century the highest prices still prevailed in the North, much change had occurred in the South. The Yangzi Delta, still the country's center of economic gravity, was superseded by the two southern coastal provinces of Fujian and Guangdong as the region of dear rice because the Taiping Rebellion took a heavy toll of lives in the delta. In the interior, Sichuan and Hubei became overpopulated, raising the price of rice, while Hunan, Anhui, and Jiangxi remained an area with large amounts of food for export. The ratio of prices between the two extremes stood at 1.5 to 1 in the South in 1909, or 2.3 to 1 if the North is included; both ratios are lower than around 1740. What this brief survey of price history suggests is that, given the inexpensive network of water transportation that radiated from the Yangzi Delta, China had a more integrated economy than Europe did in most of the seventeenth century. However, the emergence of the North Atlantic economy moved Europe along at an accelerated pace. By the middle of the eighteenth century the position of the two continents had been unequivocally reversed.

Economic historians consider population and the quantity of money to be the prime factors affecting the secular trend in prices. In addition, some scholars note the causal relationship between climatic changes and food supply, which may produce a significant impact on prices. We may observe these relationships with prices by the use of the well-known equation of exchange

$$MV_t = PT \text{ or } MV_y = PY$$

where P stands for the price level, M for the stock of money, T for the volume of transactions, Y for real output, and V_t and V_y for transaction velocity and income velocity respectively. If T or Y increases with no change in the money stock or in velocity, P will decline. On the other hand, given T or Y, if MV_t or MV_y increases, P will rise.

What follows in this section is a historical review of the major variables—population, the stock of silver (the primary component of money for most of the period), and climate cycles—that, individually or in combination, may in large measure account for the two long price swings noted above. However, our present state of knowledge on any of the variables is so incomplete that most estimates are subject to a wide margin of error. Accordingly, any conclusions we may reach cannot but be tentative.

Population affects prices in a variety of ways. Malthusians have long stressed the imbalance between population growth and food supply. Since cultivated land cannot be expanded indefinitely, population growth will inevitably result in the decrease of per capita acreage. Increased input of labor and capital may raise the yields of land per hectare and thus compensate for its shortage. Given the state of technology, however, the marginal productivity of land will eventually diminish. From then on, the food supply will not increase in proportion to population growth. Food prices cannot but rise; the level of general prices must rise too. On the other hand, not only does population increase mean more labor, but it may also contribute to capital formation and technological progress. At the same time, higher population density may stimulate an intensification of the marketing system, leading to crop specialization and division of labor and thereby raising agricultural productivity. Higher productivity means more abundant goods and services, which may in turn bring down the general level of prices.

Nonetheless, in a historical study of English population and prices Peter H. Lindert does find a strong correlation between the two prior to 1815, that is, before industrialization. Specifically, he observes that prices rose greatly in periods of rapid population growth (1526–1603 and 1760–1801) but climbed less or fell "in the period of less dramatic population increase between the early seventeenth century and the middle of the eighteenth." He offers two theories to explain how population growth affects prices. According to the first theory, rapid population growth may bring about a higher ratio of children to adults. With more children to support, a household generally has fewer savings. Lower savings relative to household income implies a greater demand for consumer goods and services relative to demand for money holdings, raising the price level. The second theory is what Lindert calls the "Goldstone variation." According to Jack A. Goldstone, population growth brings increased population density, urbanization, and specialization within agriculture. Monetized transactions will increase at the expense of production for home consumption. In an economy where the marketplace is underdeveloped, more frequent and smaller individual transactions should bring economies in the holding of cash, leading to a rise in the velocity of monetary circulation and higher prices.[15]

Despite the pioneer works of Ping-ti Ho and Dwight H. Perkins, the size of China's population before the 1953 census is still a matter of much debate. At the end of the sixteenth century the total number of people in the country was, according to Ho's estimate, around 150 million.[16] After studying the data on famine relief in Henan for 1593–94, Shu-yuen Yim concludes that official statistics on population are substantially understated and that the total population in the empire was no less than 200 million in 1600.[17] Mass uprisings and unprecedented droughts hit the greater part of the country in

---

15. Peter H. Lindert, "English Population, Wages, and Prices, 1541–1913," *Journal of Interdisciplinary History* 15, no. 4 (Spring 1985): 609–34.

16. Ping-ti Ho, *Studies on the Population of China, 1368–1953* (Cambridge, Mass., 1959), p. 264.

17. Shu-yuen Yim, "Famine Relief Statistics as a Guide to the Population of Sixteenth-Century China: A Case Study of Honan Province," *Ch'ing-shih Wen-t'i* 3, no. 9 (November 1978): 1–30.

the second quarter of the seventeenth century, causing a drastic decrease in population. Scholars are still far apart as to the extent of loss in lives during the time of the Ming-Qing transition. Estimates of the number of people at the beginning of the Manchu period vary from 70 million to 100–150 million,[18] though I am inclined to think that the upper range, or, say, 120 million, is probably a better approximation.

Following the Manchu conquest in 1644, political and economic order gradually returned. Before the pacification of the Three Feudatories and Taiwan in the early 1680s, however, bitter fighting continued in one part of the country after another because of Chinese resistance to foreign rule. Therefore, economic recovery proceeded slowly in the latter part of the seventeenth century. By 1700 China's population was most likely still quite below the level attained a century before, and perhaps something around 150 million is not far off the mark.

The eighteenth century is one of a few periods in Chinese history in which the country enjoyed prolonged peace and prosperity, and its population grew as never before. The *baojia* system for annual registration of population started in 1741 and was to last until 1850. Nevertheless, the statistics before 1776 are incomplete, and some of those close to the mid-nineteenth century are believed to be much inflated. We are left with only those for the last quarter of the eighteenth century and perhaps the first two decades of the nineteenth century that can be considered relatively reliable. According to official reports cited by Ho, the number of people totaled 353 million in 1820. By 1850 it had risen to 430 million. But, after a thorough investigation of the county data of Sichuan and a survey of apparently exaggerated figures for several other provinces, G. William Skinner concludes that China's population then was around 380 million instead.[19]

In the third quarter of the nineteenth century probably as many as 40 million people perished in the Taiping Rebellion and other social upheavals that devastated a large part of the empire and particularly the populous Lower Yangzi Valley. However, by the end of the century China had apparently regained the population lost several decades before. Despite political instability that characterized the last years of Manchu rule and the early Republican period, the country witnessed an expansion of population. In the early 1930s the total reached 500 million.[20]

It is interesting to note that grain price movements and population move-

18. Dwight H. Perkins, *Agricultural Development in China, 1368–1968* (Chicago, 1969), p. 216; Kang Chao, *Man and Land in Chinese History* (Stanford, 1986), p. 40.

19. Ho, *Studies on Population*, pp. 281–82; G. William Skinner, "Sichuan's Population in the Nineteenth Century: Lessons from Disaggregated Data," *Late Imperial China* 8, no. 1 (June 1987): 68–76. In the light of Perkins's and Skinner's evaluations, official population data for the early nineteenth century are in all probability exaggerated.

20. For the 1933 population, see Perkins, *Agricultural Development*, p. 16.

TABLE 1.2 Trends of Population, Silver Stocks, and Rice Prices in China, 1650–1930

Year	Population Total (millions)	Population Annual Growth (%)	Silver Stocks Total (millions of silver yuan)	Silver Stocks Annual Growth (%)	Rice Prices Price (taels per *shi*)	Rice Prices Annual Change (%)
1650	120	—	290–330	—	—	—
1655	—	—	—	—	2.11	—
1680	—	—	300–350	0.16	0.95	-3.24
1700	150	0.45	—	—	—	—
1820	353	0.72	—	—	2.55	0.70
1830	—	—	1,140–1,330	0.89	—	—
1850	380	0.25	900–1,100	-1.06	—	—
1870	—	—	—	—	—	—
1875	340	-0.45	—	—	—	—
1880	—	—	1,500–1,600	1.47	1.91	-0.48
1920	—	—	—	—	7.01	3.30
1930	500	0.70	3,200	1.46	—	—

NOTE: Silver stocks for 1680 and 1880 are estimated by extrapolation.

ments in China appear to be in line with what Lindert finds in the English case. As shown in Table 1.2 and Figure 1.3, a fairly strong correlation between population and prices is observable over nearly three centuries. Moreover, periods of rising prices happened to be periods of relatively rapid population growth (the 1700s and 1880–1930), whereas downward movements in prices were mostly accompanied by slower or negative growth in population (1650–80, 1820–80).

China's monetary system in the Qing period was bimetallic, with silver and copper cash. Paper notes issued by native banks (*qianzhuang*), pawnshops, and other merchants appeared in the late eighteenth century. After the Treaty of Nanjing (1842) foreign banknotes began to circulate in treaty ports. China established its first modern bank half a century later. Not until the early twentieth century did banknotes and demand deposits constitute the largest component of the money supply. To observe the possible relationship between the stock of money and prices, I have made an estimate of the total stock of silver, the most important monetary metal in China, for a number of years in the three centuries under study.

Although China did not possess rich silver mines, it was able to cope with the growing demand for specie by importing silver from abroad for most of the period. The arrival of Westerners in the Indian and Pacific oceans following the Great Discoveries opened a new era in relations between the East and

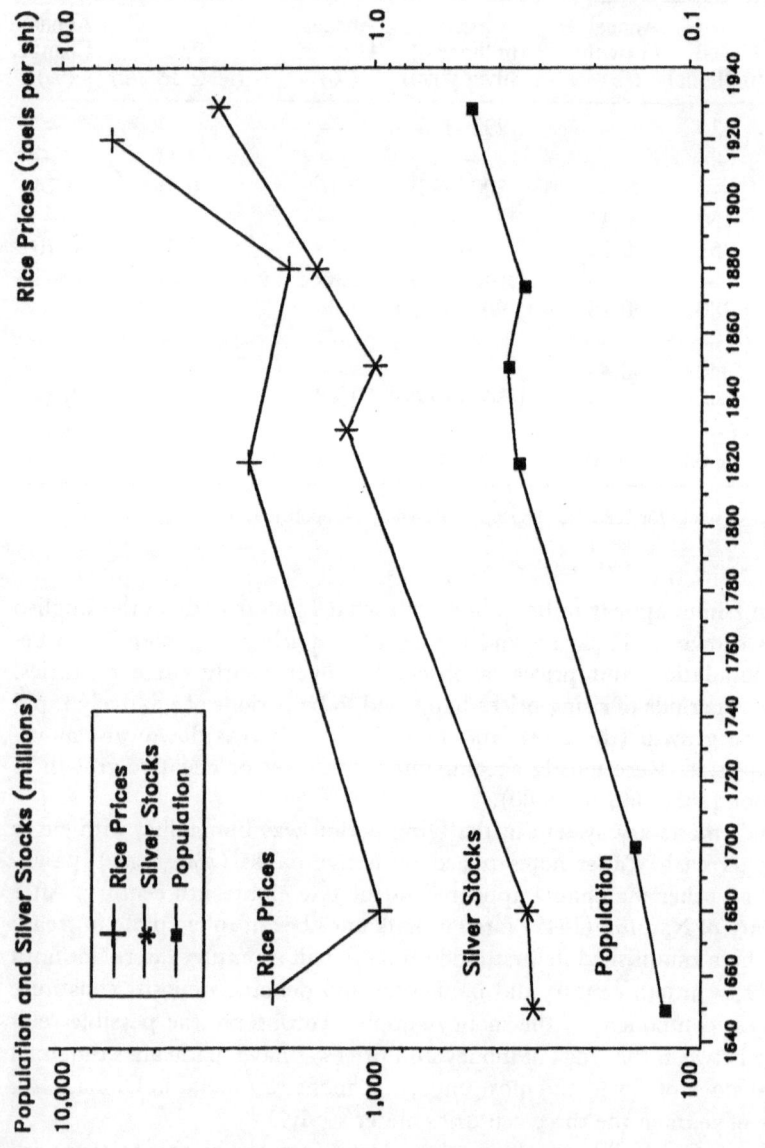

Fig. 1.3. Trends of Population, Silver Stocks, and Rice Prices in China, 1650–1930

the West. Several Chinese products, such as silk, tea, and porcelain, were in great demand in Europe, America, and Japan, though manufactures from abroad struck little enthusiasm in the Middle Kingdom. Nor could the products—spices, ivory, sandalwood, etc.—from Southeast Asia, then under the domination of Western powers, offset the trade deficit incurred. To settle the balance, foreign merchants could offer only one thing, silver, that hardly any Chinese would refuse to accept. Meanwhile the discovery of rich silver mines in Japan, Peru, and Mexico provided a timely means of payment. Portuguese, Spanish, Dutch, British, and American, as well as Chinese, merchants all took part in this thriving trade, and large quantities of silver were thus brought into the country.

From the latter part of the nineteenth century China's economy was more closely integrated with the world market. When prices of silver were lower in the world market than in China, large amounts of specie would find their way through arbitrage into its trading ports, and vice versa. Since other countries had demonetized silver one after another, while China continued to use it as a medium of exchange and means of payment until 1935, it commanded a premium in the country for most of the period. The result is that China continued to be one of the largest recipients of silver even though it suffered a perennial trade deficit from the 1870s on.

How much silver did China possess over the three centuries under discussion? Let us begin with the most recent holdings. Eduard Kann, an expert on China's finance, estimated in early 1931 that there was about 2.5 billion ounces of silver in the country, including 1.7 billion in the form of silver dollars, sycee, and subsidiary coins and 0.8 billion in ornaments and household objects.[21] At the rate of 1.30 silver dollars or *yuan* to an ounce this would amount to 3,250 million *yuan*, which accords well with the Bank of China estimate in the early 1930s.[22] During the next five years, however, China incurred a net loss of 650–700 million *yuan*, largely because of the United States Silver Purchase Act. On the eve of China's monetary reform in early November 1935 its total silver stocks probably stood in the neighborhood of 2,600 million *yuan*.[23]

Between 1893 and 1930, according to Maritime Customs statistics, China

---

21. Eduard Kann, "How Much Silver Is There in China?" *Chinese Economic Journal* 8, no. 4 (April 1931): 410–20.

22. See Thomas G. Rawski, *Economic Growth in Prewar China* (Berkeley and Los Angeles, 1989), pp. 363–65.

23. The net outflow through Maritime Customs amounted to 292 million Haikwan taels, or 456 million silver dollars, in 1931–35. In addition, somewhere between 225 million and 250 million *yuan* was smuggled out of the country in 1934–35. Liang-lin Hsiao, *China's Foreign Trade Statistics, 1864–1949* (Cambridge, 1974), p. 129; Lin Weiying, *Zhongguo zhi xinhuobi zhidu* (Changsha, 1939), pp. 4–5; Yu Jieqiong, *1700–1937 nian Zhongguo yinhuo shuchuru de yige guji* (Changsha, 1940), p. 3.

received from abroad 1,284 million silver *yuan* (823 million Haikwan taels).[24] Such being the case, it may not be far off to put the accumulated amount of specie at 1,900–2,000 million *yuan* at the end of the nineteenth century.

For earlier periods we are on a far less certain ground. In 1643 Jiang Chen, a scholar interested in fiscal and monetary matters, submitted to the falling Ming government a proposal for the adoption of paper money. He figured the total silver stocks then held in the private sector to be around 250 million taels, or 350 million *yuan*.[25] In an essay on the crisis of silver drain in the Daoguang period (1821–50), Taiping Shanren maintained that before the crisis unfolded, the country must have possessed something more than a billion silver *yuan*.[26] Both figures appear to be plausible.

In a broad survey of the influx of silver between the 1570s and 1830s Sun Yutang gives the following breakdown: 100 million silver *yuan* from the Spanish Philippines (1571–1821), over 500 million from England and other European countries (1700–1828), 100 million from the United States (1784–1833), and 140 million from Japan (seventeenth through early nineteenth centuries).[27] It should be pointed out, however, that the second item most probably includes amounts imported from the Philippines and the United States,[28] and so it should be revised downward to 300 million. According to Ch'üan Han-sheng, however, the total shipment from the Philippines during that same period was likely to have been 200 million or more instead of 100 million.[29] Moreover, there were fairly regular shipments of Japanese bullion in the latter part of the sixteenth century. A. Kobata notes, for instance, that the Portuguese carried 500,000–600,000 taels out of Japan annually to finance their trade with China.[30] Therefore, the silver inflow may reasonably be assumed to be around 800 million for the two and a half centuries in question.

Of the 800 million, how much was imported before the fall of the Ming dynasty in 1644? Liang Fangzhong estimates the amount at more than 100 million.[31] But Arai Hakuseki's study shows that Japan alone exported over

24. Hsiao, *China's Foreign Trade Statistics*, pp. 128–29.
25. Cited in Peng Xinwei, *Zhongguo huobishi* (Shanghai, 1965), p. 736.
26. Taiping Shanren, "Daoguangchao yinhuang wenti," in *Zhongguo jin sanbainian shehui jingjishi lunji* (Hong Kong, 1974), 5:41–45.
27. Sun Yutang, "Ming Qing shidai de baiyin neiliu yu fengjian shehui," *Jinbu ribao*, Feb. 3, 1951.
28. Momose Hiromu, "Shindai ni okeru Supein doru no ryūtsū," *Shakai keizai shigaku* 6, no. 2 (May 1936): 22.
29. Quan Hansheng (Ch'üan Han-sheng), "Ming Qing jian Meizhou baiyin de shuru Zhongguo," in *Zhongguo jingjishi luncong* (Hong Kong, 1972), 1:435–50.
30. A. Kobata, "The Production and Uses of Gold and Silver in Sixteenth- and Seventeenth-Century Japan," *Economic History Review*, 2d ser., 18, no. 2 (Nov. 1965): 245–66.
31. Liang Fangzhong, "Mingdai guoji maoyi yu baiyin di shuchuru," *Zhongguo shehui jingjishi jikan* 6, no. 2 (Dec. 1939): 324.

100 million (748,000 *kan*) in the first half of the seventeenth century, most of which ended up in China.[32] When the shipments from the Philippines between 1571 and 1644 and those from Japan before 1600 are added, the amount should, in the light of the foregoing discussion, be around 200 million instead.

While domestic production of silver played a secondary role in the supply of monetary metals, silver mining in Yunnan was in operation for most of the Ming-Qing period. Wei Yuan, one of the foremost scholars in the statecraft school and a keen observer of the nation's economy, wrote in 1842 that "of all silver stocks [in the country] 30–40 percent comes from mining and 60–70 percent from foreign vessels."[33] On the basis of his observation and the quantities of silver inflow, we may readily estimate the amount of bullion held in China to be in the range of 290–330 million silver *yuan* in the mid-seventeenth century and 1,140–1,330 million in the 1820s.

In the second quarter of the nineteenth century the balance of trade turned against China primarily because of the growing opium trade. According to H. B. Morse, there occurred a net drain of silver to the amount of 200 million *yuan* over the period.[34] On the eve of the Taiping Rebellion the country's holdings probably fell to the level of 900–1,100 million. In the latter half of the century, nonetheless, China resumed importing bullion from abroad. J. Laurence Laughlin notes that between 1852 and 1875 alone, at least 1 billion *yuan* of silver had been shipped from England and Mediterranean ports to India and the East.[35] So vast was the influx that China found its stocks of silver doubling in the half-century.

However rudimentary the estimate of silver stocks, the direction of change in the amount of bullion that China held over the three centuries is quite clear. We may, in light of the data presented in Table 1.2 and plotted in Figure 1.3, make two observations. First, not unlike prices and population, silver stocks in China generally followed a rising trend. Second, during the latter part of the seventeenth century and the second quarter of the nineteenth century, when the country's holdings of the white metal changed little or decreased, prices were on the decline. It appears, then, that silver stocks can serve as a crude indicator of the secular movements of prices.

To be sure, the stock of money included not only silver but also copper cash, paper notes, and, later, bank deposits. In the twentieth century, in particular, banknotes and bank deposits soon overtook silver as the dominant components of money. Nor did all silver stocks circulate as money; a

---

32. Cited in Otake Fumio, "Min Shin jidai ni okeru gaikoku gin no ryūnyū," in *Kinsei Shina keizaishi kenkyū* (Tokyo, 1942), p. 57.

33. Wei Yuan, *Shengwuji* (1927), 14:33.

34. Cited in Taiping Shanren, "Daoguangchao," pp. 45–46.

35. J. Laurence Laughlin, *The History of Bimetallism in the United States* (New York, 1897), p. 125.

good part was hoarded in safes or underground or used for jewelry by the well-to-do. Therefore, other components of money as well as the velocity of circulation should, if possible, be taken into consideration when specific periods are examined.

Climatic conditions significantly affect the state of harvest and food supply. Various empirical studies show that relatively warmer temperature increases crop output by lengthening the growing season and by making uplands cultivable, and vice versa. Referring to sixteenth- and seventeenth-century Europe, for example, Andrew B. Appleby, G. Parker, and L. M. Smith suggest that a one-degree-centigrade decline in temperature will shorten the growing season by three to four weeks and is equivalent to raising land elevation by 500 feet.[36] A recent study by Wang Shaowu indicates, moreover, that low summer temperatures in a number of years between 1954 and 1976 reduced harvest yields by a third in Manchuria.[37] It was precisely because of concern for food supply in the empire that the Qing government required all local officials to submit regular weather reports along with reports on grain prices.

The degree of correlation between harvest yields and grain prices is nevertheless not so clear, because prices also depend on such other factors as access to food supply from other areas or from other parts of the world, grain storage, speculation, and government policy. To observe the possible relationships between climate, harvest yields, and secular prices, let us first look into climate cycles and harvest fluctuations in the delta over the centuries in question. Two groups of scientists in China have conducted original research on the long-term temperature changes in the Middle and Lower Yangzi Valley. One group, under the leadership of Zhang Peiyuan, has focused its attention on phenodata for the Qing period; the other, led by Yan Jiyuan, has made a historical investigation of the years when the Huangpu River and Lake Tai froze. They derived virtually the same climate cycles for the area.[38] Between the mid-1600s and the 1970s the country went through three long cycles. The cold period of the first cycle lasted through the first decade of the eighteenth century; the warm period that followed prevailed until 1780. The second cycle extended for almost a century (1781–1882), with 1830 as the turning point between the cold and warm periods. In the early 1870s another cycle started. It was also evenly split, with the 1920s as the transition years

36. Andrew B. Appleby, "Epidemics and Famine in the Little Ice Age," *Journal of Interdisciplinary History* 10 (Spring 1980): 658; G. Parker and L. M. Smith, ed., *The General Crisis of the Seventeenth Century* (London, 1978), cited in Patrick G. Galloway, "Long-term Fluctuations in Climate and Population in the Preindustrial Era" (Paper read at the Ninth International Economic History Congress, Bern, Switzerland, 1986).

37. Wang Shaowu, "Jin sibainian dongya de lengxia" (unpublished manuscript, 1988).

38. Zhang Peiyuan, "Qingdai hannuan bianhua ji qi dui nongye de yingxiang" (Paper read at the Workshop on Qing Population History, Aug. 1985, California Institute of Technology, Pasadena, Calif.); Yan Jiyuan et al., "Changjiang sanjiaozhou de lengnuan tedian yu qushi zhanwang," in *Quanguo qihou bianhua xueshu taolunhui wenji* (Beijing, 1981), pp. 71–77.

TABLE 1.3 Price Trends, Climate Cycles, and Harvest Conditions in the Yangzi Delta, 1653–1920

Period	Price Trend	Climate Cycle	No. of Normal Harvests	No. of Good Harvests	No. of Deficient Harvests	Average Deviation of Harvests (%)
1653–1682	Down	Cold (1650–1710)	5	17	8	-7.89
1683–1780	Up	Warm (1711–1780)	48	29	21	-1.09
1781–1820	Up	Cold (1781–1830)	8	15	17	0.23
1821–1882	Down	Warm (1831–1872)	25	22	9[a]	-7.10
1883–1920	Up	Cold (1873–1920s)	15	21	2	-9.83
Total/ Average			101	104	57	-5.14

[a] The skyrocketing prices in 1861–66 were caused mostly by the Taiping Rebellion, and therefore these years are excluded.

between the cold and warm periods (see Table 1.3). It is worthy of note that in the nineteenth and early twentieth centuries secular prices moved downward in the warm period (1831–72) but upward in the cold periods (1780–1830, 1873–1920), whereas the opposite is true in the seventeenth and eighteenth centuries.

I have not yet compiled data on harvest yields. In my study of grain prices in the Yangzi Delta, however, I do find a very strong association between harvest yields and grain prices. Over the half-century between 1738 and 1789 eleven cycles in both rice prices and wheat prices can be readily identified, and all peaks of these cycles occurred in years of crop failure or poor harvests caused by floods, droughts, or epidemics in the delta or in a large part of the country in the same year or the year before.[39] It is, however, another matter whether fluctuations in local harvests affect the secular movement of prices in an area with easy access to the food-exporting provinces of the country. We may take the deviations of annual prices from their trend values (31-year moving averages) as a measure of harvest fluctuations in the delta and then compare them with changes in secular prices. Assuming that years of normal harvests are those with rice prices within plus or minus 10 percent of the trend, that years of good harvests are those with prices 10 percent or more below the trend, and that years of deficient harvests are those with prices 10 percent or more above the trend, we find that years of good and normal

39. Wang, "Food Supply and Grain Prices."

harvests outnumber years of poor harvests almost 4 to 1 and that average deviations are within the range for normal harvests for all periods (see the last four columns in Table 1.3). Accordingly, cyclical fluctuations in local harvests did not, in my judgment, have a significant impact on the long-term trends of prices, although grain prices were very sensitive to fluctuations in local harvests in the short run.

After reviewing the literature on population, silver stocks, and climate cycles, I can now offer some tentative explanations of the long-term trends of rice prices for the three centuries in question. The high level of prices at the time of the Ming-Qing transition clearly reflects the inflation and the shortage of food consequent to large-scale warfare and a series of natural catastrophes.[40] After the establishment of Manchu rule in 1644, peace and order were gradually restored in the country. Economic reconstruction followed, albeit slowly, with a concomitant improvement in the man-land ratio (depopulation had been drastic between 1600 and 1650). The supply of grain became plentiful relative to the demand for food, despite the cold climate that prevailed in the latter part of the seventeenth century.

During the same time the increase in the stock of money was at best moderate because the new Manchu regime imposed a total ban on coastal trade until the pacification of Taiwan in 1683. The shortage of exchange media received some relief, for the new government issued 1–2 million strings of copper cash annually between 1647–57; but the issuance was later progressively reduced to 200,000–300,000 strings a year.[41] The transaction velocity of money most probably fell after the decades-long inflationary spiral attending the demise of the Ming dynasty. When MV either decreased or remained rather stable and T expanded, prices could not but decline.

In the next phase of the price swing—from the early 1680s to 1820—silver stocks increased at an annual rate of about 0.9 percent, while the central government resumed the policy of expansion in the issuance of copper cash, which was facilitated by rising copper output from Yunnan. In 1724 the production from Yunnan copper mines was about 1 million catties; from the early 1740s through the first decade of the next century the annual output always went beyond the 10 million mark. Meanwhile, the quantity of cash issued by the two mints in the capital jumped from less than 0.5 million strings to well over 1 million a year, and counterfeit coins flooded a greater part of the country.[42] Furthermore, to put down the White Lotus Rebellion (1796–1804) the government spent 200 million taels, an amount equivalent

40. Zhang Xiangong, "Zhongguo dongbanbu jin wubainian ganhan zhishu de fenxi," in *Quanguo qihou bianhua*, p. 48.
41. Wang Yeh-chien, *Zhongguo jindai huobi yu yinhang de yanjin, 1644–1937* (Taibei, 1981), p. 25.
42. See Yeh-chien Wang, "Evolution of the Chinese Monetary System, 1644–1850," in *Modern Chinese Economic History*, ed. Chi-ming Hou and Tzong-shian Yu (Taibei, 1979), p. 442.

to its budget expenditures for six or seven years in normal times, which added greater inflationary pressure to the economy.[43]

During the period 1680–1820 China's population grew at 0.72 percent a year, the highest rate in the three centuries under discussion (see Table 1.2). Moreover, eighteenth-century China was a time not only of rapid population growth but also of unprecedented commercialization. Cash crops, such as cotton, mulberries, sugar cane, and tobacco, were planted more widely in various provinces. Markets and towns proliferated as never before.[44] These developments would most likely, in view of Lindert's analysis, noted above, lead to a rise in the velocity of money. Thus both the growth of the money supply and the growth of population were building up strong pressures for inflation. At the same time the cultivated acreage expanded by a half or so; new food crops (sweet potatoes, corn, and peanuts) were spreading, and double-cropping was increasingly practiced.[45] Given generally warm climate the agriculture sector also experienced rather vigorous growth. Without large increases of real output the rate of the price rise would have been much higher during the upswing, which lasted for more than a century.

The second price swing followed a generally downward trend from about 1820, but turned sharply upward in the early 1880s and continued to rise through the 1920s. We may divide the half-century of downswing into two subperiods, with 1850 at the dividing line. Before 1850 warmer climate in combination with the silver drain had the effect of depressing prices. But the money supply may not have decreased because of the multiplication of paper notes issued privately by local banks, money shops, and various commercial stores and because of the increase of copper cash by debasement and counterfeiting.[46] What was more likely to bring prices down was, besides warm climate, the possible decline in the velocity of monetary circulation caused by the apparent drop in the rate of population growth and by the increased holding of silver by the public. Before 1850 the value of silver appreciated steadily in relation to commodities and copper cash.[47] In the expectation that its value was to rise, "wealthy people and rich merchants are striving to hoard silver"; thus observed Bao Shichen, a contemporary scholar with a great interest in political economy.[48] Not only did the silver crisis slow down the velocity of circulation, but it also severely strained the issue of private notes. (Without central banking, private notes were backed by the credit of the individual issuing banks or by the merchants themselves.)

---

43. Wei Yuan, *Shengwuji*, 10:16.
44. See, for example, Liu Shiji, *Ming Qing shidai Jiangnan shizhen yanjiu* (Beijing, 1987).
45. Perkins, *Agricultural Development*, chaps. 2–3; Yeh-chien Wang, *Land Taxation in Imperial China, 1750–1911* (Cambridge, Mass., 1973), p. 7.
46. See Wang, "Evolution of the Chinese Monetary System," pp. 425–52.
47. Ibid.
48. Bao Shichen, *Anwu sizhong* (1872), 26:8.

In the third quarter of the century mass uprisings took place in many parts of the country. Most virulent was the Taiping Rebellion, which lasted 15 years and devastated a large part of the Yangzi Valley, particularly the delta area. It cost the government more than 400 million taels to bring these peasant and minority revolts to an end.[49] Hyperinflation followed immediately, as is shown distinctly in Figure 1.2. But the war-induced inflation proved to be just an aberration, for the level of prices sank as quickly as it rose following the return of peace and order in one part of the country after another.

As in the late seventeenth century, economic reconstruction proceeded with an improved man-land ratio, but the pace of economic recovery was faster. For one thing, however ruinous were the mid-nineteenth-century uprisings, they were not accompanied by the natural calamities and the consequent famine that attended the fall of the Ming dynasty (the droughts that hit China four years in a row in 1641–44 were the worst in the last 500 years). For another, continued warm climate further aided agricultural production. Prices were going down as more and more land was brought back under cultivation and more irrigation works were restored or built.

Extending from the 1880s to 1920s, the second upswing was the most inflationary period of the three centuries. While rice prices rose annually at 0.7 percent in the first upswing, they ascended at the rate of 3.3 percent a year in the second (see Table 1.2). During the half-century before the Great Depression the money supply grew at a very rapid rate. In 1930 the total stock of money (currency and deposits) amounted to about 6 billion *yuan*, of which one sixth were metal currencies.[50] How much money was in circulation 50 years earlier? We can only hazard a guess. China's silver stocks then stood probably around 1.5–1.6 billion *yuan* (see Table 1.2). Assuming that a quarter of the silver was then in circulation and that the ratios of circulating silver stocks to copper cash and to paper notes were 2 to 1 and 5 to 1 respectively, the total amount of money in circulation would be in the range of 600–700 million silver *yuan*. It was probably not more than 800 million.[51] Accordingly, the money supply may have increased by eight to ten times, or at an annual rate of 4.2 percent to 4.7 percent in the half-century. Without doubt the accelerating growth of the money supply contributed significantly to the price inflation in the period.

On the other hand, the volume of transactions also grew at an unprecedented rate. The pace of commercialization sped up as the country was increasingly integrated with the world economy from the latter part of the

---

49. Peng Zeyi, *Shijiu shiji houban de Zhongguo caizheng yu jingji* (Beijing, 1983), p. 136.
50. Rawski, *Economic Growth*, p. 163.
51. The ratios between the three components of money are quite close to Peng Xinwei's estimate for the last decades of the Qing period; see Peng Xinwei, *Zhongguo huobishi*, pp. 888–89. For the ratio of silver in circulation to its total stock, see Wang, *Zhongguo jindai huobi*, p. 35n.57.

nineteenth century on. Many local products, such as soybeans, straw mats, tung oil, and bristles, found their way into the world market. The introduction of steamships and railroads lowered the cost of transportation and also contributed greatly to market expansion. Consequently, China's trade, external as well as internal, experienced a rapid expansion. The Nankai indexes show that both imports and exports tripled in volume between 1881 and 1930.[52] The interprovincial trade in real terms was, according to Perkins's estimate, more than three times in the 1920s what it was in the late nineteenth century.[53] In view of these facts, a rate of growth in the volume of transactions of 2 percent a year is probably a good approximation. Then, the transaction velocity of money must, by implication, have risen annually by around 0.5–1.0 percent over the period.[54]

There is good reason to believe that the velocity of transactions rose in the latest phase of secular price movements. First, population increased almost as fast as in the eighteenth century. Since the proportion of self-consumed farm output still approached nearly a half of farm output in prewar China,[55] Goldstone's thesis is applicable, perhaps more than ever before. Second, the development of telegraph communication and modern banking, as well as the continued growth of native banks, greatly facilitated business transactions and thereby had the effect of allowing merchants to conduct their business with reduced holdings of cash.

To recapitulate, the secular movements of rice prices in the Yangzi Delta exhibit two long swings over the three centuries prior to World War II. Starting in the 1640s, prices followed a steep downward trend until the 1680s; afterward they moved up gradually, at 0.7 percent a year, to peak around 1820. The second swing went downward at first, for more than half a century. At the beginning of the 1880s it once again shifted direction, rising swiftly, at the rate of more than 3 percent a year, through 1930.

Given the fact that the delta occupied a position of economic centrality in the country, it is reasonable to regard the trends exhibited by the price series as reflecting supply and demand forces at work in the country. Population, the stock of money, and climate cycles are the three principal variables affecting the long-term trends. I found, among other things, that inflation was

---

52. Hsiao, *China's Foreign Trade Statistics*, pp. 274–75.
53. Perkins, *Agricultural Development*, pp. 119–24.
54. According to Thomas G. Rawski, the income velocity declined by 32–46 percent between 1914–18 and 1934. I consider the transaction velocity a better measure of monetary circulation for the reason that nearly one-half of farm output was still self-consumed in prewar China. But as Michael D. Bordo and Lars Jonung point out in their study of secular trends in the velocity of circulation in various countries, a fall in income velocity may coincide with a rise in transaction velocity. See Rawski, *Economic Growth*, pp. 161–65; Bordo and Jonung, *The Long-term Behavior of the Velocity of Circulation* (Cambridge, 1987), chaps. 2–3.
55. Buck, *Chinese Farm Economy*, p. 199.

nearly always accompanied by substantial expansion of the money supply, deflation by stagnation in monetary growth. The same was true for population. Rapid population growth appears to have contributed to inflation most likely because of changes in the age structure and because of the population-induced rise in the velocity of money. On the other hand, a decrease in population or a slowing down in its growth rate correlates strongly with deflation. Gradual changes in the climate probably helped moderate price inflation in the eighteenth century, pushing prices down in the nineteenth century and up in between; but the impact of falling temperatures on market transactions and hence on prices was neutralized or overbalanced by other factors in the latter part of the seventeenth century.

TWO

Grain Prices in Zhili Province, 1736–1911: A Preliminary Study

Lillian M. Li

The recent availability of grain price data for the Qing period now provides historians with an unprecedented opportunity to develop their understanding of the agricultural economy of every region of China. This study represents a preliminary attempt to apply the Qing period grain price data to an ongoing study of agriculture, food crises, natural disasters, and government relief in North China.[1] This rich series of data allows us to gain insight into the nature of the agricultural regime in the North, the long-term trends in the agricultural economy, the nature of short-term changes, the economic and social impact of natural disasters, and the extent of market integration and development. Because this is a first attempt, the methodology employed is exploratory, and the conclusions drawn should be regarded as tentative. In the future, completion of the data set and refinement of the methodology may

---

Many people have given me invaluable assistance with this project. In particular I would like to acknowledge the substantial contribution made by Keith Head (Swarthmore, '86), who helped analyze these data during the summers of 1986 and 1987 with the support of the Joel Dean Fund of Swarthmore College. Gudmund Iversen, Professor of Statistics at Swarthmore, has been generous with his time and expertise. A number of other Swarthmore colleagues have also generously offered guidance or assistance: John Boccio, Stefano Fenoaltea, Robinson Hollister, Jody Ann Malsbury, Frederic Pryor, F. M. Scherer, and Leah Smith. Several Swarthmore students have diligently assisted in the entering of data or with graphics: Patrick Awuah, Donald McMinn, Karen Neumer, Bonnie Spear, and Paul Talcott. I have benefited greatly from the comments of both economists and historians who participated in the Workshop and Conference on Economic Methods for Chinese Historical Research, held in January 1987 in Honolulu, Hawaii, and January 1988 in Oracle, Arizona.

1. This essay is part of a projected book on this region, *Flood and Famine in China: State Policy and Ecological Disaster in the Hai River Basin, 1690s–1990s*. The present study should be regarded as preliminary in part because the set of grain price data that I have collected thus far, though extensive, is still incomplete.

alter the conclusions, but in the interim these tentative results will, hopefully, generate some hypotheses for further analysis and research.

North China is the birthplace of China's civilization and the location of its imperial capitals throughout most of its history. Yet in recent centuries North China has also suffered unfavorable natural conditions and economic hardships. Unlike the fertile rice-growing regions of South China, the North practices mixed cultivation of dry-land grains under climatic conditions that have made the fate of each year's crop extremely uncertain.

Zhili Province (roughly equivalent to modern-day Hebei Province), the subject of this article, best embodies these contradictory characteristics. As the site of the imperial capital of Beijing since the thirteenth century, Zhili had economic advantages that derived more from its political centrality than from its natural resources. The emperors of the Qing dynasty (1644–1911), like their predecessors of the Yuan and Ming dynasties, sought to bring some of the material benefits of the South to the North. The Grand Canal was maintained specifically for the purpose of transporting rice and other products from the South to the capital. The grain tribute was intended to feed the court and officialdom, but it had the unintended consequence of linking the economies of North and South. It was the only significant North-South thoroughfare until railroads were introduced in the twentieth century. The strategic importance of Beijing also dictated that the court pay special attention to stocking both civilian and military granaries in the capital area as well as to the maintenance of the waterways in the province.

The care and protection of the Qing imperial court and its retainers took place, however, in the context of natural conditions that seem to have deteriorated through the centuries. The river system in particular has been a source of ongoing headaches. In ancient times many rivers flowed down from the Taihang mountain range, which forms a boundary between Zhili and Shanxi, its neighbor to the west. But the construction of the Yuan dynasty Grand Canal severed the normal channels of these waterways to the ocean, forcing them to flow into the canal itself. From that time on, the only outlet of five major waterways—the Bei, Yongding, Daqing, Ziya, and Nanyun rivers—was a single, short channel flowing from Tianjin to the ocean, known as the Hai River. This entire river system is known today as the Hai River Basin and is one of China's major river conservancy concerns.

Although smaller in scale, the Hai River Basin has many of the same characteristics as the larger Yellow River Basin, with which it became more closely linked after the Yellow River changed course in the 1850s to the north side of Shandong peninsula. Both have extremely shallow beds, which over the centuries have risen with increased siltation. In recent times deforestation in the mountains has accelerated the silting process. The control of these rivers requires intensive dredging, diking, and other engineering efforts. Over time, the vulnerability of these rivers to flooding has greatly increased, as has

Map 2.1. Zhili Province in the Qing Period. Adapted from the end-map in *Qingdai Haihe Luanhe honglao dang'an shiliao* (Beijing, 1981).

their tendency to waterlog the soil, particularly given the flat, even concave, topography of the land in their lower reaches.

The uneven pattern of rainfall in North China further contributes to the danger of flooding. Most of the annual rainfall in the region is concentrated in the summer months of July, August, and September. It does not take very much rain to cause the rivers to overflow. Ironically the danger of flooding occurs in the context of the overall scarcity of rainfall in the North. As a rule, drought is a more pervasive and potentially serious problem than flood, but it is the river system, the nature of the topography, and the soil that make flooding such a frequent danger and waterlogging a near-chronic condition in some low-lying areas.

Throughout the Qing dynasty, the court and bureaucracy paid close attention to the dual threats of flood and drought. In part this reflected a general bureaucratic concern with disaster prevention that was empirewide, but Zhili Province clearly posed special problems because of its political importance. The bureaucratic record reflects the tremendous concern of the court and officials with river conservancy and with the stocking of granaries to guard against shortages. In the eighteenth century these efforts appear to have been quite successful in both the prevention and relief of famines, but vigilance was constantly required. During the nineteenth century, however, especially from mid-century, either the efforts were less successful or nature was harder to control. Starting with the great drought of the 1870s, North China was periodically beset by one disaster after another until the 1960s. In the 1890s there was hardly a year in which flooding did not occur somewhere in this region. In 1917 there was a massive, provincewide flood, followed closely by the North China drought of 1920–21. Since 1949 the government of the People's Republic has assigned high priority to the management of land and water resources in the area. The sinking of tube wells for irrigation in many parts of the province has proceeded together with engineering projects to prevent the recurrence of major floods, such as that of 1963.

Despite this somewhat unstable context, North China in general, and Zhili/Hebei in particular, have been able to sustain a large population increase in the last two centuries. In 1749 the population of Zhili was reported to be about 14 million.[2] In 1790 the population was recorded as 23.5 million.

---

2. This 1749 figure almost certainly represents an underestimate. Before the *baojia* system of population registration was reformed in 1775, underestimation was common. See Ping-ti Ho, *Studies on the Population of China, 1368–1953* (Cambridge, Mass., 1959), pp. 36–48. Ho concludes that the population figures of the 1741–1775 period were on the average underestimated by 20 percent. By that formula, Zhili's 1749 population may have been close to 16.8 million. Zhili did not submit its first detailed population return under the reformed system until 1778. If Zhili's population was 16.8 million in 1749 and 23.5 million in 1790, it experienced a 40 percent increase over 41 years.

The rate of growth slackened in the next half-century; in 1850 the reported population was only 23.4 million. In 1933 Hebei's population was about 38.4 million, and in 1953, 46.6 million. In 1982 the population of the province, together with that of the independent municipalities of Beijing and Tianjin, was about 70 million.[3]

The history of the Zhili/Hebei area of North China poses questions of enormous consequence. How could this area maintain its political centrality for so many centuries despite a relatively weak economic base? How could substantial population growth be sustained in the face of what appear in the historical record to be frequent and regular occurrences of drought and flood?

THE PRICE DATA

During the Qing dynasty each provincial governor was required to submit to the throne a monthly report of grain prices in his province. This became a regular bureaucratic practice by the beginning of the Qianlong period in 1736. The Qing archives in Beijing and Taibei have a rather complete set of reports from Zhili for the eighteenth century and a more scattered sampling from the nineteenth century. I have collected approximately 609 of these monthly lists, including 233 monthly lists for 1738–64, 171 lists for 1765–95, and 205 lists for 1796–1910.[4]

In the first subperiod, 1738–64, the lists give the low and high prices of seven types of grain from each prefecture (*fu*) or independent department (*zhilizhou*) in the province: rice (*daomi*), high-grade millet (*shang sumi*), ordinary millet (*cisumi* or *zhongsumi*), white wheat (*baimai*), red wheat (*hongmai*), black beans (*heidou*), and sorghum, or kaoliang (*gaoliang*). After 1765 only five grains were reported: millet (*sumi*), sorghum (*gaoliang*), a type of panicum millet (*nimi*), wheat (*mai*), and black beans (*heidou*).[5]

Prices from seventeen prefectures or independent departments were reported by the governor-general of Zhili, although not all were reported in every period. Shuntian Prefecture (where Beijing was located) was not included until 1771. Chengde Prefecture was not included in the reports until

---

3. The Qing figures are taken from Philip C. C. Huang, *The Peasant Economy and Social Change in North China* (Stanford, 1985), p. 322. The 1982 figure is reported in Judith Banister, *China's Changing Population* (Stanford, 1987), pp. 298–99, among other places.

4. I am indebted to the staff of the Ming-Qing archives of the National Palace Museum in Taibei and the First Historical Archives in Beijing for allowing me access to these grain price lists.

5. *Sumi* was *Setaria italica*, sometimes called foxtail millet, which was the most common type of millet grown in north China. *Nimi* was *Panicum milaceum*, sometimes called broomcorn millet. *Heidou*, lit. "black bean," was a type of soybean. See Francesca Bray, *Agriculture*, vol. 6, pt. 2 of Joseph Needham et al., *Science and Civilization in China* (Cambridge, Eng., 1984), pp. 434–48.

1778. From 1736–68, the prices for Baoding Prefecture, the location of the provincial capital, were reported a month in advance of the other provinces.

These grain price reports were submitted monthly, according to the Chinese lunar calendar—with intercalary months ("leap months") added from time to time to make the lunar year catch up to the solar year. Since any given lunar month might lag behind its corresponding solar month by up to two months, solar months might be more appropriate to use in studying the agricultural cycle. In this study lunar-month prices have been used where aggregated data for year or multiyear periods would cancel out the variations in the months. However, where seasonality is an important concern, data are converted to correspond with the solar months.

AGRICULTURE AND FOOD AVAILABILITY IN ZHILI

As the above lists suggest, many grain crops were grown in Zhili. Although rice was the subject of experimentation in the early eighteenth century, it was never very widely grown.[6] Wheat was the luxury grain in the North. Planted in the fall, it was harvested the following summer. Millets of various types were the staple of the poor people's diet. Like sorghum, millet was planted in late spring and harvested in the fall. It was hardy, having a tolerance for heat and drought. Sorghum, on the other hand, was more flood-resistant. Less desirable than millet as a food, sorghum was also used in making wine, and its stalks were burned for fuel.

Other crops were important too. Black beans, reported in the Qing grain price reports, were used both as a feedgrain for horses and as food for humans. They also became a cash crop, used in the production of oil. In the twentieth century corn became a major food crop, but it is not at all clear how extensively it was grown in the Qing period. Finally, cotton was the most important nonfood commercial crop in Zhili in Qing and later times, but the extent of its cultivation before the twentieth century is a matter of some uncertainty.[7]

There were numerous cropping systems in North China, with great variation within regions. One system was a three crop rotation over two years. As Philip C. C. Huang describes it, sorghum and millet were planted in May or June and harvested in September or October. Wheat was planted in the fall and harvested in July, too late for the planting of sorghum or millet, so soy-

---

6. See Timothy Brook, "The Spread of Rice Cultivation and Rice Technology into the Hebei Region in the Ming and Qing," in *Explorations in the History of Science and Technology in China* (Shanghai, 1982), pp. 659–89, for an exhaustive study of experimentation in rice cultivation in North China.

7. Philip C. C. Huang, pp. 111–14, asserts that cotton cultivation was widespread in Zhili by the late Ming period, but others have disputed this. See, for example, Loren Brandt's review of Huang, *Peasant Economy*, in *Economic Development and Cultural Change* 35 (April 1987):670–82.

beans were planted for harvesting in October and November, after which the land would be left fallow. Other systems involved interplanting.[8]

It is not until the twentieth century that we have some idea of the acreage devoted to each of these major crops. John Lossing Buck's well-known 1929–33 farm study reports that in the winter wheat–kaoliang region, which included Hebei, wheat accounted for 45.5 percent of crop area, millet for 23.1 percent, sorghum for 18.5, corn for 16.3, soybeans for 13.4, and cotton for 8.6.[9] A survey conducted by Zhang Xinyi reports the following crop areas for Hebei in the 1930s: wheat, 31.3 million *mu* (28 percent), millet, 24.3 million *mu* (22 percent), sorghum, 21.7 million *mu* (20 percent), and corn, 15.5 million *mu* (14 percent). Beans (*dadou*) accounted for 9.8 million *mu* (9 percent), and cotton for 8.1 million *mu* (7 percent).[10]

These two estimates are similar in that they show the primary importance of wheat, millet, and sorghum, in that order. There is, of course, every reason to believe that the situation in the Qing period differed in significant ways. Corn almost certainly played a lesser role, and perhaps the proportions of wheat, millet, and sorghum were different from the twentieth century. Unless further research uncovers new sources, it is unlikely that we shall ever have an exact picture of the production of these crops during the Qing period, but this general picture of the relative importance of these crops is unlikely to be changed.

This study analyzes the prices of three of the grains reported in the Qing memorials—wheat, millet (*sumi* or setaria millet), and sorghum—because of their centrality in the agriculture and the diet of the North. Black beans probably did not constitute a significant portion of the caloric content of the average diet. Panicum millet and rice were unlikely to have been of critical importance either.

Two additional factors probably influenced the price structure, although they were exogenous to Zhili's agricultural production. First, a significant portion of the grain consumed in Zhili during the Qing was not grown in the province but was imported from the South through the grain tribute system. During the Qing, 3–4 million *shi* of grain were transported annually to the metropolitan area.[11] Most of this was destined for the consumption of the court, bannermen, and soldiers stationed in the province. But it is quite likely

---

8. Philip C. C. Huang, *Peasant Economy*, p. 61.

9. John Lossing Buck, *Land Utilization in China* (Chicago and Nanking, 1937; repr. New York, 1956), 1:211–12. Because there was some double cropping, the percentages exceed 100.

10. Cited in *Shina nōgyo kiso tōkei shiryo*, comp. Tōa kenkyūjo (Shanghai, 1941), 1:41–43.

11. The *shi* was a measure of grain volume. According to an authoritative estimate, "the likely weight of an imperial shih [*shi*] of milled rice in the eighteenth century was about 185 pounds, with a margin of error unlikely to have been more than 5 percent either way (that is, the likely range was roughly 175 to 195 pounds)." Han-sheng Chuan and Richard A. Kraus, *Mid-Ch'ing Rice Markets and Trade: An Essay in Price History* (Cambridge, Mass., 1975), p. 98.

that some quantity of grain reached the market, through either direct or indirect sales. Pierre-Etienne Will has estimated that 0.5 million *shi* a year was not used for direct consumption in Beijing.[12] Whether this amount was sufficient to have an impact on general grain price levels is not clear, and is a matter that deserves further investigation.

The second factor was an extensive state granary system, which flourished in the eighteenth century. The system included three types of granaries: the "ever-normal" granaries, the community granaries, and the charity granaries. During the eighteenth century these granaries were well stocked. In 1767, for example, the governor-general of the province reported that 3,534,536 *shi* of grain were actually stored in the province, 2,549,566 *shi* of which were in the ever-normal granaries.[13] By the nineteenth century, however, all granary holdings were down, especially those of the ever-normal granaries. In 1833, for example, the governor-general reported holdings of only about 616,000 *shi*, of which 275,719 *shi* were held in ever-normal granaries.[14]

LONG-TERM TRENDS

The Zhili price series affords an important opportunity to learn about the long-term behavior of prices over two centuries. This is important not only because of its relevance to a study of Zhili's economy in particular but also because it can serve as a general indicator of overall economic trends in North China. The price trend of these three major grains has several major characteristics. As Figure 2.1 shows, the overall price rise from 1738 to 1910 was not steep. During the eighteenth century prices rose very gradually. In the early part of the nineteenth century, there was a sharp increase in the price of wheat, followed by rises in the prices of millet and sorghum. From the 1830s to 1850, roughly during the Daoguang reign, prices fell precipitously, only to climb back up by 1870 and fall again. From 1890, prices rose steeply and steadily until the end of the dynasty. When these same prices, again grouped by four-year averages, are indexed to their base-period (1738–41) prices, the trends can be seen more clearly, as in Figure 2.2. At the end of the eighteenth century, the prices of wheat, millet, and sorghum were respectively only 134 percent, 122 percent, and 133 percent of the base-period prices. By the end of the dynasty, the three grains had risen to 258 percent, 243 percent, and 272

---

12. Pierre-Etienne Will, *Bureaucratie et famine en Chine au 18e siècle* (Paris, 1980), pp. 241–44. Will points out that tribute grain surpluses were rarely used outside Zhili.

13. Gongzhongdang, Palace Memorial Archives (Taibei), Qianlong 023616, 1767/12/12. These figures represent the actual holdings at the time of the report; the theoretical holdings, which took into account amounts loaned out but not yet paid back to the granaries, were larger.

14. Junjidang, Grand Council Archives (Beijing), Daoguang 63339, 1833/4. These figures represent actual, not theoretical, holdings.

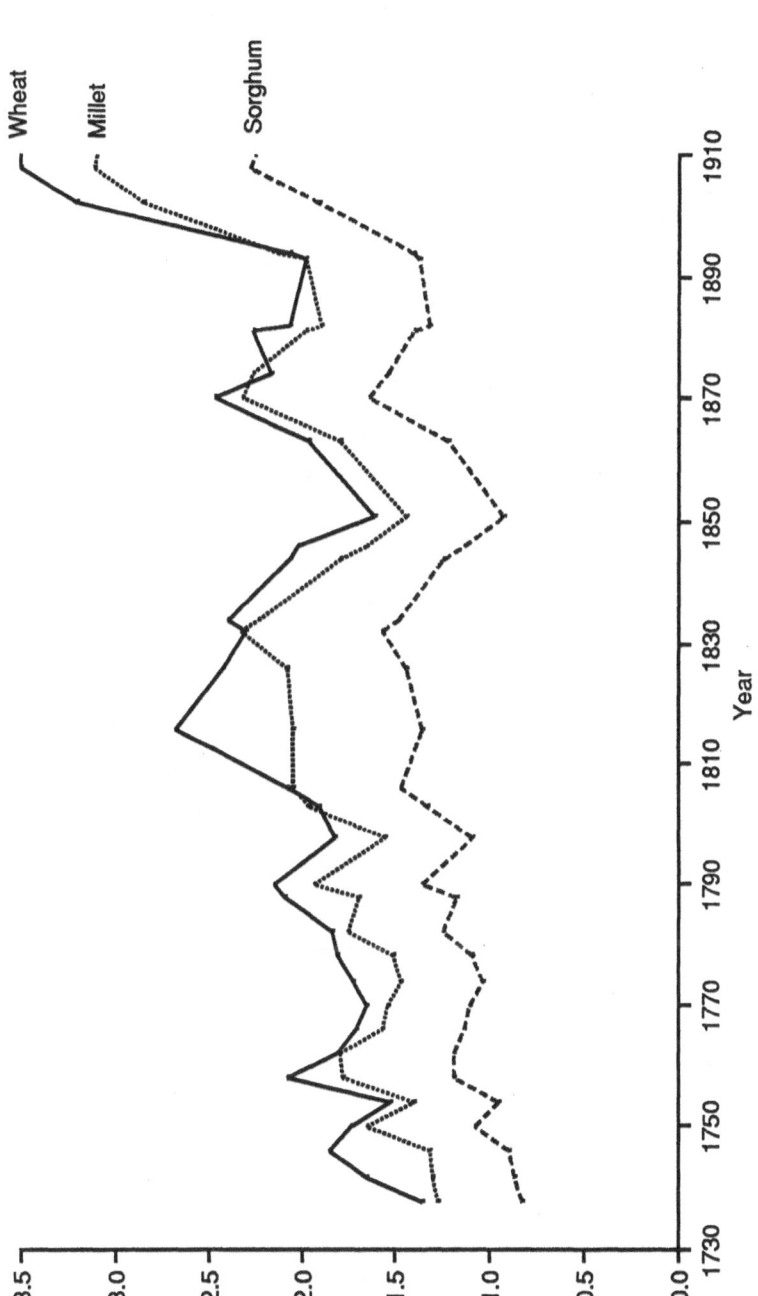

Fig. 2.1. Grain Prices in Zhili Province, 1738–1910 (four-year averages, in taels per *shi*)
Note: See text for a description of the data used in this study. In Figs. 2.1, 2.2, and 2.4, there is a substantial amount of missing data for the nineteenth century.

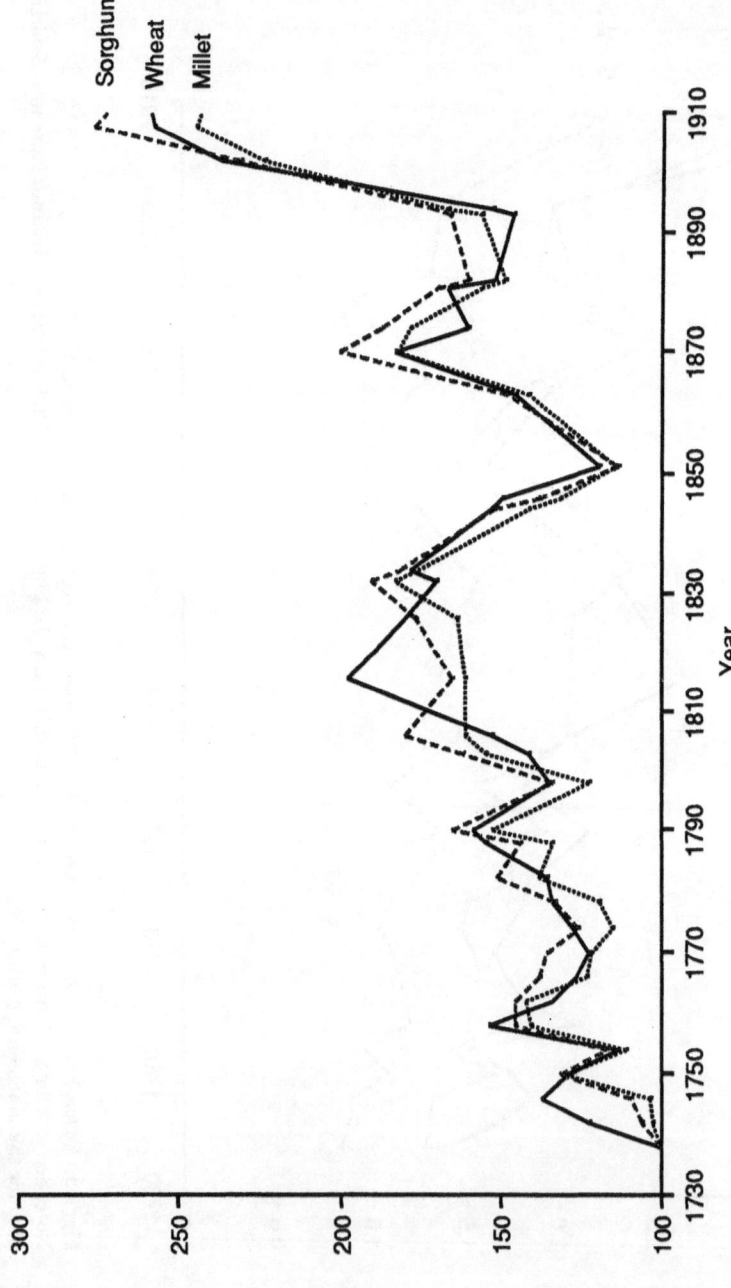

Fig. 2.2. Grain Prices in Zhili Province, 1738–1910: Indexed to the Base Period (four year averages; 1738–1741 = 100)

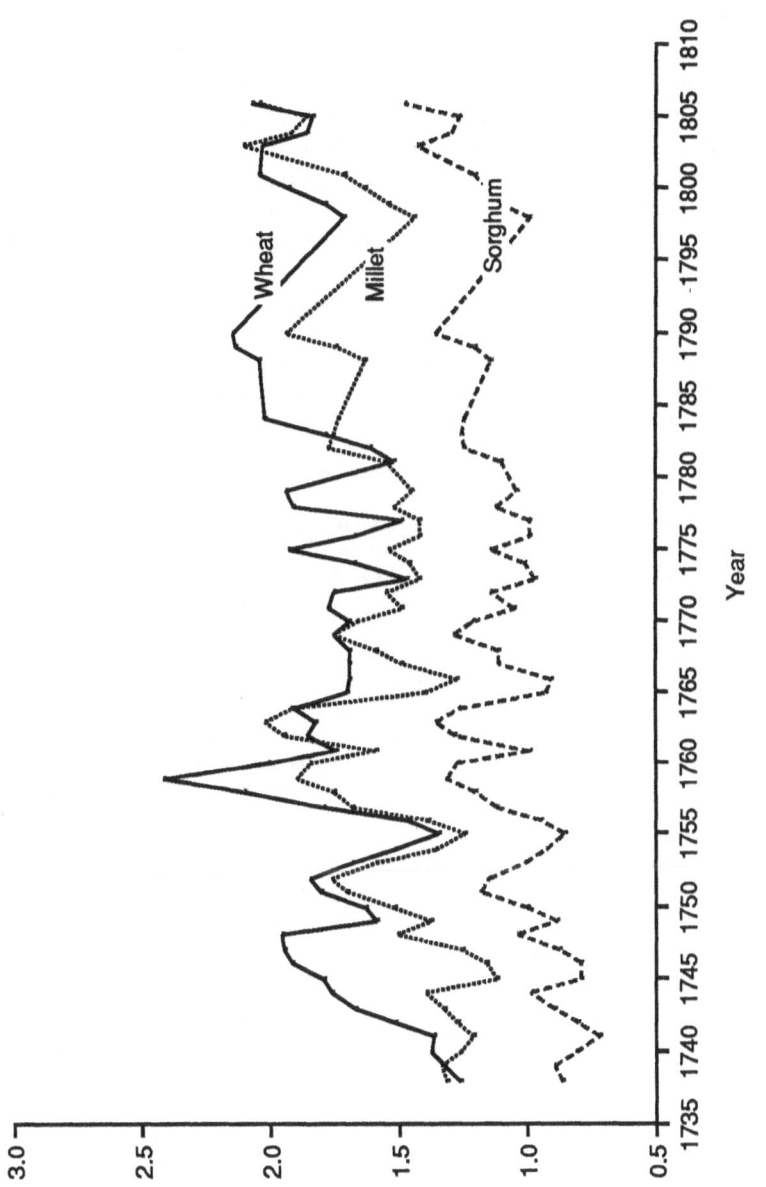

Fig. 2.3. Annual Grain Prices in Zhili Province, 1738–1806 (taels per *shi*)

percent of the base-period prices respectively, but if the final two decades of the dynasty are omitted, the increases are only 146 percent, 155 percent, and 165 percent respectively of the base-period price.

To show more clearly what the annual trends looked like, in Figure 2.3 I present the annual averages (unadjusted) for 1738–1806.[15] Here once again it is apparent that the trend for the eighteenth century was not very steep and that there seem to be cycles of about four to five years for millet and sorghum and possibly longer cycles in the price of wheat. Further, it appears that the prices of all three grains followed roughly the same trend, but there was at least one period—in the 1740s—in which the rise in the price of wheat was not accompanied by a rise in the prices of the coarse grains. A contrary trend is seen in the early 1760s, when a rise in the prices of the coarse grains was not accompanied by a continuous rise in the price of wheat.

15. Only the eighteenth century is presented because that is the century for which the data are most complete. In this essay I have used the mean of the high and low prices reported from each prefecture each month. In analyzing the high and low prices separately, I found that their behavior generally followed the same pattern. This was true of all three grains. There seemed, then, little point in studying either high or low prices separately, particularly in a preliminary study.

The adjustment of annual averages to account for the seasonal variations in the missing data presents a greater challenge. Although it would be preferable to adjust the annual averages, in fact each possible procedure for adjustment produces its own problems. One way is to estimate, or "predict," missing data by using all the known data in combination with the seasonal coefficients produced by the regression equation discussed in the next section. Another method is to adjust each known piece of data by its relevant monthly coefficient. This creates not an annual average but an estimated January price based on all known data. Until a more accurate method of adjusting data can be found, however, leaving the data unadjusted does not, I believe, produce large distortions, because the annual seasonal range of prices in Zhili was not more than 0.14 tael in the extreme case of wheat (from a high of +0.08 taels in April to a low of −0.06 taels in September in the regression on data excluding Baoding, as presented in Table 2.1). For example, in 1740, a year for which there are no missing data, the mean price was 1.38 taels. If data were missing for the three low-price months of July, August, and September, the unadjusted mean of the other nine months of data would be 1.40, a distortion of only 0.02 tael, or 1.4 percent. If I use the regression coefficients to estimate the missing data, the annual mean would come to 1.39. The difference between adjusting or not adjusting the data is only 0.01 tael, or less than 1 percent of the actual mean price of 1.38. This example presents one of the worst possible cases since the mean price was rather low in comparison to the rest of the period 1738–1910. In a year when the prices were relatively high—over 2.50 taels, for example—the use of a seasonal coefficient would tend to underestimate the missing data (e.g., 0.06 tael would make less difference). The only time that a larger distortion might be introduced by not adjusting the data would be in a crisis year for which we have only one month of data in the early part of the year not yet affected by the crisis. In such a case, the price level would be very much underestimated. If, instead of "predicting" the price where data are missing, we use the seasonal coefficients to adjust the known data, the result in this example would be 1.37, only 0.01 less than the actual mean price. The fact that this hypothetical January price is close to the mean is somewhat accidental; the actual January price for that year was 1.42, which reflects the fact that the previous year was a crisis year (see n. 21 below) and that the price of wheat was abnormally high in the winter months.

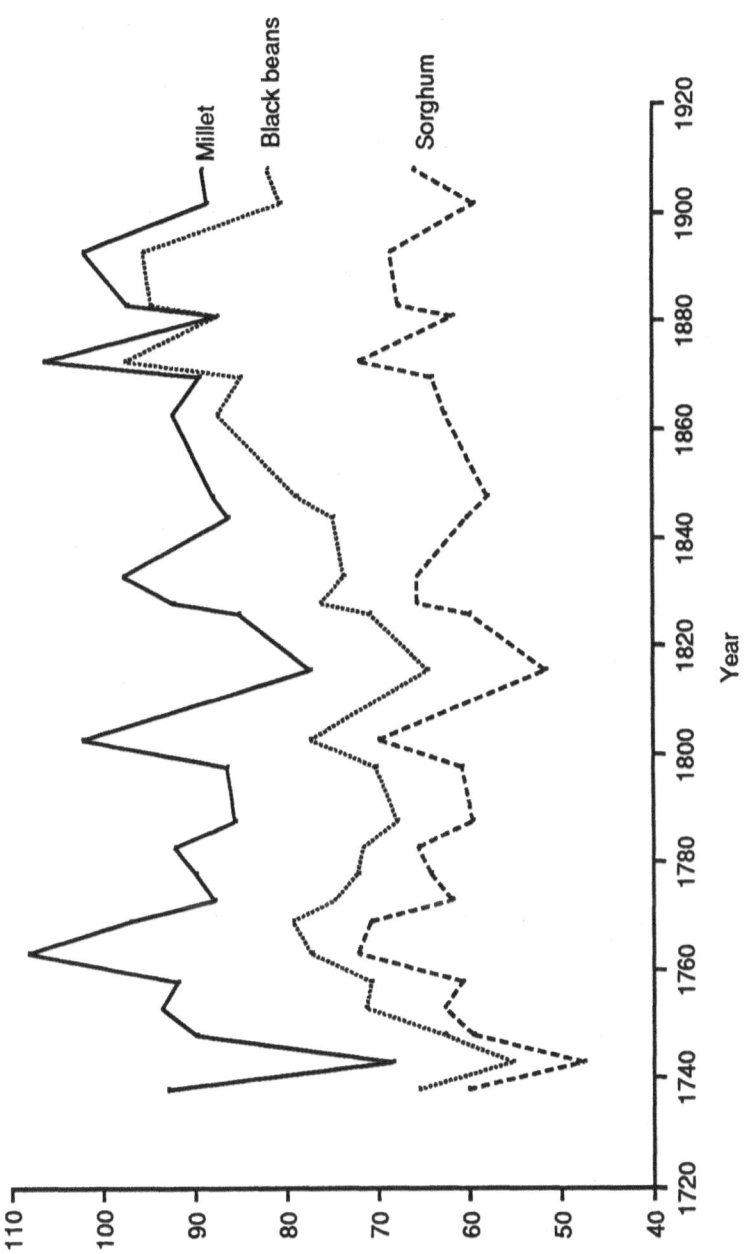

Fig. 2.4. Prices of Coarse Grains Relative to Wheat in Zhili Province, 1738–1910 (5-year averages; price = % of wheat price in concurrent period)

On the whole these graphs show that the prices of millet and sorghum followed each other very closely, with sorghum consistently being the cheaper of the two. Although millet was a less desirable grain than wheat, the figures show that there were years when its price approached that of wheat (and even exceeded it in the early 1760s, early 1780s, and early 1800s). Figure 2.4 charts the five-year averages of millet, sorghum, and black bean prices as a percentage of wheat price averages for the concurrent periods. This shows more clearly the few periods in which millet prices exceeded those of wheat (around 1760, 1800, 1870, and 1890). And it also shows that while millet, sorghum, and black bean prices maintained a spread in the eighteenth century, during the next century the price of black beans relative to wheat and millet steadily increased.

These trends suggest certain hypotheses about the roles played by these commodities in Zhili's agricultural markets. First, the generally higher price of wheat confirms that it was the luxury grain and suggests the possibility that its markets were relatively well developed. Second, the price trends of millet and sorghum seem to parallel each other, suggesting that they were responding to the same cropping cycle and weather patterns. On the other hand, millet's consistently higher price confirms our impressions from the twentieth century that millet was the staple grain and was valued more highly than sorghum. However, the fact that millet prices occasionally reached, and even surpassed, those of wheat raises the question of the extent to which it was a commercialized agricultural commodity and the extent to which it was considered a substitute for wheat. Finally, the price of black beans rose relative to wheat prices in a clear secular trend, probably because of a growing nationwide, perhaps even international, market for bean oil and other bean products produced primarily in Manchuria but also in North China.[16]

REGRESSION ANALYSIS

At any given month, the price of grain may have reflected not only the long-term price trend but also a place in the seasonal cycle, the impact of any irregularities in the weather that would affect output, as well as any exogenous factors affecting demand. To permit us to estimate, and separate out, the effects of time, seasonal variation, and crisis years on grain prices, a multiple regression of prices was run using the following equation:

$$P = a + bT + d_2M_2 + d_3M_3 + \ldots + d_{12}M_{12} + dC$$

[16]. The extent to which Zhili/Hebei was involved in this industry is a subject that awaits further research. Certainly in the twentieth century one of Manchuria's principal industries and export commodities was soybean oil and other soybean products. See, for example, Lien-en Tsao, "The Marketing of Soya Beans and Bean Oil," *Chinese Economic Journal* 7, no. 3 (Sept. 1930): 941–71.

Here the price in any given month (P) is measured by a constant (a), plus a coefficient (b) multiplied by time (T), plus dummy variables (d) that are created for every month (M) except January and another dummy variable created for crisis years (C). The dummy variable C is entered as a 1 in a crisis year and as a 0 in noncrisis years.[17]

Since one of the purposes of this regression is to measure the effect of seasonality, all data used in the analysis were converted to solar prices using a method that weights the price by the number of appropriate lunar days in each solar month.[18] Since prices for Baoding, the seat of the provincial capital, were routinely reported a month in advance of prices from other prefectures during 1736–68, a period that represents 44 percent of my data (268 out of 609 monthly reports), I also ran the regression with Baoding prices excluded lest the months for which there are only Baoding prices unduly affect the results.[19]

The most problematic decision in setting up this regression concerned the crisis years. Although it would be ideal to use meteorological data (temperature and rainfall) to code years of crisis, I do not yet have access to such data. In their absence, I am forced to rely on reports of crises found in the historical records. Since such data represent the human (social and political) impact of natural disasters as seen through administrative lenses, they must necessarily have their limitations. The historical record itself is necessarily subjective, and our access to it is also incomplete, a function of what documents have survived in which collections and archives. In this regression analysis I selected as crisis years those years recorded in *Qingdai Haihe Luanhe honglao dang'an shiliao*[20] as having floods that affected 50 counties (*xian*) or more. Although this compilation itself may be flawed, it is drawn from a survey of local gazetteers. In addition I selected from miscellaneous records at my

---

17. This regression equation was also run with T^2 as a variable to see if there were perhaps a nonlinear relationship between time and price. The results were not statistically significant ($t < 2$), and overall did not produce a better R^2, and so we concluded that there is not a second-order relationship between time and price.

18. I am very grateful to Peter C. Perdue for providing the complex formula and table by which the lunar data have been converted to solar data and to Keith Head, who wrote the program that adapted this table to my data.

19. For example, the price list submitted by the Zhili governor-general reporting prices for the third lunar month included the fourth-month prices for Baoding Prefecture, presumably because these local prices were already available to him by the time he received the third-month prices from the outlying prefectures. Consequently, if I have the third-month provincial report but am missing the fourth-month provincial report, the Baoding price is the only one I have for the fourth month and the provincial average in fact represents only Baoding. Because there is reason to think that prices behaved differently in the capital, I have thought it wise to run the regression both with and without Baoding prices.

20. *Qingdai Haihe Luanhe honglao dang'an shiliao* (Beijing, 1981).

TABLE 2.1 Annual Trends and Seasonal Variation in Grain Prices in
Zhili Province, 1738–1910
(regression coefficients, in taels per *shi*)

Variable	Wheat Price		Millet Price		Sorghum Price	
	Excluding Baoding	Including Baoding	Excluding Baoding	Including Baoding	Excluding Baoding	Including Baoding
Crisis year	0.06	0.08	0.06	0.07	0.01	0.02
Time (1738 = 0)	0.0059	0.0056	0.0061	0.0061	0.0045	0.0045
February	0.01	0.01	0.03	0.03	0.02	0.02
March	0.04	0.03	0.05	0.04	0.05	0.04
April	0.08	0.05	0.06	0.05	0.06	0.05
May	0.06	0.05	0.06	0.06	0.06	0.06
June	0.02	0.01	0.07	0.07	0.08	0.08
July	-0.05	-0.04	0.09	0.09	0.08	0.09
August	-0.04	-0.06	0.09	0.11	0.08	0.08
September	-0.06	-0.08	0.06	0.05	0.02	0.01
October	0.02	-0.01	0.08	0.05	0.04	0.02
November	0.02	-0.02	0.03	0.01	0.01	-0.01
December	0.02	-0.02	0.00	0.02	0.01	0.01
Constant	1.56	1.62	1.30	1.33	.87	.90
R^2	.49	.44	.59	.56	.58	.55
F	40.13	37.99	61.07	61.59	57.79	58.12

disposal years in which 25 or more counties were affected by drought. This combined method yielded 54 years that were coded as crisis years.[21]

When the regression was run for 1738–1910, with Baoding prices excluded, the results (see Table 2.1) showed that the effect of time was 0.0059, 0.0061, and 0.0045 taels for wheat, millet, and sorghum respectively, meaning that for each year, the price increased by this amount for each grain. These increases confirm the impression, derived from Figure 2.1, that the inflationary trend was not very steep or significant over this long time period.

The regression results show the monthly variation of prices, using January as the base month. The results, graphed in Figure 2.5, show the effect of the multiple-crop system of Zhili. Wheat prices reached their peak in April but did not reach their lowest point until September—somewhat surprisingly, since the wheat harvest took place around July. Millet and sorghum prices, however, peaked in June, July, and August, from which point they fell until

21. 1738, 1739, 1743, 1744, 1747, 1750, 1759, 1761, 1762, 1771, 1780, 1790, 1794, 1801, 1806, 1808, 1810, 1813, 1814, 1816, 1819, 1820, 1822, 1823, 1830, 1832, 1834, 1835, 1839, 1840, 1855, 1871–73, 1876, 1877, 1879, 1882, 1883, 1886–90, 1892–1900, and 1908. Of course, I lack price data for many of these years.

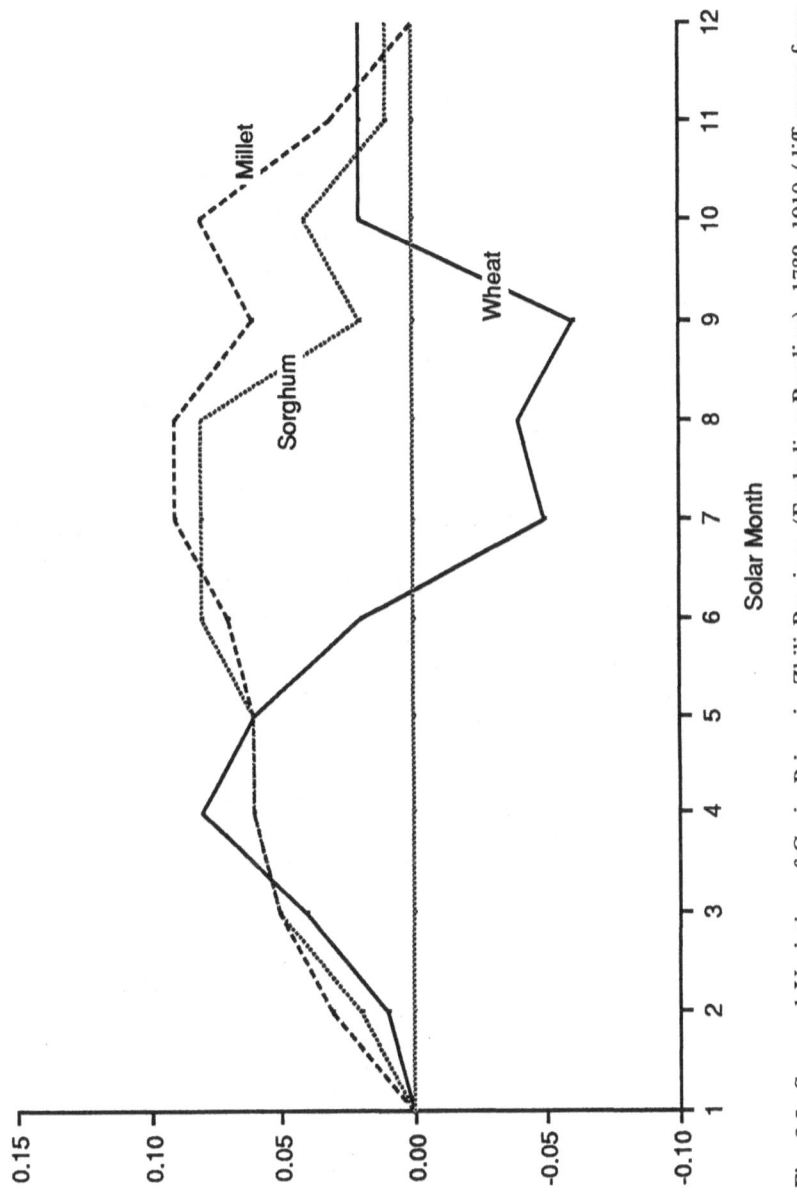

Fig. 2.5. Seasonal Variation of Grain Prices in Zhili Province (Excluding Baoding), 1738–1910 (difference from January price, in taels per *shi*)

the end of the year, with a brief jump in October. The prices of all three grains rose steadily through the early months of the year. But if Baoding is included, as in Figure 2.6, there is a smoother descent for wheat in the fall, but in October, wheat, millet, and sorghum prices peak briefly. If Baoding is included and only eighteenth-century data are analyzed, the shape of the seasonal curves is smoother, with the annual low price for wheat and the high prices for millet and sorghum all occurring in August. Preliminary analysis of price data separately for each prefecture shows that the exact patterns of seasonality vary slightly from place to place but fall within a general pattern.

The regression coefficients also vary when either eighteenth-century data or nineteenth-century data are used alone. Although the greater quantity and likely higher quality of the eighteenth-century data would suggest that its regression results would be more significant, in fact the R^2—a measure of the amount of variation in price explained by the regression as a whole—is considerably higher when both centuries of data are used together.[22] When a Chow test—a measure of the extent to which two samples may affect the regression results—was run on these regressions, no significant difference was found between the two centuries of data.[23] Consequently, the results of the regression run on both centuries of data are used throughout this paper.

These sets of monthly coefficients present several puzzles. Why does the annual low price for wheat come so much later than its presumed harvest-time? Why do the prices of sorghum and millet jump around in the autumn and early winter? Why does the seasonal pattern seem to vary depending on the time period and the number of prefectures included?

One possible explanation may be that seasonal patterns do differ from one area to another. In Buck's survey, the price of wheat in the wheat-kaoliang area was highest in January–February, and lowest in May–June. Millet had its high price in May–June and its low price in November.[24] But another 1930s study of prices in Zhengding, Hebei, found that the annual high price for wheat was in April, and the low price followed immediately in May, while the high price of millet was in June–July, and the low immediately afterward, in August–September.[25]

---

22. Running the regression on either eighteenth- or nineteenth-century data alone produced much lower R^2s than using two centuries of data together. For wheat, for example, the R^2 is 0.4859 for both centuries together, 0.2029 for the eighteenth century, and 0.1662 for the nineteenth century. These differences are undoubtedly due to the strength of the time trend, which is by far the most significant variable in any of these regressions.

23. The Chow test was developed by Gregory C. Chow, "Tests of Equality between Sets of Coefficients in Two Linear Regressions," *Econometrica* 28, no. 3 (July 1960):591–605. I am grateful to F. Michael Scherer, formerly of the Economics Department at Swarthmore College, for his help with this test. The F-ratio was insignificant for both wheat and millet (0.83 and 0.63, respectively) and marginally significant for sorghum (1.80).

24. Buck, *Land Utilization in China*, 1:335–36.

25. "The Seasonal Variation of Prices for Farm Products and the Profitability of Storage," *Economic Facts*, no. 7 (October 1937):319–42.

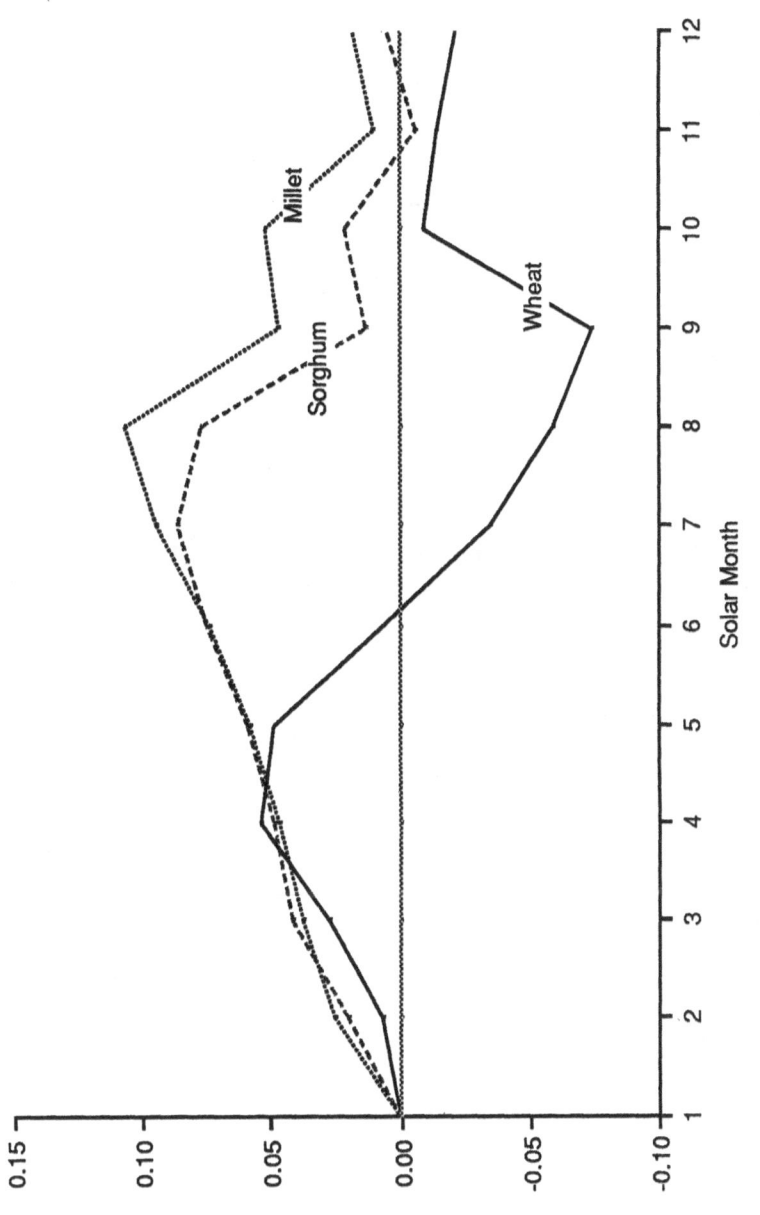

Fig. 2.6. Seasonal Variation of Grain Prices in Zhili Province (Including Baoding), 1738–1910 (difference from January price, in taels per *shi*)

The irregularities in the autumn prices could also be explained by deliveries of grain tribute to the province, which occurred before winter, or alternatively by the restocking of granaries, which was also done in the autumn. Since it was mostly unhusked millet that was stored (because wheat spoils too quickly), post-harvest prices may have risen a bit before falling to their annual low at the end of the year.[26]

Although the precise effects of seasonality seem to differ according to the way the regression is run, the overall pattern is clear. Moreover, the regression analysis reveals that the effect of seasonality was less important than the effect of crises.[27] The spread of prices within each year was less than 0.14 tael for wheat and less than 0.11 tael for millet and sorghum, no matter which way the regression is run.

Although regression analysis is a sophisticated tool for measuring the separate effects of different variables on price, it has its limitations. For the purposes of this grain price analysis, it can give us a good measure of the factors in price variability, but it is sensitive to differences in time and space and therefore cannot be absolutely accurate. It must be used as an approximate tool, not a precise measure. In future work, more accurate specification of crisis years, more complete data, and work with disaggregated prefectural data may produce more satisfactory results. Still, these preliminary results do inspire some confidence. Although the t-value for each of the monthly coefficients tends to be under 2, in using descriptive data, as opposed to sampling, t-values are not relevant. Moreover, the R^2s achieved here are not poor, and the F-values are so large that the overall strength of the regression variables can be seen to be very substantial.[28]

CRISES

One purpose of the regression analysis is to try to measure the effect of crises on price levels. The regression analysis for 1738–1910 suggests that the effect of a crisis year was, on the whole, not very dramatic. The inclusion of Baoding data raises the effect slightly (see Table 2.1). A separate regression run solely on Baoding data results in higher crisis coefficients. Moreover, if the

---

26. Pierre-Etienne Will and R. Bin Wong, *Nourish the People: The State Civilian Granary System in China, 1650–1850* (Ann Arbor, 1991), manuscript pp. 5, 132. Thirty percent of the granary stock was supposed to be sold off each year and replaced.

27. This impression was confirmed when the regression was run with only the monthly dummies as variables. The resulting R^2s were astonishingly low: 0.0099, 0.0129, and 0.0189 for the three grains, respectively. Running the regression with interaction variables ($C*M$, $C*T$, etc.) also produced very low R^2s showing that a nonlinear relationship was not a better explanation for the behavior of prices.

28. Concerning these and other statistical problems, I am grateful to Gudmund Iversen, professor of statistics at Swarthmore College, for his judgment and invaluable suggestions.

TABLE 2.2 Grain Price Increases in Crisis Years in Zhili Province, 1738–1910
(regression coefficients, in taels per *shi*)

Period	Wheat Price	Millet Price	Sorghum Price
Year, including Baoding	0.08	0.07	0.02
Year, excluding Baoding	0.06	0.06	0.01
Year, Baoding only	0.14	0.08	0.03
Crop year, including Baoding	0.09	0.15	0.11
Crop year, excluding Baoding	0.04	0.13	0.08
Crop year, Baoding only	0.12	0.14	0.13

monthly price data are divided into a "crop year," from July to the end of June, the effect of crises is seen to be far higher for the coarse grains but slightly lower for wheat. Table 2.2 summarizes the coefficients generated in these various ways. In all cases the R^2s are very similar, as are the coefficients for time. The monthly coefficients vary, but are within two standard errors of zero.

Dividing the year at July generates a higher coefficient for the crisis variable, because a crop year more closely approximates the seasonal weather pattern in the North. Since July and August are the months of greatest annual rainfall, droughts and floods have their first impact in the second half of the year and the next winter. They affect the coarse grains first. Although sorghum is known to be flood-resistant, its price seems to be the most differentially affected by the use of this technique. Overall, however, the price of millet was the most affected in a year of crisis.

The fact that Baoding prices were more affected by crises than prices in the rest of the province raises some interesting questions. As the seat of the provincial capital, Baoding Prefecture might be expected to have higher prices than outlying prefectures because of a stronger demand for grains. Its wheat prices were much more affected by crises than wheat prices in the rest of the province, suggesting a stronger demand for the luxury grain in the capital than elsewhere.

Tables 2.3, 2.4, and 2.5 attempt to evaluate the effect of natural disasters on grain prices in three crisis periods.[29] The tables compare the actual prices of the three grains with their predicted prices (for a noncrisis year), calculated with the regression coefficients presented in Table 2.1, using data for 1738–1910 but excluding Baoding.

---

29. The period 1743–44 was chosen because it is a well-studied drought, the periods 1762–63 and 1775–76 because the data were relatively complete. Although 1775–76 is identified in documentary sources as a drought period, these years are not coded as crisis years in the regression analysis (see n. 21 above) because fewer than 25 counties were apparently affected.

Predicted Price = $a + b$(Time) + Monthly effects

Time is the year minus 1738. Each case study covers the two calendar years that include the period of crisis.

In 1743–44 Zhili experienced a drought. As Table 2.3 shows, the actual prices of all three grains at the beginning of 1743 were below the predicted prices, particularly so for millet and sorghum. However, by May and June, when wheat prices should have fallen, they instead continued to rise, reflecting a poor harvest or an impending harvest. Although the data for the key months of the crisis, from summer 1743 to summer 1744, are missing, we can see that by July 1744 the prices of wheat and millet had risen 0.20 tael above the predicted price, and the price of sorghum, 0.15 tael. By the end of the calendar year, however, the price of wheat was almost down to the predicted level, and the prices of millet and sorghum had fallen to well below the predicted prices.

Although the actual prices at their peak reflected the impact of the drought more than the crisis coefficients of 0.06, 0.06, and 0.01 predicted they would, nevertheless it can certainly be concluded that the overall impact of the drought was rather limited in magnitude and duration. This substantiates to a considerable degree the picture of this crisis drawn by Pierre-Etienne Will.[30] First, the impact of the drought, according to the historical record, was limited to 27 counties, primarily in four prefectures. Second, these counties were the recipients of massive amounts of government relief, deployed from several sources, most notably the state granaries in Tongzhou. The grain prices in these prefectures taken separately show no difference from the provincial trends. The famine relief campaign mounted by the government was truly a model effort, and the price history seems to show that the efforts of the Qing officials were well rewarded.

Table 2.4 presents the predicted and actual prices during and after a flood in 1775, which had been preceded by a drought in 1774, to show what the conditions were in a crisis where the government may have played a less active role. In this case, it appears that wheat prices were the most seriously affected. By September 1775 wheat prices were 0.20 tael above the predicted price, and prices stayed high until June, when an apparently successful harvest sent prices tumbling down to well under their predicted or normal levels. Millet prices were close to their normal levels in the spring and summer of 1775, while sorghum prices rose 0.10 tael or slightly more. But after the fall 1775 harvest, which does not seem to have been much affected by the flood, both millet and sorghum prices fell and stayed below their predicted levels in 1776. So the main impact of the crisis fell on wheat, and as in 1743–44, the impact was limited in magnitude and duration.

---

30. See Will, *Bureaucratie et Famine*.

TABLE 2.3 Grain Prices during the 1743–1744 Drought in Zhili Province (Excluding Baoding)
(in taels per *shi*)

Year and Month[a]	Wheat Price			Millet Price			Sorghum Price		
	Predicted	Actual	Residual[b]	Predicted	Actual	Residual[b]	Predicted	Actual	Residual[b]
1743									
January	1.59	1.55	−.04	1.33	1.19	−.14	0.90	0.76	−.14
February	1.60	1.56	−.04	1.36	1.20	−.16	0.92	0.78	−.14
March	1.62	1.57	−.05	1.38	1.22	−.16	0.94	0.82	−.12
April	1.66	1.61	−.05	1.39	1.25	−.14	0.95	0.84	−.11
May	1.65	1.65	.00	1.39	1.28	−.11	0.96	0.86	−.10
June	1.61	1.68	+.07	1.40	1.31	−.09	0.97	0.88	−.09
July	1.54	—	—	1.42	—	—	0.98	—	—
August	1.55	—	—	1.42	—	—	0.98	—	—
September	1.53	—	—	1.39	—	—	0.92	—	—
October	1.61	—	—	1.41	—	—	0.94	—	—
November	1.60	—	—	1.36	—	—	0.91	—	—
December	1.61	—	—	1.34	—	—	0.91	—	—
1744									
January	1.59	—	—	1.34	—	—	0.90	—	—
February	1.61	—	—	1.37	—	—	0.92	—	—
March	1.63	—	—	1.39	—	—	0.95	—	—
April	1.67	—	—	1.40	—	—	0.96	—	—
May	1.65	—	—	1.40	—	—	0.96	—	—
June	1.61	—	—	1.41	—	—	0.98	—	—
July	1.54	1.74	+.20	1.43	1.62	+.19	0.99	1.14	+.15
August	1.55	—	—	1.43	—	—	0.98	—	—
September	1.53	1.71	+.18	1.40	1.32	−.08	0.92	0.91	−.01
October	1.62	—	—	1.42	—	—	0.94	—	—
November	1.61	1.68	+.07	1.37	1.09	−.28	0.91	0.77	−.14
December	1.62	1.65	+.03	1.34	1.09	−.25	0.91	0.77	−.14

[a] Months are solar. [b] Actual minus predicted price.

TABLE 2.4 Grain Prices during the 1775–1776 Drought and Flood in Zhili Province (Excluding Baoding)
(in taels per *shi*)

Year and Month[a]	Wheat Price			Millet Price			Sorghum Price		
	Predicted	Actual	Residual[b]	Predicted	Actual	Residual[b]	Predicted	Actual	Residual[b]
1775									
January	1.77	1.80	+.03	1.53	1.51	−.02	1.04	1.08	+.04
February	1.79	1.80	+.01	1.56	1.51	−.05	1.06	1.08	+.02
March	1.81	1.87	+.06	1.58	1.55	−.03	1.09	1.13	+.04
April	1.85	1.91	+.06	1.59	1.60	+.01	1.10	1.18	+.08
May	1.84	1.94	+.10	1.59	1.62	+.03	1.11	1.21	+.10
June	1.80	1.92	+.12	1.60	1.60	.00	1.12	1.21	+.09
July	1.72	1.88	+.16	1.62	1.61	−.01	1.13	1.23	+.10
August	1.73	1.89	+.16	1.62	1.60	−.02	1.12	1.24	+.12
September	1.72	1.92	+.20	1.59	1.58	−.01	1.06	1.20	+.14
October	1.80	1.93	+.13	1.60	1.46	−.14	1.08	1.08	.00
November	1.79	1.96	+.17	1.56	1.40	−.16	1.05	1.02	−.03
December	1.80	1.96	+.16	1.53	1.39	−.14	1.05	0.98	−.07
1776									
January	1.78	1.97	+.19	1.53	1.40	−.13	1.05	0.99	−.06
February	1.79	1.97	+.18	1.56	1.40	−.16	1.07	1.00	−.07
March	1.81	1.99	+.18	1.58	1.41	−.17	1.09	0.99	−.10
April	1.86	2.02	+.16	1.59	1.43	−.16	1.10	1.02	−.08
May	1.84	2.02	+.18	1.59	1.44	−.15	1.11	1.03	−.08
June	1.80	1.81	+.01	1.60	1.44	−.16	1.12	1.02	−.10
July	1.73	1.52	−.21	1.63	1.44	−.19	1.13	1.00	−.13
August	1.74	1.41	−.33	1.63	1.42	−.21	1.13	0.99	−.14
September	1.72	1.38	−.34	1.60	1.39	−.21	1.07	0.96	−.11
October	1.80	—	—	1.61	—	—	1.09	—	—
November	1.80	—	—	1.56	—	—	1.06	—	—
December	1.80	1.44	−.36	1.54	1.34	−.20	1.06	0.91	−.15

[a] Months are solar. [b] Actual minus predicted price.

In Table 2.5 the data for the latter part of the 1761–63 flood crisis are presented. According to documentary evidence, this flood affected 53 counties in the Hai River Basin. By the beginning of 1762, prices were considerably higher than normal for all three grains. With the exception of a brief dip in June 1762, wheat prices kept climbing, reaching a level about 0.21 tael above normal in March–April 1763, after which prices began to come down, reaching their normal levels by the end of the year. Millet was the most severely affected of all the grains. Its price kept climbing until winter 1762–63, when it was more than 0.60 above normal. Its prices remained high during the year. Sorghum prices also reached a level of about 0.40–0.46 above their predicted prices in January–April 1763.

As both Table 2.5 and Figure 2.3 show, this flood marked one of the few times in the Qing period when the price of millet actually exceeded the price of wheat. In an extensive flood, property is damaged and recovery may take a longer time than after a drought. The data in this case certainly show a greater impact and a much slower recovery than do the data in the two cases involving drought. These results suggest a hypothesis for future investigation, namely, that floods in the Qing period had a more pronounced effect on prices than droughts did.

On the whole, however, these three cases show that the impact of crises in the eighteenth century was relatively moderate, especially in comparison with the staggering price increases of other well-documented world famines, or even late-nineteenth- or twentieth-century famines in China. According to Andrew B. Appleby, grain prices in French subsistence crises of the seventeenth and early eighteenth centuries rose to three or four times their normal levels.[31] In Zhili, in the eighteenth century at least, prices were not generally affected more than 10–20 percent; prices rose just over 40 percent for millet in 1762–63, the worst case seen so far.

Appleby also argues that the English mixed farming system, with animal husbandry and multiple grains, worked to minimize the effects of shortages because people could choose to eat inferior grains, usually reserved for livestock, instead of wheat, the preferred grain—eating down the food chain, so to speak. In Zhili the grain prices maintained a separation from each other, except in the 1761–63 flood, when millet prices reached and then exceeded those of wheat. Separation of prices suggests either that the markets were indeed separate, and there was little substitutability in crisis times, or else that there really was not a crisis, because there was no need for substitution. In a real crisis people become unable, or unwilling, to pay the exorbitant price of an expensive grain and therefore substitute an inferior grain, which in turn drives up the price of the second grain. Consequently, the separation

---

31. Andrew B. Appleby, "Grain Prices and Subsistence Crises in England and France, 1590–1740," *Journal of Economic History* 39, no. 4 (Dec. 1979):865–86.

TABLE 2.5. Grain Prices during the Last Years of the 1761–1763 Flood in Zhili Province (Excluding Baoding)
(in taels per shi)

Year and Month[a]	Wheat Price			Millet Price			Sorghum Price		
	Predicted	Actual	Residual[b]	Predicted	Actual	Residual[b]	Predicted	Actual	Residual[b]
1762									
January	1.70	1.89	+ .19	1.45	1.85	+ .40	0.98	1.18	+ .20
February	1.71	1.89	+ .18	1.48	1.85	+ .37	1.00	1.18	+ .18
March	1.73	1.89	+ .16	1.50	1.87	+ .37	1.03	1.22	+ .19
April	1.77	1.91	+ .14	1.51	1.85	+ .34	1.04	1.22	+ .18
May	1.76	1.86	+ .10	1.51	1.83	+ .32	1.05	1.23	+ .18
June	1.72	1.75	+ .03	1.52	1.84	+ .32	1.06	1.24	+ .18
July	1.65	—	—	1.54	—	—	1.07	—	—
August	1.66	—	—	1.54	—	—	1.06	—	—
September	1.64	1.75	+ .11	1.51	1.89	+ .38	1.01	1.22	+ .21
October	1.72	1.80	+ .08	1.52	1.92	+ .40	1.02	1.26	+ .24
November	1.72	1.85	+ .13	1.48	2.01	+ .53	0.99	1.33	+ .34
December	1.72	1.88	+ .16	1.45	2.06	+ .61	0.99	1.35	+ .36
1763									
January	1.70	1.89	+ .19	1.45	2.08	+ .63	0.99	1.39	+ .40
February	1.72	1.92	+ .20	1.48	2.10	+ .62	1.01	1.44	+ .43
March	1.74	1.95	+ .21	1.50	2.12	+ .62	1.04	1.47	+ .43
April	1.78	1.99	+ .21	1.51	2.14	+ .63	1.05	1.51	+ .46
May	1.77	—	—	1.52	—	—	1.05	—	—
June	1.73	—	—	1.52	—	—	1.06	—	—
July	1.65	1.76	+ .11	1.55	2.09	+ .54	1.07	1.43	+ .36
August	1.66	1.75	+ .09	1.55	2.04	+ .49	1.07	1.40	+ .33
September	1.65	1.74	+ .09	1.52	1.97	+ .45	1.01	1.30	+ .29
October	1.73	1.74	+ .01	1.53	1.90	+ .37	1.03	1.24	+ .21
November	1.72	1.74	+ .02	1.48	1.86	+ .38	1.00	1.22	+ .22
December	1.73	1.75	+ .02	1.46	1.84	+ .38	1.00	1.20	+ .20

[a] Months are solar. [b] Actual minus predicted price.

of prices (their nonconvergence) in 1743–44 and 1775–76 suggests that there was no real crisis in those two instances, while the convergence of millet and wheat prices in 1762–63 suggests that there was a real crisis in that situation. Again, this idea, like others in this paper, is advanced as a hypothesis that must be tested, particularly with prefectural data that will focus on the particular parts of the province affected in a particular crisis.

REGIONAL VARIATION

A central question in the study of these grain prices is the extent to which they varied within the province. In a well-developed market system, the correlation of prefectural prices ought to have been high, and price variation ought to have been low. Price variation within the province should also tell us something about the impact of crises. In a well-developed market system, the impact of natural disasters ought to have been cushioned, since grain would have been able to flow from unaffected regions to the affected ones. Of course, the same effects—strong price correlations and low price variation—might also have been achieved if the granary system was highly effective in its functions of price stabilization and famine relief or if the entire province had identical weather and other environmental conditions.

In approaching the question of market integration, we first employed the statistical measure called the coefficient of variation. The coefficient of variation is the standard deviation divided by the mean, multiplied by 100. It is a measure of the extent to which prices varied among prefectures during a given period. If market integration increased over time, then the coefficient of variation should decline. If, on the other hand, markets deteriorated, then the coefficient of variation should increase. We calculated the coefficients of variation of prefectural prices for each year from 1738 to 1910 for which we had data, omitting Xuanhua and Chengde, which were in the northern sections of the province. Then we did a regression analysis of the coefficients of variation with year (T) and crisis year (C) as variables. The resulting regression coefficients for year were 0.018, 0.041, and 0.013 for wheat, millet, and sorghum respectively (with t-values of 3.8, 7.8, and 2.6). In other words, the coefficients of variation for all three grains increased over time, and millet prices experienced significantly greater increases in regional variation than the other two grains.

These results are contrary to the expectation that over time markets should have become more integrated; if so, the coefficient of variation should have decreased. They also draw attention to, and invite explanation for, the different price behavior of millet, which was the staple grain for most people and which might perhaps have been more sensitive to population growth and to crises.

In the same regression analysis, however, the regression coefficients for

TABLE 2.6 Grain Price Variation in Crisis and Noncrisis Years in Zhili Province (Excluding Xuanhua and Chengde), 1738–1910

Crop	Price in Noncrisis Years (mean of values)	Price in Crisis Years (mean of values)	Difference in Mean Price
Wheat			
Standard deviation (taels)	0.24	0.25	
Mean price (taels)	1.97	2.10	+.13
Coefficient of variation[a]	12.11	11.55	
Millet			
Standard deviation (taels)	0.22	0.24	
Mean price (taels)	1.77	1.93	+.16
Coefficient of variation[a]	11.97	11.88	
Sorghum			
Standard deviation (taels)	0.16	0.17	
Mean price (taels)	1.22	1.32	+.10
Coefficient of variation[a]	12.93	12.71	

[a] (Standard deviation / mean) * 100. Computed from standard deviations and means having more than two decimal places.

crisis years were all negative, with t-values under -2.0. That crisis years would cause variation to decline seems counterintuitive. When the various components of the coefficient of variation are separated out, however, a more plausible picture emerges. As Table 2.6 shows, the coefficient of variation declines for crisis years only because the standard deviation does not increase as much as the mean price. In other words, the lower coefficient of variation for crisis years is more a reflection of a higher mean price, totally to be expected, than diminished variation among prefectural prices. The table not only shows that the standard deviation did not increase very significantly in crisis years but also shows that the increase in the mean price was greater for millet—0.16 taels on the average—than it was for wheat or sorghum—0.13 and 0.10 taels respectively.[32] On the whole, this analysis confirms the impressions derived from the earlier case studies in supporting the view that the impact of crises, both on the level of prices and on their variation across regions, was relatively limited.

As a second step, we used Pearson correlations to study regional integration. The correlation coefficients measure the relationship between grain

32. The careful reader may note that the differences between the mean prices of crisis and noncrisis years differ somewhat from the crisis variables presented in Table 2.2. They are, however, roughly of the same order of magnitude as the last set, representing "crop year, Baoding only." Once again, it should be emphasized that regression analysis cannot produce precise results.

prices in pairs of prefectures, with 1.0 being a perfect correlation. The comparison of annual prices for the 17 prefectures of the province revealed astonishingly high degrees of correlation for most pairs of prefectures, with the unsurprising exceptions of Xuanhua and Chengde prefectures. Pearson correlations for wheat prices were mostly over 0.70, sometimes over 0.90, often above 0.80. Similar generalizations can be made for millet and sorghum.

When correlations are calculated separately for eighteenth- and nineteenth-century prices, no clear trend can be confirmed. While wheat correlations between most pairs of prefectures seem to rise, for millet the picture is more mixed. Excluding Chengde and Xuanhua, correlations for the remaining 15 prefectures show that in 59 of 105 cases, correlations declined from the eighteenth to the nineteenth centuries, while in 46 cases they increased. This partly supports the picture presented by the study of coefficients of variation, and continues to make interesting the hypothesis that millet prices experienced greater spatial variation in the nineteenth century than the eighteenth century. Clearly, the next step in pursuing this question is to study the province on a region by region basis to see which regions shared this experience and which did not.

Since the correlation of prices themselves incorporates a similar time trend for all of the prefectures, it exaggerates the extent to which prices were actually correlated. Studying the first difference of these prices (the difference between the price in a given year and the price in the previous year) omits the common time element and provides a better measure of correlation. A preliminary analysis of annual price differences for the eighteenth century reveals that for wheat and millet about two thirds of the possible correlations between prefectures were 0.60 or over; for sorghum over 55 percent of the correlations were over 0.60. These results also suggest a reasonably high degree of correlation, but understanding their significance must await further work, and comparing them to nineteenth-century correlations must await a more complete set of nineteenth-century data.

Taken together, these preliminary attempts to study price variation in Zhili suggest a relatively high degree of integration within Zhili Province south of the Great Wall, but an integration that may have declined in some sections of the province, particularly in the case of millet, from the eighteenth to the nineteenth centuries. It should not be assumed, however, that integration was necessarily the result of a well-developed market system. The relative behavior of wheat and millet prices suggests that the market for wheat, a commercial product, may have been well developed and may have become more integrated in the nineteenth century. Millet, on the other hand, was the staple grain for ordinary people. In the eighteenth century, its apparent high degree of price correlation may have been due to the fact that the Zhili granaries predominantly stocked millet. With the decline of the granary system in the nineteenth century, price correlation may also have declined, because the eighteenth-century integration of prices was probably more a function of the granary system than of the market system. Until some estimate can be made of the output and supply of each of these grains in the Qing period, and until the nineteenth-century data are more complete, these hypotheses must await testing.

CONCLUSIONS

While indicating directions for future work, this preliminary study of grain prices in Zhili Province during the Qing period also permits us to draw certain tentative conclusions. In the most general terms, this study suggests, first, that there was a relatively low inflationary trend for the Qianlong through the Xuantong reign periods (1736–1911), particularly so when the last two decades are omitted. Second, although there were distinct seasonal patterns in grain prices, they were not great in magnitude, and were offset by the multicrop system, particularly by the planting of winter wheat.

Third, crises were seen in several contexts to have been moderate in their impact, at least in the eighteenth century. Regression analysis showed the impact of crises to have been relatively contained. Crises caused the mean price of grain to rise somewhat but did not cause a very great increase in regional variation. The three eighteenth-century case studies confirm these general impressions. In fact, while these periods were deemed crises in administrative terms, and while they were triggered by natural crises, perhaps they were not really food crises if food crises are defined as periods of abnormally high food prices.[33]

Fourth, the multicrop system appears to have been a significant factor in mitigating the effect of crises, particularly because of the different seasonal patterns of the crops. Multicropping certainly helped to offset the disadvantages presented by weather and geography, and has perhaps been overlooked in previous discussions. Appleby's study concludes that in England and France "the evidence suggests that a symmetrical price structure and subsistence crises went hand in hand. When all grains were costly at the same time, food shortage had an impact on both mortality and fertility; when one or another grain remained cheap, the demographic aftereffects were absent."[34] It is too soon to conclude that such a generalization could be made for Zhili, but certainly this suggests a framework for future investigation. For North China, Buck observed in the 1920s and 1930s that farmers sold the higher-priced grain and ate inferior grain. Farmers in the wheat

---

33. I have explored these issues more fully in "Using Grain Prices to Measure Food Crises: Chihli Province in the Mid-Ch'ing Period," *The Second Conference on Modern Chinese Economic History* (Taibei, 1989), II, pp. 467–509.

34. Appleby, "Grain Prices," p. 882.

region, he said, sold half the wheat they grew, and purchased inferior grain, an estimated one quarter of their food needs, from the market.[35]

The long-term behavior of millet prices seems to be the outcome of either deteriorating economic conditions (population pressure, etc.) or the diminished role of government intervention in the grain market or, more likely, both. The greater volatility of millet in some crises, its increasing coefficients of variation over time, and its lower price correlations in some regions in the nineteenth century all suggest certain long-term changes in its role in the food supply of Zhili. On the other hand, price analysis suggests that the role of sorghum did not experience a similar change. Francesca Bray has suggested that sorghum probably became more important in the nineteenth century with increasing population pressure.[36] However, the long-term trends shown in Figure 2.4 do not support this view, since the price of sorghum continued to remain a constant percentage of the price of wheat and always remained separate from that of the higher-priced millet.

Finally, future work may confirm that prices throughout the region, with the exception of the two outlying prefectures, were remarkably well correlated, suggesting the powerful interaction of granaries and markets.

To understand better the nature of these secular changes, we need to have more complete price data for the nineteenth century and better weather data. This will permit us to understand more about long-term trends over both centuries. We also need to know more about the interaction between the grain tribute system, the granaries, and the grain markets in the determination of prices. Only then will it be possible to grasp why a region so indifferently and curiously endowed by nature could play such a large political role over centuries of history.

---

35. Buck, *Land Utilization in China*, 1:416.
36. Francesca Bray, *Agriculture*, vol. 6, pt. 2, of Joseph Needham, ed., *Science and Civilization in China* (Cambridge, 1984), pp. 434, 464, 451–52.

THREE

The Qing State and the Gansu Grain Market, 1739–1864

Peter C. Perdue

Most Chinese celebrate the eighteenth-century Qing empire for two achievements: the expansion by conquest of China's territory to unprecedented size and the growth of its population to become the largest in the world. Two major institutions of the Qing state made these achievements possible: the military supply system and the granary and famine relief systems. Both of these institutions depended heavily on extensive private grain markets. New data from the price memorials in the Qing archives allow us to examine the degree of integration of these grain markets in Gansu Province in the eighteenth and nineteenth centuries. Scholars have recognized that market exchange of basic commodities was spreading widely in the Chinese empire in the eighteenth century, especially in the densely populated rice paddy belts of the Lower, Middle, and Upper Yangzi, the Pearl River Basin in South China, and along the Grand Canal leading to the North. Nevertheless, few have yet studied the substantial progress of trade in the far northwestern periphery of Han China. I shall argue that Gansu had achieved a considerable degree of integration of its grain markets by the eighteenth century and that the Qing state, through its military-provisioning and granary systems, indirectly promoted this process of commercialization.[1]

The impact of the military was much greater in Gansu than in Coastal, Central, South, and Southwest China, because of Gansu's strategic location on the supply route to the garrisons occupying Central Asia. Continual military demands placed great stress on a fragile agrarian regime. But the efficient transport system developed by Qing governors of the province for military

---

1. I would like to acknowledge the invaluable help of my research assistants, Jiang Xiaohong and Ren Jingzhen, in preparing the statistics for this paper. The M.I.T. Provost Fund and Metcalfe Fellowship supported the data collection and analysis.

supply and the injection of cash into the economy, combined with efforts to prevent military demands from excessively burdening the local population, stimulated market exchange. By linking Gansu to its neighbors, Shaanxi to the east and Sichuan to the south, the Qing could both maintain the local population and send support through the Gansu corridor to the large military establishment on the frontiers. A full analysis of the Northwest should include its core area in Shaanxi Province, but lacking the price data for Shaanxi at present, I shall only discuss Gansu itself.

Gansu's land area in the Qing was over 600,000 square kilometers, half again as large as California or Japan today. It was one of the largest provinces in the empire, smaller only than Yunnan and Sichuan among the 18 provinces of interior China. (During the Qing dynasty Gansu also included within its borders present-day Ningxia Autonomous Region and Xining Prefecture in present-day Qinghai.) Its population density, however, only 25 per square kilometer in 1957, makes it the most sparsely populated province of Han China.[2]

Although the population was sparse, the cultivated acreage was also low, giving Gansu a ratio of cultivated land per capita close to the national average. In 1887 less than 3 percent of the total area of the province was cultivated land, the lowest in the empire next to Yunnan, Guizhou, and Guangxi in the Southwest.[3] Wheat and millet were the major crops in the province, with acreages of 16.4 million and 14.9 million *mu* respectively in 1931–37. Miscellaneous crops (field peas, broad beans, oats, buckwheat) accounted for 6.2 million *mu*, corn for 2.2 million *mu*, barley for 1.9 million *mu*, and sorghum for 1.1 million *mu*. Only very small amounts of rice were grown. This was a very stable mix of crops, typical of regions with very low rainfall, little irrigation, and frequent droughts.[4]

Dwight H. Perkins estimates Gansu's grain yields as the lowest of the 18 provinces, an estimate confirmed by Governor Huang Tinggui, who complained in 1744 that harvests were poor in Gansu because the local people failed to use manure properly or to plow deeply.[5] Private grain storage was so low, claimed Governor Wu Dashan, that the people obtained half of their

---

2. Population figures for Gansu are highly suspect: if the population was only 12.8 million in 1957, it is hard to believe that it could have attained the official figure of 15.2 million given for 1787. On the other hand, the 1749 figure of 5.71 million is a clear underestimate. (Dwight H. Perkins, *Agricultural Development in China, 1368–1968* (Chicago, 1969), pp. 207–8; Yeh-chien Wang, *Land Taxation in Imperial China, 1750–1911* (Cambridge, 1973), p. 87; *Qingchao wenxian tongkao* (hereafter *WXTK*) 36/5195, 37/5205-6.

3. Perkins, *Agricultural Development*, pp. 223, 236; Ping-ti Ho, *Studies on the Population of China, 1368–1953* (Cambridge, 1959), pp. 124–25. The reported area was, of course, much less than the actual cultivated area, but the relative standing of the provinces is roughly accurate.

4. Perkins, *Agricultural Development*, pp. 249–58.

5. Ibid., p. 19; *Zhupi zouzhe* (hereafter ZPZZ), *tunken gengzuo* 1744.3.25.

seed for planting each year from government granary loans.⁶ Within the province, the districts west of the Yellow River suffered colder weather and later harvests than those to the east. Not only frequent floods and droughts but also hail, wind, sandstorms, insect plagues, frost, and snow could easily ruin a crop.⁷

Besides its low productivity, Gansu is noteworthy for its high percentage of *tuntian*, or former military garrison lands, most of which were cultivated by civilians in the Qing. *Tuntian* formed over 37 percent of the registered land area in 1753.⁸ By 1772, the Qing had assigned 27 percent of the registered population, or perhaps three million people, to cultivate these fields. The Qing rulers relied heavily on the agricultural output of Gansu to feed not just local military forces but also the armies stationed in Xinjiang.⁹

The military presence both in Gansu and in Xinjiang strongly affected state demands on Gansu's resources. Regular garrisons in the northern, eastern, and southern military districts of Xinjiang numbered at least 25,000 men by the early nineteenth century. Including their dependents, this meant an army of at least 125,000 people to be supported by a combination of garrison lands, cash stipends, and grain shipments from the interior. Joseph Fletcher estimates that of the annual military pay in Xinjiang of 3 million taels in silver, Han China supplied 1.2 million taels.¹⁰ Gansu was not the only source of subventions for Xinjiang, but it was the route through which all cash, grain, horses, and clothing reached the frontier.

Given the heavy demands by the state on Gansu and its low level of agrarian output, it is not surprising that the tax accounts of the province were almost always in arrears. Even though its tax quota was only 250,000 taels in 1725, it still owed the central government an unpaid deficit of 290,000 taels.¹¹ The tax reforms of the Yongzheng reign (1723–35) imposed on Gansu additional annual demands of over 75,000 taels to provide for the "nourishing-virtue" supplements to magistrates' salaries, for which the ordinary source used in other provinces—meltage fees on silver collection—was insufficient. Gansu used 20,000 taels from surplus collections on frontier trade duties and 11,900 taels in customary fees from the sale of merchant licenses, but still had to request a special transfer of surpluses from Shaanxi.¹² Gansu's inability to

6. ZPZZ, *zhenji* 1759.3.10, Wu Dashan.

7. ZPZZ, *tunken gengzuo*, 1742.2.2, Huang Tinggui.

8. Yeh-chien Wang, *An Estimate of the Land-Tax Collection in China, 1753 and 1908* (Cambridge, 1973), table 24.

9. *Jiaqing chongxiu Daqing yitongzhi*, juan 251–73. Although Xinjiang was not established as a province until 1884, for convenience I use this term to refer to Chinese Central Asia in the eighteenth century.

10. Joseph Fletcher, "Ch'ing Inner Asia," in John K. Fairbank, ed., *The Cambridge History of China*, vol. 10, *Late Ch'ing, 1800–1911*, pt. 1 (Cambridge, 1978), p. 61.

11. Madeleine Zelin, *The Magistrate's Tael: Rationalizing Fiscal Reform in Eighteenth-Century Ch'ing China* (Berkeley and Los Angeles, 1984), p. 312n.13.

extract sufficient tax income from agriculture led it to rely on more imaginative and less orthodox methods, especially taxes and contributions by merchants for official degrees. The central government, primarily interested in grain supplies for the military, seems to have been slow to realize Gansu's limitations. The state lowered its demands for cash by decreasing the surcharge for salary supplements from 30 percent to 15 percent, but it maintained high demands for grain. Gansu's tax quota in cash in 1745, 299,000 taels, was the lowest in the empire except for Yunnan and Guizhou, but its quota in grain (508,000 *shi*) was the sixth highest.[13] In fact, Gansu paid less than its quota in grain and more in cash, relying on an annual income of 32,000 taels from the tea and horse trades.[14]

Gansu, like the other peripheral western and southwestern provinces (Shaanxi, Sichuan, Yunnan, Guizhou) was on the whole a low-revenue, deficit tax collection area, heavily dependent on subsidies from interior provinces.[15] Within the province, however, rates of collection varied widely. In 1908 the average collection per county (*xian*) was 3,600 taels of silver and 5,300 *shi* of grain, but Zhangye (the Ganzhou prefectural capital) and Wuwei (the Liangzhou prefectural capital) paid the enormous sums of 101,800 and 94,400 taels respectively.[16] Such regions relied heavily on merchant taxes, especially on salt shipments, to meet these demands.

Gansu, then, was one of the poorest of the Han-dominated regions of the empire, comparable in remoteness, sparseness of population, and low productivity to the recently settled Southwest. Unlike the Southwest, however, Gansu occupied a strategic military position guarding the corridor leading to Central Asia, where the Qing rulers conducted their most expansive military campaigns. Unlike the Southwest, too, it had no major mining resources, and its native non-Han peoples—Muslims, Tibetans, Mongols—were assimilated far less willingly to Chinese culture than the native peoples of the Southwest. Persistent tension, sometimes leading toward accommodation, sometimes toward violent revolt, characterized Gansu's social fabric throughout the nineteenth and twentieth centuries.[17] Economically, however, Gansu increased its ties to interior China from the eighteenth century on. Shaanxi merchants controlled much of the province's internal trade. Goods from Hebei, Shanxi, Sichuan, and Henan supplied the civilian and military needs of the population. Gansu merchants, in turn, sold furs as far south as Hunan.[18] Private markets had much to do with drawing the regions together,

12. Ibid., p. 140.
13. Yeh-chien Wang, *Estimate*, tables 26, 27.
14. Yeh-chien Wang, *Land Taxation*, p. 71; *Yongzheng zhupi yuzhi* (hereafter ZPYZ) 4.4.92b–93 (Gansu governor's report of 1725).
15. Yeh-chien Wang, *Land Taxation*, p. 101.
16. Ibid., p. 59.
17. Jonathan Lipman, "The Border World of Gansu" (Ph.D. diss., Stanford University, 1981).
18. *Ningxiang xianzhi*, 1816/8/8.

but the institutions established by the Qing founders and perfected in the eighteenth century, interacting with the market economy, played an important role. The institution with the greatest influence on the agrarian sector was the national granary system.

GRANARY RESERVES AND FOOD SUPPLY

The nationwide granary system of the Qing stored large amounts of grain for leveling annual price fluctuations. "Ever-normal granaries" (*changpingcang*) in each county built up their reserves during the eighteenth century using funds and grain obtained from a combination of regular state revenues, contributions for degrees, and transfers from surplus provinces and areas along the Grand Canal.[19] Local elites in many provinces also supplied and managed community granaries (*shecang*) and charity granaries (*yicang*). This extraordinary grain storage system, whose total reserves far surpassed the holdings of any other premodern state, did succeed for a while in amassing large amounts of grain and in using these reserves to level price fluctuations. Reserve holdings rose to a peak near the end of the eighteenth century, rising from 30 million to 45 million *shi*. This was a volume of 31 to 46 million hectoliters, equivalent to a weight of milled rice of 261 to 391 million metric tons.[20] Along with this growth in holdings, however, appeared many signs of corrupt management, rotting of grain, and ineffective use of grain for price relief. Although the official level of grain stores dropped back to 30 million *shi* in the nineteenth century, the real level declined even more rapidly. Furthermore, granary reserves were increasingly diverted to other uses. By the mid-nineteenth century, the use of granary reserves for military supplies had become a very common cause of depletion of the system.

The system functioned well in the eighteenth century as long as officials maintained adequate supervision over granary accounts, took care to prevent spoilage by turning over the stocks, and used grain only for price leveling. Gansu is an example of a province where latent destructive forces of the granary system appeared very early. Supplying military demands, in particular, was explicitly recognized as one of the functions of Gansu reserves. This made it all the more difficult to maintain high levels of reserves, despite the very great demands placed on Gansu by the center.

Since other studies have described the general functioning of the granary

---

19. This discussion relies on references provided in Pierre-Etienne Will and R. Bin Wong, *Nourish the People: The State Civilian Granary System in China, 1650–1850* (Ann Arbor, 1991).

20. The *shi* was a volume measure of grain, equivalent in the Qing dynasty to 2.94 U.S. bushels, or 103.5 liters. Its weight varied by type of grain, but one *shi* of milled rice, the most common granary holding in south China, roughly equaled 185 pounds, or 84.1 kilograms. See Han-sheng Chuan and Richard A. Kraus, *Mid-Ch'ing Rice Markets and Trade: An Essay in Price History* (Cambridge, 1975), pp. 79–98.

system, here I shall only discuss certain aspects of the system that are peculiar to Gansu. The Qing empire demanded extraordinarily high amounts of grain storage from this poor province. Nearly all grain stored in Gansu was either wheat or millet. The Yongzheng emperor (1723–1735) set no fixed quotas for Gansu granaries, but in 1735 Gansu reported reserves of 750,000 *shi*.[21] In 1748, however, when the Qianlong emperor assigned new targets to all the provinces, he gave Gansu the very high total of 2.29 million *shi*.[22] By 1763 it had actually achieved only 1.28 million *shi*. After 1748 the emperor allowed most provinces to reduce their target levels, but he increased Gansu's targets because frontier military garrisons needed provisions.[23] By 1789, he had raised Gansu's target to 3.31 million *shi*, but it actually reported only 2.2 million *shi* (all figures here are given in Qing imperial units, or *cangshi*). Gansu, a poor province whose population at best amounted to a mere 2 to 5 percent of the national total, was expected to store about 10 percent of the national aggregate in both 1748 and 1789. In fact, it accumulated stockpiles that accounted for 3.9 percent of national reserves in 1767 and 7.4 percent in 1789. This substantial rise in Gansu grain holdings raised it from thirteenth to fourth in size of holdings among the nineteen provinces storing grain.[24]

The target figures for 1748 and 1789, however, did not genuinely represent the required amount of stored grain in each province. At best, they revealed the expected role of each province in the granary system. It is unlikely that any Qing official seriously believed that Gansu would be able to collect over 3 million *shi* in 1789. Gansu's "deficit" of 1.1 million *shi* in this year did not necessarily signify severe inadequacies in its granary administration, but only the great limitations on the province's ability to extract large amounts of grain from a poor population. Since the northwestern provinces always maintained above-average levels of per capita grain reserves, they may well have stored enough grain to carry out their primary function of price leveling.[25]

Building up and maintaining such large reserves was always a difficult problem. Gansu had three important sources for grain besides the local agri-

---

21. *ZPYZ* 53.44a, 45b.
22. The grain measure used in Gansu, the *jingshi*, was equal to 0.7 *cangshi*, the standard granary measure used in the rest of the empire. Memorials in Gongzhongdang archive, Palace Museum, Taibei, Qianlong reign (hereafter *GZD-QL*), 2.25, 1751/11/22. All the grain figures given here have been converted to *cangshi*. Prices, however, are given here in taels per *jingshi*. For comparison with other provinces, these prices should be raised by 14 percent.
23. *Daqing gaozong chunhuangdi shilu* (Qianlong) (hereafter *QSL-QL*), j.330.33-35 (1749/1/30).
24. For 1748 figures, see *Qingchao wenxian tongkao*, 36.5195, 37.5205–5206, cited in Pierre-Etienne Will, *Bureaucracy and Famine in Eighteenth-Century China*, translated by Elborg Foster (Stanford, 1990), pp. 193, 196. For 1766 and 1789, see the tables in Will and Wong, *Nourish the People*.
25. Maps in Will and Wong, *Nourish the People*.

cultural population: special allocations from the central government, transfers from Shaanxi, and merchant contributions for degrees. Central government officials, when they realized that especially large deficits and restocking problems plagued the Northwest, allocated large amounts of money to the region. They gave Gansu 3 million taels to restock its granaries in 1766, a year of good harvests, and 8,000 more taels in 1767.[26] These large transfers, however, were extraordinary, one-time measures. Shaanxi, a much more productive province because of the fertile land along the Wei River, could also supplement Gansu's supply in good years. In 1756, a bumper crop year, the emperor allowed the Shaanxi governor to buy more grain than his normal quota and send it to Gansu.[27] The governor could not, however, transfer grain regularly to Gansu, for fear of straining Shaanxi's supplies. Other Shaanxi governors blamed excess government demand from Gansu for driving up prices on the Wei River by causing competition between official and merchant purchasers.[28] "Contributions" (*juan*)—fees paid by local merchants and others to obtain lower-level examination degrees, bypassing the first level of the examination system—became the most common regular source of grain for Gansu. From 1741 to 1745 Gansu reported collection of over 1 million *shi* of grain from contributions. On the other hand, this controversial policy did not always work. In 1747 Governor Huang Tinggui reported collection of only 43,900 *shi* from contributions, despite his exhortations.[29] A 1766 edict prohibited reliance on merchant grain contributions, because officials feared embezzlement and the difficulty that grain purchases created for the local population.[30] Gansu, however, soon resumed the practice, once local officials realized that the province had no other way to maintain its grain reserves.

Through merchant contributions for granary restocking, the Qing rulers used their monopoly authority over literati status to extract resources from the merchant community for the benefit of the rural population. The Qing state, in principle, derived most of its revenues from the land tax, levying very small taxes on internal trade. In practice, however, ties between the state and merchants were much closer than the formal fiscal structure suggests. For example, even though licensing fees for brokers in local markets formed a very small fraction of total revenue, the Qing rulers used these fees effectively to supervise local markets.[31] The use of merchant contributions for

26. Ibid., manuscript version, p. 72.
27. *GZD-QL* 21/9/9.
28. *GZD-QL*, Zhongyin, 1753/6/16, 1752/8/10, 1752/8/21; Yang Yingju 1763/6/11.
29. ZPZZ, *caizheng cangchu*, 1747/4/11, cited in Will and Wong, *Nourish the People*, manuscript version, p. 84n.72.
30. *GZD-QL* 13303; *WXTK* 37.5205, cited in Will and Wong, *Nourish the People*, manuscript version, p. 63n.23.
31. Susan Mann, *Local Merchants and the Chinese Bureaucracy, 1750–1950* (Stanford, 1987).

granary reserves shows that Qing officials not only accepted the presence of competitive markets but also recirculated commercial revenues back into agricultural subsidies. Price-leveling sales, loans to farmers, and relief distribution both stimulated agricultural production and facilitated the operations of the private grain market.

Allowing merchant contributions for granaries, however, led Gansu into one of the Qing dynasty's worst political scandals.[32] Wang Danwang, taking over as provincial treasurer in 1774, illegally commuted contributions from grain into cash, siphoned a sizable fraction off into his own pockets, and wrote fraudulent reports to the central authorities about the actual reserves in Gansu. He demanded that subordinate officials submit false reports of disasters to obtain famine relief funds from the central government. Those officials who cooperated donated part of these fraudulently obtained funds to Wang himself and kept the rest as a reward for collusion. The vast dimensions of this scandal were only discovered in 1781, after Wang had left the province, taking several hundred donkey loads of loot with him.[33] Grand Secretary Agui, sent to repress a Muslim rebellion there, exposed the huge deficits in granary accounts and set in motion an impeachment process that led to the execution of 56 officials and the banishment or flogging of more than 46. This scandal vividly illustrates the dangers of reliance on contributions and unorthodox methods to fill granary reserves. The early Qing suspicions of this method were justified: merchant contributions, in cash or grain, proved too tempting for wily and unscrupulous officials.[34] Wang's scheme devastated Gansu's granary reserves from 1774 to 1781, but they recovered under close supervision in the following years. Whatever the bureaucratic repercussions of the scandal, the measurable effects on prices, grain supply, and the local economy were slight.

Memorial reports on actual granary reserves in Gansu, as opposed to official quotas, confirm the great difficulty of maintaining stable grain reserves in the province (see Figure 3.1). In the late fall of each year, after restocking from the fall harvest, every provincial governor reported the total reserves held in his granaries. As the graph shows, Gansu's annual holdings fluctuated greatly, more, in fact, than almost every other province in the empire.

---

32. Sources are from *Shangyudang, QSL-QL, GZD-QL,* 1774–1781; *Qinding Lanzhou jilue.* A brief discussion is in Will and Wong, *Nourish the People.* The most complete discussion in English is now Muhammad Usiar Yang Huaizhong, "The Eighteenth Century Gansu Relief Fraud Scandal" (Paper presented to the conference "The Legacy of Islam in China: An International Symposium in Memory of Joseph F. Fletcher," Harvard University, Cambridge, Mass., April, 1989).

33. *Shangyudang,* 1781/7/12, p. 139.

34. Officials, however, disagreed on whether grain or cash was easier to steal. For discussion, see R. Bin Wong and Peter C. Perdue, "Famine's Foes in Ch'ing China," *Harvard Journal of Asiatic Studies* 43, no. 1 (June 1983):313–14.

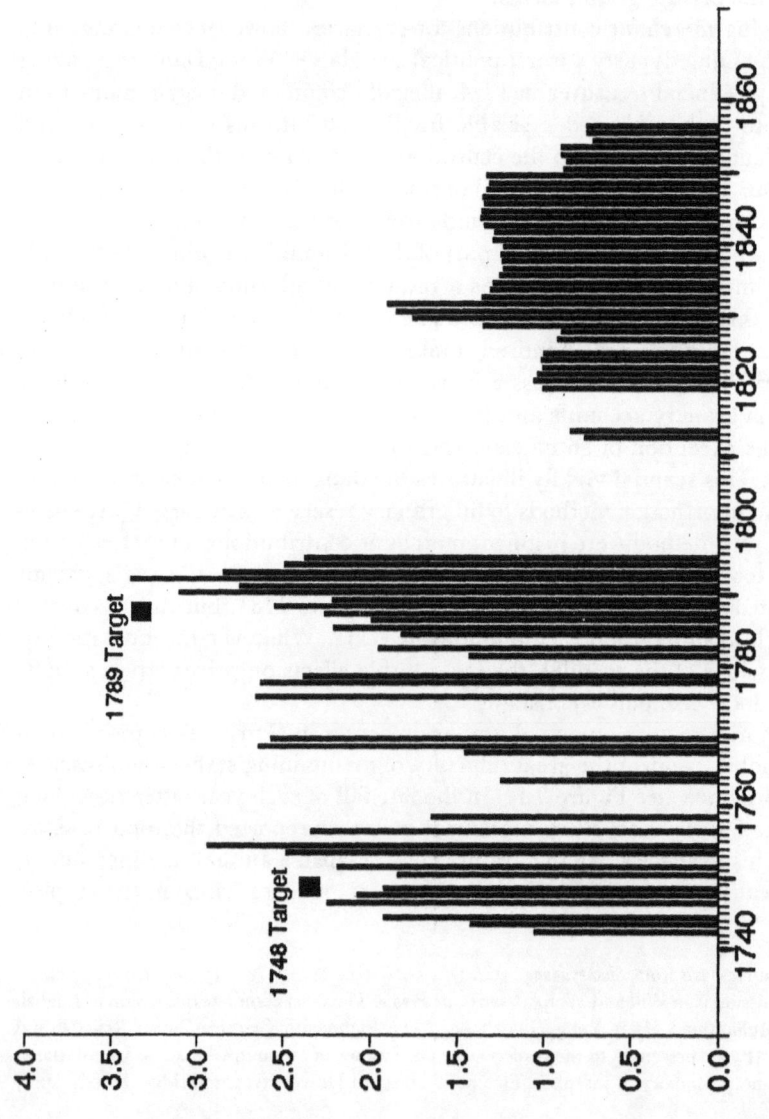

Fig. 3.1. Reported Grain Reserves in Gansu Province, 1740–1860 (millions of *shi*)
Note: "1748 Target" and "1789 Target" refer to quotas assigned to the province in these years. The bars give the actual holdings. (See text.)

Although reserves built up over the long term, from the 1740s to their peak in the 1790s, the military campaigns of the 1750s and 1760s reduced granary holdings drastically by siphoning off much of the ever-normal granary reserves to feed the troops. By 1769 the granaries appear to have recovered their level of 1753, but Wang Danwang's reign of fraudulent reporting, beginning in 1774, makes the figures for the 1770s suspect. The exposure of the relief scandal revealed that in 1781 true reserves had dropped to less than 1.5 million *shi*. Gansu experienced a genuine recovery in the 1780s and 1790s, when its granary accounts were under close scrutiny. Figures for the nineteenth century, by contrast, show that Gansu's grain holdings plummeted to a stabler but much lower level.

Gansu's granary reserves follow, in exaggerated form, the pattern of the empire as a whole. Year-to-year fluctuations were higher in the eighteenth than in the nineteenth century. Nineteenth-century granary officials undertook sporadic, short-term rebuilding campaigns, as in Gansu during the 1830s, but these campaigns did not offset a longer-term trend toward declining reserves. The figures for the nineteenth century are also more suspect, because the institutional controls over corruption, spoilage, and false reporting were looser. Rather than interpreting this drop as evidence of general decline in Qing administration, we can also view it as a shift in Qing policies away from the difficult methods of reliance on storage in kind toward greater reliance on the private market. Gansu, in this sense, pioneered moves by the Qing state toward injection of money into the regional economy. Governor Nayancheng's campaign of 1810–11 to relieve a drought that struck 30 counties exhibited further moves toward money and away from grain. He distributed 571,900 taels of silver and only 95,600 *shi* of grain to feed over 2,777,000 people.[35]

Any assessment of the Qing ever-normal granary system must distinguish between what the Qing officials expected it to do and how it really functioned. The Qing rulers designed the ever-normal granary system to serve only one goal: price leveling. In principle, each granary should have sustained itself. After an initial build-up period, during which reserves were increased through official purchases and grants, granary managers were expected to keep the granaries at a stable level without outside support. By selling at high prices in the spring and repurchasing at lower prices after the fall harvest, officials should have been able both to maintain reserves at constant levels and to use the profits to pay salaries and maintenance costs. Emperors frequently reminded local officials of their duties, required annual reports of them, and sometimes punished them for very small discrepancies in granary accounts. They expected regular and full restocking every fall. Of

---

35. The principal source for this relief operation is Nayancheng, *Zhenji* (1813). Brief discussion given in Wong and Perdue, "Famine's Foes", pp. 304–9.

course, only perfect prediction of future market conditions could have maintained absolutely stable reserves, but regions with regular harvests could much more easily keep their granaries stocked than regions suffering from frequent, unpredictable disasters. Stability also required that grain stocks be used predominantly for price-leveling sales. If reserves were diverted to other uses, either as official levies or for sales below market prices, extra funds would be required to restock in the fall.

Despite these difficulties, many provinces did succeed in keeping reserve levels stable for considerable periods of time. This stability, however, reflected a variety of relationships between regional grain markets and official purchasing activity. In the Southwest, for example, extremely stable reserves reflected a very low rate of grain turnover in regions of relatively localized markets. In the Lower Yangzi, on the other hand, stability resulted from highly commercialized, well-integrated grain markets and low per capita reserve levels.

In this paper, I stress the very wide variability of Gansu's reserves and what it reveals about Gansu's grain market. Substantial diversion of grain for military use combined with frequent poor harvests produced widely varying annual reserve levels. Still, even though Gansu's granaries fell short of the ideal design of the Qing system, they had significant economic effects. In fact, high annual fluctuations could indicate that reserves were being used effectively to relieve harvest shortages. In a region of frequent disasters, the best way to use granaries would be to accept deficits in bad years and make them up in good years, balancing the reserves over a multiyear cycle. If we could be certain that most of Gansu's reserves were used in this manner, the fluctuation in reserves would indicate highly effective management.

They could, on the other hand, indicate widespread diversion and peculation. Some provinces reported the total amount of grain purchased and sold during the year, allowing us to calculate the turnover rate, equal to the total purchases and sales divided by the end-of-year stocks. Gansu, unfortunately, is not one of those provinces, so it is difficult to determine exactly how much grain was bought and sold on the market. A more detailed examination of famine relief distributions would help resolve this question. For now, we may say that price stability after the 1760s provides at least some evidence that granary reserves were used effectively during the late eighteenth century to relieve the impact of harvest disasters. Although Gansu did not meet its targets, its high *per capita* grain holdings meant that grain distributions did have a relatively strong effect on the local grain market.

MILITARY DEMANDS ON THE GRAIN SUPPLY: THE CAMPAIGNS OF 1758–1761

The three great military campaigns of the early to middle years of the long Qianlong reign (1736–95) consolidated the Chinese hold on Central Asia, eliminated the centuries-old Mongol military threat, and expanded China's territory to unprecedented size. Only enormous logistic support from the interior made these campaigns possible. All of China's northern and northwestern provinces—Zhili, Shanxi, Shaanxi, and Gansu—bore the brunt of supplying the troops on the frontier with animals, wagons, porters, food, straw, uniforms, and weapons, but Gansu suffered the most. During the campaign against the Eleuth Mongols, from 1758 to 1761, large numbers of soldiers marched through Gansu. Even though they carried part of their rations with them, their demands on local grain markets drove up prices to spectacular heights. Grain prices doubled or tripled, but the prices of other goods also increased. Officials in Gansu had to raise the price they paid for horses from 8 to 10 taels, for cattle from 4.4 to 8 taels, in order to meet the local market price.[36]

Long pack trains marched through the province: 6,000 camels were sent from Zhili and Shanxi, many of which died of disease, requiring replacements; 12,000 horses were sent to Barkul (Balikun), of which the Eleuths stole 300.[37] Neighboring provinces received allotments of 3 million taels for grain transport to Gansu, in addition to 3 million taels given to Governor Huang Tinggui for military supplies.[38] The garrison in Hami, which increased from 10,000 to 20,000 in 1758, required at least 40,000 *shi* of grain per year.[39] Surprisingly, only 20 percent of these supplies were in kind and 80 percent in cash.

The vast distances—850 kilometers in a straight line from Lanzhou to Anxi, 300 more kilometers from there to Hami—and the high cost of transport across the steppes made it impossible to provision the troops through military pack trains alone. Expansion of garrison lands in Hami and Turfan provided valuable supplements, but only enough for 9,000 men for seven months.[40] Although Huang Tinggui instructed commanders to avoid purchases in Gansu by ordering soldiers to carry their own rations and even considered feeding the entire 20,000-man Hami garrison from Sichuan, he inevitably concluded that much of the grain had to be bought locally.[41] Of necessity, the private grain market in Gansu supplied a large share of the rations for the troops fighting on the frontier. The increase in military demand, combined with the influx of silver from government purchases, drove up local prices relentlessly.

This campaign unfortunately coincided with several years of widespread drought throughout the Northwest. Ningxia, with its irrigated fields, did send Liangzhou and Ganzhou its surplus of 112,000 *shi*, which was soon

36. *QSL-QL* 554.2b (1758/1).
37. Ibid., 576.36a (1758/12), 554.21b (1758/1), 557.31b (1758/2), 556.15 (1758/2).
38. Ibid., 512.25b (1756/5), 575.17b (1758/11).
39. Ibid., 564.19a, 564.17 (1758/6).
40. Ibid., 573.23a (1758/10).
41. Ibid., 567.27a (1758/7), 565.13a (1758/6).

exhausted. Relief needs alone were estimated at 500,000 *shi* of grain and 300,000 taels of silver.[42] Once again, the private grain market supplied much of the relief grain. In 1759 the emperor relaxed the usual rule of 50-50 distributions of relief in cash and kind to allow full cash relief where needed.[43] Where prices were low, especially east of the Yellow River in the ninth and tenth months of the year, relief in silver allowed the poor to buy food. As winter shortages exhausted market supplies, relief shifted to grain alone.[44] Besides direct distribution, the officials sold grain to reduce prices, but these sales only reduced prices by several tenths of a tael per *shi*.[45] Sales of millet at 2.4 taels per *shi* did not prevent the price from rising to 3.5 taels in Lanzhou by the end of 1759. It peaked at 4.4 taels in mid-1760 before dropping in 1761. Refugees flocked to sheds built for them in the cities, and Shaanxi shipped in 1.02 million *shi* of grain simply to provide seed loans for spring planting.[46] These are only a few signs of the major disaster inflicted on the province by the combination of the frontier military campaign and widespread drought.

In the short term, the campaigns of 1758–61 inflicted great suffering on Gansu's people, but in the long term they may have promoted Gansu's integration into the rest of the empire. Military salaries and relief allocations in cash poured large amounts of silver into the local economy. Despite its remoteness from both the copper mines of the Southwest and the silver imports on the coast, in 1761 Gansu's silver-copper ratio of 890 cash per tael was comparable with the ratio in the rest of the country.[47] Gansu officials set up government moneychanging bureaus in 1761 to help currency exchange, and they tried to standardize currency within the province.[48] We need more data on currency flows to confirm this hypothesis, but these military campaigns may well have contributed decisively to the monetization of the Northwest's economy.

The defeat of the Eleuths obviated the need for additional great military expeditions and brought relative peace to the Northwest. Of course, local unrest did not disappear. Tensions between Chinese Muslims and Han Chinese broke out in a short-lived revolt in 1781, but this had no effect on

---

42. Ibid., 565.20b (1758/6); ZPZZ, *zhenji*, 1759/6/3, Yang Yingju.
43. *QSL-QL* 567.12b (1758/7), 581.2a (1759/2).
44. ZPZZ, *zhenji*, 1758/10/17, Huang Tinggui.
45. *QSL-QL* 578.2a (1759/1).
46. ZPZZ, *zhenji*, 1760/9/9, Wu Dashan.
47. Hans-Ulrich Vogel, "Chinese Central Monetary Policy and Yunnan Copper Mining in the Early Qing (1644–1800)" (Ph.D. diss., University of Zurich, 1983); Hans-Ulrich Vogel, "Chinese Central Monetary Policy, 1644–1800," *Late Imperial China* 8, no.2 (December 1987): 27; Chen Chao-nan, *Yongzheng Qianlong nianjian de yinqian bijia biandong (1723–1795)* (Taibei, 1966).
48. Proposals to standardize currency and increase the copper supply are in *Gongzhongdang Yongzhengchao zouzhe* (Taibei, 1977–79), vol. 5, p. 230 (1725/10/1); vol. 11, p. 782 (1728/11/16); *QSL-QL* 580.13a (1759/2).

price levels. Whatever the underlying ethnic tensions in the region, Gansu's markets functioned much more stably after 1761 than they had before.

Major Qing institutions affected the grain supply in Gansu, then. In feeding armies, collecting taxes, and stocking granaries, the Qing officials had to adapt to the limitations of agricultural output in a poor peripheral province. At the same time, they stimulated market exchange by injecting cash into the economy through grain purchases and soldiers' salaries. The collection of taxes in cash also stimulated market exchange by forcing peasants to sell their surplus crops for cash.[49] The eighteenth-century conquests in Central Asia not only brought vast new territories under Chinese control; they also contributed to knitting together the interior regions of China by linking internal markets to the military supply route. The analysis of price data that follows examines the extent to which Gansu's prefectures were linked together by a system of grain markets extending from the core regions of the Southeast through the corridor into Central Asia.

PRICE DATA AND MARKET INTEGRATION

The 351 Gansu price memorials available to me cover the years 1739 to 1864. The eighteenth century is much more fully covered than the nineteenth: there are at least some data for 38 of the years 1739–99 but for only 21 of the years 1800–64. Monthly coverage is also much fuller for the eighteenth century than for the nineteenth. Some of the reports from the nineteenth century are too suspiciously constant, giving the same price three or four months in a row. My suspicions about some of the nineteenth-century data make me reluctant to draw conclusions about differences between the two centuries until more information becomes available. The Gansu price memorials report high and low prices for five major crops: millet (two varieties), wheat, beans, and barley. Here we shall analyze only the data for the primary millet crop (*sumi*). The reports cover the 13 prefectural divisions of Gansu Province, plus Hami, located in Xinjiang, and, for some years, the Jingni garrison, 100 kilometers northwest of Anxi.

Although the memorials report the highest and lowest prices within each prefecture every month, they do not tell us the locations of each high and low price. The yearly average curves of high prices and low prices within each prefecture parallel each other quite closely, but the high prices in Gongchang, for example, show occasional sharp peaks not found in the low prices (Figure 3.2). The most likely explanation for this pattern is that low prices

---

49. Compare with similar processes in England and France described by Rudolf Braun, "Taxation, Sociopolitical Structure, and State-Building: Great Britain and Brandenburg-Prussia," p. 318, and Charles Tilly, "Food Supply and Public Order in Modern Europe," pp. 380–455, both in Charles Tilly, ed., *The Formation of National States in Western Europe* (Princeton, 1975).

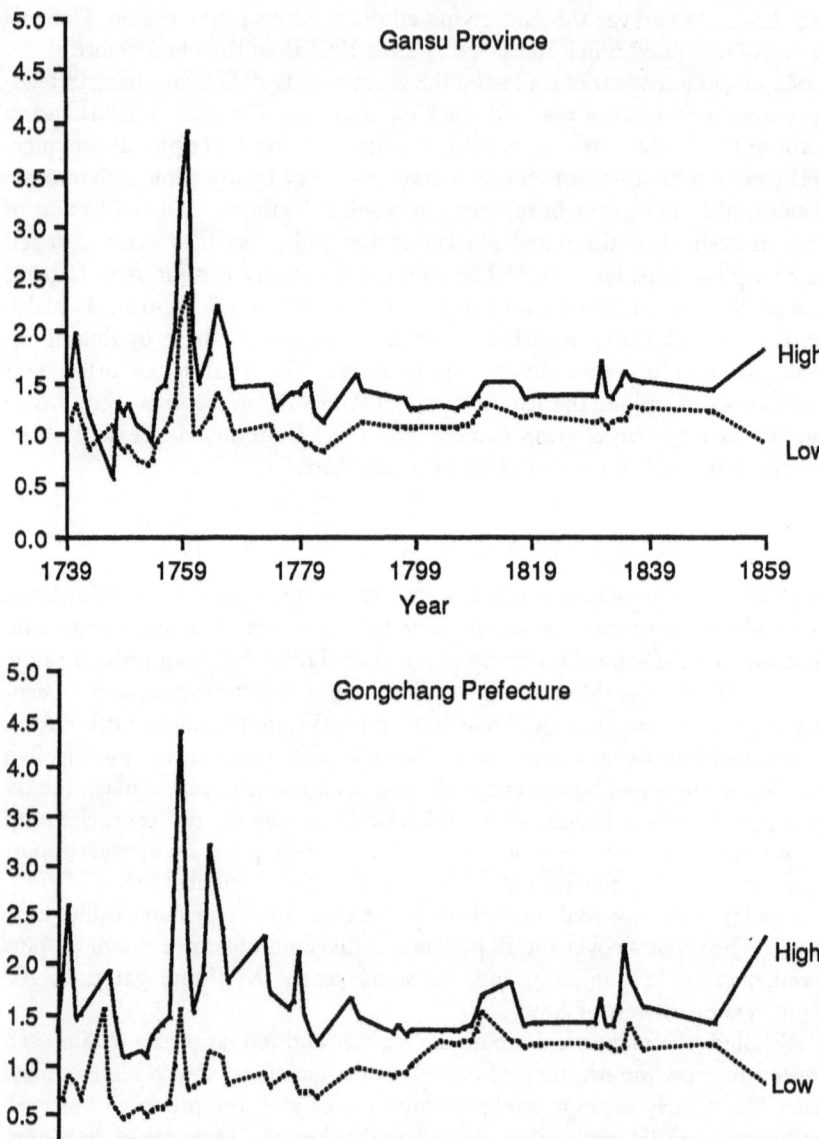

Fig. 3.2. Millet Prices in Gansu Province and Gongchang Prefecture, 1739–1864 (adjusted annual averages, in taels per *shi*)

represent the stabler patterns found in prefectural and county capitals, which were more commercialized than remote parts of the prefecture, where sporadic periods of dearth caused the sharp peaks in the series of high prices. The limited amplitude of seasonal variation in low prices compared to high prices supports our interpretation of low prices as coming from commercialized capitals (see Figure 3.3). For these reasons, analysis of the correlation between low prices is the most appropriate way, I believe, to measure market integration in this region.

Figure 3.2 shows the trends of the adjusted annual averages of millet prices for the province and one prefecture. (On the adjustment of data here and in other figures, tables, and the map, see the appendix at the end of this chapter.) As Map 3.1 demonstrates, there was a clear gradient of average prices across the province, because high transport costs raised price levels as one moved from east to west. Millet in Hami, where the mean of annual prices averaged 2.40 taels per *shi*, cost nearly twice as much as in Lanzhou, and Anxi, at 1.50 to 2.19 taels, was over 40 percent higher than Lanzhou. Low-price prefectures included Qinzhou and Jiezhou, Qingyang, and Pingliang, in the eastern end of the province, with access to Sichuan and Shaanxi supplies and the irrigated fields of Ningxia.

Several factors combined to produce the variation in grain prices among prefectures. Long-term changes in the balance of population and agricultural production, or changes in monetary supply, affected the long-term trend of prices. The cropping cycles of each region determined seasonal fluctuations from month to month. The impact of the major drought and military campaigns of 1758–61 produced drastic price changes, which swamped the impact of seasonal and annual trends. I used a multiple regression equation to analyze the relative effect, on average, of these three factors on the price for any given month.

The equation at the foot of Table 3.1 describes the monthly price as a function of a constant, the annual trend, seasonal variation due to monthly fluctuations, the disaster years of 1759–60, and an error term indicating random variation. A dummy variable (Y), whose value is 1 for the major drought years and 0 for all other years, measures how widely prices in these two years diverged from the long-term trend. The value of the coefficient (Γ) of this dummy variable given in the table shows that the combined stress of widespread drought and military campaigns in 1759 and 1760 raised the average high price by 2.10 taels, or 135 percent of the average price for the period. Prices more than doubled during these two years in nearly all prefectures, notably excepting Qinzhou and Jiezhou, in the southeast. The coefficients for both high and low prices of the dummy variable for disaster influence in Qinzhou range from 0.42 to 1.08, much less than the effect on the average of prices for the province. Jiezhou's disaster coefficient ranges from 0.22 to −0.04, showing that this prefecture, which belongs to the Sichuan

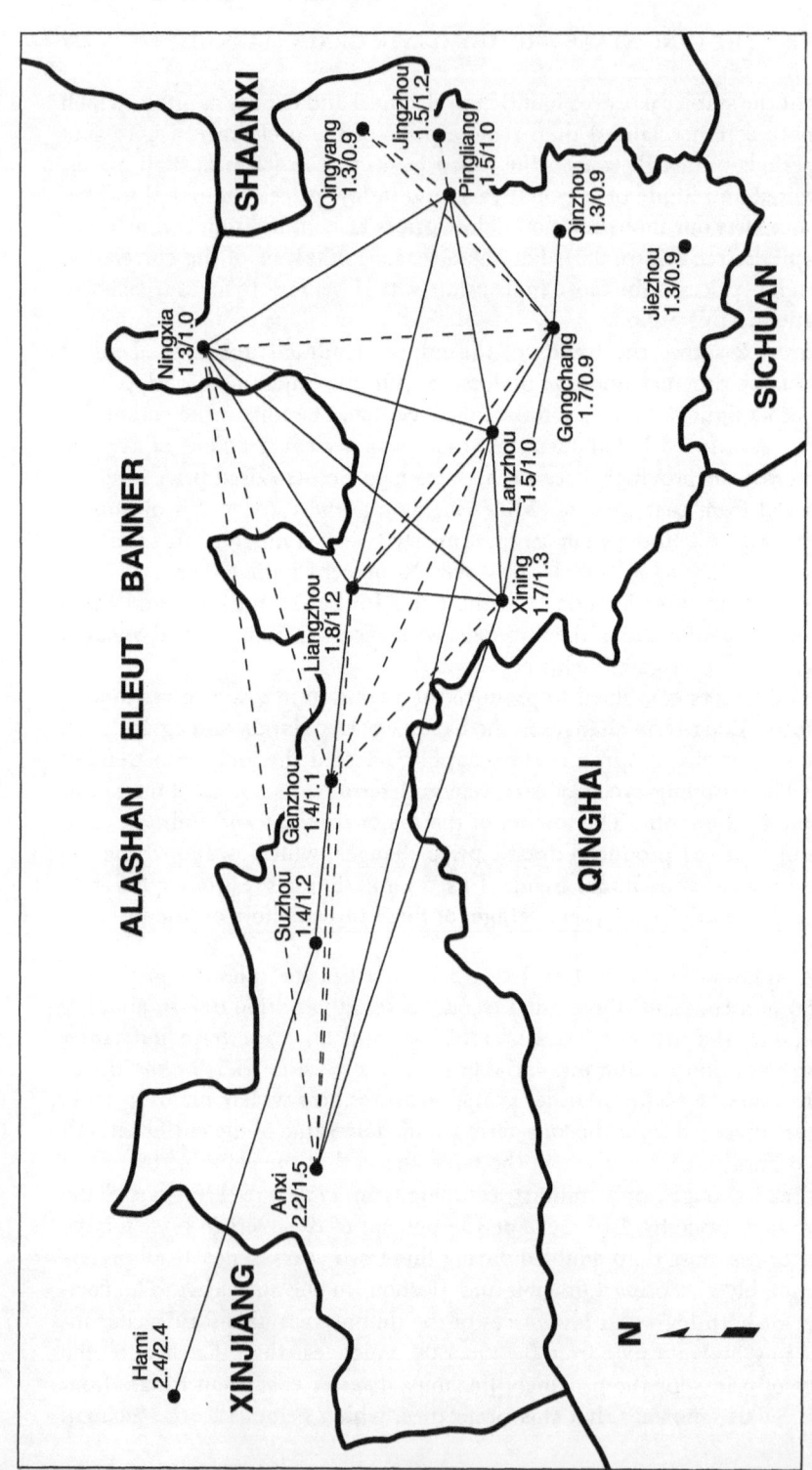

Map 3.1. Correlations and Variation of Low Millet Prices in Gansu Province, 1739–1864.
Note: Bivariate correlations of differences in adjusted annual averages are indicated by solid and dashed lines; solid lines represent r greater than 0.8, while broken lines represent r greater than 0.7 and less than 0.8. Means of high and low prices are shown for each prefecture (high prices first) in taels per *shi*.

watershed, was completely unaffected by the drought in Gansu. Drought and disaster hit hardest at the core prefecture of Lanzhou ($\Gamma = 2.82$) along with Liangzhou ($\Gamma = 3.64$) and Anxi ($\Gamma = 2.55$) on the corridor leading to Central Asia.

If we exclude the effect of these two disaster years, prices hardly rose at all over the long term. The value of α, the coefficient of the variable T for the year, gives the annual trend for each prefecture excluding the effect of the disaster years. This coefficient is negative for both high and low prices in Anxi, Ganzhou, Hami, Suzhou, and Xining and only slightly positive for the rest. (Jingni, the one exception, only provides data for a limited time period.) The ratio of α to K, the constant term, for the average for all low prices in the province, yields a long-term annual rate of increase of less than 0.1 percent per year. Gansu did not share in the rise of prices from 1780 to 1830 described by Yeh-chien Wang and Kuo-shu Hwang for the rest of the empire.[50] Its prices followed a different rhythm, determined more by military operations than by flows of silver. The high annual fluctuations up to 1762 contrast markedly with great stability after the 1770s. The price data confirm that once the early Qianlong campaigns had brought peace to the turbulent Northwest, Gansu's grain markets proved comparatively immune to sporadic attacks of rebellion, famine, and drought.

Seasonal variation from month to month was also remarkably low. Each month in the equation, except for the first month, is represented by a dummy variable, whose value is 1 for the price in that month and 0 for all other months. For example, the value of $M2$ is 1 for February prices and 0 for all other prices, the value of $M3$ is 1 for March prices and 0 for all other prices, and so forth. The coefficients of these variables indicate how much, on average, each month contributed to a change in price from the first month of the year (see Table 3.1). Month-to-month variation rarely exceeds 10 percent of the average price in each prefecture. The especially small variation of the low prices implies that grain storage in the commercialized capital cities damped out nearly all monthly fluctuations.

The monthly variations suggest that most prefectures had two major annual harvests, with a spring crop bringing low prices in April, May, or June (sometimes February or March), while the main fall crop forced prices to their low point in October (see Figure 3.3). The shapes of the curves, however, are not uniform over the region, because cropping regimes varied widely. Gansu's mix of crops and weather differed markedly from the much more uniform seasonal patterns of a rice paddy region like Hunan (see the chapter by Wong and Perdue in this volume). In Ganzhou, Suzhou, and Anxi, at the western end of the province, the fall harvest came in later than

50. Hwang Kuo-shu and Wang Yeh-chien, "Qingdai liangjia di changji biandong, 1763–1910," *Jingji lunwen* 9, no. 1 (1981).

TABLE 3.1 Annual Trends and Seasonal Variation in Millet Prices in Gansu Prefectures, 1739–1864
(coefficients of linear regression model in taels per *shi*)

Prefecture	K	α*100	Γ	Monthly Dummy Variables												R^2	N	Mean
				β2	β3	β4	β5	β6	β7	β8	β9	β10	β11	β12			
HIGH PRICES																	
Anxi	2.96	-2.10	2.55	0.03	0.02	0.12	0.05	0.00	-0.02	0.06	0.04	-0.01	-0.03	-0.13	0.50	324	2.19
Ganzhou	1.35	-0.02	1.75	-0.04	-0.05	-0.03	0.00	0.03	0.01	0.07	0.06	0.01	-0.02	0.00	0.54	326	1.44
Gongchang	1.43	0.20	2.15	-0.03	0.05	0.11	0.08	0.00	0.03	0.09	0.11	-0.06	-0.09	-0.09	0.52	326	1.68
Hami	3.20	-1.10	—	0.00	-0.02	-0.01	0.06	0.05	-0.01	0.01	-0.03	-0.04	-0.02	0.00	0.55	136	2.40
Jiezhou	1.17	0.07	0.22	0.03	0.03	0.03	0.05	0.05	0.07	0.05	0.04	0.03	-0.01	-0.04	0.07	325	1.25
Jingni	1.59	10.60	1.72	0.11	0.12	0.11	0.20	0.01	0.17	0.20	0.19	-0.09	-0.04	0.04	0.54	112	3.33
Jingzhou	1.19	0.30	—	0.03	0.09	0.12	0.05	0.09	0.06	0.05	0.07	-0.04	-0.03	0.00	0.16	163	1.50
Lanzhou	1.00	0.70	2.82	-0.01	0.07	0.10	0.10	0.06	0.07	0.08	0.10	-0.06	0.01	0.05	0.72	326	1.52
Liangzhou	1.44	0.10	3.64	-0.03	0.05	0.12	0.14	0.08	0.06	0.11	0.17	0.03	0.06	0.02	0.79	326	1.76
Ningxia	0.96	0.55	1.65	-0.04	0.06	0.04	0.10	0.06	0.07	0.10	0.11	-0.04	0.00	0.05	0.53	325	1.34
Pingliang	1.11	0.40	2.23	0.07	0.13	0.17	0.17	0.18	0.13	0.13	0.11	0.02	0.04	0.06	0.65	320	1.52
Qingyang	0.89	0.48	1.85	0.04	0.13	0.16	0.12	0.09	0.08	0.11	0.10	0.02	-0.01	0.00	0.52	325	1.28
Qinzhou	1.04	0.30	1.08	0.02	0.06	0.09	0.07	0.05	0.03	0.05	0.08	-0.01	-0.02	-0.07	0.38	324	1.28
Suzhou	1.40	-0.08	1.16	0.03	-0.07	-0.03	0.03	-0.02	-0.03	0.04	0.08	-0.03	-0.06	-0.07	0.28	323	1.42
Xining	1.79	-0.50	2.23	-0.03	0.02	-0.01	0.03	-0.02	-0.06	-0.04	0.02	-0.09	-0.06	-0.07	0.68	325	1.65
Combined	1.40	0.00	2.10	0.00	0.04	0.08	0.08	0.04	0.03	0.07	0.09	-0.02	-0.02	-0.03	0.70	314	1.56

LOW PRICES

Prefecture																	
Anxi	2.03	-1.37	1.86	-0.02	-0.11	0.00	0.02	-0.06	-0.02	0.05	-0.01	-0.05	-0.04	-0.11	0.62	326	1.50
Ganzhou	1.20	-0.25	1.30	-0.06	-0.10	-0.08	-0.04	-0.04	-0.03	-0.01	0.03	-0.01	0.01	0.02	0.57	327	1.13
Gongchang	0.60	0.65	0.51	0.01	0.00	-0.01	0.02	0.01	-0.02	-0.02	-0.01	-0.01	-0.02	0.00	0.48	327	0.90
Hami	3.20	-1.05	—	-0.01	-0.02	-0.02	0.05	0.06	-0.01	0.01	-0.03	-0.04	-0.01	0.00	0.55	137	2.40
Jiezhou	0.76	0.39	-0.04	0.00	-0.02	-0.04	-0.01	-0.01	0.00	0.00	0.02	0.01	-0.01	-0.01	0.45	326	0.92
Jingni	1.22	11.01	1.75	0.07	0.14	0.24	0.27	0.10	0.24	0.34	0.38	0.12	0.11	0.17	0.58	112	3.11
Jingzhou	1.28	-0.07	—	-0.01	-0.04	-0.03	0.00	0.02	0.02	0.00	0.00	-0.04	-0.02	0.00	-0.02	164	1.22
Lanzhou	0.79	0.40	1.69	-0.03	-0.02	-0.02	-0.01	-0.06	-0.05	-0.02	-0.03	-0.07	-0.03	-0.01	0.59	327	1.02
Liangzhou	1.16	0.01	2.28	-0.06	-0.06	-0.09	-0.06	-0.05	-0.08	-0.03	0.00	-0.04	0.03	0.03	0.76	326	0.25
Ningxia	0.81	0.23	1.06	-0.05	-0.03	-0.06	0.02	-0.02	-0.01	-0.03	-0.02	-0.02	0.01	0.04	0.45	326	0.95
Pingliang	0.59	0.77	0.69	0.02	0.03	0.02	0.00	0.04	0.00	0.01	0.01	-0.01	0.01	0.02	0.66	319	0.97
Qingyang	0.66	0.51	0.35	0.03	0.02	0.02	0.01	0.01	0.00	-0.01	-0.02	0.01	0.02	-0.02	0.33	326	0.90
Qinzhou	0.67	0.43	0.42	-0.01	-0.02	-0.04	-0.02	0.00	-0.01	-0.02	-0.01	0.00	-0.02	-0.03	0.34	325	0.88
Suzhou	1.20	-0.14	1.14	-0.02	-0.06	-0.04	-0.02	0.01	-0.03	-0.03	-0.01	-0.04	-0.04	-0.04	0.43	324	1.17
Xining	1.24	-0.11	1.77	-0.03	0.05	0.04	0.06	0.04	0.04	0.04	0.10	0.00	0.03	0.05	0.66	326	1.33
Combined	1.01	0.09	1.19	-0.02	-0.04	-0.03	-0.01	-0.02	-0.03	0.00	0.00	-0.03	-0.01	-0.01	0.71	312	1.09

NOTES: The data for Hami include only the years 1789–1864; for Jingni, only 1739–61; for Jingzhou, only 1778–1864. The data for all other prefectures include 1739–1864.

"Combined" evaluates coefficients for the average of each monthly price for all prefectures excluding Hami, Jingni, Jingzhou, and Jiezhou.

The coefficients are for the linear regression model $P = K + \alpha T + \beta_2 M_2 + \beta_3 M_3 + \ldots \beta_{12} M_{12} + \Gamma Y + \varepsilon$, where P is the monthly price (solar months): K is a constant; T is the year ($T=0$ for 1739); $M_2, \ldots M_{12}$ are dummy variables for each month excluding the first month ($M_2 = 1$ for second month, 0 for all other months, etc.); Y is a dummy variable for years of great disaster ($Y=1$ for 1759–60, otherwise $Y=0$); α is the coefficient of T (it gives the annual trend); β_2, etc. are coefficients of the monthly dummy variables; Γ is the coefficient of Y; ε is the error term; N is the number of months for which there are price data; R^2 measures the amount of variance explained by the equation; and the mean is the average of the monthly price data.

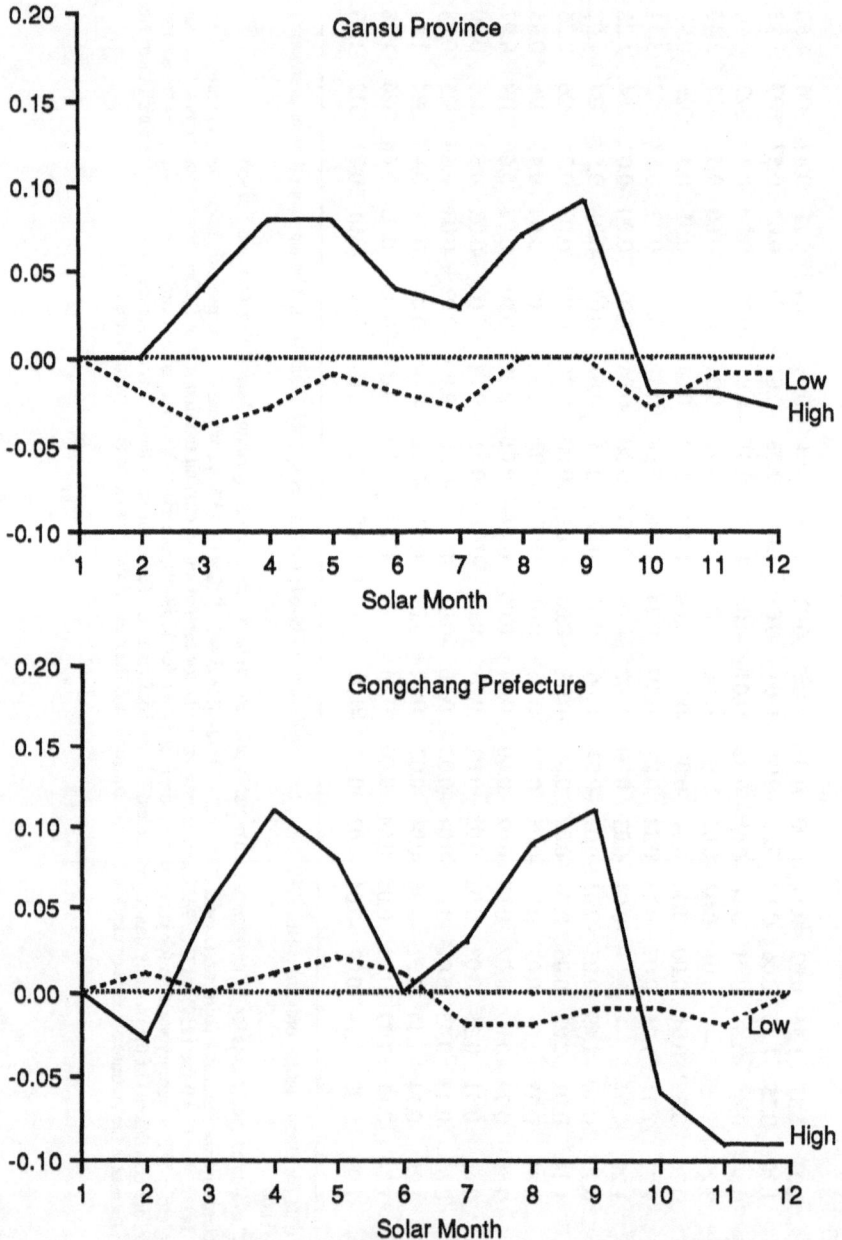

Fig. 3.3. Seasonal Variation in Millet Prices in Gansu Province and Gongchang Prefecture, 1739–1864 (difference from January price, in taels per *shi*)

elsewhere and did not produce its full effect until November and December, while the spring crop seems to have arrived as early as March. Jiezhou, Jingzhou, and Qinzhou, on Gansu's eastern periphery, had much lower variation than other prefectures and do not demonstrate the effect of double-cropping at all.

Clearly a combination of government price-leveling policies and private storage contributed to the low level of variability. Although officials thought that private storage in Gansu was too low, we cannot easily distinguish the relative contributions of private and government grain storage to price leveling. Unlike in some other provinces, grain memorials in Gansu do not report actual disbursements of grain year by year. Still, Gansu's storage costs may have been lower than other provinces' costs because there was little danger of grain rotting in the dry, cold climate.

The price data also allow us to assess the degree to which Gansu's grain markets were interconnected. Computing bivariate correlation coefficients (Pearson's r) between price series of different regions is a common method of analyzing the degree of regional market integration.[51] The possible values of this coefficient range from +1.0 to −1.0. Positive values mean some degree of synchronization between two given price series. Map 3.1 and Table 3.2 display the results of these calculations for the millet price reports from Gansu. The map uses solid lines to show correlations of greater than 0.8 and broken lines to show correlations of between 0.7 and 0.8. It uses prefectural reports of low millet prices to portray the correlations between the price differences of consecutive years from 1739 to 1864. Price differences are used to eliminate partially the influence of the annual trend: that is, the series consists of the price for 1739 subtracted from the price of 1740, the price for 1740 subtracted from the price of 1741, and so forth. (The annual average was derived from the months for which data were available after adjusting for seasonal variation. See the appendix.) Maps of correlations of monthly prices, which show short-term influences, display a similar pattern.[52]

The severe disaster years of 1759–60, however, did strongly affect all the prefectures of the province, except for Jiezhou. Removing these years from

51. See, for example, William O. Jones, *Marketing Staple Food Crops in Tropical Africa* (Ithaca, N.Y., 1972).

52. Barbara Harris has recently criticized the use of bivariate correlation coefficients to measure market integration. Recently, Martin Ravallion and Paul J. Heytens have developed more sophisticated statistical techniques to compensate for the influence of common trends and to measure more precisely the integrating effect of market exchange. Right now, missing data in the Chinese price series limit the usefulness of these techniques, but I intend to apply them to the Chinese data after obtaining more data from the archives. See Barbara Harris, "There is Method in My Madness: Or Is It Vice Versa? Measuring Agricultural Market Performance," *Food Research Institute Studies* 17, no. 2 (1979); Martin Ravallion, *Markets and Famines* (New York, 1987); Paul J. Heytens, "Testing Market Integration," *Food Research Institute Studies* 20, no. 1 (1986).

TABLE 3.2 Differences in Annual Averages of Low Millet Prices in Gansu Prefectures, 1739–1864 (Pearson's r)

Prefecture	Xining	Suzhou	Qinzhou	Qing-yang	Ping-liang	Ningxia	Liang-zhou	Lanzhou	Jingni	Jing-zhou	Jiezhou	Hami	Gong-chang	Ganzhou
Anxi	**0.810**	0.602	0.607	0.540	0.694	**0.772**	**0.792**	**0.819**	0.420	-0.101	0.101	0.375	**0.756**	**0.772**
Ganzhou	**0.788**	**0.801**	0.442	0.363	0.667	**0.792**	**0.856**	**0.700**	0.491	0.351	0.124	0.509	0.549	
Gongchang	**0.846**	0.357	**0.808**	**0.725**	**0.836**	0.763	**0.772**	**0.900**	-0.126	0.322	0.378	-0.042		
Hami	-0.060	**0.832**	0.370	0.128	0.031	-0.077	0.175	-0.281	—	0.210	0.310			
Jiezhou	0.253	0.347	0.404	0.155	0.221	0.135	0.166	0.237	-0.038	0.018				
Jingzhou	0.395	0.350	0.242	0.332	**0.707**	0.599	0.274	0.277	—					
Jingni	0.081	0.593	-0.115	-0.231	-0.273	0.239	0.095	0.113						
Lanzhou	**0.948**	0.535	0.658	0.689	**0.917**	**0.877**	**0.895**							
Liangzhou	**0.940**	0.628	0.608	0.564	**0.908**	**0.896**								
Ningxia	**0.865**	0.643	0.657	0.515	**0.823**									
Pingliang	**0.913**	0.424	0.668	**0.701**										
Qingyang	0.607	0.175	**0.702**											
Qinzhou	0.635	0.345												
Suzhou	0.606													

NOTES: Prices are adjusted on the basis of the first month (see Appendix). Coefficients > 0.700 in boldface.

the data sharply reduces the strength of interprefectural correlations, so that few coefficients exceed 0.8. At a weaker level, however, the same patterns remain. Coefficients at the level of 0.6 are still statistically significant, and they demonstrate the existence of the same network of exchange relationships.

The correlation coefficients indicate that a web of market relationships tied together the core triangle of prefectural capitals, Lanzhou, Gongchang, and Pingliang. Demands by these prefectures on the surplus production of the irrigated fields of Ningxia, to the north, tied Ningxia's prices to each. Weaker links connected Qingyang, Qinzhou, Xining, and Liangzhou to one or more of the core prefectures. A chain of trading posts linked Ganzhou, Suzhou, and Anxi to each other along the old Silk Road extending into the steppe.[53] Hami, in Xinjiang, was only weakly linked, if at all, to the Gansu markets. (Map 3.1 exaggerates its links to Liangzhou and Suzhou, probably because all of the data come from the nineteenth century.) Much of the grain supply for the Hami garrison came from *tuntian* lands in Central Asia, but a substantial portion of its supplies came through the corridor via Anxi. Conspicuously omitted from this network is Jiezhou, in the far south. Jiezhou lies on the upper reaches of the Jialing River, one of the major tributaries of the Yangzi flowing into the Sichuan Basin. If G. William Skinner is right to stress the importance of physiographic boundaries over administrative boundaries in defining economic macroregions, Jiezhou's markets should have little connection with the rest of Gansu but be linked by river transport to the Sichuan Basin. Jiezhou's isolation from the rest of Gansu confirms Skinner's theory of macroregions, attests to the overwhelming influence of river transport routes in determining Chinese grain flows, and shows that price correlations accurately define the boundaries of macroregions.[54]

Did market integration increase in Gansu from the eighteenth to the nineteenth century? An examination of graphs of average annual prices of millet from 1739 to 1864, smoothing out year-to-year fluctuations by five-year moving averages, seems to reveal some convergence between the price series of different prefectures. As expected, Hami and Jiezhou, which belong to different marketing systems, do not conform. More precisely, when we calculate the coefficient of variation (standard deviation divided by the mean) annually for 11 prefectures (excluding Jiezhou, Jingzhou, Jingni, and Hami), we find that this coefficient declines from the eighteenth to the nineteenth century (see Table 3.3). The rapid drop in the coefficient after

53. Gansu had 331 government post stations, more than any other province, stationed twenty-five miles apart along the major roads. Kono Michihiro, "Shindai no baekiro," *Jinbun chiri* 2, no. 1 (1950): 13–24, cited in Gilbert Rozman, *Urban Networks in Ch'ing China and Tokugawa Japan* (Princeton, 1973), p. 94.

54. Skinner puts Jiezhou prefecture in the Upper Yangtze macroregion, with Sichuan. G. William Skinner, ed., *The City in Late Imperial China* (Stanford, 1977), map 2, p. 214.

TABLE 3.3 Variation in Low Millet Prices in Gansu Province, 1739–1864

Year	Mean	Coefficient of Variation[a]	Year	Mean	Coefficient of Variation[a]	Year	Mean	Coefficient of Variation[a]
1739	1.13	37.0	1767	1.16	19.2	1809	1.10	11.6
1740	1.13	31.5	1768	1.00	23.1	1810	1.17	12.2
1741	1.27	28.7	—			1811	1.28	15.0
1742	1.03	41.9	1774	1.06	17.6	—		
1743	0.85	47.8	1775	0.94	16.6	1816	1.19	7.0
—			—			1817	1.15	6.1
1747	0.63	53.5	1778	0.99	12.8	1818	1.15	3.7
1748	0.89	33.4	1779	0.94	15.5	—		
1749	0.80	36.5	1780	0.90	18.3	1820	1.17	3.3
1750	0.85	50.6	1781	0.90	16.6	1821	1.16	3.6
1751	0.74	48.3	1782	0.85	14.7	—		
—			1783	0.81	16.8	1829	1.11	10.6
1753	0.68	46.7	—			1830	1.11	10.6
1754	0.75	52.1	1789	1.03	32.1	1831	1.13	14.3
1755	0.92	62.6	1790	1.06	12.2	1832	1.04	13.4
1756	1.01	53.3	—			1833	1.08	9.4
1757	1.13	59.4	1796	1.03	16.9	1834	1.12	10.4
1758	1.31	47.0	1797	1.05	16.4	1835	1.13	10.5
1759	2.09	42.6	1798	1.03	16.2	1836	1.24	6.6
1760	2.35	37.5	1799	1.05	13.2	—		
1761	0.99	53.4	—			1838	1.23	5.1
1762	1.01	52.4	1804	1.05	15.0	—		
—			—			1849	1.21	3.1
1764	1.16	34.2	1806	1.04	12.2	1850	1.20	2.5
1765	1.39	29.7	1807	1.06	12.5			
—			1808	1.08	12.6	1864	0.70	39.1

[a] (Standard deviation/mean) * 100.

NOTE: The data are for 11 prefectures, excluding Hami, Jingzhou, Jingni, and Jiezhou. Hami, Jingni, and Jiezhou are omitted because they belong to a different economic region. Jingzhou is omitted because data are missing for half of the period.

1762 supports our argument that the end of the famine and military campaign led to greater economic integration. The figure remains fairly stable for the rest of the eighteenth century but declines to a lower level from 1816 to 1850. We can tentatively conclude that the process of economic integration, although initiated by military conquest, continued under its own steam through the late eighteenth and at least into the first half of the nineteenth century.

The study of Gansu's grain markets has just begun. The archives contain much more price data; gazetteers hold information on market structure and grain flows; the markets of other major crops await analysis. Nevertheless, the information available now shows that even in the remote Northwest, Qing officials—generals, governors, and granary managers—conducted a fascinating and intricate dance with private traders—grain merchants, peasant producers, and money changers—all participating in a flourishing market economy.

APPENDIX: ADJUSTMENT OF DATA

The price memorials report the monthly high and low prices for each prefecture according to the Chinese lunar calendar. To estimate correctly the monthly variation, we first converted lunar to solar months by using a simple formula that computed each solar month's price as a weighted average of the prices in the lunar months it overlapped. For example, solar month 3 in 1739 had 9 days in lunar month 1 and 22 days in lunar month 2. The price for solar month 3 is [(9 * Price in lunar month 1) + (22 * Price in lunar month 2)] / 31.[55]

The regression equation in Table 3.1 computes each solar monthly price as a function of the year, of 11 dummy variables for the months (excluding the first month), and of a dummy variable whose value is 1 for the years 1759 to 1760. The coefficients of the 11 monthly dummy variables indicate the amount by which the price for a given month changes in relation to the first month of the solar year. Figure 3.3 displays these coefficients graphically. Subtracting these coefficients from the monthly prices for each prefecture and then averaging the months of each year for which data are available yields the seasonally adjusted annual averages displayed in Figure 3.2. These adjusted annual averages are the source for the computation of correlation coefficients in Table 3.2 and Map 3.1. To test whether the choice of base month affects the calculation of correlation coefficients, we also adjusted the monthly data using regression coefficients based on the tenth month of the year. This alternate procedure yielded few significant differences from the results discussed in the paper.

55. The source for conversion of solar to lunar months is Zheng Hesheng, *Jinshi Zhongshi shiri duizhaobiao* (Taibei, 1978).

FOUR

Grain Markets and Food Supplies in Eighteenth-Century Hunan

R. Bin Wong and Peter C. Perdue

By the sixteenth century, recent immigrants to Hunan had begun to open new lands, from which rice surpluses were shipped to the growing metropolis of Hankou and the handicraft centers of the Lower Yangzi.[1] The late Ming proverb "When Huguang [Hunan and Hubei] harvests are plentiful, all under Heaven are fed" demonstrates that Hunan had become an important producer of rice. During the Qing dynasty, the province's rice exports grew. The importance of the Hunan rice trade was stressed some 30 years ago by Abe Takeo in his classic study of food supplies in the Yongzheng period (1723–35).[2] More recent studies of empirewide grain movements have confirmed the importance of the province's exports, the volume of which totaled 8 million (plus or minus 2 million) *shi* in normal harvest years.[3] The strong demand for Hunan rice in eighteenth-century China forged important commercial ties between the province and other parts of the empire. But what about the impact of Hunan's rice export trade on the province itself? Earlier studies of Hunan's rice export trade offer some answers by focusing princi-

---

R. Bin Wong wrote this essay on the basis of qualitative data he assembled over the past several years and quantitative data he collected in Beijing supplemented by data collected by James Lee and Peter Perdue. Perdue kindly supplied the technical expertise and helped prepare the data and do some of the initial calculations; he also edited an earlier draft.

1. For a broad analysis of Hunan's settlement and agricultural expansion, as well as a nuanced portrait of the state's role in shaping these developments, see Peter C. Perdue, *Exhausting the Earth: State and Peasant in Hunan, 1500–1850* (Cambridge, 1987).

2. Abe Takeo, "Beikoku jukyū no kenkyū: Yōseishi no isshō to shite mita," *Tōyōshi kenkyū* 15, no. 4 (1957): 484–577.

3. See Guo Songyi, "Qingdai de liangshi maoyi," *Pingzhun xuekan*, 1985, no. 1:289–314; Han-sheng Chuan and Richard Kraus, *Mid-Ch'ing Rice Markets and Trade* (Cambridge, 1975); and Wu Chengming, *Zhongguo ziben zhuyi yu guonei shichang* (Beijing, 1985), p. 257.

pally on two topics: (1) the institutions of the export trade and (2) the distribution of benefits from the trade among different groups of merchants, landlords, and peasants.[4] From this work we know that it was often outside merchants who bought Hunan's surplus rice, that landlords could be major suppliers to local markets, and that all producers of surpluses could benefit from the expansion of the trade. We need, however, a sharper picture of the spatial dimensions of the trade in order to push forward our understanding of this trade's impact on the province more generally.

This paper reconstructs the spatial structure of rice marketing within Hunan Province. Which parts of the province were linked together by the rice export trade? How large were these areas—did they form narrow bands along trade routes or were the hinterlands of the trade routes also part of the market? What about rice commerce and markets in areas outside the export zone? Answers to these questions help determine the significance of market integration to an agrarian economy. Our approach combines qualitative and quantitative analyses of market integration. In the first section of this paper we present qualitative evidence on commercial rice circulation in Hunan. In the second, our discussion shifts to an analysis of rice prices. Finally, in the third section we conclude with some thoughts on market integration. We shall discover that analysis of either high prices or low prices by themselves provides an incomplete guide to market integration, since there are no a priori reasons to argue that either set should represent market integration better than the other. For Hunan, separate analyses of high and low prices reveal roughly similar pictures of market integration. We shall show that analysis must include price relationships that are not addressed in other chapters in this volume; even if some of the price relationships are not intuitively obvious, we must consider relationships among high and low prices of different prefectures in order to demonstrate that the prices reflect not just similar but related pictures of the rice export market.

---

4. On Hunan's rice markets specifically, three Japanese historians published works in the 1950s that examined institutional features of market structures: Kitamura Hironao, "Shindai no shōhin shijō ni tsuite," in *Shindai shakai keizaishi kenkyū* (Kyoto, 1978); Nakamura Jihei, "Shindai Koko kome ryūtsū no ichi men," *Shakai keizaishi gaku* 18, no. 3:269–81; Shigeta Atsushi, "Shinsho ni okeru Konan komeshijō no ichi kōsatsu," in *Shindai shakai keizaishi kenkyū* (Tokyo, 1975). Evelyn Sakakida Rawski's 1972 work on sixteenth-century Fujian and eighteenth-century Hunan, *Agricultural Change and the Peasant Economy of South China* (Cambridge, 1972), partially builds on the earlier Japanese work but presents a distinct picture. Rawski links differential economic prosperity within each province to the economic opportunities created by trade in some counties but not others. Rawski and Shigeta Atsushi sharply part company on how the benefits of expanding trade were distributed among small owner cultivators, tenants, and landlords. Rawski stresses the gains made by tenants, whereas Shigeta claims landlord control of markets. The viewpoints of the two scholars are not necessarily contradictory since tenants could reap larger benefits with landlords remaining the more important suppliers.

SPATIAL STRUCTURES OF THE RICE TRADE: QUALITATIVE EVIDENCE

Hunan's eighteenth-century commerce largely followed the province's river systems. Each of the four major rivers—Xiang, Zi, Yuan, and Li—flowed into Dongting Lake, located in the northeastern part of the province. The Xiang River was by far the most important river, draining nearly half the province's land area. Not surprisingly, merchants along this river collected and shipped considerable amounts of rice destined for export out of the province. A 1753 investigation of specialized rice markets, covering 49 of Hunan's 56 counties, found 16 counties in which major rice markets existed and three additional counties where minor rice markets also served the export trade.[5] These 19 counties—Anxiang, Baling, Chaling, Changsha, Hengshan, Hengyang, Huarong, Linxiang, Liuyang, Longyang, Shanhua, Taoyuan, Wuling, Xiangtan, Xiangxiang, Xiangyin, Yiyang, Youxian, and Yuanjiang—were all located in five of Hunan's 13 prefectures; three of the prefectures (Changde, Lizhou, and Yuezhou) bordered Dongting Lake, while the remaining two (Changsha and Hengzhou) were south of Dongting Lake on the Xiang River. Major markets contained the facilities to accommodate boats, store grain, and arrange transactions; minor markets sent rice to these major markets for export. Map 4.1 displays the 16 counties with specialized rice markets and the three additional counties with export surpluses.

By adding information from other sources, we can piece together commercial rice flows in other parts of the province. Small quantities sometimes moved along Hunan's other three major rivers and their tributaries. Along the Zi River, rice moved from Wugang to Shaoyang and from this point to Xinhua; other shipments of rice reached the tea-producing county of Anhua further downstream. These shipments along the Zi River probably did not reach Dongting Lake. Protests against the trade in the early nineteenth century make clear, however, that even these small, short-distance, nonexport shipments were significant sources of food to the people who depended on them.[6] In contrast, gazetteers provide no evidence of trade crossing county borders anywhere along the Li River.[7]

---

5. *Hunan shengli cheng'an hulü* (1820), 23.2a–23b. For a discussion of the report, see Shigeta, "Shinsho ni okeru Konan komeshijō," 17–21. Rawski, *Agricultural Change*, p. 105, puts in tabular form information presented by Shigeta from the original.

6. Deng Xianhe, "Lun huangzheng," *Hunan wenzheng: guochao wen*, 29.23a–24b, *Xinning xianzhi* (1893) 20.19a–21a. Repeated struggles over this flow of grain demonstrate the social and political importance of what in economic terms may be quite minor. See Kojima Shinji, *Taihei tenkoku kakumei no rekishi to shisō* (Tokyo, 1978), pp. 117–26, and R. Bin Wong, "Food Riots in the Qing Dynasty," *Journal of Asian Studies* 41, no. 4:774–79.

7. Rice was grown in each of three counties along the Li River but was not a major food crop in any of them; more important was the combination of winter wheat, corn, and millet. Cotton

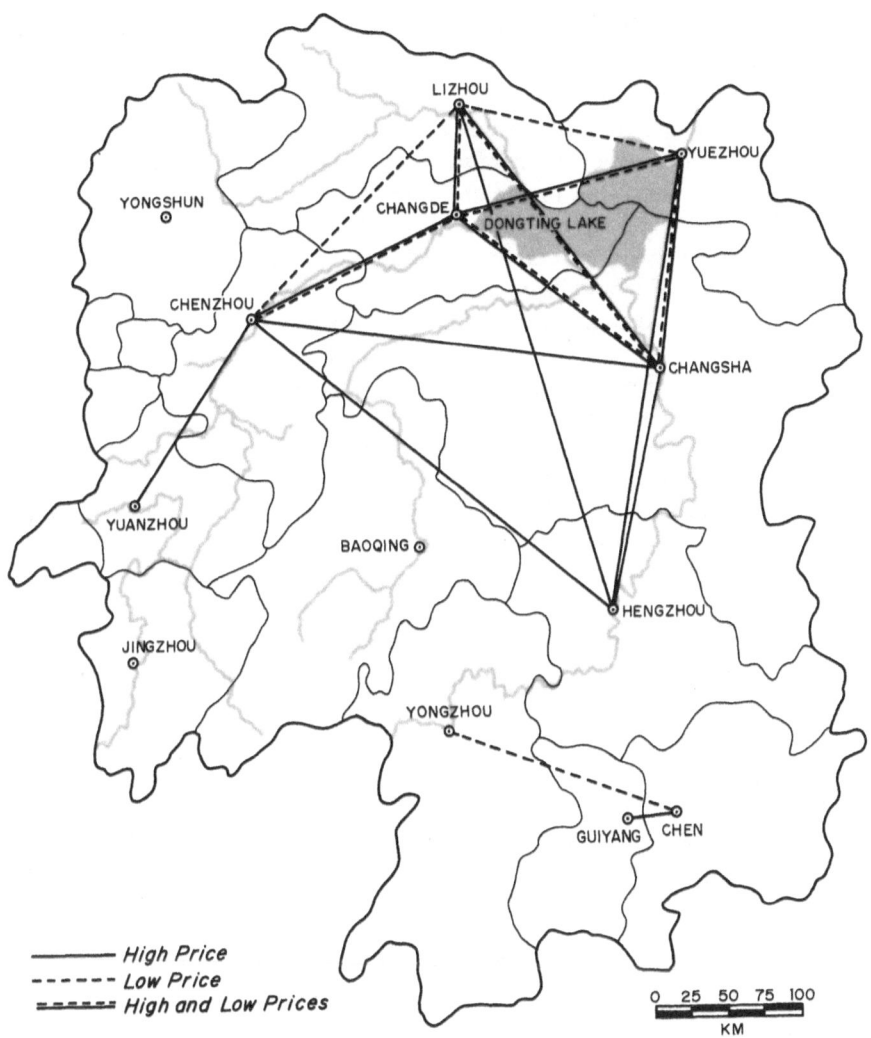

Map 4.2. Correlations of Annual Price Differences for High-Grade Rice in Qing Dynasty Hunan. (See p. 138 for Map 4.1.)

Along the Yuan River available sources allow us to reconstruct a more complex situation. Although they inform us that people in Chenzhou depended on imports from other counties, they do not tell us where the boats came from. The neighboring upstream counties of Luxi, Chenxi, and Xupu were unlikely suppliers of rice because of their own food supply limitations.[8] It appears, therefore, that the boats came upstream from the fertile paddy areas near the lake, apparently carrying rice that would otherwise flow out of the province with the export trade. Additional trade, including sales to Huitong, flourished along the upper reaches of the Yuan and its tributaries in Yuanzhou and Jianyang. These movements in southwestern Hunan, which also carried grain across the Guizhou border, were physically separate from the movements in downstream areas between the lake and Chenzhou.[9]

In southern Hunan small amounts of rice appear to have moved across prefectural boundaries. For instance, rice grown in Lanshan and Xintian fed miners in Guiyang. Sources also provide early eighteenth-century evidence of shipments of rice from Yongzhou to Hengzhou.[10] The southern mountain region within which rice was sold to feed miners also, at least for a while, sent rice into the Xiang River export trade. Map 4.1 also shows those counties outside the export zone in which rice trade is noted in gazetteer sources.

In summary, the export trade dominated rice movements in Hunan above the local level but coexisted with spatially separate movements along the Zi and Yuan rivers and in the southern mountains. Qualitative data indicate some rice trade crossing county borders in ten of Hunan's 13 prefectures, but only half of those ten participated directly in the province's Yangzi River export trade. The evidence we have just reviewed establishes the outlines of separate patterns of grain trade within the province. But this information cannot answer two important questions. Were the *physically* distinct movements of rice outside the export zone *economically* independent of the interprovincial trade? What degrees of market integration were achieved within the export zone and in areas beyond it? Our analysis of grain prices provides some answers.

---

and hemp cloth, like grain, circulated within county borders, while seed oils and mining products made their way downstream to the lake region. *Sangzhi xianzhi* (1873), 2.25–37; *Yongshun fuzhi* (1763), 10.5a; *Shimen xianzhi* (1818), 18.72a–73a, 52.49a–53a; *Shimen xianzhi* (1873), 3.48–49.

8. On Chenzhou, see *Yuanling xianzhi* (1873), 8.1a; on the counties upstream, see Fukuda Setsuo, "Shinmatsu Konan no nōson shakai," *Fukuoka joshi tandai kiyō* 8:33, 34, 51.

9. Shigeta, "Shinsho ni okeru Konan komeshijō," pp. 24–25; *Hunan shengli cheng'an hulü*, 23.2a–23b. On the route out of Hunan into the Southwest, see James Lee, *State and Economy in Southwest China, 1250 to 1850* (Cambridge, forthcoming), chap. 3.

10. *Guiyang zhouzhi* (1868), 6.18–19; *Lanshan xianzhi* (1933), 11.53. For occasional entry of Yongzhou rice into the Xiang River export trade, see *Qiyang xianzhi* (1765), 4.7a.

PRICE DATA AND THE DIMENSIONS OF MARKET INTEGRATION

From qualitative evidence we have shown a kind of market integration defined by physical movements of rice. We do not have much sense of the size of these rice shipments; we know only that some amounts of rice moved between various points within the province and to places beyond Hunan. The size of shipments, however, is not crucial to the reasoning about market integration we now develop on the basis of price data. When prices from two areas move in related ways over time, we believe the markets of these areas are integrated. There need not be very much trade between two points to cause related price movements. As long as grain merchants have enough information about prices in another area to cause them to adjust the volumes and prices of their purchases and sales accordingly, the two regions are economically integrated, regardless of the absolute size of the trade. Conversely, evidence of physical movements of grain may not signify market integration if changes in the prices do not reflect those movements. This would indicate that even though grain flows between two regions, the trade is too sporadic or localized to have a significant impact on price movements. Qualitative evidence of physical movements and quantitative price information generally complement each other, but they do not always agree completely.

The price data we use come from the monthly provincial reports to the central government of the highest and lowest county-level prices within each prefecture.[11] We have created annual series of the high prices and low prices for the most commercialized grain, high-grade rice, which we have adjusted for missing monthly data, in each of 13 prefectures reporting this information in the 63 of 68 years between 1738 and 1805 for which we have at least some observations.[12] The quantitative indicator we have chosen to guide our discussion of market integration is the bivariate correlation (Pearson's r) between differences of annual price averages. We consider any correlation between two sets of price differences that exceeds 0.65 to indicate a market relationship and thus integration of markets.[13]

---

11. Chen Jinling, "Qingchao de liangjia zoubao yu qi shengshuai," *Zhongguo shehui jingji shi yanjiu*, no. 3 (1985): 63–68.

12. Price data for a total of 693 lunar months for the years between 1738 and 1858 have been located, transcribed, and converted into solar monthly data. For the analysis in this essay we consider only high-grade rice for the years between 1738 and 1805; the coverage after 1805 is too thin to merit inclusion. Analysis of other grades of rice and other grains will be made in the future to complement this work on high-grade rice; such work will show the degree of substitution among grains, which forms yet another kind of "integration."

13. Annual averages have been created by assigning monthly weights according to the coefficients for dummy monthly variables in a regression equation for annual price by prefecture. Other studies on the Chinese Southwest (Lee, *State and Economy*, chap. 6) and on France during the eighteenth century (David Weir, "Markets and Mortality in France, 1600–1784," in *Essays in Honor of Andrew Appleby* [Cambridge, forthcoming]) have employed comparable statistical

With the prefecture as the unit of observation, two kinds of market integration are easily conceptualized: (1) *inter*prefectural integration, indicated by much of our qualitative information and by analyses of high prices and low prices separately, and (2) *intra*prefectural integration, indicated by the correlation of annual price differences of the high prices and low prices for each prefecture.[14] Obviously, market integration within each of two prefectures says nothing about integration between them. Likewise, if less obviously, measures of integration between two prefectures also say nothing by themselves about integration within each prefecture. Two separate indicators of market relationships, the correlation of differences in annual high prices and the correlation of differences in annual low prices, need not themselves be necessarily related. After examining interprefectural market integration indicated by high prices and by low prices, we shall explore the relationships between highs and lows across prefectures to demonstrate a market integration more complex than that suggested by evaluations of interprefectural correlations of highs and of lows and by intraprefectural correlations. These two independent measures are unable to capture the reality of market integration. Indeed, evaluated in light of qualitative evidence, these measures present us, in the Hunan case at least, with a serious puzzle.

Spatial Patterns of High and Low Prices

The proposition that related changes in annual price differences reflect market factors assumes that other forces are not driving the observed movements of prices. If, for instance, there was a strong and sharp trend in annual prices, due perhaps to inflation, the changes in annual price differences could not reasonably be taken as indicators of market integration. We therefore first look at an adjusted annual series of high and low prices to see what kind of long-term trend there might be. The provincial averages are displayed in Figure 4.1. Despite some fluctuations in individual years, for most of the eighteenth century prices remained between 1.1 and 1.3 taels; prices rose only modestly. In most prefectures, therefore, the rates of increase cannot help to explain the relationships among annual price changes to be analyzed below.[15]

Rice prices throughout Hunan also displayed remarkably similar seasonal patterns, compared, for instance, to those for Gansu millet examined by

---

measures and established the same kind of standard; our minimum of 0.65 is a bit higher than that used in Lee's Southwest Chinese study (0.60), but a lower standard includes many correlations that represent linkages for which we have little or no reason, judging from qualitative evidence, to expect market relationships.

14. We are grateful to James Lee for our discussions about intraprefectural price comparisons. See his essay in this volume for an example of a much fuller analysis of intraprefectural prices.

15. The annual trends are derived from the regression equation discussed in note 17.

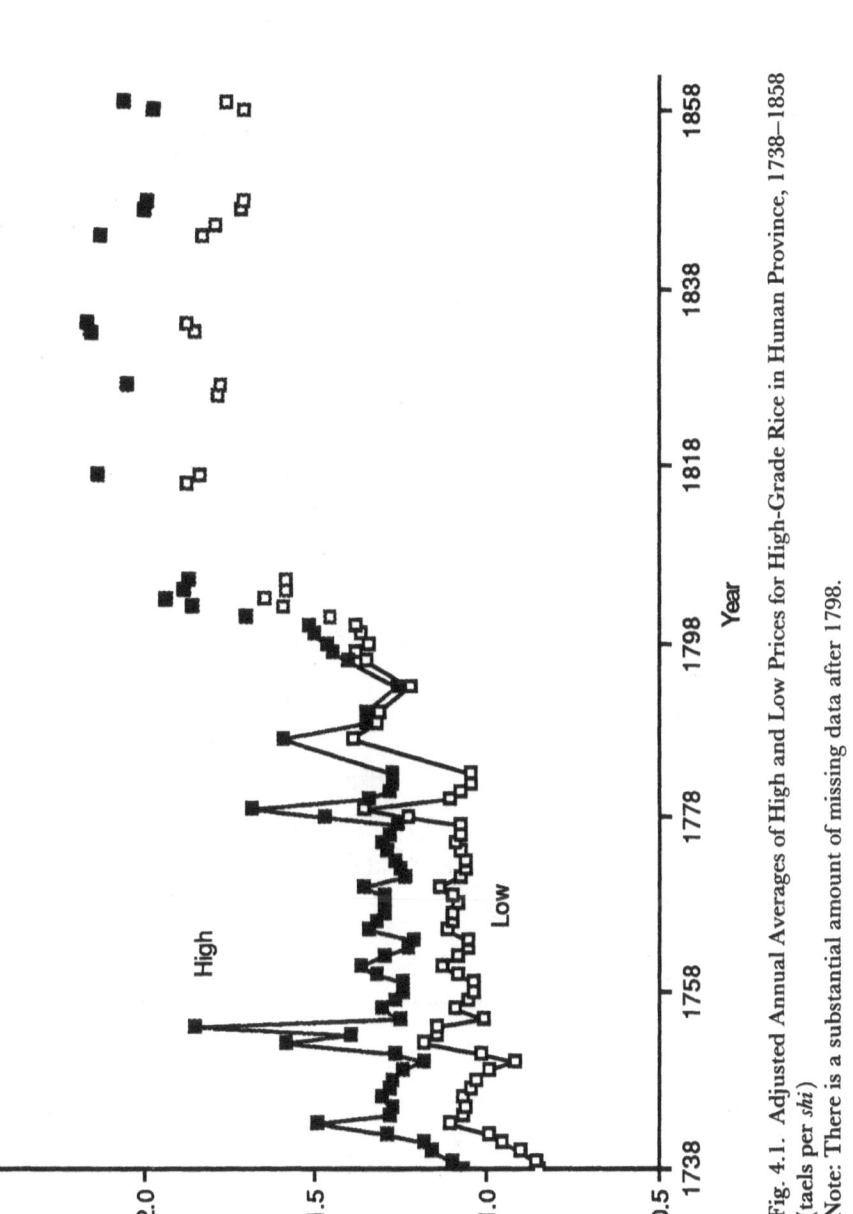

Fig. 4.1. Adjusted Annual Averages of High and Low Prices for High-Grade Rice in Hunan Province, 1738–1858 (taels per *shi*)
Note: There is a substantial amount of missing data after 1798.

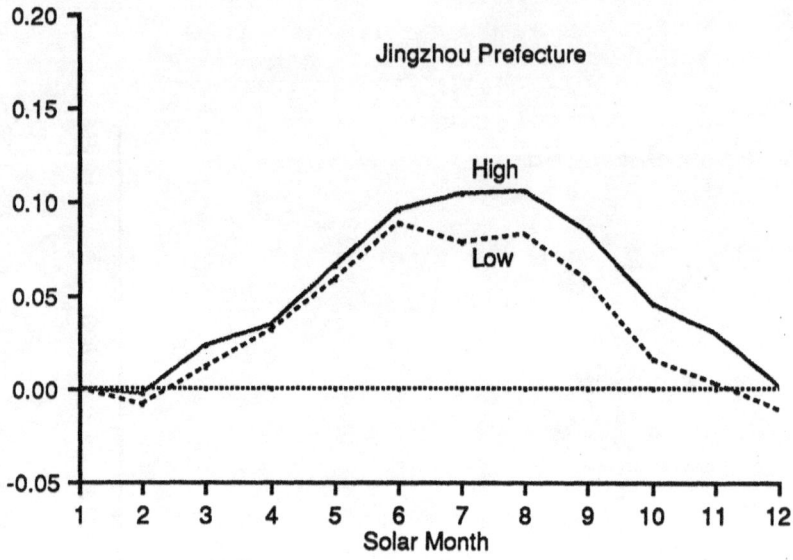

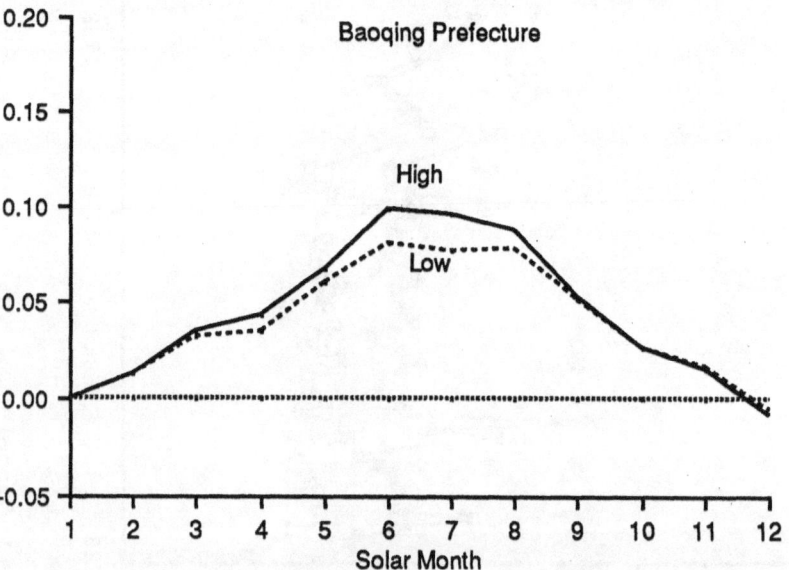

Fig. 4.2. Seasonal Variation in Prices of High-Grade Rice in Selected Hunan Prefectures, 1738–1858 (difference from January price, in taels per *shi*)

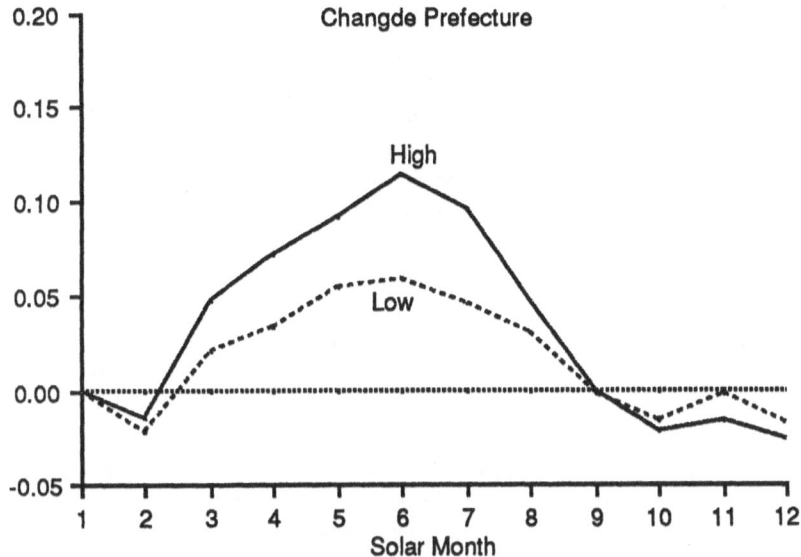
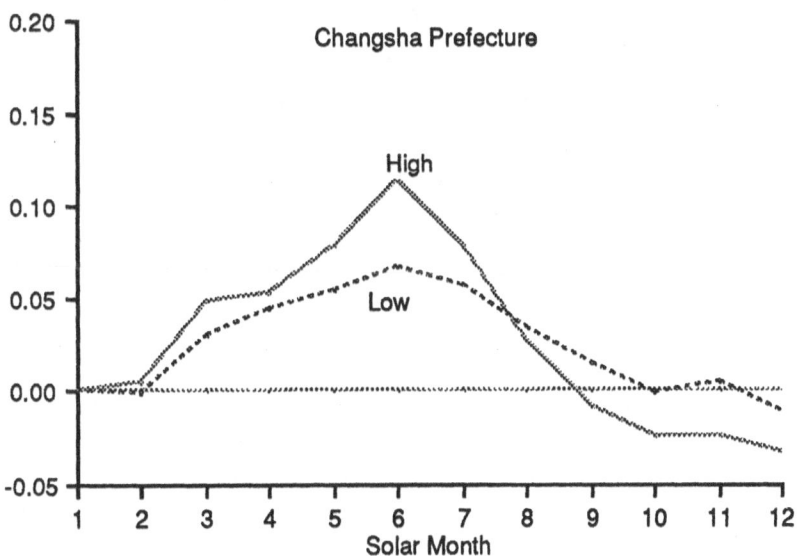

Peter C. Perdue in his essay in this volume. Figure 4.2 displays seasonal variations for four of Hunan's 19 prefectures, two representing exporting regions and two selected from the 15 non-exporting prefectures.[16] The lowest prices of the year come in December and the highest in June and July. Prices are generally low in the winter months, rise steeply in the spring, and plummet between August and September. Since these roughly symmetrical curves are similar in areas linked by rice trade as well as those that are not, trade alone cannot explain the similarities. Similar schedules of planting and harvesting are the more general reasons for the seasonal price patterns.

To use our price data to study market integration, we must remove the shared price behavior due to common annual trends and monthly variations. We obtained coefficients for each of 11 monthly dummy variables by fitting a regression equation to the price series for each prefecture, then recalculated annual averages after subtracting the coefficients from each monthly price.[17] Because the correlations discussed are calculated from the annual differences, the effect of the annual trend is nearly completely removed. The remaining correlations are a minimal set representing those price connections that are most likely caused by trade relations and not by common annual or seasonal patterns.

For the high prices in the years for which we have data between 1738 and 1805, 14 relationships show correlations of annual price differences exceeding 0.65, of which the 13 displayed in Map 4.2 confirm the basic outlines of the rice export network in eighteenth-century Hunan.[18] Nine of these links con-

16. The seasonal variations are calculated from the coefficients of dummy variables representing 11 months in a regression equation discussed in note 17.

17. The coefficients are for the linear regression model $P = K + \alpha T + \beta_2 M_2 + \beta_3 M_3 + \ldots + \beta_{12} M_{12} + \epsilon$, where P is the (solar) monthly price; K is a constant; T is the year (T = 0 for 1739); $M_2, M_3, \ldots, M_{12}$ are dummy variables for months 2 through 12 ($M_2 = 1$ for the second month and zero for all other months; no separate dummy variable is needed for the first month, during which $M_2 = M_3 = \ldots = M_{12} = 0$); α, the coefficient of T, gives the annual price trend. $\beta_2, \beta_3, \ldots, \beta_{12}$ are the coefficients of the monthly dummy variables; they indicate patterns of seasonal variation. ϵ is the error term.

18. In addition to these fourteen relationships, there are six other high price correlations present in the data from 1738 to 1805 that challenge the picture of the rice trade sketched on the basis of qualitative information. These correlations often show a link between distant areas or between remote areas and an exporting prefecture (Yongshun-Yongzhou, Baoqing-Yongzhou, Baoqing-Yongshun, Yongzhou-Yuezhou, Baoqing-Yuezhou, Chen-Lizhou). Leaving out the years after 1777, when prices become volatile because of a combination of poor harvests and political intervention, we find that five of the six dubious relationships disappear while all fourteen of the realistic ones remain. For the shorter period 1738–77, four new relationships emerge, none of which neatly fits our expectations, based on qualitative indicators, of how rice marketing worked. Links between Baoqing and the prefectures to its east (Hengzhou) and west (Yuanzhou) seem at least possible, since they are close to each other. Very difficult to consider even plausible are links between Yuanzhou and the distant export prefectures of Yuezhou and Hengzhou. Since none of these four prefectural pairs had correlations of at least 0.65 in the longer series, we reject them as likely market relationships. While harvest fluctuations or political

nected the major rice-exporting prefectures near Dongting Lake (Changde, Lizhou, and Yuezhou) and along the Xiang River (Changsha and Hengzhou). Four of these links (Changsha-Hengzhou, Changsha-Yuezhou, Hengzhou-Yuezhou, Changde-Yuezhou) lay along paths on which rice physically moved, while the other five links represent indirect price relationships without direct physical movements of rice between them. Changde's prices, for example, were connected indirectly with Hengzhou's via links to Changsha, even though no grain flowed directly from Changde to Hengzhou. Together, the nine links outline the integrated export market.

Four other links connect Chenzhou to three of the five rice-exporting prefectures and to Yuanzhou. The price data confirm the market relationship with Changde described by gazetteers. Since prices were higher in Chenzhou than in Changde, rice must have moved upstream, allowing Chenzhou to tap the export trade. Chenzhou's links to Changsha and Hengzhou further support the notion that it had ties to the export zone by showing market relationships without the connection of direct physical trade. In addition, Chenzhou prices are related to Yuanzhou prices, but Yuanzhou prices are lower, suggesting that Yuanzhou rice supplemented shipments from Changde to Chenzhou.

Completely separate from the export network is the price relationship between Guiyang and Chen. The generally higher prices in Chen suggest some small-scale trade going from Guiyang to Chen. The scanty qualitative information on this region for the eighteenth century provides no clear indication of this trade. In fact, this price relationship may not be a genuine economic link but may only represent changes due to harvest fluctuations in adjacent areas subject to similar weather conditions.

The failure of quantitative data to reveal movements of grain along the upper reaches of the Xiang, Zi, and Yuan rivers suggests that small amounts of grain can cross prefectural borders without clearly influencing price relationships. As we said above, small amounts of physical trade need not create strong economic relationships. Also, as is likely in the case of the Xiang River trade flows between Yongzhou and Hengzhou, the trade that existed in the early 1700s may have nearly disappeared by the second half of the century.

---

intervention might cause price changes in some years, sustained patterns of related price changes make the presence of a market factor more plausible. We therefore consider prefectural pairs for which the correlations of annual price differences are at least 0.65 for both the 1738–1805 and the 1738–77 periods to be the strongest candidates for market influenced price behavior, and display all but one of them in Map 4.2. The one not included is the only one of the sixty-one remaining linkages theoretically possible among Hunan's thirteen prefectures for which we find a correlation above 0.65 that cannot be explained in terms of what we know about rice marketing. Some combination of similar harvest results and political intervention presumably created this unlikely outcome. To have but one perplexing case is in fact reassuring. In general there is a good fit between our qualitative and quantitative data at the prefectural level.

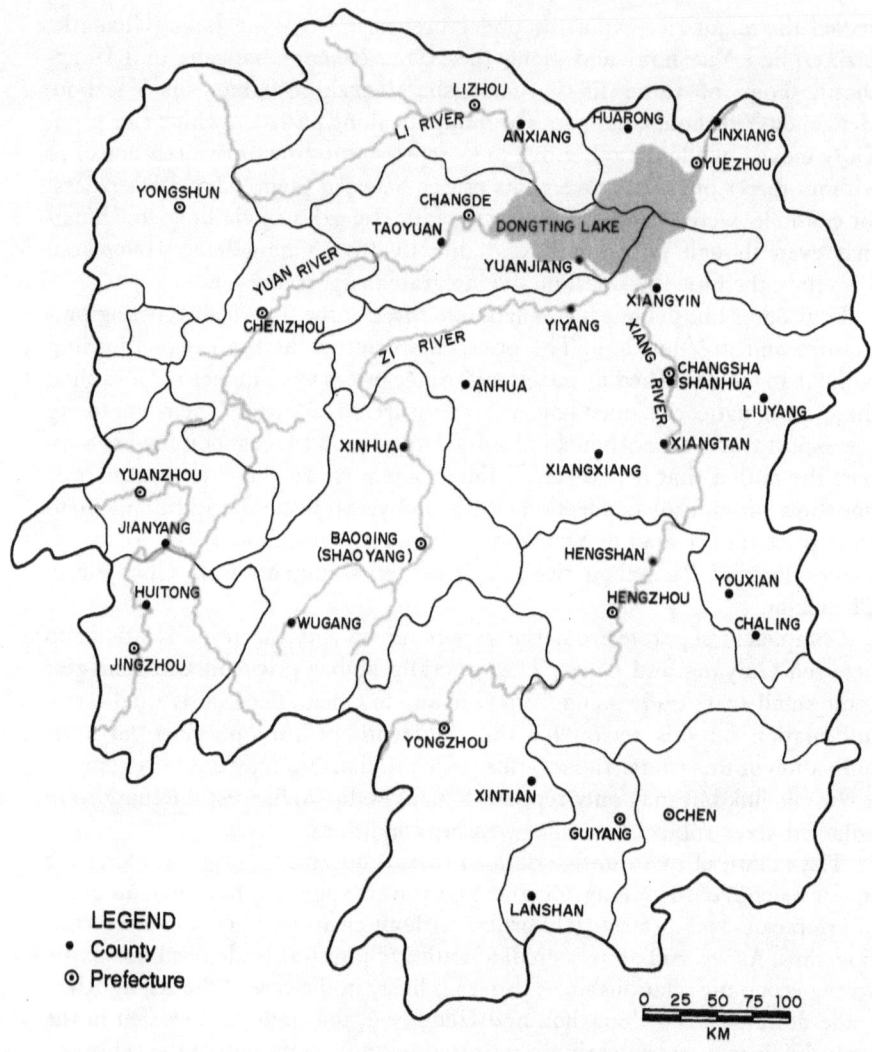

Map 4.1. Qing Dynasty Hunan. (See p. 129 for Map 4.2.)

Data on low prices again show a concentration of relationships among prefectures within the rice export zone. Map 4.2 also displays nine significant correlations of annual price differences for the low prices of high-grade rice.[19] Six of the links connect the five export prefectures, while two others connect Chenzhou to the export zone. Only the one between Yongzhou and Chen is completely separate from the export prefectures; here again, as in the Guiyang-Chen high-price relationship, a combination of trade and common weather conditions may have caused the observed connection.

A comparison of high-price correlations and low-price correlations reveals strong similarities. Both high and low prices connect the export prefectures. Six of the nine low-price relationships parallel high-price links (Changde-Lizhou, Changde-Yuezhou, Lizhou-Changsha, Changde-Changsha, Yuezhou-Changsha, Changde-Chenzhou). The Hengzhou high-price links that are lacking for low prices account for most of the differences between the high-price and the low-price relationships.

Why is Hengzhou different from the other export prefectures? Before finding an answer to this question we must first confirm that interprefectural highs and lows both represent the export market. We can generally attribute the differences between highs and lows to transport costs in the same way as we treat differences between prefectures as the product of transport cost differences. But this is not enough. For the highs and lows to be related, we must find correlations between them. The most obvious place to look for such relations with prefectural-level data is in intraprefectural correlations.

Our sources provide the highest and lowest prices within each prefecture without giving the counties these prices come from, which can in principle vary each month. Still, if the highs and lows are closely correlated, all the counties in the prefecture likely follow similar patterns. In other words, a relationship between the high and low prices in the same prefecture indicates market integration within the area, including counties reporting prices between the high and the low. The precise counties reporting the high and the low each month need not therefore necessarily be the same; we can still observe more general features of the rice market in the prefectures. We consider first the correlations of annual price changes for high and low prices

---

19. In addition, there are correlations over 0.65 for ten pairs of prefectures in only one of the two data samples (1738–1805, 1738–1777). In five of these cases prices might be related because of geographical proximity (Changsha-Hengzhou, Baoqing-Yuanzhou, Hengzhou-Baoqing, Changsha-Baoqing, Yuanzhou-Chenzhou), if low prices come from adjacent counties in different prefectures. In five other instances, however, there is no obvious explanation for the high correlations (Baoqing-Yongshun, Yuezhou-Yuanzhou, Baoqing-Yuezhou, Yuezhou-Chen, Changsha-Chen). Since market relationships are very unlikely according to our qualitative sources, we suspect that similar harvest conditions or political intervention combined to create the correlations. We consider only those links affirmed by both data samples to be ones with a strong market component; these are presented in Map 4.2.

within each prefecture (with the number of counties under its jurisdiction shown in parentheses):

Baoqing (5)	0.18	Jingzhou (4)	0.64
Changde (4)	0.75	Lizhou (6)	0.74
Changsha (12)	0.39	Yongshun (5)	0.14
Chen (6)	0.19	Yuanzhou (3)	0.08
Chenzhou (4)	0.34	Yuezhou (4)	0.53
Guiyang (4)	0.89	Yongzhou (8)	0.23
Hengzhou (7)	−0.01		

Seven of the 13 prefectures—Hengzhou, Yongzhou, Baoqing, Chenzhou, Yongshun, Yuanzhou, Chen—have no statistically significant correlations. Two of the six with significant correlations are small southern prefectures (Jingzhou and Guiyang), where short distances and low production levels allow greater impact from common weather patterns. Four export prefectures (Changsha, Yuezhou, Changde, and Lizhou) are the other four cases with statistically significant correlations, confirming the 1753 report's identification of major rice markets in these prefectures.[20] But the correlations for Changsha and Yuezhou are well below the 0.65 cutoff we use to identify strong indications of market integration. We therefore have a problem. Interprefectural highs and interprefectural lows each outline market integration for the rice export trade in a roughly similar manner (Hengzhou being the important difference), but we cannot establish convincing relations among the highs and lows by looking simply at intraprefectural relations. Further analysis of the price data is necessary.

Thus far we have considered correlations of annual price differences for high prices and low prices between and within prefectures. In other words, for prefectures A and B, we have considered those correlations of highs and lows depicted in Figures 4.3a and b. Together our measures represent the combination of intraprefectural and interprefectural market integration depicted in Figure 4.3c.

The organization of data by prefecture leads analysts to concentrate on the relations making the boxlike Figure 4.3c. But market relationships do not map neatly onto politically defined space. In economic terms, there is no reason to expect the market(s) providing the low prices in one prefecture to be more related to the market(s) providing the high prices in that prefecture than to the market(s) providing the high prices in some nearby prefecture. Market placements and transportation networks could easily link the highs of one prefecture with the lows of another. Unfortunately, since we do not know the county-level locations of the prefectural highs and lows, we can

---

20. Changsha's correlation is significant at the 0.01 level; each of the correlations for the other three is significant at the 0.001 level.

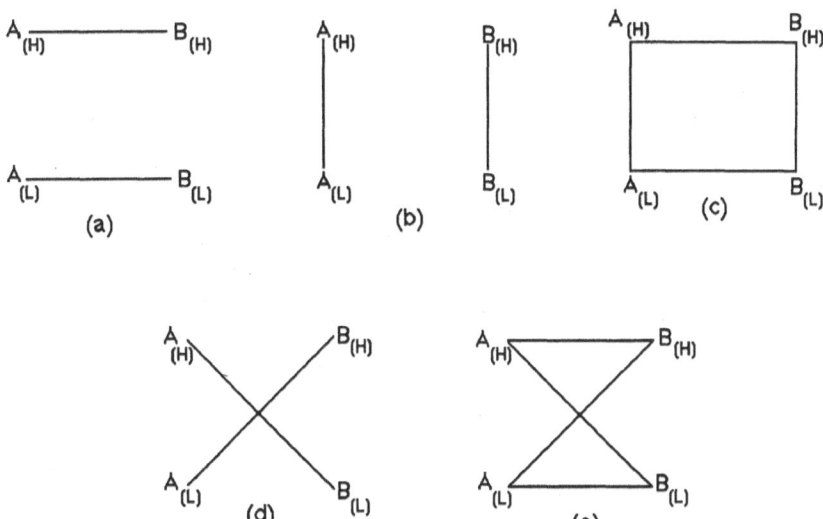

Fig. 4.3. Ways to Measure Correlations of High (H) and Low (L) Prices in Prefectures A and B

only propose this scenario as a reasonable explanation of the correlations we shall examine in a moment. When related "cross" prices, shown in Figure 4.3d, are combined with the relationships between highs and lows of two prefectures, we can argue that the two interprefectural relationships are themselves related (Fig. 4.3e); in other words, we can establish market integration between highs and lows, even in the absence of strong intraprefectural correlations.

For Changsha and Yuezhou, the two export prefectures with low intraprefectural correlations, we can demonstrate the integration of their high and low prices into a common rice export network by observing in each case their cross-price relationships with nearby Lizhou shown in Figures 4.4a and 4.4b. The correlations of high Lizhou prices with low Changsha prices (0.70) and with low Yuezhou prices (0.68) reveal a market integration by cross prices that is much broader and stronger than an examination of high and of low prices between and within prefectures would have mistakenly suggested.

The number of strong relationships between rice-exporting prefectures varies. The extreme case is Changde and Lizhou (Fig. 4.4c), where all possible relationships among high and low prices are strong, thus suggesting widespread market integration within and between prefectures. For other pairs of export prefectures, some combination of strong and weak correlations can be found. The larger the number of strong correlations, the broader

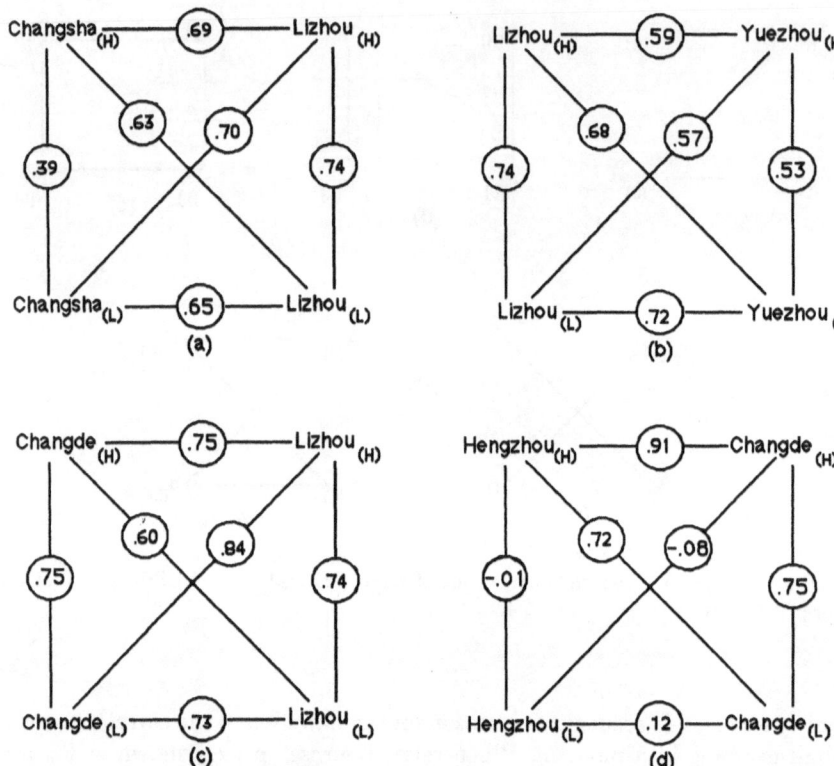

Fig. 4.4. Correlations of High (H) and Low (L) Rice Prices in Selected Rice-Exporting Prefectures in Hunan, 1739–1805

the likely degree of market integration spanning the two prefectures. This kind of analysis confirms the integration of highs and lows in the export zone and asserts that the political boundaries of prefectures are not an important guide to the possible lines of economic integration represented by cross prices. The export market encompassed more than a narrow string of places along a single major transportation route; it spanned large portions of all but one of the export prefectures.

Hengzhou is the exception. The absence of low-price correlations between Hengzhou and other prefectures is shown most clearly for the Hengzhou price relationships displayed in Figure 4.4d. We first observe, in dramatic contrast to the high-price relationships, that the low prices have no relationship. Second, in contrast to the strong connection between high Hengzhou prices and low Changde prices, low Hengzhou prices have no link to high Changde prices. Finally, low and high Hengzhou prices have no relation to each other. Figure 4.4d displays this right triangle of strong relationships (high Hengzhou prices–high Changde prices–low Changde prices), showing how high cross-price correlations strengthen our sense of highly integrated markets. The low and high prices from Hengzhou together suggest that the prefecture embraces integrated zones along the Xiang River and isolated zones toward the province's hilly eastern border. The examination of high and low prices together reveals more completely the degree to which rice-exporting prefectures are integrated into a larger marketing network than does examination of either highs or lows by themselves. Prefectures outside this network have fewer strong relationships among their prices.

MARKET INTEGRATION

We have analyzed qualitative and quantitative data on Hunan's rice trade. Our findings delineate Hunan's rice export trade and distinguish it from rice trade patterns in other parts of the province. First, price data generally confirm the outlines of the export trade based on qualitative information. The rice market within the export zone, with the important exception of Hengzhou, appears highly integrated both between prefectures and within prefectures. Second, price data reveal very little market integration outside the export zone—only a few thin connections in southern Hunan. The price data clarify movements along the Yuan River by suggesting amounts of some size going upstream from Changde and downstream from Yuanzhou. For the Zi River trade, however, Baoqing prices correlate poorly with other prefectures; this suggests that the trade identified by qualititative evidence may have been largely limited to movements within Baoqing Prefecture.

In Hunan's periphery, no rice markets, with the important exception of those in Chenzhou, were tied to the export trade. The case of Chenzhou, which tapped part of the Changde trade, demonstrates how an export market can include prefectural exports inside as well as outside the province. As is true for interprefectural integration, intraprefectural integration, except for two small isolated prefectures (Guiyang and Jingzhou), is high only in commercialized prefectures connected to interregional trade (Changde and Lizhou).

In sum, our analysis confirms the importance of commerce to eighteenth-century China's agrarian economy by combining qualitative and quantitative analyses of the spatial reach of China's grain markets within one province. The two approaches complement and correct each other: gazetteer evidence of small amounts of trade outside Hunan's export zone need not mean clear-cut market integration, while prices in export prefectures could be tied together without direct trading links. Persistent images of rural isolation and "natural" rather than commercial economy in Qing China will ultimately have to yield before the mounting evidence of active, integrated markets. But the presence of areas outside the export zone unaffected by rice market integration reminds us that any picture of China as a market society is also incomplete.

Let us not, therefore, jump to the conclusion that the kind of market activity we find in this agrarian Chinese setting implies everything that market activity does in other times and places. True, eighteenth-century China displayed some features of modern economies, but which ones? Even though additional research is clearly needed, we can provisionally propose that market integration in eighteenth-century China, as in modern economies, promoted regional specialization. Price signals informing people of the most profitable production strategy to pursue stimulated specialization according to comparative advantage then as now. But the presence of economically "rational" behavior does not necessarily mean that the resulting economic activity as a whole was "modern." Lacking were the forces that promote modern economic expansion—big capital investments, major technological advances, and new expanding markets. These forces work *through* an integrated market economy. Integrated markets may be highly desirable for economic advance, but they hardly create such developments by themselves. The Hunan rice case, like other Qing dynasty grain price examples, may represent a kind of market integration achieved without the familiar dynamics of modern economic change.

FIVE

Infanticide and Family Planning in Late Imperial China: The Price and Population History of Rural Liaoning, 1774–1873

James Lee, Cameron Campbell, and Guofu Tan

Between 1700 and 1900 China's population more than tripled, increasing from 150 million to almost 500 million. This dramatic rise in population is probably the most frequently noted achievement of Qing society. It is also one of the most important elements in any explanation of Qing economic performance.[1] Nevertheless, despite considerable research on the economic and demographic history of late imperial China, we have yet to devise precise demographic or economic measures for much of this period. In consequence, we have very little detailed quantitative knowledge about either the economy or the population; we also have little understanding about how population, as a variable, actually interacted with the economy during the eighteenth and nineteenth centuries.

Detailed population and price records do, however, survive in the historical archives of Taiwan and the People's Republic of China.[2] This paper is

---

We presented a preliminary version of this paper at the conference on Economic Methods for Chinese Historical Research organized by Thomas G. Rawski and Lillian M. Li and held in Oracle, Arizona, in January 1988. We would like to thank the participants and especially the organizers for their comments as well as George Alter, Francesca Bray, Peter H. Lindert, Donald N. McClosky, Susan Naquin, Jean-Laurent Rosenthal, Wang Shaowu, and Susan Cotts Watkins. We would also like to thank the following institutions for their financial support: California Institute of Technology, Liaoning Population Research Institute, National Academy of Sciences, National Endowment for the Humanities, and Wang Institute of Graduate Studies.

1. See Dwight H. Perkins, *Agricultural Development in China, 1368–1968* (Chicago, 1969); Mark Elvin, *The Pattern of the Chinese Past* (Stanford, 1973); and Ramon H. Myers, *The Chinese Economy Past and Present* (Belmont, 1980) for three recent influential books where population plays a key role in the analysis of Qing economic performance.

2. For a description of some of these materials and their location in China, see Michael Finegan and Ted Telford, "Chinese Archival Holdings at the Genealogical Society of Utah,"

a preliminary attempt to use such materials to reconstruct the price and population history of Daoyi District, a rural suburb of Shenyang in Liaoning Province, for approximately 100 years, from 1774 to 1873. First, we summarize the results of an ongoing study of the population history of Daoyi and demonstrate that mortality and fertility differed sharply by sex. Second, we reconstruct the price history of five food grains (rice, millet, sorghum, wheat, and soybeans) and determine the degree of price integration in the prefectural market. Finally, we analyze the relationship between grain prices and demographic rates in order to prove that the differential rates by sex were the product of a systematic pattern of infanticide according to household situation as well as economic conditions. We conclude that in Liaoning both mortality and fertility were highly responsive to changes in economic circumstances.

The study of food prices and population has, of course, long been a central topic both in the historical demography and in the economic history of the preindustrial world. This is only natural, for population was everywhere one of the most dramatic and dynamic economic variables and fluctuations in population were at least in part a function of harvest variations. Numerous studies in European history have repeatedly discovered relatively strong positive correlations between food prices and mortality and even weak negative correlations between food prices and fertility.[3] As we shall see, in Liao-

---

Late Imperial China 9.2 (Dec. 1988): 86–114; and James Lee and Bin Wong, "New Research Sources for the Study of Late Imperial China," *China Exchange News* 15.3–4 (1987): 6–8. Until the discovery of these materials most historians have had to rely largely on genealogical data. See also four articles by Ts'ui-jung Liu: "Chinese Genealogies as a Source for the Study of Historical Demography" in *Studies and Essays in Commemoration of the Golden Jubilee of the Academia Sinica* (Taipei, 1978), pp. 849–70; "The Demographic Dynamics of Some Clans in the Lower Yangtze Area, ca. 1400–1900," *Academia Economica Papers* 9.1 (Mar. 1981): 115–60; "Ming Qing renkou zhi zengzhi yu qianyi," in *Zhongguo shehui jingji shi yantao hui lunwenji* (Taibei, 1983), pp. 283–316; and "The Demography of Two Chinese Clans in Hsiao-shan, Chekiang, 1650–1850," in *Family and Population in East Asian History* (Stanford, 1985), pp. 13–61; also see three articles by Ted Telford: "Marriage and Fertility in Tongcheng County, 1520–1661" (Manuscript presented to the Workshop on Qing Population History, Pasadena, 1985); "Survey of Social Demographic Data in Chinese Genealogies," *Late Imperial China* 7.2 (1986): 80–117; and "Fertility and Population Growth in the Lineages of Tongcheng County, 1520–1661" (Manuscript presented to the Conference on Chinese Lineage Demography, Asilomar, Calif., 1987); and Stevan Harrell, "The Rich Get Children: Segmentation, Stratification, and Population in Three Chekiang Lineages, 1550–1850," *Family and Population in East Asian History* (Stanford, 1985), pp. 81–109. See too, however, the important cautionary article by Harrell, "On the Holes in Chinese Genealogies," *Late Imperial China* 9.1 (Dec. 1987): 52–87.

3. Indeed Goubert has gone so far as to claim that "the price of wheat almost always constitutes a true demographic barometer. The range and frequency of the fluctuations in grain prices control the size and the frequency of the demographic crises." Pierre Goubert, "En Beauvaisis: problèmes demographiques de XVIIe siècle," *Annales ESC* 7.4 (1952): 453–68. For several recent examples of the state of this field, see Tommy Bengtsson, Gunnar Fridlizius, and Rolf

ning correlations between vital rates and prices were just as strong, but the patterns of population behavior were fundamentally different from European ones. Indeed, because of the widespread use of infanticide as a method of family planning, the strongest correlations link prices with fertility, not mortality. The Chinese apparently regarded infanticide as a form of postnatal abortion through which they could choose the number, spacing, and sex of their children in response to short-term economic conditions as well as their long-term family-planning goals.

Our demographic data for Liaoning come from an ongoing study of over 12,000 Chinese peasants who lived between 1774 and 1873. So far as we can tell, these peasants were direct descendants of an earlier Ming garrison.[4] The Qing government certainly classified the population as Han Chinese and in the early seventeenth century organized them as members of the Han banner armies.[5] Two thirds were farmers who lived in three villages (Baodao *tun*, Daoyi *tun*, and Dingjia *fangshen*) in Daoyi District, a northern suburb of Shenyang. The rest were farmers originally from Daoyi, who had since moved to nearby villages. Because almost all of these villages were located near the provincial capital, the vast majority of these farmers undoubtedly produced food for the city market as well as for their own consumption. We have, however, almost no information on the specific structure of the village economy or the nature of these market relations during the eighteenth and nineteenth centuries.

What we do have are 85,000 individual records and 12,000 household records on the demography of this population throughout this period. This information is preserved in 25 triennial registers. These registers provide a nominative list of the families that received state banner land and in turn were liable for special corvée and military banner service. Specifically, they record for each person his or her name, age, occupation, family and lineage

---

Ohlsson, eds., *Preindustrial Population Change: The Mortality Decline and Short-Term Population Movements* (Stockholm, 1981). See too the detailed analysis by Ronald Lee and others in E. A. Wrigley and R. S. Schofield, eds., *The Population History of England, 1541–1871* (Cambridge, Mass., 1981).

4. The 1566 edition of the *Quan liao zhi*, 4.3, includes a Daoyi *tun* in a list of Ming garrison villages.

5. Our registers are entitled *Zheng huangqi Daoyi tun Hanjun rending hukou ce* ("Daoyi Village population registers from the Han army of the Plain Yellow Standard"). According to Zhou Yuanlian, *Qingchao kaiguo shi yanjiu* (Shenyang, 1981), and "Guanyu baqi zhidu de jige wenti," *Qingshi luncong* 3 (1982): 140–54, these Han banners date from the Manchu conquest of Shenyang in 1625. We discuss the changing social organization and ethnicity of this population in some detail in James Lee and Cameron Campbell, "Happy Families: Household Hierarchy and Differential Vital Rates in Rural Liaoning, 1774–1873" (Forthcoming). In 1982, of the 17,792 people who lived in Daoyi District (*qu*), a suburb of present-day Shenyang, 60 were Muslim, 62 were Mongol, 343 were Xibo, 563 were Manchu, 618 were Korean, and 16,146 were Han Chinese.

TABLE 5.1 Summary of the Population Registers of Daoyi, Liaoning, 1774–1873

Year of Register	Population			Entrances				Exits			Unannotated Disappearances		
	Total	Males	Females	Births	Marriages	Immigration	Deaths	Marriages	Emigration	Total	Males	Females
1774	2,192	1,234	958	—	—	—	135	31	—	—	—	—
1780	2,548	1,467	1,081	366	115	266	118	38	2	242	109	133
1786	2,748	1,578	1,170	479	170	226	188	47	32	417	217	200
1792	2,772	1,568	1,204	357	203	60	252	60	8	283	136	147
1795	2,902	1,629	1,273	260	112	24	174	50	29	14	5	9
1798	2,951	1,642	1,309	226	95	42	213	46	7	45	19	26
1801	3,014	1,697	1,317	198	73	14	162	38	14	13	7	6
1804	3,155	1,768	1,387	317	120	22	223	72	17	8	6	2
1810	3,144	1,776	1,368	354	176	37	251	56	16	255	95	160
1813	3,181	1,782	1,399	182	97	33	207	55	8	4	3	1
1816	3,131	1,758	1,373	131	88	4	209	50	3	7	4	3
1819	3,154	1,781	1,373	124	65	11	128	39	11	6	4	2
1822	3,151	1,781	1,370	236	150	24	285	106	2	21	11	10
1828	3,270	1,869	1,401	530	215	38	196	60	15	395	185	210
1831	3,270	1,865	1,405	197	85	6	233	46	0	11	6	5
1837	3,291	1,929	1,362	400	187	17	204	65	6	309	128	181
1840	3,214	1,912	1,302	154	84	2	236	64	1	17	7	10

Year	Population Total	Population Male	Population Female	Entrances Total	Entrances Male	Entrances Female	Exits Total	Exits Male	Exits Female	Unannotated Disappearances Total	Unannotated Disappearances Male	Unannotated Disappearances Female
1843	3,125	1,889	1,236	114	54	2	195	35	2	27	6	21
1846	3,094	1,869	1,225	118	93	1	173	39	3	29	12	17
1855	3,187	1,953	1,234	**393**	**283**	**28**	190	29	6	**386**	**172**	**214**
1858	3,162	1,962	1,200	126	95	7	174	36	14	32	12	20
1861	3,199	1,997	1,202	156	99	3	177	30	3	12	6	6
1864	3,132	1,997	1,155	173	98	32	334	15	1	22	13	9
1867	3,156	2,012	1,144	188	109	31	244	21	8	30	17	13
1873	3,271	2,067	1,204	**316**	**225**	**35**	249	10	4	**204**	**108**	**96**
Total	12,466[a]	6,326[a]	6,140[a]	6,095	3,091	965	5,150	1,138	212	2,789	1,288	1,501

NOTES: The columns under "Population" record the number of people alive at the end of each register period. Exits include all the people who are recorded as having departed during the intercensal period through death, marriage, or emigration. Entrances list all the people who appear in the registers for the first time through birth, marriage, or immigration. People who disappeared without annotation between the previous and current register are listed under "Unannotated Disappearances." The number alive in a register is equal to the number alive in the previous register plus the entrances and minus the exits recorded in the current register. The totals under "Population" are counts of the number of individuals by sex who make at least one appearance in the data set.

Registers were compiled every three years. Most numbers, therefore, represent the cumulated events over a three-year intercensal period. Because of missing registers, some numbers, however, represent the cumulated events over six years, and in one case, over nine years. These numbers are in boldface.

[a] The number of individuals who make at least one appearance in the data set.

relationships, birth date, recent demographic events, and village of residence. The registers survive in the Liaoning Provincial Archives and were coded into machine-readable form at the Liaoning Population Research Institute and the California Institute of Technology.[6] To the best of our knowledge, no other material records a Chinese peasant population before 1900 with such continuity and detail. We present a crude summary profile of all 25 registers in Table 5.1.

The sources are a product of the Eight Banner registration system.[7] In Liaoning, Qing officials relied heavily on such records for civilian and military administration. They accordingly devised a remarkable system of internal cross-checks to ensure consistency and accuracy. First, they assigned every person in the banner population to a residential household (*linghu*) and registered them on a household certificate (*menpai*). Then they organized these households into clans (*zu*) and compiled annually updated clan genealogies (*zupu*). Every three years local authorities compared these genealogies with the household certificates to compile the population registers. Thanks to such efforts, the banner registers provide far more comprehensive and accurate data than the population registration system (*baojia*) common elsewhere in China.

These registers do not, however, record the entire population. They have two related defects. On the one hand, nine of the registers from the century under observation are damaged or lost. We therefore have incomplete information on deaths and to a lesser extent births for 27 years.[8] On the other hand, even when registers do exist, registration is still incomplete in the very early age groups. Almost no one below 2 *sui* is registered. Indeed, the mean age at first appearance for both sexes is 6 *sui*, which is slightly less than five Western years of age.[9] Many children who died before 6 *sui* simply do not

---

6. The process has been very labor-intensive, requiring several thousand hours over five years, and would not have been completed without the assistance of many people. Registers were transcribed by James Lee (1774, 1792), Robert Eng (1780, 1786), Julie Sun (1798, 1819), Liu Guiping (1855), Wang Yuanqing (1861), He Ti (1864), Anna Chi (1795, 1843, 1846, 1858, 1873), and Alice Suen (1801, 1804, 1810, 1813, 1816, 1822, 1828, 1831, 1837, 1840). Lawrence Anthony, Cameron Campbell, and Martin Hunt wrote machine programs to identify transcription errors. Anna Chi and James Lee repeatedly "cleaned" the entire data set. We would like to thank all the participants for their help, in particular Anna Chi and Alice Suen.

7. See Fu Kedong, "Baqi zhidu huji chutan," *Minzu yanjiu* 6 (Dec. 1983): 34–43, for a more complete description of the banner registration system. We would like to thank Pamela Crossley for bringing this article to our attention.

8. We are missing nine registers, dated 1777, 1783, 1789, 1807, 1825, 1834, 1849, 1852, and 1870.

9. By *sui* the Chinese meant to indicate the number of calendar years during which a person had lived. People are accordingly 1 *sui* at birth and 2 *sui* at the next New Year. *Sui* are, therefore, on average one and a half years higher than Western years of age. The mean age at first appearance for all 25 registers was 6.1 *sui* for females and 5.8 *sui* for males. Age at first appearance by family relationship was similarly consistent: 6 *sui* for children in the generation below the head and 5 *sui* for grandchildren.

appear in our records. Girls are more likely than boys not to be registered, especially after 1840. Our estimations of vital rates accordingly fall considerably short of the actual levels of fertility and mortality.

Fortunately, with the exception of female underregistration, these omissions, at least before 1840, do not appear to follow any selective bias. Such bias as there is appears to be uniform over time and household position. Thus, mean age at first appearance is quite consistent by sex, time, and household relationship, so that the data, although incomplete, are nevertheless sufficient to document a variety of distinct patterns of mortality and fertility behavior in Daoyi.[10] These patterns by sex, age, household type, and family relationship, as well as economic condition, are far too consistent to be the product of underregistration. We summarize three particularly pertinent examples.

First, although the level of mortality during this century was moderate, deaths were distributed highly unevenly by sex. We contrast the overall mortality experiences of males and females in Table 5.2. We then present the experiences of the two sexes in periods of high and low overall mortality in Tables 5.3 and 5.4. The contrasts reveal significantly higher levels of mortality among females than among males but also far greater fluctuations in mortality among males than among females. The pattern of mortality, in other words, suggests a system of resource allocation wherein the female share, although relatively constant, was smaller than the male share. Males consumed more resources; but because they relied on the harvest surplus for their larger share, they were more vulnerable to harvest fluctuations than females. In Daoyi, in other words, the price of privilege was economic insecurity.

Second, the patterns of birth spacing and birth stopping strongly suggest that most married couples controlled their fertility to a considerable extent. Two very useful indications of such conscious limitation are the length of time between births and the age of women at the birth of their last child. Studies of many historical European populations show that in the absence of fertility control, birth intervals beginning with the second birth are rarely

---

10. These findings derive from a number of conference papers that elaborate on their significance. See Lawrence Anthony, James Lee, and Alice Suen, "Adult Mortality in Rural Liaoning 1795 to 1819," California Institute of Technology Working Paper 115 (1985); James Lee and Robert Eng, "Population and Family History in Eighteenth Century Manchuria: Preliminary Results from Daoyi, 1774–1798," *Ch'ing-shih wen-t'i* 5.1 (June 1984): 1–55; James Lee and John Gjerde, "Comparative Household Morphology of Stem, Joint and Nuclear Household Systems: Norway, China, and the United States," *Continuity and Change* 1.1 (May 1986): 89–112; John Gjerde, Anita Tien, and James Lee, "Comparative Household Processes of Stem, Joint, and Nuclear Household Systems: Scandinavia, China, and the United States" (Manuscript presented to the annual meeting of the Social Science History Association, 1987); James Lee, Cameron Campbell, and Lawrence Anthony, "A Century of Mortality in Rural Liaoning, 1774–1873," *Le peuplement du monde avant 1850*, ed. Antoinette Fauve-Chamoux (Paris, 1990).

TABLE 5.2 Male and Female Life Expectancy in Daoyi, 1792–1867

Age Group	Male Life Expectancy	Female Life Expectancy	Difference in Life Expectancy	Standard Deviation of Difference in Life Expectancy
1–5	35.2	28.0	-7.2	0.8
6–10	43.3	35.8	-7.5	0.7
11–15	42.9	35.0	-7.9	0.6
16–20	39.7	33.2	-6.5	0.6
21–25	36.4	33.2	-3.2	0.5
26–30	32.7	31.1	-1.6	0.4
31–35	28.9	28.6	-0.3	0.4
36–40	25.2	25.9	0.7	0.4
41–45	21.8	23.4	1.6	0.4
46–50	18.3	20.7	2.4	0.4
51–55	15.4	17.5	2.1	0.3
56–60	12.6	14.6	2.0	0.2
61–65	10.4	11.5	1.1	0.2
66–70	8.1	8.6	0.5	0.2
71–75	5.7	6.2	0.5	0.2
76+	3.5	3.7	0.2	0.2

SOURCE: Computed from intercensal life tables for 1792–1795–1798–1801–1804, 1810–1813–1816–1819–1822, 1828–1831, 1837–1840–1843–1846, 1855–1858–1861–1864–1867. See James Lee, Cameron Campbell, and Guofu Tan, "A Century of Mortality in Rural Liaoning, 1774–1873" in Antoinette Fauve-Chamoux, ed. *Le peuplement du monde avant 1850* (Paris, 1990).

NOTE: All ages are in *sui*, on average one and a half years higher than Western years of age.

much more than two years long.[11] Moreover, the mean age at last birth is almost always within one year of age 40. In our population, by contrast, the mean age at last birth was only 34 (35.5 *sui*). Furthermore, the mean birth interval beginning with the second birth was almost five years. As we can see in Figure 5.1, in striking contrast with European populations, where birth intervals increase by order of child, birth intervals in Daoyi actually decrease. According to these data, most couples decided to have fewer children than their natural limit and tended to space these children far apart.

Third, people in Daoyi appear to have used some form of sex-selective fertility control.[12] Table 5.5 analyzes the birth histories of almost 1,000 com-

11. Most of our information for Europe comes from Michael W. Flinn, *The European Demographic System, 1500–1820* (Baltimore, 1981); and Ansley J. Coale and Susan Cotts Watkins, *The Decline of Fertility in Europe* (Princeton, 1986).

12. Apparently the Chinese did not consider children during the first year of life to be fully human. This was a traditional concept. An imperial edict recorded in the *Tang huiyao* (Important documents of the Tang; Beijing, 1955) for the year 623 says: "People when they are first born are just young animals [*huang*]. At four *sui* they become minors [*xiao*]. At 16 *sui* they become youths

TABLE 5.3 Female Life Expectancy in Daoyi during Good and Bad Periods, 1792–1867

Age Group	Life Expectancy in Good Periods	Life Expectancy in Bad Periods	Difference in Life Expectancy	Standard Deviation of Difference in Life Expectancy
1–5	30.2	18.4	11.8	2.2
6–10	42.8	23.8	19.0	2.0
11–15	42.1	24.9	17.2	1.9
16–20	39.6	23.3	16.3	1.8
21–25	36.4	28.4	8.0	1.4
26–30	33.7	26.9	6.8	1.2
31–35	30.6	24.6	6.0	1.1
36–40	28.0	22.4	5.6	1.1
41–45	26.2	20.2	6.0	1.0
46–50	23.7	18.3	5.4	0.9
51–55	20.6	15.5	5.1	0.9
56–60	16.8	13.6	3.2	0.8
61–65	12.8	11.0	1.8	0.7
66–70	9.3	8.3	1.0	0.6
71–75	7.1	6.0	1.1	0.5
76+	4.2	3.2	1.0	0.3

NOTE: Good and bad periods are those intercensal periods when life expectancy was at least one standard deviation higher or lower than average life expectancy during the century under consideration. For females 1816–19 and 1828–31 were good periods and 1795–98, 1861–64, and 1864–67 were bad periods. See James Lee, Cameron Campbell, and Guofu Tan, "A Century of Mortality in Rural Liaoning, 1774–1873" in Antoinette Fauve-Chamoux, ed. *Le peuplement du monde avant 1850* (Paris, 1990).

pleted marriages and computes the sex ratios by birth order and completed family size, that is, the total number of births registered to the parents by the time the mother reached age 45. The numbers are certainly exaggerated because of the underregistration of females, but it is the unusual pattern that is important. In single-child families there were 576 boys for every 100 girls. For families with two children ever born there were 211 boys per 100 girls at

---

[*zhong*]. At 21 *sui* they become adults [*ding*]. At 60 *sui* they become old [*lao*]." *Tang huiyao*, 85.1555. According to a famous passage from the *Rites of Zhou*, a compendium of statements on early political institutions and policies probably completed in the second century B.C., "people should be registered after they have grown their teeth." In a well-known commentary on this passage, Qiu Jun, a fifteenth-century statesman, explained: "The human body is not fully developed until teeth are grown. Boys grow their first set of teeth in their eighth month and their second set in their eighth year. Girls grow their first set of teeth in their seventh month and their second set in their seventh year. They should then all be recorded in the population register." See Qiu Jun, *Daxue yanyi bu* (The Supplement to the exposition of the Great Learning, 1792), 13.14.

TABLE 5.4 Male Life Expectancy in Daoyi during Good and Bad Periods, 1792–1867

Age Group	Life Expectancy in Good Periods	Life Expectancy in Bad Periods	Difference in Life Expectancy	Standard Deviation of Difference in Life Expectancy
1–5	45.0	28.9	16.1	1.8
6–10	53.0	36.4	16.6	1.3
11–15	51.0	36.4	14.6	1.2
16–20	47.6	33.2	14.4	1.1
21–25	43.7	30.4	13.3	1.1
26–30	40.6	27.2	13.4	1.0
31–35	36.4	23.8	12.6	0.9
36–40	32.8	20.0	12.8	0.9
41–45	28.8	17.3	11.5	0.8
46–50	24.8	13.8	11.0	0.8
51–55	21.3	11.4	9.9	0.7
56–60	17.3	9.7	7.6	0.7
61–65	13.3	8.3	5.0	0.6
66–70	9.6	6.3	3.3	0.6
71–75	6.9	4.6	2.3	0.5
76+	4.1	3.1	1.0	0.3

NOTE: For males 1798–1801 and 1816–19 were good periods and 1795–98, 1819–22, and 1861–64 were bad periods. See James Lee, Cameron Campbell, and Guofu Tan, "A Century of Mortality in Rural Liaoning, 1774–1873" in Antoinette Fauve-Chamoux, ed. *Le peuplement du monde avant 1850* (Paris, 1990).

TABLE 5.5 Sex Ratios by Birth Order and Completed Family Size (male births per 100 female births)

| Birth Order | Completed Family Size | | | | |
	1	2	3	4	5+
1	576	211	156	158	88
2	—	450	294	229	139
3	—	—	324	278	149
4	—	—	—	422	138
5+	—	—	—	—	162
N	115	328	428	401	599

NOTE: These calculations include only children born between 1792 and 1840 to the 883 completed first marriages that began before 1840. Births after 1840 are included in the completed family size, but are not included in the computations of sex ratios because of the decline in female registration after 1840. Inclusion would show even more lopsided sex ratios in later parities.

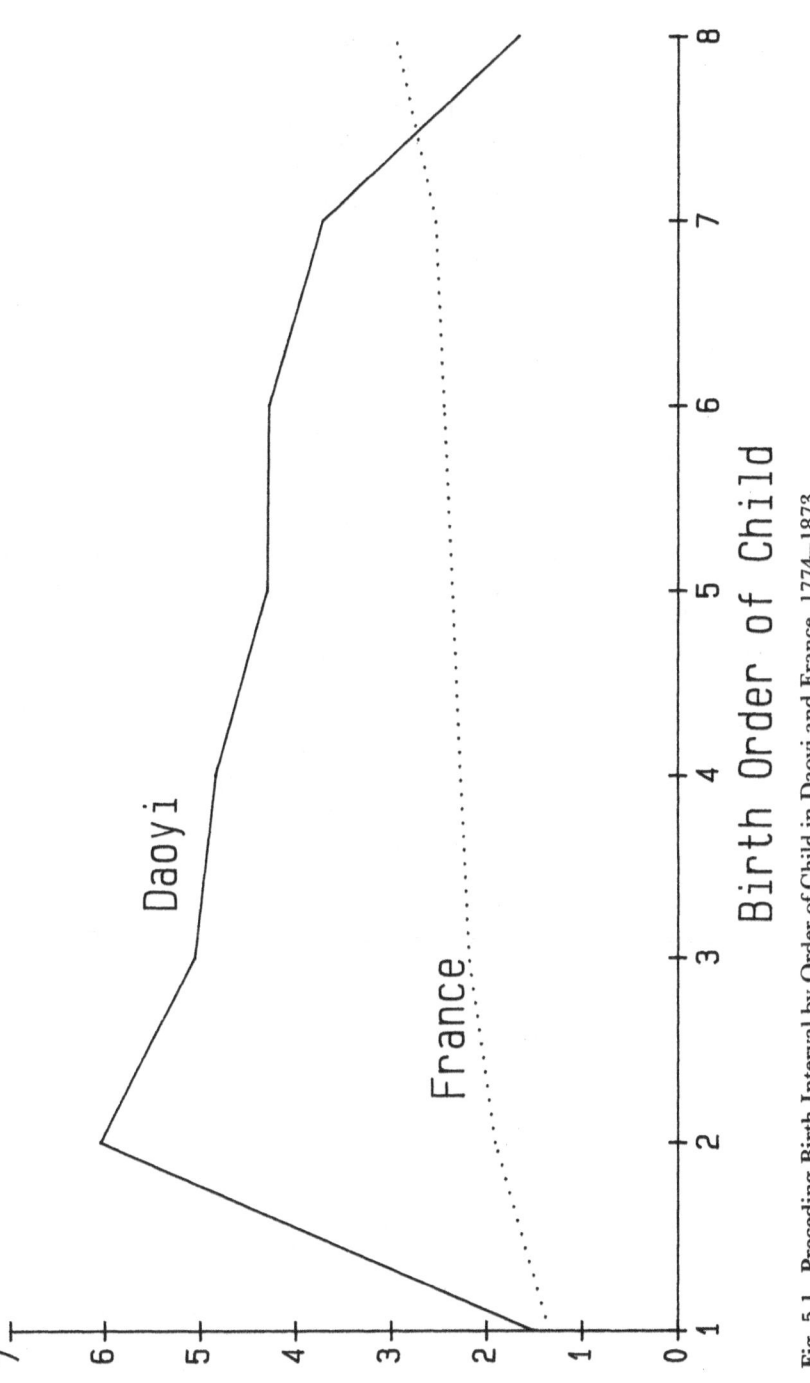

Fig. 5.1. Preceding Birth Interval by Order of Child in Daoyi and France, 1774–1873
Note: Based on 1774–1873 data for Daoyi and 1500–1820 data for France. Data for France are from Michael W. Flinn, *The European Demographic System* (Baltimore, 1981), p. 330.

the first birth and 450 boys to 100 girls at the second birth. For families with three children ever born the ratio was 156 boys to 100 girls at the first birth, 294 boys to 100 girls at the second birth, and 324 boys for every 100 girls at the last birth. This highly unnatural pattern continues through all other completed family sizes. The closer a girl's birth order was to the completed family size, the less likely she was to survive to registration. The pattern is too systematic to be explained by random underregistration.

Daoyi peasants, in other words, used sex-selective methods of fertility control to determine the number and sex of their children. Generally there was a strong preference for boys, since sons had a higher utility, especially during their parents' old age. Couples targeted the number of boys they wanted and stopped having children after the desired number had been reached. This behavior produced both the low mean age at last birth and the unusual pattern in Table 5.5, where sex ratios increase steadily with birth order. Whether or not a girl born before the cutoff would be allowed to live depended on many factors, one of the most important of which was wealth. Poorer couples who only planned on one or two boys would be less willing to be burdened with girls. Wealthier couples, however, would want more children and would be more likely to allow early girls to live. As a result, the sex ratios in Table 5.5 for couples who had few children are comparatively high, while the ratios for couples who had more children are comparatively moderate.[13]

A study of age-specific fertility by household position underlines the strong relationship between wealth and fertility. Most peasants in Daoyi lived in highly hierarchical, complex households, where resources depended to a large extent on their position within the household.[14] We would therefore expect fertility patterns to reflect two well-known Confucian principles of household organization, whereby household heads took precedence over other family members and senior relatives took precedence over junior relatives. Indeed, the calculation of fertility by household position, presented in Figure 5.2, confirms that, at least in Daoyi, most Chinese families obeyed such principles. The hierarchy of fertility begins with the head at the top, followed by the head's brothers and sons, then his uncles, brothers' sons, cousins, and cousins' sons. The marital fertility rate of household heads is

---

13. We would like to thank George Alter for his illuminating analysis of Table 5.5. Stevan Harrell, "The Rich Get Children," pp. 81–109, shows clearly that in late imperial China fertility was tied to wealth. He studied three lineages in Xiaoshan County, Zhejiang, from 1550 to 1850 and found that members of the richer branches of the lineages had more children than members of the poorer branches. This behavior can be attributed to a long natalist tradition in Chinese society.

14. We discuss the structure of household hierarchy as well as the patterns of household progression and calculate differential vital rates by household structure and household position in James Lee and Cameron Campbell, *Happy Families*.

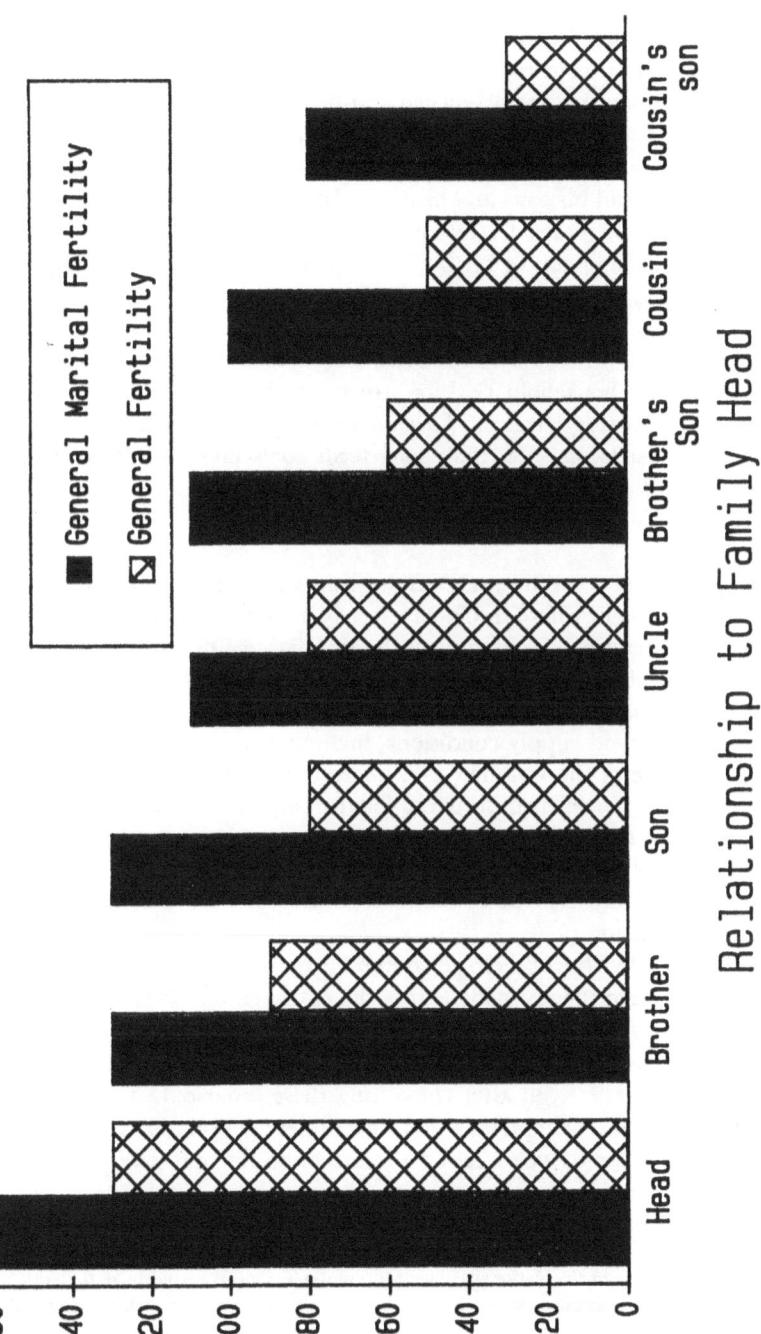

Fig. 5.2. Male Fertility in Daoyi by Family Relationship, 1792–1873 (births per 1,000 person-years)
Note: General male marital fertility equals male births over married men 15–35. General male fertility equals male births over all men aged 15–35.

twice that of cousins' sons. The marital fertility of sons is not only higher than that of brothers' sons, it is almost as high as that of brothers and far higher than that of cousins. Removing the control for marriage accentuates the differences between the privileged and the dispossessed. Because chances of marrying depended on household position as well, not only does the gap between the head and cousins' sons widen considerably: so do the gaps between the head and his sons and brothers. In both cases as distance from the household head increases, fertility decreases.

Given the technology of birth control available in late imperial China, such distinctive sex-selective patterns of family planning could only arise if parents consciously chose the number and sex of their children at least in part through infanticide. The patterns according to birth order, completed family size, and household position are too rational and systematic to be explained by underregistration. Parents' decisions to use infanticide were, of course, not based solely on their long-term goals and household position. Couples must have been influenced by short-term conditions. Indeed, as we shall see, couples were influenced in the short term by the price of food.

The price data come from an empirewide system to monitor food conditions that began elsewhere in China as early as the late seventeenth century but did not extend to Liaoning until the late eighteenth century. Thereafter until well into the twentieth century, magistrates in each of Liaoning's two prefectures, Fengtian and Jinzhou, reported every ten days to the provincial government on food supply conditions, including the price of all major food grains, the state of the weather, and harvest yields when appropriate. The provincial governor in turn prepared for the emperor a brief summary each lunar month of the lowest and highest prices reported in each prefecture for five food grains (rice, husked and unhusked millet, sorghum, wheat, and soybeans). It is these monthly summaries that provide our price data for Fengtian prefecture.

The principal virtue of these price summaries is the systematic spatial and temporal coverage they provide across the entire empire for over 200 years. To date, we have collected over 1,500 of these monthly price reports for the prefecture, almost two thirds of which are from the century under consideration in this paper.[15] Even after converting these lunar data to solar-month equivalents, we have complete or almost complete information (nine months' worth or more) for 65 years and no information for only five years (1791,

---

15. James Lee collected 1,200 of these memorials from the First Historical Archives in Beijing in 1985, 1986, and 1987. Yeh-chien Wang kindly provided the 300 remaining memorials from his own research in the National Palace Museum in Taibei. We would like to thank Yeh-chien Wang for his gracious assistance to us here and elsewhere. Anna Chi transcribed the material into machine-readable form. We gratefully acknowledge her assistance.

1815, 1822, 1823, and 1825).[16] Figures 5.3 and 5.4 illustrate the price curves of the monthly lowest reported price and the monthly highest reported price for all five grains from 1774 to 1873 in taels of silver per *shi* of grain. These price data provide a systematic measure of food availability in Daoyi and, by extension, of economic conditions, which we can correlate with vital rates. They also enable us to identify which grains were most closely tied to specific changes in population and which grains may therefore have loomed largest in individual decision making on fertility and mortality.

It is important to remember, however, that these price materials also have a number of deficiencies, especially for microanalysis at the subprefectural level.[17] They are denominated in silver and accordingly do not accurately reflect the retail market, which commonly used copper cash. They only provide us with the highest and lowest prices in each month and tell us nothing about the overall distribution of prices within each prefecture. Finally, they do not tell us the location of the reported prices. We consequently cannot calculate an average prefectural price. We cannot even assume that the monthly low and high prices were necessarily related. We can only assume that the data represent general price trends over time. For the purposes of this analysis we shall therefore separately analyze all ten types of price at our disposal.

Correlation coefficients between annual averages of different grain prices, summarized in Table 5.6, reveal a high degree of substitutability among most grains. This was especially true for the monthly low and high prices of husked and unhusked millet, as well as the monthly low and high prices of millet, rice, and sorghum. Monthly low and high prices for the same grain, however, are less strongly correlated than low-priced and high-priced grains by themselves. We suspect that this pattern occurred because these two sets of prices may represent two different regions within the prefecture.[18] Our analysis, in other words, confirms that monthly low-priced and high-priced grains were not always substitutable.

---

16. Peter C. Perdue produced the programs that converted monthly prices from lunar to solar dates. We gratefully acknowledge his repeated assistance and encouragement as we converted our data. We would also like to note that Anna Chi helped supplement this program to cover fully the period from 1736 to 1911.

17. Although subprefectural data for Fengtian exist in the Liaoning Provincial Archives, all the weekly and monthly reports that we have found to date are from the very early twentieth century. We would like to thank the Liaoning Provincial Archives for making these data available.

18. For the moment we have no direct information on where the monthly low and high prices come from. Unless we can find the subprefectural price reports for the eighteenth and early nineteenth centuries, our analysis will always be incomplete. We do not know if these price data consistently originate from the same region. We consequently cannot guarantee that our results always accurately reflect the historical realities.

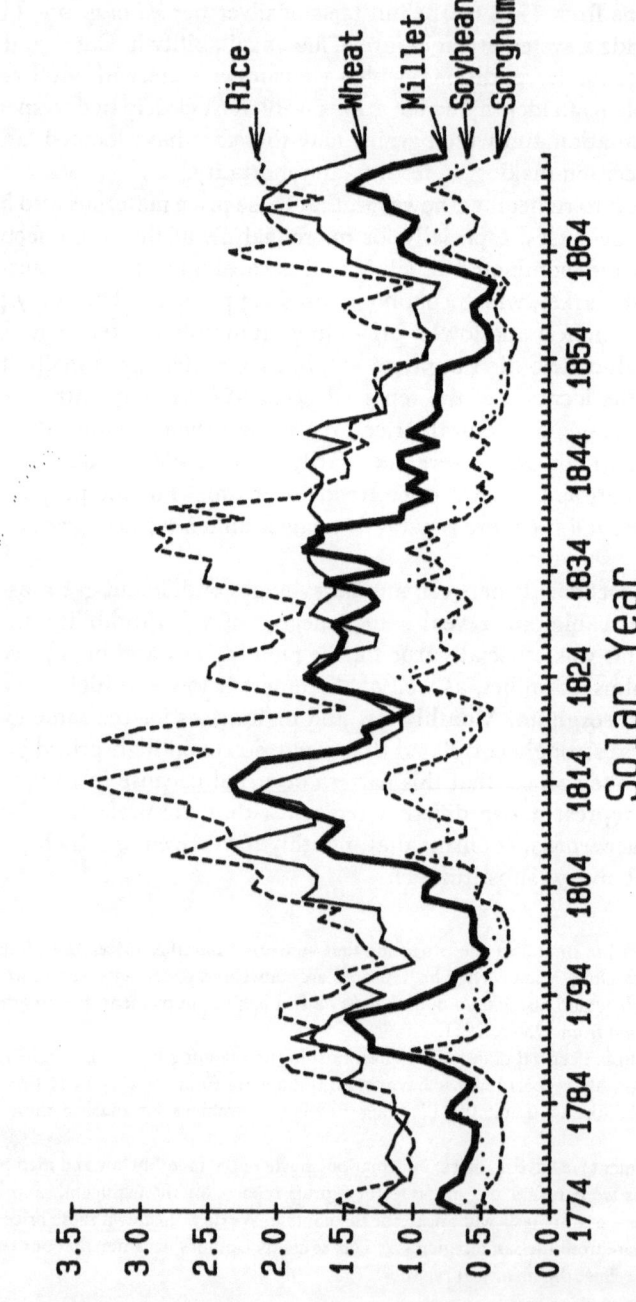

Fig. 5.3. Low Grain Prices in Fengtian Prefecture, 1774–1873 (annual averages in taels per *shi*)

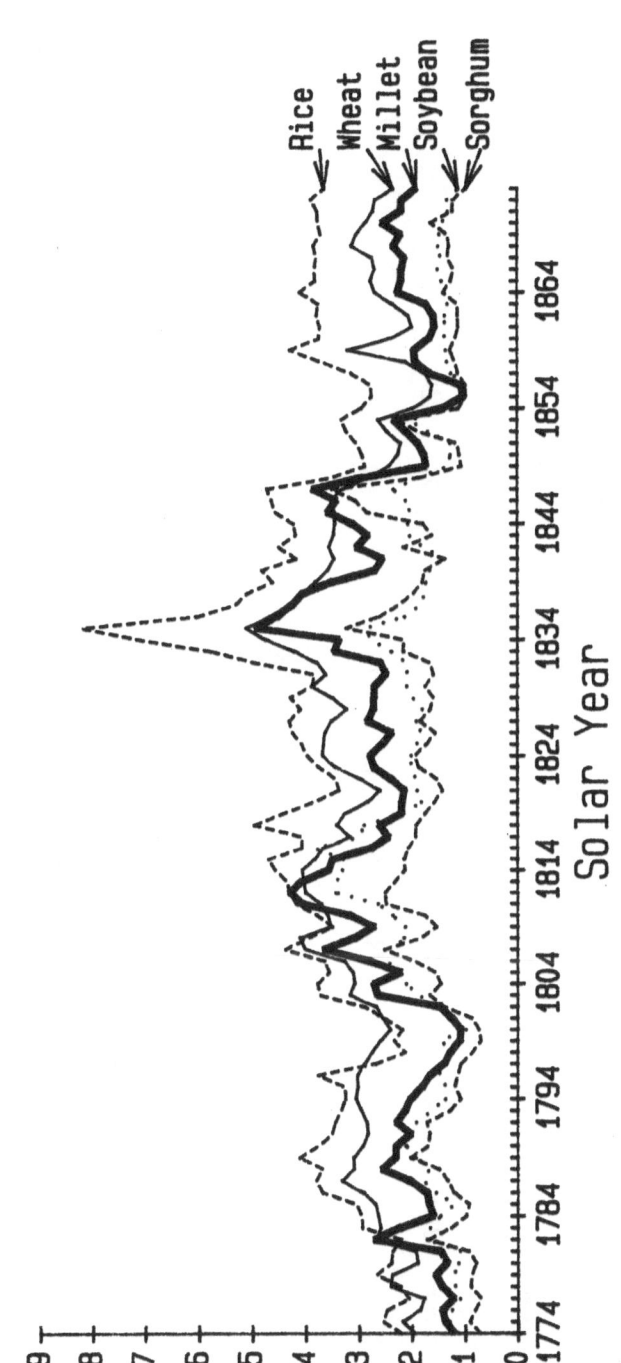

Fig. 5.4. High Grain Prices in Fengtian Prefecture, 1774–1873 (annual averages in taels per *shi*)

TABLE 5.6 Correlations of High and Low Grain Prices in Fengtian Prefecture, 1774–1873

	Mean Price	Standard Deviation	High Prices					Low Prices					
			Rice	Husked Millet	Unhusked Millet	Sorghum	Wheat	Rice	Husked Millet	Unhusked Millet	Sorghum	Wheat	Soybeans
Low Prices													
Soybeans	0.625	.194	.60	.66	.66	.48	.72	.80	.83	.83	.89	.65	
Wheat	1.465	.341	.48	.67	.66	.53	.69	.63	.69	.69	.68		
Sorghum	0.565	.234	.62	.76	.77	.62	.75	.81	.91	.91			
Unhusked Millet	0.536	.232	.56	.74	.75	.63	.74	.84	1.00				
Husked Millet	1.073	.463	.56	.74	.75	.62	.74	.84					
Rice	1.858	.605	.66	.69	.69	.54	.75						
High Prices													
Soybeans	1.809	.591	.60	.74	.75	.75	.73						
Wheat	3.047	.712	.82	.87	.87	.75							
Sorghum	1.568	.564	.76	.89	.90								
Unhusked Millet	1.208	.424	.81	1.00									
Husked Millet	2.406	.846	.81										
Rice	3.785	.958											

Nevertheless, virtually all prices rose and fell usually in tandem and occasionally by as much as a factor of two or three within the space of just one or two years. A recent study by Wang Shaowu of the climate and harvest history of Manchuria indicates that fluctuations in summer temperature were responsible for most of these sharp price variations through their impact on crop yields.[19] Even as recently as 1954, 1957, 1969, 1972, and 1976, low summer temperatures reduced harvest yields by as much as one third. According to Wang, there were at least 26 similarly cold summers between 1774 and 1873, concentrated in the 1780s, 1810s, and 1830s.[20] Given the low level of agricultural technology in the late eighteenth and early nineteenth centuries, the impact of these low temperatures on harvests may have been even more severe than in the twentieth century.[21] Indeed, an examination of Figures 5.3 and 5.4 reveals that these three decades were characterized by rapid price increases. Prices, in other words, appear to accurately reflect the availability of food within Daoyi and should have had great impact on population behavior.

To what extent, then, did grain prices affect vital rates? Figures 5.5 and 5.6 summarize what information we have on annual crude birth and death rates for the century under observation. Again these data suffer from two limitations. On the one hand, we cannot calculate reliable birth or death rates for several years due to missing registers. On the other hand, because of the limitations of the registration system, we can only compute average death rates over three-year periods.[22] We cannot compute actual annual death rates for either sex. Our mortality statistics therefore appear deceptively stable. Given the incompleteness of the vital data and the volatility of the price data, we should anticipate that the correlations of prices to population will be weaker on paper than they were in reality.

19. Wang Shaowu, "Jin sibainian dongya de lengxia" (Unpublished manuscript, 1988), reconstructs the temperature history of Manchuria by using a time series from the Japanese island of Hokkaido, which, he explains, was dominated by the same pressure system and therefore subject to the same large-scale fluctuations in temperature.

20. According to Wang, these unusually cold summers were 1774, 1776, 1778, 1782, 1783, 1785, 1786, 1789, 1793, 1813, 1815, 1825, 1830–33, 1835–38, 1841, 1846, 1856, 1857, 1866, and 1869.

21. For example, again according to Wang, a mean summer temperature just 1.5 to 2 degrees centigrade below normal in 1902 and 1913 resulted in 50 percent and 80 percent reductions in harvest yields respectively, compared in each case to the average yield of the five previous years.

22. Female death rates cover only 25 intercensal periods and therefore include only 75 years of the century under observation. Male death rates, by contrast, include 30 intercensal periods and cover virtually the entire century. It is important to remember that these crude rates are unadjusted for deaths missing because of late registration. We estimate elsewhere that as many as one fourth of all deaths are missing in every population register (Lee, Campbell, and Anthony, "A Century of Mortality"). Since the proportion of underregistration appears to have been consistent, the temporal pattern illustrated in Figure 5.6 should be substantively correct.

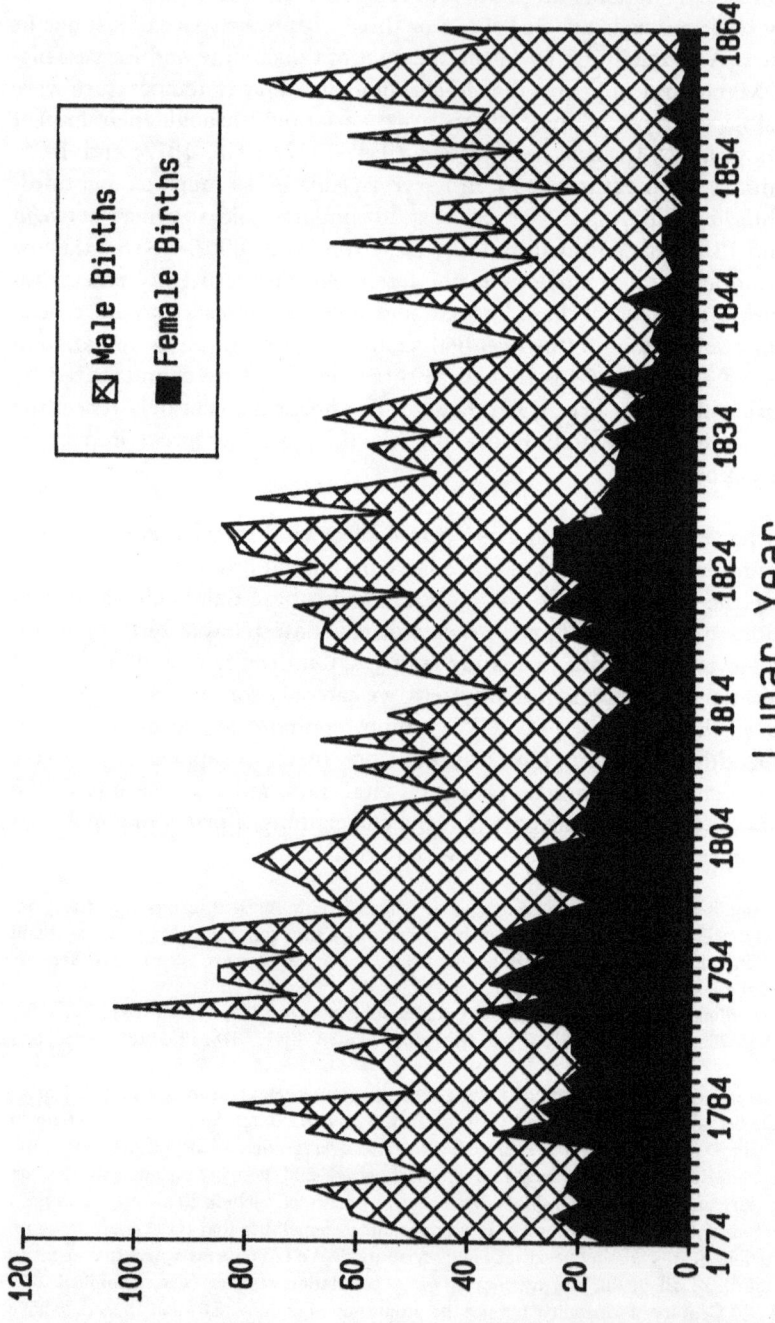

Fig. 5.5. Crude Birth Rates in Daoyi, 1774–1864 (per 1,000 married women aged 15–45)

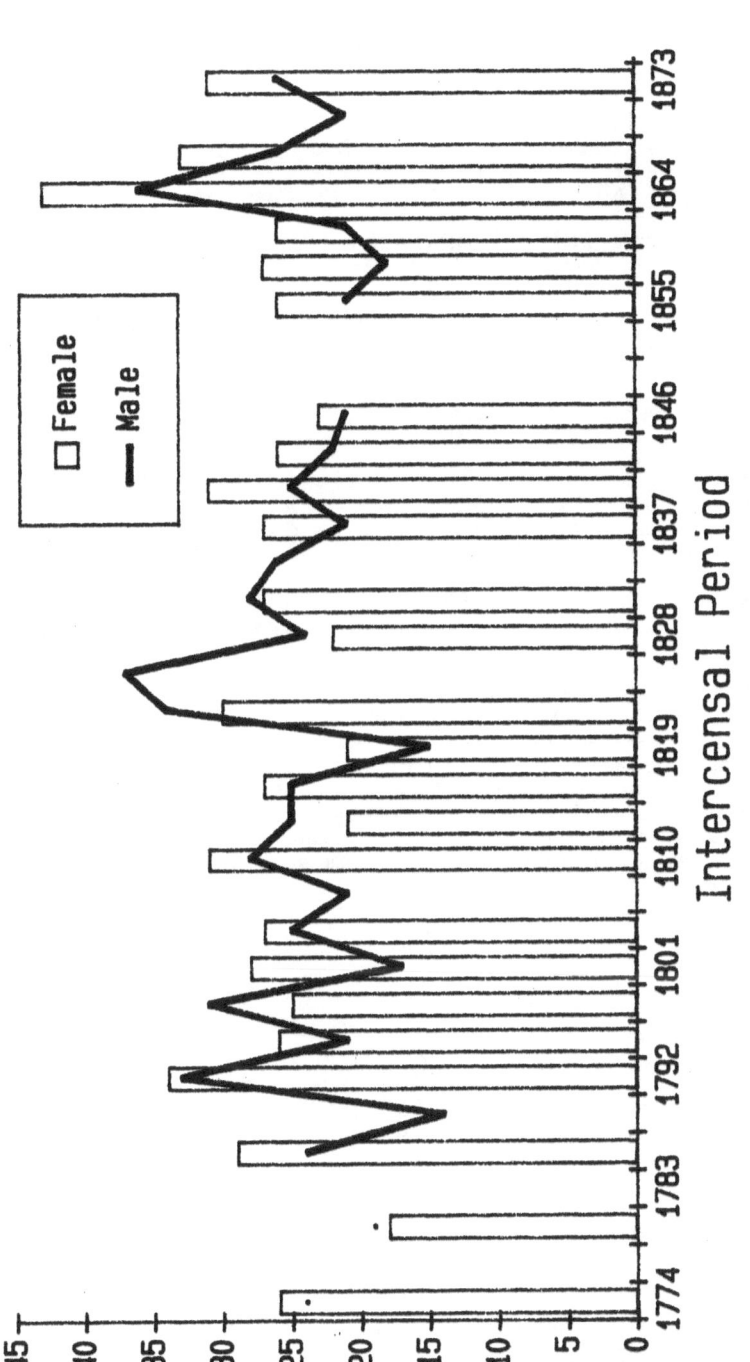

Fig. 5.6. Crude Death Rates in Daoyi, 1771–1873 (per 1,000 population, by intercensal period)

TABLE 5.7 Correlations of Grain Prices and Death and Birth Rates in Daoyi, 1774–1873

| | Household Death Rate | | Household Birth Rate | | | | | |
| | All | | All | | Complex[a] | | Simple[b] | |
Grain Price	Female	Male	Female	Male	Female	Male	Female	Male
Rice								
High	—	—	- 0.62	—	- 0.46*	—	- 0.46*	- 0.36
Low	—	—	- 0.60	- 0.37*	- 0.48	—	- 0.54	- 0.46
Millet								
High	—	—	- 0.65	- 0.37	- 0.55	- 0.33*	- 0.50*	- 0.56
Low	—	0.32	- 0.49	—	- 0.42*	—	—	- 0.45
Sorghum								
High	—	—	- 0.57	—	- 0.46*	- 0.33*	- 0.39*	- 0.39
Low	—	0.26	- 0.58	- 0.40*	- 0.54	—	- 0.46*	- 0.49
Wheat								
High	—	—	- 0.68	—	- 0.36*	—	- 0.54	- 0.34
Low	—	0.43	- 0.44	- 0.38*	- 0.48	—	—	- 0.39
Soybean								
High	—	—	- 0.45*	—	- 0.63	—	—	- 0.51
Low	—	0.39	- 0.57	- 0.40*	- 0.36	—	- 0.40*	- 0.47

NOTE: All correlations have a significance of 0.001 unless marked with an asterisk, in which case the significance is 0.01. Correlations with a significance of less than 0.01 have been omitted. Our calculations begin from 1774 for all households and from 1789 for the breakdown by simple and complex households, and end in 1840 for female births and in 1873 for male births. The prices are adjusted annual averages from Fengtian prefecture; the birth and death rates are annual rates from Daoyi.

[a] Households with two or more conjugal units.

[b] Households with only one conjugal family unit.

Nevertheless, in spite of these limitations, the comparison of annual birth and death rates with annual average grain prices yields a number of truly significant results. In keeping with our previous analysis of mortality, the correlations between food prices and death rates are far stronger for men than for women. Indeed, as we can see from Table 5.7, there are no significant correlations between food prices and female death rates. The only meaningful relationships we can find are between male death rates and the annual average of monthly low prices. There are no correlations between the annual averages of monthly high prices with mortality. From these findings we can infer that the monthly low prices for the prefecture somehow reflect the availability of food in Daoyi during subsistence crises. We can also identify which of the five reported grains were the most important subsistence crops for our population. Rice prices, for example, were uncorrelated with mortality and can be considered relatively unimportant. All other grains had significant if weak correlations with mortality. Wheat was the most important of these food crops.

However, in keeping with our analysis of fertility and family planning, correlations between grain prices and birth rates are not only far stronger than correlations between grain prices and death rates, they are also stronger for females than for males, especially in complex households. Strong negative correlations exist for virtually all grain prices regardless of the type of price (monthly low or monthly high) or the variety of grain. Figure 5.7, which plots birth rates by sex against low millet prices—millet being a common food staple—graphically illustrates the relationship between prices and fertility. When food prices were high, people had fewer children, especially fewer girls.

Fetal wastage and standard methods of family planning would have produced dramatically different results. Spontaneous abortions would have affected males as well as females.[23] Contraception would have produced strong correlations with lagged prices as well as current prices. In fact, though, correlations between prices and fertility are not only stronger for females than for males, they are stronger for current prices than for lagged prices.[24] Parents, in other words, made their fertility decisions in response to conditions at time of birth rather than conditions at time of conception. The unnatural response of birth rates by sex to immediate economic conditions, therefore, strongly suggests that in Daoyi many peasants limited their fertility through sex-selective neglect or infanticide.

Parents, of course, were most likely to make such drastic decisions in response to extreme economic conditions, only adjusting their fertility when prices were exceedingly high or exceedingly low. As a result, the correlations between birth rates and food prices in Table 5.7 may not accurately reflect the full responsiveness of fertility to economic conditions. We therefore calculate the percent changes in birth rates between years of medium prices (within one standard deviation of the mean) to years of unusually high or low prices (above or below one standard deviation) in order to measure the sensitivity of birth rates to high and low price extremes. According to these calculations, summarized in Figures 5.8 through 5.11, virtually all households

---

23. According to Henri Leridon, *Human Fertility* (Chicago, 1977), p. 15, the natural sex ratio for stillbirths is 120–30 dead boys per 100 dead girls.

24. If the peasants were limiting their fertility though sexual restraint rather than infanticide, we would expect even more pronounced correlations between births and prices, with a lag of one year or more. In fact we discovered that the relationship remains strong, although the values for both sexes decrease rather than increase. Therefore, although some couples may have practiced restraint, others preferred to rely on infanticide as a means of fertility control in times of economic pressure.

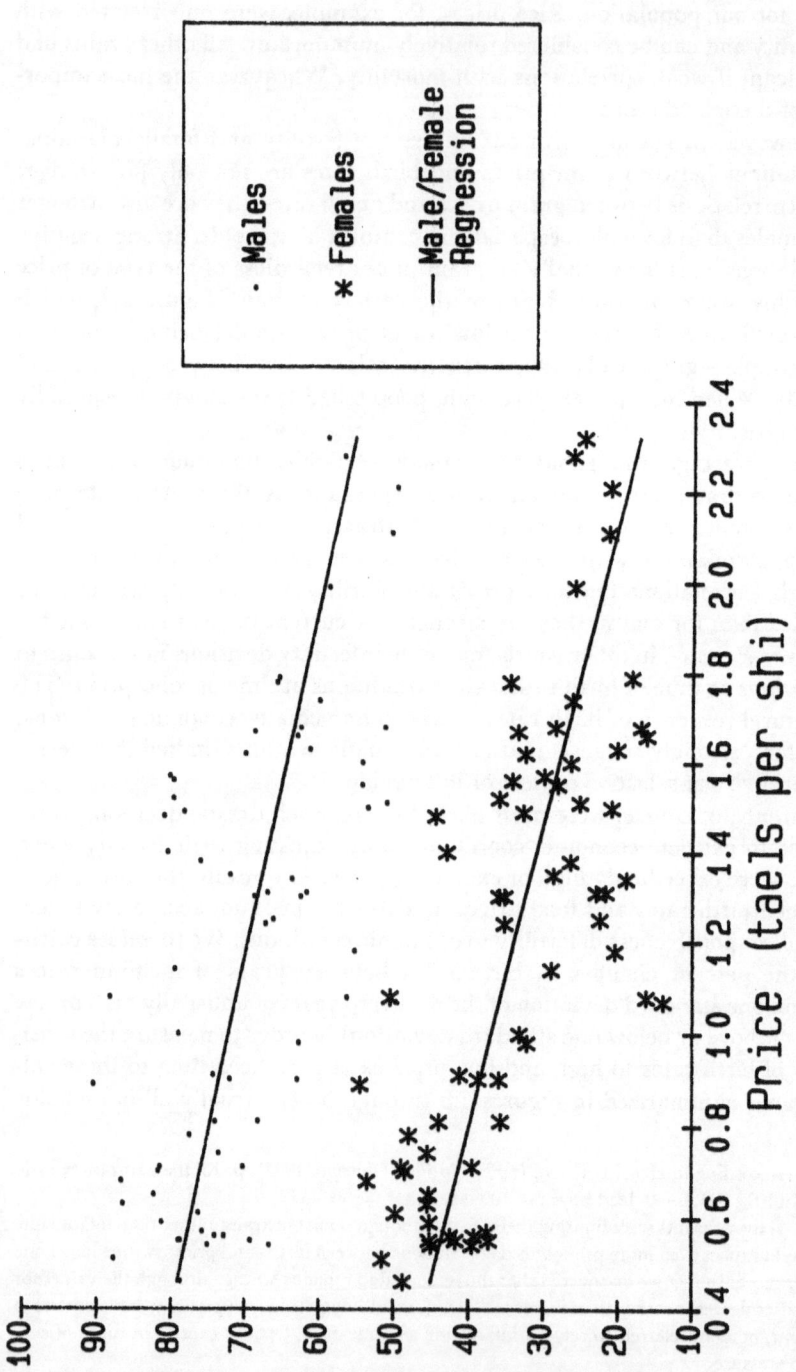

Fig. 5.7. Birth Rates by Sex in Daoyi as a Function of Low Millet Prices, 1775–1840 (per 1,000 population)
Note: Male correlation coefficient = −0.59. Female correlation coefficient = −0.69

responded to high prices by reducing fertility and to low prices by increasing fertility.

Household wealth, and, by extension, household type, played a key role in the decision to let a daughter survive. Wealthy households, which were generally complex, were less affected by economic conditions than were poorer households, which were usually simple. Indeed, as we can see in Figure 5.8, when prices were high, parents in complex households reduced their female birth rate by one quarter, while parents in simple households cut theirs in half. In contrast, when prices were low, parents in complex households increased their female birth rate by one third, while parents in simple households did not change theirs at all. Simple households, therefore, were so impoverished relative to complex households that they not only kept far fewer girls than normal when times were bad but they allowed no extra ones to live when times were good.

The decision to keep a daughter depended, of course, on whether or not the couple already had a child. Indeed as we saw in Table 5.5, a girl was most likely to be kept if she was the first of several children. According to Figure 5.8, however, this was especially true in complex households. When times were bad, the birth rate for girls without older siblings dropped by less than one tenth while the rates for girls with older siblings dropped by four-tenths. In contrast, when times were good, the rate for girls without older siblings almost doubled while the rates for girls with older siblings went up only by one tenth. That complex-household parents were willing in bad times as well as good times to support a daughter so long as she was their firstborn reflects a desire to keep first children regardless of their sex. In spite of the widespread practice of infanticide, in other words, primordial affection could triumph over material concerns.

A girl's chances of surviving in a complex household, however, depended on household position as well as birth order. Figure 5.9 reveals that the less incentive parents had to produce a male heir, the more girls they allowed to live when prices were low. In good years, therefore, brothers and nephews, who were the furthest from the line of inheritance, had 50 percent more girls than usual. Heads, however, had only as many girls as they did in normal times. In contrast, all parents, whatever their relationship to the head, had at least one-third fewer girls in bad times than normal. Even in complex households, while some parents were willing to support more female children than normal in times of plenty, girls were still enough of a luxury that few parents were willing to save them when times were hard.

But baby girls were by no means the only victims of infanticide. Some parents also neglected or perhaps even killed their sons as well as their daughters when times were bad. According to the correlations for male births in Table 5.7, this was especially true in the simple, that is, poorer, households. Male birth rates had uniformly strong negative correlations with all

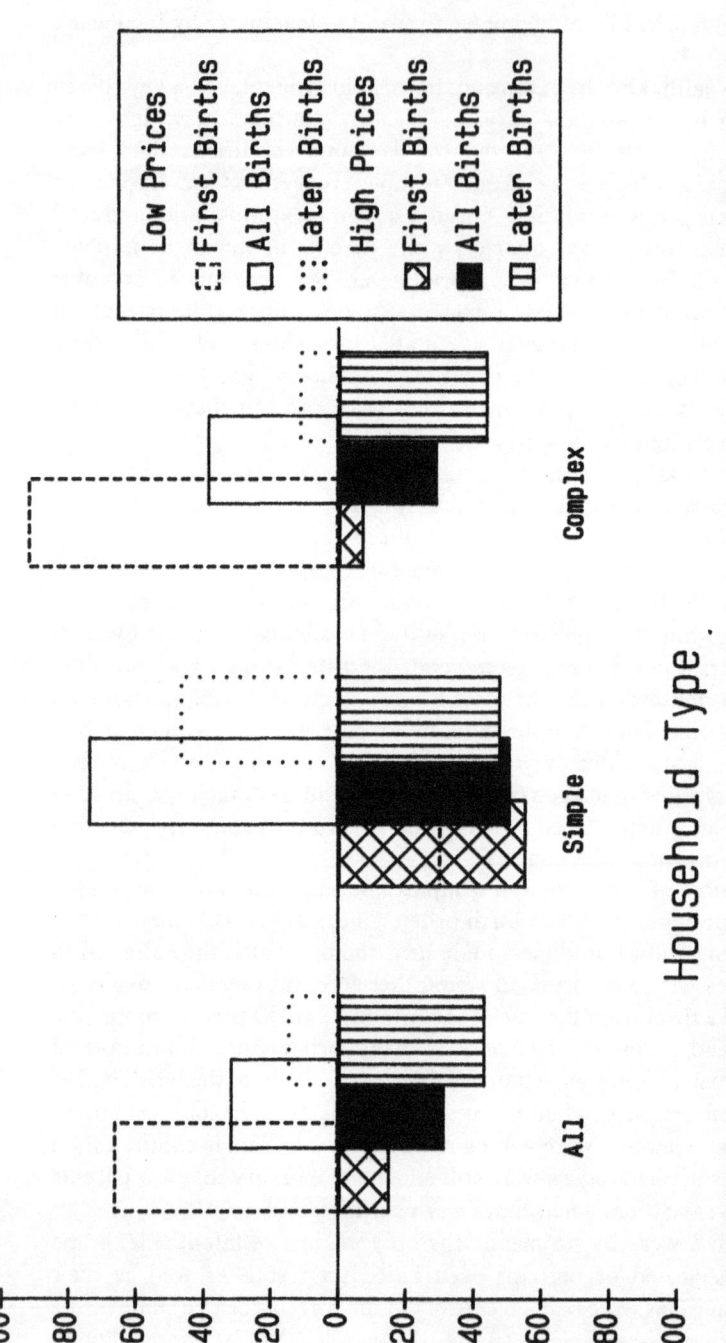

Fig. 5.8. Female Births by Household Type in Daoyi in Periods of High and Low Grain Prices, 1792–1840 (% change from normal rate)

Notes: Marital fertility only. For boys, periods of high and low grain prices are years where the price is more than one standard deviation above or below the mean for the period 1792–1873. For girls, periods of high and low grain prices are years where the price is more than one standard deviation above or below the mean for the period 1792–1840. Different years were selected for boys and girls because the mean and standard deviation of grain prices for the period 1792–1873 were different from the mean and standard deviation for the period 1792–1840. The years of high prices were therefore 1812–1816 for girls and 1807–1817, 1823–1827, 1829, 1833, and 1836–1838 for boys. The years of low prices were 1795–1802 and 1805 for girls and 1797–1801 and 1854–1862 for boys.

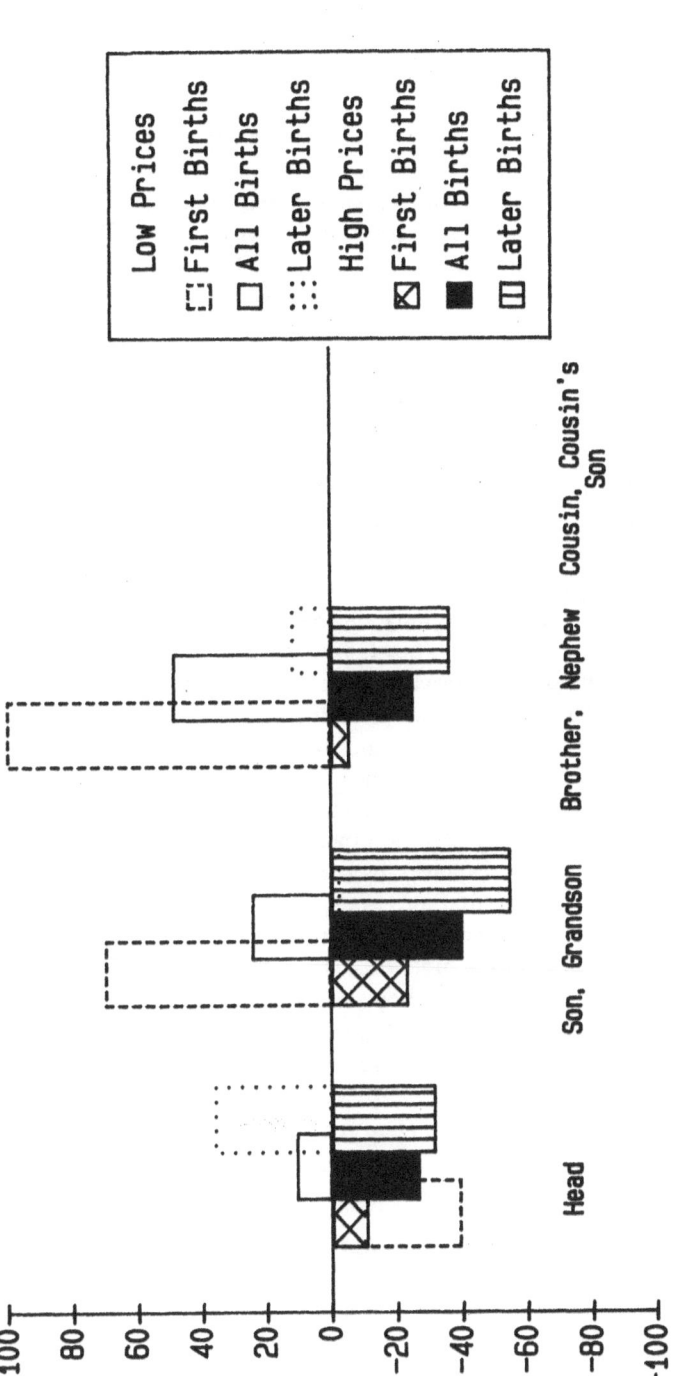

Fig. 5.9. Female Births by Family Relationship in Daoyi in Periods of High and Low Grain Prices, 1792–1840 (% change from normal rate)

Note: See notes in Fig. 5.8.

food prices. Indeed, the correlations with male fertility were almost as strong as the correlations with female fertility. When prices were high, in other words, parents in these households neglected their sons as well as their daughters. In Fengtian, at least, the common assumption that Chinese parents neglected only their daughters may be untrue.[25]

Even in simple households, of course, parents only made the decision not to keep a son under extreme economic pressure. As we can see in Figure 5.10, when prices were high, the male birth rate in simple households declined by one third, but when prices were low, it increased by only one sixteenth. Parents, in other words, did not regard their boys as luxury goods. They thought of them as necessities. As a result, male birth rates remained relatively constant so long as there was no crisis. Parents in simple households only gave up their sons when they did not have the resources to support them.

Male infanticide, however, was not restricted to simple households. Figure 5.11 indicates that in complex households parents at the very top and very bottom of the household hierarchy also reduced their male birth rate in response to economic pressure. Indeed, when prices were high, cousins, who were at the bottom of the hierarchy, only allowed half as many boys to live as when prices were normal. Similarly, heads who were at the top of the household hierarchy had one quarter fewer boys. Evidently, just as men paid for their privileged position relative to women with greater increases in mortality in times of crisis, so household heads paid for their privileged position by lowering their fertility to the levels of other relations. Here too the price of privilege was greater vulnerability to economic fluctuation.

Just as with girls, birth order was an important consideration for boys in complex households, but the response to economic conditions differed considerably. The birth rates for firstborn sons, unlike those for their female counterparts, were more responsive to high prices than the birth rates for later sons. Thus when prices were high, the rate for firstborn sons declined by one fifth while the rate for later-born boys changed hardly at all (see Figure 5.10). This was especially true for the children of co-resident sons, brothers, and nephews, who were neither at the top nor at the bottom of the household hierarchy. Mid-ranking couples apparently had extra boys only if they were wealthy enough to be relatively immune to economic pressure. Heads, on the other hand, were under constant pressure to produce more sons regardless of wealth. It was poorer heads who responded to economic crisis by delaying or canceling plans for extra sons.

---

25. According to Hanley and Wolf, eds., *Family and Population*, p. 5: "Although female infanticide was common in some parts of China in difficult times, there is no evidence that the Chinese ever tried to limit the number of sons. . . . In Japan, in sharp contrast, infanticide and abortion were commonplace, not only as a response to natural and social catastrophes, but as a kind of family planning with long-range objectives."

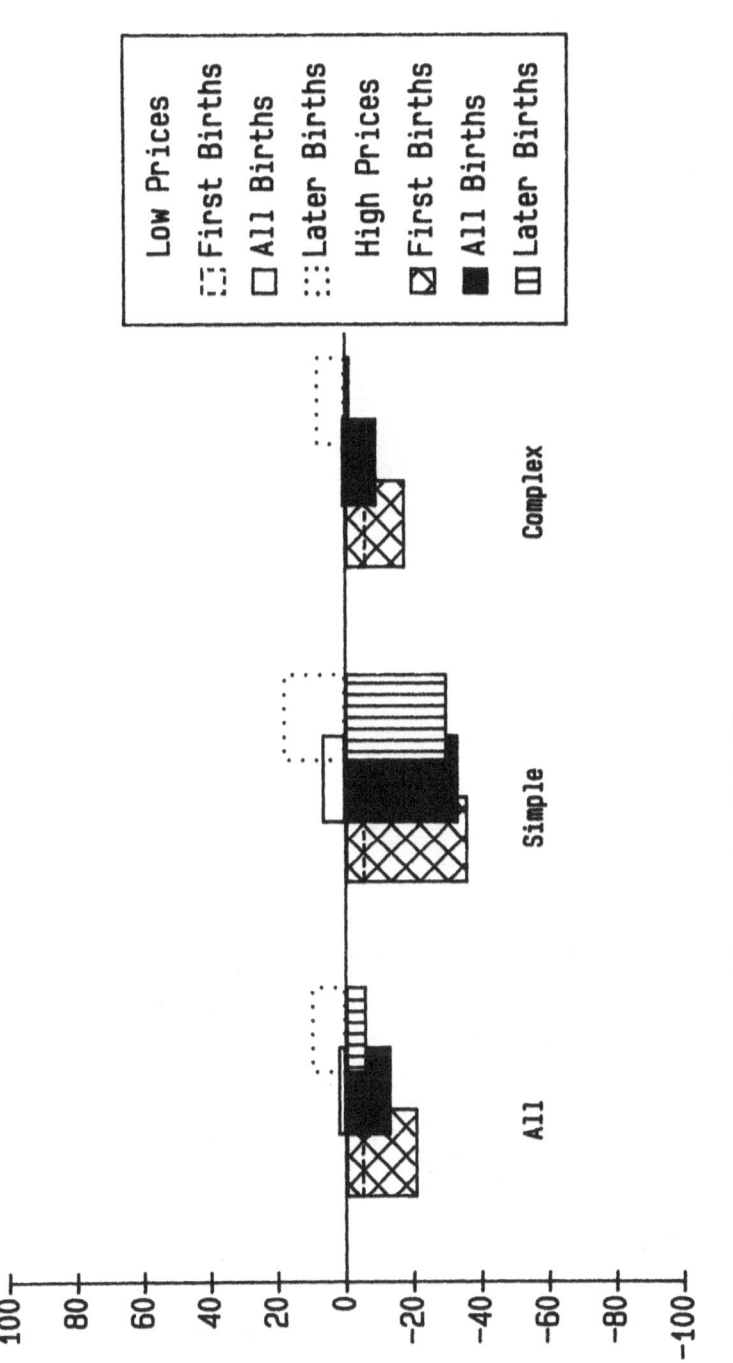

Fig. 5.10. Male Births by Household Type in Daoyi in Periods of High and Low Grain Prices, 1792–1873 (% change from normal rate)

Note: See notes in Fig. 5.8.

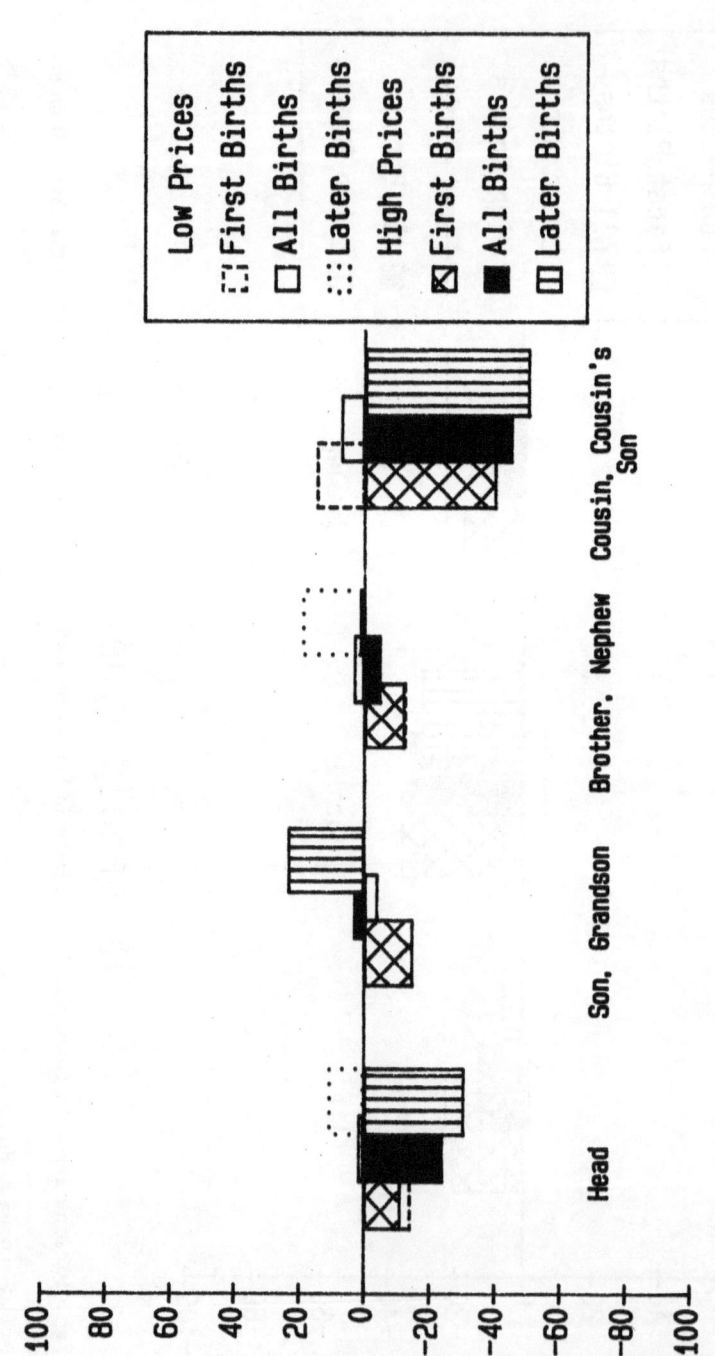

Figure 5.11. Male Births by Family Relationship in Daoyi in Periods of High and Low Grain Prices, 1792–1873 (% change from normal rate)

Note: See notes in Fig. 5.8.

But while male birth rates were not as responsive as female birth rates to changes in food prices, we should remember that male death rates were more strongly correlated with prices than female death rates. Girls, in other words, were apparently considered such luxuries that, like wives, they were permitted only when parents were confident that they could support them, albeit at a very low level. Boys, on the other hand, were valued so highly that in even the most marginal of household circumstances they were often allowed to live. Thus while females who survived infancy were unaffected by price fluctuations, males were vulnerable even as adults precisely because they were allowed to survive in poor as well as wealthy households.

Until recently virtually the only attempt at precise demographic measures of a "traditional" rural Chinese population has been the reexamination by G. W. Barclay, A. J. Coale, M. A. Stoto, and T. J. Trussell of the data collected by John Lossing Buck in his 1929–31 survey of Chinese agriculture.[26] Relying very heavily on a body of indirect techniques of demographic estimation, these distinguished demographers concluded that in China, although marriage was both early and universal, fertility was nevertheless extremely low. They furthermore suggested that such low fertility may well have been characteristic of the late imperial period. The problem that then confronted historians of late imperial China was how to explain the sustained rapid rise of Qing population in the face of such low "natural" fertility. The present study, in relying on direct analysis of eighteenth and nineteenth century materials, suggests that such low fertility may well have been the result of fertility control and that the level of "natural" fertility in eighteenth- and nineteenth-century China may in fact have been higher.

This study further suggests that if all Chinese peasants controlled their fertility in response to economic conditions, then the rise in population during the eighteenth and nineteenth centuries may well have been a direct response to significant advances in economic growth. Our findings, in other words, seem to corroborate recent claims by Western as well as Chinese historians of unprecedented agrarian expansion beginning in the eighteenth century and increasingly rapid commercialization beginning in the nineteenth century.[27]

26. See Buck; G. W. Barclay, A. J. Coale, M. A. Stoto, and T. J. Trussell, "A Reassessment of the Demography of Traditional Rural China," *Population Index* 42.4 (1976): 606–35.

27. In English see, for example, Yen-p'ing Hao, *The Commercial Revolution in Nineteenth-Century China*, (Berkeley and Los Angeles, 1986); Peter Perdue, *Exhausting the Earth: State and Peasant in Hunan, 1500–1800* (Cambridge, Mass., 1987); William T. Rowe, *Hankow: Commerce and Society in a Chinese City, 1796–1889* (Stanford, 1984). In Chinese see Guo Songyi, "Qingchu fengjian guojia kenhuang zhengce fenxi," *Qingshi luncong* 2 (1980): 111–38; Guo Songyi, "Qingdai de renkou zengzhang he renkou liuqian," *Qingshi luncong* 5 (1984): 103–38; Wu Chengming, *Zhongguo ziben zhuyi yu guonei shichang* (Beijing, 1985); and Xu Dixin and Wu Chengming, *Zhongguo ziben zhuyi de mengya* (Beijing, 1985).

Finally, this study provides some insights into the complexity of household decision making in eighteenth- and nineteenth-century Daoyi and perhaps by extension (a very wide one to be sure) in China at large. Peasants based their decisions about infanticide on a complex combination of interrelated factors, including economic conditions, household type, position within the household, number and sex of previous children, sex of child, and long-term goals for family size and composition. Food prices were an important factor in this decision-making process, but the equation differed considerably for each individual depending on the other variables. The relative importance of these factors has yet to be determined. We can already appreciate that the study of prices and population ultimately leads to a better understanding of Qing society as well as the Qing economy.

PART TWO
Market Response

SIX

Land Concentration and Income Distribution in Republican China

Loren Brandt and Barbara Sands

> *There is reason to think that in the (last) twenty years . . . occupying ownership has lost ground. . . . The fact of concentration can hardly be questioned. . . . Over a large part of China, tenancy of one kind or another undoubtedly predominates and it appears everywhere to be increasing.*
> RICHARD TAWNEY, *AGRARIAN CHINA* (1938)

These remarks by the British historian Richard Tawney typify much of the thinking both in China and in the West about the growing concentration of landholdings in late nineteenth- and early twentieth-century rural China. Perceptions of widening disparities in land ownership in turn underlie a nearly endless list of critical assessments of the changing distribution of incomes and economic welfare during the same period. Carl Riskin, for example, argues: "Chinese rural society was hardly egalitarian with respect to the distribution of income and wealth: and although characterized by substantial social mobility, the predominant direction for the latter was downward, at least in relative terms."[1] Harry Harding similarly notes: "Though still prone to drought, flood, and plague, China's rural economy could, in most years, also produce the surplus to support one of the world's most advanced urban civilizations and most highly bureaucratic states. But the distribution of that output was increasingly unequal."[2]

Quite often these concerns of widening inequality are accompanied by observations of increasing population pressure and the lack of technological change; indeed, the received economic story of late nineteenth- and early twentieth-century agrarian China is one of increasing immiseration for the populace in general and a relative worsening for the rural poor. Political events in the first half of the twentieth century involving two major regime

---

1. Carl Riskin, *China's Political Economy* (New York, 1986), p. 32.
2. See Harry Harding, *China's Second Revolution: Reform after Mao* (Washington, D.C., 1987), p. 13.

changes have only strengthened these views of China's recent troubled past, if not fired them directly.³

Empirical support for this history is, however, quite limited. This is particularly true for questions concerning the distribution of land ownership and economic welfare. Despite the keen interest in the development literature concerning questions of distribution and their obvious historical relevancy to the case of China, they have been largely neglected.⁴ Moreover, China's distributive record prior to 1949 has rarely been put in any kind of comparative perspective.

The purpose of our paper is to reexamine a number of issues relating to the distribution of land ownership and economic welfare in the pre-1949 economy. Because the historical data on distribution are spotty at best and China itself is so diverse, this paper is largely exploratory, and some of its findings preliminary in nature. Despite these limitations, based on data presently at our disposal, we make the following points.

First, we have failed to find convincing evidence that land ownership became more concentrated during the late nineteenth and early twentieth centuries. Second, even if concentration increased, it cannot be inferred that the increase necessarily heralded increasing immiseration or welfare inequality. A number of alternative processes can underlie increasing concentration in land ownership with opposing interpretations for the behavior of economic welfare. Third, drawing on survey materials for the 1930s, some of them covering all of China and others relating only to a select number of North China villages, we have calculated measures of income distribution that suggest income inequality was much lower in rural early twentieth-century China than has been previously inferred on the basis of data on land distribution alone; in fact, when compared with other low-income countries, China actually appears to be on the moderate side. Moreover, the estimates of income inequality that we have obtained fall within the limits some Chinese officials have recently recommended for their rural sector.

These observations suggest that the current view of China's modern economic history is uncertain at best and yet to be firmly established by contem-

---

3. Philip C. C. Huang, in fact, argues that these imbalances underlay the social and political upheavals of the nineteenth and twentieth centuries. See his *Peasant Economy and Social Change in North China* (Stanford, 1985), p. 293. Exceptions to this conventional wisdom include two books: Thomas G. Rawski, *Economic Growth in Prewar China* (Berkeley and Los Angeles, 1989), and Loren Brandt, *Commercialization and Agricultural Development: Central and Eastern China, 1870–1937* (Cambridge, 1989).

4. C. Robert Roll's unpublished Ph.D. dissertation (Harvard University, 1974) represents the only empirical investigation of income distribution in pre-1949 rural China that we are aware of. Ramon H. Myers, in *The Chinese Peasant Economy: Agricultural Development in Hopei and Shantung, 1890–1949* (Cambridge, Mass., 1970), on the other hand, examines changes in land distribution in North China from the 1890s to the 1940s.

porary quantitative evidence. In the sections below, we take each of the above points in turn and discuss our findings.

INCREASING CONCENTRATION OF LANDHOLDINGS?

Concerns over a rise in the concentration of landholdings and growing tenancy were voiced in China prior to the early twentieth century. During the late Ming and Qing, for example, government officials regularly expressed alarm over what appeared to be an increasing accumulation of land by the wealthy and a decline in the holdings of smaller farm households. These developments are frequently linked to the commercialization and market development of the period.[5] Are data consistent with views of a secular rise in land concentration?

Reasonably good data on land ownership exist for the early twentieth century. On the basis of data compiled by the National Land Commission in 1934 on almost 1.75 million rural households residing in 16 provinces, Table 6.1 presents an estimate of the size distribution of landholdings for rural China.[6] These aggregate data are complemented by many village-level surveys undertaken during the 1920s and 1930s.[7] Both kinds of data confirm what others have long argued—the distribution of land ownership in rural China was highly unequal—and on the surface are consistent with the view that distribution may have been worsening. For the distribution in Table 6.1, the Gini coefficient, a frequently used measure of inequality, is 0.72.[8] The top 1 percent of rural households owned approximately 18 percent of the land;

---

5. See, for example, Yang Yi, "Qingchao qianqi de tudi zhidu," *Shehui yuekan* 7 (1958): 21–26, and Fu Yiling, "Guanyu Mingmo Qingchu Zhongguo nongcun shehui guanxi de xin guji," *Xiamen daxue xuebao* 6 (1959): 57–70.

6. These data suffer from a number of omissions that have been overlooked. These problems are discussed in more detail in Brandt, *Commercialization and Agricultural Development*, chap. 6.

7. The results of 47 surveys carried out between 1931 and 1941 are reported in Chao Kang [Zhao Gang] and Chen Chung-yi [Chen Zhongyi], *Zhongguo tudi zhidu shi* (Taibei, 1982), pp. 234–38. A majority of these are the product of the research efforts of the South Manchurian Railway Company and can be found in Minami Manshū Tetsudō Kabushiki Kaisha, *Mantetsu chōsa geppō*.

8. The Gini coefficient is equal to 1 minus 2 times the area under the Lorenz curve. The Lorenz curve, based on an arrangement of households in ascending order of income, relates the cumulative proportion of households to the cumulative proportion of income received. The Gini coefficient can assume a value between 0 and 1 with a measure of 0 implying a uniform distribution of incomes (or assets) across the population and the measure 1 implying extreme inequality. It can also be interpreted as the expected gain—measured as a percentage of the mean for the population—of a lottery in which each person is allowed to draw an income at random from the population and compare it with his or her own. Thus, when incomes are uniformly distributed, the expected gain is 0, as would be the Gini coefficient. The more concentrated incomes are, the larger the expected gain will be. See Graham Pyatt, "On the Interpretation and Disaggregation of Gini Coefficients," *Economic Journal* 86 (June 1976): 243–55.

TABLE 6.1 Size Distribution of Land Owned by 1.75 Million Rural Households in China, 1930s

Size of Holding (mu)	Average Size (mu)	Percentage of Households (mu)	Percentage of Land Owned (mu)
Landless	0.00	25.80	0.00
0–5	2.65	26.42	6.21
6–10	7.23	17.80	11.42
11–15	12.25	9.77	10.63
16–20	17.42	5.93	9.17
21–30	24.33	6.10	13.17
31–50	38.01	4.60	15.54
51–70	58.59	1.61	8.38
71–100	82.61	0.98	7.16
101–150	120.21	0.54	5.71
151–200	171.97	0.18	2.76
201–300	240.95	0.14	3.17
301–500	378.40	0.08	2.63
501–1,000	671.87	0.01	2.30
1,001+	1,752.60	0.01	1.75
Total	11.04	100.00	100.00

SOURCE: Tudi Weiyuanhui, *Quanguo tudi diaocha baogao gangyao* (Nanjing, 1937), tables 21 and 23.

the top 5 percent owned nearly 39 percent; and the top 10 percent owned around 53 percent. By contrast, slightly more than a quarter of all rural households were landless, and an additional quarter owned less than 5 *mu*. Similar percentages are suggested by the village-level data.

The problem is that comparable information on the previous distribution of landholdings, be it 25 years earlier or 200, presently does not exist. For the Qing we are limited to a handful of observations at the county and village level that simply are too few to generalize about. Table 6.2, nonetheless, documents one such case: the distribution of landholdings in the early eighteenth century for several subdivisions in Huailu County, Hebei, and village-level data in the same county 200 years later.[9] At least for this North China village the distributions are very similar, though, not unexpectedly, average farm size in 1939 was slightly lower than in either 1706 or 1736.

While data on landholdings are also seriously deficient for the late nineteenth century, additional information on such things as the percentage of land that was rented out and the hiring of long-term labor, either or both of which typically accompany an increasing concentration of landholdings,

9. Additional pre-twentieth-century data can be found in Kang Chao, *Man and Land in Chinese History* (Stanford, 1986), chap. 6.

TABLE 6.2 Size Distribution of Land Owned by Households in Huailu County, Hebei, 1706, 1736, and 1939

Size of Holding (mu)	1706 Households (%)	1706 Land (%)	1736 Households (%)	1736 Land (%)	1939 Households (%)	1939 Land (%)
Landless	18.4	0.0	25.5	0.0	19.5	0.0
0–10	37.6	12.4	35.3	11.3	42.2	13.8
11–20	22.7	22.0	18.4	18.4	19.2	18.8
21–30	10.8	17.6	8.3	14.3	7.8	14.2
31–40	4.5	10.5	4.4	10.3	4.9	12.3
41–50	1.8	5.4	2.2	6.8	1.9	6.4
51–100	2.9	12.1	4.2	19.0	3.2	17.8
101–150	0.5	3.7	0.5	5.3	0.3	3.0
151+	0.8	16.4	1.2	15.6	1.0	13.7
Total	100.0	100.0	100.0	100.0	100.0	100.0

SOURCES: The data for 1706 and 1736 are taken from Jiang Taixin, "Qingchu kenhuang zhengce ji diquan fenpei qingkuang de kaocha," *Lishi yanjiu* 5 (1982), pp. 167–82; for 1939, Minami Manshū tetsudō kabushiki kaisha, Kitō nōson jittai chōsahen, *Nōka keizai chōsa hōkoku, Hokushi keizai shiryō*, no. 32, p. 85.

NOTE: The calculations for 1706 are based on data for 29 *jia*, 7,652 households; those for 1736, on data for 4 *jia*, 1,094 households; and those for 1939, on data for 308 households in Macun, Huailu County.

suggests no long-term rise in the half-century between the 1880s and 1930s. Estimates of land rental, for example, reveal that in both periods approximately a third of cultivated acreage was rented, two thirds of which was owned by absentee landlords.[10] We have not uncovered estimates of the number of long-term agricultural laborers for the 1880s—though qualitative evidence suggests their numbers were substantial—but of the 1.75 million rural households surveyed by the National Land Commission in the 1930s, only 1.57 percent were classified as landless, laboring households, that is, households earning a living as long-term contract agricultural laborers.[11] Finally, over the 25-year period between 1912 and 1937, the percentage of households classified as owner-operators failed to decrease, as we might expect had tenancy been on the rise.[12]

On the basis of these very limited data we do not want to push any view very far, especially one suggesting that the degree of concentration of landholdings remained constant for several hundred years. As we will explain

10. Chung-li Chang has estimated that about a third of all land was rented in the 1880s, or roughly the same percentage as in the 1930s. See Chung-li Chang, *The Income of the Chinese Gentry* (Seattle, 1962), p. 145.

11. Tudi Weiyuanhui, *Quanguo tudi diaocha baogao gangyao* (Nanjing, 1937), p. 34.

12. *Nongqing baogao* 5, no. 12 (Dec. 15, 1937): 330.

below, over the long run there were a number of alternative processes simultaneously influencing land concentration; and indeed, it would be odd if these processes offset one another exactly. Nonetheless, the point needs to be made that data presently at out disposal simply cannot support the popularly held view that the high degree of concentration of landholdings observed in the 1930s was the product of several decades (or centuries) of increasing inequality.

Finally, although in the 1930s 10 percent of the population owned over half the farmland in China, can this be considered extreme compared to landholding patterns in other countries? Interestingly, data compiled by Peter H. Lindert suggest that it was not extreme. Concentration in China is markedly less than in Mexico in the 1920s, where 10 percent of the households owned an estimated 64–99 percent of the land and 79 percent were landless, or in Victorian England (excluding London), where 85 percent of all households owned no land and 10 percent owned 82 percent of the land; and it is actually slightly better than that estimated separately for farming households and the entire rural population (whites only) in the United States—certainly not noted for its extreme concentration—in both 1798 and 1860.[13] In many respects, land distribution in China in the 1930s is very similar to that estimated for post-independence India.[14]

HISTORICAL PROCESSES

From the perspective of many observers, land sales by indebted smallholders were the major underlying cause for the increasing concentration of landholdings. Farm households borrowed for a variety of reasons: to obtain working capital, to meet consumption needs in times of emergency, and in some cases to help cover major ceremonial expenses, such as weddings and funerals. To secure these loans, land was frequently pledged as collateral. In still other cases, the rights of land use were ceded to the lender, with the income generated from the land serving as the interest. Once the loan was repaid, rights of land use reverted back to the original owner. This land was commonly referred to as *diandi*.

In many cases, borrowers were unable to service these loans. Han-seng Chen's description is typical: "When a poor peasant in China mortgages his bit of land, he has practically no hope of ever getting it back. Everything conspires against him in his frantic effort to meet the interest charges, and eventually he loses not only the land but also this additional fruit of his

---

13. Peter Lindert, "Who Owned Victorian England? The Debate over Landed Wealth and Inequality," *Agricultural History* 61, no. 4 (1987): 25–51.

14. I. Z. Bhatty, "Inequality and Poverty in Rural India," in *Poverty and Income Distribution in India*, ed. T. N. Srinivasan and P. K. Bardhan (Calcutta, 1974).

labor."[15] These difficulties were invariably attributed to declining economic fortunes caused by high taxes and land rents, local disaster, depressed agricultural conditions, and so forth. If land was used as collateral, it might simply be forfeited; if an asset other than land secured the loan, land still might have to be sold to make repayment. If land-use rights were ceded to the lender, the possibility of redeeming the land in the near future became even more remote.[16] With the loss of their land, small cultivators were invariably forced either to rent back the same land from the new owners or possibly to hire out as wage laborers. This explains the link implicit in the opening quote from Tawney between rising tenancy (or perhaps wage labor) and a growing concentration of landholdings.

Although some small farm households were unquestionably forced to relinquish ownership of their land during times of economic duress, this analysis suffers from several weaknesses; moreover, there are a number of equally compelling explanations for increasing concentration of landholdings and a rise in tenancy with alternative implications for the secular behavior of incomes.[17]

For example, in asserting that the loss of land through debt-sales gives rise to an increasing concentration of land ownership, there is an implicit assumption of who the borrowers and lenders were, the lenders typically being larger landowners/landlords, frequently absentee, the borrowers, on the other hand, being primarily poorer, small farm households that had earlier exhausted all personal financial resources. Although larger landowners were usually heavily involved in the credit market, a detailed examination of land and credit arrangements in three diverse villages in North China reveals that lending activity was more diversified among households than previously believed; in other words, lending activity was not limited to a class of big landowners. In fact, in a majority of those cases involving *diandi*, farm households with less than 30 *mu* were the creditors. The borrowers were frequently larger landowners themselves in need of capital.[18] Data compiled by John Lossing Buck on lending activity in 151 localities in 16 provinces are very

15. Han-seng Chen, *Landlord and Peasant in China* (New York, 1936), p. 95.

16. In some cases, the rights of land use were actually rented back to the original owner. According to Madeleine Zelin, failure to fulfill the rental agreement could mean the total alienation of the original owner from the land. See Zelin, "The Rights of Tenants in Mid-Qing Sichuan," *Journal of Asian Studies* 45, no. 3 (May 1986): 499–526.

17. Please recall, however, our earlier remarks regarding the uncertainty over the intertemporal behavior of land distribution.

18. Based on an examination of contracts involving *diandi* in the surveys cited in n. 33. In the villages we examined, the amount of land that villagers had obtained the farming rights to through *diandi* exceeded the amount of land that they had ceded the rights *to*. The likely explanation for this is that some of the former was owned by absentee landlords or perhaps village members who had migrated yet wanted to retain some claim to village resources should they decide to return.

consistent with the village-level data for North China: for only 8 percent of all loans were landlords and other wealthy households cited as the source of credit. Much more important were relatives and neighbors.[19]

Observations such as these make generalizations about the relationship between forced land sales and increasing concentration difficult without much more careful examination of credit and land markets in rural China. Moreover, even if it is true that land ownership was increasingly concentrated, this does not necessarily mean that income became more concentrated as well. John R. Shepherd has recently pointed out that there are alternative historical processes capable of simultaneously generating an increasing concentration of landholdings and a rise in tenancy which do not necessarily imply increasing immiseration of the rural poor.[20] These include an expansion in cultivated area through investment by wealthy households in land reclamation, migration of landless households into such areas because of better economic opportunities, and shifts in forms of landlord farm management. These processes could operate during periods of economic growth and expansion just as well as in times of economic decline. More generally, a rise in real wages and an increase in labor's share of national income could offset the influence on income distribution of any increased concentration of landholdings.

Each process can be adduced for many parts of China. Between the seventeenth and nineteenth centuries, for example, the increase in the demand for rice in the Lower Yangzi drew the capital of wealthy landowners into land reclamation projects in the Dongting Lake area of Hunan. Immigrant households supplied much of the labor for reclaiming and later for tenanting this land.[21] This process contributed to a relatively high degree of land concentration and tenancy in the area, which persisted into the 1930s.[22] Similar kinds of investments occurred in the Jiangnan area and in some of the more commercialized areas of the North China Plain. During the last half of the Qing, cultivated area increased by roughly half, much of it through investments such as these.[23]

19. John L. Buck, *Land Utilization in China: Statistical Volume* (Chicago, 1937), p. 404. If the loans extended by landlords and other wealthy households were larger than average, they may have been more important than their percentage of the total number of loans otherwise suggests.

20. John R. Shepherd, "Rethinking Tenancy: Spatial and Temporal Variation in Land Ownership Concentration in Late Imperial and Republican China," *Comparative Studies in Society and History* 30.3 (July 1988): 403–31.

21. See Peter C. Perdue, *Exhausting the Earth* (Cambridge, Mass., 1987).

22. According to the National Land Commission survey, 47.8 percent of cultivated area in Hunan was rented. The high degree of land rental and estimates of the concentration of cultivated holdings provided in Table 6.3 suggest a highly concentrated land ownership.

23. By the early twentieth century, if not before, much of the potential for expanding cultivated area in China proper (excluding Manchuria) had been exhausted. In eastern Jiangsu, however, an estimated 5 million to 6 million *mu* of land in abandoned salt farms (or a 25 percent

There was also migration, most notably in the eighteenth century into Sichuan, in the mid-to-late nineteenth century into highly fertile areas of the Lower Yangzi depopulated by the Taiping Rebellion, and in the twentieth century into Manchuria.[24] In each case, individuals or entire households moved into these areas to take advantage of better economic opportunities. Even without land exchanging hands, migration under these conditions can lead to an increasing concentration of landholdings (because of an increase in the number of landless households) and a rise in tenancy in the area experiencing the in-migration.[25] In fact, one observes a higher degree of concentration of land ownership in Manchuria for the early twentieth century than in other parts of China.[26]

The historical role of these alternative processes throughout much of China points to the shortcomings in many earlier interpretations of land concentration and tenancy in the early twentieth century. The concentration of landholdings cannot simply be viewed as the cumulative product of a single process. Rather, the degree of concentration observed in a locality at any given time needs to be seen as the legacy of several, possibly interrelated, economic/historical processes including migration, reclamation, and commercialization as well as forced land sales that may or may not have been weakened over time by other forces operating on the rural economy.[27]

---

increase over existing cultivated area in eastern Jiangsu) was reclaimed for agricultural use. In these counties we typically find a relatively high degree of tenancy. Information on tenancy and the landholdings of land reclamation companies in the area can be found in the Ministry of Industry survey of Jiangsu for 1933. See Zhongguo Shiyebu, Guoji Maoyiju, *Zhongguo shiye zhi: Jiangsu sheng* (Shanghai, 1933), pp. 231–32.

24. On the migration to Manchuria, see Thomas R. Gottschang, "Economic Change, Disasters, and Migration: The Historical Case of Manchuria," *Economic Development and Cultural Change* 35.3 (Apr. 1987): 461–90.

25. A possible reduction in concentration in the area experiencing the out-migration may have kept inequality, in the aggregate, from worsening.

26. For a sample of villages settled after the turn of the century, Myers has found an average Gini coefficient for landholdings equal to 0.86. This is 15–20 percent higher than the average for the 47 villages cited in n. 7. See Ramon H. Myers, "Socioeconomic Change in Villages of Manchuria during the Qing and Republican Periods: Some Preliminary Findings," *Modern Asian Studies* 10, no. 4 (1976): 591–620. Interestingly, the Gini coefficient for villages settled before the turn of the century is not markedly less than for those settled afterward, thus suggesting the legacy of the initial pattern of settlement.

27. One of these other forces we have in mind here is family division. Since Adam Smith, there has been a presumption that over the course of several generations family division helps to reduce the inequality of landholdings. Lavely and Wong argue that this need not be the case and demonstrate how the impact of partible succession on land concentration is influenced by both inter- and intra-landclass differences in reproductivity. See William Lavely and R. Bin Wong, "Family Division, Reproductivity, and Landholding in North China," Research Report no. 84–65, Population Studies Center, University of Michigan, Nov. 1984.

LAND AND INCOME DISTRIBUTION IN RURAL CHINA

Data on land distribution have long served as the key indicator of the degree of economic welfare inequality in the rural sector. Yet how accurate are landholdings as such a measure? There exist data sources from the 1930s that allow estimates of the degree of dispersion of both land and income in the rural sector. These include the survey of the National Land Commission used earlier that provides provincial-level data, and village-level surveys carried out by the South Manchurian Railway Company in North China. Although these data sources differ in a number of key respects and the latter are confined to North China, together they provide new insights into the relationship between the degree of concentration of incomes and land ownership in China's rural sector.

In estimating the degree of inequality in an economy, several important methodological questions immediately arise. These are related to the selection of the measure of economic well-being and the unit of observation (individual, family, income earner, etc.).[28] We have selected income as our measure of well-being, although other indicators of welfare, such as consumption or expenditures, could also be used and might actually be preferable. All the income data are provided at the household level, but rather than rank households by total household income as has frequently been done, we have elected to rank them by per capita household income. In this regard, we are following Simon Kuznets, who concludes in a comparison of the two methods:

> It makes little sense to talk about inequality in the distribution of income among families or households by income per family or household when the underlying units differ so much.... Before any analysis can be undertaken, size distributions of families or households by income per family must be converted to distributions of persons (or consumer equivalents) by size of family or household income per person (or per consumer).[29]

Kuznets's remarks would seem to have a particular relevancy for rural China, where the range of household sizes was enormous. With many households consisting of one or two people and others including up to 20, the potential for differences in measures of inequality based on household rather than individual income or wealth is obviously large.

Before reporting provincial-level estimates of the degree of income in-

---

28. These issues are discussed in R. Albert Berry, "Evidence on Relationships among Alternative Measures of Concentration: A Tool for Analysis of LDC Inequality," *Review of Income and Wealth* 33.4 (Dec. 1987): 417–30.

29. Simon Kuznets, "Demographic Aspects of the Size Distribution of Income: An Exploratory Essay," *Economic Development and Cultural Change* 25, no. 1 (Oct. 1976): 87. See also Gautam Datta and Jacob Meerman, "Household Income or Household Income per Capita in Welfare Comparisons," *Review of Income and Wealth* 26, no. 4 (Dec. 1980): 401–18.

TABLE 6.3 Distribution of Cultivated Holdings and Incomes per Household in China, 1930s

Province	Gini Coefficient		Percentage of Land Rented (mu)
	Cultivated Holdings	Incomes	
Jiangsu	0.570	0.430	42.23
Zhejiang	0.569	0.416	51.31
Anhui	0.538	0.473	52.64
Jiangxi	0.530	0.339	45.10
Hunan	0.601	0.428	47.70
Hubei	0.525	0.393	27.79
Hebei	0.596	0.458	12.89
Shandong	0.541	0.454	12.63
Henan	0.598	0.437	27.27
Shanxi	0.528	0.517	—
Shaanxi	0.562	0.415	16.64
Chahar	0.437	0.648	10.20
Suiyuan	0.641	0.497	8.75
Fujian	0.557	0.345	39.33
Guangdong	0.423	0.335	76.95
Guangxi	0.542	0.445	21.20
Arithmetic average	0.547	0.439	32.84
Entire sample	0.615	0.458	30.73

SOURCE: Tudi weiyuanhui, *Quanguo tudi diaocha baogao gangyao* (Nanjing, 1937), tables 15 and 33.

equality, we first look at the concentration of landholdings reported in the National Land Commission survey. Unfortunately, the summary report of the National Land Commission only provides a distribution of landholdings for the country as a whole (see Table 6.1). Provincial-level information, however, is provided on the distribution of operational holdings, the sum of owned and rented land that a household cultivates. The survey reports the number of households in each of 13 size categories. We have modified these data slightly to include households that did not farm, that is, had no operational holdings, and then calculated Gini coefficients for the new distributions.[30] These estimates are provided in Table 6.3.

It is widely agreed that land rental increased access to land; thus, the distribution of operational holdings should be more equal than the distribu-

---

30. Most computational formulas for the Gini coefficient based on grouped data such as these underestimate the degree of inequality because they ignore intragroup inequality. We have followed Kakwani in correcting for this, using the midpoint of each interval as an estimate of its mean. See Nanak Kakwani, "On the Estimation of Income Inequality from Grouped Observations," *Review of Economic Studies* 43, no. 3 (Oct. 1976): 483–92.

tion of land ownership. This is borne out by the data: the Gini coefficient for landholdings is 0.72, while that for cultivated holdings is 0.62. For a majority of provinces the Gini coefficient for operational holdings is between 0.53 and 0.60.

In general, we expect the difference between the Gini coefficient for owned and cultivated holdings to be positively correlated with the percentage of land rented; in other words, the more land that is rented out to tenants, the lower the concentration of operational holdings associated with any given level of inequality of land ownership. Since the Gini coefficient for operational holdings for the provinces of North China and the Yangzi Valley are almost the same, the greater prevalence of tenancy in the Yangzi Valley than in North China would suggest that land ownership was more widely distributed in North China than in the Yangzi Valley.[31] The Gini coefficient for landholdings in the Yangzi was probably in excess of 0.75, while that for North China was nearer to 0.65.

But what about incomes? Were they just as concentrated as land ownership? Again drawing on data compiled by the National Land Commission, we have calculated Gini coefficients for household incomes in each of the 16 provinces. These estimates also appear in Table 6.3. Without exception, they reveal a degree of income inequality much lower than that suggested by the land data alone. For a majority of the provinces the Gini coefficient for household income was in the vicinity of 0.40–0.45, while the Gini coefficient for the entire sample is 0.46.[32] These estimates are 35 percent to 40 percent lower than what the provincial Gini coefficients for landholdings probably are. Geographically, the degree of income dispersion appears to be slightly below the national average in the more densely populated areas of the Yangzi and South China and modestly higher in the North and Northwest.

DATA FROM NORTH CHINA

In a number of respects these estimates are not entirely satisfactory. On the one hand, it is not exactly clear from the summary report which measure of income was used: net or gross, cash or total (which includes cash income plus income in kind). C. Robert Roll has argued that households probably re-

31. Approximately 45 percent of land was rented out in the Yangzi region, as compared to 15–20 percent in North China. These estimates are based on Tudi Weiyuanhui, *Quanguo tudi diaocha*, pp. 26–27.

32. In calculating the Gini coefficient for the entire sample, we have pooled the data by taking a weighted average of the percentage of households in each province in each size category, using as weights the percentage of the total rural population in each province. Rural population estimates are based on provincial population estimates contained in Dwight H. Perkins, *Agricultural Development in China, 1368–1968* (Chicago, 1969), p. 212, and estimates of the percentage of population classified as rural are provided in Wu Baosan, *Zhongguo guomin suode, 1933 nian* (Shanghai, 1947), 1:151.

ported their total net income, yet the difficulty of accurately estimating all in-kind income and production expenditure cannot be underestimated. On the other hand, if household incomes and family size are systematically related, the distribution of household income may provide a misleading indicator of income distribution on a per capita basis. From a welfare perspective, it is the latter distribution with which we are concerned. Again, we need to know how the distributions for household income and household income on a per capita basis are related to each other.

Three village surveys undertaken by the South Manchurian Railway Company in 1936 in Hebei Province provide important information on each of these questions.[33] These surveys are unique because they enumerate every household in the village and give information on both in-kind and cash incomes and expenditures, thus allowing comprehensive estimates of household incomes.[34] The village data allow us to compare the degree of inequality in the distribution of assets and income by households and in per capita terms. The difference between these two measures of village inequality can be combined with the information in Table 6.3 to make a tentative estimate of the degree of income inequality in rural China at the household level on a per capita basis, which can then be compared with estimates for other low-income countries. These surveys also provide important clues as to why the concentration of incomes observed in Table 6.3 was so much lower than that suggested by the data on land ownership alone.

The three villages selected by the South Manchurian Railway Company for detailed examination include Michang Village in Fengrun County, Dabeiguan in Pinggu County, and Qianlianggezhuang (Lianggezhuang for short) in Changli County. All three were located in northeastern Hebei within 100 kilometers of each other and were less than several hundred kilometers from Tianjin. Despite some obvious similarities, there were marked differences between the villages, some of which are captured in Table 6.4.

Dabeiguan was a relatively poor, only moderately commercialized farming village that was first settled in the early Ming dynasty (1368–1644). At the time of the survey it was made up of 98 households and had a total population of 601. Much of its acreage was devoted to food crop production

---

33. See Minami Manshū Tetsudō Kabushiki Kaisha, Kitō Nōson Jittai Chōsahan, *Dainiji kitō nōson jittai chōsa hōkokusho: tōkeihen; Dai ichiban: Heikoku ken; Dai sanban: Hōjun; Dai yonban: Shorei ken* (Dairen, 1937). These surveys are part of an enormous collection of materials on social and economic life in China compiled by the South Manchurian Railway Company during the late 1930s and early 1940s. For an introduction to these materials, see Philip C. C. Huang, *Peasant Economy*.

34. An earlier estimate of the degree of income inequality in a North China village made by Marc Blecher suffers in both regards because it is based on a stratified sample in which larger farms are overrepresented and because household income is measured simply by the gross agricultural output of each household. See Marc Blecher, "Income Distribution in Small Rural Chinese Communities," *China Quarterly* 68 (Dec. 1976): 795–816.

TABLE 6.4 Market Exchange in Three Hebei Villages, 1936

Market Exchange	Michang	Lianggezhuang	Dabeiguan
Percentage of land rented	32.07	49.08	5.09
Hiring-in/out of labor			
Annual basis (no. of laborers)	34/17	8/0	18/11
Monthly basis (no. of months of labor)	10/10	1/0	12/19
Daily basis (no. of days of labor)	807/2,959	561/4,096	342/2,610
Net labor importer (-) or exporter (+) (expressed in terms of labor hired annually)	- 8.04	+ 9.65	+ 3.03
Labor hired as a percentage of total village labor	14.80	5.67	10.12
Number of village members who migrated	37	19	4
Number of households borrowing/lending	49/27	65/47	44/43
Net borrowing (+) or lending (-) (*yuan* per year)	+ 4,185.00	+ 1,267.30	- 3,510.00
Draft animal rental (days)	132	0	10
Percentage of agricultural output marketed	47.00	11.00	13.00
Percentage of self-sufficiency in grain production	69.00	28.00	90.00
Percentage of gross income earned in cash	76.00	69.00	35.00

SOURCE: Based on data contained in Minami Manshū Tetsudō Kabushiki Kaisha, Kitō Nōson Jittai Chōsahan, Dainiji kitō nōson jittai chōsa hōkokusho: tōkeihen. *Dai ichiban: Heikoku ken; Dai sanban: Hōjun; Dai yonban: Shōrei ken* (Dairen, 1937).

NOTE: In calculating the net import or export of labor by each village, we have converted daily labor into monthly at the rate of 24 days equal 1 month, and monthly to annual at the rate of 10 months equal 1 year.

for village consumption, although approximately 15 percent of the total cultivated area was used to grow cotton and sesame primarily for market sale. Slightly less than 15 percent of agricultural output was marketed. Animal husbandry represented an important, but perhaps declining, sideline for some households.[35]

Every household in the village was engaged in agriculture, and all but five actually owned some land. Farms averaged almost 25 *mu*, or 1.67 hectares (15 *mu* equals 1 hectare). Only five percent of the land in the village, however, exchanged hands through the rental market. In contrast, the labor market

35. According to the preface to the survey, population pressure had reportedly begun to crowd out animal husbandry. Some households (the poorer ones) were forced to abandon animal husbandry altogether, whereas others switched to rearing smaller animals.

was very active. Villagers employed substantial amounts of labor from inside and outside the village on an annual and seasonal basis. Villagers also worked outside the village primarily on a daily basis. In this regard, the labor market appears to have been the primary mechanism through which households offset imbalances in resource endowments. On the whole, Dabeiguan was a small net exporter of labor. In all likelihood because of more lucrative opportunities outside the village, Daibeguan was, at the same time, a net lender of capital.

Michang, in contrast, typifies the richer, more highly commercialized villages of North China. It was made up of 114 households and had a total population of 753. Because of its rail links to the region's major urban centers, agriculture had become highly specialized in the course of the early twentieth century. In the process, farm households replaced the cultivation of basic foodgrains, like sorghum and millet, with cash crops, such as cotton, and purchased larger amounts of grain from outside sources. By the mid-1930s more than a third of the cultivated area was in cotton, and almost half of agricultural output was marketed. Commercial fertilizers also began to be widely used and represented a significant expenditure item for almost all farming households.

Although agriculture was the primary source of income in Michang, 15 households were engaged solely in nonagricultural activities. An additional 22 households were engaged in nonfarm sidelines. These activities included peddling, carpentry, food processing, and local government service. Three households reported no income and were classified by surveyors as "beggar households." A total of 19 village members had also migrated (primarily to Tangshan and Tianjin, and mostly as shopkeepers) and, through remittances, represented a key source of income for some households.

Cash-cropping and the commercialization of the local economy substantially increased productivity and the demand for labor.[36] Only a portion of this increase, however, was accommodated by an increase in labor supply from within the village, and Michang looked increasingly outside its boundaries for labor. In the 1930s, Michang was a net importer of labor. This was complemented by a very active land rental market, in which almost a third of all land exchanged hands. Yet most of this exchange was due to villagers cultivating land owned by village outsiders (absentee landlords). Within Michang, households cultivated most of the land they owned. Unlike Dabeiguan, Michang was a net borrower of capital.

Situated on the Bei-Ning Railroad, Lianggezhuang was also a highly commercialized village, although more closely tied to Manchuria than to North

---

36. The annual labor requirement for cotton, for example, was 12 days per *mu*, or double the requirement for grain crops. The demand for marketing and auxiliary services also increased labor demand.

China. With 101 families and a total population of 574, it was slightly smaller than either Michang or Dabeiguan. Through the first three decades of the twentieth century, Manchuria had provided a rapidly expanding market for farm products and employment for some village members. Lianggezhuang's chief agricultural export was pears. Much of the profit from these exports was reportedly reinvested in land, and by the 1930s almost one third of total acreage was in pear orchards.

With the establishment of the puppet state of Manchoukuo in 1932, however, exports and seasonal migration were sharply curtailed. These difficulties were further compounded by a series of poor harvests. In 1936 pear output contributed only one-seventh to the gross value of agricultural output despite representing almost a third of cultivated area. This had profound ramifications for the labor market, for this one crop had formerly absorbed over one half of agricultural household labor and had drawn in much labor from outside the village.[37] As these opportunities dried up, many villagers now sought short-term work in the nearby prefectural capital, and Lianggezhuang actually became a net exporter of labor. Reflecting these difficulties, in 1936 agriculture contributed only 58 percent of total gross village income.

What can we say about the distribution of land and income in these three villages, and how does it compare to the aggregate estimates for Hebei? Table 6.5 reports Gini coefficients for asset holdings (land, draft animals, and labor power) and incomes, both on a household and household per capita basis for each of the three villages. Mean values of each variable are reported in parentheses.[38] In Michang and Lianggezhuang average landholdings were smaller, and land ownership much more concentrated, than in Dabeiguan. The same is also true of household ownership of draft animals. In the two more highly commercialized villages the degree of concentration of landholdings was 20–25 percent higher than in Dabeiguan. The average Gini coefficient for the three villages was 0.70, only slightly higher than the average (0.65) for 32 villages also surveyed in Hebei in 1936.[39] In all three villages, however, land rental helped to equalize access to land among households; this effect is most pronounced in Michang and Lianggezhuang, where a third and a half of the land were leased to tenants, respectively. In Michang, for example, the Gini coefficient for landholdings was 0.75, while that for operational holdings was 0.55; in Lianggezhuang the coefficients were 0.75 and 0.53, respectively. The mean operational holding in Michang was also much larger than the mean landholding because of the substantial

---

37. This was the opinion of the surveyors as expressed in the preface to the survey.

38. Here, and throughout this paper, we apply the term "per capita" to data on landholdings, incomes and other variables that we obtain by dividing household figures for these variables by the number of persons per household.

39. See *Mantetsu chōsa geppō* 18, no. 1 (1939): 39–73 and 18, no. 4 (1939): 21–31.

TABLE 6.5 Asset and Income Distribution in Three Hebei Villages, 1936
(Gini coefficients)

Components of Asset and Income Distribution	Michang	Lianggezhuang	Dabeiguan
Household size	0.30 (6.44)	0.27 (5.29)	0.26 (6.09)
Labor power[a]	0.33 (2.86)	0.32 (2.09)	0.24 (4.11)
Male laborers	0.29 (2.20)	0.33 (1.73)	0.25 (2.13)
Female laborers	0.64 (1.07)	0.64 (0.55)	0.32 (3.22)
Draft animals	0.72 (0.50)	0.81 (0.30)	0.49 (0.80)
Land owned	0.75 (15.30)	0.75 (19.47)	0.58 (23.57)
Land cultivated	0.55 (21.40)	0.53 (15.49)	0.51 (24.87)
Capital borrowed	0.82 (93.91)	0.76 (151.84)	0.76 (49.50)
Capital lent	0.90 (57.20)	0.85 (164.39)	0.77 (85.32)
Net cash income	0.60 (153.81)	0.52 (101.07)	0.60 (37.38)
Net in-kind income	0.46 (98.84)	0.56 (61.40)	0.45 (123.21)
Net income	0.49 (252.65)	0.41 (162.47)	0.44 (160.59)
Net income per capita[b]	0.39 (37.28)	0.35 (32.81)	0.35 (26.36)
Consumption expenditure	0.44 (178.42)	0.35 (139.80)	0.39 (129.91)
Consumption expenditure per capita	0.30 (27.02)	0.29 (29.59)	0.33 (24.62)

NOTES: Village averages are in parentheses. Land is measured in *mu* and incomes and expenditures in *yuan*. Unless otherwise noted, the Gini coefficients are for distributions at the household level.

[a] The number of laboring males plus 0.65 times the number of laboring females in the household.

[b] The reported figures are the average net incomes per capita for all households. Net income per capita for each village (in the order they appear in the table) is 39.23, 30.71, and 26.50.

holdings of absentee landlords. In Lianggezhuang the situation was the exact opposite, because a quarter of the land was rented out to nonvillagers, who were not included in the survey.

Table 6.5 also shows Gini coefficients for household income and household income on a per capita basis.[40] The Gini coefficients for household income are very consistent with the estimate suggested by the National Land Commission data for Hebei. As reported in Table 6.3, the Gini coefficient for the distribution of rural incomes in Hebei was 0.46. We also observe that for two of the three villages net household incomes were much more evenly distributed than cash incomes.

Yet for reasons spelled out above, it is the distribution of household income on a per capita basis that concerns us. And here we observe in every case a much lower degree of inequality on a per capita basis than on a household basis: Michang, 0.488 versus 0.391; Lianggezhuang, 0.409 versus 0.346;

---

40. The details of the income calculations are included in a lengthy appendix available from either author on request.

and Dabeiguan, 0.436 versus 0.349. The average difference between the Gini coefficients is 0.08. If this relationship held throughout the province, it would suggest a Gini coefficient for per capita rural household incomes in Hebei of 0.38, that is, 0.46 − 0.08. We also note that when measured on a per capita basis, the differences in the degree of income inequality between the villages are very small. Moreover, although overall inequality was slightly higher in Michang, average per capita income was also more than a fifth higher than in either of the other villages. With differences in consumption expenditure per capita even smaller, much of the higher income in Michang obviously took the form of higher savings.

Several questions immediately arise: (1) why is the inequality of incomes on a per capita basis much lower than the inequality at the household level? (2) why are household incomes distributed so much more equitably than landholdings? and (3) what diluted the influence of the much higher inequality in landholdings in Michang and Lianggezhuang and produced a dispersion in incomes similar to that observed for Dabeiguan?

Until the recent work of Kuznets, the influence of the size distribution of households on income disparities was neglected. Most estimates of income inequality were calculated using income per household. Since households differ in size, this can provide a very misleading indicator of the degree of dispersion of incomes on a per capita basis. In general, family size and family incomes are highly positively correlated. In the three villages we examined, the households with the highest incomes are usually those with ten or more members. The most obvious reason for this is that larger families typically have more members of working age who can add to the household's income. In China these households were typically extended, multigenerational households that had not recently divided.

If incomes increase more than proportionally with household size, the dispersion of incomes on a per capita basis will actually exceed their dispersion on a per household basis. But this is typically not the case; rather, incomes increase less than proportionally, and family size and per capita incomes are negatively associated. Indeed, some of the poorest households on a per capita basis in these villages are among those identified as having the highest total household incomes. Although it need not always be the case, under such conditions the dispersion of household incomes on a per capita basis can be less than that for total household incomes. This is in fact what we observe for all three villages.[41]

---

41. The tendency for the dispersion of household incomes on a per capita basis to be lower than their dispersion on a household basis appears to be much more common for developing than for developed countries. For a sample of six developing countries (Colombia, India, Malaysia, Nepal, Sri Lanka, and Taiwan), the average difference between the Gini coefficient for household incomes or expenditures and the same measure on a per capita basis was 0.05. The largest difference was observed for Malaysia, where the Gini coefficient for households

The second and third questions concerning the link between land ownership and income earnings benefit from a brief examination of what we mean by income. Conceptually, income can be thought of as a stream of earnings generated by all factors of production owned by an individual or household (current technology defining what is and is not a factor of production). In a primarily agrarian economy, the key factors of production are land, labor, and capital (the last including such things as farm implements and draft animals). Letting H, L, and K represent these three factors, and r, w, and t their returns, for household i, income, Y, is figured by the equation

$$Y^i = r^*H^i + w^*L^i + t^*K^i,$$

where H^i, K^i, and L^i denote household i's ownership of land, labor, and capital. A household's income, therefore, is positively related to how much of each factor it owns and to the return to each factor.

Yet where do r, w, and t come from? The returns to the various factors of production depend on the nature of the rural economy—most importantly, existing production technology, factor proportions, and the workings of markets or exchange. If all households had access to the same production technology, but each household simply used the resources that it possessed, r^i, w^i, and t^i would differ among households, with the return to each factor negatively correlated with its relative availability within the household. Exchange alters all this. Allowing households to buy and sell the services of the factors of production frees them from their particular endowments and allows them access to all factors of production within the village. Exchange effectively coordinates all households' demands for and supplies of all factors of production, so that the return to each factor is determined by its relative availability within the village rather than within the household.[42] That is, r, w, and t would be the same across households.

Looking at incomes from this perspective, it becomes clear why many observers thought income distribution within China was highly unequal. For a majority of rural households agriculture was the primary source of income, only modestly supplemented by income from subsidiary activities, such as

---

ranked by incomes was 0.52, whereas that for households ranked on a per capita basis was 0.43. The data also suggest a slightly larger difference between the two measures in rural than in urban areas. These estimates are taken from Pravin Visaria, "Demographic Factors and the Distribution of Income: Some Issues," in International Union for the Scientific Study of Population, *Economic and Demographic Change: Issues for the 1980's* (Helsinki, 1979), 1:289–320; and Berry, "Evidence on Relationships." On the relationship more generally between household size and income distribution, see Simon Kuznets, "Size of Households and Income Disparities," *Research in Population Economics* 3 (1981): 1–40.

42. If factors are mobile, their returns will depend on relative availability within an even wider marketing area, not just availability within the village.

handicrafts. Thus, household incomes in the rural sector were systematically tied to income from agriculture and land ownership. At the same time, farming in China was highly labor-intensive; the land-labor ratio, in fact, was one of the lowest in the world. Modern inputs into agriculture had yet to be introduced in any quantity. As a result, the marginal productivity of labor, the level of rural wages, and the percentage of output captured by labor tended to be low relative to the return to land. A direct result of the limited off-farm opportunities, low relative returns to labor, and high concentration of land ownership was an unequal distribution of rural incomes.[43]

Yet perceptions were that income inequality was becoming more severe. Why? On the one hand, both Chinese and Western observers believed that land ownership had become much more concentrated; on the other hand, they observed a falling land-labor ratio and associated with that a marked decline in wages relative to land rents.[44] This fall was only exacerbated by the imperfectly working factor markets, which prevented households from rationally redistributing factors among themselves.[45] A concurrent decline in off-farm employment opportunities, which small farm households disproportionately relied on, was also perceived to have occurred.[46] What all this seemed to mean was that landowners, who were becoming an even smaller minority, appeared to be capturing an increasing percentage of the net product of the rural sector.

43. This discussion can be formalized through a decomposition of the Gini coefficient for household income. Let G_k ($k = L, H,$ and K in all cases) be the concentration index (or Gini coefficient) for earnings, y_k, from labor, land, and capital, respectively; u be mean total household earnings; u_k be the mean earnings of each factor; s_k be the earnings of each factor as a percentage of total earnings; and C_k be the correlation between y_k and the ranking of Y, total income. G^Y, the concentration index for total incomes, is then equal to

$$G_Y = (1/u) \sum_{\text{all } k} (s_k * C_k * G_k * u_k)$$

A high degree of concentration for income from landholding tends to increase income inequality, as does a high share of income from land. Incomes are also more concentrated the more highly correlated income from land is with income from other factors. In the expression for the concentration index, the correlation of incomes among the factors of production is reflected by C_k. A more even distribution of income from labor and the other factors of production helps to lower income inequality, as does a higher share of labor earnings in total income. If the returns to each factor were roughly constant across households in a village—and there is empirical reason for believing it was in rural China—the concentration index for earnings from each factor would be the same as the index for the factor itself, i.e., the Gini coefficient for earnings from landholdings would be equal to the Gini coefficient for landownership. We will make use of this fact in the discussion that follows.

44. Estimates by Dwight H. Perkins suggest that the land-labor ratio in China proper declined by roughly 15 percent between the 1890s and the 1930s. See *Agricultural Development in China*, pp. 212 and 236.

45. See Philip C. C. Huang, *Peasant Economy*, esp. chaps. 4–12.

46. See, for example, Fan Baichuan, "Zhongguo shougongye zai waiguo zibenzhuyi qinruhou de zaoyu he mingyun," *Lishi yanjiu* 3 (1962): 88–115.

The evidence on land and income distribution presented earlier belies much of this story. To see why, recall that income distribution depends not only on the distribution of land ownership but also on the distribution of the other factors of production in the rural economy, most importantly, labor power and, to a lesser extent, draft animals and other forms of capital. It also depends on the returns to these factors and on the correlation of factor ownership across households. A high correlation of landholdings with ownership of other factors of production would only reinforce the influence of a high concentration of landholdings on incomes. The distributive impact of a high degree of concentration in land ownership could, however, be partly or entirely offset by the effects of more even distribution of ownership for other factors of production, by a rise in the share of total income earned by other factors, or by a weak or inverse correlation between ownership of different productive factors by different households.

In Table 6.5 we observe that labor power (and therefore income from labor) was indeed much more evenly distributed among households than was land. The Gini coefficients for labor power per household were 0.33, 0.32, and 0.24, for Michang, Lianggezhuang, and Dabeiguan, respectively. Draft animal ownership, on the other hand, was about as unequally distributed as landholdings in the three villages.

Yet the strength of this influence clearly depends on the portion of output that labor captures. If labor power is evenly distributed among households, but the portion of output going to labor is relatively small, the equalizing effect would itself be modest. In rural North China, land captured about half of agricultural output, labor a third, and the remainder represented the return to draft animals and other forms of farm capital.[47] These estimates are misleading, however, because agriculture was not the only source of income. In all three villages there were a variety of sidelines that offered subsidiary sources of incomes that primarily represented returns to labor. Our calculations, based on the three village surveys, show that land rents (including rents attributed to owner-operated farm land as well as cash or in-kind payments by tenants to landlords) amounted to about a third of total village income, while labor incomes accounted for more than half of all income.

Intervillage differences along these same lines helped to diminish the influence of the much higher concentration of landholdings on incomes in Michang and Lianggezhuang. In Michang, land rents averaged between 4 and 5 *yuan* per *mu*, while a long-term laborer could expect to earn 45–50 *yuan* in cash, plus an in-kind component of perhaps equal value. In Dabeiguan, by contrast, land rents were modestly less, at 3–3.50 *yuan* per *mu*, but wages paid long-term agricultural laborers were only about half the rate in Michang. In

---

47. These estimates are taken from Loren Brandt, "Farm Household Behavior, Factor Markets, and the Distributive Consequences of Commercialization in Early Twentieth-Century China," *Journal of Economic History* 47.3 (September 1987): 731.

Lianggezhuang, land rents averaged even less, between 2 and 2.50 *yuan* per *mu*, while wages (cash component only) paid long-term agricultural laborers were 30–35 *yuan*. The same relationship is reflected in output shares; the share of agricultural output going to land in Michang and Lianggezhuang was roughly 40 percent, while in Dabeiguan it exceeded 50 percent.[48] The significantly higher return to labor relative to land in both Michang and Lianggezhuang helped to reduce the influence of a more concentrated land ownership in these villages and produce a degree of income inequality not much different from that in Dabeiguan.

Nonagricultural activities and remittances played a similar role. In both Michang and Lianggezhuang, 40 households were engaged in nonagricultural activities either as a sideline or on a full-time basis.[49] From both villages there was also substantial out-migration—37 household members from Michang, and 19 from Lianggezhuang had migrated—and the outmigrants in turn typically remitted a healthy portion of their earnings back to the villages. The higher the percentage of income generated from nonagricultural sources and received in the form of remittances, the weaker the influence of land concentration on the overall dispersion of incomes. In Lianggezhuang, nonagricultural activities and remittances produced 42 percent of gross household income, while in Michang they amounted to 17.4 percent; in Dabeiguan they totaled only 6.1 percent.

Finally, Table 6.6 reveals that the correlation between land ownership and the other factors of production was also much weaker in Michang and Lianggezhuang than in Dabeiguan. The same is also true for the relationship between labor power and draft animal ownership. While factor ownership was positively correlated, the probability that a household with substantial landholdings simultaneously had more than average labor power and draft animals was significantly lower in either Michang or Lianggezhuang than in Dabeiguan. This partially reflects the higher degree of specialization in the local economy of the first two. As a result, even though land was distributed more unequally in Michang and Lianggezhuang than in Dabeiguan, the

---

48. Average land rents were computed from detailed land contract information provided by the survey. Land's share was then calculated by dividing average land rent by average output per unit of land.

49. The percentage of households in Michang and Lianggezhuang engaged in nonagricultural activity on a full-time basis (3.5 percent and 7.4 percent, respectively) was low compared to that in other North China villages. The average for 30 villages examined by the South Manchurian Railway Company was 13.7 percent. In a number of localities, 20 percent or more of households was classified solely as nonagricultural. These include Macun in Huailu County, 21.8 percent; Zhongliangshan in Changli County, 26.8 percent; Huzhang in Ninghe County, 31.2 percent; and Dongjiao, located just outside Shijiazhuang, 46.8 percent (see Huang, *Peasant Economy*, pp. 314–20). In a sample of 22 villages in southern Manchuria, 16 percent of all labor (not households) was classified as nonagricultural; see Kokumuin Jitsugyōbu Rinji Sangyō Chōsakyoku, *Kōtoku gannendo nōson jittai chōsa*, 4 vols. (Changchun, 1936).

TABLE 6.6 Correlations of Factor Holdings by Households
in Three Hebei Villages, 1936
(Pearson's r)

Factors of Production	Draft Animal Ownership	Landholdings	Female Agricultural Labor
Landholdings			
Lianggezhuang	0.10		
Debeiguan	0.80[a]		
Michang	0.55[a]		
Labor power			
Lianggezhuang	0.32[a]	-0.03	
Debeiguan	0.57[a]	0.61[a]	
Michang	0.38[a]	0.49[b]	
Male agricultural labor			
Lianggezhuang			0.32[a]
Debeiguan			0.49[a]
Michang			0.54[a]

NOTE: Labor power is measured in adult male equivalents.
[a] Statistically significant at 1 percent.
[b] Statistically significant at 10 percent.

superior market access and non-farm employment opportunities available to residents of Michang and Lianggezhuang produced distributive outcomes that displayed no more inequality than we observe in Dabeiguan.

These calculations show, then, that the distribution of landholdings can be a very misleading indicator of the degree of income inequality in the rural economy. There is no direct line of causality running from higher concentration of landholdings to a higher concentration of income. What is true for several villages at a single time is probably true for a single village over a long period of time. Unfortunately, we do not have earlier data on distribution for these villages, and so the origins of the higher concentration of landholdings in Michang and Lianggezhuang remain a bit of a mystery. Nevertheless, even if landownership in the latter two villages became more concentrated, no widening of income differentials can be inferred.

INCOME DISTRIBUTION IN CHINA
IN A COMPARATIVE PERSPECTIVE

If household-level data for our small sample of North China villages are an accurate indication of the difference between the Gini coefficient for household incomes and household incomes on a per capita basis in other parts of the country—the Gini coefficient for the rural sector as a whole was probably in the vicinity of 0.38.[50] What tentative conclusions can we draw about the degree of inequality in the rural sector and China more generally on the basis of these data? In other words, how does the distribution of incomes in China compare with that in other low-income countries? Are there reasons to believe that incomes in rural China were exceptionally unequal? Given recent suggestions in the People's Republic of China that the degree of rural inequality, as measured by the Gini coefficient, be controlled within 0.30 to 0.40, perhaps not.[51]

Although much more work is required before these questions can be answered exhaustively, some comments are in order. Ideally, we would like to compare the distribution of income observed for China with that estimated for other low-income countries in the 1930s. Short of this, we would like to compare our estimate with contemporary estimates for low-income countries similar in key respects to the China of the 1930s. India is an obvious candidate. Comparisons such as these are hampered by data limitations, however.

On the one hand, estimates of the degree of dispersion of rural incomes are almost always for households rather than households on a per capita basis. As we argued earlier, the latter is the preferred basis for measuring the distribution of economic welfare. Unless one is willing to assume that the influence of the size distribution of households on income distribution is constant over time and space, comparisons on a household basis can be misleading.

With this caveat in mind, in Table 6.7 we report Gini coefficients for rural household incomes in several Asian countries. And here we observe a degree of dispersion very similar to that estimated for China. Only in the case of Taiwan, which after World War II benefited from an income-leveling land reform, is it consistently markedly lower. Moreover, for nine of the 16 provinces that we provide estimates for (see Table 6.3), the degree of concentration compares even more favorably. In light of this finding, it seems highly unlikely that inequality was rising over time; if it was, extrapolation would imply a degree of concentration of incomes before the turn of the century that would be considered exceptionally low by international standards.

50. This estimate was obtained by subtracting the average difference between the Gini coefficient for household incomes and household incomes on a per capita basis for the three Hebei villages from the Gini coefficient for the pooled sample in Table 6.3. One indication that in the aggregate household incomes on a per capita basis were more evenly distributed than household incomes is that cultivated area per household on a per capita basis was more evenly distributed than cultivated area per household. This is reflected in data provided by Buck on the size distribution of farms. The fact that Buck oversampled larger farms is not a point here. While the largest farms were almost 20 times larger than the smallest, on a per capita basis the difference was only one third of this. The same is true for data on land ownership. These relationships also hold separately for each of the eight regions Buck surveyed. See Buck, *Land Utilization in China: Statistical Volume*, pp. 289, 291, 300.

51. "Nongcun you meiyou liangji fenbu?" *Banyuetan* 22 (1987): 20–21.

TABLE 6.7 Distribution of Household Incomes in Selected Low-Income Countries
(Gini coefficients)

Country	Rural Sector		Urban and Rural Sectors
	Income per Household as a Whole	Income for Household per Capita	Income for Household per Capita
Brazil			
1968			0.424
Colombia			
1974			0.461
India			
1961–62	0.410		
1964–65	0.350		
1967–68	0.460		
1968–69	0.430	0.397	
Malaysia			
1957	0.421		
1970	0.464		0.428
Philippines			
1961	0.397		
1965	0.423		
1971	0.462		
Singapore			
1966	0.447		
1975	0.436		
Taiwan			
1972	0.344		
1975	0.363		
Thailand			
1962–63	0.361		
1968–69	0.381		
1971–73	0.466		

SOURCES: For all countries except India, estimates of rural sector inequality are taken from *Income Distribution by Sectors and Overtime in East and Southeast Asian Countries,* Harry Oshima and Toshiyuki Mizoguchi, eds. (Quezon and Tokyo, 1978). The estimates for India are taken from I. Z. Bhatty, "Inequality and Poverty in Rural India," in *Poverty and Income Distribution in India,* T. N. Srinivasan and P. K. Bardhan, eds. (Calcutta, 1974). Remaining estimates are taken from R. Albert Berry, "Evidence on Relationships Among Alternative Measures on Concentration: A Tool for Analysis of LDC Inequality," *Review of Income and Wealth* 43.3 (October 1987), pp. 483–92.

On the other hand, the few estimates that we have for the dispersion of household incomes on a per capita basis are for the rural and urban sectors combined, while our estimate for China is for the rural sector alone. This is not as great a problem as at first it might seem. In the 1930s, the rural sector—the focus of the National Land Commission survey—constituted between 85 percent and 90 percent of the entire population. The urban sector, although growing at a rate of 2–3 percent per annum, was still very small. The critical question is, how does the addition of data for household incomes in the expanding urban sector influence our overall assessment of income distribution in the Chinese economy? Is there any reason to believe that the distribution for the entire economy differs markedly from that for the rural sector alone?

It was once widely believed that income distribution tends to worsen initially with the growth of the modern/urban sector. Kuznets cites two primary reasons for this belief: (1) a tendency to pay substantially higher wages in the modern/urban sector than in the rural sector and (2) an increasing concentration of capital in the modern/urban sector.[52] More recent work on a host of countries casts some doubt on this relationship. Nevertheless, for China Kuznets' hypothesis would seem to imply that incomes were more concentrated nationally than they were in the rural sector.

Data on the distribution of incomes in the urban sector presently do not exist. Nonetheless, it seems to us that any upward revision to the estimates obtained separately for the rural sector would actually be relatively modest. Despite the absolute doubling of China's urban population in the early twentieth century, it still amounted to no more than 10–15 percent of the total. As for incomes, it is important to remember here the small size of China's modern sector, almost all of which was located in the cities. Estimates by Ta-chung Liu and Kung-chia Yeh suggest that even as late as the mid-1930s the modern sector constituted no more than 6–8 percent of the gross domestic product.[53] Because agriculture's contribution to total GDP was two thirds and rural households earned an additional 20–25 percent of their income from nonfarm sources, the percentage of national income going to the urban population could not have been much more than 20 percent and was probably slightly less.[54] Moreover, an examination of budgetary surveys for

---

52. Simon Kuznets, "Economic Growth and Income Inequality," *American Economic Review* 45 (Mar. 1955): 1–28.

53. Ta-chung Liu and Kung-chia Yeh, *The Economy of the Chinese Mainland* (Princeton, 1965), p. 66.

54. Assuming that 10 percent of income from agriculture went to absentee landlords residing in urban areas (based on the assumptions that 35 percent of land was rented, 60 percent by absentee landlords, and that rental payments constituted 45 percent of output on rented land), then 60 percent of total gross domestic product would have been going to rural households in the form of income from farming. If we add to this the income earned by farming households from

working-class households in such cities as Shanghai, Wuxi, and Tianjin reveals a level of per capita income very similar to that observed for the rural sector.[55] This is consistent with empirical work of Thomas B. Wiens, who found that "despite considerable regional variation in the monetary wage levels of farm laborers and industrial workers in various industries... nationally... farm wages appear to be slightly below the level of wages of the least skilled urban occupations, as might be expected."[56]

Although examples can be provided of accumulation of great wealth by some Chinese families, the above considerations lead us to believe that the Gini coefficient for household incomes on a per capita basis for all of China was probably not much in excess of 0.40. How does this compare to that for other countries? In Table 6.7, we report estimates of the Gini coefficients for the distribution of household incomes on a per capita basis for several countries. The sample is small, but the degree of concentration of incomes in China does not appear to be high by comparison.

Finally, what can we say about the concentration of incomes and landholdings in the aggregate? Excluding the holdings of absentee landlords, the Gini coefficient for rural landholdings was 0.72. Making allowances for these landholdings by assuming an average holding of 100 *mu* suggests a Gini coefficient for rural landholdings in the vicinity of 0.80. This, of course, excludes urban landholdings, which, by all indications, were even more concentrated, implying a still higher degree of concentration. Compared to the Gini coefficient for incomes, it becomes obvious that even in a primarily agrarian economy like China's, the link between land concentration and income distribution is tenuous at best.

SUMMARY

In this paper we have reexamined the links between land concentration and income distribution in rural China. From our perspective, much of the conventional wisdom regarding distribution in late nineteenth- and early

---

nonagricultural activities—estimated by Buck to have been approximately 15 percent of total household income—plus the income earned by the 10–15 percent of the rural population classified as nonagricultural (under the assumption that their average incomes equaled that of the farming population), the percentage of total income going to the urban sector would have been roughly $1 - \{((0.90*0.67) / 0.85) / 0.125\} = 0.165$, or 16.5 percent. With slightly in excess of 10 percent of the population classified as urban, the ratio of average urban-to-rural incomes would have been approximately 1.5 to 1.

55. See Bureau of Social Affairs, City Government of Shanghai, *Shanghaishi gongren shenghuo chengdu* (Shanghai, 1934); Bureau of Statistics, Ministry of Industry, *Wuxi gongren shenghuofei ji qi zhishu* (Nanjing, 1935); H. N. Feng, "An Enquiry into the Family Budget of Handicraftsmen in Tientsin, 1927–28," *Quarterly Journal of Economics and Statistics* 1, no. 3 (Sept. 1932).

56. Thomas B. Wiens, "The Microeconomics of Peasant Economy: China, 1920–40" (Ph.D. diss., Harvard University, 1973), p. 169.

twentieth-century China is badly in need of reexamination. Certainly on the basis of the exploratory examination we have carried out, the views of Tawney and many other observers now seem very difficult to sustain. The many questions that do remain can only be answered through more detailed empirical work of the kind we have attempted here.

Income distribution in rural China has always been a highly charged issue. Perhaps inevitably, views on the subject are difficult to divorce from individual perceptions of the events leading up to and including the 1949 Communist takeover. Yet to say that incomes were no more concentrated—perhaps even less so—than they were in other low-income countries is not, of course, to deny that there was extreme poverty in China or that the number of people living on the margin of subsistence might have possibly increased during the early twentieth century. Given that between the 1890s and 1930s the Chinese population expanded by almost 125 million, an increase in the absolute number of poverty-stricken people can be reconciled almost as easily with the view that incomes became less concentrated as it can be with the view that income distribution worsened. Nonetheless, once we free ourselves from the established paradigm of a secular worsening of inequality and begin to entertain notions of more complicated behavior for land and income distribution, it will be easier to analyze objectively the long-term evolution of the Chinese economy, including the post-1949 changes in the rural sector.

SEVEN

Farming, Sericulture, and Peasant Rationality in Wuxi County in the Early Twentieth Century

Lynda S. Bell

Peasant decision making is a subject of interest to a wide range of social science theorists as well as policy planners. A compelling reason for this interest is that in the third world, improving the productive capacity of the rural sector is an important component of development. Not only is a larger food supply necessary to support a growing population of industrial workers, but peasants must have improved standards of living so that they can transform themselves into investors and consumers to support fledgling industry. Therefore, understanding how and why peasants decide production and resource-allocation issues has become an important theme in economic decision theory.

Within this context, there has been a debate about whether or not peasants behave rationally. For example, Samuel Popkin has argued vehemently in favor of the idea, stating that peasants constantly take risks to improve their profit-making potential. This is a purist approach to the issue of rationality, and makes no concessions to other circumstances that may affect the peasant's decision-making processes.[1] However, many economists who study peasant economies have come to accept a slightly modified view of peasant rationality. Rather than seeing peasants as pure profit maximizers, they observe that even when markets are well developed and functioning

---

1. Samuel Popkin, *The Rational Peasant: The Political Economy of Rural Society in Vietnam* (Berkeley and Los Angeles, 1979). Popkin argues specifically against James C. Scott, *The Moral Economy of the Peasant: Rebellion and Subsistence in Southeast Asia* (New Haven, 1976). Scott claimed that peasants operate according to the principle of safety first and that patron-client ties figure prominently in peasants' efforts to avoid risk. Scott's work was influenced by the earlier social theorist Karl Polanyi, who made the important point that social institutions other than the marketplace greatly affect peasant decision making in precapitalist societies. See Scott; Polanyi, *The Great Transformation* (New York, 1944).

smoothly, peasants often lack the education and information necessary to take full advantage of them. Moreover, peasants also face the constraints of environment, low land-labor ratios, adverse land tenure relationships, and low levels of technological development.[2]

Under these circumstances, the concerns of most peasants involve not only profit maximization but also the satisfaction of the immediate consumption demands of all household members. To accomplish this second goal, peasants often work at many sorts of supplementary tasks in addition to their principal crop-producing activity, a strategy that spreads risk and provides additional household income. Perhaps the best way to describe this behavior in the language of economics is to say that peasant families act simultaneously as both profit-maximizing producers, or firms, and income-maximizing consumers. Consequently, individual peasant households sometimes display behavior that in their role as producers could be considered irrational, since their supplementary activities often bring far fewer returns per unit of labor than prevailing market wages in agriculture. However, if there are a number of institutional and environmental constraints at work and satisfaction of basic consumption needs can be fulfilled in no other way, adopting such behavior helps to maximize the total real and future income of the family as a whole and becomes a consumer-specific form of economic rationality.

As described here, my analysis builds on the work of A. V. Chayanov and of Philip Huang, who uses Chayanov's arguments to elaborate a model of China's long-term development. Because Huang believes that one of the principal characteristics of China's economy in the late imperial period was diminishing returns to labor, he calls his model "economic involution," or alternatively, "involutionary growth," terms meant to convey the importance of increasing labor intensification and the propensity for per capita incomes to stagnate even as total output increased. Although I cannot fully address here all the issues raised by the concept of involution, I should note that I follow both Chayanov and Huang in my analysis of peasant decision making.[3]

---

2. Michael Lipton, "The Theory of the Optimizing Peasant," *Journal of Development Studies* 4, no. 3 (April 1968): 327–51.

3. A. V. Chayanov's main works are *Peasant Farm Organization* and "On the Theory of Noncapitalist Economic Systems," both translated and edited by Daniel Thorner, Basile Kerblay, and R. E. F. Smith, in *A. V. Chayanov on the Theory of the Peasant Economy* (Homewood, Ill., 1966). For an excellent summary of Chayanov's arguments, see Mark Harrison, "Chayanov and the Economics of the Russian Peasantry," *Journal of Peasant Studies* 2.4 (July 1975): 389–417. Philip C. C. Huang has written two books, *The Peasant Economy and Social Change in North China* (Stanford, 1985) and *The Peasant Family and Rural Development in the Yangzi Delta, 1350–1988* (Stanford, 1990) advancing his argument on involution. I will discuss the pros and cons of Huang's concept of involution at much greater length in a book manuscript now in preparation.

Specifically, I use Chayanov's idea that the producer-consumer dualism of peasant households affects their approach to both labor allocation and marketing activity. In my view, however, this dualism did not prevent some Chinese peasants from introducing innovative production techniques or from achieving higher levels of consumption; for this reason, the term *involution* used by Huang to describe the late imperial economy may be misleading, seeming to connote an inevitable process of universal, inward-looking decline. Nevertheless, I do share Huang's view that the producer-consumer dualism of peasant households precluded substantial gains in material welfare for the vast majority of Chinese peasants by the early twentieth century. Under conditions of declining land-labor ratios coupled with little technological change, most Chinese peasants approached markets as vehicles to improve their short-term consumption needs and found no leeway to pursue the expanded circulation and accumulation of capital that could have led to innovative long-term investment.

In this chapter, I will present early twentieth-century evidence from the Lower Yangzi county of Wuxi that supports this producer-consumer view of peasant rationality. I shall show that Wuxi peasants engaged in sericulture as a form of supplementary-income-earning activity under conditions of extensive commercialization, dense population, and unfavorable land-labor ratios. Cash-cropping in mulberry has often been analyzed as a way that some rural districts increased their wealth in the early twentieth century, and I do not dispute that Wuxi was one of China's most rapidly developing counties at that time. I shall also show, however, that most peasants who produced mulberries and raised silkworms in Wuxi did so out of economic necessity, that the income per labor day earned from those activities was far smaller than for rice/wheat farming, and that it was difficult to make improvements in silk production overall as long as relatively poor peasant households were responsible for innovations in sericulture technique. For these reasons, although peasants in Wuxi behaved quite rationally, they had trouble contributing to long-term plans of silk industry leaders for the improvement of silk quality and became an important obstacle to long-term silk industry growth.

QING TRENDS IN COMMERCIALIZATION AND DEMOGRAPHIC GROWTH

To understand the dynamics of farming and sericulture in Wuxi in the early twentieth century, it is useful to explore trends already under way in Wuxi's local economy. Situated in the heart of the Lower Yangzi regional core, Wuxi had been experiencing a long process of commercial growth and population increase for at least two centuries before 1900.[4] This prior experience set the stage for the rapid spread of sericulture as a supplementary income-earning activity among Wuxi peasants.

The dynamics of Qing period commercialization in Wuxi had two parts. First of all, Wuxi became an important rice-marketing center from the Qianlong period (1736–95) onward. Second, Wuxi peasants became heavily involved in cotton cloth production and marketing to supplement the income-earning capacity of their households. I shall explore these two forms of commercial activity in turn.

During the early eighteenth century, Wuxi was well on its way to becoming a major center of rice trade and transport within the Lower Yangzi region.[5] By the early Qianlong years, areas to the west and south of Wuxi, in Anhui and Jiangxi provinces, were experiencing grain surpluses, while areas to the southeast of Wuxi, in Jiangsu and Zhejiang provinces, were evolving as a grain-deficit region because of escalating population growth, arable land becoming fully occupied, and regional urbanization.[6] Under these conditions, Wuxi's strategic position on the Grand Canal, just south of its confluence with the Yangzi, and on the northeast bank of Lake Tai, an important transport link to northern Zhejiang, made the county a place where large-scale grain shipping, storage, and marketing began to take place.[7]

At this point, state policy was also a dynamic factor, as Wuxi became an important concentration point in central China for the collection of tribute grain (*caoliang*) before it was sent via the Grand Canal northward to Beijing. This had two consequences. First of all, as surcharges on tribute grain mounted and certain portions of the total tax were converted to cash equivalents, officials responsible for these levies increasingly collected them in cash.

---

4. The term "Lower Yangzi regional core" is derived from G. William Skinner's influential work on economic "macroregions" in China as they developed in the late imperial period. The Lower Yangzi macroregion encompassed parts of Jiangsu, Zhejiang, and Anhui provinces and was one of China's richest agricultural areas from the tenth century onward. The "regional core" centered on the highly commercialized and densely populated area extending from the Shanghai-Ningbo coastal region inland to the area straddling the Jiangsu-Zhejiang-Anhui border. For a more detailed discussion of China's macroregions, see G. William Skinner, ed., *The City in Late Imperial China* (Stanford, 1977).

5. I am indebted to Zhou Guangyuan of the Institute of Economics, Chinese Academy of Social Sciences, Beijing, for help in locating several sources dealing with eighteenth-century trends and in developing an overall picture of Wuxi's early patterns in commercialization and demographic growth.

6. Shehui Jingji Yanjiusuo, *Wuxi mishi diaocha* (Shanghai, 1935), preface, pp. 1–2; Dwight H. Perkins, *Agricultural Development in China, 1368–1968* (Chicago, 1969), pp. 140–51.

7. Sun Jingzhi et al., *Economic Geography of the East China Region (Shanghai, Kiangsu, Anhwei, Chekiang)*, published in Chinese, Nov. 1959, citation from the English translation by JPRS (Washington, D.C., 1961), pp. 4, 98; Wuxi Difangzhi Bianji Weiyuanhui, ed., *Wuxi gushixuan* (Wuxi, 1959), pp. 36–40.

They then purchased grain to meet the portion of the total tax still demanded in kind by the central government in Beijing. Thus, rice circulated ever more freely as a commodity for purchase and sale in various central China locales, and Wuxi emerged as a leading center for this activity.[8] Second, the development of an extensive regional shipping network also proceeded at a faster pace as tribute grain came toward the Grand Canal via adjacent river routes from the eight central provinces responsible for providing it. Strategically placed at a regional transport hub, Wuxi took full advantage of this situation.[9]

As commercial opportunities increased, so too did population. Estimating the precise rate of population growth in the eighteenth century is difficult because of China's methods of enumeration. In a study of Chinese population from the Ming dynasty through the mid-twentieth century, Ping-ti Ho explains that the prevailing system of population reporting in Qing times was based on the *ding*, a unit of taxation that originally referred to all adult males of working age. As is typical for the era, the only existing population figure for Wuxi in the early eighteenth century is a gazetteer report of 142,509 *ding* in 1726.[10] Ho also points out that during the eighteenth century, the *ding* figures no longer bore any relation to the number of adult males in a given population, but rather had evolved over the two centuries or so of their usage into pure fiscal units corresponding only to a locale's total tax liability. On the basis of extensive examination and evaluation of such figures, Ho concludes that the *ding* represented "substantially less than one-half" the real population.[11]

By the late eighteenth century, population reporting was beginning to correspond to reality more closely. Earlier in the century, the Kangxi emperor introduced a series of tax reforms referred to as *tanding rudi* or *tanding rumu*, literally, "spreading the *ding* into the land," with the intention of eliminating the *ding* system of tax accounting and instituting a tax based purely on land ownership at a permanent fixed rate.[12] These reforms spread slowly, however, and were only brought to fruition by the Qianlong emperor in the mid 1770s, with decrees that permanently ended the *ding* assessment and called for an annual accounting of true population figures and real grain

---

8. Harold C. Hinton, *The Grain Tribute System of China (1845–1911)* (Cambridge, Mass., 1956), pp. 1–15.

9. The eight provinces responsible for tribute grain payments were Shandong, Henan, Anhui, Jiangsu, Zhejiang, Jiangxi, Hubei, and Hunan. See Hinton, *Grain Tribute System*, p. 7. On Wuxi's role as a transport and marketing center in this process, see Shehui Jingji Yanjiusuo, *Wuxi mishi diaocha*, preface, 1–2.

10. *Wuxi-Jinkui xianzhi* (A gazetteer of Wuxi and Jinkui counties), 1881 edition, 8:5.

11. Ping-ti Ho, *Studies on the Population of China, 1368–1959* (Cambridge, 1959), p. 35.

12. I am grateful to Chen Qiguang of the Institute of Economics in Beijing for explaining Kangxi's reforms that began in 1712; Ping-ti Ho also discusses the reforms in *Studies*, p. 25.

output.[13] The effect of imperial reforms on population enumeration in Wuxi was that the revised *ding* figures reported for 1795 totaled 566,217, a closer measure of the true number of males within the county.[14]

To derive population figures and to calculate a rate of demographic growth for Wuxi, I follow Ho's guidelines for the early eighteenth century and the suggestions of Chinese population expert Liang Fangzhong that male *ding* figures for Lower Yangzi region around the turn of the nineteenth century were approximately 53 percent of the total population.[15] Therefore, I consider the 1726 *ding* figure to have been only around 30 percent of the real population, a rough estimate to achieve Ho's description of the *ding* as being "substantially less than one-half" the population, to arrive at an approximate population of 475,030; and following Liang, I take the 1795 *ding* figure to be 53 percent of the total, for an estimated population in that year of 1,068,334. This translates into an annual rate of population growth of 1.2 percent for the period 1726 to 1795.[16] For China as a whole, Ho has estimated the rate of annual increase to have been 0.9 percent during this period.[17] It is also useful to compare my calculations with Dwight H. Perkins's estimate that population doubled in Jiangsu from the mid-eighteenth century into the early nineteenth, a rate of increase that corresponds roughly to his national-level estimate that the country reached an all-time high in population, increasing from 200–250 million in 1750 to 400 million by the early years of the nineteenth century. When translated into an annual rate of population growth, Perkins's figures produce estimates very similar to Ho's, from 0.8–0.9 percent. Because of Wuxi's special conditions of rapid commercialization and the development of rural industry, it is possible that population there grew more quickly than either Ho's or Perkins's estimate suggests. But for lack of better population data for the early eighteenth century, it seems impossible for the moment to provide any more accurate calculations than these.[18]

13. Ping-ti Ho, *Studies*, pp. 47–48.
14. *Wuxi-Jinkui xianzhi*, 8:5–6.
15. Liang Fangzhong, *Zhongguo lidai hukou, tiandi, tianfu tongji* (China's dynastic statistics on household population, land, and land taxes) (Shanghai, 1980), pp. 440–41. Liang's figures are for Songjiang prefecture immediately to the east of Wuxi.
16. Calculations follow George W. Barclay, *Techniques of Population Analysis* (New York, 1958), pp. 28–33, for continuous population growth.
17. Ping-ti Ho, *Studies*, p. 64.
18. Perkins, *Agricultural Development*, pp. 202–9. On trying to answer why Wuxi's annual rate of population growth may have been higher during the eighteenth century, studies of demographic growth conducted for various European locales offer intriguing hypotheses. The work of Franklin F. Mendels on Flanders in the eighteenth century, for example, argues that rapid commercialization and the development of rural industry altered nuptiality patterns—people married earlier because they could afford to—thus accelerating the regional rate of population growth (*Industrialization and Population in Eighteenth-Century Flanders* [New York, 1981]). Historians

In any case, the rate of growth of Wuxi's population is not as important to the argument at hand as the degree of population density that Wuxi experienced by the end of the eighteenth century. In the 1790s, when figures on population and land had become far more reliable, Wuxi had only 1.3 *mu* of arable land per capita, just 0.1 hectare, or slightly more than one sixth of an acre.[19] At the same time, as Perkins has demonstrated, there were no radically new developments occurring in agricultural technology during this period that would have led to substantial gains in grain output.[20] Therefore, to comprehend how peasants in densely populated regions such as Wuxi continued to support themselves, we must turn to an exploration of trends in subsidiary activities designed to raise the potential earning power of the peasant household.

Significantly, it was also during the eighteenth century that gazetteer reports for Wuxi began to note the importance of *mianbu* or *huabu*, handicraft cotton cloth, which Wuxi peasants produced in order to secure additional grain supplies. A 1752 gazetteer explains how these exchange relationships operated among Wuxi peasant households:

> Of five counties in Changzhou prefecture, Wuxi is the only one that does not cultivate cotton of its own; yet cotton cloth is even more important here than in the other counties. Wuxi peasants get only enough grain from their fields for three winter months' consumption. After they pay their rents, they hull the rice that is left, put some in bins, and take the rest to pawnshops to redeem their clothing. In the early spring, entire households spin and weave, making cloth to exchange for rice to eat because by then, not a single grain of their own is left. When spring planting is underway in the fifth month, they take their winter clothing back to the pawnshops in order to get more rice to eat.... In the

---

of Qing China have been interested in testing such theories for various regions of China, but the reconstruction of the demographic data is a formidable task due to the problems in population enumeration that I have discussed here. Ongoing work by James Lee, R. Bin Wong, and William Lavely promises to shed future light on China's unresolved demographic issues.

19. Land per capita is calculated from a population figure estimated from the *ding* statistics for 1795 in *Wuxi-Jinkui xianzhi*, 8:5–6, and land statistics for the mid 1770s in *Wuxi-Jinkui xianzhi*, 9:1 and 10:1.

20. Perkins, chaps. 3, 4. Perkins's main argument is that for China as a whole during the fourteenth through the twentieth centuries, grain output rose steadily, but mainly through the better use of "traditional" technology—the opening of new lands, the use of better and more extensive irrigation techniques, the introduction of double-cropping to new areas, and the use of a few new crops such as sorghum, sweet potatoes, and corn. Twentieth-century surveys show that no double-cropping of rice was attempted in Wuxi (although another form of double-cropping was achieved through planting a winter crop of wheat, which was treated as a cash crop) and that early-ripening varieties of rice were rarely used. As I shall argue below, the preferred method of supporting a burgeoning population in Wuxi seems to have been for peasants to develop various methods to earn cash income to purchase rice imported from surrounding areas.

autumn, with the slightest rainfall the sound of looms permeates the villages once again and the peasants take their cloth [to market] to exchange it for rice to eat. Although there are sometimes bad crop years in Wuxi, as long as other places have good cotton harvests, our peasants have no great difficulties.[21]

From this passage, we can see that by the middle of the eighteenth century, Wuxi peasants had developed a complex pattern of cotton spinning and weaving, pawning of clothing items made of cotton, selling of cotton cloth, and rice buying. As commercialization proceeded and population grew, it was important for peasant families to develop methods that would adequately support their consumption demands. Although it is difficult to document the process of peasant decision making more precisely for the eighteenth century (I shall be more exact with twentieth-century data), it is likely that household labor was used more effectively by combining cotton spinning and weaving with the regular farming enterprise. Especially important was that the labor of women and children could be tapped and also that spinning and weaving could proceed during the slack agricultural periods of late fall, winter, and early spring. Even though peasants had to use relatively scarce rice resources immediately after the harvest to redeem their winter clothing and to acquire cotton, operating in this fashion must have meant that the income-earning potential of the family as a whole, or, stated another way, the "total product" of their labor, was raised. With an active and growing rice market within the county, the possibility that peasant demand for grain could be satisfied by rice imported from other areas helped to promote this particular pattern of agrarian development.[22]

With this brief sketch of Qing period commercialization in Wuxi, I shall turn now to a discussion of changing conditions in the late nineteenth century. I shall argue that the large-scale undertaking of sericulture by Wuxi peasants at this time should be seen not only as an adaptation to the new market demand for Chinese raw silk but also as a continuation of seeking ways of supplementing household income through diversification.

SERICULTURE AFTER THE TAIPING REBELLION

Sericulture became an attractive option for Wuxi peasants around 1870 because of two converging sets of circumstances: the "opening" of Shanghai by the British as a result of the Opium War and subsequent developments in the international silk market, and the chance for peasants to make innovative

---

21. *Xi-Jin shi xiaolu* (A brief record of what is known about Wuxi and Jinkui counties) (Wuxi, 1752), 1:6–7.

22. Further discussion of these developments in *Xi-Jin shi xiaolu*, 1:8, refers to the rice purchased by peasant households in Wuxi as *kemi*, literally "guest rice," meaning that this rice was coming into the county from other areas.

adaptations in their patterns of subsidiary activity following the devastation of central China in the Taiping period. I shall begin this discussion with the international situation.

In the 1840s, Shanghai became a port open to foreign trade, and an international community of foreign businessmen and Chinese merchants began to congregate there. Among the foreigners were men interested in promoting the development of machine-based spinning of silk yarn and its export to expanding silk markets in both Europe and the United States. The first modern steam-operated silk filatures, plants where this yarn was processed, were built in Shanghai in the early 1860s, with capital and equipment provided by European investors.[23] A chronic problem plagued these early filatures, however. A marketing network to secure cocoons for filatures had not yet been established in rural areas adjacent to Shanghai. Moreover, silk filatures faced an uphill battle in establishing such a network, because they were thrown into direct competition for cocoons with well-entrenched production and marketing networks for handicraft silk products. For lack of adequate cocoon supplies, all of Shanghai's early filatures had great difficulties remaining open.[24]

Meanwhile, just to the west of Shanghai, a domestic war of great intensity was building. In 1861, the Taiping rebels made their way to Nanjing, and a four-year period of intense warfare within the immediate environs ensued. The consequences of this war for many rural areas were devastating. Peasants and landlords alike fled the region, while many tens of thousands who stayed behind died as a result of the fighting. After the Taiping defeat in 1865, the area was badly in need of resettlement and restoration to its full productive capacity.[25]

Because of these converging circumstances, the time was now ripe for peasants in Wuxi to act. As the Taiping period ended and peasants migrated to the area, they converted portions of former paddy land to mulberry fields and began to raise cocoons each spring for sale to newly developing Shanghai filatures. Although data for this period are insufficient to determine the precise start-up costs of these activities, we do know that members of elite society in Wuxi often encouraged this switch to sericulture. In some cases, gentry

23. Yin Liangying, *Zhongguo canye shi* (A history of Chinese sericulture) (Nanjing, 1931), p. 12; E-tu Zen Sun, "Sericulture and Silk Textile Production in Ch'ing [Qing] China," in W. E. Willmott, ed., *Economic Organization in Chinese Society* (Stanford, 1972), pp. 103–4; Lillian M. Li, *China's Silk Trade: Traditional Industry in the Modern World* (Cambridge, 1981), p. 164.

24. Yin Liangying, *Zhongguo canye shi*, p. 12; Wuxi Difangzhi Bianji Weiyuanhui, ed., *Wuxi gushixuan*, p. 41. For an extended discussion of the competition for cocoons between producers of handicraft silk and the new steam-powered filatures in Shanghai, see Lynda S. Bell, "Merchants, Peasants, and the State: The Organization and Politics of Chinese Silk Production, Wuxi County, 1870–1937" (Los Angeles, 1985), chap. 2.

25. Li Wenzhi, "Lun Qingdai houqi Jiang-Zhe-Wan sansheng yuan Taiping Tianguo zhanlingqu tudi guanxi de bianhua," *Lishi yanjiu* 6 (Dec. 15, 1981): 82–86.

members bore the initial costs of mulberry purchase and early dissemination of sericulture technique. Undoubtedly, they did this in the hope that they could attract new tenants to their land with the promise of substantial cash earnings.[26] From this point onward, sericulture replaced cotton cloth production as the primary subsidiary activity of peasant households, and Wuxi began to develop as the cocoon-marketing capital of the central China region.[27]

Although ecologically it was possible to raise both mulberries and cocoons in Wuxi, it also became clear as sericulture developed that there were relatively higher risks there than in other locales. Spring weather in Wuxi was not quite as warm as in older sericulture areas closer to the coast and further south, and so Wuxi peasants often experienced seasons in which they lost their silkworm crops entirely to the vagaries of rapidly changing humidity, cool snaps, and the subsequent growth of incurable bacterial infections.[28] Moreover, sericulture in Wuxi was tied directly and solely to the international market for machine-spun raw silk. None of its cocoons entered into the domestic handicraft market, making Wuxi peasants especially vulnerable to drops in the international price of raw silk and the filature closings that inevitably resulted.[29] A kind of boom-bust atmosphere prevailed within the Wuxi cocoon market, and the risks associated with cocoon production in Wuxi were likewise relatively high.[30]

26. Yan Jinqing, ed., *Yan Lianfang yigao* (Wuxi, 1923), 10:9; Gao Jingyue and Yan Xuexi, "Wuxi zuizao de sangyuan,"' *Wuxi xianbao* (Aug. 20, 1980): 4; Zhang Kai, "Mantan lishishang Jiangsu de canye," *Canye keji* 3 (Oct. 1979): 53; Li, *China's Silk Trade*, pp. 131–38.

27. On cocoon marketing in Wuxi, see Bell, "Merchants, Peasants, and the State," chap. 3.

28. "Sican zhaiyao," *Jiangnan shangwu bao* 9 (Apr. 21, 1900), commercial raw materials section, p. 2; and Dierlishi Dang'anguan, file no. 3504, "Liangnianlai bensheng [Zhejiang] canzhong zhizao ji qudi jingguo gaikuang, Minguo ershinian—Minguo ershiernian," p. 4; Sun Guoqiao, "Wuxi zhidao yu yangcan shiye zhi yaodian," *Nongye zhoubao* 1, no. 25 (Oct. 16, 1931): 985; "Wuxi jianshi jianse," *Minguo ribao*, May 21, 1916, sec. 3:10; "Canxun yin yushui guoduo shousun," *Minguo ribao*, May 11, 1921, sec. 3:11; "Wuxi chunjian shoucheng jianse," *Minguo ribao*, June 5, 1921, sec. 2:8.

29. The link between the Wuxi cocoon market and the central China filature industry is treated at length in Bell, "Merchants, Peasants, and the State," chaps. 1 and 3. For the problem of periodic filature closings, see Minami Manshū Tetsudō Kabushiki Kaisha, Shanhai Jimusho Chōsashitsu (hereafter SMR, Shanghai Office), *Mushaku kōgyō jittai chōsa hōkokusho* (Shanghai, 1940), pp. 85–87, 94; *Yinhang zhoubao* 13, no. 34 (Sept. 3, 1929), weekly commerce section, pp. 2–3, and 13, no. 37 (Sept. 24, 1929), weekly commerce section, p. 4; *Gongshang banyuekan* 2, no. 17 (Sept. 1, 1930), legislation section, pp. 4–6; and *Shenbao*, Jan. 19, 1937, sec. 4:14. For filature closings in Wuxi during the depression, see *Gongshang banyuekan* 2, no. 3 (Feb. 1, 1930), commercial news section, p. 16, and 4, no. 19 (Oct. 1, 1932), national economy section, pp. 1–2; He Bingxian, "Minguo ershiyinian Zhongguo gongshangye de huigu," *Gongshang banyuekan* 5, no. 1 (Jan. 1, 1933), articles section, p. 18; and Chūshi Kensetsu Shiryō Seibi Jimusho, ed., *Mushaku kōgyō jijō* (Shanghai, 1941), p. 40.

30. This aspect of the modern silk industry in central China is often referred to in the literature as its speculative nature. See, for example, Wuxi Difangzhi Bianji Weiyuanhui, ed. *Wuxi*

Despite the riskiness of the endeavor, once Wuxi peasants plunged into sericulture, they persisted with great tenacity. Throughout the decades of the late nineteenth and early twentieth centuries, the proportion of land devoted to mulberries climbed steadily in Wuxi, to reach peaks of 20–30 percent in various locales by the early 1920s.[31] And yet in many ways, such a decision on the part of Wuxi peasants remained something of an anomaly. Why did they continue to engage in sericulture, even after it became obvious that serious uncertainties existed both in weather and marketing conditions? Were the profits they reaped in good years enough to offset the possibility that, in bad years, they would lose their cocoon crop entirely? Or were there some other, even more compelling reasons for Wuxi peasants to persist in sericulture?

In the remainder of this chapter, I shall try to answer these questions using detailed survey materials on twentieth-century Wuxi agriculture. As I introduce the world of peasant-household decision making, I shall attempt to relate this discussion to the earlier trends I have described as evolving in Wuxi since the eighteenth century—a high level of commercialization, dense population, and the consequent need for peasants to develop strategies to supplement their income-earning potential through subsidiary household activity.

LAND AND LABOR ALLOCATION IN THREE WUXI VILLAGES

Three villages in Wuxi were surveyed in 1940 by the Shanghai Office of the Japanese South Manchurian Railway Company (SMR), a research organization active in areas of China then occupied by the Japanese government.[32] These villages lay within a one kilometer radius of the market town of Rongxiang *zhen*, approximately eight kilometers from the west gate of Wuxi City.[33] This was a highly commercialized and densely populated area, yet the large majority of households still depended primarily upon rice/wheat agriculture and household-based subsidiary activities, with sericulture the

---

gushixuan, pp. 45–46; Chen Tingfang, "Juyou fengjian de maiban xingzhi de Zhongguo saosiye," in Chen Zhen, et al., eds., *Zhongguo jindai gongyeshi ziliao* (Beijing, 1959–61), 4:113; Zhuang Yaohe, interview with author, Wuxi, May 27, 1980; Chūshi Kensetsu Shiryō Seibi Jimusho, ed., pp. 39–43; and SMR, Shanghai Office, *Mushaku kōgyō jittai chōsa hōkokusho*, pp. 85–87.

31. Lu Guanying, "Jiangsu Wuxixian ershinianlai zhi siye guan," *Nongshang gongbao* 8, no. 1 (Aug. 15, 1921), articles and translations section, p. 45; *Gongshang banyuekan* 2, no. 15 (Aug. 1, 1930), investigation section, p. 3; and SMR, Shanghai Office, *Kōsoshō Mushakuken nōson jittai chōsa hōkokusho* (Shanghai, 1941), p. 11.

32. SMR, Shanghai Office, *Kōsoshō Mushakuken*. For a broader discussion of the research activities of the South Manchurian Railway Company in China, see Philip C. C. Huang, *The Peasant Economy and Social Change in North China* (Stanford, 1985).

33. SMR, Shanghai Office, *Kōsoshō Mushakuken*, pp. 14–15.

most important among these, for the bulk of their yearly incomes. Of the 80 households in these villages, 75 engaged in farming; they constituted the sample with which the Japanese researchers worked.[34]

Although there is some cause for concern as to whether or not the conditions in these villages still reflected economic patterns as they had evolved before the effects of the depression and the Japanese occupation, the researchers themselves were highly sensitive to this issue. They explored available secondary sources on the percentage of land devoted to mulberries before the depression and found estimates ranging from one fifth to one third for various locales.[35] In the survey villages in 1940, 22.5 percent of arable land was devoted to mulberries, a finding within the range of predepression figures.[36] Even though mulberry acreage declined during the years when the depression affected silk prices most severely, that is, from 1930 to 1932, by 1940 peasants were restoring mulberry fields to their former position within the agrarian cropping regime.[37] On the issue of prices for agricultural goods, the researchers reported not only 1939 data but also 1933 data collected in Wuxi by the Nationalist government in an effort to determine effects of inflationary trends caused by the Japanese occupation.[38]

As elsewhere in Wuxi, most families in the Japanese-surveyed villages combined rice/wheat farming with mulberry cultivation and cocoon rearing. Rice was grown once yearly during the summer months. Then, after the fall harvest, peasants pumped their rice paddies dry and planted winter wheat on all or some of the land. Mulberries were planted in "field fashion" in Wuxi. Trees were not grown on embankments between rice fields, as in the older sericulture districts to the south of Wuxi, in Jiangsu and Zhejiang. Rather, a portion of arable land that could have been used for grain cultivation was used instead for mulberry trees. While the trees could be pruned and fertilized in off-peak periods of late fall, winter, and early spring, the first monthlong busy period for mulberries, during which the trees were stripped of their leaves for silkworm feeding, came from late April to late May, coinciding precisely with rice seedling preparation. In June, cocoons were marketed, wheat harvested, and rice seedlings transplanted, giving the peasants no time to recover from their extremely busy monthlong period of silkworm feeding and cocoon raising. Peasants raised a second cocoon crop in summer or, ideally, in early fall, when the mulberry regrowth was fuller. Fall crops

---

34. Ibid., pp. 25–26.
35. Ibid., p. 11.
36. Ibid., table 1, following the text.
37. Ibid., pp. 9–11, 18–19. Figures reported by the SMR research group indicate that about 378,000 *mu* were devoted to mulberry in 1927, 30 percent of all cultivated land in Wuxi. This figure fell steadily until 1932, when only 84,000 *mu* were cropped to mulberries. By the late 1930s, mulberry land was up again to 240,000 *mu*.
38. Ibid., pp. 9–10. I shall also say more about the reconstruction of prices in note 43 below.

first became possible in Wuxi in the late 1910s, with the introduction of refrigeration and delayed incubation of silkworm eggs. The fall round of silkworm raising usually came in late August and ended in mid-September, long before the late October rice harvest. Since late summer/early fall was a less busy time for grain cultivation, this round of cocoon raising was not nearly as taxing for peasant families as in the spring.[39]

To relate data from the Japanese survey to the previous discussion of peasant rationality, let me pose the question I am most interested in exploring: Precisely what did peasant families gain by engaging in this particular work regime? When considering this issue, I found it useful to construct Table 7.1, comparing income, production costs, and labor usage for rice/wheat farming and mulberry culivation combined with silkworm raising.[40] The main point I wish to make with the comparison is that mulberry cultivation with silkworm raising brought slightly higher returns per *mu* than rice/wheat farming (9.25 *yuan* for rice/wheat versus 11.96 *yuan* for cocoons) but fewer returns per labor day (0.27 *yuan* for rice/wheat versus 0.19 *yuan* for cocoons). Moreover, earnings from wage labor in agriculture were also higher, averaging 0.25 *yuan* per labor day.[41] We see a situation, therefore, much like that observed by economists elsewhere—peasants who worked at certain tasks, in this case those of sericulture, for less than optimal returns to labor.[42] Should we conclude from this finding that peasants were "irra-

39. Ibid., pp. 55, 61, 69–70, 72, 74.
40. Table 7.1 originally appeared in Bell, "Merchants, Peasants, and the State," p. 122; most of the data are derived from the SMR survey report. For a full accounting of all the calculations, see "Merchants, Peasants, and the State," pp. 122–24. Philip C. C. Huang (*Peasant Family and Rural Development*, p. 127) has argued that my original calculation for labor days spent in sericulture in this table was too low because I failed to take into account a sufficient number of days for pruning the trees and also the days in the growing cycle of silkworms when they rested. He then adds 28 days to my original estimate of 52 days to come up with a total of 80 days for mulberry cultivation and silkworm raising. I agree with Huang that the days silkworms rested (an additional 11 days for the spring and fall cycles combined) should be added to the total and I have done this in my calculations here. However, I am less sanguine about his decision to add an additional 17 days for pruning the trees. Villagers in neither survey discussed here (for more on the second survey, see the next section) said that they spent a total of 30 days yearly (Huang's estimate) working the mulberry fields; by contrast, they regularly gave a number in the range of five to thirteen days (see Table 7.1 and Table 7.5, labor for mulberry cultivation). What the villagers did say very often when questioned about their work in sericulture is that they spent 30 days in the spring season raising silkworms, an estimate which I interpret to have included *all* the work involved, including the stripping (or "pruning") of the trees to get leaves to feed to their silkworms. What seems to have happened in Huang's method of calculating, therefore, is that he counts the days during the silkworm raising cycles when leaves were stripped from the trees as labor days for both sericulture *and* work in the mulberry fields, to get a total of 80 days rather than my estimate of 63.
41. The figure of 0.25 *yuan* for day labor in agriculture is the average found for central China's rice/wheat region by John Lossing Buck's 1929–33 survey of agricultural conditions throughout China. It is cited in SMR, Shanghai Office, *Kōsoshō Mushakuken*, p. 93.
42. Chayanov, *Peasant Farm Organization*.

TABLE 7.1 Annual Income, Production Costs, and Labor Usage per *Mu* for Rice/Wheat Cultivation and Silkworm Raising in Wuxi County, Jiangsu, 1939

	Summer Rice/ Winter Wheat		Spring/Fall Silkworm Raising	
Income *(yuan)*				
Rice			Spring silkworms	
(1.48 *shi* x 7.00 *yuan*)		10.36	(0.27 *dan* x 42.00 *yuan*)	11.34
Wheat			Fall silkworms	
(0.53 *shi* x 4.50 *yuan*)		2.39	(0.11 *dan* x 42.00 *yuan*)	4.62
Total		12.75	Total	15.96
Production costs *(yuan)*				
Fertilizer		2.00	Fertilizer	2.80
Irrigation		1.50	Irrigation	0.00
			Silkworm egg cards	1.20
Total		3.50	Total	4.00
Net income *(yuan)*				
Income minus production costs		9.25	Income minus production costs	11.96
Labor *(days)*				
Rice		20	Mulberry cultivation	13
Wheat		14	Spring silkworm feeding	30
			Fall silkworm feeding	20
Total		34	Total	63
Net income *(yuan)* per labor day		0.27		0.19

NOTE: All labor day values are rounded to the nearest whole number.

tional"? I would argue that we should not, and at this point, take into careful account the problems of population density and scarcity of other options for earning cash income to understand why peasant families in Wuxi undertook sericulture.[43]

43. In order to dispel doubts that price figures in Table 7.1 may have been atypical and hence relevant only for the postdepression period in Wuxi, I have also computed price figures for a sample of 146 households in Wuxi in 1928 and 1929, selected from the Guoli Zhongyang Yangiuyuan survey. This second survey is explained more fully in the next section. Prices for rice, wheat, and cocoons were all slightly higher in 1928 and 1929 than in 1939, but the crucial comparison of earnings per labor day between rice/wheat farming and cocoon rearing remains valid. In fact, it tips even more dramatically in favor of rice/wheat farming producing higher

First of all, let us consider population issues and average size of farm holdings. Although gazetteer figures indicate that Wuxi lost as much as one half to two thirds of its population during the Taiping period, by the 1920s former levels of population density had been completely restored.[44] The amount of available arable land per capita in Wuxi in 1929 stood at 1.3 *mu*, a figure identical to that reported for the late eighteenth century. This made Wuxi the second most densely populated county within Jiangsu Province.[45] An important by-product of dense population was the small size of peasant farming units. In the SMR-surveyed villages, average farm size was 2.5 *mu*, approximately 0.2 hectare, or slightly more than one-third of an acre. Moreover, no single farm was larger than 7 *mu*, and 72 percent of the farming households owned 3 *mu* or less.[46] Even by the standards of the Lower Yangzi region, where land was fertile and well irrigated and thus capable of supporting larger populations than in many other areas, these were very small farming units.[47]

The small size of farms in Wuxi caused the Japanese researchers to consider carefully what other methods were used to augment family incomes. What they found was a fairly consistent pattern of subsidiary activities undertaken by village households. In terms of income-generating capacity, sericulture was most important, usually accounting for 50 percent or more of a family's cash earnings.[48] There were other important trends under way as

---

returns to labor, with the average being 0.71 *yuan* as opposed to 0.28 *yuan* for cocoons. The even larger margin arises primarily because wheat prices were higher by about 55 percent in 1928–29 than in the postdepression period, while the prices for rice and cocoons were higher by only about 20 percent. Another point worth noting concerning calculations in Table 7.1 is that I have purposely excluded land price as a production cost, because price figures for rice/wheat land and mulberry land were nearly identical. I have confirmed this fact via an analysis of variance test on land prices from the Guoli Zhongyang Yanjiuyuan survey of 1929, which showed no significant difference between prices for the two types of land. Finally, interplanting mulberry with other crops, a strategy that might have lowered land costs for mulberry culture by raising total yield, was rare in Wuxi because local farmers planted their mulberry trees close together, leaving no room for other crops. This is substantiated by the Guoli Zhongyang Yanjiuyuan survey, which demonstrates that other crops such as peas, beans, and potatoes were not grown with mulberries, but rather were raised on small supplemental plots.

44. The estimate of population loss in Wuxi during the Taiping period is calculated from cadastral figures found in *Wuxi-Jinkui xianzhi* 8:6–7. For a more precise accounting of the figures involved, see Bell, "Merchants, Peasants, and the State," p. 84.

45. Chen Huayin, "Jiangsusheng renkou yu yiken tianmu zhi xilian," *Tongji yuebao* 1, no. 3 (May 1929):44–48.

46. SMR, Shanghai Office, *Kōsoshō Mushakuken*, pp. 23, 88.

47. The SMR researchers had already surveyed villages in three other Jiangsu counties, where they found the average size of landholdings to be 6.4 *mu* (Jiading), 5.3 *mu* (Changshu), and 9.6 *mu* (Songjiang). They were quite surprised by the small size of farming units they observed in Wuxi. See SMR, Shanghai Office, *Kōsoshō Mushakuken*, p. 23.

48. SMR, Shanghai Office, *Kōsoshō Mushakuken*, pp. 103–4.

well, with a high proportion of village men working away from home on a permanent basis, often as clerks or factory workers in Shanghai. But their yearly cash incomes were still lower on average than those generated through cocoon sales.[49] Men could also remain in the villages to hire themselves out as agricultural wage labor, but because land was scarce, this was done only at peak seasons among village households as a means of satisfying temporary labor needs. The number of days men could work at such tasks was extremely limited and, in comparison to sericulture, provided only small amounts of supplementary cash income.[50]

Given the constraints of peasant life in Wuxi, it thus appears that sericulture enabled peasants to better meet their subsistence requirements by increasing the total product of their family labor. First of all, sericulture employed women in an occupation that produced relatively higher cash earnings than cotton cloth production. When we compare the daily income from sericulture with that from cotton weaving, we see, on average, that women were able to earn only 0.02 *yuan* per day making cotton cloth versus 0.19 *yuan* from sericulture.[51] In turn, peasants used most of their cash income from sericulture to purchase rice and other items necessary to satisfy immediate household consumption demands. Sixty percent of all cash income was spent on food, and most of the rest went to purchase clothing and other household goods. There is no evidence to suggest that these households had accumulated any substantial savings, and only 0.8 percent of cash income went to productive investments in agriculture.[52] Rent obligations also figured into this picture for many families, putting a further strain on the capacity for self-sufficiency in grain production. Overall, about 25 percent of the land in these villages was rented, and 10 percent of the rice produced yearly went to rent payments.[53]

The issue of what constitutes "survival capacity" for peasant households, or, put another way, their relative level of subsistence, is a highly volatile topic in the literature on peasant decision making. I cannot attempt to give the definitive answer to the question here. But to get at least some sense of the importance of sericulture in Wuxi in assuring what I would call "basic subsistence," I shall consider evidence concerning grain consumption both in China at large and in Wuxi in particular.

In the early 1930s, John Lossing Buck documented yearly adult grain consumption for China as a whole: it ranged from 390 to 952 *jin*. His figures

---

49. Ibid., pp. 99–104.
50. Ibid., pp. 88–95; tables 2 and 3, following the text.
51. The figure for cotton weaving comes from Guoli Zhongyang Yanjiuyuan, selected questionnaires, table 11. The sericulture figure is found in Table 7.1 above.
52. SMR, Shanghai Office, *Kōsoshō Mushakuken*, pp. 122–24; table 15, part 2, following the text.
53. Ibid., pp. 25, 144–47.

include not only the main cereal grains of rice, wheat, and millet but also potatoes, beans, and peas. In many areas of China, these latter three items often made up a large proportion of daily consumption for many peasant households. This could be because of the relative infertility of the land or because rent payments were usually demanded in the highest quality grain a given locale produced, leaving the poorest of local peasant families to consume coarser foodstuffs. Commenting on these figures and comparing them to provincial-level data for the 1950s, Dwight H. Perkins has concluded that about 400 jin of grain per adult per year is a fairly accurate estimate of China's "minimum subsistence" requirements.[54]

In the SMR-surveyed villages in Wuxi, the preferred pattern of grain management and consumption for most households was to preserve as much of the rice they produced themselves as they could for their own use. As we have seen, rent obligations took about 10 percent of the rice produced, so that overall the village households had about 29,550 jin of their total production of 32,833 jin left for consumption purposes. They also purchased rice with cash income from sericulture, wheat sales, and other subsidiary employments, amounting to an additional 32,250 jin. When converted to the average amount of rice consumed yearly, this works out to approximately 824 jin of rice per household. Since the average household size was 4.1 members, this meant an average per capita rice consumption figure of only 201 jin. If we convert this to an adult equivalent for purposes of comparison with Buck's data (using Buck's estimate of 77 adult equivalents for a total population of 100), we arrive at a figure of 261 jin for the yearly rice consumption per adult villager. To come up to the minimum subsistence levels suggested by Perkins, Wuxi peasants supplemented their diets with broad beans and peas, which were both locally grown.[55]

When viewed from this comparative perspective, we find that in terms of quantity of grain consumed, Wuxi villagers were quite near the lower end of the consumption range observed by Buck for China as a whole in the 1930s. Of course, their diet, which had a large proportion of white rice, was of quite high quality by Chinese standards. Relatively speaking, then, just how well off were these peasant households?

It seems fairly clear that as long as the market for Chinese raw silk was doing well, Wuxi peasants would rarely have faced hunger. Moreover, the

---

54. This discussion of "minimum subsistence" is drawn from Perkins, *Agricultural Development*, pp. 14–15, 300–301. In the latter pages, Perkins cites Buck, *Land Utilization in China: Statistical Volume* (Nanking, 1937), at length.

55. SMR, Shanghai Office, *Kōsoshō Mushakuken*, pp. 144–49. The average size of a farming household is found in this same work, table 1 following the text. For Buck's "adult equivalent," see Perkins, *Agricultural Development*, p. 301. According to Guoli Zhongyang Yanjiuyuan, selected questionnaires, table 1, broad beans (*candou*) and peas (*wandou*) were both grown in Wuxi in 1929, broad beans being far more common.

grain they had available to them was of high quality, and they themselves must have felt quite satisfied that these sorts of options were available to them. However, when the market for raw silk was doing poorly, this rather fragile, near-subsistence-level system would have collapsed. To demonstrate this, we can consider what would have happened if all mulberry land within the SMR-surveyed villages had been converted back to rice/wheat farming, and sericulture abandoned. Many families in Wuxi took this option during the worst years of the depression. The additional rice that could have been produced on former mulberry land amounted to only 12,300 *jin*, a figure that falls far short of the 32,250 *jin* that villagers normally purchased.[56] This means that if sericulture had been abandoned, peasant families would have had to find other ways to earn supplementary cash income to continue purchasing grain at their accustomed levels. Options that provided returns comparable to sericulture were not readily available within the village itself and, as we have seen, often meant out-migration for male members of individual farming families.[57]

What I would argue on the basis of these considerations is that in Wuxi by the early twentieth century, sericulture had become a crucial link in a complex system that, in good years, provided moderate levels of subsistence for most farming families. Even though individual workers' earnings were below those to be had through rice/wheat farming, the total product of peasant family labor was raised via sericulture. Peasants tolerated this situation because under conditions of dense population and scarce land, finding ways to better employ peasant women had become essential. Since financial reserves were small or nonexistent and most cash income was spent on food and other basic living expenses, a sudden drop in income caused by falling silk prices would depress living standards for many peasant families in Wuxi and would push some households below basic subsistence requirements.[58]

A FURTHER LOOK AT WUXI VILLAGES

To substantiate this picture of peasant family farming, some additional evidence can be garnered from a second rural survey in Wuxi. This second survey was carried out in the summer of 1929 by Chinese researchers of the Social Science Research Institute of the newly formed Academia Sinica. I

---

56. I have made this calculation from figures on average rice output per *mu* and the number of *mu* currently cropped to mulberry. See "Merchants, Peasants, and the State," pp. 148–49.

57. For a discussion of relative returns to various kinds of subsidiary occupations, see the next section of this paper.

58. I have argued elsewhere that accounts of rural destitution during the 1930s in Wuxi reflect the impact of a collapsing world silk market on a regional economy that had become increasingly dependent on revenues from the production of cocoons and raw silk. See Bell, "Explaining China's Rural Crisis."

will present a more extensive analysis of these materials in a future book manuscript. Here I give only preliminary findings from a small sample of the total number of households surveyed. What is quite useful about these data is that they were collected before the depression, yet they reveal a nearly identical pattern of land and labor usage to that seen in the SMR survey.[59]

When working with this second data set, my first concern has been to compare land and labor productivity in rice/wheat farming with mulberry cultivation and silkworm raising. If my original hypothesis is correct, then we would expect the results of Table 7.1 to be duplicated—namely, that overall cash earnings of the family might be raised via mulberry cultivation and silkworm raising but that labor productivity would be lower. We would also expect to see a preponderance of small peasant family farms operating on small plots, using primarily their own family labor for a combined effort in rice/wheat farming, silkworm raising, and other subsidiary occupations. In order to specify more precisely the significance of the size of farming units, I have also tried to introduce another comparative dimension into the data analysis, that is, between larger and smaller farming units, to see if there were any economies of scale at work and, if so, what size of farm produced the most efficient use of land and labor resources.

I have constructed a set of six tables from a 31-household sample selected from the three villages of Suxiang, Maocun, and Baishuidang.[60] Table 7.2 presents the size distribution of farming units. Although these farms were slightly larger on average than those in the SMR survey, even the very largest farms worked only between 20 and 38.5 *mu*. In fact, in the entire sample of 800 households, only 25 households worked 20 *mu* or more. Where size did seem to make some difference was in the decision of what proportion of farmland would be planted in mulberry. Very small farms sometimes planted all of their land in mulberry, an indication that they may have hoped that a more intensive effort in sericulture would increase their overall earning

---

59. Guoli Zhongyang Yanjiuyuan, selected questionnaires from Suxiang (Beiyanxia Township), Maocun (Kaiyuan Township), and Baishuidang (Yangming Township). In the 1950s and 1960s, the Chinese scholar Zhang Zhiyi was working through these materials; however, during the Cultural Revolution his manuscript was lost. Since that time, the materials have been housed at the Institute of Economics in Beijing. I am grateful to Professor Chen Hansheng, who led the original survey, for telling me that the materials were still at the Institute, and to Professors Dong Fureng and Peng Zeyi for arranging access to them. Shang Lie of the Modern History Section of the Institute also has helped to sort the materials, and Professor Liu Kexiang has helped familiarize me with much of the special terminology used, especially in matters of landholding.

60. I have chosen the 31-household sample using three criteria. First, I have aimed for roughly the same proportions of large, medium, and small farms found in the entire group of 800 survey questionnaires. Secondly, these 31 households came from three ecologically different villages. And finally, these households had no missing data in the categories relevant to the argument I present below.

TABLE 7.2 Land Usage for Rice/Wheat Farming and Mulberry Cultivation in Three Wuxi Villages, 1929

Village, Household ID No., and Size Category[a]	Size of Farm (mu)	Mu per crop			Rice/Wheat Land		Mulberry Land	
		Rice 1[b]	Rice 2[c]	Wheat	No. of Mu	Percentage of Total	No. of Mu	Percentage of Total
Suxiang								
318–M	7.0	5.0	1.0	6.0	6.0	86	1.0	14
322–M	8.8	7.0	0.5	7.5	7.5	85	1.3	15
324–M	6.0	4.0	0.0	4.0	4.0	67	2.0	33
346–M	12.5	10.0	0.5	10.5	10.5	84	2.0	16
316–S	2.0	1.7	0.0	1.7	1.7	85	0.3	15
320–S	4.0	3.0	0.0	3.0	3.0	75	1.0	25
321–S	5.0	3.0	0.0	3.0	3.0	60	2.0	40
334–S	4.3	3.5	0.0	3.5	3.5	81	0.8	19
342–S	3.7	1.7	0.3	2.0	2.0	54	1.7	46
343–S	5.0	3.8	0.2	4.0	4.0	80	1.0	20
Maocun								
361–L	26.5	19.0	1.5	17.5	20.5	77	6.0	23
368–L	20.0[d]	14.0	1.0	12.0	15.0	75	5.0	25
382–L	38.5[d]	27.1	1.1	23.2	28.2	73	10.3	27
352–M	7.0	4.2	0.8	4.0	5.0	71	2.0	29
353–M	8.0	6.0	0.0	5.5	6.0	75	2.0	25
358–M	11.5	8.5	0.5	7.5	9.0	78	2.5	22
359–M	13.0	10.0	0.0	9.0	10.0	77	3.0	23
362–M	12.0	9.5	0.5	9.0	10.0	83	2.0	17
354–S	5.0	3.5	0.5	3.3	4.0	80	1.0	20
357–S	3.0	2.0	0.0	2.0	2.0	67	1.0	33
360–S	1.0	0.0	0.0	0.0	0.0	0	1.0	100
363–S	1.5	0.0	0.0	0.0	0.0	0	1.5	100
366–S	2.7	2.0	0.0	2.0	2.0	74	0.7	26

388–S	1.3	1.0	0.0	1.0	1.0	77	0.3	23
397–S	5.0[d]	0.0	0.0	0.0	0.0	0	5.0	100
Baishuidang								
450–M	6.0	3.6	0.4	4.0	4.0	67	2.0	33
421–S	1.0	0.0	0.0	0.0	0.0	0	1.0	100
444–S	2.4	2.0	0.0	2.0	2.0	83	0.4	17
446–S	1.0	0.0	0.0	0.0	0.0	0	1.0	100
447–S	1.5	1.0	0.0	1.0	1.0	67	0.5	33
448–S	3.1	1.6	0.0	1.6	1.6	52	1.5	48

[a] S, small household, working 0.1–5.0 *mu* of land; M, medium household, working 5.1–19.5 *mu*; L, large household, working 20.0–38.5 *mu*.
[b] *Gengdao*, a short-grained, late-ripening rice.
[c] *Nuodao*, a glutinous rice.
[d] Also rented out land.

TABLE 7.3 Land Productivity in Three Wuxi Villages, 1929

Village, Household ID No., and Size Category[a]	Yields per Mu (jin)				Net Income per Mu (yuan)[b]			
	Rice 1	Rice 2	Wheat	Mulberry	Rice 1	Rice 2	Wheat	Mulberry
Suxiang								
318–M	300.0	255.0	78.0	300	11.50	7.10	4.20	3.00
322–M	280.0	135.0	84.0	1,200	17.30	7.20	4.00	6.00
324–M	210.0	—[c]	28.0	600	17.00	—	1.60	6.00
346–M	280.0	280.0	78.0	1,000	10.41	10.41	3.87	5.00
316–S	238.0	—	70.0	500	8.90	—	3.09	3.50
320–S	272.0	—	84.0	1,000	12.30	—	4.20	5.00
321–S	280.0	—	70.0	800	23.50	—	3.50	4.00
334–S	224.0	—	108.0	800	6.20	—	0.80	4.80
342–S	217.5	217.5	70.0	500	12.50	12.50	3.75	10.00
343–S	290.0	300.0	55.2	700	12.40	12.40	2.40	7.00
Maocun								
361–L	352.0	320.0	140.0	1,500	12.98	19.18	3.24	- 3.50
368–L	387.5	310.0	126.0	1,500	12.73	11.23	5.40	22.00
382–L	288.0	240.0	126.0	900	11.50	10.30	4.39	- 1.50
352–M	384.0	320.0	140.0	700	18.10	20.50	5.50	0.10
353–M	300.0	—	84.0	800	9.37	—	2.28	2.40
358–M	320.0	288.0	140.0	1,000	13.40	18.80	5.50	- 4.00
359–M	288.0	—	112.0	1,300	11.60	—	4.00	- 0.10
362–M	352.0	256.0	168.0	1,000	15.30	18.30	7.50	3.00
354–S	352.0	224.0	112.0	800	16.10	11.70	5.00	2.40
357–S	320.0	—	112.0	1,000	13.25	—	0.00	3.00
360–S	—	—	—	2,000	—	—	—	2.00
363–S	—	—	—	1,500	—	—	—	- 1.50
366–S	180.0	—	70.0	800	7.30	—	3.25	2.00

388–S	240.0	—	140.0	400	12.30	—	5.60	0.30
397–S	—	—	—	1,300	—	—	—	4.10
Baishuidang								
450–M	192.0	160.0	70.0	500	7.30	9.50	3.75	5.00
421–S	—	—	—	600	—	—	—	5.30
444–S	208.0	—	70.0	1,000	9.70	—	3.75	3.00
446–S	—	—	—	500	—	—	—	5.00
447–S	272.0	—	28.0	700	13.70	—	1.50	2.10
448–S	320.0	—	56.0	600	14.30	—	3.00	6.00

[a] S, small household, working 0.1–5.0 *mu* of land; M, medium household, working 5.1–19.5 *mu*; L, large household, working 20.0–38.5 *mu*.
[b] Costs of fertilizer, draft animal usage, and mechanized pumping are subtracted from these amounts.
[c] The symbol "—" means that this household did not raise this crop.

potential despite the riskiness of such a venture. This never happened among medium-size or larger farms.

Table 7.3 looks at yields per *mu* of different types of farmland—a rough measure of land productivity. The results among different-size farms are ambiguous, indicating that economies of scale probably did not apply in this system. Larger farms did not get consistently higher yields per *mu* than small farms in any crop. But what does seem of importance in this table is a higher degree of variance in both physical yields and monetary returns for mulberry cultivation as opposed to rice/wheat farming. Physical returns for Rice 1 for Maocun, for example, varied by roughly a 2 to 1 ratio, whereas physical returns for mulberry varied by 5 to 1. Likewise, financial returns varied by less than 3 to 1 for Rice 1 but varied from −4.00 *yuan* to 22.00 *yuan* for mulberry, a range that included the possibility of negative returns for some households. The reason for the greater variance in financial returns to mulberry can be attributed to at least two factors: the difficult climatic conditions for silkworm raising that prevailed in Wuxi and the vagaries of daily market prices for both cocoons and mulberries. We have seen that Wuxi's springs were cold and damp, often leading to bacterial infection among silkworms and the total destruction of some households' yearly crops. In addition, prices for cocoons and mulberry leaves varied widely from one day to another and also among marketing locations. Both these factors meant that some families spent more fertilizing their mulberry fields and buying silkworm eggs than they were able to earn by selling their cocoon crop.[61] The result was that mulberry cultivation, with its widely varying financial returns, was much riskier than devoting land to a combination of rice and wheat farming.

Tables 7.4, 7.5, 7.6, and 7.7 explore questions of labor usage and labor productivity. Tables 7.4 and 7.5 summarize labor usage. In Table 7.5 we see that the majority of labor days in silkworm raising were performed by household labor, especially that of women.[62] Comparisons among villages are also important. We see in Baishuidang, for example, that all households put more total labor days into mulberry cultivation and cocoon rearing than into rice/

---

61. On daily and hourly fluctuations in cocoon prices see "Jianshi zaxun" [Miscellaneous reports on cocoon markets], *Minguo ribao*, June 4, 1917, sec. 2:7; "Wuxi—shiju bujing zhi shangshi" [Wuxi—markets in chaos], *Minguo ribao*, June 4, 1917, sec. 2:7; and "Zhijie shouhai zhi shangkuang" [Trade experiences immediate adverse effects], *Minguo ribao*, June 5, 1917, sec. 3: 10; on problems in the erratic pricing of mulberry leaves according to widely fluctuating demand, see Wang Xuexiang, "Gaishan sangye maimai jigou zhi guanjian" [My opinions on reforming marketing mechanisms for mulberry leaves], *Zhongguo canci* 2, no. 7 (Jan. 1937): 92–93.

62. In the Suxiang households, there are slightly more labor days in silkworm raising performed by men. This is an unusual aspect of the labor distribution among the ten households sampled here. Calculations for a larger sample of 141 households across 13 villages show that 69 percent of silkworm raising days were performed by household women. See Lynda S. Bell, "Chinese Women and the Value of 'Surplus Labor,'" (Los Angeles, 1990) pp. 12–13.

wheat farming. This suggests that in future work with these data, it will be worth testing intensity of labor effort in sericulture against size of landholdings as well as the availability of other kinds of subsidiary employment in various villages. Each of these factors probably influenced a peasant family's decision to work more intensively at sericulture. If there was too little land or too few opportunities for other outside employment, a family would have no choice but to work more intensively at their sericulture effort.

Table 7.6 examines the composition of family labor units. Three things are striking about this table. First is the number of adult males by size of farm. Small farms almost always had only one adult male, suggesting that division of household property in each generation (*fenjia*) was an important downward leveling force. Second, only the largest farms hired laborers by the year. Since large farms were very rare in Wuxi, this is an indication that the demand for full-time agricultural laborers was quite small. Finally, most farms, regardless of size, hired some day labor. However, as in the villages of the SMR survey, this method was used only to fill temporary labor needs, usually at peak periods of planting and harvesting. The most intensive period came in May and early June, when peasants were tending to delicate rice seedlings, raising silkworms, marketing cocoons, and harvesting winter wheat. Overall, this table shows that with the conjugal family as the principal unit of production, most farms remained quite small and hired additional labor only as short-term labor needs dictated.

Finally, Table 7.7 looks at the important issue of labor productivity. The most conclusive data of the analysis thus far are found in the final column of this table: returns per unit of labor were, as anticipated, almost always lower for mulberry cultivation and silkworm raising than for rice/wheat farming. This duplicates in more precise terms my former analysis of the SMR data, confirming that participation in sericulture raised family income overall even as it lowered labor productivity in terms of net income per labor day for the household as a whole. Thus, as before, I would argue that sericulture was a form of labor intensification in which peasant families engaged to allow their continued survival under conditions of high population density and a relatively low land-labor ratio.

What this analysis has not yet provided is an answer to why sericulture was chosen over other forms of subsidiary work, including factory employment and other handicraft options. It is true, for example, that factory work brought relatively high cash returns. Data from the 1929 survey on factory wages indicate that child female factory workers could earn about 0.10 *yuan* per day while women made 0.40 to 0.50 *yuan* per day. Comparing these sums to those observed for returns to sericulture in the final column of Table 7.7 shows that earnings per day for work in sericulture were often roughly comparable to factory wages but not as reliable, with a great deal of variation possible. Despite the better wage-earning conditions, the survey also indicates

TABLE 7.4 Labor Days in Rice/Wheat Farming in Three Wuxi Villages, 1929

Village, Household ID No., and Size Category[a]	Rice 1		Rice 2		Wheat		Total Labor Days
	Labor Days per Mu	Total Labor Days	Labor Days per Mu	Total Labor Days	Labor Days per Mu	Total Labor Days	
Suxiang							
318–M	20	100	20	20	6	36	156
322–M	15	105	15	8	10	75	188
324–M	25	100	—[b]	—	10	40	140
346–M	6	60	6	3	5	53	116
316–S	20	34	—	—	5	9	43
320–S	18	54	—	—	6	18	72
321–S	13	39	—	—	10	30	69
334–S	29	102	—	—	10	35	137
342–S	10	17	10	3	7	14	34
343–S	8	30	8	2	5	20	52
Maocun							
361–L	10	190	10	15	4	70	275
368–L	10	140	10	10	5	60	210
382–L	12	312	12	13	5	116	440
352–M	12	50	12	10	6	24	84
353–M	10	60	—	—	4	22	82
358–M	12	102	12	6	7	49	157
359–M	12	120	—	—	6	54	174
362–M	12	114	12	6	5	45	165
354–S	12	42	12	6	6	20	68
357–S	12	24	—	—	6	12	36
360–S	—	—	—	—	—	—	—
363–S	—	—	—	—	—	—	—
366–S	10	20	—	—	5	10	30

388–S	12	12	—	—	5	5	17
397–S	—	—	—	—	—	—	—
Baishuidang							
450–M	12	43	12	5	6	24	72
421–S	—	—	—	—	—	—	—
444–S	12	24	—	—	6	12	36
446–S	—	—	—	—	—	—	—
447–S	12	12	—	—	7	7	19
448–S	12	19	—	—	6	10	29

NOTE: All labor day values are rounded to the nearest whole number.

[a] S, small household, working 0.1–5.0 *mu* of land; M, medium household, working 5.1–19.5 *mu*; L, large household, working 20.0–38.5 *mu*.

[b] The symbol "—" means that this household did not raise this crop.

TABLE 7.5 Labor Days in Mulberry Cultivation and Silkworm Raising in Three Wuxi Villages, 1929

Village, Household ID No., and Size Category[a]	Mulberry Cultivation		Silkworm Raising[b]						Total Labor Days
	Labor Days per Mu	Total Labor Days	Spring				Summer/Fall		
			Women F	Men F	Men H	Children F	Women F	Men F	
Suxiang									
318-M	8	8	30	60	15	30	20[c]	—[d]	163
322-M	7	9	30	10	—	—	—	—	49
324-M	11	22	30	20	—	—	—	—	72
346-M	7	14	30	—	9	—	—	—	53
316-S	7	2	30	30	—	—	25[e]	—	87
320-S	5	5	30	24	—	—	30[e]	24[e]	113
321-S	11	22	30	20	11	—	—	—	83
334-S	6	5	30	20	—	10	—	—	65
342-S	5	9	—	60	—	—	—	—	69
343-S	5	5	—	30	—	—	—	—	35
Maocun									
361-L	8	48	90	10	5	—	—	—	168[f]
368-L	8	40	30	—	—	—	30[e]	—	100
382-L	10	103	60	60	15	—	80[g]	60[h]	398[i]
352-M	10	20	40	20	—	—	—	—	80
353-M	12	24	40	20	—	—	—	—	84
358-M	11	28	50	20	15	—	—	—	113
359-M	10	30	40	20	—	—	—	—	90
362-M	8	16	30	15	15	—	—	—	76
354-S	10	10	40	15	—	—	—	—	65
357-S	10	10	40	10	—	—	—	—	60

360–S	12	12	40	20	—	—	—	—	—	72
363–S	10	15	30	30	15	—	—	—	—	90
366–S	8	6	—	—	—	—	—	—	—	6[i]
388–S	8	2	—	—	—	—	—	—	—	2[j]
397–S	12	60	30	—	30	—	—	—	—	120
Baishuidang										
450–M	10	20	30	15	5	—	—	20[e]	10[e]	100
421–S	10	10	30	15	—	—	—	—	—	55
444–S	10	4	30	5	—	—	—	20[e]	—	59
446–S	10	10	40	—	—	—	—	—	—	50
447–S	10	5	30	10	—	—	—	—	—	45
448–S	10	15	30	15	—	—	—	—	—	60

NOTE: All labor day values are rounded to the nearest whole number.

[a] S, small household, working 0.1–5.0 *mu* of land; M, medium household, working 5.1–19.5 *mu*; L, large household, working 20.0–38.5 *mu*.
[b] F, family labor days; H, hired labor days.
[c] These were fall season labor days.
[d] The symbol "—" means that this household had no labor days in this category.
[e] These were summer season labor days.
[f] This total includes 15 days of hired female labor for the spring season (not listed separately).
[g] Forty of these days were in the summer season, 40 in the fall season.
[h] Thirty of these days were in the summer season, 30 in the fall season.
[i] This total includes 10 days of hired male labor in the summer season and 10 days of hired male labor in the fall season (not listed separately).
[j] This household did not raise silkworms; it only cultivated mulberries.

TABLE 7.6 Labor Units in Three Wuxi Villages, 1929

Village, Household ID No., and Size Category[a]	Resident Family Labor (no. of people)				Long-term Hired Labor (no. of people)[b]	Short-term Hired Labor[c] (no. of days)		
	Men	Women	Children	Total		FW	SR	Total
Suxiang								
318–M	2	1	2	5	—[d]	10	15	25
322–M	2	1	1	4	—	—	—	—[e]
324–M	1	1	1	3	—	50	—	50
346–M	2	2	1	5	—	119	9	128
316–S	1	1	0	2	—	—	—	—[e]
320–S	1	1	1	3	—	—	—	—
321–S	1	1	0	2	—	—	11	11
334–S	1	1	1	3	—	—	—	—[e]
342–S	1	1	1	3	—	7	—	7
343–S	1	1	0	2	—	6	—	6
Maocun								
361–L	2	3	2	7	1	50	—	65[f]
368–L	1	1	2	4	1	150	—	150
382–L	2	5	2	9	2	100	—	100
352–M	2	3	0	5	—	15	—	15
353–M	2	1	1	4	1	—	—	—
358–M	3	2	1	6	—	—	—	—
359–M	1	1	1	3	—	—	—	—
362–M	1	2	1	4	—	132	15	147
354–S	2	3	0	5	—	—	—	—
357–S	1	1	0	2	—	12	—	12
360–S	1	1	0	2	—	10	15	25
363–S								

366–S	1	1	0	2	—	—	—
388–S	1	0	0	1	—	—	—
397–S	1	2	1	4	60	30	90
Baishuidang							
450–M	1	1	3	5	25	5	30
421–S	1	1	0	2	10	—	10
444–S	1	1	1	3	—	—	—
446–S	1	1	0	2	—	—	—
447–S	1	1	0	2	—	—	—
448–S	1	2	0	3	—	—	—

[a] S, small household, working 0.1–5.0 *mu* of land; M, medium household, working 5.1–19.5 *mu*; L, large household, working 20.0–38.5 *mu*.
[b] All male.
[c] FW, labor hired to work in the fields, all male; SR, labor hired to raise silkworms, all male.
[d] The symbol "—" means that this household had no labor days in this category.
[e] This household exchanged labor with a neighbor.
[f] This total includes 15 days of hired labor worked by women raising silkworms (not listed separately).

TABLE 7.7 Labor Productivity in Three Wuxi Villages, 1929 (yuan)

Village, Household ID No., and Size Category[a]	Daily Cash Wages to Short-term Hired Labor			Net Income per Labor Day[c]	
	Farm Work[b]	Silkworm Raising Male	Silkworm Raising Female	Rice/Wheat	Mulberry/Silkworms
Suxiang					
318–M	0.33	0.33	—[d]	0.58	−0.15
322–M	—	—	—	0.83	0.98
324–M	0.30	—	—	0.53	0.47
346–M	0.60	0.55	—	1.30	0.81
316–S	—	—	—	0.48	0.12
320–S	—	—	—	0.69	0.16
321–S	—	0.50	—	1.17	0.41
334–S	—	—	—	0.18	0.32
342–S	0.30	—	—	0.96	0.35
343–S	0.50	—	—	1.14	0.37
Maocun					
361–L	0.30	—	0.25	1.21	0.55
368–L	0.26[e]; 0.35	—	—	1.21	1.13
382–L	0.50	—	—	0.96	0.52
352–M	0.33	—	—	1.36	0.42
353–M	—	—	—	0.84	0.42
358–M	—	—	—	1.06	0.64
359–M	—	—	—	0.87	0.54
362–M	0.26[e]; 0.33	0.26[e]	—	1.35	0.73
354–S	—	—	—	1.21	1.04
357–S	—	—	—	0.74	0.38
360–S	0.30; 0.50[f]	—	—	—	0.43

363–S	0.50[f]	0.30	—	—	0.21
366–S	—	—	—	0.70	0.36
388–S	—	—	—	1.05	-1.26
397–S	0.33[f]	0.37	—	—	0.25
Baishuidang					
450–M	0.40	0.40	—	0.63	0.49
421–S	0.30	—	—	—	0.33
444–S	—	—	—	0.75	-0.01
446–S	—	—	—	—	0.41
447–S	—	—	—	0.78	-0.02
448–S	—	—	—	0.96	0.05

[a] S, small household, working 0.1–5.0 *mu* of land; M, medium household, working 5.1–19.5 *mu*; L, large household, working 20.0–38.5 *mu*.
[b] All male.
[c] "Net income" deducts production costs as in Table 7.3.
[d] The symbol "___" means that this household hired no one in this category.
[e] Per day rate for labor hired for monthly wage (*duangong*).
[f] Work in mulberry fields.

that relatively few females were employed in factories in Wuxi in 1929, a situation that may be explained by factors other than cash-earning considerations. When peasant girls and women were sent to factories, their prolonged absence meant that families were deprived of their work in domestic services such as cooking, child-care, and animal tending. For many peasant households, therefore, the loss in female services offset the benefits of a reliable cash wage from factory work. As for the possibility of substituting other cash-earning options within the household setting, compared to sericulture they all brought far fewer returns to labor: only 0.03 *yuan* per day for making hemp rope, 0.02 *yuan* per day for weaving cotton, and 0.03 *yuan* per day for making lace. These meager amounts made such options far less attractive than sericulture as cash-earning alternatives within the household setting.[63]

PEASANT FARMING AND PROBLEMS OF SILK INDUSTRY GROWTH

Given the constraints of environment, demography, and available options for earning cash income, the Wuxi peasant decision for sericulture was entirely rational. At the same time, however, Wuxi peasants did not earn exceptionally high incomes through this route. As they intensified their labor effort in sericulture, they remained fairly close to subsistence-level living conditions, spending most of their cash income to satisfy yearly consumption demands. These facts allow me to comment briefly on the pitfalls of assuming any close relationship between peasant rationality and the potential for new forms of economic growth.

Because sericulture was primarily a method used to augment family income to satisfy immediate consumption demands, little surplus income was available for technical improvements. Although the most modern methods of silkworm breeding were known in Wuxi, the majority of small peasant family farms were not able to introduce them. These techniques included crossbreeding of silkworm egg varieties to strengthen disease resistance; refrigeration of silkworm eggs to allow for more efficient timing of summer and fall cocoon raising; close regulation of temperature during the silkworm-raising process; and use of bacterial disinfectants to protect delicate silkworms in their early stages of growth.[64] Some households had access to improved egg cards via state-supported and privately run egg breederies, but these improved cards had to be purchased by the peasant households. They were rarely given free of charge even on an experimental basis and thus required

---

63. Guoli Zhongyang Yanjiuyuan, selected questionnaires, table 11.
64. For further discussion of problems of silkworm raising and methods of sericulture improvement, see Bell, "Merchants, Peasants, and the State," pp. 49–50, and chap. 4; and Dierlishi Dang'anguan, file no. 3504, "Jiang-Zhe-Wan-Hu qudi canzhong qingxing."

yearly cash outlays that peasant households often did not or could not make.[65] Methods of temperature control and disinfectant use were even more difficult to implement because silkworms were reared within peasant family living quarters. The most efficient way to implement these improved methods would have been to build separate facilities designed especially for silkworm rearing.[66] This option was simply not within the means of most Wuxi peasant households. The results were clear enough: the 1929 survey data from Wuxi show a high rate of yearly cocoon crop failure, with many households routinely losing an entire season's efforts. Moreover, the quality of cocoons remained low compared to rapidly improving Japanese varieties, and the quantity of cocoons needed to make equivalent amounts of raw silk remained high.[67]

Poor raw material supply does not tell the whole story of the problems encountered by China's silk industry. I raise this issue here only to suggest that the purist approach to peasant rationality does not do much to explain the larger developmental issues at stake. Ultimately, a fuller analysis of silk industry growth should also include discussion of capital markets, the behavior of new bourgeois investors, political institutions, and the interrelationships of all such factors to the rural base.[68] To begin such an analysis, a modified understanding of peasant rationality is useful as a first step. We should realize that small peasant family farming in Wuxi, a perfectly rational system of peasant behavior, may have been more of a hindrance than a help to silk industry growth.

65. Guoli Zhongyang Yanjiuyuan, selected questionnaires, table 8, shows only a moderate rate of improved silkworm egg usage in Wuxi in 1929, far less than I believed previously on the basis of information available for the mid-1930s. See Bell, "Merchants, Peasants, and the State," p. 234.

66. When I visited sites of silkworm raising in Wuxi in 1980, I observed that temporary thatched, windowless structures put up within mulberry fields and collectively managed by groups of peasant women were quite efficient for maintaining temperature and draft control. Coal stoves were kept burning inside constantly, and the temperature was carefully monitored. See also Dierlishi Dang'anguan, file no. 3504, "Liangnianlai," p. 4, for a discussion of the construction of silkworm rearing facilities within sericulture experimental stations designed to control drafts and temperature change. A report on a trip by a U.N.-sponsored group to sericulture areas in central China in 1979 also discussed the relative success of collective silkworm-rearing enterprises in maintaining conditions of constant temperature and humidity. See Food and Agriculture Organization of the United Nations, *China: Sericulture. Report on a FAO/UNDP Study Tour to the People's Republic of China, 6 May to 4 June 1979* (Rome, 1980), pp. 38–42.

67. According to personal accounts of former sericulture improvement specialists, it took 6 *dan* of dried cocoons to make 1 *dan* of Chinese raw silk. In Japan, because improved silkworms produced cocoons with fibers of increased length and strength, only 3.5–4·*dan* of dried cocoons were needed during the 1920s to produce 1 *dan* of raw silk. See Bell, "Merchants, Peasants, and the State," p. 217.

68. This fuller analysis will appear in a book now in preparation.

In this chapter, I have provided a long-term view of peasant decision making in Wuxi. By looking at trends in rural development over three centuries, the switch to sericulture in Wuxi can be seen as a product not only of new opportunities brought about through world market integration but also of long-term demographic trends and the development of subsidiary activities to increase the income-earning potential of individual peasant families. Another focus here has been on the internal workings of farm households to understand more precisely what motivates their actions. I have shown that under conditions of a low land-labor ratio and few options for nonfarm employment, peasants were willing to work at sericulture despite the low and unreliable income that it provided. What they gained was a chance to better employ peasant women and increase the income-earning potential of the family as a whole. Although these actions were entirely rational, peasant families in Wuxi worked close to subsistence levels so that surplus earnings for investment were slim. These findings suggest that future studies of Chinese development should take into careful account the evolution of peasant family farming systems in various regions and the nature of their impact on long-term patterns of economic growth.

EIGHT

Women's Work in the Ningbo Area, 1900–1936

Susan Mann

The economy of nineteenth-century Chinese farm households depended on the combined labor of men and women. How did the growth of foreign trade and the rise of industrialization affect women's work? This chapter argues that, in one coastal area, foreign trade and early industrialization increased the importance of women's work in the household economy. However, each woman's access to new sources of income was constrained by class, by locality, by household composition, and by her point in the life cycle.[1]

In the late empire, agricultural treatises and local custom attest to a clear gender division of labor in Chinese peasant households: "men plow, women weave" (*nan geng nü zhi*). This gender division of labor reflected beliefs about women's work that were widely shared in late imperial society. First, Chinese women were supposed to work inside the home; on the eve of industrialization, the bulk of farm labor in China was performed by men.[2] Second,

---

1. The author acknowledges with thanks critical comments from Jon Cohen, Emily Honig, Lillian M. Li, Thomas G. Rawski, G. William Skinner, Richard Sutch, and the anonymous readers. The original research for this chapter was supported by a faculty research grant from the Academic Senate, University of California, Santa Cruz. For invaluable new data collected during a research trip to China in 1988, I am grateful to the Committee on Scholarly Communication with the People's Republic of China, which sponsored the research, and to members of my host institution, the Economics Institute of the Shanghai Academy of Social Sciences, especially Yao Xinrong.

2. Strong taboos on women's going "outside" implied that those who could be seen on the streets or in the fields—working or not—were of questionable reputation or at least of lower-class background. In most parts of China, public opinion held that except at the peak of the harvest season, it was proper for women to stay out of the fields. Extensive evidence is presented in John Lossing Buck, *Land Utilization in China* (Nanking, 1937; repr. New York, 1956), 1:240, 290–92, 307. In an article published in 1935, Luo Qiong quotes a couplet recited in double-crop rice areas: "Men look forward to gathering the grain; women look forward to transplanting the

women's work "inside" and men's work "outside" were seen as complementary and mutually supportive, essential not only to the welfare of the household itself but to the economic health of the entire society as well.[3]

Increased exposure to foreign markets and the advent of industrialization profoundly affected the normative division of labor in the Chinese peasant household, but did not diminish the household's dependence on the combined labor of women and men.[4] In fact, the importance of women's work increased. New markets drew the products of some domestic cottage industry into foreign trade, raising the income women could expect to earn from, say, mat weaving or embroidery. Some women's handicraft industries (notably cotton spinning) did collapse, in some areas, in the face of competition with cheaper manufactured goods. But textile factories and other light industries also offered a new generation of women jobs outside the home.[5]

Studies of early industrialization have drawn conflicting conclusions about its effects on women and their work. On the negative side, for instance, cottage industry may suffer when competing factories produce better quality goods at lower prices.[6] The decline of protoindustry may also be harder on women than on men, because factory competition is keenest in light industries—spinning and weaving—where women make most of their in-

---

seedlings." She observes that for women in these areas, transplanting rice presented one of very few opportunities to venture outside the home. See Luo Qiong, "Zhongguo nongcunzhong de laodong funü," *Funü shenghuo* 1, no. 4 (October 1935): 21.

3. See, for example, Yin Huiyi, "Jing chen nongsang siwu shu," in Wei Yuan, comp., *Huangchao jingshi wenbian* (Preface dated 1826/27, repr. Taibei, 1963), 36:15b.

4. See Gary S. Becker, "A Theory of Marriage," *Journal of Political Economy* 81 (1973): 813–46; 82 (1974): 911–16; and Fredericka Pickford Santos, "The Economics of Marital Status," in Cynthia B. Lloyd, ed., *Sex, Discrimination, and the Division of Labor* (New York, 1975), pp. 244–68. Both stress the impact of changing work opportunities on the gender division of labor within the household.

5. Albert Feuerwerker, "Economic Trends in the Late Ch'ing Empire, 1870–1911," in John K. Fairbank and Kwang-ching Liu, eds., *The Cambridge History of China*, vol. 11, pt 2 (Cambridge, 1980), pp. 15–28. In this respect, China's economic development resembles patterns found in Europe on the eve of industrialization. However, the Chinese case examined here differs from the European case in two important respects: there was no pastoral economy along China's coast, and nuptiality was early and nearly universal for women. In China, as in Europe, access to new markets and the rising importance of putting-out systems played an important role in shifting patterns of women's work. See, e.g., Louise A. Tilly and Joan W. Scott, *Women, Work, and Family* (New York, 1978), and Lindsey Charles and Lorna Duffin, eds., *Women and Work in Pre-Industrial England* (London, 1985). Early industrialization in the Ningbo area is discussed in Yoshinobu Shiba, "Ningbo and Its Hinterland," in G. William Skinner, ed., *The City in Late Imperial China* (Stanford, 1977), pp. 411–13; and Nyok-Ching Tsur, "Forms of Business in the City of Ningpo in China," trans. Peter Schran, *Chinese Sociology and Anthropology* 15, no. 4 (1983).

6. See Hans Medick, "The Proto-Industrial Family Economy," in Peter Kriedte, Hans Medick, and Jurgen Schlumbohn, *Industrialization before Industrialization*, trans. Beate Schempp (London, 1981).

come. New factories may have other negative consequences for peasant women, as their menfolk depart for urban factory jobs, leaving women to assume the full burden of agricultural labor.[7] Finally, even where women enter factories alongside men, they are still likely to be shunted into the lowest-paying, least-skilled jobs, cut off from avenues to upward mobility that new industry provides for men.[8]

But there are ways in which women may benefit from early industrialization. Some studies show that new job opportunities outside the home enable young women to earn money that may contribute toward their dowries, enhance their economic value in the household, or even permit some independence from family authority.[9] A recent analysis has argued, in this vein, that the growth of foreign trade associated with China's early industrialization benefited women by increasing their earning power and their economic value, leading to a rise in the bride-price families were willing to pay.[10] Finally, there is evidence that even the lowest-paying, most arduous factory jobs were more appealing to many young women than the tedium and drudgery of farm work. Combined with the lure of "city lights," so this argument goes, a factory job that offered three meals a day, a bed of one's own, and freedom from parental supervision was better than anything down on the farm.[11]

Clearly, there is no simple or single answer to questions about the impact of industrialization on women's work in the household economy. Nonetheless, this chapter draws some conclusions from data on Chinese women's work in one particular region, the Ningbo area of northeastern Zhejiang

7. See Ester Boserup, *Woman's Role in Economic Development* (New York, 1970).

8. For a critical discussion of these issues, see Nancy Folbre, "Cleaning House: New Perspectives on Households and Economic Development," *Journal of Development Economics* 22, no. 1 (1986): 5–40; Laurel Bossen, "Women in Modernizing Societies," *American Ethnologist* 2, no. 4 (1975): 587–601.

9. See, e.g., Tilly and Scott, *Women, Work, and Family*, pp. 94–95; Thomas Dublin, *Women at Work: The Transformation of Work and Community in Lowell, Massachusetts, 1826–1860* (New York, 1979). Dublin argues that in Lowell, women workers enjoyed more autonomy from family authority than found in Europe by Louise A. Tilly and Joan W. Scott. In Lowell, he suggests, women workers did not have to send their money home, and mill work was not "simply an extension of the traditional family economy as work for women moved outside the home" (p. 40). The jury on this issue is still out. For a summary of the issues in debate, see Dublin, *Women at Work*, pp. 36–42.

10. Marshall Johnson, William L. Parish, and Elizabeth Lin, "Chinese Women, Rural Society, and External Markets," *Economic Development and Cultural Change* 35, no. 2 (1987): 257–77.

11. City lights and youthful autonomy are a powerful theme in many studies of early industrialization, including Alice Clark's work on England. See Alice Clark, *The Working Life of Women in the Seventeenth Century* (London, 1919). Even without city lights, factory dormitories offered better accommodations for many young women than their own families could or would provide. See Mikiso Hane, *Peasants, Rebels, and Outcasts: The Underside of Modern Japan* (New York, 1982), pp. 180–81. Emily Honig, *Sisters and Strangers: Women in the Shanghai Cotton Mills, 1919–1949* (Stanford, 1986), pp. 168–71, comments briefly on all these issues. See also Elisabeth Croll, *Feminism and Socialism in China* (New York, 1980), pp. 174–75.

Province. The Ningbo data show how Chinese households responded to changes introduced by foreign market exposure and industrialization and how these changes affected women's place in the household economy.

In Ningbo, with its long history of commercialization, the gender division of labor in the household was well developed around women's handicraft or domestic work long before industrialization. Moreover, the importance of women's work in Ningbo household economies increased during the early stages of industrialization. We see this not only in expanding overseas markets for traditional crafts but also in new factory jobs for women, and even in wages paid to women farm workers. In other words, it is certain that the earning power of many Ningbo women did improve as a direct or indirect result of commercialization and industrialization. At the same time, the Ningbo data underscore the importance of local custom in shaping women's work experience. For instance, Ningbo women claimed a reputation for fine domestic service and fine handwork that privileged them (by comparison with women from other localities) as they entered new job markets, particularly in Shanghai. Their entry into new job markets was eased by kin and native-place ties that created networks to help migrating workers. But the significance of reputation and networks varied by region and by class within the Ningbo area.

My analysis asks two intersecting questions to address these issues. First, how did community norms and local custom affect household responses to new female labor markets? Second, how were women of different classes affected by new economic opportunities? Answers to these questions shed light on other aspects of early industrialization and its effects on women. For example, how did female labor markets and household responses vary across regional space? How effectively did factory jobs compete with cottage industries for women's labor? Did new economic opportunities have an impact on women's status inside or outside the home?

In many ways, as we shall see, local custom lay at the heart of all of these problems in the Ningbo area. Women's work outside the home was considered a mark of low status by Ningbo people, and respectable families went to great lengths to sequester their women. As a result, few of the economic changes associated with industrialization in Ningbo improved the status of women relative to men. Upper-class families hired maids to give their womenfolk more leisure. Middle-class households reorganized to make money from home embroidery arts. Poor families relied increasingly on income from female labor to tide them over crises or to supplement the meager earnings of male workers. Only as a last resort did families send a mother or a daughter or a daughter-in-law out to work in a factory. The result was that whereas access to jobs, education, and training outside the home—in factories, banks, shops, on the docks—expanded continuously for Ningbo men during the period of this study, relatively few Ningbo women were able, or willing, to move beyond the household. Instead, the preferred pattern among Ningbo families was for women to maintain the Ningbo home for sojourning male kinfolk.

Women from well-off households in Ningbo, especially those households at the peak of the domestic cycle with many adult women, managed to comply with local custom while earning income at home. They even had an advantage in the home handicraft market, because of economies of scale associated with housework and child care in the home.[12] Within large joint families, young unmarried women and able-bodied widows also had special advantages: they could expect to earn more from handicrafts than new mothers and mid-life housewives, because their energies were not divided by the demands of in-laws, spouse, and children. And all women in upper-class and middle-class households had servants. Women in well-off families, in other words, could make choices about work, which set them apart from the women who went out as servants or as factory workers, taking on a double burden.

Class differences in women's work showed up in regional space as well. Families in the affluent suburbs of Ningbo cultivated the gentle art of embroidery; women in remote villages wove hats from razor-sharp grasses that lacerated fingers. Whatever their class and wherever they lived, however, Ningbo women experienced dramatic changes in the uses of female labor during the first decades of the early twentieth century.

THE NINGBO AREA, NORTHEASTERN ZHEJIANG

The city of Ningbo lies south of Shanghai and Hangzhou, near the coast, in the northeast corner of Zhejiang Province (see Map 8.1). It is part of the Lower Yangzi macroregion, the most highly urbanized and affluent section of the country on the eve of the twentieth century.[13]

Ningbo was a historic seaport. A leading center of foreign and coastal

---

12. The term "domestic cycle" refers to the expansion and contraction of the household unit resulting from births, adoptions, marriages, and deaths. Thus in a joint family system, the nadir of the domestic cycle may find a household reduced to a single married couple and their very young offspring. By contrast, at the peak of the domestic cycle this same household may expand to encompass three or more generations, including a senior married couple, several married sons and their wives, and the offspring of those marriages. Although most Chinese families aspired to the Confucian ideal of a joint family, in which parents shared a household with married sons and their offspring, in reality, both class and the domestic cycle modified household composition. For the classic discussion of the domestic cycle, see Maurice Freedman, "The Chinese Domestic Family: Models," in *The Study of Chinese Society: Essays by Maurice Freedman* (Stanford, 1979), pp. 235–39. Susan Greenhalgh develops an empirically based model of the economic advantages accruing to large households in her article "Is Inequality Demographically Induced? The Family Cycle and the Distribution of Income in Taiwan," *American Anthropologist* 87, no. 3 (1985).

13. See G. William Skinner, "Regional Urbanization in Nineteenth-Century China," in G. William Skinner, ed., *The City in Late Imperial China* (Stanford, 1977), pp. 211–49, esp. 236–43.

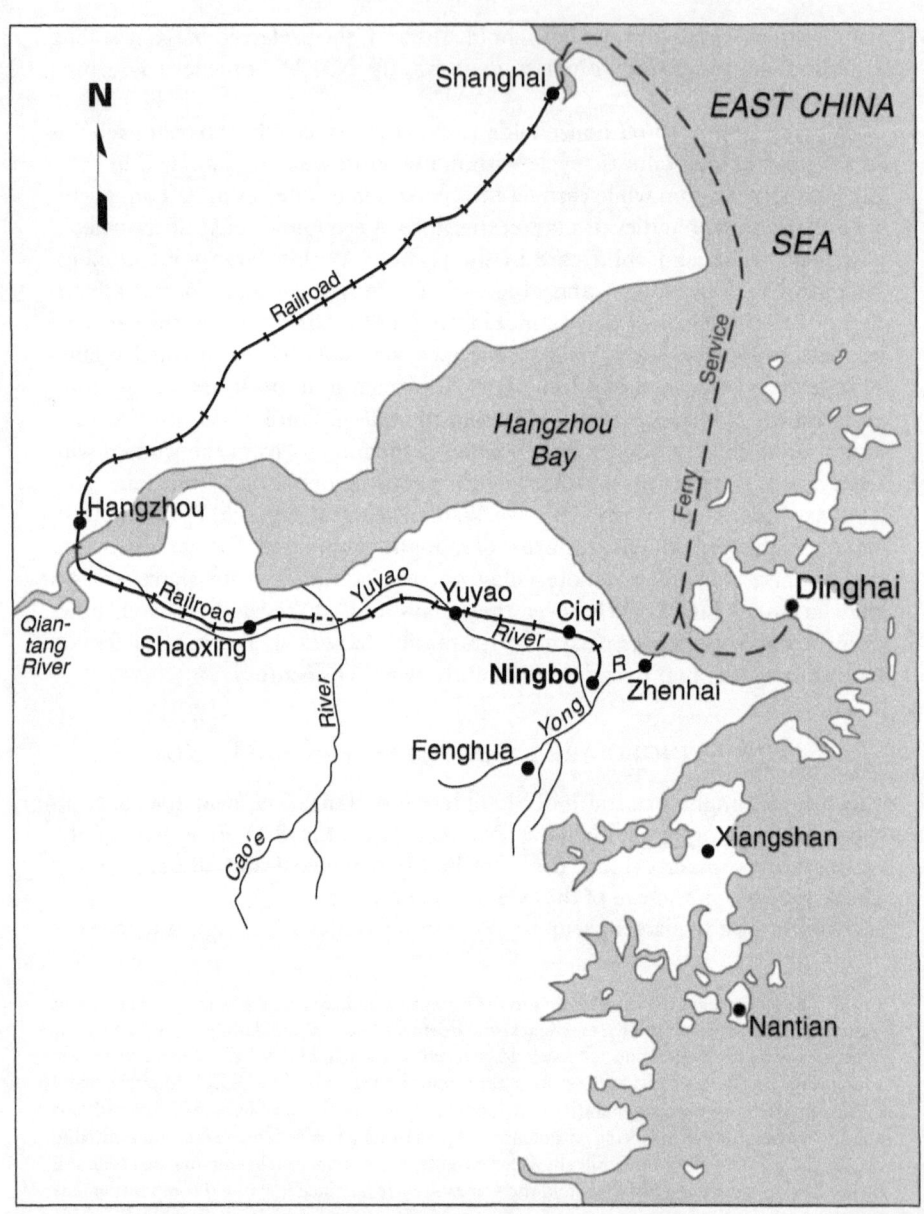

Map 8.1. Ningbo and Its Hinterland, ca. 1930.

trade as early as the Tang dynasty (618–906), it prospered in the late eighteenth century as a port for the coastal trade in local fish, salt, and rice. A history of Yin County, of which Ningbo was the seat, says that Ningbo trade began a new phase of growth early in the nineteenth century, as merchants from Fujian, Guangdong, and the Lower Yangzi Delta "gathered there like the clouds," while Ningbo traders left home for Hangzhou, Shaoxing, Suzhou, Shanghai, Hankou, Niuzhuang, and cities along the southeast coast, sometimes sojourning for years at a time. They also took up residence in Japan, Luzon, Singapore, Sumatra, and what is now Sri Lanka, opening shops and intermarrying with local women.[14] The Ningbo diaspora coincided with the growth of foreign trade along the China coast.[15] By 1800, Ningbo traders had established a foothold in Shanghai, founding a well-endowed native-place association to look after the needs and interests of its sojourning population there.

During the late imperial period, the Ningbo region (including the counties of Fenghua and Yuyao) was the home of manufactured goods sold all over China, as well as in Southeast Asia. Ningbo furniture, Fenghua woodcarvings, and Yuyao iron pans took their place beside Hangzhou scissors and Shaoxing wine as the best of their kind in the interregional domestic market. These were artisanal crafts, produced by masters and their apprentices in homes and small shops. Some traced their origins to a famous founder (Yu Xiaoxia, the late Qing bamboo carver of Fenghua, for instance) or shop (the Renhe iron pan forgery in Yuyao, founded in 1662).[16]

In late Qing times, Ningbo women's handwork was also famous throughout the country and in Southeast Asia. Ningbo women produced handwoven cloth, rush mats and matting, hats made of straw or bamboo splints, and the canopies of oiled-paper umbrellas. All were counted among the local specialties that made Ningbo famous. Women also staffed the elegant mansions of the famous Ningbo elite: the bankers, financiers, and shipping magnates whose life-style matched their money: "there were more maids in the homes of wealthy Ningbo families than anywhere else in the empire."[17] In sum, a complex division of labor, balancing agriculture, industry, and service and

14. See *Xinxiu Yin xianzhi* (1877), 2:5b–6b. On the history of the port of Ningbo, see Shiba, "Ningbo and Its Hinterland," pp. 391–439. On Ningbo's development since the mid-eighteenth century, see Susan Mann Jones, "Finance in Ningpo: The *ch'ien-chuang*, 1750–1880," in William E. Willmott, ed., *Economic Organization in Chinese Society* (Stanford, 1972), pp. 52–55, and literature cited therein.

15. On the history of European trade at Ningbo before the nineteenth century, see H. B. Morse, *The Trade and Administration of China* (London, 1921), pp. 226, 271–72.

16. See *China Industrial Handbooks: Chekiang* (hereafter *CIH:C;* Shanghai 1935, repr. Taibei, 1973), pp. 739, 680. A detailed account of local protoindustrial specialties appears in Shiba, "Ningbo and Its Hinterland," pp. 424–27.

17. See Tang Kangxiong, "Ningbo de niumu," in Zhang Xingzhou, comp., *Ningbo xisu congtan* (Taibei, 1973), p. 255.

based on the complementary spheres of male and female production, supported a flourishing local economy in Ningbo and its hinterland.

After the treaty of 1842 that opened Chinese ports to European trade, Shanghai became the central port of foreign trade for the Lower Yangzi region. Ningbo lost its preeminence as a port of foreign trade and became part of Shanghai's greater metropolitan trading system. But by then the city already had a well-honed financial connection to Shanghai. Ningbo bankers and financiers in Shanghai helped their home region ride the coattails of Shanghai's success. In 1877 the same currency exchange rates linked the economies of the Lower Yangzi cities of Suzhou, Hangzhou, Ningbo, and Shanghai.[18] Until the end of the period of this study, Ningbo's economic fortunes rose and fell with Shanghai's.[19]

Meanwhile, the local economy of the Ningbo region was also changing. By the early twentieth century, the region had become part of a commercial cotton belt stretching along the coastal edge of the province. Ningbo City, located at the mouth of the Yong River and (after 1914) at the terminus of the Shanghai-Hangzhou-Ningbo railway, grew into an important cotton center.[20] Widespread conversion of paddy land to cotton cultivation turned six of Ningbo Prefecture's seven counties into net rice importers. Market dependency throughout the area increased because of specialization in commercial cotton growing.[21] Additional commercial crops produced in the area included medicinal herbs, peaches and plums, salt (manufactured under government control), tong oil, silk, and tea, while fishing remained the mainstay of the southeastern portion of Yin County and coastal Zhenhai and Dinghai counties.[22] Traditional crafts—metal and leather work, shipbuilding, woodcarving, furniture making, and mat and hat weaving in the city and its hinterland—also continued to draw members of peasant households into the commercial economy, either as male apprentices in artisans' shops or as home handicraft workers.

French, English, and American missionaries arrived, accompanied by merchant compatriots eager to export local crafts. Exposure to new international markets varied within the Ningbo region, depending upon local trans-

---

18. *Xinxiu Yin xianzhi* (1877), 2:5b–6b.
19. *Yin xian tongzhi* (1936), "Shihuo zhi," p. 277.
20. The railroad, begun in 1909, was partially completed in 1914, except for a critical bridge link over the Cao'e River, which was not in place until after 1933. The city of Ningbo in 1933 was home to 20 cotton firms, each handling between $0.5 million and $1.5 million worth of cotton fiber yearly. See *CIH:C*, p. 218.
21. *CIH:C*, p. 1943.
22. See Himeda Mitsuyoshi, "Chūgoku kindai gyogyōshi no hito koma—Kanpō hachi nen Kin ken no gyomin tōsō o megutte," in *Tōyō shigaku ronshū* 8 (Tokyo, 1967): 66–67; on the commercial economy of Zhenhai, see *Zhenhai xianzhi*, suppl. *Xinzhi beigao* (Preface dated 1924, published 1931), 42:30a, 55–57; on Dinghai County, see *Dinghai xianzhi*, "Yuyan zhi" (Preface dated 1923, repr. Keelung, 1963).

port and location. For example, by the turn of the century the counties along the steamer route connecting Ningbo to Shanghai—Zhenhai and Dinghai—were drawn into migration and occupational networks flowing to Shanghai. Ningbo's inexpensive coastal access to Shanghai meant that local people of all classes could travel regularly to the economic center of the realm.[23]

In Ningbo's interior, the impact of foreign trade spread more slowly, first into Yuyao County, to the west of Ningbo City, with the partial completion of a rail line through the county that linked Hangzhou to Ningbo City. By the 1920s Yuyao had become the central producer of cotton for new local industry. Fenghua County, by contrast, remained a relative backwater. Situated off to the southwest, at the head of a shallow network of waterways that drained into the Yong River Basin, the county drew scornful comments from visiting foreigners in 1918. They complained about its cobblestoned streets (hard even to walk on), its shallow waterways, and the high cost of overland transport (a macadam road linking Fenghua to Ningbo was completed only in 1929).[24]

These differences in regional economic change show up sharply in survey data from the early 1930s. Consider, for instance, three of the counties just mentioned and compare the mix of agriculture and industry in each. In 1933 the county of Yin, where Ningbo was the county seat, ranked third in industrial development among administrative units in Zhejiang Province (after Hangzhou, the provincial capital, and the coastal county of Wenzhou to the south). Yin County was home to more than 20 kinds of local industry: cotton weaving (including towels), knitting, oil pressing, brewing (soy sauce and wine), cotton spinning, rice husking, tea firing, flour milling, food canning, printing, ice making, ironmongery and related industries, glass, soap, lacquer, matches, brass and tin wares, straw matting and hats, rattan and bamboo wares, wooden furniture and implements, umbrellas, electricity, dry-cell batteries, and tinfoil (used mostly for making what foreigners called joss paper to be burned in sacrifices and at funerals). Yuyao County, by contrast, listed only 12 specialties; and Fenghua, six.[25] Three of Fenghua's six local

23. On the efficient steamer launches connecting Yuyao, Ningbo, and Zhenhai with the Chusan Islands (Dinghai County) as early as 1904, see the *North-China Herald*, May 27, 1904: 1097. Steamer traffic between Shanghai and Ningbo was carried by a French line catering to "middle and upper class" Chinese travelers, causing the China Merchants Steam Navigation Company to upgrade its own facilities for Chinese travelers in order to compete (*North-China Herald*, March 15, 1907: 548–49). The triumphal entry of the first Ningbo-owned and Ningbo-operated steamer into Shanghai in 1909 is described in the *North-China Herald*, July 10, 1909: 123–24. The Ning-Shao Steamship Company's Shanghai-Ningbo route carried up to 3,000 passengers in steerage (*North-China Herald*, June 12, 1909: 609).

24. On the road, see *Yin xian tongzhi*, "Yudi zhi," p. 719; on earlier conditions, see *Shina shōbetsu zenshi* (hereafter *SSZ*), vol. 13, Zhejiang Province (Tokyo, 1919), pp. 100–101.

25. See Zhongguo Shiyebu, Guoji Maoyiju, *Zhongguo shiye zhi: Zhejiang sheng* (hereafter ZSZZ; Chinese industrial handbook: Zhejiang province; Shanghai, 1933), section *geng*: 6–10; *CIH:C*, p. 477.

industries—tea firing, handmade paper making, and bamboo and stone carving—were cottage industries catering to a domestic market. A small power plant and a factory for canning bamboo shoots (opened after 1920 and closed in 1931, in a pattern characteristic of the early local industries during this period) were the lone outposts of industrialization in Fenghua. In 1933 Fenghua was still exporting 65 percent of its rice to other areas, while Yuyao, the most important cotton-producing county in the region, imported 95 percent of its rice in the same year.[26]

In this commercialized part of Zhejiang Province, then, after the impact of foreign trade and early industrialization, three types of local economy coexisted, dominated respectively by an urban industrial and commercial labor market (Yin), a mixed economy of commercial agriculture and cottage industry (Yuyao), and a preindustrial economy based on rice agriculture and traditional crafts (Fenghua).

FEMALE FARM LABOR

Opportunities for women's work were affected by the same patterns of local variation. Take farm labor as an example. The *Chinese Industrial Handbook for Zhejiang Province*, published in 1933, supplies farm wage data for both male and female workers in the counties of Yin, Yuyao, and Fenghua. Table 8.1, where the data are displayed,[27] dramatizes gender differences in the farm labor market. Wage rates for males were relatively integrated across county boundaries; wage rates for females were not. The highest farm wages for men were reported in Yin County, the most urbanized county, where seasonal variation was also sharpest; farm wages for women were highest in Yuyao, the county where commercial cotton was king. What accounts for these differences?

The lack of integration in female wage labor markets was partly due to local variation in the norms forbidding female farm labor. In urbanized Yin County, the home of Ningbo City, women never took jobs as farm workers—

---

26. *CIH:C*, p. 193.

27. Data from *ZSZZ* 1933, section *yi*, pp. 42–45. Though it is not relevant to this table, readers should take note that men and women received different kinds and amounts of food when they performed agricultural labor on the *gong shan* system that included board and sometimes room (see Luo Qiong, p. 21). Also, wage rates presented in Feng Hefa, ed., *Zhongguo nongcun jingji ziliao* (Materials on the Chinese rural economy; Shanghai, 1933), 2:746–47 for all long-term farm workers in the three counties show Yin County wages ranging from 41 to 90 *yuan* per year; from 35 to 61 in Fenghua; from 30 to 72 in Yuyao; all figures are based on a system where meals were supplied in addition to a cash wage. The Feng Hefa figures cast some doubt on the veracity of the relatively high wage rate shown for female workers in Yuyao. The figures for Yin County presented in *ZSZZ* may also be misleading because they present a low and high range, while the other numbers probably represent means. Notes appended to the table state that the top figure of 1 *yuan* for day labor was paid at peak season only.

TABLE 8.1 Farm Wages *(yuan)* in Three Counties in Zhejiang Province, 1933

Wage Factors	Yin	Fenghua	Yuyao
Day			
Male	0.35–1.00	0.50	0.60
Female	—[a]	0.20	0.40
Month			
Male	8.00[b]	12.00	15.00
Female	—	3.50	8.00
Year			
Male	20.00–100.00[c]	100.00	120.00
Female	—	30.00	80.00

[a] No data available; females appear not to have participated in farm work in Yin County.
[b] Plus meals valued at 4 *yuan* per month.
[c] Plus food and lodging valued at 10–50 *yuan* per year.

at least so noted the statisticians who reported wages in the *Chinese Industrial Handbook for Zhejiang Province*. Moreover, women did not travel far from home to work in the fields; otherwise female wage rates would have been comparable across counties. With urban jobs competing for long-term male workers, and with families reluctant to send women out to do hard labor in the fields,[28] it appears that Yuyao farmers were forced to offer higher wages to attract female workers. They were needed: cotton, Yuyao's major commercial crop, was a labor-intensive crop that consumed more labor days per year than any other commercial crop grown in the area.[29]

Differences in wage rates for male and female farm workers in Fenghua and Yuyao dramatize the limited mobility of female farm workers. Wages for male farm workers in Fenghua ranged from 80 percent to 83 percent of wages in Yuyao. But female farm workers in Fenghua could expect to earn only half as much as their Yuyao counterparts for day labor. In Fenghua, a female farm worker paid by the month made only 44 percent of what local women

28. On the generally high wages for farm labor in this competitive labor market, see Feng Hefa, ed., *Zhongguo nongcun jingji ziliao* (Shanghai, 1933), 2:741, 753. Historically, the growth of the home weaving industry has been shown to draw female labor away from agriculture. See Evelyn Sakakida Rawski, *Agricultural Change and the Peasant Economy of South China* (Cambridge, Mass., 1972), pp. 46–47, 54–55.

29. John Lossing Buck, *Land Utilization in China: Statistical Volume* (Nanking, 1937), pp. 314–19, reports that cotton cultivation consumed 225 labor days; only garlic consumed more labor per crop hectare in Yuyao, and garlic occupied less than 1 percent of seasonal crop area, as against more than 90 percent for cotton (pp. 193–99). The next contender for crop acreage in Yuyao, broad beans (occupying more than 66 percent of seasonal crop area), consumed only 102 days of labor a year. Most of the work in cotton cultivation went to harrowing and cultivating (43 percent) and harvesting (38 percent). See p. 320.

earned in Yuyao; and for Fenghua women who contracted their labor by the year, wages were scarcely more than a third of comparable rates in Yuyao. If women had moved out of Fenghua to Yuyao for farm work, these wage differentials would have disappeared. At the other end of the spectrum, in Yin County, where city influence on village custom was greatest, and where commercial cropping took second place to fishing and handicrafts (especially furniture making, woodworking, and straw mat and hat making), "virtually no women hired out for farm labor."[30]

In short, a young woman's prospects in the labor market were constrained not only by class but also by the location of her town or village in the spatial economy of the region. Whether these different labor markets were due to taboos on women's travel and farm labor or to a lack of information about the job market, or to a combination of these, is not clear from wage data alone. But examining other sectors of the female labor market shows that taboos were important.

OTHER FEMALE LABOR MARKETS

Given the absence of women from the agricultural wage labor force in Yin County, and the high wages required to lure women into field labor in Yuyao, we would expect to find a thriving market for female labor outside agriculture in the Ningbo region. Prostitution, domestic service, and home handicrafts all were options open to women in the preindustrial economy, depending on the needs and the sensibilities of their families. Prostitution was not respectable, though it could be lucrative. By contrast, respectable women of many skills and backgrounds worked part-time or full-time as Ningbo maids. And at the pinnacle of the female employment structure stood home handicrafts, crowned by that prestigious craft that was really an art, embroidery.[31] We shall examine each in turn.

Prostitution and Domestic Service

Prostitution supported untold numbers of women in Ningbo, but information on the conditions of their work, employment, and recruitment is scanty in sources that were written primarily to celebrate the virtues of local residents. The 1877 Yin County gazetteer does include a description of prosperous brothels, under the heading "Odious Customs."[32] A former resident of Ding-

---

30. *ZSZZ, yi*, p. 44. A survey conducted in the 1930s notes: "As for long-term labor in eastern Zhejiang, few women do it, because the women are not good at working in the fields [*bushan yu congshi tianjian laodong*]. Children commonly do field labor, their jobs being limited to tending cattle and feeding pigs, chickens, and ducks." See Feng Hefa, ed., *Zhongguo*, 2:739.

31. On the prestige of embroidery work, see comments in Feng Hefa, ed., *Zhongguo*, 1:243, 301–2, citing a report dated 1930.

32. *Xinxiu Yin xianzhi*, 1877, 2:9a.

hai County reported disapprovingly in his memoirs that prostitutes (not local women) descended on his native place three times a year during the peak fishing season.[33] A government tax survey conducted in Yin County in 1939 listed three classes of prostitutes in Ningbo: "first-class" prostitutes paid the state 12 *yuan* a month in taxes, and third-class prostitutes were assessed from 4 to 6 *yuan*.[34] First-class prostitutes' taxes alone may have matched the total monthly earnings of a male farm laborer.

Respectable women scorned prostitution even in the face of dire poverty.[35] But domestic work as a cook, servant, or nursemaid was acceptable for both married and unmarried women. The memoirs of a long-time resident of Ningbo fondly recall eight famous types of "Ningbo maids," ranging from scullery maids, who did the cooking, washing, and cleaning, to the more genteel household helpers, who catered to the intimate personal needs of their employers. Those who labored as scullery maids came from poor families, performing heavy work for low wages, but other servants were drawn from across the spectrum of working-class households. For many, domestic service did not involve onerous physical labor. It doubtless had hidden costs: upper-class women were notorious for abusing their female servants, and male employers often expected free sexual access to the household help. Still, job descriptions for some of these maids (even allowing for the undeniable bias of the informant, who clearly felt they were paid too much for doing too little) suggest that theirs was mainly a seller's market.[36] Competing opportunities for women in other sectors of the economy may actually have improved the wages of Ningbo maids in their local area as the industrial and commercial economy expanded.[37]

At the same time, the range of female domestic work in Ningbo hints at the immense gaps that separated rich and poor women. The servant who ground rice, hauled water, and spent mealtimes hunched over charcoal burners lived a world apart from her mistress and even from the body servant who attended her employer. At marriage a leisured young lady was accompanied to her spouse's residence by a "dowry maid," specially chosen by her

---

33. See Jin Limen, "Lüetan Zhoushan de hunjia fengsu," in Zhang Xingzhou, ed., *Ningbo xisu congtan*, p. 222.

34. See *Yinxian yiban xingzheng gaikuang*, cited in *Nimpō chiku jittai chōsasho* (1941).

35. Ning Lao T'ai T'ai, the subject of Ida Pruitt's *Daughter of Han* (New Haven, 1945), became a beggar and finally a domestic servant when she went out to work for the first time (p. 73) to keep her family from starving. She never considered prostitution. But see Gail Hershatter, "Prostitution and the Market in Women in Early Twentieth-Century Shanghai," in *Marriage and Inequality in Chinese Society*, ed. Rubie S. Watson and Patricia Buckley Ebrey (Berkeley and Los Angeles, 1991), p. 18, on defining respectability and its problems. As she points out, we still know very little about how prostitution was viewed by peasant families.

36. The account that follows is based on Tang Kangxiong, "Ningbo de niumu," pp. 256–57.

37. The *Dinghai xianzhi, fangsu*: 51a, remarks that by the early 1920s, textile factory jobs were becoming more important than domestic service to emigrating female workers.

parents from their own household servants. Such a servant had to be both young and very capable, for she might serve her young mistress for life. Her position was like that of a sister or confidante: "these maids were exactly like the body servants found in official families in the old days." At holiday time, or during funerals or weddings, household servants, including the dowry maids, got help from "temporaries"—women recruited from poor families where small children and domestic chores prevented them from taking full-time jobs. After working two or three days, a temporary maid took home a daily wage and usually a generous bonus. In the words of one observer (evidently a former employer of temporary help): "Although they do not work so many days, their income does not necessarily reflect this."

As for status, a body servant enjoyed leisure and even luxury, though at the price of servitude. Her economic status may have been higher than that of the temporary help, but her formal social status was beneath that of married women from commoner households who worked as temporary maids or nursemaids. Maid service gave the well-to-do leisure; it gave poor women jobs that were less arduous and better paying than farm work; it offered alternatives to prostitution; and it provided long-term security in a market where most farm and factory jobs were both seasonal and unstable. Working as a maid could be a respectable prelude to marriage in Ningbo. And maid takers were in some cases also maid givers; for instance, nursemaids who attended Ningbo mothers after childbirth hired their own nursemaids during confinement. All these factors make it difficult to generalize about the impact of domestic service on women's status. In any case, maid service remained both a secure and a widely accepted form of respectable work for commoner women—a clear step above prostitution, a cut below the most respectable form of women's work, home handicrafts.

Home Handicrafts

Women's work in family enterprises crossed class lines in Ningbo. Descriptions of "middle-class" households[38] demonstrate the crucial role of women's work in the preindustrial household and also underscore the advantages enjoyed by households commanding a large female labor force. A survey of Ningbo industry conducted in 1907 by Nyok-Ching Tsur, a Ningbo native, identified a distinctive mode of production unique to Ningbo's middle-class families. During the period of his study, home production supplied each family's needs for preserved foods, cotton cloth, and yarn, with some to spare for the market. At the turn of the century, in fact, well-off households in

---

38. See Tsur, "Forms of Business." During this period, references to the Ningbo "middle class" were common in the press. For instance, in 1907 a new French steamer line became a financial success by catering to the needs of middle- and upper-class travelers between Ningbo and Shanghai, according to the *North-China Herald,* March 15, 1907: 548–49.

Ningbo were growing, storing, and processing their own rice, either for cakes or for rice flour. It was common for such families to process their own cotton. Tsur estimated that 40 percent of households that supplied their own cloth even grew their own raw cotton: men did the cleaning and drying, women the spinning and weaving.[39]

Women spun together in an enclosed courtyard, working late into the night unless they had to stop to put young children to bed. The division of labor among them was elaborate: "almost every woman spins a special quality yarn for a particular cloth." Weavers used several different kinds of loom, one type requiring the labor of three or four women working with both hands and feet; the simplest loom, a hand loom, calling for only one pair of hands. In one apparently lineage-scale enterprise, 60 to 70 women were producing 40 different kinds of cloth. Individuals within the household also specialized in the products they made: scarves and shawls using coarse cotton were the preserve of the nearsighted or the novice; young girls whose eyesight was still sharp worked on the fine multicolored embroidery.[40]

Women's work brought income to these households, and it had sentimental value as well—at least to the men. The elaborate division of labor was an emblem of the organic unity—Tsur called it the "harmonic congeniality"—of the grand Chinese family. "While the girls and women sit working diligently, the men read aloud some amusing poem or tell the news from the city, so that the evening passes in a hurry."[41] The gender division of labor in these exemplary Chinese families represented a perfect synthesis of Confucian family values and profit-making enterprise. Hierarchies of gender, age, and skill were reproduced and displayed every day in the work performed by women.

But during the early twentieth century, household economies were changing in response to new markets. Though the majority of families continued producing goods for their own use, saving extra income for the dowries of their daughters,[42] some households were attracted to more entrepreneurial ventures. In cotton-growing areas, weaving households could engage in barter, with two families exchanging their own products (towels for clothing, for instance) through a female broker well known to both parties. Family production systems also lost ground to imported factory goods. Cloth woven at home, for instance, was threatened by the import of British, American, and Japanese textiles.[43] Increasingly, the test of survival for any home industry appeared to be its ability to compete in international markets. Consequently,

---

39. Tsur, "Forms of Business," pp. 45–46.
40. Ibid., p. 46.
41. Ibid., p. 47.
42. Large farm families preserved great quantities of meat and vegetables—especially salted pork and fish and pickled cabbages—selling what they could not use. Ibid., p. 49.
43. Ibid., p. 99.

even those households already producing for local or regional markets were forced to adopt new approaches to marketing.

Brokers employed by foreign companies and by new Chinese firms moved quickly to meet the needs of households trying to tap the commercial market; they also solicited and even trained contract workers in the home.[44] In many handicraft industries, contractors hired brokers to go house to house, linking individual household enterprises with the shifting domestic and international demand for their products. Brokers collected finished and semifinished goods manufactured in the home, under contract or on commission: paper umbrellas, straw hats, mats made from the local esparto grass (hundreds of *mu* of these rushes were planted in fields outside the city), and embroidery. Women were the mainstay of all these home industries.[45]

Under these new market conditions, demand stayed high for bamboo umbrella frames made at home by men and women (women sorting the pieces, men building the frames).[46] Female mat weavers, using rushes grown only in China, also kept their customers both at home and abroad. But something had changed. Mat weavers now began working to order, following the exact specifications of a contractor: "now every woman knows at once how long, how thick, and how smooth the individual threads of bast must be to correspond with the contractor's wishes."[47]

Embroidery arts entered the market for the first time as a result of foreign demand. Silk embroidery—the emblem of refined womanhood—was discovered by foreign missionaries during the 1860s, and by the end of the century, contractors were purchasing huge quantities for customers at home and in Europe. Embroiderers bought their own supplies and worked their own designs, while 16 "embroidery collectors" vied for their output. The new commercial market for fine embroidery in Ningbo "found welcome support among the women and girls of the middle class. Whereas women formerly had embroidered just to pass the time, they now were offered a rewarding side occupation by the embroidery collectors."[48]

---

44. On brokers and their role in the economy of this period, see Susan Mann, "Brokers as Entrepreneurs in Presocialist China," *Comparative Studies in Society and History* 26, no. 4 (1984): 614–36.
45. Tsur, "Forms of Business," pp. 23, 25, 29.
46. Ibid., pp. 96–97.
47. Ibid., p. 100.
48. Ibid., p. 101. Jane Schneider has shown that in nineteenth-century Sicily, the commercial availability of manufactured cloth freed women of nonelite families to pursue the noble art of embroidery for the first time. Obviously Tsur drew a different conclusion about the relationship between class and embroidery in Ningbo, and his data do not permit me to press Schneider's questions. The case of the lace makers, discussed below, demonstrates that at least some women began doing commercial needlework for the first time during Ningbo's early industrialization. In China, as in Sicily, embroidery was both a status symbol and an emblem of female seclusion, but I have seen no evidence that lace making conferred similar prestige. The bride's trousseau in

Sometime after the turn of the century, a new group of middlemen entered this market as well. Professional contractors began supplying the embroiderers with silk, designs, and embroidery frames, paying piece rates for finished work. Commissioned pieces invited yet a new division of labor, as households began to specialize in different designs (animals, figures, flowers). Within the household, each female embroiderer cultivated her own specialty, so that work on an individual piece might be divided up among members. In this market, the families who divided their skills most efficiently produced the best work and made the most money. "The more clever the distribution [of labor], the more beautiful the work, and the higher also the wage paid by the contractor."[49]

Women in the embroidery business divided their labor according to age, skill, and leisure. In the largest family enterprises, the most productive workers were widows under 60 and girls under 20—that is, unmarried or unattached women who could devote most of their time to their work. Some of their income was set aside for their own use. Young girls did embroidery and made silk shoes to earn money for their dowries; widows used their income to supplement the allowance they received from lineage trusts before they became eligible for full support. Married women with husband and family to attend, by contrast, were able to work only part-time at handicraft enterprises, and the disposition of their income is less clear.[50]

Household production on this scale required managerial as well as manual skills. Small embroidery projects, for instance, took 15 days; a wall hanging or curtain required up to three months. The mother or the senior female in the household negotiated contracts for daughters, daughters-in-law, and other workers (who might include concubines, adopted girls, and live-in servants).[51] She also supervised the labor and took responsibility for meeting deadlines and other specifications. She negotiated terms with the embroidery contractors, who employed collection agents to check on work, deliver raw materials and orders, and collect and pay for orders. The marketing center for this home-based embroidery business was likely to be a wholesale outlet located in a large city, with branches elsewhere for retail sales. Traveling salesmen sold the embroidery in towns where there were no permanent

---

accounts I have read did not include handmade lacework. See Jane Schneider, "Trousseau as Treasure: Some Contradictions of Late Nineteenth-Century Change in Sicily," *Women and History*, 1985, no. 10:81–119. A detailed description of trousseaux in Ningbo appears in Tang Kangxiong, "Peijia zhuanglian," in Zhang Xingzhou, ed., *Ningbo xisu congtan* (Taibei, 1973), pp. 212–14.

49. Tsur, "Forms of Business," p. 103.
50. Ibid., p. 121.
51. See Ibid., pp. 33–36, for a description of the "service-children" purchased by "mandarins and rich merchants" from families unable to support them.

stores. Women's embroidery, the hallmark of late Qing domesticity, had entered the world market.

Lace making, unlike embroidery, was a new women's handicraft industry, introduced during the mid-nineteenth century when Roman Catholic sisters began teaching it to Chinese peasant girls. Lace making eventually employed 1,000 women making handkerchiefs, cushion covers, and other items for export. Though the French managers of the fledgling lace industry conducted their affairs "with some secrecy," Chinese women in neighboring villages soon took up the art and local businessmen got wind of it. By 1936 more than 2,000 Ningbo lace makers were at work supplying over 30 contractors, with perhaps another 1,000 women making lace in the neighboring counties of Zhenhai and Ciqi. Piece rates in 1936 ranged from 0.30 *yuan* to 4 *yuan* for each article; monthly earnings averaged over 10 *yuan* per person, placing lace making well within the range of male farm wages and far above even the best-paid female farm jobs.[52]

Straw hat weaving was one of the Ningbo area's oldest home crafts. Before the opening of foreign trade, the Ningbo region was known for a special grass known as "mat grass," which is still grown in the Ningbo area as a third crop and is exported to Japan for tatami. This grass could also be woven into sturdy, weather-resistant, broad-brimmed hats for farm work. Easily made (one weaver could make up to five in a day), these hats were a major sideline in farm households.[53]

Unfortunately, the only detailed data on the production of straw hats dates from the early twentieth century, well after new marketing systems and raw materials had created a European market for Ningbo hats. The first major change came in the 1880s, when a market for Ningbo-made farmers' hats first developed in London and Paris; it developed somewhat later in New York. In 1908 Ningbo women were already producing 6 million straw and woven bamboo hats for export abroad and shipping an equal number inland to Chinese customers in the interior. Locally grown straw was picked and cleaned by workers employed by a contractor, then delivered to home weavers in huge bundles, along with samples to copy. The largest market for these hats was in farm villages in present-day Vietnam.[54]

52. *Yinxian tongzhi*, 1936, "Shihuo zhi," pp. 57a–b. This commission work, in which the contractor supplied the design (drawn by male designers), produced hundreds of thousands of pieces for export each year. Exposure to this market meant risk: the local lace-making industry went on to peak between 1923–27; thereafter, a slide in production brought prices and volume down from 80 cents a meter in 1923 to 22 cents a meter in 1933. See *CIH:C*, pp. 539–40.

53. Unless otherwise specified, the information on hat weaving that follows is drawn from a preprint of a volume in a new series on Chinese domestic industry and commerce currently in preparation at the Shanghai Academy of Social Sciences. The volume I cite is titled *Shanghai Huashang guoji maoyi ye*, first draft, fourth section, third volume (*chugao, disi zhang, sanci*) in the series Zhongguo ziben zhuyi gongshangye shiliao congkan.

54. Tsur, "Forms of Business," pp. 104–5.

Major changes in the hat industry followed during World War I, when a French company based in Shanghai introduced two grasses—a type of ramie (*macao*) and a fine pale grass called "gold thread" (*jinsi*)—from the Philippines. To train women to weave with these imported materials, the French company sent a delegation of women workers to Manila in 1914 to observe Filipina workers.[55] Between 1914 and 1923, Shanghai exports of Ningbo hats made from ramie and gold thread increased tenfold. To popularize the new materials and new weaving techniques, the company, Yongxing (Eternally Flourishing), set up weaver-training centers in Roman Catholic churches. Successful education of local weavers made it possible for Yongxing to develop a putting-out system in which (male) company agents distributed raw materials and samples to women workers at their homes. Two or three women workers at the company's Ningbo branch worked at a shop in the city, stamping the shape of the hats with a machine and finishing off the edges and trimming.

These new materials and new markets brought home weavers higher prices for hats. But the new hats were harder to fashion. Whereas ordinary straw hats could be made in a few hours, a gold-thread hat took up to a week to finish. The new grasses were razor-sharp, and they easily cut fingers. Japanese women weavers, according to some sources, refused to use them, and even in the Ningbo area, gold-thread hat weaving moved quickly from the protoindustrial center "Outside West Gate," where most of the weaving was concentrated, to counties where poverty made women willing to tolerate the pain. Within a few years, Yuyao County, together with Huangyan County to the south of the Ningbo area—considered peripheral counties by Ningbo cityfolk—became the major production center for gold-thread hats.[56]

The production side of this hat market, which was at its peak in 1927 and declined steadily during the 1930s, looked something like this. Hat companies (one in Ningbo, which monopolized the local sale of raw materials and the purchase of finished hats; five or more in Shanghai, which sold raw materials or purchased finished hats direct from brokers operating in the countryside) relied on a brokered putting-out system. Each company supervised up to 20 brokers, the broker himself being a skilled hat weaver. The broker supplied women with straw and collected hats on a piece-rate basis from about 50 households with which he was well acquainted. An experienced worker earned between 1.50 and 2.00 *yuan* for every hat she could make. Since one hat took the best workers about five days, hat weaving was more profitable than farm labor for women, except in Yuyao.[57] A weaver

---

55. *Shanghai Huashang guoji maoyi ye*, p. 6.
56. Ibid., pp. 13, 16.
57. Output for less experienced workers was about three hats a month. *CIH:C*, p. 687. See *SSZ*, 13:657–58, which reports ordinary straw hats that could be made in half a day or less, selling for between two and four American copper coins each.

could expect up to 20 *yuan* a month when business was good; 10 *yuan* per month was the average.[58] Though in Yuyao female farm workers could earn more than hat weavers, the stigma attached to women's farm work compromised the value of the income.[59] Hat weaving was easier than farm work; it could be done year-round; and it kept women indoors (a prestige factor as well as a practical advantage, because it allowed women at home to manage household chores, child care, and other tasks at the same time). The advantages of hat weaving even without wage incentives are obvious.

Raw materials and orders for hats came through brokers, but training was generally in-house, supplied by female family members. Mothers, or mothers-in-law, purchased straw and grasses and collected payments. Hat-weaving women had only limited access to information, and of course they had no mobility in the market. They never left home; they believed that going out was immoral, improper, and impermissible.[60]

Hat weaving was peasant work. Training was short ("An ordinary person can learn to make hats in two weeks," commented one observer). Children could do it: young girls started weaving at the age of 8 *sui*, that is, between six and seven years old. And the work was rough: hat weavers developed thick calluses to protect their fingers against the sharp grass. By contrast, home embroidery was elite women's work, more art than craft. Training was long, requiring years of leisure: young girls began practicing at the age of 10 so they could turn out elegant pillowcases by the age of 16. The tiny needles and delicate fabrics demanded small, fine hands and smooth fingers—hands only a woman free from hard labor could aspire to. Embroidery thus marked a distinctive class line in home craft production, a line underscored by a close look at the work of hat weavers.

Whether they were embroiderers or hat weavers, however, women with access to the handicraft market subscribed to the same values: they were working respectably at home. Nyok-Ching Tsur opined, in fact, that one of the main reasons for the rise of contracting in the Ningbo area was its popularity among women who preferred to work at home rather than accept jobs outside.

58. *Yinxian tongzhi* (1936), "Shihuozhi," p. 58a. In interviews with eight retired hat weavers in Ciqi County, November 1988, I heard complaints about the effect of the war on their business. One woman told us that in the 1940s, when hat prices fell by more than half, she measured her income in bowls of rice: one hat bought three bowls.

59. See the figures in *ZSZZ, yi*, pp. 43–48.

60. During interviews with eight retired hat weavers in Ciqi County in November 1988, I asked about going out. "Did you go to plays?" "Never." "Did you ever go to Shanghai?" "Shanghai?! We never heard of going to Shanghai!" These women obtained materials from and sold their products to a broker from the same company every week or month, at rates set by the standards of the company. So removed were they from the city at the center of the prefecture where they lived that when asked what the special traits of Ningbo women were, they replied, "We don't know: we aren't from Ningbo."

A special characteristic of Chinese women and girls is their great shyness. They are not fond of serving in strange, distinguished houses, the more so since the earnings there are small. They prefer to remain at home, where they can find better-paying work without being deprived of their family life. Naturally, there are also women and girls in China who are employed in factories or who earn their livelihood as wage workers; but these are exceptional cases.[61]

Even the famous "Ningbo maids," by remaining in the confines of the domestic realm, escaped some of the stigma attached to "going out." Work in the home was a mark of female respectability in Ningbo, and it was a mark recognized by women of all classes.[62]

In sum, the early twentieth century saw a commercial revolution in women's home industries in the Ningbo area, a commercial revolution based on contracting to household workers. Contemporary observers criticized contractors for driving independent artisans out of business.[63] But contracting, it appears, actually expanded economic opportunities for a wide range of female home workers, precisely because local custom confined them to the household, where they had no mobility and limited access to materials and information.[64]

Factory Jobs

Ningbo belonged to a region in China where women entered the factory work force in large numbers during the early twentieth century.[65] Within the Ningbo area itself, taboos on women's work outside the home were strong,

---

61. Tsur, "Forms of Business," p. 92.

62. Other ethnographers have noted the relationship between women's home handicraft industry and middle class status. See, for example, Fei Hsiao-tung and Chang Chih-i, *Earthbound China: A Study of Rural Economy in Yunnan* (Chicago, 1945), p. 240.

63. See Tsur, "Forms of Business," p. 93. Independent craftworkers could no longer survive, because of the need for capital to purchase raw materials in bulk to meet market demand and because of the problem of acquiring information about rapidly changing market conditions. Overall, Tsur complains (p. 91), the image of China as a land of domestic workers and independent artisans was—in his area, at that time—a figment of the uninformed observer's imagination. Most of those seemingly independent workers, he stresses, were actually employed by contractors.

64. Women, of course, paid the price of dependency in other ways. For example, my informants complained bitterly that during the war, after Japan occupied the Philippines, imports of gold-thread grass were cut off, and they had to find some other source of income.

65. The region referred to here is the Lower Yangzi macroregion, including the cities of Shanghai, Nanjing, Suzhou, Hangzhou, and Ningbo (see n. 13 above). Most of the workers in Shanghai's cotton mills in the early twentieth century were women, and women workers were hired by the thousands as new factories opened elsewhere in the region. By contrast, in North China, female factory workers made up only a negligible part of the urban work force until much later. On north-south differences and temporal change in patterns of female factory work, see Gail Hershatter, *The Workers of Tianjin, 1900–1949* (Stanford, 1986), esp. pp. 54–57. On women cotton mill workers in Shanghai, see Honig, *Sisters and Strangers*.

and only the poorest households sent women to factories. Yet even where women remained at home, new factories altered the household division of labor.

In the first place, the increasing availability of factory-made goods meant that in 1908 "items which the women in Ningpo produced themselves as recently as thirty years ago, e.g., shoes, finer fabrics, and bags, are in most cases bought in shops today."[66] Added this contemporary observer, "Only one generation ago, the women made shoes, hats, shirts, and other apparel for their husbands and for themselves. It caused much attention in Ningpo at that time when a young woman bought from a merchant something that she could have manufactured herself through the diligence of her hands. Today this has become very different."[67] Because factory products made some forms of housework obsolete, in short, factories brought well-to-do women more leisure. Factory-made products for the home also freed women to devote more energy to home handicraft production for the market.

For the poorest households, on the other hand, factories offered new jobs. By 1919 the city of Ningbo boasted four factories large enough to command the attention of Japanese investigators surveying the local economy: two cotton-spinning mills, an electric power plant, and an oil-pressing plant.[68] Tongjiuyuan, a Chinese-owned cotton mill and the first of its kind in the province, was founded in 1895 as a patriotic enterprise by two prominent local businessmen, after China's defeat in the war with Japan. It opened as a cotton-ginning plant and gradually expanded into spinning after 1900.[69] Tongjiuyuan employed 1,300 workers, 1,000 of them women. The 300 male employees received monthly wages of 4–10 American dollars in 1919; women were paid by the day, from 8 to 20 cents in American copper pennies.[70] The coarse yarn the plant produced, used only in local cloth manufacture, was sold mostly within Zhejiang Province. The other cotton mill, Hefeng, was founded in 1905 as a Sino-Japanese joint venture, originally organized along Japanese lines under the protection of the Japanese consulate. The company opened with 23,000 American-made spindles in 1907, spinning raw cotton grown in Yuyao and Shaoxing counties to the west. Seventy percent of its 2,600 workers were women, paid by the day or on a piece-rate basis. The company supplied temporary housing in a dormitory for all workers.

Women factory workers in Ningbo suffered the stigma attached to women who went out to work in a public place. Moreover, their wages were relatively

66. Tsur, "Forms of Business," p. 33.
67. Ibid., p. 61.
68. *SSZ*, 13:45.
69. For a time the company also tried weaving cloth, but in 1919, in the wake of a fire and a takeover by a rival company, textile production in the plant was abandoned.
70. *SSZ*, 13:636–42; *CIH:C*, p. 482. The Tongjiuyuan and Hefeng mills both paid wages in American currency, for reasons I have not yet been able to determine.

low. Although pay rates in the Ningbo mills were said to be "about the same" as those in Shanghai, an experienced female worker could earn only between 20 and 25 cents (American copper coins) a day twisting thread or carding cotton. Reelers were paid about 8 cents a day. Floor supervisors fared better, earning monthly wages of 32 *yuan*.[71] In other words, at Hefeng and at Tongjiuyuan, local factory wages and terms (with the exception of the privileged job of supervisor) paid no more than home handicrafts for many workers. And by removing women from the home, factory jobs exacted a premium that discounted the real value of their wages. Sending a woman "out" not only compromised a family's status but also forced it to forgo her domestic services or replace them with the labor of someone else.[72]

Irregular hours and plant closings were as common as low wages in Ningbo's factories. The cottonseed oil–pressing plant with financial ties to the Tongjiuyuan cotton mill catered to a limited provincial market, and shut its doors during the first four months of every year to await the new cotton harvest. Workers in the mill, when it was open, earned about 10 *yuan* a month, working 12-hour shifts.[73] A small match factory, a candle factory, a shop that made towels, and a feeble electric plant (closed more often than not) also kept erratic schedules. The Zhengdaxin Match Factory, established in 1912 (some sources say 1909) by a French missionary and subsequently taken over by Chinese managers, employed about 70 male workers at 30 cents a day, along with 150 female workers who packaged the matches on a piece-rate basis. Women workers earned 1 cent for 100 boxes, with efficient workers turning out 2,400–2,500 boxes a day. Making boxes smeared with phosphorous paste for striking matches paid 2 cents for 60 but took longer, so that daily earnings peaked at about 20 cents. Here again contractors opened doors by helping women respond to erratic factory schedules: efficient women workers could earn daily wages comparable to those of relatively skilled mill workers by making match boxes at home under contract to the match factory.[74]

---

71. See *SSZ*, 13:47. Again, it is not clear why floor supervisors were paid in Chinese currency while line workers were paid in American money.

72. Stephen Hymer and Stephen Resnick, "A Model of an Agrarian Economy with Nonagricultural Activities," *American Economic Review* 59, no. 4, pt. 1 (1969): 493–506, present an economist's model of these domestic services, which they call Z goods. Z goods are "nonagricultural nonleisure activities" designed to meet the household's needs for food, clothing, shelter, entertainment, and ceremony. Although Hymer and Resnick's analysis makes no specific reference to gender roles, their description of Z goods makes it clear that women's work accounts for the bulk of these activities.

73. *SSZ*, 13:47–48. The sex of these workers is not specified in the source, but if female workers were included, this would have been noted. I have yet to identify a source specifying monthly wages for female factory workers in Ningbo. Females, with the exception of supervisors, appear to have received exclusively day rates.

74. Ibid., 13:653–54.

No wonder that even as these new factories came into being, women's home handicraft industries remained vigorous. Work at home offered numerous advantages for women, and the demand for home-manufactured goods remained strong. At the close of World War I, the market for traditional handicrafts still flourished, with some commodities even expanding their foreign or domestic markets. Home-woven textiles, for instance, succumbed to competition from factory-made goods, as "local cloth" (*Yong bu*), once widely sold in North China, was displaced by Japanese imports. However, home weavers turned to new types of cloth, which they marketed successfully up the Yangzi for a wider clientele. Straw hats and mats remained at the top of the list of local specialties, along with embroidery, fishnets, and joss paper.[75]

In sum, as long as factories did not offer competitive wages or steady employment, and as long as female seclusion remained a mark of status, Ningbo women who had a choice would have seen no reason to abandon home handicrafts for jobs outside the home.[76] Home handicrafts made on contract continued to flourish on a large scale alongside Ningbo's small but growing industrial sector. Local factories could not compete for workers against domestic employment for many reasons. They employed mostly day labor and closed periodically. They required women to work outside the home among strangers. They demanded new skills. Home handicraft industries, by contrast, did not take women away from their homes or from their customary work there—cooking, cleaning, caring for the sick, bearing children, babysitting, mending and making clothes, and keeping their menfolk company. Nyok-Ching Tsur's ideal of "harmonic congeniality" in the household economy survived for both practical and sentimental reasons.

Which Ningbo women did take factory jobs? Not middle-class women, who remained respectably at home. The few thousand women who entered local factories in Ningbo came from poor households strategizing to keep their menfolk afloat. Part-time women workers from such households, recruited locally—usually through female relatives—made up the female labor force that staffed Ningbo's earliest factories.[77] They were paid by the day.

---

75. According to the *Yinxian tongzhi* ("Shihuozhi," pp. 57–58), the volume of exports of straw hats fell from nearly 5 million units in 1927 to about 1.5 million in 1930 and 1931; it was still falling in 1932.

76. Writing in 1908, after one factory had already been operating for a decade, Nyok-Ching Tsur ("Forms of Business," p. 111) saw no threat to the household enterprises and their contractors, though he praised the patriotism of factory founders.

77. See *CIH:C*, pp. 490, 495. In interviews with eight retired women workers from the Hefeng mill, conducted in Ningbo in November 1988, informants commonly named a mother or a mother-in-law as the person who got them their jobs. Some worked to put brothers through school, others to support male kin who were apparently unemployed.

Their output served mainly the domestic market.[78] They remained under the close supervision of their families, a world apart from the women who migrated to Shanghai to labor in the mills. Moreover, since they worked close to home, workers in Ningbo factories were always at the beck and call of the family if their labor was needed urgently at home. High absentee rates meant they were readily fired. And they carried the classic double burden, arriving home after a 12-hour day to find menfolk hungry for a meal and complaining about the late hour.[79]

MIGRATION AND THE FEMALE LABOR FORCE

Only the poorest Ningbo families seem to have sent women to work in local factories. But women workers in Ningbo factories seem to have had no access to the Shanghai factory labor market.[80] Though it remains unclear which families sent women to Shanghai to work and what their status was, the gazetteer for Dinghai County, an island, claims that thousands of its own men and women migrated to Shanghai to work during the early twentieth century. And it is possible that jobs outside the home in Shanghai carried less of a stigma among Ningbo women who migrated there to work far from the prying eyes of local gossips.[81]

The reasons for Shanghai's appeal are not difficult to find. Shanghai factories—regardless of Ningbo factory owners' claims—paid better wages than the Ningbo mills. According to a 1930s survey, female textile workers in Shanghai could expect to earn an average of slightly over 12 *yuan* per month; in Ningbo, as we have seen, monthly factory jobs for women during that time

---

78. The Hefeng Cotton Spinning Mill, for instance, paid most of its workers—1,343 of 1,785 employees—by the day, only 20 by the month, and none by the year. *CIH:C*, p. 483. Yarn from the mill continued to supply local home weavers; it was too coarse to compete in the international market. Yarn from the Hefeng mill was sold in Guangxi, Guangdong, Sichuan, and Tianjin, as well as within Zhejiang Province (p. 485). Perhaps thousands more women were also employed by the factories to do piecework at home under contract, using raw materials supplied by their employers (p. 532).

79. Comments by retired Hefeng mill workers, Ningbo, November 1988.

80. Retired Hefeng mill workers told me that they were aware at the time that many Ningbo women went to Shanghai to work, but they had no way to get there themselves: "You had to have a relative, someone you knew, a connection, a route [*yao you luzi*]."

81. Abundant evidence for the presence of Ningbo women and men in the Shanghai work force suggests that the taboo on women going out to work may have been honored in the breach, at least by many women. See, for example, *Dinghai xianzhi, fangsu*: 51a, which mentions thousands of men and women from Dinghai County working in Shanghai and in Hankou. On Ningbo workers in Shanghai, see also references in Yuen Sang Leung, "Regional Rivalry in Mid-Nineteenth Century Shanghai: Cantonese vs. Ningpo Men," *Ch'ing-shih wen-t'i* 4, no. 8 (1982): 40; and Emily Honig, "The Politics of Prejudice: Subei People in Republican-Era Shanghai," *Modern China* 15, no. 3 (1989): 250–51.

were available only to supervisors.[82] Moreover, many Ningbo workers had easy access to the Shanghai job market, following networks of kinship and friendship long since established by sojourning Ningbo entrepreneurs. In Shanghai, Ningbo's reputation for fostering discipline, hard work, and local pride made Ningbo workers desirable.[83] As male Ningbo workers joined Ningbo's merchant elite abroad,[84] their wives, daughters, sisters, and friends-of-friends followed. It was well known in Shanghai factories that Ningbo women did not have to find jobs through demeaning negotiations with labor contractors.[85] One source suggests that Ningbo workers were placed through workers' associations (*gonghui*), which guaranteed good service to the employer and screened working conditions for the employee.[86] Ningbo maids and Ningbo factory workers benefited from the reputation of their native place throughout Shanghai.[87] Women factory workers in the Shanghai cotton mills all understood that Ningbo recruits would be given the finer, higher-paying women's jobs.[88] And Ningbo prostitutes in Shanghai

82. Mukōyama Hirō, "Kyū Chūgoku ni okeru rōdō jōken," *Ajia kenkyū* 8, no. 4 (1961): 42. Honig, *Sisters and Strangers*, p. 175, reports wages ranging from 14 *yuan* to 27 *yuan* per month for the top jobs in the Shanghai mills. The 1923 gazetteer for Dinghai County reported maids' monthly wages in Shanghai at 3–4 *yuan*, implying that already the mills were luring women out of domestic work and into the factories. See *Dinghai xianzhi, fangsu*: 51a. Note that real wage rates may have been less important than the promise of stable employment. Ningbo's factories were not a source of steady income.

83. Honig, "Politics of Prejudice," pp. 258–59, argues persuasively that reputation was less important than personal connections and access to jobs in various levels of the Shanghai economy.

84. On the rise of occupational associations composed of semiskilled workers in Shanghai, see the *North-China Herald*, July 18, 1910, p. 74. On the growth of the Ningbo working class in Shanghai, see also Susan Mann Jones, "The Ningpo *Pang* and Financial Power at Shanghai," in Mark Elvin and G. William Skinner, eds., *The Chinese City Between Two Worlds* (Stanford, 1974), pp. 86–88. Ningbo women working for Westerners in private homes earned 3 to 4 taels a month. *Dinghai xianzhi, fangsu*: 51a.

85. See Honig, *Sisters and Strangers*, p. 97.

86. *Dinghai xianzhi, fangsu*: 51a, mentions recruitment through *gonghui* but does not explain exactly how it worked.

87. On regional stereotypes of factory workers in the Shanghai textile mills, see Honig, *Sisters and Strangers*, pp. 57–78 et passim; and Chu-fang Chang, "Chinese Cotton Mills in Shanghai," *Chinese Economic Journal and Bulletin* 3, no. 5 (1928): 907–8. Chang observes, "Most of the skilled hands employed in the engine rooms are Shanghai and Ningpo natives. Ningpo woman hands are more skilled than their sisters from other provinces."

88. For more on the prestige of Ningbo women workers, see Honig, *Sisters and Strangers*, pp. 71, 75, 181. In interviews conducted in Shanghai in October 1988, some middle-class Ningbo women told me that most Ningbo women working in the factories at that time were there because of connections to the Green Gang. These informants insisted that factory work for women was not considered respectable by most Ningbo people. This may explain why the main gazetteer account of female factory workers in Shanghai comes from a peripheral Ningbo county, Dinghai.

served an exclusive clientele of merchants and officials from their native place, working in hotels instead of brothels.[89]

Like the Subei region described by Emily Honig elsewhere in this volume, the Ningbo area produced its own distinctive labor market signs and linkages, channeling women workers out of the locality to jobs elsewhere. But unlike Subei people, who were consigned to the lowest-paying, most demeaning jobs, Ningbo people in Shanghai were distinguished by their ties to Shanghai's new bourgeoisie. Perhaps for that reason, it is extremely difficult to obtain precise information about the number and class background of Ningbo women factory workers. The respectable Ningbo woman was to stay at home while her menfolk went out to work to support her. Her presence in a factory was an embarrassment to her native place.

CONCLUSION

An economist called upon to "tell a story" explaining the fate of Ningbo women in the early twentieth-century household economy would have to take account not only of expanding access to international and domestic markets for the products of women's labor. The story would also have to point to region, class, and values as critical determinants of which women went out to work and where they went. While Ningbo women in better-off families clearly stood to benefit from the economic transformations of the early twentieth century, wives and daughters in poor households assumed a new double burden.[90]

This chapter has not considered how the economic changes I have described may have undermined time-honored assumptions about women's place in the home in Ningbo.[91] An untold part of my story therefore raises

---

89. Hershatter, "Prostitution," discusses the Shanghai market for female prostitutes during this period. Ningbo prostitutes in Shanghai, privileged by the native-place ties discussed in this chapter, limited their sexual services to clients from their own native place: away from home, at least, they were elite members of a marginal social category.

90. Of course a household that counted productive women among its members could not be considered the poorest of the poor, even in Ningbo. The very survival of females to maturity—the very existence of a female labor force within the domestic group—was a measure of a household's wherewithal. The poorest Ningbo families, forced to reduce expenditures, adjust family size to resources, and make plans for survival, put up their daughters for adoption as *tongyangxi* ("little daughters-in-law") and lost their labor before it became profitable. Even where the labor of mature females promised increasing income, therefore, the poorest households could not invest enough to rear daughters to maturity; among the poor, in the worst of times, even wives and mothers were expendable. During the depression years, "wife renting" was widely reported in the Ningbo area (Luo Qiong, "Zhongguo nongcunzhong," p. 22).

91. Janet Salaff's and Susan Greenhalgh's research in Hong Kong and Taiwan, respectively, suggests that changing patterns of women's work barely impinge upon persistent beliefs in pa-

another question: what were the effects of economic change on women's lives in other spheres? For example, the expansion of women's educational opportunities in the Ningbo area opened doors to some women whose place in the household and the economy was changing rapidly.[92] A few Ningbo women, we know, became politically active; some embarked on new careers in the professions.[93] But the vast majority of Ningbo women remained at the center of the household economy where, more than ever before, the nature of women's work marked the difference between economic failure and success.

---

triarchal authority and the primacy of males in the Chinese family. Honig, on the other hand, points to significant changes in the consciousness of women workers between the 1920s and 1940s, though she does not ask whether changing consciousness in the workplace led to changing domestic relations in the home. See Janet Salaff, *Working Daughters of Hong Kong* (New York, 1981); Susan Greenhalgh, "Sexual Stratification: The Other Side of 'Growth with Equity' in East Asia," *Population and Development Review* 11, no. 2 (1985): 265–314; and Honig, *Sisters and Strangers*, pp. 202–43.

92. See, for example, a report in the *North-China Herald*, Aug. 2, 1907:249, detailing local movements for women's education in Ningbo. The report mentions a women's club presided over by the wife of the local *daotai* (circuit intendant) and observes that unbound feet were becoming "quite common" among ladies from official and gentry families. In a survey of women's education in China, Ida Belle Lewis notes that the first missionary school for girls in China was opened at Ningbo in 1844 (p. 18). Her map of the distribution of Protestant mission schools in 1918 shows more than 40 day schools in Ningbo and adjacent Shaoxing Prefectures. She has no data on private and public Chinese girls' schools for the same period in the Ningbo region, but given their rapid expansion during the period of her study, we can expect there were several. See Ida Belle Lewis, *The Education of Girls in China* (New York, 1919). *Shina kaikōjōshi* (Tokyo 1922), 1:173–74, lists only two missionary schools for girls in Ningbo.

93. In 1907, the young woman revolutionary Qiu Jin was executed in adjacent Shaoxing Prefecture. See the *North-China Herald*, Aug. 2, 1907: 249–50; for a fuller discussion, see Mary Backus Rankin, "The Emergence of Women at the End of the Ch'ing: The Case of Ch'iu Chin," in Margery Wolf and Roxane Witke, eds., *Women in Chinese Society* (Stanford, 1975), pp. 39–66. On women's activism inspired by Qiu Jin, see R. Keith Schoppa, *Chinese Elites and Political Change: Zhejiang Province in the Early Twentieth Century* (Cambridge, Mass., 1982), p. 76. Research by Elizabeth Perry may show whether Ningbo women workers in Shanghai abandoned the traditional roles of their home area and threw themselves into radical political activity. Bryna Goodman's research in Shanghai has shown that professional Ningbo women's names appear in membership lists of the Ningbo guild activities in Shanghai during the 1920s and 1930s. Personal conversations with Perry, Oct. 8, 1987; with Goodman, Oct. 6, 1987. See Bryna Goodman, "The Native Place and the City: Immigrant Consciousness and Organization in Shanghai, 1853–1927" (Ph.D. diss., Stanford University, 1990).

NINE

Native-Place Hierarchy and Labor Market Segmentation: The Case of Subei People in Shanghai

Emily Honig

Both historians and economists have long been concerned with the nature of social inequalities and the processes by which they are created. This inquiry has often focused on employment opportunities, documenting the vastly different conditions of work and rewards for labor experienced by various groups of people. Recognizing that not all people have access to the same sets of jobs, institutional economists began, in the decades after World War II, to describe distinct and exclusive labor markets.[1] Peter Doeringer and Michael Piore, writing in the early 1970s, argued that labor markets were divided into a primary and a secondary sector. Jobs in the former offered relatively high wages, desirable working conditions, job stability, and potential for advancement. The secondary sector, however, was characterized by low-paying jobs, few benefits, no security, high rates of turnover, and poor working conditions.[2] Subsequent scholars insisted that this theory of "dual" labor markets overlooked the multiplicity of labor market segmentation that existed.[3] Richard Edwards, Michael Reich, and David Gordon, for example, defined three labor markets.[4]

I am grateful to the participants in the Workshop on Economic Methods for Chinese Historical Research, particularly Thomas G. Rawski, for critical comments on previous versions of this article. I would also like to thank Gail Hershatter and Christine Wong for their suggestions. Research for this article was made possible by grants from the Wang Institute for Graduate Studies and the National Endowment for the Humanities.

1. An excellent summary of this literature is in Mark Granovetter and Charles Tilly, "Inequality and Labor Processes," *New School for Social Research Working Paper Series* 29 (July 1986).

2. Peter Doeringer and Michael Piore, *Internal Labor Markets and Manpower Analysis* (New York, 1985), pp. 165–70.

3. See Richard Edwards, Michael Reich, and David Gordon, eds., *Labor Market Segmentation* (Lexington, Mass., 1975). See also David Gordon, Richard Edwards, and Michael Reich, *Segmented Work, Divided Workers: The Historical Transformation of Labor in the United States* (Cambridge, 1982).

4. The three markets are most precisely described in Richard Edwards, *Contested Terrain: The*

Despite disagreements over the number of labor markets and the exact jobs associated with each, these economists all share a recognition that no single labor market exists to which everyone enjoys equal access. Furthermore, they agree that there are vast differences among the markets: positions in some are more privileged, lucrative, and secure than in others. Finally, they share a conviction that differences in the labor markets both reflect and reinforce inequalities among different social groups, defined usually by gender, race, ethnicity, religion, or nationality.

This paper explores the relationship between divided labor markets and social inequality in Shanghai during the late nineteenth and early twentieth centuries. Although the components of the Shanghai labor market do not correlate in any precise way to those described in the United States, distinct and exclusive labor markets existed. The divisions were obvious and crucial to those who labored in Shanghai and are particularly apparent when we shift our focus beyond factory work to examine the labor market in its entirety.

Labor segmentation theory might appear unable to explain these divisions, because aside from the foreign presence, the working population of Shanghai was not divided by race, nationality, or religion as in the United States. Closer examination, though, shows that in Shanghai local origins played a role analogous to that played by ethnicity elsewhere. An analysis of the relationship between labor market segmentation and social inequality in Shanghai therefore requires an examination of the role of native-place identity.

Shanghai was a city composed primarily of immigrants, though not from across national boundaries. From 1885 to 1935, Shanghai natives accounted for an average of only 19 percent of the population of the International Concession and 26 percent of the population of the Chinese-owned parts of the city.[5] As the city developed into a large commercial and industrial metropolis, laborers, merchants, and entrepreneurs came mostly from three areas: Guangdong, Jiangnan (the Ningbo/Shaoxing region of Zhejiang and the Wuxi/Changzhou area of Jiangsu), and Subei (the area of Jiangsu north of the Yangzi River and south of the Huai, sometimes called Jiangbei; see Map 9.1).[6] Which of these areas one hailed from was critical in shaping work

---

Transformation of the Workplace in the Twentieth Century (New York, 1979), pp. 167–74. Piore accepted the notion of three labor markets, although he used slightly different labels: in addition to the secondary market, he describes an upper and a lower primary sector. See Michael Piore, "Notes for a Theory of Labor Market Stratification," in Edwards et al., *Labor Market Segmentation*, pp. 125–50.

5. Zou Yiren, *Jiu Shanghai renkou bianqiande yanjiu* (Shanghai, 1980), pp. 112–13.

6. Ibid. No standard definition of Subei exists. Most literally, it would include all of Jiangsu that lies north of the Yangzi River, from Haimen and Nantong in the south to Xuzhou in the

Map 9.1. Jiangsu Province, 1935.

opportunities, residential patterns, cultural activities, and social status. Hierarchy, in other words, was structured largely according to native-place identification: the elite was composed primarily of people from Guangdong and Jiangnan, the unskilled service sector staffed mostly by migrants from Subei. So marked was the equation of local origin and economic status that Jiangnan culture became the symbol of urban sophistication and modernity, while the language, customs, and manners of people from Subei were associated with backwardness. Their inferior status was so generally accepted that the term "Subei folk" (Subei *ren*) connoted to Shanghainese poverty, filth, and uncivilized manners.

In this paper I focus on the experience of Subei people in Shanghai to explore labor market segmentation and its relationship to social inequality. The first part of the paper examines the status of Subei people in the labor market; the second part, addressing a question overlooked by labor market segmentation theorists, analyzes the reasons that Subei people in particular were tracked into and trapped in an inferior status. The divisions in Shanghai's labor markets, we shall see, both reflected and created the prejudice against Subei people that has been so prominent throughout the twentieth century.

THE REGIONAL NATURE OF THE SHANGHAI LABOR MARKET

Subei people constituted one of the largest immigrant populations in Shanghai, by 1949 representing approximately one fifth of the city's 5 million residents.[7] Whether they had migrated from Subei themselves or were the offspring of Subei migrants, whether they were poor peasants fleeing the prospect of starvation or wealthy landowners fleeing land reform in the 1940s, Subei people in Shanghai concentrated in jobs that Shanghainese regarded as inferior. Republican period surveys of the Shanghai work force reveal three general patterns: (1) unskilled, physically demanding occupations were dominated almost exclusively by people from Subei; (2) occupa-

---

northwestern corner. Most geographers, however, consider the part of the province north of the Huai (and the former bed of the Yellow River) to belong to Huaibei, a different geographic region. The distinction between Subei and Huaibei is based on language as well as geography: Xuzhou dialect (close to Shandong dialect) predominates north of the Huai, while Yangzhou dialect prevails in almost all areas south of the Huai and north of the Yangzi.

7. It is impossible to know the exact percentage of the Shanghai population that was composed of people from Subei for other points in time, since population statistics that indicate native place specify only the province, not the district or county. According to the only available statistic, there were 1.5 million people from Subei in Shanghai in 1949. The entire population of Shanghai at that time was 5,062,878. See Xie Junmei, "Shanghai lishishang renkou de bianqian," *Shehui kexue* 3 (1980): 112.

tions attracting people from Jiangnan as well as Subei were stratified, with Subei people performing the lowest-paying, lowest-status jobs; and (3) jobs requiring high levels of skill or education were rarely available to Subei people.

The description of the labor market that follows relies on qualitative as well as quantitative data. An analysis of labor market segmentation in Shanghai would ideally include wage data, comparing the earnings of workers in different occupations. Unfortunately, such data are largely unavailable. Most of the unskilled jobs performed by Subei people were never surveyed by officials, who were more concerned with the plight of factory workers. Even when data are available, they are often unreliable. For instance, wage data for rickshaw pullers ignore the amount they had to pay for renting the rickshaw; conversely, wage data for barbers ignore the room and board that came with the job. Wage rates for most occupations fail to account for the seasonal nature of employment. Finally, wage data for any given occupation obscure the multitude of grades of workers within that enterprise, each of which had a different salary. Therefore, in the discussion that follows, wage data are used only when they may be helpful in placing the earnings of Subei workers in perspective.[8]

It was not in the ranks of the industrial proletariat but rather among coolie laborers that Subei people were most commonly found in Shanghai. Occupations most closely associated with Subei people were those that required little skill, were physically demanding, offered low pay, and promised only irregular employment. They were, in other words, precisely the kinds of job constituting the "secondary market" in the theory of dual labor markets.

Rickshaw pulling, more than any other occupation, was associated with and symbolized the status of Subei people in the Shanghai labor market. From the beginning of Shanghai's rapid development in the mid-nineteenth century, transport vehicles that depended on human labor power were considered the domain of Subei migrants. In the 1860s, well before the appearance of rickshaws, wheelbarrows used to transport both materials and people were called "Jiangbei carts," since Subei migrants were the majority of cart pullers.[9] When rickshaws began to be used in 1875, Subei people immediately took over the work of hauling rickshaws. By 1913, when there were approximately 10,000 rickshaw pullers in Shanghai, an estimated 80–90 percent were from Subei.[10] By the mid-1930s, when the number of rickshaw

8. For a more thorough discussion of the problems of wage data in Shanghai, see Shanghai Bureau of Social Affairs, City Government of Shanghai, *Wage Rates in Shanghai* (Shanghai, 1935), pp. 33–62.

9. Shanghaishi Chuzu Qiche Gongsi, "Shanghai jiedao he gonglu yingye keyun shiliao huiji" (Shanghai, 1982), p. 17.

10. Huang Renjing, *Huren baojian* (Shanghai, 1913), p. 85.

pullers had soared to 80,000, 90 percent were of Subei origin.[11] So extreme was the dominance of rickshaw pulling by people from Subei that one Republican period surveyor complained that the prevalence of Subei dialect among rickshaw pullers was an obstacle to his research work.[12] Another reporter observed that only Subei people, plagued by natural disasters and economic destruction in their home villages, would condescend to do this "bestial" and "inhuman" work.[13]

While rickshaw pulling may have been the job most immediately associated with Subei people, migrants from northern Jiangsu also dominated the ranks of freight haulers. The approximately 50,000 Shanghai dock workers in the 1930s were dominated by the so-called Subei *bang*. The predominance of Subei people among the loaders at the Shanghai docks was so extreme that, as in rickshaw pulling, the Subei dialect was the language of the trade.[14] And like rickshaw pulling, dock work did not offer stable employment. Most employees worked on a temporary basis, usually 15 to 20 days a month.[15] Most of the workers who hauled freight at the Shanghai train station were also from Subei.[16]

The final category of jobs dominated by Subei people was in the service sector. The overwhelming majority of barbers, bathhouse attendants, cobblers, and night soil and garbage collectors were from Subei.[17] Particularly the latter two jobs—quite literally "shit work"—were ones that only Subei people seemed willing to do, both confirming and reinforcing their lowly status. As one description of Shanghai Municipal Council employees notes, "Country people from Jiangbei, the Chinese who are most able to swallow hardship, are concentrated in the garbage department. Although there are individual Jiangbei people in other departments, the garbage department is

11. Shanghaishi Shehuiju, "Shanghaishi renli chefu shenghuo zhuangkuang diaocha baogaoshu," *Shehui banyuekan*, Sept. 10, 1934, p. 103.
12. Ibid.
13. Shanghaishi Renlicheye Tongye Gonghui, *Shanghai gongbuju gaige renliche jiufen zhenxiang* (Shanghai, 1934), p. 3.
14. Zhu Bangxing, Hu Lin'ge, and Xu Sheng, *Shanghai chanye yu Shanghai zhigong* (Hong Kong, 1939), p. 573. In addition to the Subei *bang*, there were also Hubei, Ningbo, and Guangdong *bang* at the docks. According to one study, workers from Subei did the heaviest jobs of transporting cargo on shoulder poles, while those from Guangdong worked aboard the boats, arranging cargo. Shanghai Gangshi Hua Bianxie zu, *Shanghai gangshi hua* (Shanghai, 1979), pp. 276–79.
15. Shanghai Gangshi Hua Bianxie zu, *Shanghai gangshi hua*, p. 276.
16. Li Cishan, "Shanghai laodong qingkuang," *Xin qingnian* 7, no. 6 (May 1920): 60.
17. On the dominance of Subei people among barbers, see Li Cishan, "Shanghai laodong qingkuang," pp. 48–49. See also *Shen Bao*, Apr. 26, 1915. For bathhouse workers, see Shanghaishi Renmin Zhengfu Gongshangju Jingji Jihuachu, ed., *Shanghai siying gongshangye fenye gaikuang* (Shanghai, 1951), p. 66; for cobblers, see *Shen Bao*, Apr. 26, 1915; for night soil collectors, see interview with Zhou Guozhen, Zhabei District Sanitation Bureau, Shanghai, Nov. 3, 1986; for garbage collectors, see Zhu Bangxing et al., *Shanghai chanye*, p. 607.

really theirs."[18] So demeaning was it to be a garbage collector that a man from Yancheng preferred the privation of unemployment. When, in order to survive, he finally had no choice but to become a garbage collector, he did not want anyone to know. "Garbage collectors employed by the city had to wear a red shirt," he recalled. "I hated wearing that red shirt because everyone could then see who I was and what I did. So as soon as we finished work each day, I would take off that shirt."[19]

The occupations dominated by Subei people were characterized by a further regional hierarchy. The most important division was between people from Yangzhou and those from the more northern areas of Yancheng and Funing. In general, people from Yangzhou had the jobs requiring slightly more skill and offering better working conditions than those employing people from farther north, reflecting perhaps the prosperity of Yangzhou compared with Yancheng. While some Yangzhou people could be found in all the occupations discussed above, they were particularly known for dominating the "three knives" occupations as barbers, bathhouse pedicurists, and cooks.[20] Yangzhou was famous as an exporter of barbers, particularly to Shanghai, and the head of the barbers' guild in 1920, Chen Sihai, was a Yangzhou native.[21] As one man who had come from a village near Yangzhou in the 1930s to work as a barber in Shanghai recalled, "My father was a barber in Shanghai; I was a barber, and my brother was a barber. In our village, at least ten out of every twenty families had members who were barbers in Shanghai!"[22] People from Yancheng and Funing, in contrast, could claim dominance of the rickshaw-pulling profession. A survey of the native place of rickshaw pullers in 1934–35 showed some 53 percent coming from Yancheng and Funing, while only 17 percent hailed from the area near Yangzhou.[23]

The hierarchy of jobs dominated by Yangzhou and by Yancheng and Funing people was confirmed by attitudes of pride and resentment expressed by people from each of those areas. People from Yancheng knew they could

18. Zhu Bangxing et al., *Shanghai chanye*, p. 607.
19. Interview with the author at the Jing'an District Sanitation Bureau, Shanghai, Nov. 18, 1986.
20. Wu Liangrong, "Shanghaishi Subeiji jumin shehui biandong fenxi," in Shanghai shehuixue xuehui, ed., *Shehuixue wenji* (Shanghai, 1984), p. 177.
21. Li Cishan, "Shanghai laodong qingkuang," pp. 48–49.
22. Interview with He Zhenghua, Xinxin Beauty Salon, Shanghai, Nov. 12, 1986. There were also a number of barbers in Shanghai from Zhenjiang, but the Yangzhou *bang* was clearly the dominant one. See Li Cishan, "Shanghai laodong qingkuang," pp. 48–49; see also *Shen Bao*, Apr. 26, 1915.
23. Shanghaishi Chuzu Qiche Gongsi, "Shanghai jiedao," pp. 127–29. This survey was of 3,517 rickshaw pullers. The predominance of people from Yancheng and Funing among rickshaw pullers is confirmed by another 1934 survey. See Shanghaishi Shehuiju, "Shanghaishi renli," pp. 104–5.

not aspire to enter the occupations controlled by the Yangzhou *bang*. "The jobs done by people from Yangzhou were much better than ours," a man from Jianhu (near Yancheng) observed bitterly. "Their work was easier and lighter. Being a barber was much better than pulling a rickshaw! The worst work was hauling night soil carts, collecting garbage, and sweeping the streets. Not many Yangzhou people did those kinds of job. They were mostly in barber shops and bathhouses."[24]

The envy Yancheng people felt for Yangzhou natives was matched by pride among the Yangzhounese. So strong was their sense of job superiority that people from Yangzhou sometimes expressed precisely the same attitudes of scorn and disgust toward Yancheng people that Jiangnan natives more frequently expressed toward Subei people as a group. Their sense of superiority was occasionally so extreme that they insisted Yangzhou was not part of Subei. For example, in explaining why the bathhouse bosses hired only people from Yangzhou, one man, himself a pedicurist from Yangzhou, said:

> It was because we people from Yangzhou know how to speak well; we speak in a rather cultivated way. It was important for the service people to speak well, or the customers would not come. Our speech is very careful and soft, while theirs [people from Yancheng] is very crude—*wawawawawawa*. We were much more picky, while Subei people were very coarse; we were very sophisticated, while they were very poor.
>
> Even though we were from Yangzhou, people still used to call us "Jiangbei folk." It was derogatory and it upset us. We knew we were from Yangzhou and were not really Jiangbei folk, but they did not know the difference.[25]

Even he admitted, however, that despite the skill required to be a barber or pedicurist, both occupations were regarded as low-class by the more elite groups in Shanghai. Moreover, although the Yangzhou natives who worked in the service trades may well have represented the elite of Subei workers, their earnings were substantially less than even those Jiangnan natives who worked in the service sector. For example, tailors, most of whom came from the Jiangnan areas of Ningbo and Changzhou, earned 3–7 *yuan* (dollars) a day in 1920, while barbers could only count on making 2–3 *jiao* (dimes).[26]

In addition to the occupations described above—ones completely dominated by Subei natives—a number of enterprises employed workers from both Jiangnan and Subei. Almost all such enterprises had a hierarchy of jobs in which Jiangnan natives were at the top and Subei people at the bottom. The most important such case, in terms of the number of Subei people employed, was factory work. As noted above, the majority of Subei migrants worked outside the ranks of the industrial proletariat. For them, factory employment

---

24. Interview with Zhou Guozhen.
25. Interview with Xu Liansheng, Yudechi Bathhouse, Shanghai, Nov. 12, 1986.
26. Li Cishan, "Shanghai laodong qingkuang," pp. 48–49.

was the highest-status work to which they could aspire. Recalled a man from Yancheng, who worked as a garbage collector, "We really wanted to work in a factory, and I was very envious of my relatives who had factory jobs. But we just couldn't get in."[27] Another man who worked for the city's sanitation bureau insisted with absolute certainty that "no people who were themselves born in Subei could get jobs in cotton mills. The only Subei people who were able to work in cotton mills were people who had been born and raised in Shanghai."[28] In fact, a sizable number of women actually born and raised in Subei worked in Shanghai's cotton mills.[29] His distorted impression shows that, for Subei people, securing a factory job was considered a step up.

The elite of Shanghai's industrial working class—those who performed highly skilled jobs, became technicians, and were employed at the highest wage rates—were primarily from Guangdong and Jiangnan. The scarce information available about the native-place origins of factory workers in the late nineteenth and early twentieth centuries suggests that Subei people were quite possibly latecomers to factory work in Shanghai.[30] The earliest groups of factory workers were from Canton, Ningbo, and Shanghai proper. For example, when the first machine-building factories were established in the 1850s, skilled workers were recruited from Canton, where a foreign-owned shipbuilding factory already operated. Peasants from Ningbo and Shanghai were employed to perform the unskilled jobs. No mention was made of any workers from Subei.[31]

When, in the early 1920s, Subei people began to appear in records of factory workers, they concentrated in industries that generally required the least skill and offered the lowest pay, such as silk reeling and cotton spinning. For example, while workers in the machinery industry earned an average of $0.85 a day in 1934, and those in shipbuilding earned $1.24, workers in silk filatures earned only $0.31, and in cotton spinning only $0.47. This gap partly reflects the difference in the earnings of male and female workers, for

---

27. Interview with the author at the Jing'an District Sanitation Bureau, Shanghai, Nov. 18, 1986.
28. Interview with Zhou Guozhen.
29. Emily Honig, *Sisters and Strangers: Women in the Shanghai Cotton Mills, 1919–1949* (Stanford, 1986), pp. 59–62.
30. The possibility that Subei people were latecomers to factory work, suggested by the scarce factory records that are available, is reinforced by the description of Subei people in a Japanese study written in 1909. The author observed a "class" comprising Subei people who worked as cobblers, coolies, cart and rickshaw pullers, night soil and garbage collectors, and peddlers. No mention was made of Subei people as factory workers at that time. This does not imply that no Subei people worked in factories but rather that their number was relatively small. See Tōa Dōbunkai, *Shina keizai zensho* (Osaka, 1908), 1:388–89.
31. Zhongguo Shehui Kexueyuan Jingji Yanjiusuo, ed., *Shanghai minzu jiqi gongye* (Beijing, 1966), 1:50–51, 58, 68. See also Yuen Sang Leung, "Regional Rivalry in Mid-Nineteenth Century Shanghai: Cantonese vs. Ningpo Men," *Ch'ing-shih wen-t'i* 4, no. 8 (Dec. 1982): pp. 39–40.

the machinery and shipbuilding industries were dominated by men, while textiles primarily employed women. Yet even within the female-dominated textile industries, those dominated by Subei natives—cotton spinning and silk reeling—offered substantially less pay than industries where the majority of workers came from Jiangnan. In underwear-knitting factories, workers earned an average of $0.79 a day in 1934; in silk-weaving factories, $0.90; in cotton-weaving factories, $0.61; and in tobacco factories, $0.57[32]—more than they earned in either cotton-spinning or silk-reeling factories.

Even within cotton mills and silk filatures, the higher-paying, skilled jobs went to people from Jiangnan. In the cotton-spinning industry—one of the largest employers of Subei workers—Subei women, considered strong, robust, and accustomed to dirt, were channeled into the workshops where the work was most arduous and dirty. Initially they dominated the undesirable jobs in the reeling workshops; in the 1930s, when mill managers began to hire women instead of men in the roving workshops, they recruited Subei women for the jobs.[33] "This was because natives of Shanghai were not willing to do that work," a mill manager explained. "The wages were not necessarily the lowest, but the work was rough. In roving there was more dust and the air was not very good. Since the work was hard, Subei people were more able to do it."[34] Women from Jiangnan villages concentrated in the weaving department, where the jobs generally required more skill and paid better: in 1934, women weavers earned an average of $0.64 a day, while women spinners earned $0.46; women rovers $0.53; and women reelers $0.43.[35] Furthermore, a number of Jiangnan women who worked in the mills eventually became factory supervisors, secretaries, or bookkeepers, advancements unimaginable to women from Subei.[36]

A similar division of labor between workers from Jiangnan and Subei was apparent in the silk-reeling industry. (The separate, and more prestigious, silk-weaving industry was dominated by workers from Zhejiang, Changzhou, and Suzhou.)[37] When the head of the YWCA Labor Bureau, Cora Deng, visited a Shanghai silk filature in the late 1920s, she was especially struck

---

32. Bureau of Social Affairs, *Wage Rates in Shanghai* (Shanghai, 1935), pp. 80–81. These wage statistics serve only as a rough index of the differences in earnings of workers in Jiangnan-dominated versus Subei-dominated industries. As averages, they represent workers in all workshops of particular industries, women, men, and children, those employed on both time and piece rates. They do not take into account the seasonal nature of some industries.

33. The division of labor according to native place in the cotton industry is discussed more extensively in Honig, *Sisters and Strangers*, pp. 72–74.

34. Interview with He Zhiguang, Putuo District Federation of Commerce and Industry, Shanghai, June 26, 1980.

35 Bureau of Social Affairs, *Wage Rates*, pp. 102–3; 108–9. This represents the wage for women in the weaving department of cotton mills, whereas the $0.61 listed earlier is for women in separate weaving mills.

36. Honig, *Sisters and Strangers*, p. 73.

37. Zhu Bangxing et al., *Shanghai chanye*, p. 125.

by the concentration of Subei women in the worst jobs, which often involved the painful work of bobbing silk cocoons in boiling water. Women from Jiangnan, on the other hand—having personal connections to the factory management—were hired to work under much better conditions.[38] Likewise, in the tobacco industry, where most of the workers were from Zhejiang, the minority of Subei workers were hired only to perform the unskilled tasks. Employed on a temporary basis, they were reportedly "maltreated and abused practically all the time, sometimes even being punched and kicked."[39] In the flour industry, dominated by workers from Ningbo, Wuxi, and Changzhou, those from Subei worked primarily as coolies, loading the heavy sacks of flour to be transported for sale.[40]

Even among prostitutes, the division between women from Jiangnan and Subei (and the further division between Yangzhou and the northern parts of Subei) was obvious to observers. The highest-class prostitutes (*changsan*), who lived in lavishly furnished brothels, acquired skills as entertainers, and catered only to wealthy businessmen and officials, came from Jiangnan. The second-class prostitutes (*yao'er*) were primarily from Yangzhou. Women (and more commonly girls) from Subei, many of whom had been kidnapped from their home villages, were the overwhelming majority of "wild chickens" (*ye ji*), who wandered the streets of Shanghai's red-light district soliciting customers.[41]

The dominance of Subei people in unskilled, low-paying jobs may obscure an equally important aspect of the work experience of Subei people in Shanghai: many never entered the formal labor market at all or worked outside it for long periods of time. Large numbers of Subei migrants eked out a living by peddling food, collecting and selling paper, hulling rice, making and selling charcoal briquettes, or doing other people's laundry. The garbage collector Zhou Guozhen spent several years supporting himself by peddling vegetables before securing a regular job in the city's sanitation bureau.[42] One man who eventually worked as a rickshaw puller survived by picking and selling garbage when he first came to Shanghai in 1925; another made shoes and repaired umbrellas; a woman helped support her family by making charcoal briquettes and by selling vegetables and occasionally fish.[43] Chen Dewang, selected as a model worker in the 1950s, recalled that upon arriving in Shanghai from Hai'an in 1944, he first lived with a group of rickshaw pullers in

38. Yuzhi Deng, "A Visit to a Silk Filature in Shanghai," *Green Year Supplement* (Nov. 1928): 9–10.
39. Shanghai Shehui Kexueyuan Jingji Yanjiusuo, *Nanyang Xiongdi Yancao Gongsi shiliao* (Shanghai, 1958), p. 74.
40. Shanghai Shehui Kexueyuan Jingji Yanjiusuo, *Rongjia qiye shiliao* (Shanghai, 1980), 1:134.
41. Honig, *Sisters and Strangers*, p. 71. See also Huang Renjing, *Huren baojian*, p. 127.
42. Interview with Zhou Guozhen.
43. Interview with retired workers at the Zhongxing Street Residence Committee, Zhabei District, Shanghai, Nov. 4, 1986.

the Nanshi District—all men from Subei who had come to Shanghai alone. "I couldn't pull a rickshaw then because I was too small. People felt sorry for me because I had no parents, so they let me wash their clothes, clean vegetables, and help them cook." When he was finally tall enough to pull a rickshaw, he still could not afford the rent, so he spent several years pulling other people's rickshaws when they were between shifts. Only after several years was Chen able to borrow enough money to rent a rickshaw with three other men and begin to work regular shifts.[44] Some women from Subei gleaned some cash by working as "poor people's seamstresses" (*feng qiong po*), sewing and mending clothes for factory workers and apprentices whose wives remained in the countryside.[45] Many people from Subei, in other words, worked for long periods of time outside or on the fringes of the formal labor market, some never securing regular jobs at all. For them, regular employment as a rickshaw puller or garbage collector was a step up.

To the extent that Subei people performed casual labor and concentrated in unskilled, low-paying jobs, the Shanghai labor market was a divided one. The labor markets that employed people from Jiangnan were almost completely inaccessible to Subei migrants. Broadly understood, then, labor market segmentation theory contributes to a description and analysis of the status of Subei people in Shanghai, where hierarchical divisions were based on native place rather than race or nationality. It explains how the Shanghai labor market reinforced and perpetuated inequalities between Subei and Jiangnan natives, as the American labor market has done between blacks and whites.

The question that remains, however, concerns the *creation* of those inequalities. Labor market segmentation theorists, writing about the United States, assume the relative status of various social groups—that white people, for example, are of a higher status than black people and are therefore more likely to be found in one of the primary sectors of the labor market. Focusing more on how the labor markets actually operate, the theorists do not offer an explanation of why certain groups are located in particular sectors. Yet the relative status of Jiangnan and Subei natives cannot be taken for granted. Understanding the status of Subei people in Shanghai requires an examination of why they, in particular, dominated the ranks of laborers in unskilled, low-paying, physically demanding jobs.

THE ORIGINS OF NATIVE-PLACE HIERARCHY

An explanation of the concentration of Subei people in the unskilled sector of the Shanghai labor market must begin with an examination of the region

---

44. Interview with Chen Dewang, Shanghai Taxicab Company, Oct. 30, 1986.
45. Tu Shipin, *Shanghai chunqiu* (Hong Kong, 1968), part 3, p. 90.

from which they emigrated and the circumstances under which they arrived in Shanghai seeking work. Conventional wisdom holds that Subei was traditionally a poverty-stricken, disaster-ridden region—representing the polar opposite of the economically advanced and prosperous Jiangnan. While poverty was the background to most migration that began in the early nineteenth century, Subei had not always been the economically inferior part of Jiangsu Province. Its prosperity, in fact, had previously rivaled that of Jiangnan. "The Grand Canal and the Huanghe [Yellow] River along with the waterways branching out from them," observes the anthropologist Hsiao Tung Fei (Fei Xiaotong), "once formed a web of canals resembling those seen south of the Changjiang [Yangzi] today."[46] The city of Huaiyin, along the Grand Canal, had been the center for the tributary grain transport administration during the Qing.[47] Yangzhou, a transshipment point on the Grand Canal, had been one of the most prosperous and famed cultural centers of China since the Tang. It "was the jewel of China in the eighth century," according to E. H. Schafer,

> a bustling, bourgeois city where money flowed easily . . . a gay city, a city of well-dressed people, a city where the best entertainment was always available, a city of parks and gardens, a very Venice, traversed by waterways, where the boats outnumbered the carriages. It was a city of moonlight and lanterns, a city of song and dance, a city of courtesans.[48]

Through the mid-Qing, Yangzhou remained a city whose wealth and prestige attracted merchants, artists, scholars, tourists, and even the Qianlong emperor himself on six occasions. Described as the "epitomy of Southern culture" and "the nerve center of domestic trade," it boasted teahouses, restaurants, literary salons, and some of the most famed artistic talents in China.[49]

Only in the nineteenth century did Subei decline in prosperity and prestige. Its impoverishment can be attributed to two interrelated events. First, the Grand Canal was replaced by sea transport, particularly for the shipment of grain from southern to northern China. Coastal ships, first used in the 1820s when Yellow River silting severely impeded the passage of boats through the canal, became the major means of transporting tribute grain

---

46. Hsiao Tung Fei, "Small Towns in Northern Jiangsu," in Hsiao Tung Fei et al., *Small Towns in China* (Beijing, 1986), p. 91.

47. Harold Hinton, "The Grain Tribute System of the Ch'ing Dynasty," *Far Eastern Quarterly* 11, no. 3 (May 1952): 345.

48. E. H. Schafer, quoted in Antonia Finnane, "Prosperity and Decline under the Qing: Yangzhou and Its Hinterland, 1644–1810" (Ph.D. diss., Australian National University, 1985), p. 34.

49. Ping-ti Ho, "The Salt Merchants of Yang-chou: A Study of Commercial Capitalism in Eighteenth-Century China," *Harvard Journal of Asiatic Studies* 17 (June 1954): 156–58. See also Finnane, "Prosperity and Decline," pp. 2, 279–304.

beginning in the 1840s.[50] This meant that certain cities and towns in Subei lost their importance as transportation and commercial centers. Mid-nineteenth-century Yangzhou, for example, was described as a "skeleton" of its former self.[51] Decline of the Grand Canal also meant that the government paid less attention to maintaining and repairing the dikes on waterways connecting with the canal, thereby leaving parts of Subei vulnerable to unprecedented numbers of floods and natural disasters.[52] Second, in 1853 the Yellow River shifted course: rather than flowing into Hongze Lake and then across Subei to the sea, it now ran northeast from Kaifeng, then crossed Shandong. The Huai River subsequently emptied into Hongze Lake with no further outlet, thereby becoming a source of treacherous flooding in Subei.[53] From the mid-nineteenth century on, then, cycles of floods, famine, and poverty characterized large portions of Subei.

The impoverishment and decline of Subei was made all the more conspicuous by the simultaneously rapid economic development of Jiangnan. By the early twentieth century, Jiangnan was as famous for its wealth as Subei was for its poverty. These differences between the two parts of the province were more than impressionistic. Modern industry as it developed in Jiangsu was centered almost entirely in the cities of Jiangnan. In 1931, for example, some 95 percent of Jiangsu's 403,152 industrial workers were employed in Shanghai and cities of Jiangnan, such as Wuxi or Changzhou. In Subei, only the city of Nantong could boast a significant number of factory workers; cities farther north, such as Yangzhou, Yancheng, and Funing, had fewer than 100 workers each.[54] Whereas industry was a growing part of the Jiangnan economy, Subei continued to depend on agricultural production—it was a major producer of cotton, salt, and pigs (thereby giving rise to the derogatory expression "Jiangbei swine" in Shanghai dialect).[55] Even when it came to agricultural production, Subei could not compete with Jiangnan, as reflected in the relative values of land in the two parts of the province. In the mid-1930s, while paddy land in Jiangnan counties such as Wuxi or Changshou sold for an average of 100 to 140 *yuan* per *mu*, they cost only 30 to 50 *yuan* per *mu* in Subei; a *mu* of dry land that cost anywhere from 55 to 120 *yuan* in Jiangnan was worth only 20 to 40 *yuan* in Subei.[56] Compared to Jiangnan,

50. Susan Mann Jones and Philip Kuhn, "Dynastic Decline and the Roots of Rebellion," in John Fairbank, ed., *The Cambridge History of China*, vol. 10 (Cambridge, 1978), p. 119.
51. Finnane, "Prosperity and Decline," pp. 4–5.
52. Charles Davis Jameson, "River Systems of the Provinces of Anhui and Kiangsu North of the Yangtzekiang," *Chinese Recorder and Missionary Journal* 43, no. 1 (Jan. 1912): 69–75.
53. David Faure, "Local Political Disturbances in Kiangsu Province, China, 1870–1911" (Ph.D. diss., Princeton University, 1976), p. 37.
54. Li Pingheng, *Zhongguo laodong nianjian* (Beijing, 1932), pp. 2–3.
55. Bureau of Foreign Trade, Ministry of Industry, *China Industrial Handbooks: Kiangsu* (Shanghai, 1933).
56. Zhao Ruheng, *Jiangsusheng jian* (Shanghai, 1935), chap. 8, pp. 17–22.

one of the wealthiest agricultural and commercial regions in all of China, Subei was indeed poor and undeveloped.

The relative wealth and poverty of the two parts of Jiangsu was reflected in patterns of migration: from the time of Subei's decline in the nineteenth century, we find records of "Jiangbei refugees" heading south to Jiangnan. Subei, it seemed, was a notorious producer of refugees. Having fled their homes because of natural disasters, or sometimes simply because it was the winter slack season, peasants congregated in Jiangsu's cities and towns, hoping to take advantage of the relief services—food, clothing, and medical care—that were often provided. Towns within Subei were the first destination for many. In 1876, for example, some 60,000–70,000 refugees were reported in Huaiyin and 42,000 in Yangzhou; in 1898, 100,000 camped in Huaiyin (arriving allegedly at the rate of 2,000 per day) and 40,000 in Yangzhou.[57] Others headed directly for Jiangnan cities, such as Suzhou, Changzhou, or Shanghai. At least as early as 1907, the Jiangbei Famine Relief Committee was established in Shanghai to attend to the problem of Subei refugees.[58]

Whether in cities of Subei or Jiangnan, Subei refugees were considered a source of disorder. As early as 1814, officials from Jiangsu and Zhejiang complained to the emperor about disruption caused by the "Jiangbei vagabonds" in such areas as Hangzhou, Jiaxing, Huzhou, Suzhou, and Changzhou. "Every year during the autumn and winter slack season," stated the edict,

> there are vagabonds from the Jiangbei places of Huaiyin, Xuzhou, and Haizhou. Usually several hundred band together as a group. They come by boat or on foot, [sometimes] pushing small carts. They are dressed in every which way and almost look like beggars. They call themselves famine victims. Whenever they pass through a village, they sit there and beg for free meals, a place to stay, or money. You must give them whatever they want so that they will leave. Otherwise they will rob you, since they have a lot of people. Everyone is afraid of their toughness; no one dares argue with them.... Some wealthy shopkeepers have moved to avoid trouble....
>
> Recently there have been more and more of these [Jiangbei people]. When they come south, they are joined by all the other unreliable elements—bandits, hoodlums, etc. I am afraid that if we let this situation continue, a major incident will occur.[59]

In his study of Jiangsu, the historian David Faure observes that throughout the second half of the nineteenth century there were constant reports of incidents—from petty thieving to conflicts provoked by "famine-begging"— involving "Jiangbei vagabonds." Officials in some Subei cities were so deter-

---

57. Faure, "Local Political Disturbances," 163.
58. *North-China Herald*, Feb. 22, 1907.
59. *Daqing shichao shengxun* (Taibei, n.d.), Jiaqing, p. 1820. The edict is dated July 9, 1814. I am grateful to Harold Kahn for calling my attention to this document.

mined to dispose of these undesirables that they actually paid for their transport to Jiangnan, where they were presumably headed anyway. And officials in Jiangnan cities, partly resigned to the seasonal influx of the refugees, waited for winter's end and then provided the refugees a "travel fee" so they would return to Subei.[60]

Not all migration was temporary or seasonal. Large numbers of people from Subei went to Jiangnan with the hope of settling there permanently. Some continued to farm, certain that even the worst circumstances in Jiangnan were better than their circumstances would be in Subei. Hsiao Tung Fei recalled often having seen, as a child, migrants from Subei cultivating the newly reclaimed land surrounding Lake Tai. Vulnerable to flooding whenever the lake water rose, this land was undesirable to natives of the area.[61] Yuji Muramatsu, in his study of landlordism in Jiangnan, corroborates this portrait of Subei immigrants forming an "underclass" among the Jiangnan peasants: they were "willing to be content with rather poor conditions to get a start in life as tenant farmers."[62] In addition to those who worked as farmers, a large number of Subei migrants settled in Jiangnan cities, living either on the boats they had brought from Subei or in shacks made of reed mats and whatever scrap materials they could find. By the 1870s the shack settlements of Subei refugees had already attracted the concern of officials in Shanghai.[63]

Although by Jiangnan standards the conditions under which Subei migrants lived and labored may have appeared intolerable, for many people from Subei these conditions were a vast improvement over what they had left behind. A man who left Yancheng in the early 1940s to work on the Wuxi docks explained that "life in Wuxi was *completely different* from life in Subei. My own opinion is that life in Subei was very tough. We ate turnips and sweet potatoes. Actually sweet potatoes were considered really good food in Subei. But when I came to Jiangnan, I ate rice. Rice was one of the best things about Jiangnan!" When asked whether having to work as a coolie lessened the desirability of Wuxi, he emphatically replied, "Of course Wuxi was still better—I was eating rice there!" Even when he moved to Shanghai, where he worked as a night soil collector and lived in one of the shack settlements, he remained certain that he was better off than in Subei. "At least we could earn some money in the shack settlements," he explained. "In the countryside we couldn't earn a cent."[64]

60. Faure, "Local Political Disturbances," pp. 279–80.
61. Hsiao Tung Fei, "Small Towns," p. 107.
62. Yuji Muramatsu, "A Documentary Study of Chinese Landlordism in the Late Ch'ing and Early Republican Kiangnan," *Bulletin of the School of Oriental and African Studies* 24, no. 3 (1966): 581.
63. *Shen Bao*, Sept. 24, 1872.
64. Interview with Zhang Ronghua, Zhabei District Sanitation Bureau, Shanghai, Nov. 3, 1986.

The picture that emerges, then, is that throughout Jiangnan, Subei refugees—whether they migrated seasonally or moved south permanently—accepted a much lower standard of living, and hence poorer working conditions, than Jiangnan natives. This at least partly explains the concentration of Subei people in the unskilled sector of the Shanghai labor market. They were, as conventional wisdom holds, fleeing poverty and willing to do jobs that no one else would do, much like the Irish who fled famine and migrated to the United States in the early nineteenth century. Furthermore, the migration experience of Subei people to Jiangnan suggests that the stereotype of them as willing to do the lowliest jobs may even have preceded Shanghai's modern development; people from Jiangnan who moved to Shanghai most likely brought with them an impression of Subei people as poor, menial laborers, for that is what they had observed in the countryside.

This alone, however, does not fully account for the concentration of Subei people in the unskilled sector of the Shanghai labor market nor for their domination of that sector. Subei was not the sole source of the poverty-stricken peasants who migrated to Shanghai. What of those who came from the Jiangnan districts of Wuxi, Changzhou, Ningbo, or Shaoxing? Despite the relative prosperity of these regions, they too were the source of many poor peasants who came to Shanghai hungry for both food and work. Why, then, do we find such little evidence of them among the ranks of Shanghai's unskilled and coolie laborers?

Scholars attempting to explain the experiences of different immigrant groups in American history have proposed a connection between the types of job experience immigrants might have acquired in their home countries and their employment patterns in the United States. A study of German and Irish immigrants in nineteenth-century Philadelphia, for instance, suggests that the Irish, coming from an underdeveloped rural economy, arrived in the United States with no industrial experience and therefore were concentrated in the unskilled sector of the labor market. The Germans, in contrast, came from an industrializing country and were able to use their previously acquired skills to obtain better jobs in Philadelphia.[65]

At least one scholar has suggested a similar connection between rural handicraft industries and the kinds of job held by people of different local origins in Shanghai.[66] At first glance this seems a compelling explanation. Jiangnan people hailed from a region famous for highly developed handicraft industries, while Subei was equally notorious for its lack of handicrafts. That men from Wuxi, known for its production of tin, dominated the tin-smithing

---

65. Bruce Laurie, Theodore Hershberg, and George Alter, "Immigrants and Industry: The Philadelphia Experience, 1850–1880," in Richard L. Ehrlich, ed., *Immigrants in Industrial America, 1850–1920* (Charlottesville, Va., 1977), pp. 123–50.

66. Wu Liangrong, "Shanghaishi Subeiji jumin shehui biandong fenxi," in Shanghai Shehuixue Xuehui, ed., *Shehuixue wenji* (Shanghai, 1984), p. 177.

jobs in Shanghai is hardly surprising. Nor should it be surprising that women from Wuxi and Changzhou, areas known for the production of handwoven cloth, dominated the weaving jobs in Shanghai's textile mills. Upon closer scrutiny, though, this explanation is problematic. First, Subei was not completely lacking in handicrafts, although their development may have been retarded compared to Jiangnan. For example, the Subei counties of Taixing and Taixian were known for the production of handwoven cloth.[67] Why, then, do we not find more women from these areas in the weaving departments of the mills? Second, there appears to have been little connection between the handicraft traditions of a region and the specific skills brought to Shanghai by peasants migrating from that area. Few women from Wuxi who were employed as weavers in the Shanghai mills had themselves engaged in cloth weaving before leaving the countryside.[68] While Yangzhou's history as a consumption center might seem to explain the predominance of Yangzhou men employed in the Shanghai barbershops and bathhouses, few had themselves ever worked as barbers or bathhouse attendants before coming to Shanghai. Rather, the majority had been peasants.[69]

An explanation of the correlation between local origins and labor market segmentation must consider how Shanghai's labor markets operated—how labor was recruited and how individuals sought employment. Previous studies have already documented the crucial role of personal and native-place connections in obtaining jobs, even in Shanghai's most modern enterprises.[70] People in management or supervisory positions tended to hire relatives, friends, or people from their home district. The important question, then, becomes the kind of connections available to migrants from Subei compared to those from Jiangnan.

An examination of the local origins of Shanghai's business community—including the owners, directors, and managers of enterprises ranging from factories to banks—indicates that people from Subei indeed had limited personal or native-place connections on which to draw in seeking jobs. Of the 2,082 individuals from Jiangsu and Zhejiang (representing nearly 90 percent of the total) listed in a commercial directory published in the 1940s, only 175 (8 percent) were from Subei. Of those from Subei, the majority were from the southernmost areas of Nantong, Haimen, and Rugao, leaving only 88 (4 percent of the total) from Yangzhou north to Funing. A closer look at the individuals from Subei listed in the directory reveals that most were involved in rickshaw companies, barbershops, bathhouses, and construction; none was

67. Cao Hui, "Jiangbei funü shenghuo gaikuang," *Nüsheng* 2, no. 10 (Feb. 1934): 10–11.
68. This observation is based on interviews I conducted with retired women cotton mill workers in Shanghai during 1979–81, as well as a survey of retirement cards at the Shanghai Number Two Textile Mill indicating each worker's personal history.
69. Interviews with He Zhenghua and Xu Liansheng.
70. See Honig, *Sisters and Strangers*, pp. 79–93.

involved in industry or banking.[71] Little wonder, then, that Subei migrants concentrated in these enterprises. Furthermore, this distribution of the Shanghai business elite explains why peasants from Wuxi, who might have at least occasionally been as poverty-stricken as those from Subei, did not end up in the unskilled sector of the Shanghai labor market. They had connections elsewhere. As a woman factory worker from Yuyao observed, "Those of us from Zhejiang could sometimes get jobs in banks because there were a lot of Zhejiang bankers. But if you were from Subei, you could never get a job in a bank."[72] (This may also help explain why poor peasants from Jiangnan areas were not the objects of social prejudice: they came from the districts that were associated with the Shanghai elite.)

We can at this point only speculate as to why merchants from Subei failed to join the ranks of the Shanghai business elite. Possibly they lacked sufficient capital to invest in Shanghai as extensively as merchants from Jiangnan did, and used what little they had to invest in enterprises, such as rickshaw companies and bathhouses, that did not require large amounts of capital. One must wonder, however, why the prosperous salt merchants of Yangzhou did not use their funds to stake a claim in the profits to be made from Shanghai's development. Perhaps, as the historian Ping-ti Ho suggests, conspicuous consumption and patronage of the arts left them with little capital for potential investments.[73] Yet another possibility is simply that individuals from Jiangnan, pushed partly by the Taiping occupation, arrived in Shanghai first and established control over the more lucrative enterprises. If there was competition over Shanghai's wealth during its early development, it was between people from Canton and Ningbo. People from Subei do not even appear to have been in the running.[74] A full explanation requires research that is beyond the scope of this paper. Nonetheless, it is clear that Shanghai's economic elite was divided according to local origin, with Jiangnan people in positions far superior to those that people from Subei attained. Subsequent migrants concentrated in the areas where they had connections; Subei people worked in precisely the enterprises that were owned or managed by individuals with whom they could claim "hometown connections" (*tongxiang guanxi*).

In addition to connections with individuals based on native-place ties, two kinds of institution played a significant role in securing jobs: the Green Gang and native-place associations. From the early twentieth century, Green Gang leaders carved out spheres of influence in Shanghai, subgroups of the gang sometimes controlling entire enterprises.[75] Connections with gang leaders,

---

71. Shanghaishi Shanghui, ed., *Shanghaishi geye tongye gonghui lijianshi minglu* (Shanghai, n.d.).
72. Interview with Shi Xiaomei, First Shanghai Textile Mill, Mar. 11, 1980.
73. Ping-ti Ho, "Salt Merchants," pp. 166–67.
74. Leung, "Regional Rivalry," pp. 29–30.
75. Xue Gengxin, "Jindai Shanghaide liumang," *Shanghai wenshi ziliao* 3 (1980): 160–78.

which often intersected native-place connections, thus assumed importance in the search for jobs. The fragmentary information currently available about the Green Gang suggests that here too the resources of Subei migrants were not as plentiful as those of their Jiangnan counterparts. Even though Subei itself was often described as a center of Green Gang activity, none of the three major Green Gang leaders in Shanghai was from Subei.[76] Du Yuesheng was a native of Pudong (part of Shanghai); Huang Jinrong hailed from Suzhou; Zhang Xiaolin came from Hangzhou. A Jiangbei *bang* existed within the Green Gang, led by Gu Zhuxuan and Jin Jiulin. Neither was ever as influential as the former three, who had "pupils" in almost every enterprise in Shanghai. Gu Zhuxuan, called the "Subei Emperor" by Subei people in Shanghai, was powerful in the rickshaw business, where thousands of workers recognized him as their master.[77] In other words, migrants from Jiangnan had a network of people from their hometowns whose position in the gang provided them access to a wide range of jobs; the gang connections available to Subei people, though, offered more limited opportunities and may indeed have contributed to the tracking of Subei migrants into jobs such as rickshaw pulling.

In addition to the Green Gang, Jiangnan migrants could draw on the influence and services provided by native-place associations. The Ningbo Guild, which existed from the 1860s, actively helped nonelite people from Ningbo find jobs in Shanghai. In the early stages of Shanghai's development, the guild recruited workers and apprentices from Ningbo for employment in Shanghai's foreign shipyards.[78] Previous scholars have assumed that no native-place associations from Subei existed in Shanghai.[79] If this was the case, Subei migrants clearly lacked a resource that benefited people from Jiangnan areas. Preliminary research suggests, however, that several Subei districts had native-place associations. In the 1910s an association of Yangzhou sojourners existed in Shanghai, and by the 1930s and 1940s most Subei districts had associations in Shanghai.[80] Unfortunately little is known about

76. Feng Hefa, ed., *Zhongguo nongcun jingji ziliao* (Shanghai, 1933), 1:359–60.
77. Interview with Gu Shuping, Shanghai Academy of Social Sciences, Nov. 19, 1986.
78. Leung, "Regional Rivalry," p. 40. Also see Susan Mann Jones, "The Ningpo Pang and Financial Power at Shanghai," in Mark Elvin and G. W. Skinner, eds., *The Chinese City between Two Worlds* (Stanford, 1974), pp. 73–96.
79. The only study that deals extensively with guilds and native-place associations in Shanghai is Negishi Tadashi, *Chūgoku no girudo* (Tokyo, 1953). Also see Negishi, *Shanhai no girudo* (Tokyo, 1951). Neither study makes reference to Subei associations in Shanghai.
80. The association was the Yangzhou Bashou Gongsuo and was reported in *Shen Bao*, Jan. 4, 1917. A Yangzhou Bayi Lühu Tongxianghui was reported in *Shen Bao*, Sept. 2, 1931; a Dongtai Lühu Tongxianghui in *Shen Bao*, Sept. 8, 1931; a Xinghua Tongxianghui in *Shen Bao*, Sept. 10, 1931; a Huai'an Liuyi Huiguan is mentioned in Shanghaishi Shanghui, ed., *Shanghaishi geye*, pp. 17, 94. In addition, there were several associations that represented larger parts of Subei. For example, a Jianghuai Lühu Tongxianghui existed at least from the mid-1920s. See *Shen Bao*, July

their activities. Many of the associations appear to have been created at the time of the 1931 flood that devastated large portions of Subei. They raised money to help refugees relocate.[81] Aside from relief work, none of the Subei migrants I interviewed could recall an instance in which they had had any contact with the native-place associations from their area. They assumed the organizations catered primarily to people of wealth. This at least suggests that the Subei native-place associations did not serve as quasi employment agencies in the way that the larger, more prestigious Jiangnan guilds did.

All these factors, then, contribute to an explanation of the concentration of Subei people in the unskilled sector of the Shanghai labor market. Migrants or refugees from an often poverty-stricken area, Subei people seemed willing to perform the most menial, lowest-status jobs in Shanghai. To them, even the worst job in Shanghai was preferable to life in Subei. Most had no non-farm skills when they arrived in Shanghai, making it difficult to secure jobs requiring other skills. More important, however, they lacked the personal and institutional connections—based on native-place ties—that might have given them access to those jobs, enabling them to move out of the unskilled sector as migrants from Jiangnan were able to do.

One question remains concerning the jobs dominated by Subei people. We observed that a number of Subei people (particularly women) worked in factories and that several industries relied heavily on Subei workers. Yet factory work was the highest to which Subei people progressed in Shanghai's job hierarchy; moreover, they never seemed to represent the majority of factory workers. How are we to explain why Subei people never dominated the ranks of Shanghai's industrial proletariat? That most factory owners and managers were from Jiangnan is only part of the answer. Given their interest in maximizing profit, one would expect them to have hired the cheapest labor available, presumably people from Subei. Why did this not happen? Supply was not at issue, particularly after the major floods of 1911, 1921, and 1931 brought massive numbers of Subei people to Shanghai, many of whom were constantly unemployed.

The failure of Subei people to dominate factory jobs requires a consideration of some of the factors that have been used to explain the scarcity of Chinese workers in California factories during the mid and late nineteenth

---

7, 1925. There was also a Subei Lühu Tongxianghui, although nothing is known about its origins or development. It is mentioned in Gu Shuping, "Wo liyong Gu Zhuxuan de yanhu jinxing geming huodong" in Zhongguo Renmin Zhengzhi Xieshang Huiyi, Shanghaishi Wei-yuanhui Wenshi Ziliao Gongzuo Weiyuanhui, ed., *Jiu Shanghai de banghui* (Shanghai, 1986), p. 360.

81. *Shen Bao*, Sept. 2, 8, and 10, 1931.

century, the initial absence of Irish immigrants in factories of the American Northeast, and the prolonged absence of black workers in factories throughout the United States.[82] In all these situations, factory owners chose not to draw on the cheapest sources of labor. The most important explanations that have been offered concern popular prejudices, among both factory managers and workers.

If popular attitudes toward and beliefs about Subei people are an indication, then they were quite possibly regarded as undesirable workers. People from Subei, as noted above, were commonly perceived as poor, dirty, backward, and uncultured. "In general, Jiangnan people are civilized, while Jiangbei people are coarse," reads a typical description.[83] "People dislike [Subei people] because they are dirty and rude," states another.[84] Yet another, slightly more specific, observes that "in terms of personality, Jiangnan people are soft and flexible, while Jiangbei people are firm and strong. ... In terms of customs, religion, and superstition, Jiangnan people tend to be more civilized and open-minded."[85]

Although it is difficult to determine how much these views affected hiring decisions, they most likely contributed to a prejudice against Subei workers among factory managers from Jiangnan, who were willing to pay a higher price for workers more familiar to them. One cotton mill engineer, recalling hiring practices in the 1920s and 1930s, stated this explicitly. "In cotton spinning," he said, "we tried to use as many natives as possible. It's hard to say why. It is not good to say that Subei people are not good workers. It's just that there are certain social attitudes. It's easier to talk to natives. Subei people are harder to handle. We did not like Subei people very much."[86] Subei women who tried to get jobs in the mills often had to dress in a way that would disguise their origins and allow them to pass as Jiangnan natives.[87] Cotton was one of the few industries that employed a large number of Subei people, but this was most likely because by the 1920s roughly half of

---

82. On Chinese workers in California factories, see Paul M. Ong, "Chinese Labor in Early San Francisco: Racial Segmentation and Industrial Expansion," *Amerasia* 8, no. 1 (1981): 69–82. On the Irish, see Clyde Griffen, "The 'Old' Immigration and Industrialization: A Case Study," in Richard L. Ehrlich, ed., *Immigrants in Industrial America*, p. 194. The failure of blacks to become a major component of the industrial proletariat in the United States until World War II is discussed in Harold Baron, "Racial Domination in Advanced Capitalism: A Theory of Nationalism and Divisions in the Labor Market," in Richard Edwards et al., *Labor Market Segmentation*, p. 201.

83. Wang Peitang, *Jiangsusheng xiangtu zhi* (Changsha, 1938), p. 369.

84. Lu Manyan, "Jiangnan yu Jiangbei," *Renyan zhoukan* 1, no. 9 (June 23, 1934): 389.

85. Zhao Ruheng, *Jiangsusheng jian*, chap. 8, p. 189.

86. Interview with He Zhiguang, Putuo District Federation of Industry and Commerce, Shanghai, June 26, 1980.

87. Honig, *Sisters and Strangers*, pp. 76–77.

Shanghai's cotton mills were owned by Japanese capitalists, who did not share the prejudice against Subei workers.[88]

It is possible that ordinary workers shared the prejudice of factory owners and managers against Subei people. While they did not necessarily play a major role in hiring decisions (except through the introduction of friends and acquaintances for new jobs), groups of workers could make it difficult for others to maintain jobs, particularly if they felt that the newcomers threatened their job security. Given that Subei people entered the factory work force after people from Jiangnan, it is possible that the latter actively resisted the recruitment of these "northerners." In the Jiangnan arsenal, for example, Guangdong and Jiangnan workers made it impossible for people from Subei to become apprentices for skilled jobs.[89] A similar phenomenon is suggested by an incident that ocurred in a cotton mill in 1920. A man from Rugao had wangled an introduction to a job as an apprentice mechanic in a Shanghai cotton mill. Enraged that he worked so hard, and fearful that he would eventually get their jobs, the other workers subjected him to physical and verbal harrassment until he finally left his job and returned to the countryside.[90] If incidents like this occurred with any degree of frequency, we might conclude that territoriality, prejudice, and quasi-ethnic conflict among workers—reminiscent of the bitter protests against the use of immigrant workers by native artisans in nineteenth-century American cities—contributed to the failure of Subei people to dominate the ranks of the industrial proletariat.[91]

CONCLUSION

Prejudice, then, combined with other factors to account for the tracking of Subei people into the unskilled sector of the Shanghai labor market. We have seen that Subei people initially came to Shanghai because of poverty and natural disasters in their home villages and therefore performed the most menial tasks to eke out a living. Because hometown connections played such a major role in securing jobs in Shanghai, subsequent waves of immigrants from Subei continued to be tracked into these jobs, for that is where they had connections. Eventually, as Shanghai industrialized and more complex and highly differentiated labor markets developed, the jobs performed by Subei people assumed an even lower status. As the attitudes toward rickshaw

---

88. Honig, pp. 30–31, 77–78.
89. Shanghai Shehui Kexueyuan Jingji Yanjiusuo, *Jiangnan zaochuanchang changshi, 1865–1949* (Jiangsu Renmin Chubanshe, 1983), p. 155.
90. Li Cishan, "Shanghai laodong qingkuang," p. 12.
91. Griffen, "The 'Old' Immigration," p. 177. Also see Ong, "Chinese Labor in Early San Francisco."

pullers indicate, the association of Subei people with unskilled, physically demanding labor created and continually reinforced the belief that they were poor, ignorant, dirty, and uncivilized.

It would be misleading to imply that a simple relationship existed between prejudice and the status of Subei people in the labor market, that there was first prejudice and subsequently an inferior economic status. Popular beliefs about Subei people they may well have prevented their entrance into preferable labor markets, but the divisions in the labor market themselves contributed to the creation of these beliefs. The propagation of negative stereotypes about Subei and Subei people was partly a product of the development of segmented labor markets in Shanghai, serving to justify the unequal access of different groups of people to job opportunities.

TEN

Local Interest Story: Political Power and Regional Differences in the Shandong Capital Market, 1900–1937

Kenneth Pomeranz

Many issues in the early twentieth-century Chinese economy hinge on the capital market. The regional capital market is central not only to the relationship between richer regions, poorer regions, and economic change but also to an understanding of the extent to which the wealth of some groups and the poverty of others was the result of power and exploitation, rather than just differences in luck and skill. And in China, where several currencies, many with limited acceptance, circulated, any analysis of supra-local capital markets must also consider domestic currency markets. Looking at currency trading raises an often overlooked set of questions concerning relationships between state and economy in early twentieth-century China.

This paper examines capital markets in one province—Shandong—between the Boxer Uprising and World War II (1900–1937). Since some but not all parts of the province experienced rapid growth in these years, we must first explain why, as interest rates declined in more prosperous areas, funds did not flow to the more "backward" regions, in which credit commanded a higher price. It is not new to note that the links between rapidly growing regions and other parts of China were weak. Much of the literature on pre–World War II China argues that the rapid growth of those areas that were stimulated by the international economy did little for the rest of the country.[1] But it is hard to prove that money made in China's "advanced" regions was rarely invested in the hinterland. Moreover, a number of scholars using aggregate national data now argue that there was an increasingly national

---

1. For reasons of brevity, a review of the literature on various controversies mentioned here has been omitted. These references are available in my Ph.D. dissertation, "The Making of a Hinterland: State, Society, and Economy in Inland North China, 1900–1937" (Yale University, 1988), chap. 1, nn. 1, 2, 5, 7, and 94.

capital market, in which coastal funds were invested in the hinterlands. This position rests on three points. First, investors seek high returns, and institutional and technological changes were making information about far-flung opportunities cheaper. Second, regional differences in interest rates were narrowing. Third, without such investment, the unbalanced trade between coastal cities and the countryside (Shanghai, for instance, sold far more than it bought) should have led to money shortages and deflation in the countryside, causing a divergence between urban and rural prices; no such divergence has been observed.

Local credit markets are also controversial. Since North China had relatively little tenancy, discussions of economic exploitation there have centered on credit and marketing. Although numerous anecdotes show moneylenders abusing local monopolies, some of the aggregate data suggest that the cheaper funds available in Shanghai, Tianjin, and overseas made their way, through intermediaries, to enough outlets to create competitive rural credit markets.

Finally, recent research has highlighted both the development of national markets in prewar China and surprising continuities between Chinese state making before and after 1949. However, relationships between these two trends have received little attention. A provincial case study cannot resolve all these issues—especially since we still lack information from below the county level[2]—but it can help us see how credit markets worked, and highlight important relationships between state making and market making.

I began by borrowing a technique used by two economic historians to estimate interest rates for medieval Europe. Using the estimates derived for each of Shandong's 12 prefectures, I did simple tests for market integration and found a surprising pattern. Not only did the province's money market not show the integration economists would likely predict where transport and information costs are low; the lines across which prices suddenly jumped did not correspond to the physiographic regions at whose boundaries most historians would expect trade networks to break down. Eventually, an investigation of traditional archival and published sources showed that this peculiar market segmentation could be traced to deliberate manipulation by certain local elites and local governments. To be more precise, the evidence suggests the following.

1. The province included three large and distinct regional capital markets (see Map 10.1). Interest rates in the poorest market (Southwest Shandong) were about 1.5 percent per month higher than in the most prosperous region (the North Coast) and approximately 0.6 percent higher than in the middle, or Heartland.

2. See, e.g., "Shandong Gaomi Wei xian zhi nongcun jiehuo," *Gong shang banyuekan* 6, no. 4 (Feb. 15, 1934): 49.

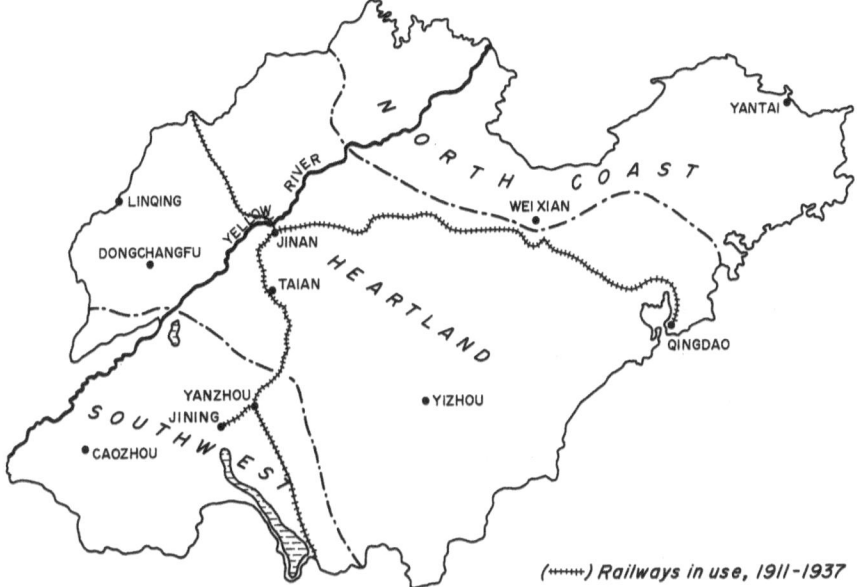

Map 10.1. Approximate Map of Shandong's Regional Capital Markets, 1911–1937.

2. The interest-rate differentials changed little between 1900–1911 and the 1930s.
3. These lasting differences were largely due to the ability of politically powerful people to restrict the flow of money in and out of their own county and to manipulate local silver-copper exchange rates while limiting others' access to the cheaper credit and silver available in more prosperous areas.
4. The artificial barriers kept the return on any hoardable or loanable asset (such as grain or money) higher in poor areas than elsewhere. Moreover, politically connected people who could cross the barriers made much greater currency-trading profits than those available either in purely local commerce or in commodities governed by national and international markets.
5. Divergence in commodity prices between the North Coast and the other regions was limited because the Heartland exported enough cash crops to avoid a silver drain and the Southwest, with fewer exports, bought few modern goods and exported laborers, who brought silver home. When Japan seized Manchuria in 1931 and curtailed migratory labor, the Southwest experienced a local deflation beyond that caused by the world depression.
6. While county governments most often obstructed currency and capital

markets, provincial officials were also caught between the advantages and disadvantages they expected from Shandong's integration into a larger economy.

7. The truncated money markets in Shandong, during a period in which many other markets became more integrated, show how politics shaped and limited market participation. These limits also handicapped governments trying to move resources, affecting state making as well as market making.

SHANDONG'S REGIONAL CAPITAL MARKETS

We have numerous interest rates from particular times and places, but most cannot be used in systematic comparisons because they omit crucial information, such as who was charged this rate or what security was put up.[3] However, we do have useful county-by-county figures for 1933.[4] For 1900–1911 we can estimate interest rates using monthly grain prices and patterns of postharvest price increases in each prefecture of Shandong, as Donald N. McCloskey and John Nash did for medieval England.[5] Over the long haul, holding grain a few months before selling it will be no more or less profitable than selling the grain immediately and holding money; otherwise, more people would turn to the more profitable activity, until it ceased being so. Thus, the average rise in grain prices after the harvest should approximate the interest rate plus other storage costs (including safeguards against theft, and provisions for losses from rotting or rats).

This method involves looking at pairs of prices a month or a few months apart. For technical reasons, the most useful quotations are the high prices from each prefecture, recorded in the prefectural capitals.[6] Ignoring pairs that end in or pass through harvest months—when prices reflected the value of the new grain rather than the accrued value of whatever little grain remained from the previous year—leaves 50 to 60 pairs for each of six grains in the 11 prefectures with reliable data. In ten, the results for the different grains are quite close, and so more trustworthy.[7] We do not know how much

---

3. E.g., *Shandong zheng su shichaji*, 1934, and *Shina shōbetsu zenshi* (hereafter *SSZ*) have many rates but no supporting details; the same is true of numerous magazine articles, gazetteers, memoirs, and so forth.

4. Zhongguo Shiyebu, Guoji Maoyiju, *Zhongguo shiye zhi: Shandong sheng* (hereafter *ZSZS*; Chinese industrial handbook: Shandong Province; Nanjing, 1934), pt. 5, pp. 91–97; for a discussion of these data, see Pomeranz, "Making of a Hinterland," app. B.

5. Donald N. McCloskey and John Nash, "Corn at Interest: The Extent and Cost of Grain Storage in Medieval England," *American Economic Review* 74, no. 1 (Mar. 1984): 174–87; this method is discussed on pp. 178–83.

6. The papers in Part One of this volume provide detailed explanations of the Qing system of grain price reporting.

7. The prefectures that do not conform to this pattern are discussed in Pomeranz, "Making of a Hinterland," chap. 1, n. 12, and app. A.

of the average price increase represents interest, but other storage costs were similar across prefectures.[8] Thus regional differences should reflect relative interest rates. The results are shown in Table 10.1.

The interest rates fall into three regional groupings; the regions are demarcated on the map. The North Coast area, which consisted of four prefectures, included the treaty ports of Yantai and Weihaiwei and had roughly 6.8 million people. With unusually strong ties to booming Manchuria, right across the Bohai Gulf, and access to the central and South China coastal regions, Shandong's North Coast had a privileged position, which gave it relatively easy access to hard currency (to be discussed later) and particularly low interest rates. Holding grain there earned less than 0.5 percent per month. At the other extreme is the second region: the Southwest, the prefectures of Yanzhou, Caozhou, and Jining, with about 6.4 million people.[9] Returns there averaged 2 percent per month.

In the remaining prefectures, ranging from Yizhou (1.2 percent) to Dongchang (1.7 percent), returns averaged 1.4 percent. This largest region, the Heartland, with 21 million people, presents the least uniform picture but still appears to have been a meaningful capital market. Moreover, these prefectures are clearly separate from the other two groups, and traded with each other much more than with those areas. They were far more involved in outside trade than the Southwest was, and more a part of the North China regional economy than the North Coast, which was instead closely tied to Manchuria.

Rates derived from 1903–11 grain prices in neighboring prefectures of Zhili Province echo this pattern.[10] Coastal Zunhua, closely tied to Manchuria, had rates like those in Shandong's North Coast (under 0.8 percent); Daming, adjoining Southwest Shandong, had rates like those in the Southwest (over 2 percent); three prefectures bordering the Shandong Heartland resembled that zone (rates were slightly over 1 percent).

Measures of dispersion for the Shandong results confirm the regional pattern. Within each individual prefecture except Laizhou, the returns from storing different grains are closely bunched around the prefectural mean for all grains. Entry and exit from local markets, storage activities, and switching between particular assets must have been fairly easy; as we shall see, this was not true of interregional money markets. To the extent that these grains are a random sample of all hoardable assets, the results suggest that in any

---

8. The kinds of storage facilities in different parts of the province were the same, and inland areas were drier. Banditry was more serious in the Southwest than elsewhere, but in the hundreds of crime reports I have reviewed, stored grain was almost never a target (grain on the road to market sometimes was). The rat population may have been unevenly distributed, but I know of no reason to think so.

9. There are a number of problems with the Jining data, which are discussed in Pomeranz, "Making of a Hinterland," chap. 1, n. 15, and app. A.

10. See ibid., chap. 1, n. 17, and app. A.

TABLE 10.1 Returns on Grain Holding in Shandong Prefectures, 1900–1911
(monthly averages, in percentages)

Region and Prefecture	Return on Wheat	Return on Sorghum	Return on Soybean (Heidou)	Return on Soybean (Huangdou)	Return on Millet	Return on Corn	Average Return
North Coast[a]							
Qingzhou	0.40	0.43	0.75	0.52	0.29	0.06	0.41
Laizhou	0.62	0.44	0.63	0.94	0.53	0.28	0.57
Dengzhou	0.49	0.60	2.25	0.89	-0.07	-0.06	0.68
Wuding	0.16	0.43	0.13	0.03	0.48	-0.10	0.19
	0.32	0.25	-0.02	0.23	0.24	0.13	0.19
Southwest[a]							
Caozhou	1.85	1.86	2.30	1.83	2.21	1.86	1.99
Yanzhou	1.57	1.73	2.12	1.81	2.39	2.07	1.95
	2.22	1.99	2.47	1.85	2.02	1.65	2.03
Heartland[a]							
Jinan	1.48	1.43	1.43	1.39	1.54	1.32	1.43
Taian	1.48	1.45	1.56	1.07	1.39	1.19	1.36
Linqing	1.49	1.73	1.55	1.36	1.93	1.37	1.57
Dongchang	1.53	1.29	1.08	1.35	1.33	1.53	1.35
Yizhou	1.96	1.54	1.67	1.64	1.98	1.62	1.74
	0.92	1.15	1.31	1.51	1.05	1.05	1.17

SOURCE: For measures of dispersion/central tendency, and further information on data and methods, see Kenneth Pomeranz, "The Making of a Hinterland: State, Society, and Economy in Inland North China, 1900–1937" (Ph.D. dissertation, Yale University, 1988), App. A.

NOTE: Jining Prefecture in the Southwest region is excluded because no reliable data are available.

[a] Average of available data for prefectures in the region.

given prefecture, there is a two-thirds probability that the average monthly return on any asset over these years would be within 0.2 percent of the mean return for all assets in that prefecture.[11]

On the other hand, specifying a grain without knowing what prefecture it was stored in has little predictive value. Thus, the concept of a functioning market in savings within each prefecture has predictive power, while the idea of a provincewide market in the storage of any particular grain—much less all grains—does not. The rates of return for different grains within each of the three regions outlined here are also tightly bunched around the regional mean for all grains, though not quite as tightly bunched as within individual prefectures. There are differences in rates of return between different prefectures in the same region, but they are much smaller than the changes that we find if we cross regional boundaries.

These divisions changed very little during the 1900–1937 period. A 1933 provincial survey presents the "highest" and "ordinary" interest rates charged by individuals, pawnshops, cooperatives, and "stores" (*shang dian*)— many of which also acted as local banks—in each county. The ordinary rates quoted for stores are probably the more reliable and more important. North Coast store rates averaged 1.95 percent; Southwest ones, 3.5 percent; and Heartland rates, 2.5 percent. In loans from individuals, the Southwest-Heartland difference is much smaller; however, it was probably easier to get an accurate picture of rates charged by stores than by the huge number of individual lenders.[12]

While the pattern of interest rates in 1933 resembles that derived for 1900–1911, the rates themselves are higher. This need not mean that real interest rates rose. The 1900–1911 figures represent what one earned simply by transferring grain into the future, without it ever leaving one's courtyard. Consequently, these rates should reflect only minimal compensation for risk. Nor would they reflect differences in bargaining power between lenders and possibly desperate borrowers. Thus, these rates should resemble those on the absolutely safest short-term money loans. Our limited evidence confirms this: the safest loans in Laizhou (North Coast) cost 0.4 percent per month, loans from trade associations to their member firms cost 0.6 percent in Jinan (Heartland), and a loan in the Southwest—the lowest rate I have found for the region—cost 1.5 percent.[13] The 1933 rates should include larger risk premiums and, after the 1910s and 1920s, may also include anticipated inflation. These higher premiums would make the rates on all the loans in the 1933 data higher than those inferred from the 1900–1911 data. What matters

---

11. See ibid., app. A, for complete figures.
12. See ibid., app. B, for a discussion of these data and a breakdown of the results.
13. *SSZ*, 4:1125, 1156; *Shandong quansheng caizheng shuomingshu*, p. 28.

for our purposes, however, is that the same pattern of regional differences persists, suggesting that similar nonmarket forces operated in both periods.

OTHER SIGNS OF REGIONAL DISTINCTNESS

The northeasternmost part of Shandong was largely cut off from the rest of the province by mountains, making trade in bulky products difficult and making the area less a part of Shandong's economy than Manchuria's. For instance, the North Coast produced only half the grain it needed; the rest came across the Bohai Gulf from Manchuria. People crossed the gulf too; until World War I, this area accounted for almost all Shandong settlers in Manchuria, while Yantai, the North Coast's largest port, handled most of Shandong's trade with Manchuria. Moreover, huge numbers of people from this area worked in Manchuria either seasonally or for several years.[14]

However, the North Coast region outlined by our statistics extends westward beyond this extreme northeastern part of the peninsula. It includes all the prefectures along the Bohai Gulf, including areas easily reached from central and western Shandong. This broader definition of the North Coast is suggested by logic as well as statistics: if access to the North Coast provided superior opportunities, people on the western part of that coast would try to join in, whether or not they were cut off from the Heartland. The question is why more of the Heartland did not become involved.

The broader definition of the North Coast is also reflected in a set of rates charged in 1911 for money transfers from Huangxian, a major banking center.[15] The ten listed destinations stretch throughout our expanded North Coast. The furthest, Xincheng, was 250 kilometers from Huangxian, but only 16 perfectly flat kilometers from the important Heartland trading center of Zhoucun and 120 flat kilometers from Jinan, Shandong's capital and largest city. However, the only destination outside the North Coast listed was foreign-controlled Qingdao. That a network with such modest costs—less than 0.5 percent of the shipment for the most expensive destination—would suddenly stop short of important markets strongly suggests that the boundaries of this trading area were set by political rather than strictly geographic factors.

Various analysts have also seen a distinct southwestern zone only loosely linked to the rest of Shandong. Its boundaries, however, are disputed, and are based on social differences—number of gentry, incidence of violence, etc.—rather than physical ones.[16] No insuperable geographic barriers sepa-

---

14. Thomas Gottschang, "Migration from North China to Manchuria, 1891–1942: An Economic History" (Ph.D. diss., University of Michigan, 1982), pp. 77–81.

15. *SSZ*, pp. 1145–47.

16. Joseph Esherick, *Origins of the Boxer Uprising* (Berkeley and Los Angeles, 1987), pp. 12–14; Sun Jingzhi, *Huabei de jingji dili* (Beijing, 1958), pp. 132–34; *Shandong minzhong jiaoyu yuekan* 5, no. 4 (May 1934), pp. 85–88.

rate the Southwest, however defined, from the Heartland.[17] After 1912, Jining and Yanzhou were also linked to Jinan by rail.[18]

DIFFERENT MARKET, SAME MAP: REGIONAL CURRENCY MARKETS

The political underpinnings of market boundaries become clear when we turn to the currency market. Like all of China, Shandong used numerous silver, copper, brass, and paper currencies during this period, with no fixed exchange rates between them.[19] In most of China, silver and silver-denominated paper were increasingly dominant,[20] but in Shandong copper remained important; consequently, so did the copper-silver market.

According to a 1933 study, copper was used for agricultural sales in five of 12 Shandong places surveyed and was the only currency farmers received in four locations. Farmers made at least some purchases with copper in eight of 13 locations. People often received loans in copper but, except in one place, had to repay in silver.[21] Prices for large items were generally quoted in silver, and taxes were always set in silver.[22]

In a unified provincial capital market, silver-copper exchange rates in different counties should have converged or at least followed parallel paths. In fact, however, exchange rates varied wildly from county to county, and trends were often far from parallel. Shanghai rates may be considered "national" prices, though Tianjin, Beijing, and Hankou rates did not always exactly track Shanghai's.[23] Prices in Yantai and other North Coast ports closely tracked Shanghai rates,[24] confirming this area's membership in a national, or perhaps littoral, economy. However, inland areas are another story.

Even within the Heartland, there were significant differences between some nearby counties, such as Jinan and Taian. In the early 1920s rates in Linqing and Qingping, two adjacent Heartland counties, diverged by as

---

17. For a brief survey of Shandong geography in English, see Esherick, *Boxers*, pp. 11–20; for greater detail, see Hou Renzhi, ed., *Xu tianxia junguo libingshu, Shandong zhi bu* (Beijing, 1940), pp. 137–216.
18. Zhongguo Jiaotongbu, Jiaotong Shi Weiyuanhui, *Jiaotong shi* (1937), pp. 3531–35.
19. Li Guijin, "Qingmo bizhi gaige ji qi shibai yuanyin de qiantan," in *Jingji shi*, 1984, no. 2, pp. 129–30, has a brief summary of the late Qing situation; by 1919, the *North-China Herald* (hereafter *NCH*), Oct. 18, 1919: 172, had counted 115 new kinds of coinage since 1912 and untold varieties of paper.
20. Leonard Hsu, *Silver and Prices in China* (Shanghai, 1935), pp. 68, 75.
21. Ibid., pp. 68, 75.
22. Ibid., p. 75; *SSZ*, pp. 260–61.
23. See, e.g., *Tongji yuebao*, Dec. 1929: 25; Dec. 1930: 52.
24. Hsu, *Silver and Prices*, p. 85; Chintao Shubigun Minseibu Tetsudōbu, *Tōhoku Santō (Bokkai Santō engan shoko Iken Chifu kan toshi) chōsa hōkokusho (Chōsa Shiryō* no. 17; Qingdao, 1919) pp. 54 (Yangjiagou), 148 (Ye County), 252 (Longkou), 286 (Huang County), 317 (Penglai).

much as 33 percent. However, after 1926 the difference hovered between 0 percent and 7 percent, only slightly above the cost of shipping copper coins between the two places.[25] Except for in Jinan, rates within the Heartland rarely differed by more than 20 percent, and sharply opposed trends do not last long.

Moreover, until 1927, trends in the Heartland (again, excepting Jinan) were similar to those in Shanghai and Yantai. After that, however, littoral rates leveled off, while those in the Shandong Heartland kept climbing. By 1933–34 silver cost about 75 percent more copper in Qingping and Linqing (the only Heartland rates available for those years) than in Shanghai.[26] In most ways, North China was less chaotic after the spring of 1928. However, since it was governments and their allies that kept the currency market divided, it is logical that with increased political stability, littoral and Heartland rates would diverge.

Evidence is scant, but it appears that the Shandong government's growing strength after 1927 allowed it to reclaim some North Coast areas, causing rates there to diverge from Shanghai's and resemble the Heartland's. A July, 1928 quotation from Longkou, a small North Coast port, is very close to rates in Jinan, Jiaozhou, Linqing, and Qingping but 27 percent above those in Shanghai.[27] However, Yantai, the largest North Coast port, escaped government control and stayed part of the littoral economy. Even three years after Japan seized Manchuria, illegal silver shipments from Yantai to Manchuria affected the local money supply enough to force the government to print more notes; this arbitrage kept the difference in silver-copper rates between Yantai and Dalian down to 8 percent,[28] far less than the North Coast–Heartland difference. Provincial state making expanded the Heartland zone, but there were limits.

The most dramatic differences, however, are between Heartland and Southwest rates. My most complete set of exchange-rate data is for Jining, the commercial center of the Southwest;[29] those data resemble nothing for the North Coast or Heartland. Jining silver prices were ordinary in 1904 but

25. Sources and calculations are in Pomeranz, "Making of a Hinterland," chap. 1, n. 40, and app. C.

26. *Xuxiu Qingping xianzhi* (1936), *jingji*: 25a–b; *Linqing xianzhi* (1934), *jingji*: pp. 22b–24a. The Shanghai data were created using the annual index numbers for copper and silver *yuan* exchange rates in Shanghai from *Tongji yuebao*, Dec. 1930, p. 51, and prices for selected dates in Hsu, *Silver and Prices*, p. 85 (for the dates at which the two series both have data, the rates coincide perfectly).

27. Quotation from *Chinese Economic Bulletin* 13, no. 3 (July 21, 1928), in *Records of Former German and Japanese Embassies and Consulates, 1890–1945* (hereafter *Records*), reel 5, p. 4618834.

28. Quotation from *Qingdao Times*, Dec. 7, 1934, in *Records*, reel 5, p. 4619093.

29. The Jining data may be found in Hai Shan, pp. 48–78. Sources for the other conversion rates appear in Pomeranz, "Making of a Hinterland," app. C.

then soared. By 1909, Jining silver commanded 40 percent more copper than in Jinan and 60 percent more than in Shanghai. By 1914, it was roughly double the price in both Taian (Heartland) and Shanghai; by 1921, almost triple; in 1929, almost six times Linqing and Qingping rates and about eight times the Shanghai rate; and in 1933, roughly double Qingping and triple Shanghai rates.[30]

Transport costs cannot explain these differences, since Jining was only 100 kilometers by rail from Heartland Taian. Nor can information problems. Currency markets in late Qing Jinan, Wei County, and Yantai generated publicly available daily prices; the same was true in early Republican Jining.[31] By this time, other commercial information regularly reached even fairly remote counties by telegraph. All the pieces were in place for lucrative arbitrage.

THE POLITICS OF ECONOMIC GEOGRAPHY: PUBLIC FINANCE

There was, however, a major obstacle to currency movements: numerous county governments banned the export of more than small amounts of certain currencies (usually silver, sometimes copper).[32] This obstructed both arbitrage and cross-county lending: if it is hard to get hard currency out of a county, it is not attractive to send money in. In setting up these barriers, county governments increased the profits of certain local money shops and, more important, their own revenues. Although peasants were often paid in copper, taxes were set in silver. In the 1800s, the exchange rate used for tax payments varied widely, in many places exceeding 5,000 copper *jing qian* per silver tael (a 1,800-to-1 rate in the units used here), but by the 1890s the market rate in cities along the seacoast was less than half that. In 1896 the Shandong governor tried to standardize the official rate at 4,800 to 1, still roughly double the Tianjin rate.[33] If county governments or their allies could enforce high rates at tax-collection time and then dispose of their copper at market rates, they would double their real revenues. As market rates shifted in favor of silver after 1905, county governments' arbitrage profits declined, but they remained significant.

High exchange rates were imposed on all direct taxes but did not enhance

---

30. Ibid., app. C and chart, pp. 52–55.

31. *Shandong quansheng caizheng shuomingshu*, p. 28; Chintao Shubigun Minseibu Tetsudōbu, pp. 462–65; *NCH*, Nov. 22, 1907: 455; Chintao Minseibu Tetsudōbu, *Chōsa Shiryo*, p. 88.

32. See, for instance, *NCH*, Nov. 10, 1905: 304; Nov. 15, 1907: 394.

33. The situation in the late nineteenth century is summarized in Esherick, *Boxers*, pp. 170–72; a post-1900 primary source that gives the government's view is Sun Baoqi's memorial of 9/25/Xuantong 1 (1909) in archives of the Huiyi Zhengwuchu, file #573, document 4802, First Historical Archives, Beijing.

national or provincial receipts. Counties collected all taxes and forwarded a fixed amount of silver to the provincial capital.[34] Thus, the profits from artificial exchange rates were retained locally. In fact, the Shandong governor complained that since Yellow River control demanded large copper expenditures, the province suffered from receiving a fixed silver income;[35] he also argued that locally imposed conversion rates led to tax resistance and so prevented the levying of necessary new taxes.[36] In 1901 the province decreed that taxes should be computed with the market exchange rate,[37] but counties continued to set their own market rates and to enforce them by restricting currency flows.

Moreover, these restrictions often led to currency shortages in inland counties, which in turn created very profitable opportunities for issuing local coins or paper. While the printing of worthless paper by various "national" governments (especially during the warlord period, 1916–28) is well known, county reports of the Shandong Office to Encourage Industry reveal a constant struggle to limit the currencies issued by local governments and merchants. These local currencies, typically denominated in copper and often issued with no financial backing, were especially common in western Shandong, most of all in the Southwest region.[38] Nearer the coast, copper coins were sometimes scarce, but a variety of foreign silver and paper rushed in to fill any vacuum.[39] It is not surprising that Jining, the Southwest trading center with the sky-high silver-copper exchange rate, had one of the worst local-currency problems, which became a major target of political insurgents.[40]

However, officials' efforts to quarantine their domains from market forces were not entirely cynical. The writings of economic officials in early twentieth-century Shandong have an almost mercantilist tone. Growth is desired, but primarily because it will help preserve China's independence, not

---

34. See, e.g., *NCH*, Nov. 15, 1907: 394. John Schrecker, *Imperialism and Chinese Nationalism* (Cambridge, 1971), pp. 213–14, says that when Germany adopted market-rate conversions in Qingdao, local tax collectors, but not the government, lost.

35. Reprinted in Wu Tongju, *Zaixu xingshui jinjian* (Taibei, 1966), 10:3748.

36. *Jining zhilizhou xuzhi* (1929), 4:14a–b; *NCH*, Mar. 18, 1904: 575.

37. *En xianzhi* (1909), 4:4a; doc. 4802 (memorial of 9/25/Xuantong 1), file 573, files of Huiyi Zhengwuchu, First Historical Archives, Beijing; *Shandong zazhi*, no. 62 (6/10/Xuantong 2): 11a–b.

38. See, e.g., *Shandong quanye huikan*, no. 4 (Jan. 1922), *ge xian shiye zhuangkuang*: 17 (on Shan County); no. 7 (May 1922), *ge xian quanye baogao*: 32–33 (Heze); no. 11 (Feb. 1923), *ge xian chengji baogao*: 20 (Heze); no. 13, *gongdu*: 41 (Tangyi), 45 (Linqing).

39. See, e.g., *Shandong zazhi*, no. 78 (11/20/Xuantong 2): 14b–15a; *NCH*, Jan. 30, 1909: 250.

40. See Tang Chengtao, "Huoguo yangmin de 'li Ji qianpiao,'" *Jining shi shiliao*, 1983, no. 1, pp. 89–91; Wu Guogui, "Yutang xinghuo—Jining Shi Yutang jiangyuan gongyun gai," *Shandong gongyun shi ziliao*, no. 16 (Feb. 10, 1985): 13.

because it will promote individual welfare.⁴¹ Import substitution and export promotion projects were conceived as ways of escaping debt, reclaiming foreign concessions, or achieving other "self-strengthening" goals that would not be best served by full integration into the coastal economy.⁴² This stress on national political goals in economic policy fit perfectly in the intellectual climate of early twentieth-century China, where even advocates of Western liberalism stressed liberating individual energies more as a stratagem in China's struggle for autonomy than as an end in itself.⁴³ The mixture of self-serving and sincere motives for impeding currency flows is exemplified in the provincial government's attempt to stop the export of copper coins from Shandong.⁴⁴

Even in the nineteenth century, copper coins had sometimes been worth more as metal than as coins, leading both Chinese and foreigners to buy coins and melt them down. During World War I, the world price of copper (as metal) climbed rapidly. Japanese merchants in Shandong aggressively bought up copper coins for use at home. After the Japanese seized Qingdao in 1914, they had little trouble evading provincial restrictions, and this trade spread along the Qingdao-Jinan railway. Between 1915 and 1919, according to the U.S. consul in Jinan, Shandong "was almost denuded of copper currency," with over 22 million *yuan* worth of copper exported. Coin exports from Shandong in these years were about 12 percent of the annual capacity of all of China's copper mints, or the equivalent of the leakage from all of China during the 1899 currency panic. Strong demand for copper coins raised their value further above the levels set by many local authorities, making restrictions even more important to county finance.

Provincial and national authorities were worried both about the symbolism of this trade—Japan used some of this copper to make bullet casings—and the control it gave Japan over the money supply along the railway. Complaints about this trade disappeared in the early 1920s but became common again after 1928.

Though provincial governments suffered from restrictions on currency

---

41. See, e.g., *Shandong zazhi*, no. 88 (4/30/Xuantong 3): 7b–8a; no. 89 (5/15/Xuantong 3): 8a–9b; no. 90 (5/30/Xuantong 3): 7a–8b; *Nong shang gongbao* 1, no. 5 (Dec. 15, 1914), *zhengshi*: 14; Lin Maoquan (head of the Shandong Office to Encourage Industry in the 1920s), *Wenji*, pp. 2a–b, 71a.

42. See, for instance, Lin Maoquan, *Wenji*, pp. 1a–7b; another, slightly different, example is the great interest by Shandong merchants and politicians in improving the harbor and otherwise building up Yantai as an alternative to foreign-controlled Qingdao and the waning of that interest when Qingdao was returned to China in 1922; see, e.g., *NCH*, Mar. 4, 1922: 576, 585.

43. See, e.g., Benjamin Schwartz, *In Search of Wealth and Power: Yen Fu and the West* (Cambridge, 1964); Joseph Levenson, *Liang Chi-chao and the Mind of Modern China* (Cambridge, 1953).

44. The following account is condensed from Pomeranz, "Making of a Hinterland," pp. 61–64.

movement between counties, they supported restrictions that kept coins from leaving the province. Provincial officials wanted a unified provincial currency and economy but were unwilling to let this happen through integration into international markets; even while they were redoubling efforts to prevent currency exports, they were (unsuccesfully) ordering all counties to abide by exchange rates for notes that would be wired from Jinan.

We have few details about how currency restrictions were enforced, but persistent exchange rate differentials suggest significant successes. In 1933 counties very close to each other, such as Shouguang (North Coast) and Linju (Heartland), and Heze and Cao (both Southwest), still quoted very different exchange rates.[45] There are also accounts of people being searched for currency at train stations and other checkpoints.[46] County governments could not fully police their borders, but policing rail and water routes greatly reduced currency arbitrage. (Postal remittances were irregular, and could be limited to firms adhering to local exchange rates.)[47] Rate differentials between Jining and the nearest Heartland points far exceeded even the costs of moving copper by wheelbarrow.

THE POLITICS OF ECONOMIC GEOGRAPHY: PRIVATE GAIN

Soldiers, however, were often exempt from inspection, and at a higher level, the politically connected could profit handsomely by evading restrictions.[48] A hint of how currency moved across counties may be gathered from the other service offered by the Huangxian currency-moving company mentioned above: convoying opium, which required either extensive official contacts or private armed forces.[49]

One revealing arbitrage story involves less privileged participants, from Fan County in far southwestern Shandong. In 1917, North China suffered huge floods. A *North-China Herald* reporter sent to the southwest Shandong–Henan–Zhili border area, near the origin of the flooding, found Japanese merchants paying 0.155 *yuan* per *jin* for copper coins worth about 0.167 *yuan* back on the coast.[50] This trade had previously been carried on elsewhere,

---

45. *Shouguang xianzhi*, 11:12a–b; *Shandong zheng su shichaji*, pp. 362, 371, 832.

46. *NCH*, Nov. 10, 1905: 304; Nov. 15, 1907: 394.

47. Clifton O. Carey, "Narrative Account of Experiences in China," p. 8, in packet labeled "Letters, Sept.–Dec., 1919," Clifton O'Neill Carey Papers, Bentley Historical Library, University of Michigan; *NCH*, Sept. 27, 1907: 720.

48. On soldiers, see *NCH*, July 29, 1916: 189. On politicians, see *NCH*, Dec. 22, 1917: 719, and Mar. 30, 1918: 752, which have examples drawn from Kaifeng, Henan, near Southwest Shandong.

49. *SSZ*, 4:1145.

50. *NCH*, Oct. 27, 1917: 216; the weight-to-value conversion ratio derived from the figures here matches figures from the American consul in Jinan quoted in Frederic Lee, *Currency, Banking, and Finance in China* (Washington, D.C., 1926), p. 32.

but high water had now allowed it to move further upstream, where silver fetched an even higher price. The Japanese were making their fourth trip to the area,

> allowing just enough interval for the natives to take their [silver] dollars upstream or inland and bring all the available [copper] cash to this shipping point. ... Last year, said the locquacious [village] headman [who was supervising the exchange], this trade did not come so far upstream *and the officials prevented the shipment of cash down to the buyers, but this year the buyers had come themselves and "bought an open road" [bribed the officials] so that all was easy,* and the impoverished countryside, under water for 3 months, was recovering, thanks to the cash trade.[51]

Several points emerge from this story. First, more people knew about this trade than could ordinarily participate; the people in this village were normally excluded. Second, who participated was determined by official prohibitions and, conversely, by bribes. Third, even after getting by the formal government, the merchants dealt, not with individual peasants, but with a village head who had organized "his" people into teams. Fourth, the biggest profits were made on the inland side of the transaction. If the copper the Japanese bought for 0.155 *yuan* was indeed worth 0.167 *yuan* on the coast, they cleared less than 8 percent between Fan County and the coast, minus their costs. The villagers who took the coins further inland (on foot) received 1,400 copper cash for silver coins that cost them roughly 1,000,[52] a 40 percent profit before accounting for their costs (largely a matter of their time). Local restrictions on currency flows created hefty profits for a favored minority of local traders, not for outside merchants.

FRAGMENTED MARKETS AND DISTRIBUTION

Weakly integrated currency and capital markets redistributed wealth from some hinterland actors to others. High interest rates benefited hinterland creditors and hurt hinterland debtors. Distorted silver-copper rates redistributed wealth from private citizens to local governments. High exchange rates hurt those who were paid in copper but bought at least some things in silver (or at silver-denominated prices), and benefited people who were paid in silver. Finally, restrictions on currency movement benefited those who had the connections to circumvent those restrictions. However, specifying the members of these groups and how much they gained or lost is very difficult.

High interest rates aided not only banks and pawnshops but also certain stores, which probably provided more credit than official financial institu-

---

51. *NCH*, Oct. 27, 1917: 216, emphasis added.
52. Ibid.

tions did.[53] Buyers of cash crops were important credit sources in the Heartland and the North Coast,[54] but not in the Southwest. In Jining, the shops that doubled as credit institutions were mostly those that sold modern or "foreign" goods: factory yarn, cloth, kerosene, matches, and cigarettes.[55] Since they often got credit from their suppliers, who were located where money was cheaper, they were major beneficiaries of the high local interest rates.[56] With their access to cheaper funds from outside the region, these "foreign goods" stores enjoyed a particularly large spread between their own cost of funds and what they charged their customers.

We have very little information on the cost of funds for these privileged firms, but to the extent that they could get outside loans from suppliers or other contacts, they stood to make very large profits. We do know that Jining's largest charity, whose directors included the city's leading gentry, merchants, and officials, received from 8 percent to 12 percent per year for its deposits at the city's leading pawnshops and merchant firms.[57] These rates were likely influenced by self-dealing, since the charity's directors were also leaders of the firms with which they deposited money; thus these rates cannot be taken as indicative of ordinary deposit rates. However, if well-connected firms were paying 1 percent per month to the charity endowment because that was even approximately what other funds would have cost them, then the spread that they enjoyed with local consumer rates at over 2 percent per month was indeed substantial.

A 1940 survey argues that yarn and foreign goods merchants had become Jining's mercantile elite and notes a sharp conflict between them and the older grain, leather, and wool merchants[58]—exporters of local products who lacked access to the importers' relatively cheap credit and were in turn surprisingly unimportant as lenders to local farmers. Unfortunately the survey does not describe this conflict. However, it does say that many importers

53. Stores had long been a major source of credit throughout China. In early twentieth-century Shandong, they became still more important, partly because of discriminatory levies on pawnshops; in fact, some pawnshops became stores with a lending sideline in order to escape these charges. See Zhang Yufa, *Zhongguo xiandaihua de quyu yanjiu: Shandong sheng, 1860–1916* (Taibei, 1982), p. 583, and *ZSZS*, pt. 10:28–31, on the small number of pawnshops remaining in the 1930s.

54. See, e.g., *Quanye huikan*, no. 12 (March 1923), *gongdu*: 30 (on Northwest Shandong in general).

55. Kokuritsu Pekin Daigaku, *Santō sainei kenjō o chūshin toseru nōsan butsu ryūtsū ni kansuru ichi kosatsu* (Beijing, 1942), hereafter *Santō sainei*, pp. 94–100.

56. On credit (in money, not just goods) from modern goods producers to their agents in the Jining area, see the letter of the British-American Tobacco agent Frank H. Canaday to A. Bassett of May 20, 1925, in the F. H. Canaday Papers, Harvard-Yenching Library, vol. 17: 92, 96. Credit was provided even though the company's Jining agent was "the richest man in the city" (vol. 15, letters of Aug. 20 and Aug. 26, 1923).

57. *Jining zhilizhou xuzhi*, 5:10b–11a, 13b, 21b.

58. *Santō sainei*, pp. 12–13.

were also local officials, while grain traders were not, and that importers, unlike exporters, got funds from Jining's two modern bank branches.[59]

These Jining importers and a few other influential firms thus appear to exemplify the politically connected oligopolists with access to cheap credit that we are looking for. This hypothesis, however, should not be confused with the claims made in some literature that such traders were parasitic "compradors," as opposed to a productive "national bourgeoisie." The foreign goods they sold, though imports to the area, were often made in Qingdao, Tianjin, or Jinan factories. Perhaps the thing these importers offered that was most genuinely foreign in origin was credit, which came to them (directly or indirectly) from suppliers and modern banks based in the treaty ports. However, the problem was not that they brought in coastal funds but that they acted as a cartel, offering less credit at higher prices than would have been available were cross-county transactions unrestrained. And, as with the currency arbitrage described above, it was the local conduits for outside credit that profited from there being few such conduits, not would-be or actual outside lenders. American complaints that hinterland retail agents passed along currency losses—but not gains—to their foreign suppliers/creditors also suggest that merchants like the Jining importers were hardly subservient to treaty port interests.[60]

Most farmers, laborers, and merchants outside the privileged circle were at least sometime borrowers—and therefore losers from the restrictions on capital mobility. However, some better-off members of these groups were also at least occasional lenders, or even net creditors, who gained from high rates. Being such did not require cash lending: farmers who did not need to sell immediately at harvesttime could hoard their crop and earn the area's high interest rate.[61] In general, though, we know very little about who could and could not afford to do this.

For government overcharges, taxpayers were the obvious losers. Local governments and money changers gained, but we do not know how much or how the spoils were divided. Some officials tried to force local money shops to accept conversion rates that would have given government all the profit, but they often failed.[62]

Cash-crop farming, which gave peasants a way to obtain silver for taxes, may have enabled some of them to escape this gouging. Several Southwest Shandong counties, however, would not let their citizens escape, even if they had silver on hand: they required that taxes be computed in silver but paid in

59. Ibid., pp. 10, 31.
60. Lee, *Currency*, p. 56.
61. *Santō sainei*, pp. 86, 92.
62. This would appear to be the case described in *NCH*, Nov. 15, 1907: 393–94, where the government itself had trouble obtaining silver. See also Schrecker, *Imperialism*, p. 213; *Shandong zazhi*, no. 62 (6/10/Xuantong 2): 11a–11b, and no. 77 (10/1/Xuantong 1): 14b.

copper.[63] Evidence about how currency restrictions affected people as consumers, workers, and so forth is even more fragmentary, though we know that at least some cash-crop farmers were paid in silver, and so gained, while virtually all casual laborers were paid in copper, and thereby lost.[64]

FRAGMENTED MARKETS AND REGIONAL ECONOMIC PERFORMANCE

The most basic effect of Shandong's highly imperfect capital market is clear. It kept capital scarcer in the Heartland and especially in the Southwest than it would have been otherwise; thus, certain projects in those regions were never carried out, even though they would have paid as well as projects that were carried out in the North Coast.

The precise effects on the Heartland of limited access to outside capital are harder to assess than those on the Southwest. The Heartland had its own access to the international economy through Qingdao. That port, however, was always dominated by one power (first Germany, then Japan) that tried to monopolize its trade, and credit and silver were never as cheap there as in Yantai, Weihaiwei, or Shanghai.[65] The northwestern Heartland was also connected to Tianjin. The Heartland sent some people to Manchuria but received fewer remittances than the North Coast; those remittances seem to have pushed interest rates to particularly low levels in the North Coast and in Zunhua, Zhili.

Significant capital infusions did reach the Heartland. Improved cotton varieties, for instance, had an enormous impact, especially on northwestern Shandong; their introduction was financed by Qingdao and Tianjin mills and by a provincial government spurred by fear of the growing influence wielded by Japanese-owned mills.[66] Once the new crop was established, the mills often advanced credit against it.[67] Little is known about the rates on these loans; at times these buyer/suppliers established local monopolies that allowed them to become quite abusive.[68] In general, however, the influx of foreign money meant that farmers got cheaper credit and did better than farmers growing for more local markets.

The growth of cash crops spared the Heartland the silver shortages common in the Southwest. As of 1933, most Heartland counties exported more

---

63. *NCH*, Nov. 15, 1907: 393–94.
64. See, e.g., *SSZ*, 4:234, 250, 260; *Records*, reel 37, pp. 4660213–19, 4660230; Wu Guogui, "Yutang xinghuo," p. 13.
65. On Qingdao rates, see *ZSZS*, pt. 5, p. 90; *Jiao-Ao xianzhi, shihuo*: 85–88.
66. For a general account, see Pomeranz, "Making of a Hinterland," chap. 2.
67. Minami Manshū Tetsudō Kabushiki Kaisha, Tenshin Jimusho Chōsaka, *Santō no mensaku* (Tianjin, 1942), pp. 47–54; Kanbe Masao, ed., *Tōa keizai kenkyū* (Tokyo, 1942), 1:118–20.
68. See, e.g., *Shandong shiye gongbao*, no. 3 (Sept. 1931), *xunling*: 27.

than they imported, which left some silver for taxes and for repaying whatever cross-county lending did occur. There is no reason to expect deflation, marked price divergence from the North Coast, or some of the peculiarities that did appear in the Southwest. Still, 30 years of persistent interest rate differences between the Heartland and the North Coast remind us that, with barriers to currency flows and conversion, the Heartland did not gain all it could have from the development of the coastal and Manchurian economies.

Having no outside loans except those financing exports may have suited Heartland officials, whose economic goals stressed the balance of payments and "independence." It did not, however, maximize growth. Capital infusions were limited by the extent to which the Heartland specialized in exports—and specialization depended on a still-backward transport network.

The Southwest was hurt much more, though. Even here, some outside capital flowed in, but only in very special circumstances.[69] We would not expect outsiders to have made retail loans to Southwest Shandong peasants for weddings, funerals, and the like; even without currency restrictions, information and collection problems would have discouraged remote lenders. What is striking is the absence of outside credit for production and marketing in the Southwest, even of crops exported to areas with cheaper money.

In the Heartland, and in nearby northern Jiangsu (just south of Shandong), trade in cash crops was financed by merchant buyers in a chain stretching back to the coastal ports and world economy.[70] However, the 1940 survey of Jining and nearby villages shows that credit for trade in Southwest Shandong came from below, not above: farmers generally borrowed from other village farmers.[71] Cash crops were brought to market by poor farmers, who borrowed from richer peasants in the village to finance their trip; they usually paid the actual producers only after returning from market.[72] The description of the market in Jining emphasizes how eager these *xiao banzi* (petty traders) were to get back to their villages;[73] time pressure probably weakened their bargaining power, and was probably partially due to pressures from producers who needed cash quickly to pay taxes and debts. These *xiao banzi* rarely borrowed from Jining grain shops, and did not—indeed, usually could not—give advances against crops.[74] Thus, even if a few received credit from above, it was not passed on.

69. See Pomeranz, "Making of a Hinterland," p. 80 and chap. 1 n. 129.

70. See, e.g., "The Peanut Trade of Tsingtao," *Chinese Economic Bulletin* 11, no. 348 (Oct. 22, 1927), pp. 213–14. On northern Jiangsu, see Chen Bozhuang, *Xiaomai ji mianfen* (Shanghai, 1936), p. 52.

71. *Santō sainei*, pp. 13, 106. This pattern is confirmed by the figures in John L. Buck, *Land Utilization in China: Statistical Volume* (1937; New York, 1982), p. 404.

72. *Santō sainei*, p. 40.

73. Ibid., pp. 33–34, 39–40.

74. Ibid., pp. 39–40.

Other potential sources also failed to relieve Southwest farmers' dependence on local credit. In 1939 most grain and most bean and nut oil firms in Jining were very small, were less than five years old, and did no business with Jining's two modern banks.[75] "Guest merchants" who came to Jining from Taian, Jinan, and elsewhere got money from modern bank branches, but only after the harvest, when they were about to purchase the crop;[76] thus they could not have passed these funds along as credit to finance production or lower levels of marketing. Southwest peasants and exporters had no chance to finance improvements with credit cheaper than that generated locally, as cash-crop growers elsewhere did. This was true even though many in the Southwest produced for ultimate buyers—Jinan flour mills and foreign buyers of peanut, cotton seed, and bean oils[77]—who could borrow more cheaply.

With even exporters cut off from cheap funds, Southwest Shandong suffered frequent, serious silver shortages. The area responded in part by making do with very few modern-sector goods. As of 1933, the Southwest imported far fewer outside goods than any other part of the province: only 35 percent as much per capita, for instance, as a sample of 18 equally remote northwestern Heartland counties.[78] Despite this austerity, however, the Southwest as a whole ran a merchandise trade deficit.[79]

With a trade deficit, taxes to pay, and little outside credit, the Southwest exported labor, particularly to Manchuria. Though Southwest Shandong was more remote from Manchuria than any part of either Shandong or Hebei (the home provinces of 95 percent of the migrants to Manchuria), it sent tens of thousands of people per year there.[80] Three years after Japan's seizure of Manchuria, remittances lost by 16 Southwest counties were estimated at 4 million *yuan* per year,[81] while Manchurian remittances to all 215 Shandong and Hebei counties were about 30 million *yuan*.[82] Jining alone may have lost 3 million *yuan* per year.[83]

Before 1931, Manchurian remittances probably covered Southwest Shandong's trade deficits, at least before we add taxes.[84] Thus, currency problems did not cause marked deflation or price divergence in the Southwest before

---

75. Ibid., pp. 13, 26–27, 68–69.
76. Ibid., p. 68.
77. Ibid., pp. 47–48, 65–72.
78. *ZSZS*, pt. 10:151–201.
79. Ibid., pt. 10:165–89, gives the county-by-county figures.
80. For estimates based on figures for 1933, see Tōā Kenkyūsho, *Santō Koshōgun chitai no chiiki chōsa*, Report no. 14, Class C, no. 158-D, pp. 127–29, based on figures for 1933.
81. "Luxi ge xian nongcun jingji xianzhuang," *Nongcun jingji* 1, no. 11 (Sept. 1, 1934), p. 75.
82. Gottschang, "Migration," pp. 137–38.
83. "Luxi jingji xianzhuang," p. 76.
84. *ZSZS*, pt. 10:156–201, has the trade figures; see also "Luxi jingji xianzhuang."

1931; the absence of outside capital is reflected instead in high interest rates, austerity, and massive temporary and permanent emigration. Even though rural elites in the Southwest sometimes prevented export growth,[85] local governments and their allies generally met their silver obligations to higher levels of government while retaining enough control to manipulate exchange and interest rates to their benefit—and to the detriment of the population as a whole.

After 1931 this balance was disrupted. Between 1930 and 1934 the Shanghai price of wheat—Southwest Shandong's major cash crop—declined 40 percent.[86] In Southwest Shandong, however, things were much worse. Of 13 Southwest counties that reported price trends in 1934, one reported a 50 percent decline in both wheat and land prices; four reported 60 percent declines; one a 75 percent decline; and seven 80 percent declines.[87] This alone does not demonstrate price divergence from other areas, but since wheat was the Southwest's biggest product and biggest export, it is suggestive. So is the price of silver money (in copper, which might serve as a proxy for all goods sold for copper) in Jining. After retreating from the dizzying heights of the mid to late 1920s, that price stabilized from 1930 to 1933, but then took off again, rising faster in Jining over the next two years than anywhere else. At the least, this shows that three years after Manchuria was closed and a silver drain began, the high rates being offered for credit and hard currency were not drawing outside funds to the Southwest. By contrast, the more open North Coast counties also had merchandise trade deficits, and traditionally received even larger remittances from Manchuria, but avoided a hard currency shortage even after Japan's takeover of Manchuria dealt a severe shock to trade and migration across the Bohai Gulf.[88]

FRAGMENTED MARKETS AND STATE MAKING

This summary of government influence on the capital market and economy leads back to the effects of economic phenomena on the state. Shandong officials announced goals of decreasing imports and increasing exports to accumulate silver. Far less attention was paid to commodities that circulated locally.[89] Meanwhile, both the province and many county governments tried

---

85. See Pomeranz, "Making of a Hinterland," chap. 2, for an extended example: the unwillingness of Southwestern village leaders to cooperate with the dissemination of new cotton varieties.

86. Wu Chengming, "Woguo banzhimindi banfengjian guonei shichang," *Lishi yanjiu*, no. 168 (April, 1984), p. 115.

87. "Luxi jingji xianzhuang."

88. *ZSZS*, pt. 10:189–201.

89. See, e.g., the discussion of development plans in *Shandong quanye huikan*, no. 10 (Jan. 1923), *lunshuo*: 1–3.

to make their jurisdictions economically meaningful units, in which they could control matters such as exchange rates and coinage free from broader market forces. Such freedom generally enhanced the particular government's short-term revenue. It also benefited merchants tied to local governments and those who could move money despite restrictions.

Many officials did seek greater economic integration. In some areas not discussed here, such as road building, important advances were made.[90] County Offices to Encourage Industry of the 1920s never tried to retire all local currency, but they often did try to centralize issuing authority, usually in the county chamber of commerce.[91] In the 1930s the provincial government tried to eliminate local paper currency, though with limited success.[92] However, these efforts aimed at concentrating control at that particular level of government; control was not to be allowed to pass to a higher government unit or broader market. Provincial efforts to standardize currency rates within Shandong while banning currency exports are a good example.

Government policies often hindered economic growth in Shandong, particularly in the Southwest. But how well did government do for itself? This is a complicated question, but some general outlines are clear. While the provincial government could not control currency trading in the rich areas near Yantai and along the Jinan-Qingdao railway, it was fairly successful elsewhere, thus protecting its own influence and revenue. However, its control was never secure.

Meanwhile, many counties maintained independent monetary policies even into the 1930s. The provincial government's greatest success against local-currency trading was probably in Zouping, where a team of outsiders was brought in to take over the entire county government; until then, numerous orders to suppress local money and adopt standard exchange rates had been ignored.[93] The 1935 national currency reform came too shortly before the outbreak of war to judge its success in Shandong, but in 1937 much of the province had very limited ties to national or international currency and capital markets, and the Southwest was still only loosely tied to the rest of the province's money markets. Unwilling to accept integration into larger markets, provincial leaders were also unable to impose full integration onto their own system.

90. See county reports in *Shandong zheng su shichaji*.
91. See, e.g., *Shandong quanye huikan*, no. 4 (Jan. 1922), *ge xian shiye zhuangkuang*: 17 (on Shan county); no. 7 (May 1922), *ge xian quanye baogao*: 32–33 (Heze); no. 11 (Feb. 1923), *ge xian chengji baogao*: 20 (Heze); no. 13, *gongdu*: 41 (Tangyi), 45 (Linqing).
92. Luo Ziwei, "Zouping sichao mianguan," *Xiangcun jianshe xunkan* 4, no. 29, pp. 26–31; *Shandong caizheng gongbao* 6, no. 3 (Dec. 1934), *mingling*: 41; *Shandong shengxianzheng jianshe shiyanqu gongbao*, no. 14 (Nov. 27, 1935): 6–7; no. 23 (Dec, 15, 1935): 3 (page numbers supplied; original is unpaginated).
93. Luo Ziwei, "Zouping," pp. 26–31.

This failure probably did not cost them much. Immediate provincial revenue increases from faster growth would have been small. The Southwest, poor and loosely tied to Jinan, was unlikely to yield more revenue. However, provincial officials could not ignore the Southwest. Two of the area's biggest problems—the Yellow River, which entered Shandong through the Southwest, and unusually serious banditry—endangered the rest of the province. Officials dealing with these problems were severely handicapped by the Southwest's economic isolation. Localities that regularly rebuilt earthen dikes balked at building cheaper stone dikes, which would have required paying hard currency to distant quarries, rather than making local expenditures for dirt, food, and labor.[94] Subcounty leaders were supposed to maintain sections of the dikes, either from local resources or a small, fixed subsidy; they received no specifications. Given very high interest rates, they often found that building and rebuilding minimal barriers every two to three years was a cheaper way to meet their formal obligations than making one large outlay for dikes that could have lasted 20 years or more. However, less permanent dikes meant more floods.[95]

After 1900, coastal areas in Shandong and elsewhere constructed fewer and fewer of their riverworks with locally levied labor and in-kind assessments (of stalks, earth, etc.) and used more cash taxes and public borrowing to buy specialized materials and hire contractors—including, sometimes, foreign contractors who brought new technology and cheaper credit. In eastern Shandong, the result was better and cheaper flood control. In the Southwest, however, reliance on local in-kind contributions increased, in part because the province forced localities to pay more of these costs than in the 1800s and because local governments preferred not to spend hard currency. In 1934 provincial officials who had just supervised Southwest Shandong's largest riverworks project in 50 years—all done with local materials and in-kind levies—explained that trying to do the project with money would have caused "panic."[96]

Flood control would have increased output enough for taxes to easily pay for the work; thus, it was a perfect project for local governments to borrow for. Local governments often borrowed money to finance flood control projects near the coast, but not in Southwest Shandong. Local riverworks officials complained that they could not arrange even the short-term credit needed for routine maintenance.[97]

---

94. This discussion of riverworks is condensed from Pomeranz, "Making of a Hinterland," chaps. 4 and 5; citations below are examples from much longer lists. On the cost effectiveness of stone dikes, see *Shandong hewu tekan*, no. 2 (Jan. 1930), *zhuanjian*: 3–5, 10–15.

95. See Pomeranz, "Making of a Hinterland," 223–35, and apps. G and H.

96. Shandong Sheng Jiansheting, *Junzhi Wan Fu Zhu Shui He zhi* (Jinan, 1934), p. 119.

97. *Shandong hewu tekan*, no. 8 (Jan. 1936), *gongdu*: 89; *Hewu jibao*, no. 1 (Apr. 1919): 117; *Shandong jianshe yuekan* 2, no. 3 (Mar. 1932), *baogao*: 45.

The failures of river control in western Shandong were not primarily due to currency problems; many other factors were involved. Nonetheless, currency policies that sacrificed economic integration to local revenues and profits made it hard to move the public's resources through time and space to get the most out of them, just as they limited most private actors' ability to do this.

In sum, one critical part of state making in early twentieth-century Shandong—the search for greater revenue—interfered with market integration. This clash contrasts sharply with the pattern in early modern Europe, where state and market making usually reinforced each other, and market integration made the extraction and movement of state revenue easier.[98] Shandong's poorly integrated markets, in turn, helped frustrate the development of an administration that could move resources to achieve things that localities could not.

Yet these problems cannot be blamed entirely on the governments involved. Government in early twentieth-century China did not consume a particularly large part of the country's income,[99] and further economic growth surely required that some governments find enough revenue to provide increased amounts of various public goods (social stability, flood control, etc.). Some local officials may have favored the methods discussed here because they were profitable for themselves and their allies, but they probably also felt these methods were less disruptive than many alternatives and may have considered them important to defending Chinese authority against foreign intrusions. Finally, the foreign intrusions that helped provoke these measures (and which also sometimes disrupted currency flows, as in 1931) were inseparable from the stimulus that made economic links to the coast so useful. Early twentieth-century Shandong saw both state making and market making, but under these circumstances, they clashed rather than meshed.

---

98. See, e.g., the discussion in Charles Tilly, "Reflections on the History of State-Making," in Tilly, ed., *The Formation of National States in Western Europe* (Princeton, 1975), pp. 17, 30–31, 52–57.

99. Most estimates place government spending at 3–5 percent of gross domestic product. See, e.g., Philip C. C. Huang, *The Peasant Economy and Social Change in North China* (Stanford, 1985), pp. 280–84.

GLOSSARY

Agui	阿桂
Anxi	安西
Arai Hakuseki	新井白石
baimai	白麥
Baishuidang (Yangming Township)	白水蕩(揚名鄉)
bang	幫
Baodao tun	包道屯
Baoding	保定
baojia	保甲
Barkul (Balikun)	巴里坤
Bei (river)	北
Beijing	北京
caizheng cangchu	財政倉儲
candou	蠶荳
cangshi	倉石
caoliang	漕糧
Changjiang (Yangzi river)	長江
Changli	昌黎
changpingcang	常平倉
changsan	長三
Changshu	常熟
Changzhou	常州
Chengde	承德
Ciqi	慈谿
cisumi	次粟米

GLOSSARY

Dabeiguan	大北關
dan	擔
Daoguang (reign period, 1821–50)	道光
daomi	稻米
daotai	道台
Daoyi tun	道義屯
Daqing (river)	大清
diandi	典地
ding	丁
Dinghai	定海
Dingjia fangshen	丁家方身
Dongtai Lühu Tongxianghui	東台旅滬同鄉會
duangong	短工
Du Yuesheng	杜月笙
Fang Xing	方行
Fenghua	奉化
feng qiong po	縫窮婆
Fengrun	豐潤
Fengtian	奉天
fenjia	分家
fu	府
Funing	阜寧
Gansu	甘肅
Ganzhou	甘州
Gao Jin	高晉
gaoliang	高粱
gengdao	梗稻
gexian chengji baogao	格縣成績報告
gexian quanye baogao	格縣勸業報告
gexian shiye baogao	格縣實業報告
Gongchang	鞏昌
gong du	公牘
gonghui	公會
gong shan	工繕
Guangxi	廣西
Guizhou	貴州
Gu Zhuxuan	顧竹軒
Hai (river)	海
Haimen	海門
Hami	哈密
Hangzhou	杭州
Hanyang	漢陽
Hebei	河北
Hefeng	和豐

GLOSSARY

heidou	黑豆
Henan	河南
He Ti	何提
hongmai	紅麥
huabu	花布
Huai (river)	淮
Huai'an	淮安
Huai'an Liuyi Huiguan	淮安六邑會館
Huaiyin	淮陰
Huang Jinrong	黃金榮
Huangpu (river)	黃浦
Huang Tinggui	黃廷桂
Huangyan	黃巖
Huguang	湖廣
huiguan	會館
Huiyi Zhengwuchu	會議政物處
jia	甲
Jiading	嘉定
Jialing	嘉陵
Jiangbei	江北
Jiangbei bang	江北幫
Jiang Chen	蔣臣
Jianghuai Lühu Tongxianghui	江淮旅滬同鄉會
Jiangnan	江南
jiao	角
Jiaqing (reign period, 1796–1820)	嘉慶
Jiaxing	嘉興
Jiezhou	階州
jin (1.1 lb., 0.5 kilogram)	斤
Jinan	濟南
jingji	經濟
Jingni	靖逆
jing qian	京錢
jingshi	京石
Jingzhou	涇州
Jin Jiulin	金九林
jinsi	金絲
juan	捐
kan	貫
Kangxi (reign period, 1662–1735)	康熙
kemi	客米
kuping	庫平
Lai	來
Lanzhou	蘭州

GLOSSARY

Liangzhou 涼州
Liaoning 遼寧
linghu 另戶
Liu Guiping 刘貴平
lunshuo 論說

macao 麻草
mai 麥
Maocun (Kaiyuan township) 毛村(開原鄉)
menpai 門牌
mianbu 棉布
Michang 米廠
Ming 明
mingling 命令
mu 畝

nan geng nü zhi 男耕女織
Nantong 南通
Nanyun (river) 南運
nimi 糜米
Ningbo 寧波
Ning-Shao 寧紹
Ningxia 寧夏
nuodao 糯稻

Pingliang 平涼
Pudong 浦東

Qianlianggezhuang 前梁各莊
Qianlong (reign period, 1736–95) 乾隆
Qing 清
Qinghai 青海
Qingyang 慶陽
Qinzhou 秦州
Qiu Jun 邱濬
Quan liao zhi 全遼志
Quanzhou 泉州

Renhe 人和
Rongxiang zhen 榮巷鎮
Rugao 如皋

Shaanxi 陝西
Shandong 山東
shang dian 商店
shang sumi 上粟米
Shaoxing 紹興

shecang	社倉
Shen Bao	申報
Shenyang	深陽
shi	石
shihuo	食貨
Shuntian	順天
Sichuan	四川
Songjiang	松江
Subei	蘇北
Subei bang	蘇北幫
Subei Lühu Tongxianghui	蘇北旅滬同鄉會
Subei ren	蘇北人
sui	歲
sumi	粟米
Suxiang (Beiyanxia township)	蘇巷(北延下鄉)
Suzhou	蘇州
Suzhou (Gansu)	肅州
Tai (lake)	太
Taiwan	台灣
tanding rudi	攤丁入地
tanding rumu	攤丁入畝
Tianjin	天津
Tongjiuyuan	通久源
tongxiang guanxi	同鄉關係
tongyangxi	童養媳
tunken gengzuo	屯墾耕作
tuntian	屯田
Turfan	吐魯番
wandou	碗豆
Wang Danwang	王亶望
Wenzhou	溫州
Wu Dange	伍丹戈
Wu Dashan	吳達善
Wuwei	武威
Wuxi	無錫
Xi'an	西安
xian	縣
xiao banzi	小販子
Xiaoshan	蕭山
Xinghua Tongxianghui	興化同鄉會
Xining	西寧
Xinjiang	新疆
Xinwen Bao	新聞報
Xuanhua	宣化

Yancheng	鹽城
Yangzhou	揚州
Yangzhou Bashu Gongsuo	揚州八屬公所
Yangzhou Bayi Lühu Tongxianghui	揚州八邑旅滬同鄉會
yao'er	么二
Yao Xinrong	姚欣榮
ye ji	野鷄
yicang	義倉
Yin	鄞
Yong bu	甬布
Yongding (river)	永定
Yongxing	永興
Yongzheng (reign period, 1723–35)	雍正
Yuan (river)	沅
yuan (approx. U.S. $0.50 in 1920)	圓, 元
Yunnan	雲南
Yu Xiaoxia	俞嘯霞
Yuyao	餘姚
Zhang Xiaolin	張嘯林
Zhangye	張掖
Zhao zhou	趙州
Zhejiang	浙江
zhen	鎮
Zhengdaxin	正大新
Zhengding	正定
Zhenhai	鎮海
zhenji	賑濟
zhi qian	制錢
Zhili	直隸
zhilizhou	直隸州
zhongsumi	中粟米
Zhongyin	鐘音
zhuanjian	轉件
Ziya (river)	子牙
zu	族
zupu	族譜

BIBLIOGRAPHY

Abe Takeo 安部健夫. "Beikoku jukyū no kenkyū: Yōseishi no isshō to shite mita" 米穀需給の研究—「雍正史」の一章としてみた [A study of the supply and demand for staple grains as a chapter in the history of the Yongzheng reign]. *Tōyōshi kenkyū* 東洋史研究 15, no. 4 (1957): 484–577.

Akerlof, George A. *An Economic Theorist's Book of Tales: Essays That Entertain the Consequences of New Assumptions in Economic Theory.* Cambridge: Cambridge University Press, 1984.

Anthony, Lawrence, James Lee, and Alice Suen. "Adult Mortality in Rural Liaoning, 1795 to 1819." California Institute of Technology Humanities Working Paper no. 115. 1985. Published in Chinese as "Liaoning sheng chengren siwang lü, 1795–1819," in *Zhongguo diyi lishi dang'an guan liushi zhounian lunwen ji* 中国第一历史档案馆六十周年论文集 [Proceedings of the Symposium on the Occasion of the 60th Anniversary of the First Historical Archives] 2:885–98. Beijing: Dang'an Chubanshe, 1988.

Appleby, Andrew B. "Epidemics and Famine in the Little Ice Age." *Journal of Interdisciplinary History*, 10 (Spring 1980): 643–63.

———. "Grain Prices and Subsistence Crises in England and France, 1590–1740." *Journal of Economic History* 39, no. 4 (1979): 865–87.

Banister, Judith. *China's Changing Population.* Stanford: Stanford University Press, 1987.

Bao Shichen 包世臣. *Anwu sizhong* 安吳四種 [Four works of Bao Shichen]. Vol. 26. 1872.

Barclay, G. W., A. J. Coale, M. A. Stoto, and T. J. Trussell. "A Reassessment of the Demography of Traditional Rural China." *Population Index* 42, no. 4 (1976): 606–35.

Baron, Harold. "Racial Domination in Advanced Capitalism: A Theory of Nationalism and Divisions in the Labor Market." In *Labor Market Segmentation*, edited by Edwards, Reich, and Gordon, 173–216.

Becker, Gary S. "A Theory of Marriage." Parts 1, 2. *Journal of Political Economy* 81 (1973): 813–46; 82 (1974): 911–16.

Bell, Lynda S. "Chinese Women and the Value of 'Surplus Labor.'" Paper presented at the All-U.C. Economic History Group Conference on Women and Work: Understanding the Gender Gap, University of California, Los Angeles, November 9-11, 1990.

———. "Explaining China's Rural Crisis: Observations from Wuxi County in the Early Twentieth Century." *Republican China* 11, no. 1 (1985): 15-31.

———. "Merchants, Peasants, and the State: The Organization and Politics of Chinese Silk Production, Wuxi County, 1870-1937." Ph.D. diss., University of California, Los Angeles, 1985.

Bengtsson, Tommy, Gunnar Fridlizius, and Rolf Ohlsson, eds. *Preindustrial Population Change: The Mortality Decline and Short-term Population Movements.* Stockholm: Almquist and Wiksell, 1981.

Berry, R. Albert. "Evidence on Relationships among Alternative Measures of Concentration: A Tool for Analysis of LDC Inequality." *Review of Income and Wealth* 33, no. 4 (1987): 417-30.

Bhatty, I. Z. "Inequality and Poverty in Rural India." In *Poverty and Income Distribution in India*, edited by T. N. Srinivasan and P. K. Bardhan, 291-336. Calcutta: Calcutta Publishing Society, 1974.

Blecher, Marc. "Income Distribution in Small Rural Chinese Communities." *China Quarterly* 68 (1976): 795-816.

Bordo, Michael D., and Lars Jonung. *The Long-term Behavior of the Velocity of Circulation.* Cambridge: Cambridge University Press, 1987.

Boserup, Ester. *Woman's Role in Economic Development.* New York: St. Martin's Press, 1970.

Bossen, Laurel. "Women in Modernizing Societies." *American Ethnologist* 2, no. 4 (1975): 587-601.

Brandt, Loren. "Chinese Agriculture and the International Economy, 1870s-1930s: A Reassessment." *Explorations in Economic History* 22 (1985): 168-93.

———. *Commercialization and Agricultural Development: Central and Eastern China, 1870-1937.* New York: Cambridge University Press, 1989.

———. "Farm Household Behavior, Factor Markets, and the Distributive Consequences of Commercialization in Early Twentieth Century China." *Journal of Economic History* 47, no. 3 (1987): 711-37.

———. Review of *The Peasant Economy and Social Change in North China*, by Philip C. C. Huang. *Economic Development and Cultural Change* 35, no. 3 (1987): 670-82.

Braudel, F. P., and F. Spooner. "Prices in Europe from 1450 to 1750." In *The Cambridge Economic History of Europe*, vol. 4, edited by E. E. Rich and C. H. Wilson, 378-486. Cambridge: Cambridge University Press, 1967.

Braun, Rudolf. "Taxation, Sociopolitical Structure, and State-Building: Great Britain and Brandenburg-Prussia." In *The Formation of National States in Western Europe*, edited by Charles Tilly, 243-327. Princeton: Princeton University Press, 1975.

Bray, Francesca. *Agriculture.* Vol. 6, part 2, of *Science and Civilization in China*, edited by Joseph Needham. Cambridge: Cambridge University Press, 1984.

Brook, Timothy. "The Spread of Rice Cultivation and Rice Technology into the Hebei Region in the Ming and Qing." In *Explorations in the History of Science and Technology in China*, edited by Guohao Li, Mengwen Zhang, and Tianqin Cao, 659-89. Shanghai: Shanghai Guji, 1982.

Buck, John Lossing. *Chinese Farm Economy*. Chicago: University of Chicago Press, 1930.

———. *Land Utilization in China*. Vol. 1. Chicago: University of Chicago Press; Nanjing: University of Nanjing, 1937. Reprint. New York: Council on Economic and Cultural Affairs, 1956.

———. *Land Utilization in China: Statistical Volume*. Chicago: University of Chicago Press; Nanking: University of Nanking, 1937. Reprint. New York: Garland Press, 1982.

Bureau of Foreign Trade. Ministry of Industry. *China Industrial Handbooks: Chekiang*. Shanghai: Bureau of Foreign Trade, 1935. Reprint. Taibei: Ch'eng Wen, 1973.

———. *China Industrial Handbooks: Kiangsu*. Shanghai: Bureau of Foreign Trade, 1933.

Bureau of Social Affairs. City Government of Shanghai. *Shanghaishi gongren shenghuo chengdu* 上海市工人生活程度 [Living standards of workers in Shanghai]. Shanghai: Zhonghua Shuju, 1934.

———. *Wage Rates in Shanghai*. Shanghai Commercial Press, 1935.

Bureau of Statistics. Ministry of Industry. *Wuxi gongren shenghuofei ji qi zhishu* 無錫工人生活費及其指數 [Consumption expenditures and index numbers for Wuxi workers]. Nanjing: Ministry of Industry, 1935.

Canaday, Frank H. Papers. Harvard-Yenching Library, Cambridge, Mass.

"Canxun yin yushui guoduo shousun" 蠶汛因雨水過多受損 [Because of heavy rain, the silkworm crop is down]. *Minguo ribao* 民國日報 May 11, 1921, sec. 3:11.

Cao Hui 曹卉. "Jiangbei funü shenghuo gaikuang" 江北婦女生活概況 [The general living conditions of women in Jiangbei]. *Nüsheng* 女聲 2, no. 10 (1934): 10–11.

Carey, Clifton O'Neill. Papers. Bentley Historical Library, University of Michigan, Ann Arbor.

Chan, Wellington K. K. *Merchants, Mandarins, and Modern Enterprise in Late Ch'ing China*. Cambridge: Harvard University Press, 1977.

Chang, Chu-fang. "Chinese Cotton Mills in Shanghai." *Chinese Economic Journal and Bulletin* 3, no. 5 (1928): 901–17.

Chang, Chungli [Zhang Zhongli]. *The Income of the Chinese Gentry*. Seattle: University of Washington Press, 1962.

Chao, Kang. *Man and Land in Chinese History*. Stanford: Stanford University Press, 1986.

Chao Kang 趙岡 and Ch'en Chung-yi 陳鍾毅. *Zhongguo tudi zhidu shi* 中國土地制度史 [A history of China's land system]. Taipei: Lianjing Chuban Shiye Gongsi Yinxing, 1982.

Charles, Lindsey, and Lorna Duffin, eds. *Women and Work in Pre-industrial England*. London: Croom Helm, 1985.

Chayanov, A. V. "On the Theory of Non-capitalist Economic Systems." In *A. V. Chayanov on the Theory of the Peasant Economy*, edited by Daniel Thorner, Basile Kerblay, and R. E. F. Smith, 1–28. Homewood, Ill.: Irwin, 1966. Originally published in Russian.

———. *Peasant Farm Organization*. In *A. V. Chayanov on the Theory of the Peasant Economy*, edited by Daniel Thorner, Basile Kerblay, and R. E. F. Smith, 29–277. Originally published in Russian.

Chen Bozhuang 陳伯莊. *Xiaomai ji mianfen* 小麥及麵粉 [Wheat and wheat flour]. Shanghai: Jiaotong Daxue Yanjiusuo, 1936.

Ch'en Chao-nan 陳昭南. *Yongzheng Qianlong nianjian de yinqian bijia biandong* (1723–1795) 雍正乾隆年間的銀錢比價變動 [Changes in the silver-copper ratio in the Yongzheng and Qianlong years]. Taibei: Zhongguo Xueshu Zhuzuo Jiangzhu Weiyuanhui, 1966.

Chen, Han-seng. *Landlord and Peasant in China*. New York: International Relations Publishers, 1936.

Chen Huayin 陳華寅. "Jiangsusheng renkou yu yiken tianmu zhi xilian" 江蘇省人口與已墾田畝之系聯 [Correlation between population and cultivated land in Jiangsu]. *Tongji yuebao* 統計月報 1, no. 3 (1929): 44–48.

Chen Jinling 陈金陵. "Qingchao de liangjia zoubao yu qi shengshuai" 清朝的粮价奏报与其盛衰 [The flourishing and decline of the Qing dynasty grain price reports]. *Zhongguo shehui jingjishi yanjiu* 中国社会经济史研究 no. 3 (1985): 63–68.

Chen Tingfang 陈廷芳. "Juyou fengjian de maiban xingzhi de Zhongguo saosiye" 具有封建的买办性质的中国缫丝业 [China's feudalistic, comprador-nature silk-reeling industry]. In *Zhongguo jindai gongyeshi ziliao* 中国近代工业史资料 [Materials on China's modern industrial history], vol. 4, edited by Chen Zhen 陈真 et al., 111–13. Beijing: Sanlian Shudian, 1961.

Chen Zhaonan, *see* Ch'en Chao-nan.

Chen Zhen 陈真 et al., eds. *Zhongguo jindai gongyeshi ziliao* [Materials on the history of China's modern industry]. 4 vols. Beijing: Sanlian Shudian, 1959–61.

Chenery, Hollis. "Introduction." In *Redistribution with Growth*, by Hollis Chenery et al., xiii–xx. London: Oxford University Press, 1974.

Chintao Minseibu Tetsudōbu 青島民政部鐵道部. *Chōsa shiryō* 調査資料 [Investigative materials] no. 3. Qingdao: Minseibu Tetsudōbu, 1918.

Chintao Shubigun Minseibu Tetsudōbu 青島守備軍民政部鐵道部. *Tōhoku Santō (Bokkai Santō engan shoko Iken Chifu kan toshi) chōsa hōkokusho* 東北山東(渤海山東沿岸商港濰縣芝罘間都市)調査報告書 [Northeast Shandong (all ports on Shandong's Bohai coast, and cities between Wei County and Yantai) research report]. *Chōsa Shiryō* 調査資料 [Investigative materials] no. 17. Qingdao: Chintao Shubigun Minseibu Tetsudōbu, 1919.

Chow, Gregory C. "Tests of Equality between Sets of Coefficients in Two Linear Regressions." *Econometrica* 28, no. 3 (1960): 591–605.

Ch'üan Han-sheng [Quan Hansheng] 全漢昇. "Ming Qing jian Meizhou baiyin de shuru Zhongguo" 明清間美洲白銀的輸入中國 [Inflow of American silver to Ming and Qing China]. In *Zhongguo jingjishi luncong* 中國經濟史論叢 [Collected papers on China's economic history], vol. 2, by Ch'üan Han-sheng, 435–50. Hong Kong: Xinya Yanjiusuo, 1972.

Chuan, Han-sheng, and Richard A. Kraus. *Mid-Ch'ing Rice Markets and Trade, an Essay in Price History*. Cambridge: East Asian Research Center, Harvard University, 1975.

Chūshi Kensetsu Shiryō Seibi Jimusho 中支建設資料整備事務所, ed. *Mushaku kōgyō jijō* 無錫工業事情 [Wuxi industry]. Shanghai: Chūshi Kensetsu Shiryō Seibi Jimusho, 1941.

Chūshi no minsengyō: Soshū minsen jittai chōsa hōkoku 中支の民船業蘇州民船實態調査報告 [The junk trade of central China: Survey report on junk conditions in Suzhou]. 2 vols. Tokyo: Hōbunkan, 1943.

CIH:C, see Bureau of Foreign Trade, Ministry of Industry, *China Industrial Handbooks: Chekiang.*

Clark, Alice. *The Working Life of Women in the Seventeenth Century.* London: Routledge, 1919. Reprint. New York: Kelley, 1968.

Coale, Ansley J., and Susan Cotts Watkins. *The Decline of Fertility in Europe.* Princeton: Princeton University Press, 1986.

Cochran, Sherman. *Big Business in China: Sino-Foreign Rivalry in the Cigarette Industry, 1890–1930.* Cambridge: Harvard University Press, 1980.

Cohen, Jon. "Institutions and Economic Analysis." Paper prepared for the Workshop on Economic Methods for Chinese Historical Research, Honolulu, January 1987.

Crafts, N. F. R. *British Economic Growth during the Industrial Revolution.* Oxford: Oxford University Press, 1985.

Croll, Elisabeth. *Feminism and Socialism in China.* New York: Schocken Books, 1980.

Daqing Gaozong Chunhuangdi shilu (Qianlong) 大清高宗純皇帝實錄(乾隆) [Historical records of the Qing dynasty] (Qianlong). Reprint. Taibei: Huawen Shuju, 1964.

Daqing shichao shengxun 大清十朝聖訓 [Imperial edicts of the Qing dynasty]. Taibei: Wenhai Chubanshe, 1965.

Datta, Gautam, and Jacob Meerman. "Household Income or Household Income per Capita in Welfare Comparisons." *Review of Income and Wealth* 26, no. 4 (1980): 401–18.

Deane, Phyllis, and W. A. Cole. *British Economic Growth, 1688–1959.* 2d ed. Cambridge: Cambridge University Press, 1967.

Decennial Reports, 1892–1901. Vol. 2. Shanghai: Inspectorate General of Maritime Customs, 1904.

Decennial Reports, 1902–1911. Vol. 2. Shanghai: Inspectorate General of Maritime Customs, 1913.

Deng Xianhe 鄧顯鶴 "Lun huangzheng" 論荒政 [On famine relief]. In *Hunan wenzheng* 湖南文徵 [A Hunan literary collection], edited by Luo Ruhuai 羅汝懷, *guochao wen* 國朝文: 29. 23a–24b. 1872.

Deng, Yuzhi. "A Visit to a Silk Filature in Shanghai." *Green Year Supplement,* November 1928: 9–10.

Diaerlishi Dang'anguan 第二历史档案馆 [Second Historical Archives, Nanjing]. File no. 3504. Main heading: "Jiang-Zhe-Wan-Hu qudi canzhong qingxing" 江浙皖沪取缔蚕种情形 [The regulation of silkworm eggs in Jiangsu, Zhejiang, Anhui, and Shanghai]. Subfile: "Liangnianlai bensheng [Zhejiang] canzhong zhizao ji qudi jingguo gaikuang, Minguo ershinian–Minguo ershiernian" 两年来本省蚕种制造及取缔经过概况,民国二十年－民国二十二年 [The manufacture and regulation of silkworm eggs in Zhejiang for the past two years, 1931–33].

Dinghai xianzhi 定海縣志 [Gazetteer of Dinghai County]. 1923. Reprint. Keelung, 1963.

Doeringer, Peter, and Michael Piore. *Internal Labor Markets and Manpower Analysis.* New York: Sharpe, 1985.

Dublin, Thomas. *Women at Work: The Transformation of Work and Community in Lowell, Massachusetts, 1826–1860.* New York: Columbia University Press, 1979.

Edwards, Richard. *Contested Terrain: The Transformation of the Workplace in the Twentieth Century.* New York: Basic Books, 1979.

Edwards, Richard C., Michael Reich, and David M. Gordon, eds. *Labor Market Segmentation*. Lexington, Mass.: Heath, 1975.

Elvin, Mark. *The Pattern of the Chinese Past*. Stanford: Stanford University Press, 1973.

En xianzhi 恩縣志 [Gazetteer of En County]. 1909.

Esherick, Joseph W. *Origins of the Boxer Uprising*. Berkeley and Los Angeles: University of California Press, 1987.

Etzioni, Amitai. *The Moral Dimension: Toward a New Economics*. New York: Free Press, 1988.

Fan Baichuan 樊百川. "Zhongguo shougongye zai waiguo zibenzhuyi qinruhou de zaoyu he mingyun" 中国手工业在外国资本主义侵入后遭遇和命运 [The fate and destiny of China's handicraft industry after the incursion of capitalism]. *Lishi yanjiu* 历史研究 3 (1962): 88–115.

———. *Zhongguo lunchuan hangyunye de xingqi* 中国轮船航运业的兴起 [The rise of China's steamship transport industry]. Chengdu: Sichuan Renmin Chubanshe, 1985.

Faure, David. "Local Political Disturbances in Kiangsu Province, China, 1870–1911." Ph.D. diss., Princeton University, 1976.

Fei, Hsiao Tung. "Small Towns in Northern Jiangsu." In Fei Hsiao Tung et al., *Small Towns in China*, 88–122. Beijing: New World Press, 1986.

Fei, Hsiao-t'ung and Chih-i Chang. *Earthbound China: A Study of Rural Economy in Yunnan*. Chicago: University of Chicago Press, 1945.

Fei Xiaotong. *See* Hsiao Tong Fei, Hsiao-t'ung Fei.

Feng, H. N. "An Enquiry into the Family Budget of Handicraftsmen in Tientsin, 1927–28." *Quarterly Journal of Economics and Statistics* 1, no. 3 (1932).

Feng Hefa 馮和法, ed. *Zhongguo nongcun jingji ziliao* 中國農村經濟資料 [Materials on the Chinese rural economy]. 2 vols. Shanghai: Liming Shuju, 1933.

Feuerwerker, Albert. *China's Early Industrialization: Sheng Hsuan-huai (1844–1916) and Mandarin Enterprise*. Cambridge: Harvard University Press, 1958.

———. "Economic Trends in the Late Ch'ing Empire, 1870–1911." In *The Cambridge History of China*, vol. 11, part 2, edited by John K. Fairbank and Kwang-ching Liu, 1–69. New York: Cambridge University Press, 1980.

Field, Alexander J., ed. *The Future of Economic History*. Boston: Kluwer-Nijhoff, 1987.

Finegan, Michael, and Ted Telford. "Chinese Archival Holdings at the Genealogical Society of Utah." *Late Imperial China* 9, no. 2 (1988): 86–114.

Finnane, Antonia. "Prosperity and Decline under the Qing: Yangzhou and Its Hinterland, 1644–1810." Ph.D. diss., Australian National University, 1985.

Fletcher, Joseph. "Ch'ing Inner Asia." In *The Cambridge History of China*, vol. 10, part 1, edited by John K. Fairbank, 35–106. New York: Cambridge University Press, 1978.

Flinn, Michael W. *The European Demographic System, 1500–1820*. Baltimore: Johns Hopkins University Press, 1981.

Fogel, Robert, and Stanley Engerman. *Time on the Cross: The Economics of American Negro Slavery*. Boston: Little, Brown, 1974.

Folbre, Nancy. "Cleaning House: New Perspectives on Households and Economic Development." *Journal of Development Economics* 22, no. 1 (1986): 5–40.

Food and Agriculture Organization. United Nations. *China: Sericulture. Report on a FAO/UNDP Study Tour to the People's Republic of China, 6 May to 4 June 1979*. Rome: FAO, 1980.

Freedman, Maurice. "The Chinese Domestic Family: Models." In *The Study of Chinese Society: Essays by Maurice Freedman*, 235–39. Stanford: Stanford University Press, 1979.
Fu Kedong 傅克东. "Baqi zhidu huji chutan" 八旗制度户籍初探 [A preliminary study of the eight banner household registration system]. *Minzu yanjiu* 民族研究 [Ethnic studies] 6 (1983): 34–43.
Fu Yiling 傅衣凌. "Guanyu Mingmo Qingchu Zhongguo nongcun shehui guanxi de xin guji" 关于明末清初中国农村社会关系的新估计 [New assessment of rural social relationships in late Ming and early Qing China]. *Xiamen daxue xuebao* 厦门大学学报 6 (1959): 57–70.
Fukuda Setsuo 福田節生. "Shinmatsu Konan no nōson shakai" 清末湖南の農村社会 [Rural society in late Qing Hunan]. *Fukuoka joshi tandai kiyō* 福岡女子短大紀要 8 (1974): 31–55.
Galloway, Patrick G. "Long-term Fluctuations in Climate and Population in the Preindustrial Era." Paper presented at the Ninth International Economic History Congress in Bern, Switzerland, 1986.
Gamble, Sidney. *Ting Hsien: A North China Rural Community*. Stanford: Stanford University Press, 1968.
Gao Jingyue 高景岳 and Yan Xuexi 严学熙. "Wuxi zuizao de sangyuan" 无锡最早的桑园 [Wuxi's first mulberry tract]. *Wuxi xianbao* 无锡县报 [Wuxi County news], Aug. 20, 1980: 4.
Gjerde, Jon, Anita Tien, and James Lee. "Comparative Household Processes of Stem, Joint, and Nuclear Household Systems: Scandinavia, China, and the United States." Paper presented at the 1987 annual meeting of the Social Science History Association.
Gongshang banyuekan 工商半月刊 [Bimonthly journal of industry and commerce]. Shanghai, 1929–35.
Gongzhongdang 宫中檔. Palace Memorial Archives, Qianlong reign. National Palace Museum, Taibei.
Gongzhongdang Qianlongchao zouzhe 宫中檔乾隆朝奏摺 [Memorials from the Palace Memorial Archives, Qianlong reign]. 75 vols. Taibei: National Palace Museum, 1979–89.
Gongzhongdang Yongzhengchao zouzhe 宫中檔雍正朝奏摺 [Memorials from the Palace Memorial Archives, Yongzheng reign]. 32 vols. Taibei: National Palace Museum, 1977–79.
Goodman, Bryna. "The Native Place and the City: Immigrant Consciousness and Organization in Shanghai, 1873–1927." Ph.D. diss., Stanford University, 1990.
Gordon, David M., Richard Edwards, and Michael Reich. *Segmented Work, Divided Workers: The Historical Transformation of Labor in the United States*. Cambridge: Cambridge University Press, 1982.
Gottschang, Thomas R. "Economic Change, Disasters, and Migration: The Historical Case of Manchuria." *Economic Development and Cultural Change* 35, no. 3 (1987): 461–90.
———. "Migration from North China to Manchuria, 1891–1942: An Economic History." Ph.D. diss., University of Michigan, 1982.
Goubert, Pierre. "En Beauvaisis: Problèmes démographiques de XVIIe siècle." *Annales ESC* 7, no. 4 (1952): 453–68.
Granovetter, Mark, and Charles Tilly. "Inequality and Labor Processes." New

School for Social Research Working Paper Series, no. 29. New York, July 1986.

Greenhalgh, Susan. "Is Inequality Demographically Induced? The Family Cycle and the Distribution of Income in Taiwan." *American Anthropologist* 87, no. 3 (1985): 571–94.

———. "Sexual Stratification: The Other Side of 'Growth with Equity' in East Asia." *Population and Development Review* 11, no. 2 (1985): 265–314.

Griffen, Clyde. "The 'Old' Immigration and Industrialization: A Case Study." In *Immigrants in Industrial America, 1850–1920*, edited by Richard L. Ehrlich, 123–50. Charlottesville: University Press of Virginia, 1977.

Gu Shuping 顾叔平. "Wo liyong Gu Zhuxuan de yanhu jinxing geming huodong" 我利用顾竹轩的掩护进行革命活动 [I used the cover of Gu Zhuxuan to conduct revolutionary activities]. In *Jiu Shanghai de banghui* 旧上海的帮会 [Gangs of old Shanghai], edited by Zhongguo Renmin Zhengzhi Xieshang Huiyi Shanghaishi Weiyuanhui, Wenshi Ziliao Gongzuo Weiyuanhui 中国人民政治协商会议上海市委员会文史资料工作委员会, 360–66. Shanghai: Shanghai Renmin Chubanshe, 1986.

Guiyang zhouzhi 桂陽州志 [Gazetteer of Guiyang Prefecture]. 1868.

Guo Songyi 郭松义. "Qingchu fengjian guojia kenhuang zhengce fenxi" 清初封建国家垦荒政策分析 [An analysis of the state policy of land reclamation during the early Qing]. *Qingshi luncong* 清史论丛 2 (1980): 111–38.

———. "Qingdai de liangshi maoyi" 清代的粮食贸易 [The grain trade in the Qing dynasty]. *Pingzhun xuekan* 平准学刊 1 (1985): 289–314.

———. "Qingdai de renkou zengzhang he renkou liuqian" 清代的人口增长和人口流迁 [Population growth and population movement during the Qing]. *Qingshi luncong* 清史论丛 5 (1984): 103–38.

Guoli Zhongyang Yanjiuyuan Shehui Kexue Yanjiusuo 國立中央研究院社會科學研究所. *Jiangsu Wuxi nongmin dizhu jingji diaocha* 江蘇無錫農民地主經濟調查 [A survey of the peasant-landlord economy in Wuxi County, Jiangsu Province]. Wuxi, 1929.

GZD-QL, *see* Gongzhongdang.

Hai Shan 海山. "Yutang qunqiu—Jining shi Yutang Jiangyuan jianshi" 玉堂春秋—济宁市玉堂酱园间史 [Chronicles of Yutang—A short history of Jining Municipality's Yutang Soy Sauce Factory]. *Jining shi shiliao* 济宁市史料 1 (1983): 48–78.

Hane, Mikiso. *Peasants, Rebels, and Outcastes: The Underside of Modern Japan.* New York: Pantheon Books, 1982.

Hanley, Susan B., and Arthur P. Wolf, eds. *Family and Population in East Asian History.* Stanford: Stanford University Press, 1985.

Hao, Yen-p'ing. *The Commercial Revolution in Nineteenth-Century China.* Berkeley and Los Angeles: University of California Press, 1986.

———. *The Comprador in Nineteenth-Century China: Bridge between East and West.* Cambridge: Harvard University Press, 1970.

Harding, Harry. *China's Second Revolution: Reform after Mao.* Washington, D.C.: Brookings, 1987.

Harrell, Stevan. "On the Holes in Chinese Genealogies." *Late Imperial China* 9, no. 1 (1987): 52–87.

———. "The Rich Get Children: Segmentation, Stratification, and Population in

Three Chekiang Lineages, 1550–1850." In *Family and Population in East Asian History*, edited by Hanley and Wolf, 81–109.

Harris, Barbara. "There Is Method in My Madness: Or Is It Vice Versa? Measuring Agricultural Market Performance." *Food Research Institute Studies* 17, no. 2 (1979): 197–218.

Harrison, Mark. "Chayanov and the Economics of the Russian Peasantry." *Journal of Peasant Studies* 2, no. 4 (1975): 389–417.

He Bingxian 何炳賢. "Minguo ershiyinian Zhongguo gongshangye de huigu" 民國二十一年中國工商業的回顧 [A review of China's industry and commerce in 1932]. *Gongshang banyuekan* 工商半月刊 5, no. 1 (Jan. 1, 1933), articles sec.: 1–39.

Hershatter, Gail. "Prostitution and the Market in Women in Early Twentieth-Century Shanghai." In *Marriage and Inequality in Chinese Society*, edited by Rubie S. Watson and Patricia Buckley Ebrey. Berkeley and Los Angeles: University of California Press, 1991.

———. *The Workers of Tianjin, 1900–1949*. Stanford: Stanford University Press, 1986.

Hewu jibao 河務季報. Beijing.

Heytens, Paul J. "Testing Market Integration." *Food Research Institute Studies* 20, no. 1 (1986): 25–41.

Himeda Mitsuyoshi 姬田光義. "Chūgoku kindai gyogyōshi no hito koma—Kanpō hachi nen Kin ken no gyomin tōsō o megutte" 中国近代漁業史の一駒咸豊八年鄞縣の漁民闘争をめぐって [An incident in the recent history of the Chinese fishing industry: The fishermen's riot in Yin County in 1858]. *Tōyōshigaku ronshū* 東洋史学論集 8 (1967): 65–108.

Hinton, Harold C. *The Grain Tribute System of China (1845–1911)*. Chinese Economic and Political Studies. Cambridge: Harvard University, 1956.

———. "The Grain Tribute System of the Ch'ing Dynasty." *Far Eastern Quarterly* 11, no. 3 (1952): 339–54.

Ho, Ping-ti. "The Salt Merchants of Yang-chou: A Study of Commercial Capitalism in Eighteenth-Century China." *Harvard Journal of Asiatic Studies* 17 (1954): 130–68.

———. *Studies on the Population of China, 1368–1953*. Cambridge: Harvard University Press, 1959.

Honig, Emily. "The Politics of Prejudice: Subei People in Republican-Era Shanghai." *Modern China* 15, no. 3 (1989): 243–74.

———. *Sisters and Strangers: Women in the Shanghai Cotton Mills, 1919–1949*. Stanford: Stanford University Press, 1986.

Hoskins, W. G. "Harvest Fluctuations and English Economic History, 1480–1619." *Agricultural History Review* 12 (1964): 28–46.

Hou Renzhi 侯仁之, ed. *Xu tianxia junguo libingshu, Shandong zhi bu* 續天下郡國利病書山東之部 [A continuation of the Book of Strengths and Weaknesses of the Areas and Commanderies of China, Shandong section]. Beijing: Yanjing Daxue Yanjiuyuan, 1940.

Hou, Chi-ming. *Foreign Investment and Economic Development in China, 1840–1937*. Cambridge: Harvard University Press, 1965.

Hsiao, Liang-lin. *China's Foreign Trade Statistics, 1864–1949*. Cambridge: East Asian Research Center, Harvard University, 1974.

Hsu, Leonard S. *Silver and Prices in China*. Shanghai: Commercial Press, 1935.

Huang, Philip C. C. *The Peasant Economy and Social Change in North China*. Stanford:

Stanford University Press, 1985.

———. *The Peasant Family and Rural Development in the Yangzi Delta, 1350–1988*. Stanford: Stanford University Press, 1990.

Huang Renjing 黃人鏡. *Huren baojian* 滬人寶鑑 [What the Chinese in Shanghai Ought to Know]. Shanghai: Methodist Publishing House, 1913.

Hunan shengli cheng'an hulü 湖南省例成案戶律 [Legal cases from Hunan involving the Board of Revenue]. 1820.

Hwang Kuo-shu 黃國樞, and Yeh-chien Wang 王業鍵. "Qingdai liangjia de changqi biandong, 1763–1910" 清代糧價的長期變動, 1763–1910 [Long-term grain price fluctuations during the Qing, 1763–1910]. *Jingji lunwen* 經濟論文 9, no. 1 (1981): 1–27.

Hymer, Stephen, and Stephen Resnick. "A Model of an Agrarian Economy with Nonagricultural Activities." *American Economic Review* 59, no. 4, part 1 (1969): 493–506.

Jameson, Charles Davis. "River Systems of the Provinces of Anhui and Kiangsu North of the Yangtzekiang." *Chinese Recorder and Missionary Journal* 43, no. 1 (1912): 69–75.

Jiang Taixin 江太新. "Qingchu kenhuang zhengce ji diquan fenpei qingkuang de kaocha" 清初墾荒政策及地權分配情況的考察 [An investigation into land reclamation policy and the distribution of land ownership in early Qing China]. *Lishi yanjiu* 历史研究 5 (1982): 167–82.

"Jianshi zaxun" 繭市雜訊 [Miscellaneous reports on cocoon markets]. *Minguo ribao* 民國日報 June 4, 1917, sec. 2: 7.

Jiao-Ao xianzhi 膠澳縣志 [Gazetteer of Jiao-Ao County]. 1928.

Jiaqing chongxiu Daqing yitongzhi 嘉慶重修大清一統志 [Revised comprehensive gazetteer of the Qing dynasty, Jiaqing reign (1796–1820)]. Shanghai: Shangwu Yinshuguan, 1934.

Jin Limen 金禮門. "Lüetan Zhoushan de hunjia fengsu" 略談舟山的婚嫁風俗 [A brief account of marriage customs in Chusan]. In *Ningbo xisu congtan* 寧波習俗叢談 [Collected accounts of Ningbo local customs], edited by Zhang Xingzhou 張行周, 220–22. Taibei: Minzhu Chubanshe, 1973.

Jining zhilizhou xuzhi 濟寧直隸州續志 [A continuation of the gazetteer of Jining Independent District]. Jining, 1929.

Johnson, Marshall, William L. Parish, and Elizabeth Lin. "Chinese Women, Rural Society, and External Markets." *Economic Development and Cultural Change* 35, no. 2 (1987): 257–77.

Jones, Susan Mann [*see also* Susan Mann]. "Finance in Ningpo: The *Ch'ien-chuang*, 1750–1880." In *Economic Organization in Chinese Society*, edited by W. E. Willmott, 47–77. Stanford: Stanford University Press, 1972.

———. "The Ningpo *Pang* and Financial Power at Shanghai." In *The Chinese City between Two Worlds*, edited by Mark Elvin and G. William Skinner, 73–96. Stanford: Stanford University Press, 1974.

Jones, Susan Mann, and Philip Kuhn. "Dynastic Decline and the Roots of Rebellion." In *The Cambridge History of China*, vol. 10, part 1, edited by John K. Fairbank, 107–62. New York: Cambridge University Press, 1978.

Jones, William O. *Marketing Staple Food Crops in Tropical Africa*. Ithaca: Cornell University Press, 1972.

Junjidang 軍機檔. Grand Council Archives. First Historical Archives, Beijing.
Kakwani, Nanak. "On the Estimation of Income Inequality from Grouped Observations." *Review of Economic Studies* 43, no. 3 (1976): 483–92.
Kanbe Masao 神戶正雄, ed. *Tōa keizai kenkyū* 東亞經濟研究 [Research on Far Eastern economies]. Vol. 1. Tokyo, 1942.
Kann, Eduard. "How Much Silver Is There in China?" *Chinese Economic Journal* 8, no. 4 (1931): 410–20.
Ke Wuchi 柯悟遲. *Louwang yongyu ji* 漏網喁魚集 [Recollection of a man who escaped from disaster]. Beijing: Zhonghua Shuju, 1986.
Kitamura Hironao 北村敬直. "Shindai no shōhin shijō ni tsuite" 清代の商品市場について [On commercial markets in the Qing dynasty]. *Keizaigaku zasshi* 経済学雑誌 28, nos. 3–4 (1953). Reprinted in *Shindai shakai keizaishi kenkyū* 清代社会経済史研究 [Studies of Qing dynasty social and economic history]. Kyoto: Hōyū Shoten, 1978.
Kobata, A. "The Production and Uses of Gold and Silver in Sixteenth- and Seventeenth-Century Japan." *Economic History Review*, 2d ser., 18, no. 2 (1965): 245–66.
Kojima Shinji 小島晋治. *Taihei tenkoku kakumei no rekishi to shisō* 太平天国革命の歴史と思想 [The history and thought of the Taiping Rebellion]. Tokyo: Kenbun Shuppan, 1978.
Kokumuin Jitsugyōbu Rinji Sangyō Chōsakyoku. 國務院實業部臨時產業調查局. *Kōtoku gannendo nōson jittai chōsa* 康德元年度農村實態調查 [Report on a survey of village conditions in 1934]. 4 vols. Changchun: Kokumuin Jitsugyōbu Rinji Sangyō Chōsakyoku, 1936.
Kokuritsu Pekin Daigaku Fusetsu Nōson Keizai Kenkyūsho 國立北京大學附設農村經濟研究所. *Santō sainei kenjō o chūshin toseru nōsanbutsu ryūtsū ni kansuru ichi kosatsu* 山東濟寧縣城を中心とせる農產物流通に関する一考察 [An investigation of matters relevant to Shandong, Jining County and City, as center and controller of the circulation of agricultural commodities]. Beijing: Pekin Daigaku, 1942.
Kono, Michihiro 河野通博. "Shindai no baekiro" 清代の馬驛路 [Qing dynasty roads with horse stations]. *Jinbun chiri* 人文地理 2, no. 1 (1950): 13–24.
Kuznets, Simon. "Demographic Aspects of the Size Distribution of Income: An Exploratory Essay." *Economic Development and Cultural Change* 25, no. 1 (1976): 1–94.
——— . "Economic Growth and Income Inequality." *American Economic Review* 45 (1955): 1–28.
——— . "Size of Households and Income Disparities." *Research in Population Economics* 3 (1981): 1–40.
Landa, Janet T. "The Political Economy of the Ethnically Homogeneous Chinese Middleman Group in Southeast Asia: Ethnicity and Entrepreneurship in a Plural Society." In *The Chinese in Southeast Asia*, vol. 1, edited by Linda Y. C. Lim and Peter L. A. Gosling, 86–116. Singapore: Maruzen Asia, 1983.
Lanshan xianzhi 藍山縣志 [Gazetteer of Lanshan County]. 1933.
Laughlin, J. Laurence. *The History of Bimetallism in the United States*. New York: Appleton, 1897.
Laurie, Bruce, Theodore Hershberg, and George Alter. "Immigrants and Industry: The Philadelphia Experience, 1850–1880." In *Immigrants in Industrial America*,

1850–1920, edited by Richard L. Ehrlich, 123–50. Charlottesville: University Press of Virginia, 1977.

Lavely, William, and R. Bin Wong. "Family Division, Reproductivity, and Landholding in North China." Research Report no. 84-65. Ann Arbor: Population Studies Center, University of Michigan, November 1984.

Lee, Frederic. *Currency, Banking, and Finance in China.* Washington, D.C.: U.S. Government Printing Office, 1926.

Lee, James. *State and Economy in Southwest China, 1250 to 1850.* Cambridge: Harvard University Press, forthcoming.

Lee, James, and Cameron Campbell. "Happy Families: Household Hierarchy and Differential Vital Rates in Rural Liaoning, 1774–1873." Forthcoming.

Lee, James, Cameron Campbell, and Lawrence Anthony. "A Century of Mortality in Rural Liaoning, 1774–1873." In *Le peuplement du monde avant 1850*, edited by Antoinette Fauve-Chamoux. Paris: CNRS, 1990.

Lee, James, and Robert Eng. "Population and Family History in Eighteenth Century Manchuria: Preliminary Results from Daoyi, 1774–1798." *Ch'ing-shih wen-t'i* 5, no. 1 (1984): 1–55.

Lee, James, and Jon Gjerde. "Comparative Household Morphology of Stem, Joint and Nuclear Household Systems: Norway, China, and the United States." *Continuity and Change* 1, no. 1 (1986): 89–112.

Lee, James, and R. Bin Wong. "New Research Sources for the Study of Late Imperial China." *China Exchange News* 15, nos. 3–4 (1987): 6–8.

Leung, Yuen Sang. "Regional Rivalry in Mid-Nineteenth Century Shanghai: Cantonese vs. Ningpo Men." *Ch'ing-shih wen-t'i* 4, no. 8 (1982): 29–50.

Leridon, Henri. *Human Fertility.* Chicago: University of Chicago Press, 1977.

Levenson, Joseph R. *Liang Ch'i-ch'ao and the Mind of Modern China.* Cambridge: Harvard University Press, 1953.

Lewis, Ida Belle. *The Education of Girls in China.* New York: Teacher's College, Columbia University, 1919. Reprint. San Francisco: Chinese Materials Center, 1974.

Li Cishan 李次山. "Shanghai laodong qingkuang" 上海勞動情況 [The condition of labor in Shanghai]. *Xin qingnian* 新青年 7, no. 6 (May 1920): 1–83.

Li Guijin 李貴勤. "Qingmo bizhi gaige ji qi shibai yuanyin de qiantan." 清末币制改革及其失败原因的浅探 [A preliminary discussion of late Qing monetary reform and the reasons for its failure]. *Hebei caimao xueyuan xuebao* 河北财贸学院学报 4 (1983). Reprinted in *Jingji shi* 经济史 no. 2 (1984): 129–37.

Li, Lillian M. *China's Silk Trade: Traditional Industry in the Modern World.* Cambridge: Harvard University Press, 1981.

———. "Using Grain Prices to Measure Food Crises: Chihli Province in the Mid-Ch'ing Period." In *The Second Conference on Modern Chinese Economic History*, 2:467–509. Taibei: Institute of Economics, Academia Sinica, 1989.

Li Pingheng 李平衡. *Zhongguo laodong nianjian* 中國勞動年鑑 [The China labor yearbook]. Beijing: Shehui Diaochaju, 1932.

Li Wenzhi 李文治. "Lun Qingdai houqi Jiang-Zhe-Wan sansheng yuan Taiping Tianguo zhanlingqu tudi guanxi de bianhua" 论清代后期江浙皖三省原太平天国占领区土地关系的变化 [On changes in land tenure in the late Qing in areas of Jiangsu, Zhejiang, and Anhui formerly occupied by the Taipings]. *Lishi yanjiu* 历史研究 6 (1981): 81–96.

Li Xu 李煦. *Li Xu zouzhe* 李煦奏摺 [The memorials of Li Xu]. Beijing: Zhonghua Shuju, 1976.

Liang, Ernest P. *China: Railways and Agricultural Development, 1875–1935*. Chicago: University of Chicago Press, 1982.

Liang Fangzhong 梁方仲. "Mingdai guoji maoyi yu baiyin de shuchuru" 明代國際貿易與白銀的輸出入 [International trade and the import and export of silver during the Ming]. *Zhongguo shehui jingjishi jikan* 中國社會經濟史集刊 6, no. 2 (1939): 267–324.

———. *Zhongguo lidai hukou, tiandi, tianfu tongji* 中国历代户口, 田地, 田赋统计 [China's dynastic statistics on household population, land, and land taxes]. Shanghai: Shanghai Renmin Chubanshe, 1980.

Lieu, D. K. *The Growth and Industrialization of Shanghai*. Shanghai: China Institute of Pacific Relations, 1936.

Lin Maoquan 林茂泉. *Wenji* 文集 [Collected works]. Preface dated 1926.

Lin Weiying 林維英. *Zhongguo zhi xinhuobi zhidu* 中國之新貨幣制度 [China's new monetary system]. Changsha: Commercial Press, 1939.

Lindert, Peter H. "English Population, Wages, and Prices, 1541–1913." *Journal of Interdisciplinary History* 15, no. 4 (1985): 609–34.

———. "International Economics and the Historian." Revision of a paper prepared for the Workshop on Economic Methods for Chinese Historical Research, Honolulu, January 1987.

———. "Who Owned Victorian England? The Debate over Landed Wealth and Inequality." *Agricultural History* 61, no. 4 (1987): 25–51.

Linqing xianzhi 臨清縣志 [Gazetteer of Linqing County]. 1934.

Lipman, Jonathan. "The Border World of Gansu, 1895–1935." Ph.D. diss., Stanford University, 1981.

Lipton, Michael. "The Theory of the Optimizing Peasant." *Journal of Development Studies* 4, no. 3 (1968): 327–51.

Liu Shiji 刘石吉. *Ming Qing shidai Jiangnan shizhen yanjiu* 明清时代江南市镇研究 [A study of Jiangnan cities and towns during the Ming and Qing]. Beijing: Zhongguo Shehui Kexue Chubanshe, 1987.

Liu, Ta-Chung, and Kung-Chia Yeh. *The Economy of the Chinese Mainland*. Princeton: Princeton University Press, 1965.

Liu, Ts'ui-jung 劉翠溶. "Chinese Genealogies as a Source for the Study of Historical Demography." In *Studies and Essays in Commemoration of the Golden Jubilee of the Academia Sinica*, 849–70. Taibei: Academia Sinica, 1978.

———. "The Demographic Dynamics of Some Clans in the Lower Yangtze Area, ca. 1400–1900." *Academia Economica Papers* 9, no. 1 (1981): 115–60.

———. "The Demography of Two Chinese Clans in Hsiao-shan, Chekiang, 1650–1850." In *Family and Population in East Asian History*, edited by Hanley and Wolf, 13–61.

———. "Ming Qing renkou zhi zengzhi yu qianyi" 明清人口之增殖與遷移 [The growth and migration of population during the Ming and Qing]. In *Dierjie Zhongguo shehui jingjishi yantao hui lunwenji* 第二屆中國社會經濟研討會論文集 [Papers from the Second Seminar on Chinese Social and Economic History], 283–316. Edited by Hsü Cho-yün 許倬雲, Mao Han-kuang 毛漢光, and Liu Ts'ui-jung 劉翠溶 Taibei: Center for Chinese Studies, 1983.

Lu Guanying 盧冠英. "Jiangsu Wuxixian ershinianlai zhi siye guan" 江蘇無錫縣二十年來之絲業觀 [An overview of the Wuxi silk industry during the last 20 years]. *Nongshang gongbao* 8, no. 1 (Aug. 15, 1921), articles and translations sec.: 45–47.

Lu Manyan 陸曼炎. "Jiangnan yu Jiangbei" 江南與江北 [Jiangnan and Jiangbei]. *Renyan zhoukan* 人言週刊 1, no. 9 (June 23, 1934): 389–400.

Luo Qiong 羅瓊. "Zhongguo nongcunzhong de laodong funü" 中國農村中的勞動婦女 [Women workers in China's peasant villages]. *Funü shenghuo* 婦女生活 1, no. 4 (1935): 17–23.

Luo Ziwei 羅子為. "Zouping sichao zhi mianguan" 鄒平私鈔之面觀 [A look at private currency in Zouping]. *Xiangcun jianshe xunkan* 鄉村建設旬刊 4, no. 29 (1936): 26–31.

"Luxi ge xian nongcun jingji xianzhuang" 魯西各縣農村經濟現狀 [The current economic situation in the rural villages of each county of western Shandong]. *Nongcun jingji* 農村經濟 1, no. 11 (Sept. 1, 1934): 75–77.

McCloskey, Donald N. *Econometric History*. Basingstoke, Eng.: Macmillan, 1987.

———. "The Economics of Choice." Paper prepared for the Workshop on Economic Methods for Chinese Historical Research. Honolulu, January 1987.

McCloskey, Donald N., and John Nash. "Corn at Interest: The Extent and Cost of Grain Storage in Medieval England." *American Economic Review* 74, no. 1 (1984): 174–87.

The Manchuria Year Book, 1932–33. Tokyo: Tōa Keizai Chōsakyoku, 1932.

Mann, Susan [*see also* Susan Mann Jones]. "Brokers as Entrepreneurs in Presocialist China." *Comparative Studies in Society and History* 26, no. 4 (1984): 614–36.

———. *Local Merchants and the Chinese Bureaucracy, 1750–1850*. Stanford: Stanford University Press, 1987.

Medick, Hans. "The Proto-industrial Family Economy." In *Industrialization before Industrialization*, edited by Peter Kriedte, Hans Medick, and Jurgen Schlumbohn, translated by Beate Schempp, 38–73. Cambridge: Cambridge University Press, 1981.

Minami Manshū Tetsudō Kabushiki Kaisha 南滿洲鐵道株式會社 Kitō nōson jittai chōsahan 冀東農村調查班 *Dainiji Kitō nōson jittai chōsa hōkokusho: tōkeihen* 第二次冀東農村實態調查報告書統計篇 [Report on the second survey of village conditions in northeastern Hebei: statistics]. *Dai ichiban: Heikoku ken* 第一班平谷縣 [Part 1: Pinggu County]; *Dai sanban: Hōjun ken* 第三班豐潤縣 [Part 3: Fengrun County]; *Dai yonban: Shōrei ken* 第四班昌黎縣 [Part 4: Changli County]. Dairen: Minami Manshū Tetsudō Kabushiki Kaisha, 1937.

———. *Mantetsu chōsa geppō* 滿鐵調查月報 [Monthly survey report of the South Manchurian Railway]. 1931–1944.

———. *Nōka keizai chōsa hōkoku—Kakurokuken, 1939* 農家經濟調查報告獲鹿縣 [Report on the investigation of farm household economy—Huailu County, 1939]. Hokushi keizai shiryō 北支經濟資料 [Materials on the economy of north China] no. 32. Beijing: Minami Manshū Tetsudō Kabushiki Kaisha, 1940.

———. Shanhai Jimusho Chōsashitsu 上海事務所調查室. *Kōsoshō Mushakuken nōson jittai chōsa hōkokusho* 江蘇省無錫縣農村實態調查報告書 [Report on an investigation of rural conditions in Wuxi County, Jiangsu Province]. Shanghai: Minami Manshū Tetsudō Kabushiki Kaisha, 1941.

———. ———. *Mushaku kōgyō jittai chōsa hōkokusho* 無錫工業實態調查報告書 [Report on an investigation of industry in Wuxi]. Shanghai: Minami Manshū Tetsudō Kabushiki Kaisha, 1940.

———. Tenshin Jimusho Chōsaka 天津事務所調查課. *Santō no mensaku* 山東の棉作 [The cotton production of Shandong]. Tianjin: Minami Manshū Tetsudō Kabushiki Kaisha, 1942.

Momose Hiromu 百瀬弘. "Shindai ni okeru Supein doru no ryūtsū" 清代における西班牙弗の流通 [Trade in Spanish dollars during the Qing]. *Shakai keizai shigaku* 社會經濟史學 6, no. 2 (1936): 1–25. Reprinted in *Minshin shakai keizaishi kenkyū* 明清社會經濟史研究 [Studies on the social and economic history of Ming and Qing China], edited by Momose Hiromu, 71–131. Tokyo: Kenbunsha, 1980.

Morse, H. B. *The Trade and Administration of China*. 3d rev. ed. London: Longmans, Green, 1921.

Mukōyama Hirō 向山寬夫. "Kyū Chūgoku ni okeru rōdō jōken" 旧中国における労動条件 [Labor conditions in Republican China]. *Ajia kenkyū* アジア研究 8, no. 4 (1961): 37–49.

Muramatsu, Yuji. "A Documentary Study of Chinese Landlordism in the Late Ch'ing and Early Republican Kiangnan." *Bulletin of the School of Oriental and African Studies* 29, no. 3 (1966): 566–99.

Myers, Ramon H. *The Chinese Economy Past and Present*. Belmont, Calif.: Wadsworth, 1980.

———. *The Chinese Peasant Economy: Agricultural Development in Hopei and Shantung, 1890–1949*. Cambridge: Harvard University Press, 1970.

———. "Socioeconomic Change in Villages of Manchuria during the Qing and Republican Periods: Some Preliminary Findings." *Modern Asian Studies* 10, no. 4 (1976): 591–620.

Nakamura Jihei 中村治兵衛. "Shindai Kokō kome ryūtsū no ichi men" 清代湖広米流通の一面 [An aspect of rice circulation in Qing dynasty Huguang]. *Shakai keizai shigaku* 社会经济史学 18, no. 3 (1952): 269–81.

Nayancheng 那彦成. *Zhenji* 賑紀 [Record of famine relief], 1813.

NCH. See *The North-China Herald and Supreme Court and Consular Gazette*.

Negishi Tadashi 根岸佶. *Chūgoku no girudo* 中国のギルド [The guilds of China]. Tokyo: Nihon Hyōronsha, 1953.

———. *Shanhai no girudo* 上海のギルド [The guilds of Shanghai]. Tokyo: Nihon Hyōronsha, 1951.

Nimpō chiku jittai chōsasho 寧波地區實態調查書 [A survey of actual conditions in the Ningbo area]. Compiled by Kōain Kachū Renrakubu 興亞院華中連絡部. 1941.

Ningxiang xianzhi 寧鄉縣志 [Gazetteer of Ningxiang County]. 1816.

"Nongcun you meiyou liangji fenhua?" 农村有没有两极分化 [Are villages polarized?]. *Banyuetan* 半月谈 22 (1987): 20–21.

Nongqing baogao 農情報告.

Nongshang gongbao 農商公報 [Bulletin of the Ministry of Agriculture and Commerce].

The North-China Herald and Supreme Court and Consular Gazette. Shanghai. 1850–1941.

Ong, Paul M. "Chinese Labor in Early San Francisco: Racial Segmentation and Industrial Expansion." *Amerasia* 8, no. 1 (1981): 69–92.

Oshima, Harry, and Toshiyuki Mizoguchi, eds. *Income Distribution by Sectors and Over-*

time in East and Southeast Asian Countries. Quezon City: Council for Asian Manpower Studies, 1978.

Otake Fumio 小竹文夫. "Min Shin jidai ni okeru gaikoku gin no ryūnyū" 明清時代における外国銀の流入 [Importation of foreign silver during the Ming and Qing]. In *Kinsei Shina kezaishi kenkyū* 近世支那經濟史研究 [Studies on the economic history of modern China], by Otake Fumio. Tokyo: Kobundo, 1942.

Parker, William N., ed. *Economic History and the Modern Economist.* Oxford: Blackwell, 1986.

"The Peanut Trade of Tsingtao." *Chinese Economic Bulletin* 11, no. 348 (Oct. 22, 1927): 213–14.

Peng Xinwei 彭信威. *Zhongguo huobishi* 中國貨幣史 [The monetary history of China]. Shanghai: Shanghai Renmin Chubanshe, 1965.

Peng Zeyi 彭澤益. *Shijiu shiji houban de Zhongguo caizheng yu jingji* 十九世纪后半的中国财政与经济 [Public finance and the economy of China in the latter part of the nineteenth century]. Beijing: Renmin Chubanshe, 1983.

Perdue, Peter C. *Exhausting the Earth: State and Peasant in Hunan, 1500–1850.* Cambridge: Harvard University Council on East Asian Studies, 1987.

Perkins, Dwight H. *Agricultural Development in China, 1368–1968.* Chicago: Aldine, 1969.

Piore, Michael. "Notes for a Theory of Labor Market Stratification." In *Labor Market Segmentation,* edited by Richard C. Edwards, Michael Reich, and David M. Gordon, 125–50. Lexington, Mass.: Heath, 1975.

Polanyi, Karl. *The Great Transformation.* New York: Holt, Rinehart and Winston, 1944. Reprint. Boston: Beacon Press, 1957.

Pomeranz, Kenneth. "The Making of a Hinterland: State, Society, and Economy in Inland North China, 1900–1937." Ph.D. diss., Yale University, 1988.

Popkin, Samuel. *The Rational Peasant: The Political Economy of Rural Society in Vietnam.* Berkeley and Los Angeles: University of California Press, 1979.

Pruitt, Ida. *A Daughter of Han: The Autobiography of a Chinese Working Woman.* New Haven: Yale University Press, 1945. Reprint. Stanford: Stanford University Press, 1967.

Pyatt, Graham. "On the Interpretation and Disaggregation of Gini Coefficients." *Economic Journal* 86 (1986): 243–55.

Qinding Lanzhou jilue 欽定蘭州紀略 [Officially compiled chronicle of Lanzhou], Qianlong reign. Reprint. Taibei: Shangwu Yinshuguan, 1976.

Qingchao wenxian tongkao 清朝文獻通考 [Qing dynasty general history of institutions]. Reprint. Taibei: Xinxing Shuju, 1958.

Qingdai Haihe Luanhe honglao dang'an shiliao 清代海河滦河洪涝档案史料 [Historical materials concerning Qing period floods of the Hai and Luan rivers]. Compiled by Shuili Shuidian Kexue Yanjiuyuan 水利水电科学研究院. Beijing: Zhonghua Shuju, 1981.

Qiu Jun 邱濬. *Daxue yanyibu* 大學衍義補 [The Supplement to the exposition of the Great Learning]. Japanese facsimile of 1792 edition.

Qiyang xianzhi 祁陽縣志 [Gazetteer of Qiyang County]. 1765.

Quan Hansheng. *See* Han-sheng Ch'üan.

QSL-QL. See *Daqing Gaozong Chunhuangdi shilu (Qianlong).*

Rankin, Mary Backus. "The Emergence of Women at the End of the Ch'ing: The Case of Ch'iu Chin." In *Women in Chinese Society,* edited by Margery Wolf and Roxane Witke, 39–66. Stanford: Stanford University Press, 1975.

Ransom, Roger. "Social Returns from Public Transport Investment: A Case Study of the Ohio Canal." *Journal of Political Economy* 78 (1970): 1041–60.
Ravallion, Martin. *Markets and Famines*. New York: Oxford University Press, 1987.
Rawski, Evelyn Sakakida. *Agricultural Change and the Peasant Economy of South China*. Cambridge: Harvard University Press, 1972.
Rawski, Thomas G. "China's Republican Economy: An Introduction." Joint Centre on Modern East Asia, Discussion Paper 1. Toronto: Joint Centre on Modern East Asia, 1978.
——. *Economic Growth in Prewar China*. Berkeley and Los Angeles: University of California Press, 1989.
Records of Former German and Japanese Embassies and Consulates, 1890–1945. National Archives Microfilm RG 242 T-179. Washington, D.C., 1962.
Riskin, Carl. *China's Political Economy*. New York: Oxford University Press, 1986.
Rockoff, Hugh. "Money, Banking and the Historian." Paper prepared for the Workshop on Economic Methods for Chinese Historical Research, Honolulu, January 1987.
Roll, Charles R. "The Distribution of Rural Income in China: A Comparison of the 1930s and the 1950s." Ph.D. diss., Harvard University, 1974.
Rowe, William T. *Hankow: Commerce and Society in a Chinese City, 1796–1889*. Stanford: Stanford University Press, 1984.
Rozman, Gilbert. *Urban Networks in Ch'ing China and Tokugawa Japan*. Princeton: Princeton University Press, 1973.
Salaff, Janet, *Working Daughters of Hong Kong: Filial Piety or Power in the Family?* New York: Cambridge University Press, 1981.
Santos, Fredericka Pickford. "The Economics of Marital Status." In *Sex, Discrimination, and the Division of Labor*, edited by Cynthia B. Lloyd, 244–68. New York: Columbia University Press, 1975.
Santō sainei, see Kokuritsu Pekin Daigaku Fusetsu Nōson Keizaikenkyūsho.
Sangzhi xianzhi 桑植縣志 [Gazetteer of Sangzhi County]. 1873.
Scherer, F. M. "Merger in the Petroleum Industry: The Mobil-Marathon Case (1981)." In *The Antitrust Revolution*, edited by John E. Kwoka, Jr., and Lawrence J. White, 19–45. Glenview, Ill.: Scott, Foresman, 1989.
Schneider, Jane. "Trousseau as Treasure: Some Contradictions of Late-Nineteenth-Century Change in Sicily." In *Beyond the Myths of Culture*, edited by Eric Ross, 325–56. New York: Academic Press, 1980. Reprinted in *Women and History*, no. 10 (1985): 81–119.
Schoppa, R. Keith. *Chinese Elites and Political Change: Zhejiang Province in the Early Twentieth Century*. Cambridge: Harvard University Press, 1982.
Schrecker, John. *Imperialism and Chinese Nationalism: Germany in Shantung*. Cambridge: Harvard University Press, 1971.
Schwartz, Barry. *The Battle for Human Nature: Science, Morality and Modern Life*. New York: Norton, 1986.
Schwartz, Benjamin. *In Search of Wealth and Power: Yen Fu and the West*. Cambridge: Harvard University Press, 1964.
Scott, James C. *The Moral Economy of the Peasant: Rebellion and Subsistence in Southeast Asia*. New Haven: Yale University Press, 1976.
"The Seasonal Variation of Prices for Farm Products and the Profitability of Storage." *Economic Facts*, no. 7 (October 1937): 319–42.

Shandong caizheng gongbao 山東財政公報. Jinan.
"Shandong Gaomi Wei xian zhi nongcun jiehuo" 山東高密濰縣之農村借貨 [Village borrowing in Gaomi and Wei counties, Shandong]. *Gongshang banyuekan* 6, no. 4 (Feb. 15, 1934): 49–52.
Shandong hewu tekan 山東河務特刊. Jinan.
Shandong jianshe yuekan 山東建設月刊. Jinan.
Shandong minzhong jiaoyu yuekan 山東民衆教育月刊. Jinan.
Shandong quansheng caizheng shuomingshu. 山東全省財政說明書 [A book explaining the finances of Shandong Province]. Jinan, 1913.
Shandong quanye huikan 山東勸業滙刊. Jinan.
Shandong Sheng Jiansheting 山東省建設廳. *Junzhi Wan Fu Zhu Shui he zhi* 濬治萬福朱水河誌 [Report on dredging and repairing the Wan Fu and Zhu Shui rivers]. Jinan, 1934.
Shandong shengxianzheng jianshe shiyanqu gongbao 山東省縣政建設實驗區公報. Jining.
Shandong shiye gongbao 山東實業公報. Jinan.
Shandong zazhi 山東雜誌. Beijing.
Shandong zheng sushi chaji 山東政俗視查記 [A report of an investigation of government and customs in Shandong]. Jinan, preface dated 1934.
Shanghai Gangshi Hua Bianxie zu 上海港史话编写组. *Shanghai gangshi hua* 上海港史话 [Stories of the history of the Shanghai docks]. Shanghai: Shanghai Renmin Chubanshe, 1979.
"Shanghai Huashang guoji maoyi ye" 上海华商国际贸易业 [The role of Chinese merchants in Shanghai in international trade]. 1st draft of vol. 3, sec. 4, in the series Zhongguo ziben zhuyi gongshangye shiliao congkan 中国资本主义工商业史料丛刊 [Collected historical materials on China's capitalist industry and commerce]. Unpublished manuscript. Shanghai: Shanghai Academy of Social Sciences.
Shanghai Shehui Kexueyuan Jingji Yanjiusuo 上海社会科学院经济研究所. *Jiangnan zaochuanchang changshi, 1865–1949* 江南造船厂厂史 [History of the Jiangnan arsenal, 1865 to May 1949]. Yancheng: Jiangsu Renmin Chubanshe, 1983.
———. *Nanyang Xiongdi Yancao Gongsi shiliao* 南洋兄弟烟草公司史料 [Historical materials of the Nanyang Brothers Tobacco Company]. Shanghai: Renmin Chubanshe, 1958.
———. *Rongjia qiye shiliao* 荣家企业史料 [Historical materials of the Rong family enterprises]. 2 vols. Shanghai: Shanghai Renmin Chubanshe, 1980.
Shanghaishi Chuzu Qiche Gongsi 上海市出租汽车公司. "Shanghai jiedao he gonglu yingyekeyun shiliao huiji" 上海街道和公路营业客运史料汇集 [Compendium of historical materials on the Shanghai street and road business and public transport]. Unpublished manuscript. Shanghai, 1982.
Shanghaishi Renlicheye Tongye Gonghui 上海市人力車業同業工會. *Shanghai gongbuju gaige renliche jiufen zhenxiang* 上海公部局改革人力車糾紛真相 [The true nature of disputes about reforming rickshaws in the Shanghai Municipal Council]. Shanghai, 1934.
Shanghaishi Renmin Zhengfu Gongshangju Jingji Jihuachu 上海市人民政府工商局经济计划处, ed. *Shanghai siying gongshangye fenye gaikuang* 上海私营工商业分业概况 [The general condition of each privately owned business and industrial enterprise in Shanghai]. Shanghai, 1951.
Shanghaishi Shanghui 上海市商会, ed. *Shanghaishi geye tongye gonghui lijianshi minglu*

上海市各业同业公会理监事名录 [Records of Shanghai guilds in various trades]. Shanghai.

Shanghaishi Shehuiju 上海市社會局. "Shanghaishi renli chefu shenghuo zhuangkuang diaocha baogaoshu"上海市人力車夫生活狀況調查報告書 [Report on an investigation of the living conditions of rickshaw drivers in Shanghai]. *Shehui banyuekan* 社會半月刊 [Social semimonthly]. Sept. 10, 1934: 99–113.

"Shanghai wushiliu nianlai mijia tongji" 上海五十六年來米價統計 [Statistics of Shanghai rice prices over the past 56 years]. *Shehui yuekan* 社会月刊 1, no. 2 (1929): 1–18.

Shangyudang 上諭檔 [Record book of imperial edicts], Qianlong reign. Original in National Palace Museum, Taibei, and First Historical Archives, Beijing. Microfilm available at Harvard-Yenching Library, Cambridge, Mass.

Shehui Jingji Yanjiusuo 社會經濟研究所 [Institue of Social and Economic Research]. *Wuxi mishi diaocha* 無錫米市調查 [An investigation of the Wuxi rice market]. Shanghai: Shehui Jingji Yanjiusuo, 1935.

Shen bao 申報 [Huangpu daily]. Shanghai.

Shepherd, John R. "Rethinking Tenancy: Spatial and Temporal Variation in Land Ownership Concentration in Late Imperial and Republican China." *Comparative Studies in Society and History* 30, no. 3 (1988): 403–31.

Shiba, Yoshinobu. "Ningbo and Its Hinterland." In *The City in Late Imperial China*, edited by Skinner, 391–439.

Shigeta Atsushi 重田德. "Kyōshin shihai no seiritsu to kōzō"鄉紳支配の成立と構造 [The origins and structure of gentry rule]. Originally two separate articles in *Jinbun kenkyū* 人文研究 22, no. 4 (1971) and *Iwanami kōza sekai rekishi* 岩波講座世界歷史 12 (1971). Reprinted in *Shindai shakai keizaishi kenkyū* 清代社會経済史研究 [Studies in Qing dynasty social and economic history], 155–206. Tokyo: Iwanami Shoten, 1975. Translated as "The Origins and Structure of Gentry Rule," in *State and Society in China: Japanese Perspectives on Ming-Qing Social and Economic History*, edited by Linda Grove and Christian Daniels, 335–85. Tokyo: University of Tokyo Press, 1984.

———. "Shinsho ni okeru Konan komeshijō no ichi kōsatsu" 清初における湖南米市場の一考察 [An investigation of early Qing rice markets in Hunan]. *Tōyō bunka kenkyūjo kiyō* 東洋文化研究所紀要 10 (1956): 427–98. Reprinted in *Shindai shakai keizaishi kenkyū* 清代社会経済史研究 [Studies in Qing dynasty social and economic history], 1–65. Tokyo: Iwanami Shoten, 1975.

"Shihuo zhi" 食貨志 [Monograph on the economy]. *Yin xian tongzhi* 鄞縣通志 [Comprehensive gazetteer of Yin County]. 1936.

Shimen xianzhi 石門縣志 [Gazetteer of Shimen County]. 1818; 1873.

Shina kaikō jōshi 支那開港場誌 [A gazetteer of China's treaty ports]. 2 vols. Tokyo: Tōa Dōbunkai Chōsa Hensanbu, 1922.

Shina nōgyō kiso tōkei shiryō 支那農業基礎統計史料 [Historical materials on Chinese agricultural statistics]. Vol. 1. Compiled by Tōa Kenkyūjo 東亞研究所. Shanghai: Tōa Kenkyūjo, 1941.

Shina no kōun 支那の交運 [China's shipping]. Tokyo: Tōa Kaiun Kabushiki Kaisha, 1944.

Shina shōbetsu zenshi 支那省別全誌 [A comprehensive gazetteer of China, arranged by province]. Vols. 4 (Shandong Province), 13 (Zhejiang Province). Tokyo: Tōa Dōbunkai Chōsa Hensanbu, 1919.

Shouguang xianzhi 壽光縣志 [Gazetteer of Shouguang County]. 1934.

"Sican zhaiyao" 絲蠶摘要 [Brief notes on raising silkworms]. *Jiangnan shangwu bao* 江南商務報 9 (Apr. 21, 1900), commercial raw materials sec.: 2.

Skinner, G. William. "Introduction: Urban Development in Imperial China." In *The City in Late Imperial China*, edited by Skinner, 3–31.

———. "Marketing and Social Structure in Rural China." *Journal of Asian Studies* 24, no. 1 (1964): 3–43; no. 2 (1965): 195–228; no. 3 (1965): 363–99.

———. "Presidental Address: The Structure of Chinese History." *Journal of Asian Studies* 44, no. 2 (1985): 271–92.

———. "Regional Urbanization in Nineteenth-Century China." In *The City in Late Imperial China*, edited by Skinner, 211–49.

———. "Sichuan's Population in the Nineteenth Century: Lessons from Disaggregated Data." *Late Imperial China* 8, no. 1 (1987): 1–79.

———, ed. *The City in Late Imperial China*. Stanford: Stanford University Press, 1977.

SMR, Shanghai Office, *see* Minami Manshū Tetsudō Kabushiki Kaisha, Shanhai Jimusho Chōsashitsu.

SSZ, see *Shina shōbetsu zenshi*.

Stigler, George J., and Robert A. Sherwin. "The Extent of the Market." *Journal of Law and Economics* 28 (1985): 555–85.

Sun, Ching-chih. *See* Jingzhi Sun.

Sun E-tu Zen. "Sericulture and Silk Textile Production in Ch'ing China." In *Economic Organization in Chinese Society*, edited by W. E. Willmott, 79–108. Stanford: Stanford University Press, 1972.

Sun Guoqiao 孫國喬. "Wuxi zhidao yu yangcan shiye zhi yaodian" 無錫植稻與養蠶事業之要點 [The essentials of rice cultivation and sericulture in Wuxi]. *Nongye zhoubao* 農業週報 [Farm weekly] 1, no. 25 (Oct. 16, 1931): 982–85.

Sun Jingzhi 孫敬之. *Huabei die jingji dili* 华北的经济地理 [Economic geography of North China]. Beijing: Kexueyuan Chubanshe, 1958.

Sun Jingzhi [Ching-chih Sun] 孫敬之 et al. *Economic Geography of the East China Region (Shanghai, Kiangsu, Anhwei, Chekiang)*. Translated by Joint Publications Research Service. JPRS publication no. 11,438. Washington, D.C.: U.S. Government Printing Office, Dec. 7, 1961. Originally published as *Huadong diqu jingji dili* 華東地区经济地理. Beijing: Zhongguo Kexueyuan Dili Yanjiusuo, 1959.

Sun Yutang 孫毓棠. "Ming Qing shidai de baiyin neiliu yu fengjian shehui" 明清时代的白銀内流与封建社会 [Influx of silver and the feudal society of Ming and Qing]. *Jinbu ribao* 進步日報 [Progress daily], Feb. 3, 1951.

Taiping Shanren 太平山人. "Daoguang chao yinhuang wenti" 道光朝銀荒問題 [The problem of silver shortage in the Daoguang period]. In *Zhongguo jin sanbainian shehui jingjishi lunji* 中國近三百年社會經濟史論集 [Essays on the past 300 years of China's social and economic history], 5:41–55. Hong Kong: Chongwen Shudian, 1974.

Tanaka Issei 田仲一成. "Shindai Settō sōzoku no soshiki keisei ni okeru sōshi engeki no kinō ni tsuite" 清代浙東宗族の組織形成における宗祠演劇の機能について [A study on the function of ritual drama in reconstructing family relationships in eastern Zhejiang during the Qing period]. *Tōyōshi kenkyū* 東洋史研究 44, no. 4 (1986): 47–50.

Tang Chengtao 唐承涛. "Huoguo yangmin de 'li Ji qianpiao'" 祸国殃民的利济

钱票 [The 'benefit Jining copper notes' that brought calamity to the nation and disaster to the people]. In *Jining shi shiliao* 济宁市史料 [Historical materials of Jining Municipality] 1 (1983): 89–91.

Tang huiyao 唐會要 [Important documents of the Tang]. Beijing: Zhonghua Shuju, 1955.

Tang Kangxiong 湯康雄. "Ningbo de niumu" 寧波的阿姆 [Ningbo's maids]. In *Ningbo xisu congtan* 寧波習俗叢談 [Collected accounts of Ningbo local customs], edited by Zhang Xingzhou 張行周, 255–57. Taibei: Minzhu Chubanshe, 1973.

———. "Peijia zhuanglian" 陪嫁粧奩 [Dowry processions]. In *Ningbo xisu congtan* 寧波習俗叢談 [Collected accounts of Ningbo local customs], edited by Zhang Xingzhou 張行周, 212–14. Taibei: Minzhu Chubanshe, 1973.

Telford, Ted. "Fertility and Population Growth in the Lineages of Tongcheng County, 1520–1661." Paper presented at the Conference on Chinese Lineage Demography, Asilomar, Calif., 1987.

———. "Marriage and Fertility in Tongcheng County, 1520–1661." Paper presented at the Workshop on Qing Population History, California Institute of Technology, Pasadena, 1985.

———. "Survey of Social Demographic Data in Chinese Genealogies." *Late Imperial China* 7, no. 2 (1986): 80–177.

Tilly, Charles. "Food Supply and Public Order in Modern Europe." In *The Formation of National States in Western Europe*, edited by Charles Tilly, 380–455. Princeton: Princeton University Press, 1975.

———. "Reflections on the History of European State-Making." In *The Formation of National States in Western Europe*, edited by Charles Tilly, 3–83. Princeton: Princeton University Press, 1975.

Tilly, Louise A., and Joan W. Scott. *Women, Work, and Family*. New York: Holt, Rinehart and Winston, 1978.

Tōa Dōbunkai 東亞同文會. *Shina keizai zensho* 支那經濟全書 [The complete book of the Chinese economy]. Vol. 1. Osaka: Tōa Dōbunkai, 1908.

Tōa Kenkyūsho 東亞研究所. *Santō koshōgun chitai no chiiki chōsa* 山東湖沼郡地帶の地域調查 [Area report on the lake region of Shandong Province]. Report no. 14, Class C, no. 158-D. Jinan: Tōa Kenkyūsho, 1940.

Tongji yuebao 統計月報. Nanjing.

Tsao, Lien-en. "The Marketing of Soya Beans and Bean Oil." *Chinese Economic Journal* 7, no. 3 (1930): 941–71.

Tsur, Nyok-Ching. "Forms of Business in the City of Ningpo in China." Translated by Peter Schran. *Chinese Sociology and Anthropology* 15, no. 4 (1983). Originally a doctoral dissertation in German, *Die gewerblichen Betriebsformen der Stadt Ningpo* [Industry in Ningbo]. Tübingen: H. Laupp, Jr., 1909.

Tu Shipin 屠诗聘. *Shanghai chunqiu* 上海春秋 [Shanghai annals]. Hong Kong: Zhongguo Tushu Bianjiguan, 1968.

Tudi Weiyuanhui 土地委員會. *Quanguo tudi diaocha baogao gangyao* 全國土地調查報告綱要 [A summary report of the national land survey]. Nanjing: Tudi Weiyuanhui, 1937.

Visaria, Pravin. "Demographic Factors and the Distribution of Income: Some Issues." In *Economic and Demographic Change: Issues for the 1980's*, vol. 1, by International Union for the Scientific Study of Population, 289–320. Liege, Belgium:

International Union for the Scientific Study of Population, 1979.

Vogel, Hans Ulrich. "Chinese Central Monetary Policy, 1644–1800." *Late Imperial China* 8, no. 2 (1987): 1–52.

———. "Chinese Central Monetary Policy and Yunnan Copper Mining in the Early Qing (1644–1800)." Ph.D. diss., University of Zurich, 1983.

Wang Peitang 王培棠. *Jiangsusheng xiangtu zhi* 江蘇省鄉土志 [Local records of Jiangsu Province]. Changsha: Commercial Press, 1938.

Wang Shaowu 王紹武. "Jin sibainian dongya de lengxia" 近四百年東亞的冷夏 [Cold summers in East Asia during the last 400 years]. Unpublished manuscript. 1988.

Wang Xuexiang 王學祥. "Gaishan sangye maimai jigou zhi guanjian" 改善桑葉買賣機構之管見 [My opinions on reforming marketing mechanisms for mulberry leaves]. *Zhongguo cansi* 中國蠶絲 2, no. 7 (Jan. 1937): 92–96.

Wang, Yeh-chien 王業鍵. *An Estimate of the Land-Tax Collection in China, 1753 and 1908.* Cambridge: Harvard University Press, 1973.

———. "Evolution of the Chinese Monetary System, 1644–1850." In *Modern Chinese Economic History*, edited by Chi-ming Hou and Tzong-shian Yu, 425–52. Taibei: Institute of Economics, Academia Sinica, 1979.

———. "Food Supply and Grain Prices in the Yangtze Delta in the Eighteenth Century." In *Proceedings of the Second Conference on Modern Chinese Economic History*, 423–61. Taibei: Institute of Economics, Academia Sinica, 1989.

———. "Food Supply in Eighteenth-Century Fukien." *Late Imperial China* 7, no. 2 (1986): 80–117.

———. *Land Taxation in Imperial China, 1750–1911.* Cambridge: Harvard University Press, 1973.

———. "Spatial and Temporal Patterns of Grain Prices in China, 1740–1910." Paper presented at the Conference on Spatial and Temporal Trends and Cycles in Chinese Economic History, Bellagio, Italy, 1984.

———. *Zhongguo jindai huobi yu yinhang di yanjin, 1644–1937* 中國近代貨幣與銀行的演進 [The development of money and banking in modern China, 1644–1937]. Taibei: Institute of Economics, Academia Sinica, 1981.

Wang Yeh-chien 王業鍵 and Hwang Kuo-shu 黃國樞. "Shiba shiji Zhongguo liangshi gongxu de kaocha" 十八世紀中國糧食供需的考察 [Study of grain supply and demand in eighteenth-century China]. Paper presented at Jindai Zhongguo nongcun jingjishi yantaohui 近代中國農村經濟史研討會 [Conference on the History of China's Rural Economy in Modern Times]. Institute of Modern History, Academia Sinica, Taibei, August 1989.

Wei Yuan 魏源. *Shengwuji* 聖武記 [Record of imperial military exploits]. 1927.

Weir, David. "Markets and Mortality in France, 1600–1784." In *Essays in Honor of Andrew B. Appleby*, edited by Roger S. Schofield and John Walther. Cambridge: Cambridge University Press, forthcoming.

Wiens, Thomas B. "The Microeconomics of Peasant Economy: China, 1920–40." Ph.D. diss., Harvard University, 1973.

Will, Pierre-Etienne. *Bureaucracy and Famine in Eighteenth-Century China.* Translated by Elborg Forster. Stanford: Stanford University Press, 1990.

———. *Bureaucratie et famine en Chine au 18e siècle.* Paris: Mouton, 1980.

Will, Pierre-Etienne, and R. Bin Wong. *Nourish the People: The State Civilian Granary System in China, 1650–1850.* Ann Arbor: University of Michigan Press, 1991.
Wong, R. Bin. "Food Riots in the Qing Dynasty." *Journal of Asian Studies* 41, no. 4 (1982): 767–88.
Wong, R. Bin, and Peter C. Perdue. "Famine's Foes in Ch'ing China." *Harvard Journal of Asiatic Studies* 43, no. 1 (1983): 291–332.
Wrigley, E. A., and R. S. Schofield, eds. *The Population History of England, 1541–1871.* Cambridge: Harvard University Press, 1981.
Wu Baosan 巫寶三. *Zhongguo guomin suode, 1933 nian* 中國國民所得, 1933 年 [China's national income, 1933]. 2 vols. Shanghai: Zhonghua Shuju, 1947.
Wu Chengming 吳承明. "Woguo banzhimindi banfengjian guonei shichang." 我国半殖民地半封建国内市场 [The internal market of our country in the half-colonial, half-feudal period]. *Lishi yanjiu* 历史研究, 4 (1984): 110–21.
―――. *Zhongguo ziben zhuyi yu guonei shichang* 中国资本主义与国内市场 [Chinese capitalism and the domestic market]. Beijing: Zhongguo Shehui Kexue Chubanshe, 1985.
Wu Guogui 吴国桂. "Yutang xinghuo—Jining Shi Yutang jiangyuan gongyun gai" 玉堂星火—济宁市玉堂酱园工运概 [Yutang sparks: An outline of the labor movement at the Jining Soy Sauce Factory]. In *Shandong gongyun shi ziliao* 山东工运史資料 [Materials on the history of the Shandong labor movement], no. 16 (Feb. 10, 1985): 12–17.
Wu Liangrong 吴良蓉. "Shanghaishi Subeiji jumin shehui biandong fenxi" 上海市苏北籍居民社会变动分析 [An analysis of social mobility among Subei natives who reside in Shanghai]. In *Shehuixue wenji* 社会学文集 [Sociological essays], edited by Shanghaishi Shehuixue Xuehui 上海市社会学学会, 170–90. Shanghai, 1984.
Wu Tongju 武同舉, ed. *Zaixu xingshui jinjian* 再續行水金鑑 [A further continuation of the Mirror of Water Works]. Vol. 10. Taibei: Wenhai Chubanshe, 1966.
"Wuxi chunjian shoucheng jianse" 無錫春繭收成減色 [The spring cocoon crop in Wuxi is down]. *Minguo ribao* 民國日報 June 5, 1921, sec. 2:8.
Wuxi Difangzhi Bianji Weiyuanhui 无錫地方志编辑委员会, ed. *Wuxi gushixuan* 无錫故事选 [Selected stories from Wuxi]. Wuxi: Wuxi Renmin Chubanshe, 1959.
"Wuxi jianshi jianse" 無錫繭市減色 [Cocoon marketing in Wuxi is impaired]. *Minguo ribao* 民國日報 May 21, 1916, sec. 3:10.
Wuxi-Jinkui xianzhi 無錫金匱縣志 [A gazetteer of Wuxi and Jinkui counties]. Wuxi, 1881.
"Wuxi—shiju bujing zhi shangshi" 無錫時局不靖之商市 [Wuxi—markets in chaos]. *Minguo ribao* 民國日報 June 4, 1917, sec. 2:7.
Xie Junmei 谢君美. "Shanghai lishishang renkoude bianqian" 上海历史上人口的变迁 [Historical changes in the population of Shanghai]. *Shehui kexue* 社会科学 3 (1980): 107–13, 124.
Xi-Jin shi xiaolu 錫金識小錄 [A brief record of what is known about Wuxi and Jinkui counties]. Wuxi, 1752.
Xinning xianzhi 新寧縣志 [Gazetteer of Xinning County]. 1893.
Xinxiu Yin xianzhi 新修鄞縣志 [Gazetteer of Yin County, newly compiled]. 1877.
Xu Dixin 许涤新 and Wu Chengming 吳承明. *Zhongguo ziben zhuyi de mengya*

中国资本主义的萌芽 [The history of nascent capitalism in China]. Vol. 1. Beijing: Renmin Chubanshe, 1985.

Xue Gengxin 薛耕莘. "Jindai Shanghaide liumang" 近代上海的流氓 [Gangsters in modern Shanghai]. *Shanghai wenshi ziliao xuanji* 上海文史资料选集 3 (1980): 160–78.

Xuxiu Qingping xianzhi 續修清平縣志 [A further revision of the Qingping County gazetteer]. 1936.

Yan Jinqing 嚴金清, ed. *Yan Lianfang yigao* 嚴廉訪遺稿 [The posthumous manuscripts of Yan Lianfang (Yan Ziqing)]. Wuxi, 1923.

Yan Jiyuan 严济远, Xu Weitong 许卫桐, Shi Xuchun 石熙春, and Zhu Jingyan 朱靜燕. "Changjiang sanjiaozhou de lengnuan tedian ji qi qushi zhanwang" 长江三角洲的冷暖特点及其趋势展望 [Special features and trends of warm and cold climate in the Yangtze Delta]. In *Quanguo qihou bianhua xueshu taolunhui wenji* 全国气候变化学术讨论会文集 [Collected essays from the National Symposium on Meteorological Changes], 71–77. Beijing: Kexue Chubanshe, 1981.

Yang Yi 楊儀. "Qingchao qianqi de tudi zhidu" 清朝前期的土地制度 [The land system of early Qing China]. *Shixue yuekan* 史学月刊 no. 7 (1958): 21–26.

Yang, Muhammad Usiar Huaizhong. "The Eighteenth-Century Gansu Relief Fraud Scandal." Paper presented at the conference "The Legacy of Islam in China: An International Symposium in Memory of Joseph F. Fletcher," Harvard University, Cambridge, Mass., April 1989.

Yao Tinglin 姚廷遴. *Linianji* 历年記 [Annals]. In *Qingdai riji huichao* 清代日記滙抄 [Collected Diaries for the Qing Period]. Shanghai: Renmin Chubanshe, 1982.

Ye Mengzhu 葉夢珠. *Yueshi bian* 閱世編 [Reminiscences]. Shanghai. Shanghai Wenwu Baoguan Weiyuanhui, 1981.

Yim, Shu-yuen. "Famine Relief Statistics as a Guide to the Population of Sixteenth-Century China: A Case Study of Honan Province." *Ch'ing-shih wen-t'i* 3, no. 9 (1978): 1–30.

Yin Huiyi 尹會一. "Jing chen nongsang siwu shu" 敬陳農桑四務疏 [Respectfully submitted explication of the four foundations of agriculture and sericulture]. In *Huangchao jingshi wenbian* 皇朝經世文編 [Collected essays on statecraft of our august dynasty], compiled by Wei Yuan 魏源. Preface dated 1826–27. Reprint. Taibei, 1963.

Yin Liangying 尹良瑩. *Zhongguo canye shi* 中國蠶業史 [A history of Chinese sericulture]. Nanjing: Guoli Zhongyang Daxue Cansang Xuehui, 1931.

Yinhang zhoubao 銀行週報 [Banker's weekly]. Shanghai, 1917–37.

Yinxian tongzhi 鄞縣通志 [Comprehensive gazetteer of Yin County]. 1935; 1936.

Yongshun fuzhi 永順府志 [Gazetteer of Yongshun Prefecture]. 1763.

Yongzheng zhupi yuzhi 雍正硃批諭旨 [The Yongzheng emperor's edicts and vermilion endorsements]. Compiled in 1738. Reprint. Taibei: Wenyuan Shuju, 1965.

Yu Jieqiong 余捷瓊. *1700–1937 nian Zhongguo yinhuo shuchuru de yige guji* 1700–1937 年中國銀貨輸出入的一個估計 [An estimate of China's imports and exports of silver, 1700–1937]. Changsha: Commercial Press, 1940.

Yuanling xianzhi 沅陵縣志 [Gazetteer of Yuanling County]. 1873.

"Yudi zhi" 域地志 [Monograph on geography]. *Yin xian tongzhi* [Comprehensive gazetteer of Yin County]. 1936.

"Yuyan zhi" 魚鹽志 [Monograph on fish and salt]. *Dinghai xian zhi* [Gazetteer of

Dinghai County]. 1923. Reprint. Keelung, 1963.

Zelin, Madeleine. *The Magistrate's Tael: Rationalizing Fiscal Reform in Eighteenth-Century Ch'ing China*. Berkeley and Los Angeles: University of California Press, 1984.

―――. "The Rights of Tenants in Mid-Qing Sichuan." *Journal of Asian Studies* 45, no. 3 (1986): 499–526.

Zhang Kai 章楷. "Mantan lishishang Jiangsu de canye" 漫谈历史上江苏的蚕业 [An informal history of Jiangsu sericulture]. Parts 1, 2. *Canye keji* 蚕业科技 2 (July 1979): 54–56; 3 (October 1979): 53–56.

Zhang Peiyuan 張丕遠. "Qingdai hannuan bianhua ji qi dui nongye de yingxiang" 清代寒暖变化及其对农业的影响 [Temperature change in the Qing period and its impact on agriculture]. Paper presented at the Workshop on Qing Population History, California Institute of Technology, Pasadena, 1985.

Zhang Xiangong 張先恭. "Zhongguo dongbanbu jin wubainian ganhan zhishu de fenxi" 中国东半部近五百年干旱指数的分析 [Analysis of a drought index for eastern China over the past 500 years]. In *Quanguo qihou bianhua xueshu taolunhui wenji* 全国气候变化学术讨论会文集 [Collected essays from the National Symposium on Meterorological Changes], 46–51. Beijing: Kexue Chubanshe, 1981.

Zhang Yufa 張玉法. *Zhongguo xiandaihua de quyu yanjiu: Shandong sheng, 1860–1916* 中國現代化的區域研究:山東省 [Regional studies of Chinese modernization: Shandong Province, 1860–1916]. Taibei: Zhongyang Yanjiuyuan, Jindai Shi Yanjiusuo, 1982.

Zhang Zhongli. *See* Chung-li Chang.

Zhao Gang. *See* Kang Chao.

Zhao Ruheng 趙如衡. *Jiangsusheng jian* 江蘇省鑑 [Jiangsu Province yearbook]. Shanghai: Xin Zhongguo Jianshe Xuehui, 1935.

Zheng Hesheng 鄭鶴聲. *Jinshi Zhongxi shiri duizhaobiao* 近世中西史日對照表 [Concordance of modern Chinese and Western dates]. Taibei: Shangwu Yinshuguan, 1978.

Zhenhai xian zhi 鎮海縣志 [Gazetteer of Zhenhai County]. Supplement *Xinzhi beigao* 新志備稿 [Complete draft of a new gazetteer]. Preface dated 1924; published 1931.

Zhenghuangqi Daoyitun Hanjun rending hukouce 正黃旗道义屯漢軍人丁戶口冊 [Daoyi village population registers from the Han army of the Plain Yellow Standard]. 1867.

"Zhijie shouhai zhi shangkuang" 直接受害之商況 [Trade experiences immediate adverse effects]. *Minguo ribao* 民國日報 June 5, 1917, sec. 3:10.

Zhongguo Jiaotongbu. Jiaotong Shi Weiyuanhui 中國交通部交通史委員會. *Jiaotong shi* 交通史 [History of transportation]. Nanjing: Jiaotongbu, 1937.

Zhongguo jin wubainian hanlao fenbu tuji 中国近五百年旱涝分布图集 [Maps showing the distribution of drought and flood in China over the past 500 years]. Compiled by Zhongyang Qixiangju Qixiang Kexue Yanjiuyuan 中央气象局气象科学研究院 [Academy of Meteorology, Central Bureau of Meteorology]. Beijing: Ditu Chubanshe, 1981.

Zhongguo Shehui Kexueyuan Jingji Yanjiusuo 中国社会科学院经济研究所, ed. *Shanghai minzu jiqi gongye* 上海民族机器工业 [The national machine industry in Shanghai]. Vol. 1. Beijing: Zhonghua Shuju, 1966.

Zhongguo Shiyebu 中國實業部. Guoji Maoyiju 國際貿易局. *Zhongguo shiye zhi: Jiang-*

su sheng 中國實業誌江蘇省 [Chinese industrial handbook: Jiangsu Province]. Shanghai: Guoji Maoyiju, 1933.

———. *Zhongguo shiye zhi: Shandong sheng* 中國實業誌山東省 [Chinese industrial handbook: Shandong Province]. Nanjing: Guoji Maoyiju, 1934.

———. *Zhongguo shiye zhi: Zhejiang sheng* 中國實業誌浙江省 [Chinese industrial handbook: Zhejiang Province]. Shanghai: Guoji Maoyiju, 1933.

Zhou Yuanlian. 周远廉. "Guanyu baqi zhidu de jige wenti" 关于八旗制度的几个问题 [Some problems concerning the banner system]. *Qingshi luncong* 清史论丛 [Essays in Qing history] 3 (1982): 140–54.

———. *Qingchao kaiguoshi yanjiu* 清朝开国史研究 [Research on the founding of the Qing state]. Shenyang: Liaoning Renmin Chubanshe, 1981.

Zhu Bangxing 朱邦興, Hu Lin'ge 胡林閣, and Xu Sheng 徐聲. *Shanghai chanye yu Shanghai zhigong* 上海產業與上海職工 [Enterprises and workers in Shanghai]. Hong Kong: Yuandong Chubanshe, 1939.

Zhu Sihuang 朱斯煌, comp. *Minguo jingjishi* 民國經濟史 [Economic history of the Republic of China]. Shanghai: Shanghai Yinhang Gonghui, 1948.

Zhuang Yaohe 庄么鶴. Interview with Lynda S. Bell. Number One Silk Factory in Wuxi. May 27, 1980.

Zhupi zouzhe 硃批奏摺. Palace Memorial Archives. First Historical Archives, Beijing.

Zou Yiren 邹依仁. *Jiu Shanghai renkou bianqian de yanjiu* 旧上海人口变迁的研究 [Research on changes in the population of old Shanghai]. Shanghai: Shanghai Renmin Chubanshe, 1980.

ZSZS. See Zhongguo Shiyebu, Guoji Maoyiju, *Zhongguo shiye zhi: Shandong sheng*.

ZSZZ. See Zhongguo Shiyebu, Guoji Maoyiju, *Zhongguo shiye zhi: Zhejiang sheng*.

INDEX

Academia Sinica, 224
Agriculture
  expansion of, 175
  and food availability in Zhili, 74–76
  survey of, 175
Akerlof, George A., 10
Alter, George, 156n13
Appleby, Andrew B., 62, 93, 98
Arai Hakuseki, 60–61
Asiatic mode of production, 2–3

Baishuidang (Wuxi), 225
Bamboo umbrella frames, 258
Banknotes, 61
Banks
  lack of jobs for Subei people in, 289
  native, 57
Bao Shichen, 65
Barbers, 276–77
Barclay, G. W., 175
Beijing, influence of as capital, 70, 72
Bell, Lynda S., xvii, 207–42
  on rural income, 27–28, 30
Black beans (*heidou*), 73
  prices of, 82
Blecher, Marc, 191n34
Brandt, Loren, xvii, 30, 179–206
  on land concentration and income, 26–27, 179–206
  on Yangzi rice markets, 11, 22
Brass, as currency, 303
Bray, Francesca, 99

Broad beans, 223
Brokers
  contracting by, 263
  and home handicrafts, 258
Buck, John Lossing, 75, 86, 98, 176
  on grain consumption, 222–23
  on incomes, 202n50
  on lending on land, 185–86

California, lack of Chinese in factories of, 191–92
California Institute of Technology, 150
Campbell, Cameron, xvii, 25, 26, 31, 145–76
Capitalism, and Marxism, 2
Changshu, rice prices in, 49
Chayanov, A. V., 27, 208–9
Chen Dewang, 281–82
Chen, Han-seng, 184–85
Chen Hansheng, 225n59
Chen Sihai, 277
Chi, Anna, 158n13, 159n16
Child labor, in factories, 231
China
  distribution of income in, 201–5
  monetary policy and independence of, 307
Chinese Industrial Handbook for Zhejiang Province, The, 252, 253
Chinese Maritime Customs Service, rice prices from, 49
Chow test, 86
Ch'üan Han-sheng, 60
Class, social, and employment, 29

Climate
  cycles in, 62–63
  effect on food supply, 62, 163
  and grain prices, 62–64
Cliometrics, 5
Coale, A. J., 175
Coastal waters, transport on, 38
Cohen, Jon, xv
Cole, W. A., 17
Commercialization
  and concentration of land holdings, 181
  pace of, 66–67
  Qing trends in Wuxi, 209–14, 217
  and women's work, 246
Contents of present volume, 21–30
  conclusions concerning, 30–32
Contributions (*juan*), fees paid for degrees, 106–7
Copper
  as currency, 303, 306
  exchange rate with silver, 305, 306
  as metal, 307
Copper cash, 57
Corn, 75
Cotton, 36, 74
  cash crop, 65
  Ningbo as center for, 250
  in Shandong Heartland, 312
  in Wuxi, 213–14
  in Yangzi Delta, 38
Cotton mills
  jobs for Subei women in, 280
  Subei people in, 292–93
Crafts, Nicholas, 17
Credit markets, regional, 303–5
Crises
  effect on prices, 88–95, 98
  in Gansu, 102
  infanticide during, 169–72
  and multicrop system, 98
  See also Droughts; Flooding
Crisis years, effect on prices, 83, 88, 89
  in 1743–44, 90
  in 1761–63, 93
  in 1774–75, 90
Currencies
  manipulated for private gain, 308–9
  restrictions on export of, 308
  in Shandong, 303
  shortages of, 306
  See also Brass; Copper; Copper cash; Paper currency; Silver

Currency trading, and capital markets, 295, 303

Dabeiguan (Hebei), 191–93, 199–200
Daoyi (Liaoning)
  food prices in, 163
  household decisions in, 176
  population history of, 146, 147
Deane, Phyllis, 17
Deng, Cora, 280
Depression, peasant decisions during, 224
diandi, land as guarantee for loan, 184
ding, population reporting based on, 211–12
Distribution
  and fragmented money markets, 309–12
  of income in China, 201–5
  of land ownership and economic welfare, 180, 188–90, 201
Doeringer, Peter, 271–72
Domestic cycle, 247
Domestic handicrafts. *See* Home handicrafts
Domestic service, 254, 255–56
  status of, 256
Dong Fureng, 225n59
Double-cropping, 65
Draft animals, 199–200
Droughts, 66
  during military campaigns in Gansu, 111
  in North China, 72
  and prices, 63, 84
  in Yangzi Delta, 49
  in Zhili, 90
Du Yuesheng, 290

Economic geography
  politics of, 305–9
  private gain, 308–9
  public finance, 305–8
Economic methods and the data problem, 16–20
Economic theory
  choice, 5–6
  economic methods and the data problem, 16–20
  economists and historians, 20–21
  entry and exit, 7
  equilibrium, 6
  objections to, 7–10
  opportunity cost, 6
  principles of, 5–7
  rationality, 6, 8

theoretical reasoning, 10–16
treatment of in present volume, 21–30
Economic welfare, and land concentration, 180
Economics
 links with history, 1, 5, 20–21
 and noneconomic factors, 9–10
 and the state, 315–18
Economics and the Historian, xv
Economy
 inequalities in, 188
 and population, 145
 studied by social historians, 5
Education, of Ningbo women, 270n92
Edwards, Richard, on labor markets, 271–72
Eight Banner registration system, 150–51
Eleuth Mongols, 111
Elvin, Mark, 3
Embroidery
 division of labor for, 259
 foreign demand for, 258
 prestige of in Ningbo, 254, 257, 258
 women's work, 244
Employment
 domestic vs. factory in Ningbo, 266
 gender, class, and social factors in, 29, 243–67
 in Shanghai factories, 267–69
Engerman, Stanley, 5
England
 grain prices in crises, 93, 98, 298
 land holding in, 184
 population and prices in, 55, 57
 silver from, 60
Equilibrium, in economic theory, 6
Etzioni, Amitai, 8
Europe
 birth intervals in, 151–52
 rice prices in premodern, 51, 52, 54
Exports
 of Hunan rice, 130
 of Wuxi silk, 216–17
 See also Embroidery; Foreign trade; Hats; Silk

Factor markets, data from, 32
Factories
 vs. cottage industries, 244n5, 246
 hours and closings, 265
 jobs for women in, 263–67
 lack of Subei people in, 278–80
 output for domestic market, 267
 return on labor in, 231
 status of Subei people in, 291
 wages in, 264–65
 See also Employment; Ningbo; Shanghai
Family, as primary unit of production, 231
Famines
 danger of in North China, 72
 in Subei, 285
Fan, I-chun, xv
Farming
 female labor for, 231–40, 252–54
 subsidiary activities, 221–22
 wages in, 252
 in Wuxi, 207–42
Faure, David, 285–86
Fei Xiaotong (Fei, Hsiao-tung), 283, 286
Females
 in Eight Banner registration, 250–51
 farm labor of, 231–40, 252–54
 food prices and numbers of, 167
 and infanticide, 169–75
 lower survival rates of, 152–56
 See also Women
Fenghua County
 farm wages in, 252–53
 products of, 251–52
 See also Ningbo
Fengtian
 food prices in, 158
 See also Liaoning
Fertility
 and birth intervals, 151–52
 control of, 151, 152–53, 175
 effect of food shortages on, 98
 and food prices, 167–69
 by household position, 156–58
 low in China, 175
 and wealth, 156
First Historical Archives, Beijing, 21, 35n, 73n4
Fletcher, Joseph, 102
Flooding
 in North China, 72
 and prices, 63, 83, 93
 in Subei, 191
 in Yangzi Delta, 49
 of Yellow River, 70, 72, 317
Fogel, Robert, 5
Foreign goods, merchants of, 310
Foreign imperialism, and Marxism, 2
Foreign trade
 effect on home market, 257

Foreign trade (cont.)
  effect on women's work, 243, 244, 246
  in home handicrafts, 258–62
  in Ningbo, 250–51
  See also Exports; Imports
France, grain prices in crises, 93, 98
fu (prefecture), 21

Gansu
  area of, 101
  effects of military campaigns, 112
  granary reserves and food supply, 104–10
  military demands on grain supply, 110–13
  population of, 103
  price data and market integration, 113–25
  sources of grain in, 106
  taxes in, 102–3
Gansu grain market, 22–23, 31, 100–125, 136
  adjustment of data for, 125
  market relationships in, 123
  and Qing state, 100–125
  variability in reserves, 110, 121
Gao Jin, Governor, 39
Gender
  and division of labor, 243–44
  in employment, 29
  and work in Ningbo, 246, 257
  and work in Wuxi, 231–40
  See also Females; Males; Women
Gini coefficient, 181n8, 189–90, 194–95
  for rural sector as a whole, 202
Goldstone, Jack A., 55, 67
Gordon, David, on labor markets, 271–72
Gottschang, Thomas R., 13
Goubert, Pierre, 146n3
Government policies and the economy
  fragmented markets and state making, 315–18
  grain storage, 100–125, 210
  military preparedness, 100–102, 110–13
  obstructing flows of commodities and money, 305–9, 316
Grains
  data on prices of, 21, 31
  in Gansu, 101
  markets for varieties of, 25
  prices of, and infanticide, 176
  reports on prices of, 39
  returns from storing of, 299–301
  storage of reserves, 22, 24, 299n8
  studies on prices of, 22
  system of Qing, 32

  in Yangzi Delta, 38
  See also Fengtian; Gansu grain market;
    Hunan; Millet; Rice; Sorghum;
    Suzhou; Wheat; Wuxi; Yangzi Delta;
    Zhili
Granaries
  and food supply, 104–10
  interactions of, 99
  kinds of, 104
  in the Qing state, 100–125
  state system of, 76
  See also Gansu grain market; Government
    policies and the economy
Grand Canal, 38, 283
  and transport of rice, 36, 70, 210, 283–84
Green Gang, Subei connections with, 289–90
Gu Zhuxuan, 290

Hai River Basin, 70
  floods in, 93
Handicrafts. See Home handicrafts
Harding, Harry, 179
Harrell, Stevan, 156n13
Harris, Barbara, 121n52
Harvests
  and climate, 62
  and demographic patterns, 163–75
  and prices, 62–63
Hats
  foreign markets for, 260, 261
  making of, 247, 249, 258–62
  new materials for, 261
  prices for, 261
  production of, 261–62
  weaving of straw, 260
Head, Keith, 83n18
Heartland of Shandong, 299, 301
  and fragmented markets, 312–15
  money markets in, 303–4
  scarcity of capital in, 312
Hebei
  incomes vs. landholdings in, 196
  inequalities of income per capita, 196
  land and income in three villages of, 194–96
  See also Zhili
Hefeng Cotton Mill, 264
  wages at, 265
Hierarchy
  of native place, 274
  origins of, 274–92
History, links with economics, 1, 5, 32

INDEX   355

Ho, Ping-ti, 4, 289
  on population, 56, 211
Home handicrafts
  embroidery, 258–60
  vs. factory work, 266–67
  and industrialization, 243–45
  lace making, 260
  of Ningbo, 249
  role of brokers in, 258
  straw hats, 260–61
Honig, Emily, xvii, 16, 269, 271–94
  on hierarchy in labor market, 28–29, 30
Horse trade
  in Gansu, 103
  for military campaigns, 111
Hoskins, W. G., 51
Households
  complexity of, and infanticide, 169
  data on incomes from in N. China, 190–206
  decision making in, 176
  incomes per capita, 196, 202
  labor allocation in Wuxi, 217–40
  in Ningbo, 269
  size of and inequalities of income, 188
  and women's work, 243, 246
  in Wuxi, 207–9, 214–40
Huai River, source of flooding in Subei, 284
Huang Jinrong, 290
Huang, Philip C. C., 207
  on cropping systems, 74–75
  on land tenure, 4
Huang Tinggui, Governor, 101, 106, 111
Hunan
  analysis of rice prices in, 127, 131
  grain markets of eighteenth century, 23, 25, 31, 126–44
  market integration in, 127, 131, 143–44
  qualitative evidence on commercial rice circulation, 127, 128–30, 143
  rice export network in, 136–37n18
  spatial patterns of high and low prices, 132–44, 136n18
Hwang, Kuo-shu, 117

Iconoclasm, 252–54
  Levenson on, 306n77
Imports
  access to credit by dealers in, 310–11
  as threat to home weaving, 257
  See also Foreign trade
Income
  defined, 197

  distribution and land concentration, 26–27, 179–206
  distribution of in China, 201–5
  inequalities in, 180
  and land in rural China, 188–201
  overestimate of inequalities, 180
  per labor day in Wuxi, 238–39
  per mu in Wuxi, 220
  See also Distribution; Households
India, 184
Industrialization
  benefits from, 245
  effect of on women's work, 243, 244
Infanticide
  and birth order, 169, 172
  and family planning in Liaoning, 145–76
  and fertility control, 167
  and food prices, 26, 147, 158
  and household position, 156–58, 172
  and household wealth, 169
  of males, 169–72
Inflation, 64
  in eighteenth century, 65, 66, 98
  in late nineteenth century, 66
  and population, 68
Integration
  of female wage labor markets, 252–53
  within provinces, 318
Integration, of grain markets, 52, 95–98, 121–25, 143–44
  interprefectural, 95–98, 121–25,132, 140–43
  intraprefectural, 132, 139–43
  and price data, 131–43
  See also Grains; Millet; Rice; Sorghum; Wheat
Interest rates
  and market integration theory, 15
  regional differences in, 296–97, 301
Investment, in land, 186
Involution, 208–9
Irrigation, in North China, 72

Japan
  and currency markets in Shandong, 306–8
  and currency problems in China, 307, 309
  and foreign imperialism in China, 2
  silver from, 59, 60
Jiang Chen, 60
"Jiangbei vagabonds," 284–86
Jiangnan
  jobs of people from, 278, 283

Jiangnan (*cont.*)
   rise of wealth in, 284
   See also Ningbo; Shanghai
Jin Jiulin, 290
Junk trade, 17–19

Kann, Eduard, 59
Kaoliang (*gaoliang*), 52, 73
   See also Sorghum
Kitamura Hironao, 127n4
Kobata, A., 60
Krulwich, Robert, 9n19
Kuperberg, Mark, 10n22
Kuznets, Simon, 188, 196
   on income distribution in urban sector, 204

Labor
   in Dabeiguan, 193, 199
   hierarchy in, 28–29
   of immigrant households, 186
   in Lianggezhuang, 194, 199
   in Michang, 199
   power of, 199
   usage of in Wuxi, 230–40
   See also Factories; Females; Ningbo; Shanghai; Women; Wuxi
Labor markets
   jobs and personal connections, 288
   regional nature of in Shanghai, 274–82
   segmentation of, 271–94
   Subei people in, 287
   See also Ningbo; Shanghai
Labor markets for females
   factories, 263–67
   farm, 252–54
   home handicrafts, 256–63
   prostitution and domestic service, 254–56
   See also Ningbo; Shanghai; Women
Lace
   as new industry, 260
   pay for making, 240, 258n48
Land, 26
   allocation of, in Wuxi, 217–30
   concentration of ownership, 26
   land-labor ratio, 196
   productivity of, in Wuxi, 230
   rental of, 189, 222
   rents from, 199–200
   tax on, 4
Land concentration
   during the Qing, 182–83
   evidence for increase, 181–84
   historical processes, 184–87
   and income distribution, 26–27, 179–206
   in late nineteenth and early twentieth centuries, 180
   in rural China, 188–90
Land tenure, 4
   under Marxism, 2
Landa, Janet T., 29
Landlords, farm management by, 186
Laughlin, J. Laurence, 61
Lee, James, xvii, 25, 26, 31, 126n, 132n14, 145–76
Li, Bozhong, xv
Li, Lillian M., xvii, 1–32, 69–99
Li River, grains near, 128n7
Liang Fangzhong
   on population, 212
   on silver stocks, 60
Lianggezhuang. *See* Qianlianggezhuang
Liaoning, 26, 31
   demographic data for, 147–51
   infanticide and family planning in, 145–76
   mortality and fertility in, 146
   price history, 146
   See also Fengtian
Liaoning Population Research Institute, 150
Lieu, D. K., 6
Lindert, Peter H., xv, 27
   on land holding, 184
   on money, 65
   on population, 55, 57
Liu Kexiang, 225n59
Liu, Ta-chung, 204
Low-income countries, distribution of household income in, 202–3
Lower class
   factory jobs for, 266
   women of, 246–47

McCloskey, Donald N., xv, 17
   on choice in economics, 5–6
   on interest rates, 15, 298
Males
   effect of food prices on mortality of, 166–67
   farm wages of, 252–53
   and industrialization, 246–47
   and infanticide, 169–72
   mortality rates of in Liaoning, 151
   number of, on farms of different sizes, 231
   preference for, 156
Manchoukuo, 194

Manchuria
  bean crops in, 82
  food from, 38
  labor exported to, 314
  migration into, 186
  population data from, 26
  ties to Shandong, 299, 302
Mann, Susan, xvii, 16, 243–70
  on female labor, 28–29, 30
  on taxes, 4
Maocun (Wuxi), 225
Marathon Oil Company, 16
Market integration, 13–16, 22–23, 31
  in China and Europe, 50–54
  difficulties of measuring, 15–16
  in Gansu, 113–24
  historians and economic theory on, 13, 32
  in Hunan, 23, 131–44
  and interest rates, 15
  and labor, 14–15
  in Shandong, 295–318
  in Zhili, 95–98
Markets
  capital, 241, 295–318
  cocoons, 215–17, 218, 241
  effect of international in Ningbo, 257–58
  for female labor, 252–67
  fragmented, and distribution, 309–12
  grain, and integration of, 143–44
  integration disrupted by politics, 303
  labor, 14
  international, 214, 224, 250–51
  See also Credit markets; Foreign trade; Integration; Labor markets; Millet; Money markets; Rice; Shandong; Sorghum; Wheat
Marxism, Chinese, 2–3
Matches, manufacture of, 265
Mats
  special grass for, 260
  weaving of, 244, 249, 258
Merchants
  contributions by for degrees, 105–7
  from Subei in Shanghai, 289
Mexico, 184
  silver from, 59
mianbu (handicraft cotton cloth), 213
Michang Village (Hebei), 191, 193, 199–200
Middle class
  in Ningbo, 256–57
  women of, 246–47, 266

Migration
  during the Depression, 224
  and female labor force, 267–69
  and landless households, 186, 187
  of refugees from Subei, 285
  seasonal and permanent, 286
Military supply system
  in campaigns of 1758–61, 110–13
  in Gansu, 100–102, 110–13
  use of granary reserves, 104
Millet (*sumi*), 52, 73
  in crisis years, 89–95
  high grade (*shang sumi*), 73
  importance of, 75
  long-term trend in prices, 76–82
  market for, 25, 97
  ordinary (*cisumi*), 73
  price data for Gansu, 113–25
  prices of, 22
  prices of and fertility, 167
Mining, of silver, 61
Mobil Corporation, 16
Mobility, limited for female workers, 253
Modernization, Chinese, and the West, 3
Monetary system, Chinese, 57
  See also Banks; Silver
Money markets, fragmented
  and distribution, 309–12
  and regional economic performance, 312–15
  and state making, 315–18
Money stocks, 31, 54–62
  and population, 25, 65
Morse, H. B., 61
Mortality
  effect of food shortage on, 98
  infant, 26
  and infanticide in Liaoning, 101
  See also Females; Fertility; Infanticide; Males
Mulberries, 36
  after Taiping Revolution, 215–16
  cash crop of, 65, 109
  labor productivity in, 231
  in Wuxi, 218, 230
Multicrop system, and seasonality, 98
Muramatsu, Yuji, 286
Myers, Ramon H., 4

Nakamura Jihei, 127n4
Nash, John, 15, 298
National Land Commission, 188, 189

National Palace Museum, Taibei, 21, 35n, 73n4
Native-place associations (*huiguan*), 29, 290n80, 291
Native-place hierarchy
 and labor market segregation, 271–94
 origins of, 282–94
Nayancheng, Governor, 109
Ningbo
 as cotton center, 250
 data from, 245–46
 description of, 247–52
 factories in, 264, 265
 female farm labor in, 252–54
 female non-farm labor markets, 254–67
 gender division of work in, 246
 in international trade, 250–51
 links with Shanghai, 250
 products of, 249
 and regional differences, 251
 women's education in, 270n92
 women's labor in, 28, 243–70
North China
 data on household income in, 190–201
 disasters in, 72
 growing conditions in, 70
 land ownership in, 27, 30, 190
 nonagricultural pursuits in villages of, 199–201
 See also Hebei; Shandong; Zhili
North Coast of Shandong, 299, 301
 and fragmented markets, 312–15
 money market rates in, 304
 ties to Manchuria, 299, 302

Opium trade, and stock of silver, 61
Opportunity cost, in economic theory, 6

Paper currency, 303, 306, 316
Paper umbrellas, 258
Parker, G., 62
Pawnshops, 310
Peas, 223
Peasant rationality
 and choice of sericulture, 220–40
 and new economic growth, 240
 work regime, 218–19
 in Wuxi, 207–42
Peasants
 decision making by, 207
 goals of, 208
 hat making by, 262

 minimum subsistence for, 222–23
 studies of in North China, 27
 use of sericulture by, 222, 240
Peng Zeyi, 225n59
Perdue, Peter C., xvii, 25, 100–125, 117, 159n16
Perkins, Dwight H., 67
 on Chinese agriculture, 20
 on Gansu, 101
 on minimum subsistence, 223
 on population, 55, 212
Peru, silver from, 59
Philippines
 material for hats from, 261
 silver from, 60, 61
Piore, Michael, 271–72
Polanyi, Karl, 7, 207n1
Political unrest, economic consequences of, 26
Politics
 of economic geography (private finance), 308–9
 of economic geography (public finance), 305–8
 and money markets, 303
 and Shandong capital market, 297–98
 See also Government policies and the economy
Pomeranz, Kenneth, xvii, 295–318
 on politics and economic change, 29–30
Popkin, Samuel, on peasant rationality, 207
Population
 of China, 55–56, 145
 of Gansu, 101
 and inflation, 65, 68
 and price of rice, 54–55, 57
 in rural Liaoning, 145–76
 and trends in food prices, 25
 in Yangzi Delta, 36
 of Zhili, 72–73
Population, in Wuxi
 density, 212, 217, 221
 link with cropping patterns, 220
 reliability of data, 211–12
Porcelain, 59
Portuguese, and silver stocks, 60
Potatoes, 223
Poverty
 in Ningbo, 225–26, 266–67
 rural, 26
 in Subei, 283–86
 among Subei migrants in Jiangnan, 281–82, 287

urban, 26
in Wuxi, 222–24
Price behavior
  data on grain, 21–26
  data on rice, 21, 26
  Qing, 21
  on rice in Yangzi Delta, 35–68
  See also Gansu; Hunan; Liaoning; Millet; Rice; Shandong; Shanghai; Suzhou; Wheat; Yangzi Delta; Zhili
Prices
  and conversion of resources to commodities, 6
  copper, 305, 306
  effect of crises on, 88–95
  leveling of ever-normal granary system, 109
  See also Grains; Rice
Profit
  maximization of by peasants, 206–7
  vs. risk, 8
Prostitution, 254–55, 268–69, 281

Qianlianggezhuang (Hebei), 191, 193–94, 199–200
  pear crops in, 194
Qing bureaucracy, price data of, 31
Qing state
  famine relief system, 100
  and Gansu grain market, 100–125
  granaries of, 100, 105
  land distribution under, 182–83
  and tax, 4
Qiu Jun, 153n12

Railways
  economic and social consequences, 12, 13
  effect on rice prices, 52, 54
Rainfall, and flooding in North China, 72
Rationality
  in economic theory, 6, 8
  of Wuxi peasants, 207–9, 216–20, 240–42
  See also Peasant rationality
Rawski, Evelyn Sakakida, 127n4
Rawski, Thomas G., xvii, 1–32
Regression analysis
  of grain prices, 82–88, 115–23, 136–43
  limitations of, 88
Reich, Michael, 271
Republican China, land concentration and income in, 179–206
Rice
  area of study, 38

data on prices of, 21, 39–52, 73–74
equation of exchange, 54
harvests of, 62–63
in Hunan, 126
labor productivity in, 231
and mortality in Daoyi, 167
and population, 54–57
prices of, 22, 35–68, 117
significance of prices of, 35
and silver stocks, 61–62
during Taiping Rebellion, 54
in Wuxi, 210, 218, 223
in Yangzi Delta, 25, 35–68
in Zhili, 73–74
See also Grains; Yangzi Delta
Rickshaw pulling
  and the Green Gang, 290
  by Subei people, 275–76
Riskin, Carl, 179
Road building, 316
Roll, C. Robert, 190–91
Rowe, William T., 4
Rubin, Julius, xv
Rural areas, land and income distribution in, 188–90

Sands, Barbara, xvii, 179–206
Schafer, E. H., 283
Schneider, Jane, 258n48
Scott, James C., 8, 207n1
Seasonality
  effects of, 83, 88
  in Gansu, 117
  in grain prices, 98
  in Hunan, 132
  in Zhili, 84–88
Segmentation of labor market, 271–94
Sericulture
  reasons for, in Wuxi, 220–22
  after Taiping Rebellion, 214–24
  in Wuxi County, 207–42
Sex, and fertility control, 152–56, 152n12
  See also Fertility; Gender; Mortality
Shaanxi Province, 101
Shandong, politics and economic change in, 29–30, 32
  See also Heartland of Shandong; North Coast of Shandong; Southwest region of Shandong
Shandong capital market
  fragmented markets and distribution, 309–12

Shandong capital market (*cont.*)
  fragmented markets and regional
    performance, 312–15
  fragmented markets and state making, 315–18
  Heartland, 299, 301
  North Coast, 299, 301
  political power and regional differences in, 295–318
  politics of economic geography, public finance, 305–8
  private finance, 308–9
  regional capital markets in, 296, 298–302, 303–5
  signs of regional distinctness, 302–3
  Southwest, 299, 301, 302–3
Shang Lie, 225n59
Shanghai
  as international market, 215, 250
  jobs for Subei people in, 287
  money market rates in, 304
  Ningbo traders in, 249
  Ningbo workers in factories of, 267–69
  population of, 272
  regional nature of labor market in, 274–82
  rice prices in, 49
  shack settlements in, 286
  social inequalities in, 272
  Subei people in, 271–94
Shen Bao, rice prices in, 50
Shepherd, John R., 186
shi, a measure of grain, 104n20
Shigeta Atsushi, 127n4
Shipbuilding, 17–18
Sichuan, 101
Silk industry, 27–28, 59, 207–42
  international market in, 214
  jobs for women from Subei in, 280–81
  problems of growth, 240–42
  in Wuxi, 209, 214–24
  in Yangzi Delta, 38
  See also Sericulture
Silkworms, 209
  labor productivity in raising, 231
  modern techniques for raising, 240–41
  raising of in Wuxi, 219, 240
Silver
  as currency, 303
  import of, 57, 59
  mining of, 61
  and prices, 57, 61–62
  stocks of, 25, 31, 57–61, 66
  substitute for grain in crises, 109
Skinner, G. William, 210n4
  on economics and politics, 4
  on grain market boundaries, 123
  on grain prices, 22, 31
  on market integration, 13
Smith, Adam, 7
Smith, L. M., 62
Social class, and women's work, 243, 246
Social forces, and economic history, 4, 20–21, 32
Sorghum (*gaoliang*), 73
  effect of crises on, 88–95
  importance of, 75
  long-term trend in prices, 76–82
  market for, 25
  prices of, 22
  See also Kaoliang
South Manchurian Railway Co.
  surveys in Hebei Province, 191
  surveys in Wuxi, 217, 225
  village surveys by, 27, 188
Southwest region of Shandong
  exports of labor from, 314
  and fragmented markets, 312–15
  local currencies in, 306
  money market rates in, 304–5
  reports of labor from, 314
Soybeans, international trade in, 67
Spatial structure of the rice trade, 128–30
Spinning of cotton, in Wuxi, 213–14
"Sprouts of capitalism," 2
Steamers, traffic between Ningbo and Shanghai, 251
Steamships, effect on rice prices, 52, 54
Stigler, George J., 8n19
Storage of grains
  private, 24, 121
  state, 24
  See also Gansu; Zhili
Stores, as source of credit, 309–10, 310n53
Stoto, M. A., 175
Straw mats, trade in, 67
Subei
  contacts in Shanghai, 288–89
  cycles of disasters in, 284
  decline in prosperity of, 283–84
  and the Green Gang, 289–90
  refugees from, 285
Subei people
  employment of, 28–29, 32

in factories, 279–80, 291
as freight handlers, 276
jobs available to, 288–92
origins of native-place hierarchy, 282–94
outside labor market, 281–82
place in hierarchy, 274–75
prejudice against, 293
as rickshaw pullers, 275–76, 277
in service sector, 276–77
in Shanghai, 271–94
Sugar cane, as cash crop, 65
sui, 150n9
Sun Yutang, 60
Sutch, Richard, xv
Suxiang (Wuxi), 225
Suzhou
  rice prices in, 38
  sources of data, 39

Tailors, wages of, 278
Taiping Rebellion
  casualties during, 56
  effect on sericulture, 215
  and migration, 187
  rice prices during, 49, 51, 54, 66
Taiping Shanren, 60
Taiwan, 202
  and China's economic development, 3
  pacification of, 64
  population and price records in, 145
Tan, Guofu, xvii, 25, 26, 31, 145–76
Tawney, Richard, 179, 185
Tax surcharges, 4
Taxes
  basis of collection, 211–12
  collected by merchants, 4
  in Gansu, 102–3
  on land, 4
  paid in silver, 303, 305
Tea
  in Gansu, 103
  trade in, 59
Temperature, long-term changes in, 62
Tenancy
  and land sales, 184–86
  and other historical processes, 186–87
Textiles, in Yangzi Delta, 36, 38
Theoretical reasoning, 10–16
  examples of, 12–13
  market integration, 13–16
  uses of for historians, 10–11
Tobacco, as cash crop, 65

Tongjiuyuan Cotton Mill, 264
Transportation, effect on rice prices, 52, 54
Trussell, T. J., 175
Tsur Nyok-Ching, 256–57, 258n48, 262, 266
Tung oil, 67
tuntian (former military garrison lands), in Gansu, 102

United States
  labor markets in, 272
  silver from, 60
  social class in, 282
  status of immigrants to, 287
U.S. Silver Purchase Act, 59
Upper class, women of, 246–47
Urbanization
  and income distribution, 204–5
  and prices, 55

Wages
  in factories, 264
  interrelations of, 13–14
  in Shanghai, 267, 275
  in textiles, 280
  of women during industrialization, 246
Wang Danwang, scandal by, 107, 109
Wang Shaowu, 62, 163
Wang, Yeh-chien, xvii, 25, 32, 35–68
Warfare, effect on rice prices, 64
Wealth, and infanticide, 169
Weaving
  collapse of as household work, 244
  of cotton in Wuxi, 213–14
  income from, 222, 240
  by middle-class women in Ningbo, 257
Wei Yuan, 61
West
  historians of, on China, 3
  trade with, 59
Wheat (*mai*), 73
  effect of crises on, 88–95
  importance of, 75
  long-term trend in prices, 76–82
  market for, 25, 52, 97
  and mortality in Daoyi, 167
  prices of, 22, 315
  red (*hongmai*), 73
  white (*baimai*), 73
  in Wuxi, 218
  See also Grains; Rice

Will, Pierre-Etienne, 31, 76, 90
Women
　changes in status of, 246
　economic value of labor by, 28
　in factory jobs, 263–67, 268, 280, 292
　as farm laborers, 252–54
　and home handicrafts, 258–63
　and industrialization, 243–44, 246
　labor of in cotton weaving, 214, 222
　limited mobility of, 253
　new labor markets and community norms for, 246
　in sericulture, 27–28, 224, 230
　taboos on working "outside," 243n2
　wages in factories, 231, 240, 264–65
　work of in Ningbo area, 243–70
　See also Females; Gender; Home handicrafts; Labor; Labor markets
Wong, R. Bin, xvii, 117
Wu Chengming, 38
Wu Dashan, Governor, 101–2
Wuxi, 32
　cotton cloth in, 210
　further look at villages of, 224–40
　land and labor allocations in villages of, 217–24
　peasant farming and silk industry growth, 240–42
　Qing trends of commercialization in, 209–14
　rice trade in, 210
　sericulture in, 27–28, 207–42
　tin production in, 287–88

xian (county), 21
Xiang River, and rice trade, 128, 143
Xiaoshan, rice prices in, 49
Xinwen Bao, rice prices in, 50

Yan Jiyuan, 62
Yancheng, jobs of people from, 277–78
　See also Subei

Yangzhou
　heyday of, 283
　jobs of people from, 277–78
Yangzhou Bashou Gongsuo, 290n80
Yangzi Delta
　data on, 39–52
　harvest yields and prices, 63
　importance of, 36
　land ownership in, 190
　market integration in, 52
　rice prices in, 25, 35–68
　Taiping Rebellion in, 66
Yeh, Kung-chia, 204
Yellow River, 70
　dikes along, 317
　shifting course of, 284
Yim, Shu-yuen, 55
Yin County, 251
　farm wages in, 252–53
Yongxing, 261
Yu Xiaoxia, 249
Yuan River, rice trade on, 130, 143
Yunnan, silver mining in, 61
Yuyao County, 251
　farm wages in, 252–53
Yuyao River, 251

Zelin, Madeleine, on tax surcharges, 4
Zhang Peiyuan, 62
Zhang Xiaolin, 290
Zhang Xinyi, 75
Zhang Zhiyi, 225n59
Zhili
　agriculture and food availability in, 74–76
　effect of crises in, 88–95
　grain markets in, 23, 69–99
　long-term trend of prices in, 76–82
　price data from, 73–74
　regional variations, 95–98
　seasonal patterns, 82–88
Zhou, Guangyuan, xv, 210n5
Zhou Guozhen, 281
Zi River, 128, 143

Compositor: Asco Trade Typesetting Ltd., Hong Kong
Text: 10/12 Baskerville
Display: Baskerville

www.ingramcontent.com/pod-product-compliance
Lightning Source LLC
Chambersburg PA
CBHW031419230426
43668CB00007B/357